Evidence and Proof

The International Library of Essays in Law and Legal Theory
Series Editor: Tom D. Campbell

Schools

Natural Law, Vols I & II   *John Finnis*
Justice   *Thomas Morawetz*
Law and Economics, Vols I & II   *Jules Coleman and Jeffrey Lange*
Critical Legal Studies   *James Boyle*
Marxian Legal Theory   *Csaba Varga*
Legal Reasoning, Vols I & II   *Aulis Aarnio and Neil MacCormick*
Legal Positivism   *Mario Jori*

American Legal Theory   *Robert Summers*
Law and Language   *Fred Schauer*
Sociological Theories of Law   *Kahei Rokumoto*
Rights   *Carlos Nino*
Law and Psychology   *Martin Levine*
Feminist Legal Theory   *Frances Olsen*
Law and Society   *Werner Krawietz*

Areas

Criminal Law   *Thomas Morawetz*
Tort Law   *Ernest Weinrib*
Contract Law, Vols I & II   *Larry Alexander*
Anti-Discrimination Law   *Christopher McCrudden*
Consumer Law   *Iain Ramsay*
International Law   *Martti Koskenniemi*
Property Law, Vols I & II   *Elizabeth Mensch and Alan Freeman*
Constitutional Law   *Mark Tushnet*
Procedure   *Denis Galligan*
Evidence and Proof   *William Twining and Alex Stein*

Administrative Law   *Denis Galligan*
Child Law   *Harry Krause*
Family Law, Vols I & II   *Harry Krause*
Welfare Law   *Peter Robson*
Medicine and the Law   *Bernard Dickens*
Commercial Law   *Ross Cranston*
Communications Law   *David Goldberg*
Environmental Law   *Michael Blumm*
Conflict of Laws   *Richard Fentiman*
Law and Religion   *Wojciech Sadurski*
Human Rights Law   *Philip Alston*
European Community Law, Vols I & II   *Francis Snyder*

Legal Cultures

Comparative Legal Cultures   *Csaba Varga*
Law and Anthropology   *Peter Sack*
Hindu Law and Legal Theory   *Ved Nanda*
Islamic Law and Legal Theory   *Ian Edge*
Chinese Law and Legal Theory   *Michael Palmer*
Socialist Law and Legal Theory   *W. Butler*

Japanese Law and Legal Theory   *Koichiro Fujikura*
Law and Development   *Anthony Carty*
Jewish Law and Legal Theory   *Martin Golding*
Legal Education   *Martin Levine*

Future Volumes
Labour Law, Common Law and Legal Theory, Civil Law and Legal Theory,
African Law and Legal Theory, Legal Ethics and Cumulative index.

Evidence and Proof

Edited by

William Twining

Quain Professor of Jurisprudence
University College, London

and

Alex Stein

Senior Lecturer, Faculty of Law
Hebrew University, Jerusalem

NEW YORK UNIVERSITY PRESS
REFERENCE COLLECTION

First published in the U.S.A. in 1992 by
NEW YORK UNIVERSITY PRESS
Washington Square
New York NY 10003

Library of Congress Cataloging-in-Publication Data
Evidence and proof / edited [by] William Twining and Alex Stein.
     p. cm. – (The International library of essays in law and legal theory. Areas)
  "New York University Press reference collection."
  Includes bibliographical references and index.
  ISBN 0-8147-8196-9
  1. Evidence (Law) 2. Burden of proof. I. Twining, William L.
II. Stein, Alex, 1957-   . III. Series.
K2261.Z9E92 1992
347′.06–dc20
[342.76]   92-4120
                                                                    CIP

Contents

PART VII AUXILIARY PROBATIVE POLICY

PART VIII EXTRINSIC PROBATIVE POLICY

PART IX PROTECTION OF THE ACCUSED

Acknowledgements

The editors and publishers wish to thank the following for permission to use copyright material.

Adelaide Law Review for the essay: Philip McNamara (1985), 'The Canons of Evidence – Rules of Exclusion or Rules of Use?', *The Adelaide Law Review*, **10**, pp. 341–64.

American Bar Association Journal for the essay: Kenneth Culp Davis (1964), 'An Approach to Rules of Evidence for Non–Jury Cases', *American Bar Association Journal*, **50**, pp. 723–7. Reprinted with permission from the August 1964 issue of the ABA Journal, the Lawyer's Magazine, published by the American Bar Association.

Basil Blackwell Ltd for the essay: G.E.M. Anscombe (1958), 'On Brute Facts', *Analysis*, **18**, pp. 69–72.

Boston University Law Review for the essay: Adrian A.S. Zuckerman (1986), 'Law, Fact or Justice?', *Boston University Law Review*, **66**, pp. 487–508.

Charles Frederick Chamberlayne (1908), 'The Modern Law of Evidence and its Purpose', *American Law Review*, **42**, pp. 757–73.

L. Jonathan Cohen (1983), 'Freedom of Proof', in William Twining (ed.), 'Facts in Law', *Archiv für Rechts–und Sozialphilosophie*, **16**, pp. 1–21. Copyright © L. Jonathan Cohen.

Columbia Law Review Association, Inc. for the essay: Jack B. Weinstein (1966), 'Some Difficulties in Devising Rules for Determining Truth in Judicial Trials', *Columbia Law Review*, **66**, No. 2, pp. 223–46. Copyright © 1966 by the Directors of the Columbia Law Review Association, Inc. All Rights Reserved. This article originally appeared at **66** *Colum. L. Rev.* 223 (1966). Reprinted by permission.

Rupert Cross (1974), 'An Attempt to Update the Law of Evidence', *Israel Law Review*, **9**, No. 1, pp. 1–23. Copyright © Rupert Cross.

Deborah Charles Publications for the essay: William Twining (1980), 'Debating Probabilities', *The Liverpool Law Review*, **II**, pp. 51–64. Copyright © Deborah Charles Publications.

The Journal of Philosophy for the essay: Edna Ullmann–Margalit (1983), 'On Presumption', *The Journal of Philosophy*, **LXXX**, No. 3, pp. 143–63.

The Law Book Company Limited for the essay: The Honourable Sir Richard Eggleston (1987), 'Focusing on the Defendant', *The Australian Law Journal*, **61**, pp. 58–64.

Law and Contemporary Problems for the essay: Judith Jarvis Thomson (1986), 'Liability and Individualized Evidence', *Law and Contemporary Problems*, **49**, No. 3, pp. 199–219. Reprinted in Judith Jarvis Thomson (1986), *Rights, Restitution, and Risk*, Harvard University Press.

Law and Society Association for the essay: David A. Schum and Anne W. Martin (1982), 'Formal and Empirical Research on Cascaded Inference in Jurisprudence', *Law & Society Review*, **17**, pp. 105–51. Reprinted by permission of the Law and Society Association.

Northwestern University School of Law for essays: John H. Wigmore (1913), 'The Problem of Proof', *Illinois Law Review*, **VIII**, No. 2, pp. 77–103. Reprinted by special permission of Northwestern University School of Law, Illinois Law Review, Volume **VIII**, No. 2, pp. 77–103 (1913). John H. Wigmore (1908), 'Book Review of C. Moore, "A Treatise On Facts, or the Weight and Value of Evidence"', *Illinois Law Review*, **3**, pp. 477–8. Reprinted by special permission of Northwestern University School of Law, Illinois Law Review, Volume **3**, pp. 477–8, (1908).

Gerald J. Postema (1983), 'Fact, Fictions, and Law: Bentham on the Foundations of Evidence', in William L. Twining (ed.), 'Facts in Law', *Archiv für Rechts–und Sozialphilosophie*, **16**, pp. 37–64.

The Stockholm Institute for Scandinavian Law for the essay: Per Olof Ekelöf (1964), 'Free Evaluation of Evidence', *Scandinavian Studies in Law*, **8**, pp. 47–66.

Sweet & Maxwell Limited for the essay: J.L. Montrose (1954), 'Basic Concepts of the Law of Evidence', *The Law Quarterly Review*, **70**, pp. 527–55.

University of California Press Journals for the essay: George F. James (1941), 'Relevancy, Probability and the Law', *California Law Review*, **29**, pp. 689–705. Copyright © 1941 by California Law Review Inc. Reprinted from California Law Review, Vol. **29**, pp. 689–705, by permission.

The University of Chicago Press for the essay: David Kaye (1982), 'The Limits of the Preponderance of the Evidence Standard: Justifiably Naked Statistical Evidence and Multiple Causation', *American Bar Foundation Research Journal*, pp. 487–516. Copyright © The University of Chicago Press.

University of Illinois at Urbana–Champaign for the essay: Michael H. Graham (1983), '"Stickperson Hearsay": A Simplified Approach to Understanding the Rule Against Hearsay', *University of Illinois Law Review*, No. 4, pp. 887–923. Copyright © Board of Trustees of The University of Illinois.

The Washington Law Review and Fred B. Rothman and Co. for essays: Arval A. Morris (1982), 'The Exclusionary Rule, Deterrence and Posner's Economic Analysis of Law', *Washington Law Review*, **57**, pp. 647–67, and Richard A. Posner (1982), 'Excessive Sanctions for Governmental Misconduct in Criminal Cases', *Washington Law Review*, **57**, pp. 635–46. Copyright © The Washington Law Review Association.

Series Preface

The International Library of Law and Legal Theory is designed to provide important research materials in an accessible form. Each volume contains essays of central theoretical importance in its subject area. The series as a whole makes available an extensive range of valuable material which will be of considerable interest to those involved in the research, teaching and study of law.

The series has been divided into three sections. The Schools section is intended to represent the main distinctive approaches and topics of special concern to groups of scholars. The Areas section takes in the main branches of law with an emphasis on essays which present analytical and theoretical insights of broad application. The section on Legal Cultures makes available the distinctive legal theories of different legal traditions and takes up topics of general comparative and developmental concern.

I have been delighted and impressed by the way in which the editors of the individual volumes have set about the difficult task of selecting, ordering and presenting essays from the immense quantity of academic legal writing published in journals throughout the world. Editors were asked to pick out those essays from law, philosophy and social science journals which they consider to be fundamental for the understanding of law, as seen from the perspective of a particular approach or sphere of legal interest. This is not an easy task and many difficult decisions have had to be made in order to ensure that a representative sample of the best journal essays available takes account of the scope of each topic or school.

I should like to express my thanks to all the volume editors for their willing participation and scholarly judgement. The interest and enthusiasm which the project has generated is well illustrated by the fact that an original projection of 12 volumes drawn up in 1989 has now become a list of some 60 volumes. I must also acknowledge the vision, persistence and constant cheerfulness of John Irwin and the marvellous work done by Mrs Margaret O'Reilly and Mrs Sonia Bridgman.

TOM D. CAMPBELL
Series Editor
The Faculty of Law
The Australian National University

Introduction

This volume brings together leading theoretical writings on legal fact–finding which are dispersed and not readily accessible. It contains a collection of essays written in English, largely about evidence and proof in the Anglo–American systems, and published in various legal and non–legal periodicals. These essays have been selected primarily on the basis of their significance for the general theory of evidence. However, as a result of space limits and other constraints, we had to exclude from this volume several important publications which are either widely accessible or too long, or which appeared in special collections of essays and *festschrifts* rather than journals. References to these and other important sources are to be found in the endnotes.

The issues selected reflect what we consider to be the most important trends in the theory of evidence. Perhaps the most important recent development in that field has been a shift from a rule-oriented and court-centred approach to legal evidence towards the interdisciplinary study of various processes of legal fact–finding. This shift has gradually emerged in the past three decades and can be viewed as part of a decline of law as an autonomous object of study.[1] It has a number of important currents. First, it has become recognized that evidentiary rules, although not unimportant, are both exceptional and subject to many exceptions. They cannot therefore be the main object of the general study of proof. Rather, it is the nature of reasoning about facts in situations to which these rules do not apply that should be dealt with first and foremost.[2] The logic of proof is always antecedent to evidentiary rules. Furthermore, attention should be paid not only to the determination of facts in contested trials, but also to the processes of proof which take place in various administrative settings. Being by and large unconstrained by evidentiary rules, administrative officials and tribunals decide many important matters and determinations of fact which form part of these decisions deserve attention. The same is true of uses of factual information in pre–trial and post–trial decisions.

Second, the ways in which judges and other legal officials reason about facts, largely ignored by orthodox scholars as matters that belong solely to 'common sense', have become an important object of study. Inquiries into these ways of reasoning have generated controversies, the most significant of which concern probability and induction applied in legal contexts (the 'probability debate') and the tension between atomistic and holistic approaches to reasoning about facts. This broad and expanding agenda which characterizes the 'New Evidence Scholarship'[3] has introduced into the study of legal proof epistemology, statistics, psychology, semiotics and several other extra-legal disciplines.

Third, the processes of legal fact–finding, including procedural rules that shape some of these processes, rest on certain moral and political assumptions. Orthodox scholars tend to marginalize these assumptions by linking them with exceptional extraneous policies such as those that underlie the exclusion of illegally obtained evidence and immunities from disclosing probative information. It has, however, been established that political and moral choices affecting different processes of proof go far beyond that. Thus, in a seminal article which, unfortunately, could not be reproduced in this volume, Ronald Dworkin has demonstrated that principles of political equality and fairness have a significant impact on legal proof and procedure.[4]

These trends rest on several common assumptions about the role of reason in legal fact–finding and the hierarchy of its objectives. These assumptions belong to the Rationalist Tradition of Evidence Scholarship which has dominated the specialized study of evidence and proof since early times. They are summarized in the following table:[5]

Table 1 The Rationalist Tradition: Basic Assumptions

Model 1 A Rationalist model of adjudication

A. *Prescriptive*
1. The direct end
2. of adjective law
3. is rectitude of decision through correct application
4. of valid substantive laws
5. deemed to be consonant with utility (or otherwise good)
6. and through accurate determination
7. of the true past facts
8. material to
9. precisely specified allegations expressed in categories defined in advance by law i.e. facts in issue
10. proved to specified standards of probability or likelihood
11. on the basis of the careful
12. and rational
13. weighing of
14. evidence
15. which is both relevant
16. and reliable
17. presented (in a form designed to bring out truth and discover untruth)
18. to supposedly competent
19. and impartial
20. decision-makers
21. with adequate safeguards against corruption
22. and mistake
23. and adequate provision for review and appeal.

B. *Descriptive*
24. Generally speaking, this objective is largely achieved
25. in a consistent
26. fair
27. and predictable manner.

Note: Prescriptive rationalism: acceptance of A as both desirable and reasonably feasible. No commitment to B.

Complacent rationalism: acceptance of A & B *in re* a particular system.

Model II   Rationalist theories of evidence and proof: some common assumptions

1. Knowledge about particular past events is possible.
2. Establishing the truth about particular past events in issue in a case (the facts in issue) is a necessary condition for achieving justice in adjudication; incorrect results are one form of injustice.
3. The notions of evidence and proof in adjudication are concerned with rational methods of determining questions of fact; in this context operative distinctions have to be maintained between questions of fact and questions of law, questions of fact and questions of value and questions of fact and questions of opinion.
4. The establishment of the truth of alleged facts in adjudication is typically a matter of probabilities, falling short of absolute certainty.
5. (a) Judgments about the probabilities of allegations about particular past events can and should be reached by reasoning from relevant evidence presented to the decision-maker; (b) The characteristic mode of reasoning appropriate to reasoning about probabilities is induction.
6. Judgments about probabilities have, generally speaking, to be based on the available stock of knowledge about the common course of events; this is largely a matter of common sense supplemented by specialized scientific or expert knowledge when it is available.
7. The pursuit of truth (i.e. seeking to maximize accuracy in fact-determination) is to be given a high, but not necessarily an overriding, priority in relation to other values, such as the security of the state, the protection of family relationships or the curbing of coercive methods of interrogation.
8. One crucial basis for evaluating 'fact-finding' institutions, rules, procedures and techniques is how far they are estimated to maximize accuracy in fact-determination – but other criteria such as speed, cheapness, procedural fairness, humaneness, public confidence and the avoidance of vexation for participants are also to be taken into account.
9. The primary role of applied forensic psychology and forensic science is to provide guidance about the reliability of different kinds of evidence and to develop methods and devices for increasing such reliability.

Among these homogeneous assumptions, the most striking one is faith in the possibility of ascertaining past events by empirical methods, coupled with the belief that this possibility can usually be realized in legal fact–finding despite its inherent scarcities of time, resources and information. Although some sceptical views about legal fact–finding have, from time to time, been expressed, they are regarded as exceptional. The most prominent advocate of such views was Jerome Frank.[6] His main concern was the unreachability of fact; that is, the obstacles – some inevitable, some avoidable – to reaching objectively true judgments about past events, as well as the difficulties of predicting the outcomes of adjudicative fact–determination. But on close examination even Frank turns out not to be a radical fact–sceptic. He had never denied the possibility of objective knowledge about particular past events nor subscribed to a strong epistemological relativism. Rather, he was a reformer whose aim was not merely to dispel the implausible myth of adjudicative certainty, but to implement changes in legal procedures, fact–finding and education which would make decision–making fit more closely to a rationalist model of truth-seeking.[7] This volume contains an important essay of Edmond Cahn which discusses Frank's scepticism and its implications.

Although the rationalist foundations of legal fact-finding appear to be unimpaired and remarkably homogeneous, the possibilities of scepticism in this area have yet to be explored. A tentative list of such possibilities is presented in the following table:[8]

Table 2   Rationalist Theories of Evidence and Proof, with Selected Variants

Aspirational rationalism (ideal type)	Selected variants
1. Cognitivist epistemology.	Epistemological scepticism.
2. Correspondence theory of truth.	Coherence theory of truth.
3. Rational decision–making as aspiration.	(a) Scepticism about the possibility of rationality in (a) any context, (b) adjudication (this cannot be the aspiration);
	(b) claims to aspire to rationality in adjudication are a pretence or a delusion (this is not in fact the end which is pursued);
	(c) some other end should be pursued (this should not be the aspiration).
4. Decisions based on relevant evidence.	(a) Relevance a meaningless concept;
	(b) lawyers' conceptions of relevance are unduly narrow or otherwise strange.
5. Common sense appeals to a shared social stock of knowledge about the common course of events.	(a) Scepticism about common sense;
	(b) scepticism about general cognitive consensus;
	(c) scepticism about general cognitive competence.
6. Inductive reasoning the norm.	(a) Scepticism about the possibility of rationality in (a) any context, (b) adjudication;
	(b) scepticism about induction;
	(c) mathematical (Pascalian) reasoning the only valid kind of reasoning;
	(d) alternative conceptions of 'rationality' (e.g. holistic rather than atomistic; Hegelian rather than Baconian).
7. The pursuit of factual truth (as part of rectitude of decision) commands a high priority (as a means to justice under the law).	(a) Scepticism about all claims to 'truth' (cognitivist epistemology);
	(b) fact and value cannot be separated in normative enquiries (anti-positivism);
	(c) truth is (largely) irrelevant in conflict–resolution;
	(d) the adversary system does not give a high priority to the attainment of truth.
8. Justice under the law.	(a) Ethical relativism or subjectivism;
	(b) other ends should be or are in fact pursued.

These trends in theorizing about fact–finding in law, highlighted by the materials reproduced in this volume, will now be outlined.

Rules v. Reasons in Legal Fact–Finding

Specialized writings on evidence in Anglo-American legal systems have a long tradition, with many treatises expounding the existing evidentiary rules and their judicial interpretations. This tradition can be traced back to Gilbert's *The Law of Evidence* which first appeared posthumously in Dublin in 1754. Since then, specialized treatises on the law of evidence have become a standard source of reference and study. Due to their expository competence, clarity and analytical rigour, some of these works have become influential and survived several editions. The most famous of these works (in chronological order) have been by Peake,[9] Phillipps,[10] Starkie,[11] Greenleaf,[12] Taylor,[13] Best,[14] Stephen,[15] Phipson,[16] Thayer,[17] Wigmore,[18] Chamberlayne,[19] McCormick,[20] Cross[21] and Weinstein.[22]

In the shadow of this vast literature, the attempts to develop a theory of legal reasoning about facts appear to be modest. The most significant of such attempts was that made by Bentham in the nineteenth century.[23] Maintaining that the primary objective of judicial proof is rectitude of decision which leads to correct application of the substantive law, he called for an abolition of all mandatory rules of evidence. According to Bentham, rectitude of decision can be secured only by reason, by considering the concrete circumstances of each case, and never by rules. Bentham endorsed what can be described as a cognitivist empirical epistemology, arguing that mandatory precepts addressed to the will of the trier of fact have to be replaced by flexible guidelines instructing his understanding.[24] Bentham's robust utilitarianism and, at a more specific level, his call for a removal of some proof–related protections given to criminal defendants, have never been accepted universally. They have even been strongly criticized.[25] Despite this, his contribution to the shift from rules to reasons in the theory of judicial fact–finding is most significant. The epistemological foundations of Bentham's theory are discussed in Postema's essay reproduced in the present volume.[26]

Other early attempts associated with the transition from rules to reasons have been made by Burrill,[27] Thayer[28] and Chamberlayne.[29] Chamberlayne's arguments in favour of this transition were normative rather than descriptive and, broadly speaking, similar to those of Bentham. Thayer's theory was expository. He viewed evidentiary rules as a mixed group of disparate exceptions to the principle of free proof. Thayer's view has been helpfully elaborated on by Philip McNamara in an essay reproduced in this volume.[30]

These and other attempts in that direction[31] have been dwarfed by Wigmore's *Principles of Judicial Proof*.[32] Arguing that the science of proof is both anterior to and more important than evidentiary rules, Wigmore made an attempt to develop a systematic framework for legal reasoning about facts. His method, incorporating 'logic, psychology and general experience', was based on a rigorous analysis of all inferential chains linking forensic evidence with its ultimate probanda. Since human beings cannot normally keep all these chains and their underlying generalizations constantly in mind, they all ought to be charted so as to enable the trier of fact

[t]o perform the logical (or psychological) process of conscious juxtaposition of detailed related ideas, for the purpose of producing rationally a single final idea. Hence, to the extent that the mind is unable to juxtapose consciously a larger number of ideas, each coherent group of detailed constituent ideas must be reduced in consciousness to a single idea; until at last the mind can consciously juxtapose them with due attention to each, so as to produce its single final idea.[33]

In contrast to his famous *Treatise*, Wigmore's *Principles* exerted no significant influence on his contemporaries and it is only in recent years that its importance has become recognized.[34] Wigmore's essay 'The Problem of Proof' (reprinted in this volume) was meant to be a preliminary exploration of what later appeared in that work.

We have also included in this volume Wigmore's short but devastating review of Moore's *Treatise on Facts*[35] which purported to derive rules for weighing evidence from reported cases. According to Wigmore, evidentiary weight can never be subject to any rules predetermined by the law; those endeavouring to subject it to such rules, thus limiting the authority of the jury, are 'committing moral treason to our system'.

Other works which exhibit the shift from rules to reasons include those of Gulson,[36] Michael and Adler[37] and Jonathan Cohen.[38] However, none of these authors set out to produce a full–fledged theory of legal fact–finding as ambitious or comprehensive as those developed by Bentham and Wigmore.

As predicted by those two thinkers, rigid evidentiary rules which previously dominated the process of judicial fact–finding are now being steadily abrogated and replaced by more flexible guidelines and standards. The centrality of discretionary choices has become more explicit, and this fact, recognized long ago in general jurisprudence, has added its contribution to the shift from evidentiary rules to principles of proof. More attention is now being paid to the nature of inferential reasoning and the determination of evidentiary weight; admissibility of evidence and other technical matters are becoming less and less important.[39] Ekelöf's essay reprinted in this volume exemplifies this shift, showing *inter alia* that Continental legal systems have in that respect preceded their Anglo-American counterparts.[40]

The 'black–letter–man'[41] could say about weight and evaluation of evidence very little that would go beyond stating that 'this is a matter of common-sense which should normally be decided by the jury'. Nor has he illuminated the discretionary choices that take place when the remaining mandatory precepts run out. This, of course, is not to say that writing about evidentiary rules is futile or uninteresting, or that these rules are unimportant. Although it is a mistake to regard them as central to the process of proof, their significance – especially in criminal trials – must not be underestimated. Applied with varying degrees of rigidity, many of these rules are founded on important probative and extra-probative policies. These policies should be integrated in, rather than segregated from, the study of proof. Writers like McCormick, Cross, Morgan, Maguire[42] and, more recently, Zuckerman[43] are among those who have analysed evidentiary rules from this perspective.[44] Some of these writers can indeed be criticized for exaggerating the role played by these rules in the process of proof, but this should not detract from their actual contribution to the study of that process.

We have therefore included in the present volume, in addition to the legal–philosophical and other interdisciplinary inquiries into the process of proof, a number of essays about evidentiary principles and rules. It was not our objective to include discussions of the specifics of these rules, nor to explore their variants in different jurisdictions. The essays which deal with evidentiary rules have been reproduced primarily with a view to highlighting issues of general importance, such as different auxiliary and extraneous policies pursued by the law of evidence (Graham, Morris and Posner); the meaning of the basic evidentiary concepts (James and Montrose); legal distribution of the risk of error (Thayer);[45] the role of presumptions in legal reasoning as a species of practical reasoning (Ullmann-Margalit),[46] and special measures taken to safeguard criminal defendants which have been the subject of ongoing debates between civil libertarians and supporters of law and order (Cross).[47] These issues are closely related to the more general debate about both form and substance of legal regulation that should apply to judicial and other legal fact-finding. The most important contributions to this debate (Chamberlayne, Davis, Cohen, Weinstein and McNamara) are also included in this volume.[48]

Interdisciplinary Studies of Legal Fact-Finding

Although considerably affected by existing normative constraints and other contextual factors, judicial fact–finding can hardly be claimed to possess a peculiar rationality of its own distinguishable from that employed in non–legal settings. Specialized legal methods applied in ascertaining the validity of disputed propositions of law can certainly not be sufficient in adjudicating between contested factual accounts. At the same time, it is now widely accepted that fact–finding cannot be disposed of by identifying it with 'ordinary common sense', or by skills that can only be acquired through practice and experience which should therefore not be regarded as an appropriate academic subject.

It is therefore not surprising that specialists in different areas of study have increasingly become involved in exploring the possibilities of understanding and improving the methods of legal fact–finding through a variety of extra-legal disciplines. Within this constantly expanding framework, major roles have so far been played by psychologists, forensic scientists, decision theorists, sociologists, statisticians and philosophers of knowledge.[49] One of the most significant advances in the study of fact–finding has been made by empirical psychologists who cast serious doubts on some of the existing assumptions about eyewitness identification, testimony of victims of sexual offences and children's testimony.[50] Forensic scientists[51] have contributed significantly to the study of the ways in which real evidence and its probative value should be analysed. Decision theorists have explored ways of making rational decisions in conditions of uncertainty.[52] Sociologists have explored the ideas of linking the fashion in which forensic information is gathered, processed, moulded into institutional categories and evaluated to existing social attitudes and ideologies. This involves an examination of what passes for 'knowledge' in society, ending in some cases with a rather sceptical view that reality is socially constructed and that different social processes therefore produce different 'realities'.[53]

A great amount of literature has been devoted to questions about the nature of probability and induction to be employed in judicial determinations of fact. Lawyers, statisticians and philosophers have taken part in this important debate[54] which has focused on the following main questions. Should triers of fact employ any of the methods of making decisions under uncertainty on the basis of mathematical calculation of the risk of error (the 'aleatory models')? Should any of such models replace the present framework of decision-making which operates without recourse to mathematics and is largely reliant upon context-specific or 'individualized' forms of inductive support?[55] Can the distinction between 'aleatory' and 'inductivist' types of reasoning be sustained, and if yes, what are the principles which determine whether we endorse one of those types in preference to another?

These questions arise since facts in adjudication are normally determined in terms of probabilities and scarcely, if at all, in terms of absolute certainties. Since risks of error in adjudication are inevitable, why not approach their distribution scientifically by substituting the exactitude of mathematics for untutored intuitions of the triers of fact? Is it not the case that inductivism in judicial fact–finding merely obfuscates the aleatory character of decisions? Far from reaching an agreement on any of these issues, the participants in the probability debate have extended them by setting forth a number of more specific questions over which they disagree. First, what, if any, moral values intrinsic to the judicial process would be violated by applying aleatory models in ascertaining the probability of contested facts? This question is especially pertinent in criminal trials where the presumption of innocence obtains. By assigning positive probability estimates to unknown facts (under the principle of indifference, frequency and propensity theories and the like), aleatory models disregard this presumption and thus posit a tangible threat to civil libertarian values. In civil cases, where risks of error are normally allowed to be distributed equally between the parties, this problem tends to be less acute but does not disappear entirely. The possibility that cases can be won or lost on the ground of 'naked statistics' rather than 'individualized' evidence about actual events implies that a person's rights and duties can be determined merely by his/her association with some class which is held to be statistically significant. This, arguably, tends to undermine the acceptability of judicial verdicts by the public at large. In reply, it has been argued that convictions should require the highest feasible degree of certainty (as in the case of fingerprints, for instance) and that any such certainty is ultimately probabilistic and aleatory. As to the moral values that, allegedly, disallow statistical inferences in adjudication, these values have nothing to do with the veracity of verdicts and are thus ritualistic. Instead of endorsing them uncritically, one should ask whether they are more important than overall rectitude of decisions. In any event, judicial reasoning based on subjective estimates of the probability can, when necessary, account for the fact that the evidence produced by one of the parties was nakedly statistical. Thus, if this party could reasonably be expected to produce evidence that highlights the particularities of the case, non-production of that evidence should decrease the probability of his/her allegations. Given that subjective probabilities obey the ordinary rules of probability calculus, their use in adjudication would maintain a rigorous framework for analysing evidence and at the same time escape the critique of naked statistics.

Second, is it correct that probability calculations propounded by aleatory models – the complementational principle for negation and the multiplicative principle for conjunction – generate, as argued by Jonathan Cohen,[56] legally anomalous outcomes? According to the first principle, on a scale ranging from 0 (an impossibility) to 1 (an absolute certainty), the cumulated probability value of any proposition and its negation must be 1, so that plaintiffs should win their cases even when the allegations of fact brought forward by their opponents have been proved to be true at as high a probability level as 0.49999. Under the second principle, when two or more events need to be proved as co–occurring, the probability of each of them must be multiplied by those of the rest. Hence, even when a plaintiff succeeds in establishing that the probability of each of such events is as high as 0.7, his case as a whole would nevertheless not be regarded as preponderantly true.[57] Arguably, these and other difficulties establish that aleatory models are intrinsically inappropriate for adjudicative purposes.

The adherents of aleatory models have confronted these objections by arguing that their mathematical methods can be adjusted to fit the adjudicative frameworks within which they are to be employed. Furthermore, one of the parties in dispute has always to carry the risk of error. Hence, although to allow for the possibility of a defendant losing his case where it was attested to be as probable as 0.4999 is not desirable, to decide in his favour would be even less attractive. Alternatively, the idea of apportionment of what is at stake has been propounded as a right solution in cases of uncertainty. This idea has become especially influential in those areas where individualized evidence is unavailable or unsuitable, as in the establishment of causation in mass torts[58] as well as in proof of consumers' confusion, brand-name 'genericness' and acquisition of 'secondary meaning' in disputes involving trademarks or passing-off.[59] Statistics about ethnic or gender composition of the workforce have also been shown to be probatively significant in cases of employment discrimination,[60] and the same is true about school-desegregation litigation in the US.[61] In cases where paternity is in dispute, the use of statistical methods has become almost routine.[62] In at least some of those cases, the use of statistical evidence is no longer regarded as controversial. Yet the probability debate has not been resolved, and probably cannot be resolved once and for all, in favour or against the incorporation of statistical methods into judicial fact-finding.

A number of essays reflecting this debate will be reproduced, as part of the present series, in the volume on Legal Reasoning.[63] In our volume, which includes some of the other representative works, Twining's essay should be read as an introduction to the debate. It focuses primarily on Jonathan Cohen's critique of 'misplaced mathematicization', his support of non-mathematical inductivist reasoning and the responses to Cohen's thesis written by Glanville Williams and Sir Richard Eggleston. A recent paper by Eggleston adds to his support of statistical methods and David Kaye's work, focusing on tort causation, approaches these methods and their uses in litigation from an economic perspective. Judith Jarvis Thompson maintains, with some reservations, that there are independent considerations of morality militating against judicial use of 'naked statistical evidence', whilst Adrian Zuckerman opposes statistical methods of fact–finding from an entirely different angle. In his view, fact–finding in law must not be equated with an empirical inquiry into 'What happened?'. It also entails an evaluative transformation of 'bare facts' into legally significant categories of 'constitutive facts' which give rise to various rights, duties and liabilities. Such value–judgements involve 'immeasurable merits' of individual cases and thus can never be verified by any probabilistic method. Hence, the possibility of using statistics in adjudication hinges upon the possibility of distinguishing between empirical gathering of facts and their evaluative categorization. Zuckerman is sceptical about the latter and, consequently, about the former possibility.

Other interdisciplinary studies of judicial proof are represented here by an inquiry into human inferences conducted by decision theorists (Schum and Martin) and by different writings of philosophers of science, morality and practical reasoning (Cohen, Thompson and Ullmann-Margalit). Economic analysis of different evidentiary problems is exemplified by works of Posner and Kaye.[64]

Another theoretical issue antecedent to the probability debate and other aspects of judicial fact–finding is the tension between holistic and atomistic fashions of reasoning. The general assumption that judicial reasoning about facts is a predominantly analytical enterprise has been challenged by writers who have stressed the impact of 'stories',[65] 'the case as a whole',[66] 'coherence'[67] and 'gestalt'[68] on the outcome of decisions. These holistic views draw heavily upon psychology, philosophy and the study of rhetoric. We could not, however, reproduce in this collection any essay that directly reflects these views. This exclusion is a result of space limits and other editorial constraints that have nothing to do with the quality of excluded materials.

Legal Fact–Finding and Moral Theory

Another important trend in contemporary theorizing about evidence is the growing appreciation that the role of morality in judicial (and other legal) fact–finding is greater than had previously been acknowledged. First, it has become recognized that rectitude of decisions is the main, but by no means the overriding, objective of legal proof and procedure. This is so not only due to exceptional cases where probative evidence is excluded because illegally obtained, or where such evidence is not allowed to be unveiled in order to protect privacy, confidentiality or state security. There are also, as has been powerfully argued, certain 'process values' – amongst them fairness, integrity and parties' participation – which should be maintained throughout all fact–finding processes independently of their effect on the accuracy of outcomes. These values emanate from political morality and should, arguably, shape the standards of admitting and examining evidence to which individuals affected by official decisions are to be entitled.[69] Furthermore, judicial verdicts, especially in criminal cases, are not solely resolutions of immediate legal disputes. In addition, they convey, and should convey, more general normative messages to the public at large. For this and other related reasons, general acceptability of these judicial verdicts ought to be sought; this would once again require that various pre-trial and trial procedures of gathering and examining evidence, as well as judicial reasoning about facts, be morally legitimate. The criteria for moral legitimacy of verdicts need therefore to be articulated, and evidence theorists have made numerous attempts in that direction.[70]

Second, judicial determination of disputed facts is typically conducted in conditions of uncertainty and thus involves risks of error. The ways in which such risks are and should be distributed between the litigants are important. Evidence theorists have thus to devise criteria for distributing such risks and to scrutinize the ways in which they are in fact distributed in different civil and criminal trials. Any such criterion is bound to rest on political morality. For example, the requirement that criminal allegations be proved 'beyond reasonable doubt' reflects certain risk-related preferences usually associated with the protection of an innocent individual from wrongful conviction. This protection, however, is granted only where the existing doubts are 'reasonable' – that is, noticeable or perceptible. The law appears to have differentiated between accidental convictions of innocent persons (which have to be tolerated as a matter of necessity) and deliberate impositions of the risk of error on the accused, which should not be allowed. However, the risk of accidentally mistaken conviction could also be reduced if, instead of channelling public funds into education, health, roads and other amenities, these funds were devoted to attaining maximum accuracy in criminal trials. Hence, the extent of the risks of error presently assumed in criminal trials is, after all, a matter of political choice.

This choice, when it emanates from a democratic process of making decisions, is regarded as fair so long as each person taking part in that process is antecedently as likely as any other to benefit from the amenities supported by public resources and accidentally to share the harm generated by the under–funded criminal procedures. Hence, when a risky legal system works to somebody's disadvantage and an innocent person is occasionally found guilty, this regrettable outcome would not undermine the fairness of that system.[71] By contrast, if a person known to be possibly innocent were *deliberately* convicted, this would amount to a fresh political decision which imposed on that person an extra risk not shared by others. Such a decision would violate the principle of equality and fairness. In other words, although the prior determination of the protection given to the defendant is bound to be affected by some utilitarian considerations, his right to be acquitted as a result of any perceptible doubt is a genuine right which overrides utility. Like any other citizen, criminal defendants are entitled to equal concern and respect, and it is the violation of their entitlement to equality that renders any deliberate imposition of the risk of error on any of them morally unjustifiable.[72]

This requirement of equality has many important implications. One of them is the need to re-examine the traditional opinion that the 'presumption of innocence' is a mere restatement of the rule that guilt should be proved beyond reasonable doubt.[73] As has recently been argued, this presumption has to be understood comparatively; it requires that those charged with crimes be given the same amount of protection as all other presumptively innocent persons. This requirement would entail a larger set of rights which derive from the treatment of others.[74] These rights would affect not only the standard of proof practised in criminal trials, but also the ways of gathering evidence, its forensic examination and many other important matters.[75]

Since political morality cannot be neglected in theorizing about fact–finding in law, some of the essays reproduced in this volume deal with specific evidentiary issues from this perspective. They do not, however, provide a comprehensive account of political and moral issues that arise in connection with different fact–finding processes. Some of these issues have been outlined above; that summary, along with its endnotes, must suffice to provide a starting point for a more detailed reading on this subject.

Turning to a different issue, morality might also be relevant for distinguishing between propositions of 'fact' – ones that ought to be proved by evidence – and questions of 'law' or 'value' which do not require any such proof. This distinction becomes difficult in cases where particular facts need to be categorized as falling or not falling within the 'ultimate probanda', the more general sets of 'constitutive facts' which give rise to substantive rights and duties.[76] This volume includes a classic paper by Elizabeth Anscombe which clarifies the meaning of 'brute facts' and Zuckerman's essay which shows that triers of fact, in making their decisions, have to resort and in fact do resort to value-judgements. All these issues remain open to further exploration.

Notes

1. Cf. R.A. Posner (1987), 'The Decline of Law as an Autonomous Discipline: 1962–1987', *Harvard Law Review*, **100**, 761.
2. See W.L. Twining (1990), *Rethinking Evidence*, Oxford, esp. chs. 2 and 6 and pp. 349ff.
3. See R. Lempert (1986), 'The New Evidence Scholarship: Analyzing the Process of Proof', *Boston University Law Review*, **66**, 439.
4. R. Dworkin, 'Principle, Policy, Procedure', in C. Tapper (ed.) (1981), *Crime, Proof and*

Punishment: Essays in Memory of Sir Rupert Cross, London, p. 193ff; later reprinted in R. Dworkin (1986), *A Matter of Principle*, Oxford, ch. 3.

5. Reproduced with permission from Twining, *supra* n. 2, p. 73. For detailed discussion see id., ch. 3.
6. J. Frank (1949), *Courts on Trial*, Princeton.
7. See Twining, *supra* n.2, pp. 109–12.
8. Reproduced with permission from Twining, *supra* n.2, p. 132. For detailed discussion see id., ch. 4.
9. T. Peake (1801), *A Compendium of the Law of Evidence*, London; reprinted in 1979.
10. S.M. Phillipps (1814), *A Treatise on the Law of Evidence*, London; 9th ed., 1843.
11. T. Starkie (1824), *Law of Evidence and Digest of Proofs in Civil and Criminal Proceedings*, London; 4th ed., 1853.
12. S. Greenleaf (1842), *A Treatise on the Law of Evidence*, Boston; 16th ed., 1899.
13. J.P. Taylor (1848), *Treatise on the Law of Evidence*, London; 12th ed., 1931.
14. W.M. Best (1849), *A Treatise on the Principles of the Law of Evidence*, London; 8th ed., 1893.
15. J.F. Stephen (1876), *A Digest of the Law of Evidence*, London; 12th ed., 1948.
16. S.L. Phipson (1892), *The Law of Evidence*, London, 14th ed., 1990.
17. J.B. Thayer (1898), *A Preliminary Treatise on Evidence at Common Law*, Boston; reprinted in 1969.
18. J.H. Wigmore (1904–1905), *A Treatise on the System of Evidence in Trials at Common Law*, Boston; 3rd ed., 1940. This work consists of 10 volumes, some of which were revised by others after Wigmore's death. The latest revision of Volume I was made by Peter Tillers in 1983.
19. C.F. Chamberlayne (1911–16), *A Treatise on the Modern Law of Evidence*, New York.
20. C.T. McCormick (1954), *On Evidence*, St Paul, Minn.; 3rd ed., 1984.
21. R. Cross (1958), *On Evidence*, London; 7th ed., 1990.
22. J.B. Weinstein and M.A. Berger (1975), *Weinstein's Evidence*, New York. This work consists of 7 volumes. Since 1975, it has been continuously updated.
23. See J. Bentham (1827), *Rationale of Judicial Evidence*, London, edited by J.S. Mill; also reproduced in J. Bowring (1838–43), *The Works of Jeremy Bentham*, Volumes VI and VII, Edinburgh. See also J. Bentham (1825), *A Treatise on Judicial Evidence*, London, edited by E. Dumont and translated into English.
24. See W.L. Twining (1985), *Theories of Evidence: Bentham and Wigmore*, ch.2, esp. 60ff, London.
25. See Twining, id., at pp. 100–108.
26. See further G. Postema (1986), *Bentham and the Common Law Tradition*, Oxford. For an earlier exposition of Bentham's views, see Twining, id.
27. A.M. Burrill (1856), *A Treatise on the Nature, Principles and Rules of Circumstantial Evidence, especially of the Presumptive Kind, in Criminal Cases*, New York.
28. *Supra* n.17.
29. See *supra* n.19 and his essay reproduced in this volume.
30. For further discussion see Twining, *supra* n.2, at pp. 188ff.
31. Such as J. Ram (1861), *A Treatise on Facts as Subjects of Enquiry by a Jury*, London.
32. J.H. Wigmore (1913), *The Principles of Judicial Proof as given by Logic, Psychology and General Experience and Illustrated in Judicial Trials*, Boston; 2nd ed., 1931; 3rd ed., 1937, under the revised title of *The Science of Judicial Proof*. Subsequent references will be to the 3rd edition of this book.
33. Ibid, at p. 48.
34. See T. Anderson and W.L. Twining (1991), *Analysis of Evidence*, Boston and London; Twining, *supra* n.24, ch. 3 and pp. 171–86; and P. Tillers and D. Schum (1988), 'Charting New Territory in Judicial Proof: Beyond Wigmore', *Cardozo Law Review*, **9**, 907.
35. C.C. Moore (1908), *A Treatise on Facts: Or the Weight and Value of Evidence*, New York.
36. J.R. Gulson (1905), *Philosophy of Proof*, London; 2nd ed., 1923.
37. J. Michael and M. Adler (1931), *The Nature of Judicial Proof: An Inquiry into the Logical, Legal and Empirical Aspects of the Law of Evidence*, New York, tentative ed; J. Michael and M. Adler (1934), 'The Trial of an Issue of Fact', *Columbia Law Review*, **34**, 1224; J. Michael and M. Adler (1952), 'Real Proof', *Vanderbilt Law Review*, **5**, 344.
38. L.J. Cohen (1977), *The Probable and the Provable*, Oxford.

39. See C. Tapper's preface to R. Cross (1985), *On Evidence*, London, 6th ed., describing the shift in the 'balance of importance of the law of evidence', as a replacement of many technical rules by discretionary principles and guidelines. See also T.M. Mengler (1989), 'The Theory of Discretion in the Federal Rules of Evidence', *Iowa Law Review*, **74**, 413.

40. For a refined version of O. Ekelöf's views, see his essay 'My Thoughts on Evidentiary Value' in P. Gärdenfors et al. (eds) (1983), *Evidentiary Value*, p. 9ff, Lund.

41. O.W. Holmes (1897), 'The Path of the Law', *Harvard Law Review*, **10**, 457, 469.

42. McCormick, *supra* n.20; Cross, *supra* n.21; E.M. Morgan (1956), *Some Problems of Proof under the Anglo-American System of Litigation*, New York; E.M. Morgan (1961), *Basic Problems of Evidence*, New York: Practicing Law Institute, revised ed.; J.M. Maguire (1947), *Evidence: Common Sense and Common Law*, Chicago.

43. A.A.S. Zuckerman (1989), *The Principles of Criminal Evidence*, Oxford.

44. See, for instance, the recent revival of the 'best evidence' principle by D.A. Nance (1988), 'The Best Evidence Principle', *Iowa Law Review*, **73**, 227 and the discussion of the hearsay rule by M. Kadish and M. Davis (1989), 'Defending the Hearsay Rule', *Law & Philosophy*, **8**, 333.

45. See also an illuminating account by J. McBaine (1944), 'Burden of Proof: Degrees of Belief', *California Law Review*, **32**, 242.

46. See also E. Morgan (1937), 'Presumptions', *Washington Law Review*, **12**, 255.

47. For civil libertarian arguments see A. Ashworth (1977), 'Excluding Evidence as Protecting Rights', *Criminal Law Review*, 723; K. Greenawalt (1981), 'Silence as a Moral and Constitutional Right', *William and Mary Law Review*, **23**, 15; W.J. Stuntz (1988), 'Self–Incrimination and Excuse', *Columbia Law Review*, **88**, 1227.

48. Some additional material on legal reasoning about facts will be reproduced, as part of the present series, in the volumes on *Legal Reasoning* edited by A. Aarnio and D.N. MacCormick.

49. The existing sources are too vast to be listed, let alone discussed, in this Introduction. Some of them have been discussed in Twining, *supra* n.2, *passim*. The main paths of academic enquiry are enumerated at p. 350 of that book. For a list of references see id., at pp. 373ff.

50. See, for instance, K.A. Deffenbacher and E.F. Loftus (1982), 'Do Jurors Share a Common Understanding Concerning Eyewitness Behavior?', *Law & Human Behavior*, **6**, 15; S.M. Lloyd-Bostock and B. Clifford (eds) (1983), *Evaluating Witness Evidence*, Chichester. Such studies have greatly benefited legal writers in exploring the possibilities of reforming some of the evidentiary rules. For a recent example, see D.J. Birch (1990), 'Corroboration in Criminal Trials: A Review of the Proposals of the Law Commission's Working Paper', *Criminal Law Review*, 667, 675–82 (examining the rationality of 'corroboration warning' in rape and sexual assault cases). For a useful overview see S.M. Lloyd-Bostock (1988), *Law in Practice*, London. See also G. Gudjonnsen and J. Drinkwater (eds) (1987), *Psychological Evidence in Court*, Leicester.

51. See, generally, A.A. Moenssens, F.E. Inbau and J.E. Starrs (1986), *Scientific Evidence in Criminal Trials*, New York, 3rd ed., and various publications in *Journal of Forensic Science* issued by the American Academy of Forensic Sciences.

52. A helpful introduction to decision theory can be found in M.D. Resnick (1987), *Choices*, Minneapolis: University of Minnesota Press. For its possible contribution to judicial fact–finding, see J. Kaplan (1968), 'Decision Theory and the Fact–Finding Process', *Stanford Law Review*, **20**, 1065.

53. P. Berger and T. Luckmann (1967), *Social Construction of Reality*, London. These writers have, however, abstained from making claims in favour of strong relativism. D. McBarnett's (1981) study, *Conviction*, London, seems to involve some relativist motifs. See also M. King and C. Piper (1990), *How the Law Thinks about Children*, Aldershot: Gower.

54. Significant publications, besides those reproduced in the present volume, are: H.M. Hart and J.T. McNaughton, 'Evidence and Inference in the Law', in D. Lerner et al. (eds) (1959), *Evidence and Inference*, 48; Free Press, New York; V. Ball (1961), 'The Moment of Truth: Probability Theory and Standards of Proof', *Vanderbilt Law Review*, **14**, 807; Kaplan, *supra* n.52; A. Cullison (1969), 'Probability Analysis of Judicial Fact–Finding: A Preliminary Outline of Subjective Approach', *University of Toledo Law Review*, **1**, 538; L. Tribe (1971), 'Trial by Mathematics: Precision and Ritual in the Legal Process', *Harvard Law Review*, **84**, 1329; R. Lempert (1977),

'Modelling Relevance', *Michigan Law Review*, **75**, 1021; Cohen, *supra* n.38; M. Finkelstein (1978), *Quantitative Methods in Law*, New York; L. Brilmayer and L. Kornhauser (1978), 'Quantitative Methods and Legal Decisions', *University of Chicago Law Review*, **46**, 116; D. Kaye (1979), 'The Laws of Probability and the Law of the Land', *University of Chicago Law Review*, **47**, 34; D. Schum (1979), 'A Review of a Case Against Blaise Pascal and His Heirs', *Michigan Law Review*, **77**, 446; C. Wagner (1979), Book Review, *Duke Law Journal*, 1071; D. Kaye (1979), 'The Paradox of the Gatecrasher and Other Stories', *Arizona State University Law Journal*, 101; G. Williams (1979), 'The Mathematics of Proof', *Criminal Law Review*, 297, 340; L.J. Cohen (1980), 'The Logic of Proof', *Criminal Law Review*, 91; G. Williams (1980), 'A Short Rejoinder', *Criminal Law Review*, 103; R. Eggleston (1980), 'The Probability Debate', *Criminal Law Review*, 678; D. Kaye (1980), 'Naked Statistical Evidence', *Yale Law Journal*, **89**, 601; L.J. Cohen (1981), 'Subjective Probability and the Paradox of the Gatecrasher', *Arizona State University Law Journal*, 627; D. Kaye (1981), 'Paradoxes, Gedanken Experiments and the Burden of Proof: A Response to Dr. Cohen's Reply', *Arizona State University Law Journal*, 635; J. Brook (1982), 'Inevitable Errors: The Preponderance of the Evidence Standard in Civil Litigation', *Tulsa Law Journal*, **18**, 79; N. Orloff and J. Stedinger (1983), 'A Framework for Evaluating the Preponderance of Evidence Standard', *University of Pennsylvania Law Review*, **131**, 1159; R. Eggleston (1983), *Evidence, Proof and Probability*, London, 2nd ed.; P. Tillers, 'Modern Theories of Relevancy', in J.H. Wigmore (1983), *On Evidence*, Vol. 1A, par.37.6 Boston, Mass.: Little, Brown & Co.; C. Nesson (1985), 'The Evidence or the Event? On Judicial Proof and the Acceptability of Verdicts', *Harvard Law Review*, **98**, 1357; L. Jaffe (1985), 'On Probativity and Probability: Statistics, Scientific Evidence, and the Calculus of Chance at Trial', *University of Pittsburgh Law Review*, **46**, 925; N. Cohen (1985), 'Confidence in Probability: Burdens of Persuasion in a World of Imperfect Knowledge', *New York University Law Review*, **60**, 385; Symposium (1986): 'Probability and Inference in the Law of Evidence', *Boston University Law Review*, **66**, Nos. 3 & 4, partly reprinted in P. Tillers and E. Green (eds) (1988), *Probability and Inference in the Law of Evidence: The Uses and Limits of Bayesianism*, Dordrecht; D. Kaye (1987), 'Apples and Oranges: Confidence Coefficients and the Burden of Persuasion', *Cornell Law Review*, **73**, 54; T. Connolly (1987), 'Decision Theory, Reasonable Doubt, and the Utility of Erroneous Acquittals', *Law & Human Behavior*, **11**, 101; F. Schoeman (1987), 'Cohen on Inductive Probability and the Law of Evidence', *Philosophy of Science*, **54**, 76; L.J. Cohen (1987), 'On Analyzing the Standards of Forensic Evidence: A Reply to Schoeman', *Philosophy of Science*, **54**, 92; L. Jaffe (1988), 'Prior Probability – A Black Hole in the Mathematician's View of the Sufficiency and Weight of Evidence', *Cardozo Law Review*, **9**, 967; D. Shaviro (1989), 'Statistical Probability Evidence and the Appearance of Justice', *Harvard Law Review*, **103**, 530; J. Koehler and D. Shaviro (1990), 'Veridical Verdicts: Increasing Verdict Accuracy through the Use of Probabilistic Evidence and Methods', *Cornell Law Review*, **75**, 247; B. Robertson and G.A. Vignaux (1991), 'Inferring Beyond Reasonable Doubt', *Oxford Journal of Legal Studies*, **11**, 431; C.R. Callen (1991), 'Adjudication and the Appearance of Statistical Evidence', *Tulane Law Review*, **65**, 457.

55. For illuminating account of the philosophical foundations of these two ways of reasoning see L.J. Cohen (1989), *An Introduction to the Philosophy of Induction and Probability*, Oxford. See also F. Schoeman (1987), 'Statistical vs. Direct Evidence', *NOUS*, **21**, 179.

56. Cohen, *supra* n.38, part two.

57. This problem would also arise when the events in question are not independent of one another as we have assumed them to be.

58. See G. Robinson (1982), 'Multiple Causation in Tort Law: Reflections on the DES Cases', *Virginia Law Review*, **68**, 713; R. Delgado (1982), 'Beyond Sindell: Relaxation of Cause–In–Fact Rules for Indeterminate Plaintiffs', *California Law Review*, **70**, 881; D. Rosenberg (1984), 'The Causal Connection in Mass Exposure Cases: A "Public Law" Vision of the Tort System', *Harvard Law Review*, **97**, 851; C. Nesson (1986), 'Agent Orange Meets the Blue Bus: Factfinding at the Frontier of Knowledge', *Boston University Law Review*, **66**, 521; R. Allen (1986), 'Rationality, Mythology, and the "Acceptability of Verdicts" Thesis', *Boston University Law Review*, **66**, 541; N. Cohen (1986), 'The Costs of Acceptability: Blue Buses, Agent Orange and Aversion to Statistical Evidence', *Boston University Law Review*, **66**, 563; S. Gold (1986–87), 'Causation in Toxic

Torts: Burdens of Proof, Standards of Persuasion and Statistical Evidence', *Yale Law Journal*, **96**, 376; J. Johnston (1987), 'Bayesian Fact–Finding and Efficiency: Toward an Economic Theory of Liability Under Uncertainty', *Southern California Law Review*, **61**, 137; T. Brennan (1988), 'Causal Chains and Statistical Links: The Role of Scientific Uncertainty in Hazardous–Substance Litigation', *Cornell Law Review*, **73**, 469; J.G. Fleming (1988), 'Mass Torts', *Denning Law Journal*, 37; C. Cranor and K. Nutting (1990), 'Scientific and Legal Standards of Statistical Evidence in Toxic Tort and Discrimination Suits', *Law & Philosophy*, **9**, 115.

59. See, for instance, R.C. Sorensen (1983), 'Survey Research Execution in Trademark Litigation: Does Practice make Perfection?', *Trademark Reporter*, **73**, 349; R.B. Boal (1983), 'Techniques for Ascertaining Likelihood of Confusion and the Meaning of Advertising Communications', *Trademark Reporter*, **73**, 405; J.P. Lipton (1988), 'A New Look at the Use of Social Science Evidence in Trademark Litigation', *Trademark Reporter*, **78**, 32; P. Weiss (1990), 'The Use of Survey Evidence in Trademark Litigation: Science, Art or Confidence Game?', *Trademark Reporter*, **80**, 71. For recent developments in England, see P.G.M. Pattison (1990), 'Market Research Surveys – Money Well Spent? The Use of Survey Evidence in Passing Off Proceedings in the UK', *European Intellectual Property Review*, **3**, 99.

60. See Finkelstein, *supra* n.54; R.M. Cohn (1980), 'On the Use of Statistics in Employment Discrimination Cases', *Indiana Law Journal*, **55**, 493; R. Belton (1981), 'Burdens of Pleading and Proof in Discrimination Cases: Toward a Theory of Procedural Justice', *Vanderbilt Law Review*, **34**, 1205; S. Willborn (1986), 'Proof of Discrimination in the United Kingdom and the United States', *Civil Justice Quarterly*, **5**, 321; J. Gardner (1989), 'Racial Discrimination and Statistics', *Law Quarterly Review*, **105**, 183; Cranor and Nutting, *supra* n.58.

61. Note (1986), 'Allocating the Burden of Proof After a Finding of Unitariness in School Desegregation Litigation', *Harvard Law Review*, **100**, 653.

62. For discussion that favours this approach see I. Ellman and D. Kaye (1979), 'Probability and Proof: Can HLA and Blood-Group Testing Prove Paternity?', *New York University Law Review*, **54**, 1131.

63. See Aarnio and MacCormick, *supra* n.48, reproducing Williams (1979), Cohen (1980), and Eggleston (1980), *supra* n.54.

64. Space constraints have prevented us from reproducing in this volume P. Gianelly (1980), 'The Admissibility of Novel Scientific Evidence. Frye v. United States: A Half-Century Later', *Columbia Law Review*, **80**, 1197; and J. Monahan and L. Walker (1986), 'Social Authority: Obtaining, Evaluating and Establishing Social Science in Law', *University of Pennsylvania Law Review*, **134**, 477. These articles helpfully discuss the role of expert knowledge and social science methods in judicial determinations of fact.

65. Twining, *supra* n.2, ch. 7. See also B.S. Jackson (1988), *Law, Fact and Narrative Coherence*, Roby, Merseyside, ch. 1.

66. See W.L. Bennett and M.S. Feldman (1981), *Reconstructing Reality in the Courtroom*, London and New York, and its discussion by E. Loftus and E. Green (1983), Book Review, *Journal of Criminal Law & Criminology*, **74**, 315. See also R. Hastie and N. Pennington (1983), *Inside the Jury*, Cambridge, Mass.; Tillers, *supra* n.54; and M. Abu-Hareira (1986), 'An Early Holistic Conception of Judicial Fact-Finding', *Juridical Review*, 79.

67. D.N. MacCormick (1978), *Legal Reasoning and Legal Theory*, Oxford, 86ff; D.N. MacCormick (1980), 'The Coherence of a Case and the Reasonableness of Doubt', *Liverpool Law Review*, **2**, 45; D.N. MacCormick (1984), 'Coherence in Legal Justification', in W. Krawietz et al. (eds), *Theorie der Normen*, Berlin, 37.

68. Frank, *supra* n.6, ch. 12.

69. For discussion see R.S. Summers (1974), 'Evaluating and Improving Legal Process – A Plea for "Process Values"', *Cornell Law Review*, **60**, 1, and M.D. Bayles (1987), *Principles of Law*, Dordrecht, ch. 2. See also M.D. Bayles (1986), 'Principles for Legal Procedure', *Law & Philosophy*, **5**, 33, where these and related ideas are discussed in a more concise fashion. Summers (1974) and Bayles (1986) will be reproduced, as part of the present series, in the volume on Legal Procedure edited by D.J. Galligan.

70. See Nesson, *supra* n.54 and I.H. Dennis (1989), 'Reconstructing the Law of Criminal Evidence',

Current Legal Problems, **42**, 21. See also A.A.S. Zuckerman (1987), 'Illegally Obtained Evidence – Discretion as a Guardian of Legitimacy', *Current Legal Problems*, **40**, 55.

71. Dworkin (1986), *supra* n.4, at pp. 84–87.
72. id.
73. See, for instance, Cross (1990), *supra* n.21, at p. 125.
74. See, for instance, A. Stein (1991), 'Criminal Defences and the Burden of Proof', *Coexistence*, **28**, 133.
75. See Twining, *supra* n.2, at pp. 207–208.
76. W.N. Hohfeld (1923), *Fundamental Legal Conceptions as Applied in Judicial Reasoning*, New-Haven: Yale U.P., 34. See also J.B. Thayer (1890–91), '"Law" and "Fact" in Jury Trials', *Harvard Law Review*, **4**, 147; N. Isaacs (1922), 'The Law and the Facts', *Columbia Law Review*, **22**, 1; W.W. Cook (1936), '"Facts" and "Statements of Fact"', *University of Chicago Law Review*, **4**, 233; C. Morris (1942), 'Law and Fact', *Harvard Law Review*, **55**, 1303; W.A. Wilson (1963), 'A Note on Fact and Law', *Modern Law Review*, **26**, 609; W.A. Wilson (1969), 'Questions of Degree', *Modern Law Review*, **32**, 361; E. Mureinik (1982), 'The Application of Rules: Law or Fact?', *Law Quarterly Review*, **98**, 587; K.L. Scheppele (1990), 'Facing Facts in Legal Interpretation', *Representations*, (The Regents of the University of California), **30**, 42; H.T. Klami, et al. (1991), 'Evidence and Legal Reasoning: On the Intertwinement of the Probable and the Reasonable', *Law and Philosophy*, **10**, 73.

Part I
General

[1]

FREEDOM OF PROOF

L. JONATHAN COHEN (THE QUEENS COLLEGE, OXFORD UNIVERSITY)

Proof of fact is inherently free, yet is everywhere (within the common law systems) in chains. The validity of a proof — its provision of adequate reasons for believing a particular conclusion — can neither be made nor unmade by the wishful thinking of lawyers or legislators. Yet courtroom argument about matters of fact is subject to a vast mass of adjective law regulating admissibility of evidence, requirements of corroboration, authentication of documents, permissive inferences, legal presumptions, judicial notice, burden of proof, and so on. How this came about has been much studied.[1] But its legitimacy — that is, the ethical standing of the present situation — has not been often discussed in recent years. It will be my topic to-day.

Within the Anglo-American context no argument for total freedom of proof could appear other than hopelessly utopian: so large are the textbooks on the law of evidence. But one possible position is that there is an ethico-political presumption in favour of freedom and that, as Bentham held,[2] each departure from this ideal has to be separately justified. On the other side it would be equally unrealistic under modern conditions to argue in favour of total regulation, because of the indefinitely large variety of evidential items and complexes of items that, in accordance with contemporary knowledge, might constitute acceptable proof or disproof of a particular kind of fact at issue. But again an argument in favour of a mere presumption would escape the taint of impracticability that discredits the more sweeping thesis. Perhaps there is just a general ethico-political presumption in favour of regulation, though various areas or levels of freedom may be separately justified.

The battle worth taking seriously lies therefore between champions of the one presumption and champions of the other. My own aim is to evaluate the relative strengths of the arguments on either side, and in particular to defend the ethico-political presumption in favour of freedom against a powerful new line of reasoning which threatens to undermine its foundations. But the relevance of this new argument can only be appreciated properly if older arguments have first been duly reviewed.

---

1 Most recently and iconoclastically by J.H. Langbein, 'The criminal trial before the lawyers', *University of Chicago Law Review* 1978, 45, pp. 263–316.

2 *Rationale of Judicial Evidence*, London: Hunt and Clarke, 1827, vol. V, p. 1 (bk. ix, pt. III, ch. i).

2   L. Jonathan Cohen

I

An initial line of argument in favour of regulating proof, wherever possible, runs like this. At the heart of the idea of justice, it can be argued, lies the principle that like cases should be treated alike. Justice substitutes the rule of law for the play of despotic caprice. And this should presumably apply to adjective, as much as to substantive, issues. If the purpose of a legal system ought to be to constitute an institutionalisation of justice, then the system ought to institutionalise the principle of *similia similibus* in all aspects of its operation. Any arbitrariness or freedom in adjectival law, which leaves a certain kind of issue to the unpredictable discretion of an unregulated trier of fact, would seem to be intrinsically as unjust as permitting different interpretations of substantive law to be applied to different people when their circumstances are alike in all relevant respects. Ideally, therefore, all the rules by which disputes are settled ought to be administered as rules of law, because triers of fact are more likely to behave uniformly and predictably when legally compelled to do so than when left to their own intellectual devices. It is hardly to be doubted that accidents of prejudice, mood, forgetfulness, inattention or stupidity will more often corrupt the rationality of legally unconstrained and unappealable decisions than of legally constrained and appealable ones.

A second argument in the same direction rests on the claim that another consideration supporting the embodiment of certain kinds of rules in substantive law has a corresponding implication for adjective law. Disputes and accusations, it may be argued, must be judged under rules that are not only uniformly administered but also publicly accessible. People ought to be able to discover in advance where they stand as regards possible adjudication in their affairs. Accordingly, just as this requirement of accessibility supports the embodiment of such rules in what is called substantive law, as determined by codes, statutes or precedents and formulated in appropriate text-books, so too all the rules applied by the courts in determining issues of fact should be equally accessible in adjective law. Of course, it might be objected that any pattern of valid reasoning employable by triers of fact will be familiar also to ordinary laymen. But this assumption of a universal cognitive competence, as we shall see later, is currently under serious challenge.

Each of these two arguments that support a presumption in favour of regulating proof owes its force to an assumption that some considerations affecting substantive law — uniformity and accessibility, respectively — should have an analogous bearing on adjective law. But there are also two arguments in the other direction which owe their force to the fact that certain considerations affect adjective law differently from substantive law.

It is a matter for political controversy how far Lockean rights to personal freedom can justify opposition to legislation that is designed to promote policies for social welfare, national security, environmental preservation, cultural enrichment, administrative economy and so on. But when such legislation affects forensic proof an additional opposing consideration must inevitably come into play – a consideration that rarely has any relevance when legislation affects substantive issues. Accuracy is at risk. A risk of inaccuracy in certain trial outcomes has to be traded off against whatever advantages are to be derived from the public policy that is operative. For example, a litigant's case may hinge crucially upon the evidence of a document belonging to some class of which disclosure is held to be against the public interest.[3] Or, if the law of evidence authorises a presumption that a child born in wedlock was fathered by the husband, it may be doing so in order to promote the institutions of marriage and the nuclear family. Or, if possession of marijuana or heroin is made to ground a permissive inference of knowledge that the drug has been illegally imported, it may be possible thereby to establish federal jurisdiction over all such cases.[4] And, obviously, innumerable other ways also exist in which the legal regulation of proof can be made to serve the ends of social expediency rather than those of adjudicative accuracy. So to prefer freedom of proof wherever possible is a way to protect the truthfulness of justice against the inroads of social expediency. The onus of justification should therefore fall on those who wish to restrict freedom of proof rather than on those who wish to defend it. Nor will it do for jurists or philosophers to take the rights and wrongs of any particular trade-off between accuracy and expediency to be a matter for majoritarian decision, as Dworkin suggests,[5] within a general framework of fairness and equality. The task of jurisprudence and philosophy here is to insist on an adequate evaluation of the arguments that might persuade such a majority, not to abdicate from rational criticism in favour of voters who are conceived of as having no ear for argument.

Another consideration that tends to affect adjective law differently from substantive law is the question of retrospective application. If a commercial or industrial practice, say, is made unlawful which many people find unobjectionable, or a practice which many people find objectionable is made lawful. the disagreement may well be put down to a difference of interests or values. This is the stuff of which political controversy is made, and, however serious it may be in a particular case, the possibility of such disagreement is a generally accept-

---

3 Cf. A.A.S. Zuckerman, 'Private and Public Interest' in Tony Honoré et al.. *Crime. Proof and Punishment: Essays in Memory of Sir Rupert Cross*, London: Butterworth, 1981, pp. 248–295.

4 Cf. C.R. Nesson, 'Reasonable Doubt and Permissive Inference: the Value of Complexity', *Harvard L.R.* 92, 1979, pp. 1187–1225.

5 Ronald Dworkin, 'Principle, policy, procedure', in Tony Honoré et al., *Crime, Proof and Punishment: Essays in Memory of Sir Rupert Cross*, London: Butterworth. 1981, pp. 193–225.

4   L. Jonathan Cohen

able hazard of citizenship in a modern state. In a democracy minorities have to learn to tolerate majorities: at least the change in substantive law will not normally be made retrospective. But disagreement about the norms of proof tends to generate a much deeper sense of injustice. This is because of the common belief in a universal cognitive competence whereby, given a proper presentation of all the relevant evidence about any particular factual issue, either every normal and unbiased person would come to the same conclusion about it or at worst everyone would agree that it was an issue about which the norms of proof are indeterminate and reasonable people might venture different conclusions. That belief supports the view that, if well-informed people continue to express serious disagreement about any norms of proof, someone is being unreasonable or dishonest. So the breathalyser or speed-detecting radar that is found to give a demonstrably incorrect reading has to be discarded and convictions already secured by it have to be reversed. Indeed many had moral qualms about the limitation to prospective effect that administrative convenience seemed to require when confessions secured prior to arraignment were ruled inadmissible by the U.S. Supreme Court in *McNabb*.[6] How many unjustly convicted men remained in prison then? Correspondingly, if a comprehensive law of proof existed, there would probably be great moral pressure to make most amendments of it operate retrospectively as well as prospectively. And the likelihood of this moral pressure is not only an important feature of negative analogy with substantive law, where retrospectiveness is rarely thought desirable. It would also often be at odds with what is administratively practicable and would accordingly generate a continuous risk of social conflict. Under the ideal of free proof, however, no question about retrospective or prospective implications arises. So far as the ideal is operative, each particular factual issue is decided on its own merits and no general rules are promulgated by a legislature or extracted from precedents. The ideal of free proof thus creates no special problem about administrative practicability or risk of social conflict. Correspondingly the desire to avoid such problems wherever possible supports accepting an ethico-political presumption in favour of free proof.

The matter is therefore rather evenly balanced if we just weigh these arguments about accuracy and retrospectiveness against those considerations of uniformity and publicity that tend in the opposite direction. As often happens with philosophical arguments that revolve around an alleged analogy, the relevant parallelism between substantive and adjective law is not decisive. The parallelism is neither sufficiently strong to establish an ethico-political presumption against free proof, nor sufficiently weak to determine one in favour of it.

There is another argument, however, that might be more conclusive. Only by producing generally acceptable verdicts on facts at issue can a legal system

6 318 U.S. 332 (1943).

ensure that in the long term it will continue to retain the respect of the informed public. Only thus will it even survive. What is crucial here is not so much
actual accuracy of trial outcomes, but rather the extent to which people believe
in this accuracy, especially in criminal cases. Moreover only by using broadly the
same fact-finding procedures as those that the informed public respects can a
legal system ensure that it will produce generally acceptable verdicts. In different
cultures, of course, different kinds of fact-finding procedure will be appropriate
in accordance with prevalent ideas about the normal sources of knowledge. But
we have to deal with our own culture. Now our culture is certainly one in which
very many people assume that, given a proper presentation of all the available
evidential data about a particular factual issue, either every normal and unbiased
person will come to the same conclusion or they will agree to the reasonableness
of suspending definite judgment because insufficient evidence is available. In
such a culture the only way to ensure that generally acceptable verdicts will be
given is correspondingly to allow as much freedom as possible for the operation
of human reasonableness, unfettered by legal constraints. Indeed the desired
result, in terms of confidence in the system, is probably best secured by allowing some substantial role in juridical fact-finding to laymen, whether as jurors,
assessors or magistrates. The employment of laymen for this task guarantees
that no extensive legal expertise is relevant, and hence that verdicts are reached
very largely by everyday processes of reasoning. In sum, without any lay participation in its administration,[7] or without at least the likelihood of lay approval
for most of its findings of fact, a modern legal system risks becoming dangerous-
ly alienated from the community to which it belongs; and so, to prevent such
alienation, proofs of fact have to be kept as free as possible from legal technicalities.

This argument turns on the bearing that popular epistemology is claimed to
have upon the acceptability of fact-finding procedures in the courts. But how
well established in that claim? If we look briefly at the changing structure of
the relationship between popular epistemology and juridical fact-finding over
the past thousand years of European history, we shall find not only that it has
not always supported a presumption in favour of free proof in the past: it is
also in danger of being transformed into a threat to that presumption in the
present. Let us see how this comes about.

---

7 There are no doubt also other reasons for lay participation. One is the need for a safety-
valve when some feature of the criminal law is grossly out of touch with public opinion:
in such a case the publicly accepted virtue of the jury lies in its readiness to bring in a
verdict that is patently contrary to the facts, rather than a verdict that most people
would regard as being in accordance with the facts.

6   L. Jonathan Cohen

II

The old Germanic system of proof by ordeal was not only totally constrained in regard to the estimation of probative value. It also, in effect, left God to produce all the evidence. Admittedly ordeal by combat, by water or by fire was often thought of as assigning jurisdiction to the Deity and substituting Divine justice for human. The outcome of an ordeal was called a 'Judgment of God'.[8] But, if God is omniscient, He knows already whether an accused is guilty or innocent without any need for a trial. God does not need to interrogate witnesses, extract confessions, evaluate circumstantial evidence or inspect the outcome of an ordeal. So the proof involved here is not a proof which persuades the Deity, acting in a judicial role, but a proof which the Deity provides, through the result of the ordeal, in order to persuade human judges. If the accused is not swallowed up by the water, that is a sign which proves his guilt.[9] Trial by ordeal is a human trial, not a Divine one. And the system was open to the objection that, so far as it sought not just to settle a dispute but to settle it in accordance with the truth, either it assumed God to be permanently at Man's disposal, as a compellable witness, or, if God's omniscience was not exploitable by the ordeal, the result of the ordeal failed to constitute evidence that could be thought relevant in any way to the administration of justice.

Public confidence in the just outcome of a trial was therefore very much at risk wherever proof by ordeal was still employed after the old Teutonic religion had disappeared. That religion had been consistent with the conception of divinity inherent in the ordeal procedure, but the procedure did not sit so easily in the context of Judaeo-Christian theology. In fact after the Fourth Lateran Council abolished trial by ordeal (in 1215) its replacement by Roman-canon procedure had the effect of secularising proof except so far as witnesses' oaths were concerned. The production of evidence was now a task for man, not God, and, even though estimation of the evidence's probative value was almost as strictly regulated as before, adherents of the received theology could now have better grounds for confidence in the administration of justice.

Indeed, the developed Roman-canon procedure, which came to prevail in most of Continental Europe, was very much in accordance with the popular epistemology of the later Middle Ages and Renaissance. For serious criminal offences a court could convict only on the testimony of two eyewitnesses or on the accused's own confession. It could not convict on the basis of circumstantial evidence, however strong. But strong circumstantial evidence, or the testimony of one eyewitness, constituted a half-proof that legitimated the use of torture (except against doctors of law and certain other privileged categories)

---

8 C. Beccaria, *An Essay on Crimes and Punishments*, London: F. Newbery, 1770, p. 62.
9 H. Goitein, *Primitive Ordeal and Modern Law*, London: Allen & Unwin, 1923, p. 55 ff.

Freedom of Proof 7

in order to extract a confession. Moreover, though the widely accepted *Constitutio Criminalis Carolina*[10] admits (article 24) that it is not possible to codify all the kinds of circumstance that raise suspicion, and hence contribute to a half-proof, it lists a substantial number of them, such as having a motive, running away from the scene of the crime, holding a bloody weapon, possessing stolen goods, and so on. At the same time, in the interest of the accused, it stipulates that two witnesses, who must be of good repute, are needed to prove each such ground for suspicion, and it requires the judge or examiners to attend to whether a witness is shifty or inconsistent in his testimony, and so on. So except for novel kinds of circumstantial evidence that are unspecified in the code tribunals are given no freedom at all in the estimation of probative value. Premises are made indisputable, and conclusions follow unavoidably.

These provisions fitted well into the context of contemporary ideas regarding the normal sources of scientific knowledge. What were those ideas? Since science was not normally thought of as a continuing enquiry but as a completed (even if partially forgotten) system,[11] every important fact had to be regarded as having been at some time accessible somewhere within the corpus of scientific writing. So whatever the theories of philosophers about the ultimate foundations of knowledge, the standard popular assumption was that knowledge about facts worth learning rested on authority — if not on the authority of the Church, or of the Early Fathers or of the scholastic writers, then at least on that of the Bible, on that of some hermetic tradition[12] or on that of the great writers of classical antiquity. To defend a claim to serious knowledge, whether about historical facts or about physical processes, people could normally appeal to the certainties available in the relevant books. They did not need to appeal to the relatively uncertain inferences that they might think capable of being drawn from the data of direct investigation. It was as if the title of authoritative writers to be believed mirrored the title of feudal overlords to the absolute loyalty of their lieges. To pursue one's own independent scientific enquiries (as a few outstanding figures, like Roger Bacon or Dietrich of Freiburg,[13] nevertheless managed to do) was as discordant with predominant cultural trends as to promote one's own political purposes. And in the judicial sphere a system of

10 A translation of relevant articles is given in J.H. Langbein, *Prosecuting Crime in the Renaissance England, Germany, France*, Cambridge, Mass.: Harvard U.P., 1974, p. 259 ff.

11 This was one of the assumptions that Francis Bacon felt he had to overturn: see, e.g. his *Cogitata et visa de interpretatione naturae, sive de inventione rerum et operum*, in *The Works of Francis Bacon*, ed. B. Montague, London: W. Pickering, 1828, vol. x, p 495.

12 Cf. Frances A. Yates, *Giordano Bruno and the Hermetic Tradition*, London: Routledge and Kegan Paul, 1964. But see also C. Trinkaus, *In Our Image and Likeness*, London: Constable, 1970, pp. 498–503.

13 Cf. A.C. Crombie, *Robert Grosseteste and the Origins of Experimental Science*, Oxford: Clarendon Press, 1953.

8   L. Jonathan Cohen

closely regulated proof was a natural corollary. Individual Continental judges
were not in a position to draw their own inferences from the facts: rather they
had to adopt those and only those inferences that the legal system authorised.
Moreover within that system the primary source of knowledge was the authority
of those who could be attributed some special claim to be directly aware of the
relevant facts — either eyewitnesses or the agent himself.

Even the English jury, in its earlier mode of functioning, was not wholly
out of keeping with this popular epistemology. The self-informing jury could be
regarded as a natural authority on the facts which the court needed to know.
Consulting such a jury obviated any need for the court to pursue its own independent enquiries. But, just as the feudal structure weakened earlier in England
than on the Continent, so too the English legal system came earlier to reflect a
conception of factual knowledge as something that each individual is capable of
achieving for himself rather than as something that has to be accepted on the
authority of a person or institution. First, the jury of trial was separated from
the jury of indictment (1352), with the result that the task of fact-finding was
spread more widely.[14] And then, from the sixteenth century onwards, after
justices of the peace and others began to launch prosecutions, juries gradually
ceased to be self-informing. Fortescue had said,[15] around 1460, that the jurors
themselves were the main witnesses: now separate witnesses began to appear
more and more, first for the Crown, later — at least on charges of felony — for
the defence. What seems to be happening is that the process of proof, instead of
remaining private to the jury, is being made public and discussable. Instead of
its just having to be assumed, on the authority of the jury, that there are evidential facts which suffice, or fail to suffice, for a verdict of guilt, the relevant
evidential facts are now available in open court so that any individual can assess
their probative value for himself. Confidence in the administration of justice can
thus be sustained against a contemporary background both of growing doubts
about the validity of dogmatic claims to authoritative certainty and of increasing
tolerance for individual judgment whether in religious, political or scientific
matters. Finally, in the seventeenth century, a direct and explicit *rapprochement*
was achieved between the prevailing epistemology and the jurisprudence of
proof. A leading judge, Sir Matthew Hale (for whose views on the subject Black-
stone later had great respect), came to agree with the prevailing opinions of
philosophers and scientists, like Locke and Boyle, that in investigating issues of
fact demonstrative or infallible knowledge was not to be insisted upon.[16] The

14 For a historical critique of this evolution cf. Glanville Williams, *The Proof of Guilt, A
   Study of the English Criminal Trial,* London: Stevens 2nd ed. 1958.
15 Quoted in J.B. Thayer, *A Preliminary Treatise on Evidence at the Common Law,* Boston: Little, Brown, 1898, p. 130 ff.
16 B.J. Shapiro, 'Sir M. Hale and the "Method of Invention" ', 34 *Isis,* 1943, p. 753.

rules for determining truth in legal matters, he held, were the same as in other areas of investigation, and it should suffice if a conclusion was beyond the doubt of any reasonable individual.

The Continental movement towards free proof owed much to the example of the English system, particularly with regard to the question of enforced self-incrimination. Except in cases of refusal to plead, torture was used in England for only a relatively brief period under the Tudors, and primarily for the investigation of supposed conspiracies against the State; and in each case warrants of immunity were issued to the torturers by the Council.[17] So far, therefore, from forming a normal part of the judicial machinery, torture was regarded instead as being normally unlawful. Moreover, in Voltaire's age there were relatively few restrictions on the kinds of evidence that an English jury could take into account.[18] So the English system would appear as one which made no use of torture because it allowed such freedom in the construction of proofs that no need arose to legitimise the enforcement of confessions as a substitute for other evidence.

One has to look rather carefully, however, at the extent to which changing attitudes to torture were influential in the Continental movement towards free proof. Langbein[19] has made out a strong case for the thesis that socio-economically induced changes in penal practice were responsible for a substantial decline in the actual use of judicial torture in Continental Europe long before the publications of those writings of Beccaria, Voltaire and others that are often supposed to have been decisive, or at least highly influential, in the movement for free proof and the abolition of judicial torture. Langbein's main argument is that the need for adequate supplies of forced labour in galleys, workhouses, etc. encouraged many western European courts in the sixteenth and seventeenth centuries to use their discretionary power to impose a *poena extraordinaria*, not for the crime itself, but on account of a sufficient accumulation of suspicion. If the crime had been proved, the *poena ordinaria* of death or maiming would have had to be imposed. But if the accumulation of suspicion had been deemed insufficient to justify torture, no proof by self-incrimination could then be obtained, therefore no execution could take place, and, if the accumulation of suspicion was nonetheless sufficient for a *poena extraordinaria*, the accused person could be sent alive and intact to join a labour force.

Nevertheless the impact of the eighteenth-century antitorture writings is not to be under-estimated. What Langbein is discussing, in regard to the earlier period, is not a change in the legal system, but a change in the relative frequency

17 J.H. Langbein, *Torture and the Law of Proof*, Chicago: University of Chicago Press, 1976, pp. 129–31.
18 Cf. J.H. Langbein, 'The criminal trial before the lawyers', loc.cit.
19 J.H. Langbein, *Torture and the Law of Proof*.

10   L. Jonathan Cohen

with which certain provisions of that system were put to work. The rules about
torture were not abolished during this period: they were just not applied as
often as they might have been. What Langbein has shown is how a practice of
somewhat freer proof – proof to justify condemnation to a *poena extraordinaria*
– grew up interstitially within the neo-Roman system. But the reforms that took
place in the latter half of the eighteenth century, and the earlier years of the
nineteenth, were of a more fundamental nature, though their acceptance was no
doubt made easier by the existence of the interstitial system. Legal stipulations
of probative value were now abolished, and torture ceased to be an authorised
method of obtaining evidence with sufficient probative value. The legal system
itself was changed. And behind the change of opinion that achieved this in
France, Prussia, Austria, Hungary and elsewhere we can recognise the considerable influence of writers like Beccaria and Voltaire.

No doubt, as Langbein points out, most of the arguments about torture
(apart from the recent cases of demonstrable injustice that were cited) were
long familiar. For example, it was an old point that torture tests endurance, not
veracity, or that it inflicts unjust suffering on those not adjudicated guilty. But
the special effectiveness of the anti-torture writings of Voltaire, Beccaria and
others was not due to any particular merit in their content. It was due rather to
the general climate of ideas amidst which they appeared – a climate that enabled
those writings also to launch a campaign for free proof. Only by such a campaign
could they undermine the positive argument for the legitimacy of torture. Only
by supporting free proof could Beccaria,[20] for example, offer a plausible alternative to an excessively restrictive system which often made full proof of a guilty
person's guilt extremely difficult unless a confession could be obtained. The
crux of the matter was that the philosophers of the Continental Enlightenment
successfully popularised in Europe those assumptions about the universal human
capacity for rational fact-finding that were presupposed by the development of
the English jury system.

Of course this modern belief in a universal cognitive capacity had already
been articulated in the writings of the great seventeenth century epistemologists,
such as Bacon, Descartes, Locke, Spinoza and Leibniz. Whatever the particular
difficulties in their several philosophical positions, whatever the controversies
which raged between empiricists and rationalists, realists and idealists, monists
and pluralists, a common theme dominated the whole epistemological scene:
knowledge may be gained by anyone working on his own. If people with the
same opportunities and desires for knowledge use just their own innate faculties
and reject every appeal to prejudice or past authority, they will all construct the
same edifice of true belief. There is a universal cognitive competence in each individual which is the only legitimate way for him or her to acquire scientific

20 C. Beccaria, op.cit., pp. 49–53, cf. pp. 57–69.

knowledge. 'We must begin anew from the very foundations', wrote Bacon;[21] and 'I could not believe that I ought for a single moment to content myself with accepting the opinions of another', wrote Descartes,[22] 'unless I had in view the employment of my own judgment in examining them at the proper time.' When Voltaire advocated[23] that the courts could, and should, follow the Roman rule requiring proof to be clearer than midday light, he was writing for a public already acquainted with Descartes' criteria of truth – clarity and distinctness.

It is immaterial here whether we regard this programme for the acquisition of knowledge as an application of protestant principles – about the supremacy of the individual conscience – to purely intellectual issues, or as a rational reconstruction of the new science of Gilbert, Galileo, Huyghens and Newton, or as the intellectual counterpart of entrepreneurial capitalism, or simply as a timely adaptation of older philosophical principles. What is relevant for present purposes is just the principle of intellectual self-confidence that the epistemological revolution seemed to warrant. Once the writings of the eighteenth century legal reformers had helped this principle to become a commonplace, it inevitably formed part of the framework within which judicial trials of fact came to be evaluated. So the Roman-canon system of regulated proof could be seen not only as suffering from the inefficiency of torture as an instrument for the discrimination of guilt and innocence, but also as lacking any defence of this practice against the argument that much more effective methods of determining guilt were available to take its place. Instead of the evidence's having to be restricted to confessions or eyewitness testimony, with exactly precalculated quanta of probative value, the tribunal itself was now intellectually entitled to estimate the probative value of whatever evidence was put forward.[24] Anyone could now see what would be the best guarantee that trials of fact would normally have an outcome which ordinary people, believing in their own capacity for estimating probative value, would find acceptable. That is to say, while the truth of the principle of universal cognitive capacity was obviously a *necessary* condition for the intellectual legitimacy of free proof, the widespread acceptance of that principle could be seen as a *sufficient* condition for free proof to be the ideal that ought to be respected.

21 Novum Organum, I, xxxi, in *The Works of Francis Bacon,* ed. J. Spedding, R. Ellis and D.N. Heath, London: Longmans, 1879, I, 162.
22 *Discourse on Method,* III, in *The Philosophical Works of Descartes,* tr. E.S. Haldane and G.R.T. Ross, Cambridge: Cambridge U.P., 1931, p. 98.
23 Voltaire, *Commentaire sur le livre des Délits et des Peines,* in *Oeuvres Complètes de Voltaire,* 1879, vol. 25, p. 576.
24 Cf. section 363 of the 1843 Hungarian code of criminal procedure, quoted by T. Király, *Criminal Procedure, Truth and Probability,* Budapest: Akadémiai Kiadó, 1979, pp. 23–4.

12   L. Jonathan Cohen

This transition to an ideal of free proof is sometimes described as involving a transition from objective to subjective criteria,[25] as if the validity of a proof under the new system consisted in its ability to persuade the trier of fact into an inner state of conviction. But any such description of the new system is bound to misrepresent the ideal of free proof, just as it would misrepresent the seventeenth-century epistemological revolution to regard it as replacing an objective conception of scientific truth by a subjective one. In a system of free proof the adversary parties (or the investigating magistrate) who are arguing for or against the validity of a particular proof are not arguing about the question whether the proof *will* persuade the trier of fact, but about whether it *ought to* persuade. Of course, in such a system the law may well require a trier of fact to be convinced of the case against an accused, before convicting. But equally under the older system it was implicit that an honest judge had to be convinced of the existence of *plena probatio* before convicting. And the validity at issue in free proof is *de jure* just as objective — just as much independent of particular prejudices, personal quirks and other mental features in the trier of fact — as the validity at issue in the older system of regulated proof. But instead of its being determined by a rather small set of permanently prescribed criteria, it is determined by a very much larger set of criteria, about the actual composition of which we may expect some occasional changes of opinion. The actual membership of this larger set is a fully objective fact: it contains norms of logic and probability, laws of nature, principles of human behaviour, and other general truths. Admittedly, whereas any reader of the *Carolina* can discover once and for all the correct criteria of validity in a particular system of regulated proof, no-one can be expected to give a correct and conclusive statement of all the criteria of validity in a system of free proof. Human knowledge improves, and a system of free proof allows its practitioners to exploit all such improvements as they arise. Nevertheless, the criteria of free proof are fundamentally objective. Even though people may not always agree at once about whether a particular item should be added to the accepted stock of known general truth, they at least regard the issue of truth or falsehood in logical, mathematical or factual matters as a wholly objective one.

III

The modern belief in a universal cognitive capacity thus supports an ideal of free proof. As Bentham held, each departure from that ideal has to be separately justified. But any such justification must also be considered subject to an im-

---

25 Cf., for example, the views of Filangieri, discussed by Király, op.cit., pp. 13–15.

portant constraint: it should not clash with the postulate of a universal cognitive capacity which supports the general presumption.

The hearsay rule, for example, may be justified within appropriate limits, as is often claimed, by the unfairness of arguing from statements that are not subject to cross-examination. The seven-year rule for presumption of death may be justified by the need to ensure uniformity of practice over cases where in each it is obvious that some duration of disappearance has to be critical but selection of any one specific duration seems relatively arbitrary. What was previously a question of fact about the reasonableness of certain standards of care, say, may quite justifiably be converted into a question of law if the legislative authority discerns a need to guide public mores rather than just to follow them. Rules for the proof of documents enjoin standard procedures that facilitate appropriate preparations for a trial. Rules allocating the burden of proof or persuasion are scarcely avoidable in an adversary system, as also are rules securing the confidentiality of the lawyer-client relationship. Justifications such as these do not impinge at all on the fundamental epistemological principle of universal cognitive capacity that helps to underwrite the ideal of free proof.

But if instead a rule is justifiable only from premisses about the credulity of lay triers of fact its adoption might appear to presuppose some universal defect in ordinary people's cognitive capacity. If the evidence of children, or of allegedly raped women, for example, does in fact always require corroboration, then this requirement, it might be supposed, is a general fact of which anyone with an adequate cognitive competence should be aware. Or if they are not aware of it, and need to have awareness of it forced on them by the law, then their ability to determine particular issues out of their general cognitive competence might seem to be called in question. And, if that competence is defective in this respect, what guarantee is there that it may not also be defective in regard to many other kinds of issue?

However, this line of argument is misdirected. Problems about corroboration do not present any real threat to the principle of universal cognitive competence. That principle does not imply that lay triers of fact can safely be assumed already to know all the causal laws and factual propensities that govern the proof of particular cases. Rather it implies that they have a natural capacity for simple deductive and probabilistic inference which has enabled them, by the time they arrive at maturity, to acquire a sufficient store of general knowledge to be in a position to evaluate the credentials of proposed additions to this store. On technical issues, for example, they may well be unaware of substantive details. But they should be in a position to evaluate the credibility of the right kind of expert evidence. Equally, if as inexperienced in legal proceedings as most modern[26] jurors are, they may well be unaware that a certain kind of testimony

26 They were often much more experienced in the seventeenth and early eighteenth centuries, according to J.H. Langbein, 'The criminal trial before the lawyers', loc.cit.

14   L. Jonathan Cohen

is intrinsically unreliable or non-probative, if indeed it is so. But they can be warned about this. Hence the real trouble with a corroboration requirement, or an exclusionary rule about hearsay, previous convictions or similar facts, is not that, where the rule is a matter of code, statute or common law, it casts any doubt on the universal cognitive competence of lay triers of fact, but rather that it may itself run contrary to fact in many cases. It may legitimate wrong conclusions' being drawn from the evidential data that are admissible. The exclusionary category of unreliable testimony may be framed in terms that are altogether too broad. Perhaps the interests of justice would be served better, therefore, not by blanket legal restrictions, but by confining exclusionary requirements to rules of practice that require judges, when not sitting alone, to warn juries about the risks inherent in placing excessive reliance on certain kinds of uncorroborated evidence, or on evidence of previous convictions, similar facts, etc., so that the ultimate freedom of factual decision remains with the lay trier of fact. Indeed, to the extent that lay juries no longer have a role in the adjudication of civil cases it would be quite natural for exclusionary law to be transformed into rules of practice wherever its motivation was fear of lay inexperience, since this motivation would not be felt to justify restrictions in courts where the trier of fact was a professional judge. Or at any rate the extent to which such rules of practice are not an acceptable alternative in criminal cases to rules of inadmissibility may be seen as a measure of the extent to which not condemning the innocent is seen as a more important social objective than not acquitting the guilty.[27]

Nevertheless, the ideal of free proof is not immune to attack. If the assumption of universal cognitive competence were shown to be false, the main foundation of the ideal of free proof would crumble. It does not matter that individual lay triers of fact are undoubtedly susceptible to various adventitious causes of error, since such factors are less likely to affect a whole plurality of jurors,

27 This preference for acquitting the guilty over condemning the innocent lies at the root of the demand for proof beyond reasonable doubt in criminal cases. How can such a preference be justified? Appeals to natural rights, such as a right to be held innocent until proved guilty, tend here to be question-begging. Perhaps it is just that in both cases – acquitting the guilty and condemning the wrong person – a guilty person is left at large to endanger the community. but if an innocent is condemned some additional harm is done. It is merely a matter for speculation whether a guilty person who has been caught and prosecuted, albeit unsuccessfully, is more, or less, likely to commit another crime than a guilty person left at large who has not been prosecuted at all. But Condorcet, *Essai sur l'application de l'analyse à la probabilité des décisions rendues à la pluralité des voix*, Paris: Imprimerie Royale, 1785, p. xxix, has a more interesting argument: cf. the discussion in L.J. Daston, 'Mathematics and the Moral Sciences: the Rise and Fall of the Probability of Judgments, 1785–1840', in H.N. Jahnke and M. Otte (eds.), *Epistemological and Social Problems of the Sciences in the Early Nineteenth Century*, Dordrecht: Reidel, 1981, pp. 287–309.

magistrates or assessors. But if mature adults cannot normally be relied upon at least to have the skills to make a more or less accurate appraisal of properly presented factual proofs, the practice of free proof would be dangerous; and without a general belief in the reliability of adult reasoning the long-term need to maintain confidence in the legal system would certainly not provide grounds for a presumption in favour of free proof. A legal system would then need to take other measures to ensure general approval for its verdicts. It would have to aim at stipulating as extensive a set of explicit criteria of valid proof as is practicable,[28] or at least at spelling out precisely the qualities or signs that on its view guarantee a person's ability to apply such criteria implicitly (nor is it easy to see how lawyers could justify their specification of those qualities or signs without being able to produce a fairly comprehensive codification of the criteria which were to be applied).

As it turns out, the principle of universal cognitive competence, which was formulated in various ways by the leading seventeenth century epistemologists, has come under two different forms of attack in recent years.

The first of these is philosophical. Contemporary epistemologists have largely succeeded in showing the untenability of what are called foundationalist programmes. That is to say, there are no self-evident or incorrigible premisses on which the edifice of scientific knowledge can be shown to rest. The interpretation of even the most elementary observation involves assumptions on which it is conceivable that we may later need to change our minds. So nobody can build up his structure of knowledge from absolute scratch, in the way that Descartes, say, or Carnap once thought possible. But, though this places some restriction on our cognitive competence, it restricts the power of that competence rather than its universality. We are all — lawyers as well as laymen — subject to the same limitation of certainty: no intellectual authority escapes it. So this inherent fallibility does not impinge in any way on the ideal of free proof. It merely reminds us that even expert evidence may one day turn out to have been mistaken.

The other attack on the principle of universal cognitive capacity is potentially more serious, however. This attack is based on the result of psychological experiments, not on philosophical arguments, and calls into question the supposed universality of human cognitive competence, not its power.

Of course, psychological experimenters began long ago to enter into a dialogue with lawyers about the other factors than objective truth, such as recency, familiarity, association, etc., that may determine the content of eye-witness

---

28 A starting-point for this might be afforded by J.H. Wigmore's *The Principles of Judicial Proof or the Process of Proof as given by Logic, Psychology and General Experience and illustrated in Judicial Trials,* 2nd ed., 1931, Boston: Little, Brown & Co.

16   L. Jonathan Cohen

testimony.[29] But lay jurors or assessors who do not know about the risks of error inherent in eyewitness identification, for example, can easily be reminded of them. This is just another issue of the type already encountered in regard to those categories of testimony that are deemed to require corroboration, and it can be dealt with analogously by a rule of practice. The ideal of free proof does not need to assume that every lay trier of fact comes into court already knowing all the relevant causal laws and propensities, without any need to be instructed or reminded in relevant respects. The principle of cognitive competence implies that adults can always add to what they already know, not that they already know all that is to be known. It implies that they can learn from suitable experts, not that they are already experts themselves.

What strikes at the root of the ideal of free proof, however, is the claim that ordinary human cognitive ability is itself subject to a considerable range of systematic defect or fallacy. The growing frequency with which this claim has been made in the past fifteen years[30] marks a major turnabout in fashions of human self-perception in the civilised world, and constitutes a long-term threat to the popular epistemology of cognitive competence. It is as if the epistemological optimism of the seventeenth century and the Enlightenment is beginning to crumble, and the failure to solve economic, political and ecological problems about industrial growth, along with a widespread interest in the psychology of the irrational or even a certain backlash of popular feeling against the whole enterprise of science, are reflected in a tendency to impose rather pessimistic interpretations on experimental data about ordinary human reasoning powers. In many different kinds of experiments lay adults are supposed to reveal their incompetence at reasoning correctly, i.e. their incompetence at reasoning in accordance with the norms of deductive logic or of standard probability-theory. So their unsuitability to be trusted with weighty inferential tasks, affecting the lives or liberty of their fellows, is not to be remedied by *ad hoc* reminders about relevant general facts. What would be needed instead, if we were to take some psychologists' claims seriously, would be either a legal codification of the relevant logical and probabilistic norms, so that their application to the decision of a particular case becomes a matter of law, or at least a legal requirement that every trier of fact should have an attested competence in the application of these specific norms. Indeed that something like this is needed is the conclusion to

29 For references see J. Marshall, *Law and Psychology in Conflict,* Indianapolis: Bobbs Merrill, 1966, and *Report to the Secretary of State for the Home Department of the Departmental Committee on Evidence of Identification in Criminal Cases,* London: H.M.S.O., 1976, pp. 71–73.

30 For a good survey of the literature see R.E. Nisbett and L. Ross, *Human inference: strategies and shortcomings of social judgment,* Englewood Cliffs: Prentice Hall, 1980.

which Saks and Kidd, for example, have arrived in their recent study of what the psychological literature implies for adjudicative procedure.[31]

Of course, no-one has ever seriously doubted that jurors or lay assessors, like everyone else, sometimes make mistakes. Such errors may be due to inattention, failure of memory, wishful thinking, emotional prejudice or a host of other factors that from time to time interfere with intellectual performance. In addition the sheer complexity of some cases may cause lay jurors to err if counsel or judge has not taken appropriate care in the presentation of the arguments;[32] and the inability of jurors to question witnesses, though it sits well enough with an adversarial system of legal procedure, may sometimes allow important misunderstandings to crystallise. Any method of proof has to accept the possibility of occasional human error. But what the psychologists claim is the existence of systematic patterns of cognitive error in ordinary lay reasoning and it is with these these that the ideal of free proof cannot co-exist.

For example, Wason and Johnson-Laird[33] claim to have obtained experimental data showing that in many kinds of situation people are prone to commit what logicians call the fallacy of illicit conversion, i.e. the fallacy of inferring from a proposition of the form 'if p, then q' to one of the form 'if q, then p'. And if such a tendency were indeed prevalent among jurors this would obviously have serious implications for the accuracy with which they are capable of interpreting evidence and assessing probative value. Similarly in another experiment[34] the subjects were told that in a certain town blue and green cabs operate in a ratio of 85% to 15%, respectively, while a witness identifies a cab in a crash as green and the court is informed that in the relevant light conditions he can distinguish blue cabs from green ones in 80% of cases. The subjects were then asked: what is the probability (expressed as a percentage) that the cab involved in the accident was blue? The median estimated probability was 20% and the investigators, Kahneman and Tversky, claim that this shows the prevalence of serious error because it implies a failure to take base rates (i.e. prior probabilities) into account. The investigators commented: 'Much as we would like to, we have no reason to believe that the typical juror does not evaluate evidence in this fashion.' Again, according to the same investigators[35] people typically

---

31 M.J. Saks and R.F. Kidd, 'Human information Processing and Adjudication: Trial by Heuristics', *Law and Society Review* 15, 1980–81, pp. 123–160, esp. p. 134.
32 Cf. P.W. Sperlich, 'The case for preserving trial by jury in complex civil iitigation', *Judicature* 65, 1982, pp. 394–419, esp. pp. 415–419.
33 P.C. Wason and P.N. Johnson-Laird, *Psychology of Reasoning: Structure and Content*, London: Batsford, 1972.
34 D. Kahneman and A. Tversky, 'On the Psychology of Prediction', *Oregon Research Institute Research Bulletin* 1972, 12, 4.
35 A. Tversky and D. Kahneman, 'Judgment under Uncertainty: Heuristics and Biases', *Science* 125, pp. 1124–1131.

judge the probability that A originates from, or belongs to, B as being high
when A is highly representative of (i.e. similar to) B and as low when the opposite is the case. On their view this is a heuristic that, though sometimes harmless, tends to foster two important computational errors. It has the consequence
both that prior probabilities, or base-rate frequencies, tend not to be taken
into account where they should be, and also that the significance of differences
in sample-size tends to be ignored. And again there is no doubt that if such
tendencies really exist the ideal of free proof has much less justification than
has commonly been supposed.

It turns out, however, that experimental data of this kind, which allegedly
show the widespread prevalence of important fallacies in ordinary human
reasoning in civilised countries, are always open to alternative interpretations.
For example, in regard to allegedly illicit conversion, we find that in typical
cases the fallacy disappears if we look not just at the sentences uttered, but
also at the implications of their utterance.[36] Similarly, in the experiment about
the blue and green cabs it would not be unreasonable for subjects to take the
overall distribution of cab-colours to be relatively unpredictive of the relevant
prior probability, which is the probability that a cab of a particular colour would
be involved in an accident of the kind that occurred.[37] And the alleged fallacy of
representativeness turns out to be a quite correct procedure if one is operating
with a non-mathematical and non-additive conception of probability – a Baconian rather than a Pascalian one.[38]

Of course, these are only three items out of the rather extensive literature
claiming to have demonstrated some systematic tendency in ordinary people
to reason fallaciously. Someone may well object, therefore, that the ideal of
free proof stands in need of a much more comprehensive defence.

We need a reason for attributing some relatively *a priori* status to the principle of universal cognitive competence. We need a reason for supposing that,
wherever experiments seem to show persistent patterns of error in some type of
lay inference, these results are to be interpreted as evidence either that the
subjects were in fact thinking in other terms than those that would convict
them of fallacy or that the error was due to the inattention or emotional prejudice of the subject, or to the unfamiliarity and artificiality of the situation, or
to some other factor that corrupts the proper exercise of native competence.
That is, we need to back up the presumption in legal theory that lies in favour

36 L. Jonathan Cohen, 'Can human irrationality be experimentally demonstrated? *Be-
    havioral and Brain Sciences* 4, 1981, pp. 326–7.

37 Ibid. p. 329 and pp. 365–6. Cf. also L. Jonathan Cohen, 'Do People Have the Wrong
    Programmes? Further Thoughts about the Interpretation of Experimental Data on
    Probability Judgment' (forthcoming in *Journal for the Theory of Social Behaviour* 12,
    1982).

38 As in L. Jonathan Cohen, 'On the Psychology of Prediction: Whose is the Fallacy?',
    Cognition 7, 1979, pp. 385–407.

of not regulating proof, by arguing for a presumption in psychological theory that lies in favour of universal cognitive competence. Otherwise the ideal of free proof lacks a strong enough intellectual foundation to weather the criticism that may be launched against it as psychological research continues.

Note first that the psychological issue here is certainly a theoretical one. We are not faced — or liable to be faced — with brute facts about which there is no room for argument (as in the case of some of the forensically relevant findings about recognition, identification or memory). The problem here concerns the nature of the explanation that should be sought for real or apparent errors in deductive or probabilistic reasoning, where experiments reveal these real or apparent errors to occur regularly and predictably in certain contexts. What is in question is not the robustness of certain kinds of experimental data, but the type of process that should be postulated to explain them. Do they result from the operation of cognitive mechanisms that are inherently valid but may nevertheless malfunction under unfavourable conditions, or do they result from the presence of some mechanisms in the human mind that are inherently invalid and tend therefore under certain conditions to deliver results which need to be edited, revised or discarded?

As it turns out there are powerful arguments in favour of the former explanation.

One argument is that, since any defence of a set of norms for ordinary deductive reasoning — norms that may be used as a basis for criticising actual performance — must rely at crucial points on the appeal to human intuition, human beings cannot coherently also suppose that they have one or more built-in mechanisms which, when functioning normally, may deliver invalid judgments of deducibility. The mechanisms have to be thought of as delivering valid judgments when functioning normally in order that the intuitions may be thought of as providing support for the norms, since without such support for the norms there is no rational basis for any criticisms of actual performance. In short you can't argue some inferential performances to be invalid, without assuming a general inferential competence that is valid.

The same point[39] can be put in another way as follows. Suppose you produce other sorts of arguments — i.e. arguments not invoking intuitions — to support a particular system of norms of deductive reasoning. How then could you be sure that your system of normative criteria applies to the particular concepts of conditionality, disjunction, negation etc with which ordinary people actually operate? Obviously you would first have to determine what

39 The argument is developed at greater length, and defended against critics, in 'Can Human Irrationality be Experimentally Demonstrated?' and 'Are there any *a priori* Constraints on the Study of Irrationality?', *Behavioral and Brain Sciences* 4, 1981, pp. 317–331 and 359–370.

those latter concepts are. But the only way to do this would be to study people's actual judgments about deducibility: unless your proposed system licenses those judgments it does not apply to ordinary people's reasoning. And so you would in the end come round to defending your system by an appeal to lay intuitions about deducibility.

It is not uninteresting to notice an alternative doctrine that is currently put forward by some contemporary philosophers who oppose the grounding of relevant norms on an appeal to intuition and thereby leave room for the principle of universal cognitive competence to be considered false. This alternative view — as advocated, for example, by Stich and Nisbett[40] — is that the proper basis for a theory of logical norms is not the intuitions of ordinary laymen but rather the consensus of experts. Thus the principle of universal cognitive competence is to be replaced by a canonisation of certain intellectual authorities, and in this general reversion to an older style of thinking the ideal of free proof also would certainly have to be sacrificed. But the position is an incoherent one. Even experts obtain a consensus only by arguing with one another and the argument that then wins, not the bare fact of the experts' agreement, is the true basis for any agreed theory that emerges.

The position regarding judgments of probability is not quite analogous to that regarding judgments of deducibility, because it may be possible to identify the nature of a person's probability-function independently of his specific strategy for evaluating it. For example, where probability is conceived of as a relative frequency alternative methods of estimation are available and where probability is conceived of as the strength of justifiable belief alternative ways of measuring this strength may be employed. Hence in the case of probabilistic reasoning it is not logically impossible that ordinary people should be discovered to employ some systematically incorrect heuristic. Nevertheless it seems highly unlikely now that any such discovery will ever be made. Alternative interpretations can be given for the various experimental results that have been alleged to show neglect of base rates, ignorance of the law of large numbers, conservatism in adjusting probabilities to new information, etc. And these alternative interpretations form a coherent pattern that makes better sense of the data than the *ad hoc* postulation of fallacious heuristics. What happens in that pattern is that in each case the subjects of the psychologists' experiments tend to be cued by the nature of the task set them to use a particular conception of probability and to formulate their responses appropriately. It is only when this principled cueing is overlooked, and subjects are assumed (without any obvious reason) to be using just the same conception of probability as the experimenters happen to have in mind, that there seems to be any evidence for attributing to them a fallacious

40 S.P. Stich and P.E. Nisbett, 'Justification and the Psychology of Human Reasoning'. *Philosophy of Science* 1980, 47, pp. 188–202.

heuristic. Indeed it generally turns out quite easy to get the 'correct' answers by altering the cues appropriately.[41]

Nor is there any difficulty for a system of free proof in accommodating technical advances in the methodology of fact-finding. Expert testimony can be heard, and its validity can be exposed to the usual opportunity for scrutiny. The value of a new statistical method, for example, has to be shown by considerations that are cogent in terms of already accepted criteria. So the ideal of free proof is not only well founded in respect of a static conception of cognitive competence. It also has no difficulty at all in coming to terms with the possibility of technical improvements. Unexciting as the conclusion may sound, when we consider how the law of a contemporary civilised country should handle evidence or proof, the presumption still remains as much in favour of freedom as in Bentham's day. There is no general need to write rules of proof into the law, nor to define a corresponding level of intellectual qualification for triers of fact. We need only a reasonable layman, not a logician or statistician, to determine what is beyond reasonable doubt.[42]

41 Details are given in L. Jonathan Cohen, 'Do People Have the Wrong Programmes? Further Thoughts about the Interpretation of Experimental Data on Probability Judgment', loc. cit.

42 I am grateful for helpful comments on an earlier draft to Professor Jonathan Adler, Professor William Twining and Mr Adrian Zuckerman, and to participants in discussions in April 1982 at the Durham conference of the U.K. Association for Legal and Social Philosophy and at the Yale Law School Legal Theory Workshop.

[2]

FACT, FICTIONS, AND LAW:
BENTHAM ON THE FOUNDATIONS OF EVIDENCE

GERALD J. POSTEMA, UNIVERSITY OF NORTH CAROLINA AT CHAPEL HILL

Bentham and the American Realists both regarded the claims of common law adjudication with deep scepticism. As so-called "rule-sceptics" both viewed common law's claim to generate rules which genuinely constrain judicial decision-making as so much window-dressing. Some Realists also seemed to entertain a scepticism about evidentiary matters, although the exact nature of that scepticism was never entirely clear. Bentham, however, clearly extended his scepticism about rules beyond his critique of common law to the law of evidence. His theory of evidence is founded on a deep scepticism regarding the possibility of constructing rules (even fully authoritative, statutory rules) regarding the admissibility, reliability, and weight of evidence. But if we cannot explain this scepticism by appeal to his rejection of common law, what does explain it? Perhaps it is grounded in a deeper epistemological scepticism. One might imagine Bentham arguing that it is impossible to construct useful or adequate rules for the admission or exclusion of evidence, or for assessing its weight or reliability, precisely because there is no objective basis for making such assessments and judgments, and consequently any such rules would be entirely arbitrary.

There is much in Bentham's discussion of the notions of the weight of evidence and of its "probative force" that would lend credence to this explanation. For example, he insists that judging the "degree of connexion" between a principal fact and an alleged evidentiary fact is strictly an "instinctive operation."[1] Not only, in his view, is the strength of evidence for a conclusion likely to be different on different occasions, but, he often insists, this degree of strength *just is* the extent to which one feels persuaded of the truth of a proposition given the evidence, and that, of course, can vary widely from person to person.

> In the case of circumstantial evidence, the probative force of the evidentiary fact, considered as indicative of the existence of the principal fact (which is as much as to say the strength of the persuasion produced by it), is susceptible of every variety of degree in the bosom of the judge (RJE vi, 224).

---

1 Jeremy Bentham, *The Rationale of Judicial Evidence*, Bowring edition, *Works of Jeremy Bentham*, vol. vi. p. 216. This is hereafter cited as: RJE vi, 216. Bentham's *Introductory View of the Rationale of Evidence* (*Bowring* vi, 1–186) will be cited as IRE, followed by page numbers.

38   Gerald J. Postema

This seems to commit Bentham to a radically sceptical view of evidence and
inference in juridical contexts. Yet, paradoxically, one of his most impressive
intellectual achievements, and perhaps his most immediately influential jurisprudential work, is his monumental *Rationale of Judicial Evidence*. This sets out in
great detail a comprehensive theory of legal evidence which shows few signs of
this epistemologically sceptical foundation.

The main objective of this essay is to explore Bentham's views regarding the
logical and epistemological foundations of the law of evidence, drawing at some
important points on materials from his so-called "theory of fictions," in order to
resolve this apparent contradiction in Bentham's views. Bentham surely was a
subjectivist regarding probability statements, I shall argue, but a subjectivist
with a difference — a difference which is, I believe, historically and philosophically significant. Although Bentham was primarily concerned with the ontology
or semantics, rather than the syntax, of probability statements, his semantic
views have important implications for our understanding of the syntax of
probability statements. Thus, discussion of these views adds a historical voice
to the chorus in current debate over the logic of probability in its primary juridical uses. Textual evidence is not unambiguous, and Bentham himself did not
view the issues in quite the sharply defined terms of the recent debate between
Pascalian/Bayesians and Baconians,[2] nevertheless the preponderance of evidence
suggests that, if he were forced to choose, he would side with the Baconians.
This is of historical interest, of course. But more interesting from a philosophical
point of view is his attempt to ground this Baconian interpretation of probability
in juridical contexts on a sophisticated subjectivist foundation.

I.

Correct adjudicative decisions must be made on the basis of particular propositions of law and particular statements of fact. The former are inferred from

---

2 The so-called Baconian attack on the standard Pascalian/Bayesian understanding of probability has, of course, been led by L. Jonathan Cohen in several papers and especially
   his book *The Probable and the Provable* (Oxford: Clarendon Press, 1977). On the American side of the Atlantic the cause has been taken up by, among others, Brilmayer and
   Kornhauser, "Review: Quantitative Methods and Legal Decisions," 46 *U. Chi. Rev.* 116
   (1978). The Pascalian case has been made by Sir Richard Eggleston in his *Evidence,
   Proof, and Probability* (London: Weidenfeld and Nicolson, 1978), and carried forward
   against Cohen by Glanville Williams, "The Mathematics of Proof," (1979) *Crim. L. Rev.*
   297, 340 and (1980) *Crim. L. Rev.* 678. See also Cohen's reply "The Logic of Proof,"
   (1980) *Crim. L. Rev.* 91 and 747. For the growing literature in American legal journals
   see David Kaye, "The Laws of Probability and the Law of the Land," 47 *U. Chi. L. Rev.*
   34 (1979).

general propositions of law, the latter are grounded on other particular statements of fact – i.e., on evidence. Evidence, according to Bentham, is some matter of fact (or statement regarding some matter of fact) which is presented to the judge (fact-finder) for the purpose of producing in the judge's mind persuasion of some other material fact necessary for decision (IRE, 7–8). Evidentiary facts persuade fact-finders of the existence of principal facts in virtue of their "probative force." Evidentiary facts "prove," or at least "probabilize" or "disprobabilize," principal facts to some degree (RJE vii, 4). The account thus far set out has two noteworthy implications. (a) Probative force comes in degrees. In its highest degree, probative force is conclusive of (makes "practically certain," in Bentham's phrase) some proposition; in some lesser degree it is said to make the proposition more (or less) probable. (b) Probative force is not a property of single facts – either evidentiary or principal – rather it is a property of an evidentiary fact *E* only insofar as *E* is evidence of principal fact *P*. More exactly, it is a *relation between* sets of facts or propositions. *P* is "probabilized" *by E* and it is probable only *relative to E*. Thus, the probability of *P* cannot logically be detached from *E*. There is no "absolute" or without-qualification probability of *P*, unless by this one refers to the probability of *P* given *all* there is to know.[3]

The central logical and epistemic questions at the foundations of the law of evidence concern this notion of probability or probative force of evidence. However, in Bentham's view our investigation of these questions is faced immediately with a difficulty concerning the semantics of probability language which threatens the entire enterprise. First, following Locke, we may wish to distinquish between the probability of a proposition and the degree of assurance we attach to the proposition.[4] But then language and our ordinary conceptual frame-work incline us to regard probability as an objective property of the facts themselves – existing with them "in nature." But this cannot be, he insists. Consider a pair of facts such that *P* is probable to some degree given (i.e., relative to) *E*. No matter how hard we look, he argues, we will not be able to find among the sensible properties of *P* or *E* the property of *P*'s probability given *E*.[5] Moreover, "Be the fact what it may, between its existence and non-existence. . . there is no medium: and thence it is that, ascribed to facts themselves, *probability* and *improbability*, with their infinity of degrees are mere figments of imagination. . ."[6]

---

3 This is the clear implication of Bentham's claim (at *Bowring* viii, 211) that to say without qualification that some proposition P is impossible or improbable is to assume omniscience.

4 Locke, *Essay Concerning Human Understanding*, IV, xx, 16.

5 Compare Hume's famous argument regarding moral properties in *A Treatise on Human Nature*, III, I, i.

6 IRE, 46. See the parallel passage at RJE vii, 78–9 where he goes on to say: "the matter of fact being, at the time in question, either in existence or not in existence, . . . neither the evidence nor the persuasion [is] capable of making any the slightest change in it. . ."

Gerald J. Postema

That is, facts either exist, or they do not; there is no such thing as a probable fact. Existing as a fact does not come in degrees, but probability does admit of degrees; therefore, probability cannot be a fact or quality of facts in nature.[7] "Upon examination," he concludes, "this quality... is a purely fictitious one..." (RJE vii, 77). But if the probability of an event is not an objective property of the event as the surface logic of probability leads us to believe, then either we are talking sheer nonsense, or some radically different semantic interpretation of the language of probability must be given. For Bentham, this semantic or ontological question must be answered first before the epistemic issues underlying the concept of evidence and proof in law can be addressed.

According to Bentham, the language of probability may be the language of fictions, but to say this is not to say that it is language we must, or even can, do away with. The language of probability is significant, not because it is used to refer to concrete material entities or actual events, but because it expresses or captures an important sort of psychological fact, viz., the degree to which one is persuaded of the truth of a proposition given the evidence for it. Subjective persuasion of the existence of facts, unlike facts themselves, does admit of degrees and, thus, naturally fits our concepts of probability better than any objective fact or property.

> Probative force, and closeness of connexion as between fact and fact, having not more than apparent and relative existence (relative, viz. relation being had to him by whom the facts are contemplated in his view) nothing more can be truly indicated by them [i.e., "probative force" and "closeness of connexion"] than strength of persuasion on his part...[8]

7 John Venn, almost sixty years later, draws the opposite conclusion from almost the same argument:

> I am about to toss one [a penny] up, and I therefore half believe ... that it will give head. Now it seems to be overlooked that if we appeal to the event, ... our belief must inevitably be wrong, and therefore the test above mentioned will fail. For the thing must either happen or not happen: i.e., in this case the penny must either give head or not give it; there is no third alternative. But whichever way it occurs, our half-belief, so far as such a state of mind admits of interpretation, must be wrong. If head does come, I am wrong in not having expected it enough; for I only half believed in its occurrence. If it does not happen, I am equally wrong in having expected it too much; for I half believed in its occurrence, when in fact it did not occur at all... The two states of belief and disbelief correspond admirably to the two results of the event happening and not happening respectively, ... but to partial belief there is nothing corresponding in the result, for the event cannot partially happen in such cases as we are concerned with.

John Venn, *The Logic of Chance*, Chapter VI, reprinted in *Studies in Subjective Probability*, Henry Kyburg and Howard Smokler eds., (New York: John Wiley & Sons, 1964), pp. 32, 33. However, Venn ignores here, as Bentham to his credit does not, that probability is always relative to evidence.

8 RJE vii, 64; see also Bentham's "Essay on Ontology," *Bowring* viii, 211.

That is, since probability is not an objective property of facts, and since probability is relative to the assessor of evidence, it must be just the degree of his persuasion of the principal fact which he expresses when he attributes the quality of probability to that fact.

However, the argument implicit in these remarks seems to rest on a confusion of two different ways in which probability assessments may be said to be relative to the assessor. For from the fact that the probability of an event can be determined only with respect to a body of evidence, it follows that if John claims that it is likely to rain today, then there must be some body of beliefs which John holds which constitutes the evidence on the basis of which John makes his claim. The logic of probability warrants relativizing John's assertion to some set of beliefs which John presumably holds. But it does not follow from this that John's claim indicates nothing more than John's degree of persuasion of the truth of the statement "It will rain today." It does not follow that probability is relative to John's *persuasion* of *P* given *E,* though it does follow that it is relative to *E* which John believes.

This confusion not only affects the validity of Bentham's implicit argument, it also raises some doubt about the precise character of the account of probability he wishes to advance. It might be helpful to contrast two sharply different accounts of probability which take seriously the relativity of probability to evidence and then ask of Bentham's account with which it has greater affinity.

The first might be associated with Leibniz[9] whose views on probability, like Bentham's, were much influenced by reflection on juridical evidence and proof.[10] All juridical inference, he observed, is relative to the evidence set before the court, and thus, all probability conclusions are *"ex datis"*: i.e., conditional on, and proportional to, what we know. He noted further that evidence seldom conclusively establishes a proposition, but that it can warrant our inferences. This warrant is due, in Leibniz's view, to a *logical* relation obtaining between *propositions,* independent of anyone's beliefs about them. On this view, there might be different assessments of the weight of evidence, but there is only one correct assessment, the correctness of which is due to the logical relation between the propositions in question and is entirely independent of any personal opinion about it.

Sharply contrasting with this Leibnizian view is what I shall call the "Humean" or radical subjectivist view, which holds that probability is *nothing more* than

9 Leibniz seems to have sketched a prototype of the modern logical theory associated with Keynes, Carnap, and others. My discussion of Leibniz follows Ian Hacking, *The Emergence of Probability* (Cambridge Univ. Press, 1975), Chapters 10, 15.

10 He called the theory of probability "natural jurisprudence," and regarded juridical argument as the model of reasoning and deliberation about contingencies, as mathematics was regarded as the model of reasoning about necessary truths.

the degree of assurance which a person feels in the truth of some proposition after considering a body of evidence. This degree of persuasion is simply the *product* of the impact of the evidence on the mind of the assessor. "Inferences" drawn from evidence, then, are not open to rational assessment; such inferences neither have nor need objective warrant. Inference is merely a matter of moving from evidence to conclusion in a way paved by association or custom.[11]

Now, neither his rejection of the notion of probable facts, nor his recognition of the relativity of the probability of a proposition to evidence, forces adoption of one or the other of these two views. Yet, what we have seen of Bentham's positive view seems to commit him to something very close to the Humean view. He seems to hold that probative force of *E* regarding *P just is* the intensity of one's persuasion of *P* given *E*. "To say that the probative force of the evidence is at such or such a degree, is to say that, in the bosom of the judge, intensity of persuasion is at that degree" (IRE, 18 n.). The language of probability, he suggests, is restricted to the two functions of (a) expressing degrees of confidence, or the lack of it, in statements of fact, and (b) inducing similar attitudes towards such statements of fact in others.[12] Why, then, ascribe the qualities of probability, certainty, etc. (wrongly) to the facts themselves? For convenience, says Bentham, and because it is rhetorically effective, since one is more likely to convince another of the truth of the claim one makes if one can disguise one's own part in the "probabilizing" of it.

However, like the contemporary subjectivist theories of probability which it clearly anticipates, this view faces several serious difficulties. First, we should note that, unlike Ramsey and other recent subjectivists, Bentham fashions his account strictly in terms of degrees of persuasion, rather than degree of *belief*.

---

11 See Hume, *Treatise*, I, III, viii.

> Thus all probable reasoning is nothing but a species of sensation. 'Tis is solely in poetry and music, we must follow our taste and sentiment, but likewise in philosophy. When I am convinc'd of any principle, 'tis only an idea, which strikes more strongly upon me. When I give the preference to one set of arguments above another, I do nothing but decide from my feeling concerning the superiority of their influence. Objects have no discoverable connexion together; nor is it from any other principle but custom operating upon the imagination, that we can draw any inference from the appearance of one to the existence of another.

> It is, of course, a question of some complexity whether Hume himself was a "Humean Subjectivist." See J. A. Passmore, "Hume and the Ethics of Belief," in *David Hume: Bicentenary Papers*, ed. G. P. Morice (Edinburgh: Edinburgh Univ. Press, 1977), pp. 77–92.

12 Probative force is a fictitious quality, "a quality, having nothing of the reality connected with it but the *persuasion* ... as it hath place in the mind of him, by whom, for the more convenient expression of it, or for the more effectual spreading of the like persuasion, the fictitious quality in question is thus attributed to . . . that fact itself" (IRE, 46). See also RJE vii, 91–2, 78–9. The parallel with the Emotivist analysis of moral language is striking.

This both avoids the difficulties many have found in the notion of degrees of belief and it retains the focus of the analysis of probability on the context of argument and proof. But one might still doubt whether there are discrete degrees of persuasion, We might grant that it is possible roughly and qualitatively to grade confidence in a proposition but insist that, nevertheless, it is quite another thing to hold that persuasion comes in qualitatively measurable degrees such that talk of degrees of persuasion can qualify as an interpretation of the formal mathematical calculus of probability.[13] Two replies to this objection are available at this point. First, there is good reason to believe that Bentham did not intend his account of probability to provide a semantics of the Pascalian probability calculus.[14] Thus, his account may need no more precision than the terms he relies on allow.

But Bentham would not be content to leave the matter here, for he thought it made good sense to talk of discrete and measurable degrees of persuasion, and he sought to demonstrate this. Anticipating Ramsey and others,[15] he argued that the practice of wagering provides both the *proof of* the fact that persuasion admits of, and exists in, degrees of strength, and an adequate *measure* of the probability one assigns to a proposition.[16] This argument, however, is persuasive for the general conclusion that confidence does sometimes come in measurable quantities, but there are serious questions about its general applicability in juridical contexts. Dumont, for example, questioned the intelligibility of the notion of wagers in this context. The analogy with wagers, he argued, is mistaken because "Testimony turns on past events: wagers turn on future events: as a witness, I know, I believe, or I doubt; as a wagerer, I know nothing, but I conjecture, I calculate probabilities. . ." (RJE vi, 235, editor's note). But this does not put the objection very clearly. The key difference is not between future and past, but between wagers on which there is a clear, uncontroversially determinable outcome (which, of course, will not be known at the time of the wager) and a wager on matters which are in principle unsettlable. In the latter case, accepting reasonable odds may have no rational basis,[17] and those are just the sorts of cases which figure prominently in law.

---

13 See Venn, in Kyburg and Smokler, *Studies*, p. 21.

14 See Section IV below.

15 F. P. Ramsey, "Truth and Probability;" Bruno de Finetti, "Foresight: Its Logical Laws. Its Subjective Sources;" and Leonard Savage, "The Foundations of Statistics Reconsidered;" all in Kyburg and Smokler, *Studies*.

16 RJE vi, 223. It must be noted that this device serves for Bentham, as a measure of the degree of persuasion which has, in his view, independent existence as a psychological fact. In this respect Bentham differs from some recent subjectivists who tend to take a more behaviourist approach to the wager-measure.

17 On this problem see Clark Glymour, *Theory and Evidence* (Princeton: Princeton Univ. Press, 1980), p. 70; and Cohen, *Probable and Provable*, pp. 89–91. This problem afflicts attempts to apply the wager notion to capture probabilities in *general* theoretic state-

44   Gerald J. Postema

A second, more important, objection can be raised to the subjectivist account. If the probability of a proposition is just the degree of confidence one feels in the proposition, then either such probability statements make no assertions at all (they lose all cognitive content and cannot bear truth value), or they are merely statements about the actual state of mind of the speaker. But then disputes over probability assignments are reduced simply to disagreements in attitude; or even worse to disagreements about the accuracy of certain psychological descriptions. Rational assessment of probability assignments is completely ruled out; and this leaves their ability to warrant decisions made on the basis of them a complete mystery. Now, recent subjectivists, in order to insure that a system of wagers conforms to the standard axioms of the probability calculus, insist on coherence of the system,[18] and so countenance at least one normative constraint on probability assignments.[19] But this constraint is very weak; it gives us no guarantee that such assignments will be even minimally reasonable.[20] The coherence requirement represents a step back from radical Humean subjectivism, but it still allows not only that there may be more than one reasonable assignment of probability given some body of evidence, but also that there is no basis for assessing any assignment as unreasonable. Surely, some probability assignments are more reasonable than others, one might protest; and in the juridical context we want to guarantee that fact-finders make the most reasonable assignments of the probative force of evidence. After all, justice depends on it.

Finally, Humean subjectivism, even under the constraint of coherence, finds no place for the rational exercise of *judgment* in the *formation* of beliefs. It pays attention only to the outcome of the process of "assessment" of evidence; it ignores the fact that one attempts (more or less rationally) to *draw* this conclusion, and that one may wish to use the same evidence to construct an *argument* to persuade others of the truth or likelihood of the conclusion. Clark Glymour rightly points out that:

ments (see Henry Kyburg, *Probability and the Logic of Rational Belief* (Middleton, Con.: Wesleyan Univ. Press, 1964), p. 35). But it also afflicts probability statements regarding singular events in the past, which are the most common sort of facts that need to be proven in a court of law.

18 A system of wagers is coherent, in the current usage, if a "Dutch Book" cannot be made against the wagerer, i.e., his system of wagers does not guarantee that he will lose.

19 See Kyburg and Smokler, *Studies*, Introduction, pp. 10–11.

20 Bayesians argue that intersubjective convergence regarding probability assignments will eventually be achieved if persons are exposed to the same data and they are required to "learn from experience," revising initial probability assignments upon consideration of new data through repeated applications of Bayes' Theorem and the Inverse Probability Theorem. This prospect may relieve the burden of the above objection if our concern is with assignments of probability in scientific reasoning. But for determination of probative force of evidence in juridical contexts the reply is lame, since there is no time or opportunity to carry out the "learning" process.

> To ascribe to me degrees of belief that make my slide from my premises to my con-
> clusion a plausible one fails to explain anything... because, even if it is a correct
> assignment of my degrees of belief, it does not explain why what I am doing is
> *arguing* – why, that is, what I say should have the least influence on others, or why
> I might hope it should.[21]

And the shift from talk of degrees of belief to degrees of persuasion does not
avoid this problem. But surely, in law as in science, the objective of presenting
evidence to fact- finders is to present reasons – that is, an argument – for drawing the conclusion from this evidence.

These are powerful objections against Humean subjectivism. But Bentham was
sensitive to them, especially the last one. He sought an account of probability
which avoided the unacceptable ontological commitments of objectivism (and
even of the Leibnizian view) while leaving substantial room for the rational assessment of probability assignments. I shall argue in the remainder of this essay
that despite appearances, the view suggested above, when properly understood
against the background of Bentham's general philosophical views (his "theory of
fictions"), falls between the Humean and Leibnizian extremes. Bentham sketches
a sophisticated version of subjectivism which goes some distance towards meeting the above objections.

In light of what we have already seen of Bentham's discussion of evidence, it
should be no surprise that one can find a short outline of the central claims of
his theory of fictions prefacing early work on judicial evidence.[22] And his mature
theory of evidence clearly shows the marks of the maturing of this theory of
fictions. That theory provides the key to understanding his view of the foundations of the law of evidence. It is to a short sketch of some main elements in that
theory that I now turn.

II.

From the beginning of his long career Bentham believed that systematic reflection on language and its relationship to thought and reality was the key to understanding and improving the world.[23] He was keenly aware that language is deeply

---

21 Glymour, *Theory and Evidence*, p. 75.
22 See Bentham's University College Manuscripts, box xlvi, folios 18–22 (hereafter cited:
   U. C. xlvi, 18–22).
23 See Douglas Long, *Bentham on Liberty* (Toronto: Toronto Univ. Press, 1977), Chapter
   4. Bentham did not set out in a systematic way to develop and defend these fundamental
   views on ontology, epistemology, etc. until late in his career (beginning with the sketch
   in the Chrestomathia papers in (about) 1813). But there is overwhelming evidence in published and manuscript sources that he had firmed up in outline his basic views very early
   (with the apparent exception of the legitimacy of abstract ideas on which he seemed to
   vacillate until 1813). There are preliminary sketches of the basic position in his earliest

46   Gerald J. Postema

misleading. It seems to commit us to the existence of a host of entities which we
know do not exist.[24] Although we use language to describe and communicate
our beliefs about the world around us, that language does not accurately mirror
that world. Bentham's theory of fictions set out to explain why. He attempted
systematically to distinguish real entities (and expressions which actually connect us in some significant way to the world) from fictitious entities and language that purports to refer to them, to explore the relations that obtain between these two great classes, and to explain why we find fictions to be indispensible.

All real entities, in Bentham's view, fall into one of two classes; (i) concrete
material substances, and (ii) mental entities which, following Hume, he distinguishes into impressions and ideas.[25] All other entities to which language seems
to commit us are fictitious. Fictitious entities "reside in or about real entities"
(U. C. xlvi, 21). That is, they can be separated into groups and arranged heuris-
tically in a pattern of concentric circles progressing outward from real entities.[26]

work, e.g., U. C. clxix, 50–66; U. C. xxvii, 3–5, 25, 53; U. C. cxxxv, 1–69 *passim.*; U. C.
cvi, 2–3; U. C. lxix, 52–53, and the "Preparatory Principles Inserenda" MSS, U. C. lxix,
77–241 *passim.*, especially 140–41, 219–20, 227–8. The results of this work can be
seen, for example, in *Fragment on Government*, Chapter V, and *Of Laws in General*,
Appendix B.

24 Bentham writes in his Memorandum Book (1831):
    Wherever there is a word, there is a thing; so says the common notion – the result of
    the association of ideas. Wherever there is a word, there is a thing; hence the almost
    universal practice of confounding *fictitious* entities with *real* ones – corresponding
    names of fictitious entities with real ones (*Bowring* xi, 73).
  This is true not only of "fabulous entities" (ghosts, chimeras, witches, etc.) created by
  the imagination, the relatively harmless fictions of the poet, and the sinister fictions of
  lawyer and priest (see *Bowring* viii, 199, 126, 262; U. C. lxix, 52, 221). But it is also true
  of entities we cannot easily dispense with like rights, obligations, the will, the mind, etc.

25 Bentham liberally borrows terminology from Hume, and surely was much influenced by
  Hume's doctrines. But he often borrows terms without thereby embracing the associated
  Humean understanding of the terminology. Regarding his use of the term "impression"
  he says, "I may be permitted to borrow the nomenclature of that subtle and elegant philosopher in this instance without adopting many of his opinions . . ." (U. C. lxx (a), 52).
  He explicitly rejects two such opinions: (a) Although often throughout his writings (e.g.
  at *Bowring* viii, 224; and U. C. cxxxv, 311) he speaks of ideas as copies of impressions
  (following Hume, *Treatise*, I, III, i), he clearly rejects this notion in an early fragment on
  basic concepts of mathematics (U. C. cxxxv, 56; see also U. C. lxix, 219). (b) He also decisively rejects the Humean doctrine (*Treatise*, I, III, vii) that belief is an especially lively
  idea, insisting to the contrary that "A belief is [the product of] an act of the judgment"
  U. C. lxix, 133). The same point is made, with considerable humor, at RJE vi, 255 f.

26 See, e.g., U. C. xlvi, 21; *Bowring* viii, 197, 199–203, 325–6, 262–4; U. C. cvi, 2–3.
  The arrangements vary in detail largely because Bentham never settles on a precise statement of the principle of inclusion and dependence. He vacillates especially over the status
  (real or fictitious) of space, time, and relations.

First order (sometimes he calls them "semi-real") fictions include motion and rest, matter, form and figure, space, time, and (sometimes) relations. Second order fictions include qualities[27] and collective entities (e.g., genera, species, and collections of events, like war), which are aggregates of real entities or events all of which share some common properties. Higher orders of fictions are possible too, e.g., rights, duties, liberty, virtue and vice, and psychological entities like the will.

The principle of distinction underlying this classification is never made fully explicit and never defended by Bentham. Frequently, he seems to rely on an epistemic criterion: real entities are those objects the existence of which is made known to us directly through perception.[28] However, he admits that only mental entities (impressions and ideas) are directly apprehended and concrete material substances are perceptible only indirectly. Often he speaks of them as "inferential" entities, since their existence is determined only by inference from perceptions.[29] But this does not disqualify them as real entities for Bentham.[30] Furthermore, he is willing to allow the possibility of *incorporeal* substances (i.e., real entities) — e.g., God, angels, minds, etc.[31] Thus, the epistemic criterion is at best insufficient.

The principle that seems to be at work most often in Bentham's discussion rests on a notion of dependence and independence: fictitious entities are dependent on other entities (real or fictitious), whereas real entities are independent and self- sufficient (ontological sovereigns, as it were).[32] But the dependence re-

---

27 Here he seems to have in mind Locke's doctrine of secondary qualities (U. C. lxix, 184, 227–8). In his view, qualities are produced in us by motion of material substances (which causes the corresponding sensations) (U. C. lxix, 127, 228).

28 See e.g., *Bowring* viii, 325; U. C. xlvi, 21. At U. C. xlvi, 18 he says that real entities are "objects capable of affording impressions."

29 *Bowring* viii, 195–7, 224, 126 n*.

30 Bentham, like Locke, is a philosophical realist. At several places he is content to briskly dismiss Berkeleian idealism in a terse footnote. See, e.g., *Bowring* viii, 197, 119, 189; U. C. xlvi, 20.

31 *Bowring* viii, 195–6, 126 n*; U. C. xlvi, 20.

32 "[M]aterial substances and perceptions [are] ... substantive and independent: motions modal and dependent. For a material body may be conceived to exist without motion, but motion cannot be conceived to exist without either a perception or a material body ..." (U. C. xlvi, 20). "It is from real entities only that we get any idea at all of fictitious ones. They exist only in real ones. If a proposition be not true of them as they exist in real entities it is not true at all ..." (U. C. cxxxv, 67).

Further evidence that this principle is at work: (i) At U. C. ci, 30, Bentham says that time is a fiction as is space, but that time is dependent on place and so is *more fictitious* yet than place. (ii) At U. C. clxix, 229 he draws an analogy between real entities and Aristotle's notion of first substance. (iii) It is the principle at work in most of the discussions of the various orders of fictitious entities; e.g., at *Bowring* viii, 326, 197; U. C. cvi, 2–3; U. C. lxix, 140.

lations between real and fictitious entities hold only derivatively. A deeper dependence underlies and explains them. The deeper fact is that fictitious entities, unlike real entities, depend for their "existence" on language,[33] and even more fundamentally on what Locke had called the "active powers of the mind."[34] The key to understanding the central themes of Bentham's ontology and epistemology, and thus his theory of probability, lies in understanding this thesis regarding the dependence of fictions on language and mind.

To begin, consider Bentham's paradigm entities: concrete particular material objects (or events consisting of such objects in motion). These objects exist in nature, entirely independent of mind or language. Such substances are composed of matter, have some form or shape, are either in motion or at rest during some time and at some place; they possess qualities of various sorts and bear relations to other things. However, Bentham maintains, the matter, form, motion, time, place, qualities, relations, etc., do not really exist; they are fictitious entities ascribed, in a manner of speaking, to the concrete object.

> The word *substance* is the name of a class of real entities, of the only class which has in it any corporeal entities.
> The word *matter* is but the name of a class of fictitious entities, springing out of the sort of real entity distinguished by the word *substance*.
> And so it is in regard to the word *form*.
> The ideas respectively designated by these corresponding words are fractional results, produced from the decomposition of the word *substance*. (*Bowring* viii, 201)

The fictitious entities: matter, motion, etc., are produced by "decomposing" the concrete object. This is, of course, logical decomposition, i.e., analysis.[35] These fictitious entities are arrived at by the mental operation of analysis or abstraction. And "[a]bstract entities can no otherwise be expressed than by fiction" (*Bowring* viii, 334), that is, as an object, "the existence of which is feigned by the imagination, feigned for the purpose of discourse, and which, when so formed, is spoken of as a real one" (*Bowring* viii, 325).

The nature of this dependence of fictions on the mind and language can best be seen if we shift our attention from the ontological perspective to the epistemological. Following Locke, again, Bentham insists that all knowledge is derived from experience, observation, and perception. All ideas are derived (or have their

---

33 At *Bowring* viii, 198 he maintains: "To language, then – to language alone – it is, that fictitious entities owe their existence, their impossible, yet indispensible, existence."
34 See Locke, *An Essay Concerning Human Understanding*, II, xii. Note that the dependence is not merely dependence on the mind, for all impressions and ideas depend on the mind in the sense that they are all mental entities. The claim here is that fictitious entities depend for their existence on the active or creative powers of the intellect.
35 Bentham calls it "primaeval logical analysis" (*Bowring* viii, 121–6).

roots in) immediate sense impressions.[36] Concrete material objects (either in motion or rest) impress sensible images on the mind (U. C. lxix, 140). But the concrete object presents a vastly complex, composite impression:

> No portion of matter ever presents itself to sense, without presenting, at one and the same time, a multitude of simple ideas, of all which taken together, the concrete one, in a state more or less correct and complete, is composed. At the same time, though naturally all these ideas present themselves together, the mind has it in its power to detach. . . any one or more of them from the rest, and either keep it in view in this detached state, or make it up into a compound with other simple ideas, detached in like manner from other sources. But, for the making of this separation — this abstraction, as it is called — more trouble, a stronger force of attention, is necessary, than for the taking them up, in a promiscuous bundle, as it were; in the bundle in which they have been tied together by the hand of Nature: that is, than for the consideration of the object in its concrete state (*Bowring* viii, 26, the author's emphasis omitted).

By focusing attention on one part of the composite image presented by the object and abstracting from that composite a new, abstract, idea is formed: the idea of (some particular) colour, or shape, etc. "Being abstracted and slipt off from the individual stock, and thereupon planted in the mind, it has there taken root and acquired a separate and independent existence" (*ibid*.). And from these, even more abstract ideas, e.g., of colour itself or figure, can be formed.[37] Thus the product of the several "mental operations" (attention, analysis, abstraction) performed on the sensory manifold is not just a set of *terms*, the names of so many fictitious entities, but a new set of *ideas* to which the terms in some way correspond.[38] On these ideas further mental operations may be performed (e.g., composition, synthesis, judgment or inference, arrangement or "methodization," etc.[39]) and the resulting product will be more fictions, i.e., more ideas, some more complex, some, as we shall see, simpler. "It is only by means of the real [entities] that we can understand the nature of such as are fictitious. The fictitious are entities created, as it were, by the imagination for the purpose of discourse. . ." (U. C. xlvi, 19).

But this account of the origins of fictions is misleading in two important respects. First, it suggests that Bentham shared with Hume (and arguably Locke)

36 These doctrines are, of course, the empiricist underpinnings of Bentham's entire philosophical outlook. They are expressed frequently throughout his writing. See, e.g., *Bowring* viii, 238; U. C. xlvi, 18; U. C. cxxxv, 304–5, 311. But, as I shall argue below, there is a deep strain of pragmatism in Bentham's philosophy as well, and equally as fundamental.

37 Ibid. See also *Bowring* viii, 256–8; *Bowring* xi, 72–3.

38 See *Bowring* viii, 127: "It is by an operation of the nature of *analysis, primaeval* analysis, that the ideas designated by the several names of *fictitious entities* have been formed." See also, *Bowring* viii, 121.

39 *Bowring* viii, 225–9, 256–8, 262–6, 281–2.

50   Gerald J. Postema

the view that the total sensible impression of a concrete object is in fact a large
aggregate of discrete atomic impressions ("simple ideas") marked off and bun-
dled together, as it were, by nature.[40] On this view, the mind may be actively
involved in creating *abstract* ideas (though Hume, of course, denied even this),
but the initial, discrete, simple ideas wait to be discovered by the mind. However, in fact Bentham's mature theory assigns a more radically active role to the
mind than this view allows.

   According to Bentham, concrete material objects — or particular events in
which such objects figure — impact upon the senses, creating a complex, but undifferentiated sensory manifold. The mind, driven by its needs and interests,
analyzes this sensory manifold, carving out one part or another for special attention, and thus fashioning so many discrete, simpler, impressions or ideas. Bentham calls this operation of the mind on given undifferentiated and uninter-
preted sensory data "primaeval logical analysis."[41] It is only *after* this analysis
or partitioning of primitive sensory experience, and its subsequent synthesis,
that the images yielded by events can be regarded as bundles of determinate,
assignable simple ideas. For Bentham, simplicity is not a sign of an idea's being
primitive or basic; on the contrary, it is a sign of the idea's being the product of
a sophisticated intellectual process.[42] Simple ideas are not the work of nature,
passively received by the mind,[43] but rather the artificial products of an active
and sophisticated human mind, seeking to satisfy its needs and pursue its interests.[44] The activities of the mind here, and elsewhere, are governed throughout by rules which are not *a priori* but pragmatic in origin, according to Bentham — a sort of pragmatic logic which, in his view, derives from the ultimate

---

40 This is suggested at *Bowring* viii, 26. See also U. C. lxix, 140: "Events, that is bodies in
    motion, offer/impress certain sensible, visible (tangible) images on the mind. Situations,
    that is the same bodies at rest, impress (offer) also certain sensible images on(to) the
    mind. These images in either case, are bundles of simple ideas determinate and assign-
    able." See also U. C. lxix, 127.

41 *Bowring* viii, 121–7. Compare his discussion of analysis and abstraction in mathematics
    ("posology"), U. C. cxxxv, 34, 37, 200–205, 217–25.

42 "Every man who speaks, speaks in propositions, the rudest savage, not less than the most
    polished orator, — terms taken by themselves are the work of abstraction, the produce of
    a refined analysis: – ages after ages must have elapsed before any such analysis was ever
    made" (*Bowring* viii, 321). See also *Bowring* viii, 322–3; U. C. cii, 413–14. "Inferior
    animals speak solely in *propositions*. By the faculty of *abstraction man* has learned to
    resolve his propositions into *words*." (U. C. cii, 81, author's emphasis).

43 "Making minerals, vegetables, and animals – this is her proper work — and it is quite
    enough for her; whenever you are bid to see her doing *man's* work, be sure it is not
    Nature that is doing it but the *author*, or somebody or other whom he patronizes and
    whom he has dressed up for the purpose in the goddess's robes . . ." (*Bowring* viii, 125,
    author's emphasis).

44 See *Bowring* viii, 124 n*, 125.

principle of rationality: the principle of utility.[45] Thus, *both* the abstract ideas of colour, figure, etc., *and* the particular simple ideas from which these ideas of qualities are derived, are products of the mind, i.e., are fictitious entities. Against this background it is possible to understand Bentham's otherwise paradoxical claim that "A body (real entity) is an aggregate of fictitious entities."[46] What he means is that real entities are concrete objects which present themselves to the human senses; the sensory product of that encounter is then subjected to analysis and reconstruction — matter is distinguished from form and figure, qualities are noted, etc. In short, the sensory manifold is "decomposed" into a large number of notable fictitious entities. Hence, the real concrete object (or its primitive sensory impact on the mind) is, from the point of view of the active mind, an aggregate of fictitious entities, a "bundle of simple ideas determinate and assignable."

The above account of fictions needs amending in a second respect: we need clarification of the relationship between language and the ideas fashioned by the active intellect. The category of fictions is, for Bentham, a linguistic category, and he often speaks of fictions as *designating,* or *being signs* of, ideas.[47] This suggests that fictions are simply labels attached, *post hoc,* to ideas fashioned by the mind, labels which purport to refer to real entities, but which in fact refer to the *ideas.* This is not his considered view, however. The thesis which calls for attention here is Bentham's version of Locke's[48] doctrine that language is the

45 See the "Essay on Logic," especially *Bowring* viii, 219–22. Compare Bentham's definition of logic with the definition I. A. Richards attributes to Peirce: "Logic is the Ethics of thinking in the sense in which Ethics is the bringing to bear of self-control for the purposes of realizing desires." Richards' review of C. K. Ogden's, *Bentham's Theory of Fictions* in *Scrutiny*, vol . 1 (1932), p. 408. Richards claims that this was also F. P. Ramsey's favourite quote.

46 U. C. cxxxv, 69. The passage continues: "Bodies (Real Entities) are distinguishable by the fictitious entities (properties) they are known to be made up of (to contain) and again by the degrees of them they contain."

47 See *Bowring* viii, 121, 127, 323.

48 See Locke, *Essay*, III, 2 ("[W]ords, in their primary or immediate signification, stand for nothing but the ideas in the mind of him that uses them. . .") No doubt Bentham was influenced in this, as in so many other matters, by Locke. But it is also likely that he draws here on the same Late Scholastic tradition which had powerfully influenced Locke's theory of language. E. J. Ashworth, in her paper, "Locke on Language," (forthcoming in *The Canadian Journal of Philosophy*) demonstrates that Locke at this point echoes the views of Late Scholastic logicians Du Trieu, Burgersdijck, and Sanderson. "They all agreed," she writes, "both that concepts had a part to play in the signifying process, and that words are used to refer to things rather than concepts, but they preferred to describe the situation by saying that words signify concepts immediately whereas they signify things only mediately, by means of the intervening concept." (The connection to Locke and Bentham is made even clearer by the fact that "concepts" for these logicians were regarded not as abstract entities, but components in one's internal mental language.) Sanderson is particularly interesting because he spoke of the concept as the *immediate signi-*

52   Gerald J. Postema

sign of thought.[49]

   This doctrine is best understood against the background of Bentham's view
of the functions and origins of language. Bentham distinguishes between the
"transitive" (or social) and the "intransitive" (or solitary) uses of language (*Bowring* viii, 228–9, 301). This distinction is not meant to mark the difference between public and so-called "private" language, but that between two different
functions of the same, essentially public language. Language is used "intransitively" in the largely solitary process of shaping and fixing thoughts or ideas for
oneself; in its "transitive" use the speaker seeks to convey or communicate the
thoughts/ideas thus determined. According to Bentham, the transitive is first in
the order of time. Language developed first from the need to communicate primitive thoughts and experiences,[50] i.e., immediate perceptual experience of material objects and immediate affective or conative experience (*Bowring* viii, 322–
3). And, in his view, it is still largely for the purpose of communication that we
use language "intransitively." Nevertheless, once we move beyond mere communication of primitive experience, the capacity for which we share with animals,
to the formation of intellectually more sophisticated notions about ourselves,
our experience, and the world around us, the order of priority is reversed. Communication depends on the formation and articulation of ideas intransitively.
But, it turns out, this intransitive use of language *just is,* in Bentham's view, the
activity of the active intellect in fashioning its conception of itself and the world
around it. For this task, Bentham insists, language is not just useful, making the
process easier and more efficient, it is absolutely indispensable. Formation of
ideas beyond the most primitive is possible *only* with the use of language.[51]
Without language, most of our thoughts (recall that Bentham uses this term very
widely) not only would be incommunicable, they would be literally unthinkable
— most aspects of life and experience would be unavailable to both thought and

---

ficate of a work and individuals as *mediate significates* – language to which Bentham's
own is very close (see below). This is not surprising since throughout Bentham's writings
on logic, language, and fictions there is evident a very intimate knowledge of Sanderson's
influential logic text, *Logicae Artis Compendium* (1618, and many later editions through
1841). Sanderson was widely used in Oxford and there is no doubt that Bentham studied
it as an undergraduate. See his letter to his father 12 June 1761, *Correspondence, Collected Works* vol. i. p. 47. References to Sanderson in Bentham's work on fictions etc.,
can be found, among other places, at *Bowring* viii, 214, 231, 235, 252, 256, 261, 199,
104.

49 *Bowring* viii, 329, 320–23, 188. "Thought" here is understood very broadly by Bentham to encompass any and all constituents of the mind, from the most primitive sensory experiences to the most abstract ideas, from beliefs, judgments, and the like ("intellectual thoughts") to desires, wants, intentions, volitions, fears, and the like ("voli-
tional"/"concupiscible" thoughts). See *Bowring* viii, 329–30, 333.

50 *Bowring* viii, 228–9, 320; U. C. cii, 92.

51 *Bowring* viii, 119, 129, 174, 198, 219, 231, 320–23, 331; U. C. ci, 423.

discourse. But, further, this instrument of language, having originally been designed to communicate primitive sensory experience of concrete material bodies
in motion, is stamped with the pattern of this original design. "[O]ur ideas coming,
all of them, from our senses, from what other source can the signs of them. . .
come?" (*Bowring* viii, 329). Consequently, fictions are an indispensable part of
language and thought,

> [a] necessity to which we are subjected by the imperfection of the instrument for the
> purposes of discourse, the necessity of mixing falsehood with truth, on pain of being
> without ideas, as well as without conversation. . . (*Bowring* viii, 129n).

Thus, language is not merely a set of labels conventionally adopted to denote
objects either material or immaterial. Language is, rather, the indispensable expression or embodiment of human thought, the instrument with which we shape
our conceptions of ourselves and the external world.

Now, terms in this language sometimes actually refer, actually denote objects
in the real world (material objects or ideas), but often they stand for, that is,
express, ideas for which there is no actual referent. Bentham makes this point in
a way that has puzzled some commentators. He claims that some "thoughts,"
though not all, refer beyond themselves to entities (either real or fictitious).
Thus, he maintains, it becomes necessary to distinguish between the *immediate*
subject of communication and the indirect or *ulterior* subject. The only immediate subject of communication, he claims, is some belief, conviction, attitude,
feeling, or other "thought" (*Bowring* viii, 330). But such thoughts always have
secondary subjects as well, viz., actual events, states of affairs, or real entities in
the world.[52] What Bentham means here is that we are capable of talking about
the world, but only by way of making known, signifying, or expressing constituents of the mind. The terminology here is unapt, but the distinction seems
to be that between expressing a belief and making a report about some fact or
event (including one's believing). To *signify* some content in the speaker's mind,
for Bentham, is not to denote it but to express it — literally, to "press it out"
(*Bowring* viii, 227) — and thereby convey the thought to another person.

According to Bentham, the immediate subject of language about real entities
is a *thought* or *idea* about the real entity in question — it expresses that thought.
The ulterior subject is the real entity itself — it refers to or denotes that entity.
This is simple enough, but the matter gets more complicated when we turn to
language ostensibly referring to fictitious entities and Bentham never discusses
this case adequately. The view seems to be that the immediate subjects of language using fictitious terms are, again, thoughts or ideas, but this time ideas
which are products of the mind (or language). Because this language develops

52 *Bowring* viii, 321, 330–31, 333, 336, 187.

on the patterns established for communicating about real entities, it appears to refer to real entities too, that is, to material objects in the external world. But it does not. There are no real entities (not even ideas) which are the ulterior subjects of such discourse. But such talk is not in consequence nonsense, nor is it incapable of validation. However, validation cannot be carried out in the standard way in which discourse about real entities is tested (i.e., determining whether the appropriate correspondence between language and reality holds). Validation of the use of fictions must be carried out by tracing the fiction back to the real entities from which it was constructed or abstracted and assessing the process by which the fiction was fashioned. Since the mind in the exercise of its active powers is governed by rational principles, the fiction can be regarded as veridical or legitimate if the (rational) process through which it was created was properly followed.

Thus, *all* language is expressive of (signifies) ideas. This is not a feature peculiar to discourse about morality or probability. And this fact does not preclude rational assessment of judgments. Although the methods of testing then will vary in accord with the nature of the ideas or thoughts involved.

Thus, the following picture of Bentham's view of the relations obtaining among reality, thought, and language emerges. It is only through creation of abstract ideas with the aid of fictions that the advances of thought of which the human mind is capable can be achieved. Through the exercise of the rational faculties the human mind is capable of fashioning a framework for understanding and manipulating the world around it. This framework is embodied (though imperfectly) in language. Language directly signifies our thought and ideas; thus, it does not (cannot) mirror accurately the actual structure of the external world. Language does not provide us with a picture of reality, but with the tools needed to grasp and manipulate reality to our own purposes. For Bentham, as Ogden has noted, language "is essentially a technological apparatus for dealing with the world of things in space."[53] This is a philosophical theory, then, which is as much pragmatist as empiricist. On this view, we have sensory access to the external world to some extent, but the structure of reality *as we know it* is the artificial, "fictitious" product of the human intellect. This conceptual apparatus is determined, however, not by *a priori* principles or categories, but by the needs, interests, and purposes of human beings and the strategies they develop to meet their needs and advance their purposes.

53 C. K. Ogden, *Bentham's Theory of Fictions* (London: Routledge and Kegan Paul, 1932), Introduction, p. xlvi.

Facts, Fictions, and Law   55

III.

With this sketch of Bentham's theory of fictions in hand we can turn to the task of clarifying his account of probability. In his writings on fictions, Bentham maintains that probability, necessity, possibility, etc. are "ontological fictions" (*Bowring* viii, 120), i.e., fictions concerned with existence. Indeed, he regards existence itself as a fictitious entity, a quality predicated properly of real entities or events, and falsely (or in a manner of speaking) of fictitious entities (*Bowring* viii, 210). Unlike other fictions, however, ontological fictions are doubly fictitious; they are, he says, "fictitious qualities."

> Quality itself is but a fictitious entity, but these are all of them so many fictitious qualities. They do not, real qualities – they do not, like gravity, solidity, roundness, hardness, as belong to the objects themselves to which they are ascribed, – in the character of attributes of the objects to which they are ascribed (*Bowring* viii, 211).

The point is not that probability and its kin are qualities of qualities (i.e., second or higher order fictions), for many kinds of fictions can be regarded in this way. Rather, the point is that although all qualities are fictitiously said to exist (directly or indirectly) in real entities, *these* qualities are fictitiously (i.e., falsely) *ascribed* to events or facts, whereas in fact they are qualities of experiences or beliefs about events or facts. Probability and its kin signify a modification of belief: "a disposition, a persuasion of the mind...in relation to the state of things, or the event . . . to which these qualities are ascribed" (*ibid*.).

Bentham's argument for this subjectivist interpretation of probability should now be clear. Noting correctly that probability was not an ordinary natural property of events, he was forced by his lean ontology to regard probability language as expressive of certain ideas without direct reference to real entities. His theory of language surely encouraged this move and suggested to him the most plausible alternative analysis. One implication of his distinction between the immediate and ulterior subjects of discourse is his doctrine of elliptical expression, a doctrine which leads naturally to regarding probability language as expressive of degrees of persuasion. In his view, my utterance "Eurybiades struck Themistocles" must be regarded as elliptical, since the expression inside the quotation marks does not capture and display all that is conveyed by my utterance. In particular, it leaves out the fact that I *expressed* my belief in the event's having taken place. Thus, says Bentham, if the matter were fully to be expressed, the representation of my utterance should read: "It is my belief that Eurybiades struck Themistocles".[54] Now, accepting this doctrine for the time

54 This does not generate an infinite regress (such that 'p' means 'I believe that p' which, in turn, means 'I believe that I believe that p,' etc.) because in Bentham's notation "I be-

being, consider the utterance "Eurybades probably struck Themistocles." How should this be understood? One might try: "It is my belief that E probably struck T." But that would locate the probability as a property of the event and that has already been ruled out. A more natural analaysis would be: "I am reasonably confident that E struck T." For we say, for example, "I know E struck T," or "I think E struck T;" and in each case the qualifier modifies the opinion, not the fact. To say, "I know that E struck T" is, among other things, to say quite emphatically "E struck T." And to do so in no way changes the event referred to. Rather, it qualifies the speaker's relationship to the statement referring to that event. The use of "probably" and its kin most naturally fits this pattern.

This, then, is Bentham's argument for his subjectivist account of probability. Despite the evident weaknesses that remain, it is clear that this argument does not commit Bentham to the radical, sceptical Humean subjectivism. We have already seen that he does not believe that the expressivist or performative aspect of probability language precludes critical assessment of the ideas thereby expressed. He does insist, insofar as immediate signification is concerned, that the speaker is infallible (since he cannot, in Bentham's view, mistake the contents of his mind). But it does not follow from this that the belief or conviction is true, correct, justified, or reasonable; nor does Bentham warrant this inference. As we have seen, there is nothing in his views generally that precludes rational assessment of such expressions. And concerning probability assignments, Bentham seems to allow explicitly for rational assessment of them: "to say that such a degree of probative force is *properly belonging* to a mass of evidence in question, is to say that, upon the receipt of the same mass of evidence, the same degree of intensity of persuasion is the degree which is *fit and proper* to have place in the bosom of the judge" (IRE, 18 n).

This should come as no surprise in light of what we have learned from the discussion of Bentham's theory of fictions. His analysis of probability as a fictitious quality allowed him to put to rest questions regarding the ontological status of probabilities which constantly troubled him, while leaving open certain crucial epistemological questions. Probabilities are neither objective entities or events "in nature," nor are they mysterious abstract entities. They are, insofar as they have any reality, psychological facts of a special sort. But Bentham's subjectivism does not stop there. The "ideas" which fictitious terms signify are not merely the products of the impact of material bodies on our senses, or of the association of two or more given ideas. As we have seen, the rational faculties, according to Bentham, play an active role in the formation of such ideas. This is especially true of belief (in all its grades) which, he insists, is the product of judg-

lieve that . . .' marks the expression of the belief, it does not purport to *report that* one believes.

ment (U.C. 1xix, 133), i.e., of the exercise of the "judicial faculty." And the exercise of these faculties is open to critical assessment. Thus, although the subjective degree of confidence that a person has in a given hypothesis is a fact about the state of mind of that person (one which, Bentham believes, is capable of being directly apprehended by the person), this degree of confidence is itself subject to rational assessment insofar as the exercise of that person's rational faculties which produced it is. Such ideas have, or ought to have, a rational basis, and that basis, and the inference from it, are open to critical assessment. Hence, probability statements or assessments of the probative force of evidence (E) for some principal fact (P) must be seen to involve more than expression of the speaker's current state of mind. They also implicitly appeal to a complex fact about how (or how much) E *would* incline the speaker to embrace P when they are both regarded under certain appropriate conditions. Confidence in the inference from E to P is open to correction just as perceptual judgments or beliefs may be corrected for distance or perspective.[55]

Direct support for this reading of Bentham's subjectivism comes from several quarters. First, Bentham allows that it is not uncommon for people to express full confidence in propositions which in fact are self-contradictory (*Bowring* v.ii, 211; IRE, 47). Such propositions represent impossible states of affairs, and this is so regardless of what people think about the matter. Their confidence is ill-placed; the judgment of probability is just wrong. This mistake is to be explained, in this type of case, in terms of a failure sufficiently to attend to the meaning of the words in question, which failure results in misdirection of attention to experience and evidence. Thus, he concludes, those who seriously entertain such propositions are simply mistaken — not about their degree of confidence, but about the warrant for that confidence.

Second, immediately after asserting forcefully that probability and improbability are not real qualities inhering in the facts themselves, but only fictitious qualities expressing degrees of persuasion, Bentham turns to the question of justification. What are the causes, that is, *grounds*, of this persuasion? he asks.

> It having been shown that improbability and impossibility, applied to a matter of fact, are merely terms expressing a certain strength of persuasion of the non-existence of that fact — what remains is, to show what are the grounds on which such a persuasion is liable to be entertained: to show, in other words, in what consists the improbability or impossibility of any alleged fact.[56]

---

55 Compare Hume's views on the moral sentiments, especially in the *Enquiry Concerning the Principles of Morals*, ed. Charles W. Hendel (New York: The Liberal Arts Press, Inc., 1957), e.g., pp. 5–6, 198–9. See generally two papers by W. D. Falk, "Hume on Practical Reason," *Philosophical Studies*, 27 (1975), 1–18 and "Hume on Is and Ought," *Canadian Journal of Philosophy*, 6 (1976), 359–78.

56 RJE vii, 79. See also RJE vii, 83–4; IRE, 46.

58   Gerald J. Postema

Bentham is not content to locate the psychological source of probability claims; he finds it necessary to give an account of how such persuasion comes about and how it can be justified. Confidence, on his view, is not a brute datum; it calls for explanation and justification.

The process of arriving at rational assessments of probability is, in Bentham's rough and tentative account, divided into two parts or stages: the first concerns judgments of improbability, defining conditions under which claims may properly be disbelieved with full confidence. The primary test is whether the proposition or alleged fact conforms, or fails to conform, to "the established course of nature" as understood or judged by the speaker.[57] The judgment of the improbability of an event is based on a judgment of disconformity of the alleged event's occurring and what the speaker knows about the regular causal relations that obtain in nature. Bentham makes clear that this is a potentially complex judgment of the overall fit (or lack of it) of the alleged fact with the rest of our beliefs about nature gained from long experience. He suggests, though of course he never explicitly states, that the process involved is akin to inference to the best explanation of a large body of our beliefs. The judgment of improbability, then, will be relative to the assessor's beliefs about the established course of nature, and his best explanatory account of his beliefs, but this is still a rational assessment made on the basis of experience, and not simply the immediate response of the mind to the appearance in his field of awareness of the piece of evidence and, in close proximity, the principal fact in question.[58]

The second stage or part of this process guides assessment of the relative degree of probative force of a body of evidence for some principal fact. This Bentham calls the method of "infirmative suppositions" (RJE vii, 64−5). The method is defined roughly as follows: Suppose that one regards some evidentiary fact E as counting in favour of some principal fact P to *some* extent or other (in court of law this would be a minimal condition of relevance[59]). To determine the probative force of E with regard to P, first consider whether there are any facts which are neither impossible nor improbable as defined above, and which

---

57 IRE, 45−7; RJE vii, 83−105.

58 Bentham emphatically rejects the view that belief or persuasion is formed simply as a brute or intuitive response to experience. He calls this "nonsense psychology" or "nonsense *pisteutics*" and lumps this heresy together with "nonsense ethics" (moral sense and moral sentiments theories) which he excoriates (e.g., in Chapter 2 of the *Introduction to the Principles of Morals and Legislation*). (He attacks Hume for falling into this heresy after seeing the Utilitarian light; RJE vi, 240 n*.) All of these heresies rest on the irrationalist "principle of sympathy and antipathy." The mistake both in ethics and "pisteutics" is that the view short circuits the process of rational formation of judgments in light of experience (and utility). This process takes "thought and talent," he insists, not mere sentiment or the propensity to believe.

59 See Eggleston, *Evidence, Proof, and Probability*, pp. 64−8.

were they to obtain would be incompatible with the existence of *P* or in virtue of which the existence of *P* would be less probable. We are to think of circumstances (which are themselves, and in combination with *E*, compatible with the course of nature) which when added to *E* would make *P's* obtaining a matter contrary to *E*, given what we know of the course of nature. Now, if *no* such "infirmative suppositions" are, from one's perspective (i.e., given one's overall beliefs), conceivable, then *E* is *conclusive* of *P*. If, however, one or more such infirmative suppositions is conceivable, then the probative force of *E* on *P* falls short of practical certainty. The degree of probative force of *E* on *P* according to Bentham, is equal to the ratio expressive of practical certainty minus the probability of the infirmative supposition's actually obtaining. And where there is more than one such infirmative supposition (say, $I_1, I_2, I_3 \ldots I_n$) conceivable, the probative force of *E* on *P* is equal to practical certainty minus the probability of (I_1 or I_2 or I_3 or ... or I_n) obtaining.[60] The basic idea seems to be that that the proper degree of persuasion of *P* given *E* for a given person can be determined by measuring the shortfall from full confidence (practical certainty) produced by doubts put in the way of full confidence, qualified by the seriousness of those doubts. This is likely to be in many cases a complex matter of judgment.

The above proposal for a method of determining the strength of inference from evidentiary to principal facts, despite its sketchy character, reveals clearly Bentham's fundamental approach to the question of assessing probative force of evidence. The radical Humean version of subjectivism is decisively rejected. Confidence to some degree in *P* is not simply *produced* by reflecting on *E*. The belief is the product of a judgment arrived at by following a rule-governed strategy. But, similarly, the strictly logical, Leibnizian view of the relation between evidence and hypothesis is rejected. Nowhere, least of all in his description of the method of infirmative suppositions, does Bentham embrace the view that there is one and only objective, logical (though non-deductive) relation between evidence and conclusion such that belief in *P* is rational or justified given *E* just to the degree that that relation holds.[61] The degree of confidence which a person ought to have in a given statement is determined by application of "logical" rules, but these are not rules of logic strictly speaking. They are, rather, strategies for the direction of the mind. They are "procedural" rather than "substantive" logical rules. As we have seen, Bentham's approach to logic was essentially pragmatic. Rejecting what he regarded as the sterile syllogistic logic of the "aristotelians," he sought to bring Bacon's insights into the scientific process to

---

60 This, I believe is what Bentham means when he speaks of "the sum of their infirmative forces" (RJE vii, 65).

61 For example, J. M. Keynes, *A Treatise on Probability*, (London: Macmillan, 1921), Chapter 1; R. Carnap, *Logical Foundations of Probability* (Chicago: Univ. of Chicago Press, 1950).

bear on the whole field of intellectual and practical affairs. He sought a method
by the use of which the human mind could learn from, and build on, observation
and experience. The task of such a logic, in his view, is to define strategies for
the best use of the rational faculties, where "best use" is defined in terms, ultimately, of successfully advancing human purposes and satisfying human needs
and interests.

Thus, Bentham' account of probability, both within and outside the law, is
subjectivist and pragmatist. Sharing many features with both modern subjectivism — especially its stress on the essential connection between probability assessments and decisions, choice, and action — and the longer Leibnizian tradition
with its stress on rational assessment of assignments of probability, it calls attention to a philosophically interesting middle way. However, the picture I have
sketched of Bentham's views of the semantic and epistemological foundations of
probability may be too clean, representing Bentham's views as more coherent
and well-developed than they in fact are. It is time, now to muddy the waters
some.

We may begin by considering the relation between Bentham's modified subjectivism and relativism concerning probability assignments. Unlike modern subjectivists, Bentham sketches a method of assessing the rationality of initial probability assignments. But this account gives no guarantee that rational assignments by different people will be the same. Bentham's sophisticated subjectivism
does not rule out a vigorous interpersonal relativism. Now, Bentham seems willing to accept this, but he attributes it to the relativity of probability assignments
to evidence and background beliefs (RJE vii, 80–82, 91–98). (The King of Siam
rejects travellers' reports of "hardened water" in northern claimates as absurd
because they do not fit well with his experience and beliefs about the ordinary
course of nature (RJE vii, 95).) But Bentham also fervently believes that, given
the same store of background beliefs regarding the ordinary course of nature,
people would make the same assignments of probability, provided they follow
the procedure faithfully. Thus, in the end, Bentham's account of probability,
though subjectivist, is not radically relativist. But we have already seen that this
does not follow from anything in the account of rational assessment of probability assignments. Bentham seems to introduce a contingent assumption here
akin to Cohen's assumption of "universal cognitive competence."[62] Bentham
never explicitly defends this assumption, but motivation for it, perhaps, can be
seen in his general Enlightenment attitude toward knowledge and human improvement. In his view, the heavy blanket of ignorance, prejudice, and superstition smothers universal human potential for rational judgment in practical and
theoretical affairs. If the blanket is lifted, if obstacles to rational judgment and
human progress are eliminated, the clear and pure light of truth will shine through,

---

62 See L. Jonathan Cohen, "Freedom of Proof," in this volume, pp. 2 *et passim*.

the same for everyone, just as clearing away ignorance, prejudice, and superstition will reveal a deep and universal commitment to the simple rationality of the principle of utility. But if this is Bentham's motivation, then we have uncovered a residual and quite broad *objectivism* in his view of truth and knowledge which is not entirely consistent with his professed, though sophisticated, subjectivism, nor in his implicit pragmatism.

IV.

A few words remain to be said, in closing, regarding the relationship between Bentham's account of the semantics of probability and the current debate between Pascalians and Baconians over the syntax of probability statements. It should be clear from the above discussion that there is nothing in Bentham's general account of the semantics of probability which puts him firmly in either camp. But his remarks about the epistemology of probability and the model of rational assessment of probability assignments suggest that he would side with the Baconians if he were given the choice.

First, we should note that, despite his proposal of the wager as a device for measuring a person's degree of persuasion,[63] Bentham seems to have harbored serious doubts about the Pascalian understanding of probability (the "doctrine of chances") at least for juridical contexts. He seems to have regarded himself as providing an account not of "mathematical" probability as measured by the doctrine of chances, but of "ordinary" probability.[64] Cohen rightly points out Bentham's rejection of the Pascalian calculus, but he draws this correct conclusion from what I believe is the wrong textual evidence.[65] In the passage he cites to support his claim (RJE vi, 224) Bentham does reject what he calls the "mathematical" scale for measuring probative force, but what he has in mind in that passage is a scale of measurement which has no upper bound (the "infinite scale") which he links (wrongly?) to the doctrine of chances. He rejects *this* scale not because he believes it to be conceptually mistaken, but only because he thinks it infeasible for use in juridical contexts. The criticism rests on the assumption that, strictly speaking, no matter how strong a case has been

---

63 See above p. 43 and RJE vi, 223. This passage must not be given too much weight in determining Bentham's general views on probability. The wager, in fact, is not a good device for measuring degrees of *persuasion*, – i.e., probative force of *evidence for* a hypothesis – since it measures only one's confidence in the hypothesis (without taking into account the evidence for it). For Bentham's purposes it measures the wrong thing.

64 This is not to say that he was adverse to searching for a feasible probability scale or measure which could be expressed in quantitative terms. See RJE vi, 223–35.

65 Cohen, *The Probable and the Provable*, p. 54.

made for some proposition, the addition of even more evidence would make that case even stronger: one hundred unimpeachable witnesses to the commission of a crime make the case twice as strong (says Bentham) as fifty such witnesses. But for practical purposes we need to define some upper limit of evidence — practical certainty — and treat probative force as if it were a finite quantity finitely divisible. This, clearly, does not commit Bentham to rejection of the Pascalian probability calculus.

However, there is stronger evidence of such a rejection later in the *Rationale* (RJE vi, 240—44). The context of the passage is Bentham's attack on "innatists" who wish to explain our willingness to believe a witness to an event, the prior probability of which is extremely small, in terms of an innate propensity to believe testimony of others, even against our judgment of the near impossibility of the event's occurring. This, Bentham objects, would commit us to abandon reason and experience for sentiment, which would be irrational. Belief in the trustworthiness of witnesses, like judgments of probability generally, are based on experience of the normal course of nature. In both cases, one's degree of persuasion is not based on some judgment of relative frequency, but rather on what makes sense of experience as a whole in terms of orderly causal relations in nature. Thus, we believe witnesses in the face of mathematically or statistically improbable events because (or when) we judge that the events, though statistically improbable, are *not extraordinary*. As Mill points out in his editorial note to this passage, Bentham is distinguishing sharply between *mathematical* improbability and "ordinary" improbability. Mathematically improbable events occur all the time; we do not regard them as improbable because they conform to our views regarding the orderly behavior of nature. Although this argument is not free of confusion, it is reasonably clear that Bentham has in mind a conception of probability not reducible to the standard Pascalian conception.

Second, the model of rational assessment of probability and probative force which Bentham sketches, though admittedly rough and undefended, bears a certain kinship relation to the recently revived Baconian conception of probability. The method of "infirmative suppositions" is Baconian in spirit. It is designed to assess the strength of inferences from a body of particular facts to another particular fact, all against the background of already established or accepted (though defeasible) causal generalizations. The initial judgment of relevance of evidence is made on this basis and the inference is challenged by other hypotheses which are themselves established on the same basis. The probability of *P* given *E* is determined by locating relevant circumstances that would defeat the *prima facie* inference from *E* to *P*. This resembles, though it does not reproduce, Cohen's "method of relevant variables" and "the balancing off of favourable and unfavourable circumstances" in the assessment of inductive probabilities.[66]

66 See Cohen, *ibid.*. sections 42—44, 58—62.

One might object that Bentham's account of probability is uninformatively circular, since it defines probability of *P* given *E* in terms of the probability of the potential infirmative suppositions. But this is not a serious objection: (a) Bentham is not *defining* probability or probative force here. That definition, or an approximation to it, was given earlier — the probative force of *E* is the degree to which a person would be persuaded of *P* on the evidence of *E* were he to assess *E* in the appropriate fashion. What Bentham sets out here is the method for properly assessing probative force. (b) According to this process, the inference from *E* to *P* is a function of the strength of other inferences which are themselves based on other inferences. The warrant from any particular inference is drawn from the web of inferences and beliefs to which it is connected. This is at least plausible, though not uncontroversial, once we recognize the deep pragmatism of Bentham's epistemology.

Problems, of course, remain. One of them concerns the status of the probabilities involved in "infirmative suppositions." Once they are brought into the process two different judgments of probability are required: (a) the probability of the evidence *E plus* the infirmative suppositions yielding the complement of the principal fact *P* (or weakening the probability of *P*) and (b) the probability of the circumstances of the infirmative suppositions *and* those of *E* simultaneously obtaining. Now, clearly Bentham regards the probability assessment in (a) to be of the same kind as those already discussed. But what is the nature of the judgment in (b)? Is this also to be understood on the same model? Or does this involve a judgment of frequency? And if the latter, how does that affect the overall probative force of *E* on *P*?

Bentham's account of probability, like all of his philosophical reflections, was born out of the need to establish the foundations of a practical discipline. Both the strengths and weaknesses of his account can be traced largely to this point of origin. Its strengths lie in this sensitivity to the complex "subjective" and "objective" dimensions of legal proof — to the roles of both belief, decision and persuasion *and* rational justification in this process. Thus one often finds passages stressing the rhetorical or expressive uses of probability language alongside other passages pointing out the commitment implicit in such use to rational justification for the assignments of probability made. Out of this appreciation comes a sketch of an account of probability which is of genuine philosophical interest. But at the same time, the account tends to be eclectic, and the tensions between subjective and objective elements are not fully resolved. Perhaps because of the practical origin of the excursion into the theory of probability, perhaps also because of his own philosophical limitations, Bentham did not develop the view in detail once it was sketched out to his immediate satisfaction. Thus it remains a sketch — suggestive, but wanting fuller, detailed articulation and defense.

No doubt the rule-scepticism running through his theory of evidence is influenced by his epistemology and his conception of the probative force of evi-

64   Gerald J. Postema

dence. (Although there may be other motivations for it also.) But this is not a
sceptic's epistemology. The precise relationship between Bentham's rule-scepticism and his epistemology remains to be worked out, but the initial paradox that
motivated our excursion into Bentham's theory of probability is now resolved.

[3]

FORMAL AND EMPIRICAL RESEARCH ON CASCADED INFERENCE IN JURISPRUDENCE

DAVID A. SCHUM*

ANNE W. MARTIN

This paper reports observations from a series of formal and empirical studies of the process of assessing the probative value of evidence in the cascaded or hierarchical inference tasks commonly performed by fact finders in court trials. The formal research develops expressions that prescribe how the ingredients of various forms of evidence can be coherently combined in assessing the probative value of evidence. These expressions allow identification and systematic analysis of a wide assortment of subtle properties of evidence, many of which are commonly recognized in evidence law. The reported empirical research was designed to evaluate the consistency with which persons actually assess the probative value of evidence when they are asked to make these evaluations in several equivalent ways. Results show that persons, when required to mentally combine a large amount of probabilistic evidence, exhibit certain inconsistencies such as treating contradictory testimony as corroborative testimony and double-counting or overvaluing redundant testimony. However, when people are asked to make assessments about the fine-grained logical details of the same evidence, these inconsistencies do not occur.

I. INTRODUCTION

This paper contains an introduction to some of the results and observations we have accumulated from a series of studies on the task of assessing the probative value of inconclusive or probabilistic trial evidence. Some of these studies are formal or logical in nature and concern the manner in which the probative value of evidence *should be* assessed coherently. The other studies are empirical and behavioral in nature and concern the manner in which persons *actually do* assess the probative value of evidence. Our dual concern was voiced by Wigmore (1937: 8), who expressed interest in ". . . the reasons why a total mass of evidence does or should persuade us to a given conclusion, and why our conclusions would or should

* The research reported in this paper was supported by The National Science Foundation under Grants SOC 77-28471 and SES 80-24203 to Rice University. The authors gratefully acknowledge the advice and assistance during the planning of our research of Professor Richard Lempert, University of Michigan School of Law, and Professor L. Jonathan Cohen, The Queen's College, Oxford University. The authors also wish to thank Dr. Felice Levine, National Science Foundation, for her encouragement and support.

have been different or identical if some part of that total mass of evidence had been different." Our formal and empirical studies have proceeded hand-in-hand. Formal research helps to identify meaningful variables and measures for empirical research; empirical research, interesting in its own right, is also useful in testing the adequacy of the foundations for formal studies.

A major focus of our research has been upon inductive inference tasks, which Wigmore termed "catenated"; the modern terms for these tasks are "cascaded" or "hierarchical" (Wigmore, 1937: 13). Wigmore was the first to point out the fact that most inferential reasoning tasks are cascaded in nature. A cascaded inference task is composed of one or more reasoning stages interposed between evidence observable to the fact finder and the ultimate facts-in-issue. An example of a cascaded inference is presented by testimony from a witness of less than perfect credibility that the defendant was at the scene at the time of the crime. The testimony requires one first to assess the likelihood that the defendant was, in fact, at the scene/time. This foundational stage involves evaluation of the witness's credibility. Then, assuming the defendant at the scene/time of the crime, one must assess how strongly this event bears on the issue of whether or not the defendant committed the crime. Further difficulty is presented by intricate patterns of reasoning which require the joint consideration of current evidence with one or more previously given pieces of evidence.

The formal research discussed in this paper concerns the logical requisites of cascaded inference tasks and the manner in which these requisites should be combined. Wigmore acknowledged that logicians had found canons of reasoning in simple situations; however, he lamented the fact that (at that time) there were no such canons of reasoning from an entire mass of evidence "mixed" with respect to logical form (Wigmore, 1937: 8). Our formal work shows that, though the process is tedious and difficult, canons of reasoning can be derived for masses of mixed evidence.

The present article is meant to introduce the reader to ways in which formal analysis can be used to understand the logical demands of inference from the types of evidence presented in legal settings. As a result, the detailed mathematical arguments that form the bases for the analyses will not be described here. Interested readers are directed to our monographs dealing with these mathematical arguments.[1] Our focus in this article is on the major conclusions of our formal studies as they bear upon commonly encountered evidentiary issues in inferences made at trial. A technical appendix is included in which we illustrate the essentials of our formal process using three examples. The reader choosing to disregard this appendix is in no way disadvantaged in reading the text of this paper.

The benefits of formal reasearch on legal inference have not gone unnoticed by current scholars in jurisprudence (e.g., Lempert and Saltzburg, 1977; Lempert, 1977; Eggleston, 1978). Such research assists in efforts to illuminate and sharpen legal reasoning. The reader is, of course, interested in how our current research adds to this process.

Our empirical research concerns the reasoning processes of the ordinary citizens upon which so much depends in court trials. In fact, very little is known about human inferential reasoning, partly because of the lack of knowledge about the tasks people are asked to perform. Our formal research concerns what these tasks demand, and our empirical research concerns how well persons seem to meet these demands. Previous studies have suggested that everyone is subject to biases and errors in inferential behavior (e.g., Saks and Kidd, 1981). Unfortunately, many conclusions about human biases and error rest upon studies incorporating ill-posed problems or problems which are quite abstract. An objective in our empirical research was to present carefully posed concrete inferential problems which begin to approach the complexity of those faced by the fact finder in a court of law.

II. FORMAL RESEARCH: FOUNDATIONS

The inference tasks performed by the fact finder commonly involve the interplay of inductive and deductive reasoning processes; this fact was noted by Wigmore in his analysis (1937: 20). Our formal research generally focuses upon inductive inference, the task of revising one's opinion about the relative likelihood of rival facts-in-issue on the basis of inconclusive or probabilistic evidence. In evaluating or "weighing" evidence in an inferential task, one recognizes that items of evidence differ. in strength; for various reasons some items are persuasive and allow for substantial revision in our opinions, while other items

---

[1] Requests for reprints or preprint monographs should be sent to the authors at: 7416 Timberock Road, Falls Church, Virginia 22043.

seem to justify little or no opinion revision. Thus, a major task
in inductive inference consists of evaluating the inferential or
probative strength of evidence. Given more than one item of
evidence, one must somehow aggregate or combine the
probative weights given to each item. One major complication
is that the probative weight given to one item frequently
depends strongly upon our recollection of other items. We
explore the tasks of evaluating the probative strength of
individual items of evidence and of collections of all the items.
In essence, this research is concerned with relevance issues.

Federal Rule of Evidence FRE 401 defines *relevant*
evidence as "evidence having any tendency to make the
existence of any fact that is of consequence to the
determination of the action more probable or less probable
than it would be without the evidence." As others have noted
(Lempert and Saltzburg, 1977), there appear to be "natural"
measures within conventional probability theory for the
relevance or probativity of evidence. These measures are
termed "likelihood ratios," and they provide an indication of
the necessary opinion revision prescribed by FRE-401 for
relevant evidence. In our context, a likelihood ratio expresses
the probability of an item of evidence assuming the defendant's
guilt, relative to the probability of this same item of evidence
assuming defendant's innocence.[2] We use an upper-case Greek
lambda [Λ] to symbolize a likelihood ratio and add a subscript
when Λ applies to a certain evidence item e; thus, Λ_e means the
likelihood ratio for evidence item e. When $\Lambda_e = 1.0$, evidence e
has equal probability assuming guilt or assuming innocence,
and so e is nonprobative. When Λ_e is greater than 1.0, then e is
probative evidence favoring defendant's guilt; when Λ_e is less
than 1.0, then e probatively favors defendant's innocence.

Our first formal objective has been to formulate and study
likelihood ratio expressions for various identifiable logical
species of evidence. We have termed these species of evidence
inference structures and have used these inference structures
as the basic "building blocks" in thinking about complex
masses of evidence representing entire cases. The complexity
of a likelihood ratio depends upon the form of the evidence and
the nature of the reasoning process established by the
evidence. Once derived for the evidence in some inference
structure, likelihood ratio expressions tell us what probabilistic

---

[2] Likelihoods and likelihood ratios appear as ingredients in Bayes' rule.
Essentially, these ingredients prescribe the amount of revision, from prior
opinion to posterior opinion, which an item of evidence justifies.

ingredients are required at each step in the reasoning process and how they should be combined in a coherent manner.

To many persons, equations seem sterile and, when applied as representations for human tasks, seem almost certain to fail in capturing all of the behavioral essentials that intuition and experience suggest are features of the tasks. Consequently, the second objective in our formal research has been the study of what we have termed the "behavioral richness" of our likelihood ratio expressions (Schum, 1977a). This term does not refer to the extent to which any of our formal expressions describes or predicts the actual behavior of any person. In our usage, a likelihood ratio is behaviorally rich if it captures the essentials and subtleties of probative value assessment that recorded experience with the evidence of concern suggest are there.

A third objective in our formal research has been to relate the study and analysis of likelihood ratio expressions for various inference structures to the rules and prescriptions of evidence law, noting both similarities and differences between the prescriptions of our formal expressions and corresponding established legal prescriptions. In general we have been impressed by the many similarities, a full accounting of which appears in our specific monographs. We view this correspondence between formal and legal prescriptions concerning relevance issues as evidence for a convergence to coherence in the development of evidentiary rules and procedures.[3] In addition, our formal research provides some basis for the sharpening of the definition of legal terms. As laypersons in jurisprudence, we have observed apparent difficulties among jurists in obtaining crisp definitions of certain terms (e.g., redundancy, corroborative and cumulative evidence). Formal research forces one to be precise, or at least to settle upon definitions.

---

[3] We note that our formal approach provides just one set of standards against which the coherence of legal prescriptions can be evaluated. There are other standards which we both recognize and appreciate. Our formal research is grounded on the axioms of "conventional" mathematical probability theory. There are other axiom systems which lead to other prescriptions for "coherent" inductive reasoning. One in particular is Cohen's system of "inductive" probabilities (Cohen, 1977). Cohen claims this system to be more congenial to application in legal matters than the mathematical systems which we use; much current debate on this issue has resulted (e.g., Schum, 1979a; Kaye, 1979, 1981; Cohen, 1981). Other systems include the "belief functions" of Shafer (1976), and the "possibility" measures of Zadeh (1978). We continue to work within the mathematical system, because it is our belief that this system is the only one extant which offers the flexibility necessary to capture the rich array of subtleties in evidence.

One of our strong hopes has been that our formal research will assist us in efforts to perform empirical research of greater interest and relevance to jurists. Laboratory research on human inference is often criticized for being too abstract and for not including enough relevant aspects of tasks as they occur in natural settings (Winkler and Murphy, 1973). In our empirical research, subjects evaluated evidence having a variety of subtle properties. Likelihood ratios, derived for the evidence our subjects evaluated, contain ingredients which, far from being mathematically arcane, in fact lay bare the logical steps or stages in reasoning from the evidence to the major facts-in-issue.

III. FORMAL STUDIES: RESULTS AND OBSERVATIONS

On Inference Structures

Substantively, evidence varies in near-infinite fashion. Fortunately, however, there appears to be a manageably finite number of logically distinct forms of evidence. Various classification schemes are found in evidence law treatises, but no one scheme seems to enjoy universal acceptance. Our formal work has basically involved circumstantial evidence with a testimonial foundation; Wigmore noted that such evidence is the form most frequently encountered at trial (1937: 13). Our formal process works equally well for "real" evidence; in fact, formalizations for the probative value of such evidence are simpler than for testimonial evidence (Schum, 1980). Our interest in testimonial evidence arises partly because of an abiding interest in the nature of the relationship between the credibility of the source of evidence and the inferential or probative value of what the source reports (Schum and Du Charme, 1971).

There appears to be a relatively small number of generic types of evidence which we have termed *inference structures*. We distinguish between simple, complex, and mixed inference structures. A *simple* inference structure is a chain-like reasoning process "set in motion" by a single item of testimony. The foundation of the reasoning chain is a testimonial assertion; later stages or links in the chain represent circumstantial reasoning steps from the matter asserted to the ultimate or major facts-in-issue. In such structures the number of reasoning steps can vary. A further characteristic of a simple inference structure is that neither the testimonial assertion nor the events at subsequent reasoning stages are assumed to be probabilistically linked to previous evidence or events in their reasoning chains. Shown in Figures 1-A and 1-B below are diagrammatic representations of two simple inference structures involving testimonial evidence. The one in Figure 1-A, termed a "first-order cascaded inference," is the simplest possible case of cascaded or catenated inference. Witness W_i asserts that event D happened—for example, that the defendant was at the scene of the crime. The event D^c is the event that D did not occur. We represent the testimonial assertion that D occurred as D_i^* to distinguish it from the event D itself. Failure to distinguish between testimony about an event (D_i^*) and the event itself (D) has caused no end of difficulties in many previous studies of the impact of witness credibility upon the probative value of testimonial evidence (e.g., Eggleston, 1978). The first stage of reasoning is from testimony D_i^* to events D, D^c; this is the foundation stage of reasoning and, as formalizations for the probative value of D_i^* show, involves assessment of the credibility of W_i. The next stage of reasoning is from events D and D^c to events H_1 and H_2, representing the major or ultimate facts-in-issue (e.g., that defendant committed the crime, H_1, or did not, H_2). In this stage of reasoning the probative

Figure 1.   Example Inference Structures
A. Simple cascaded inference, first order.
B. Simple cascaded inference, second order.
C. Complex cascaded inference, corroborative testimony.

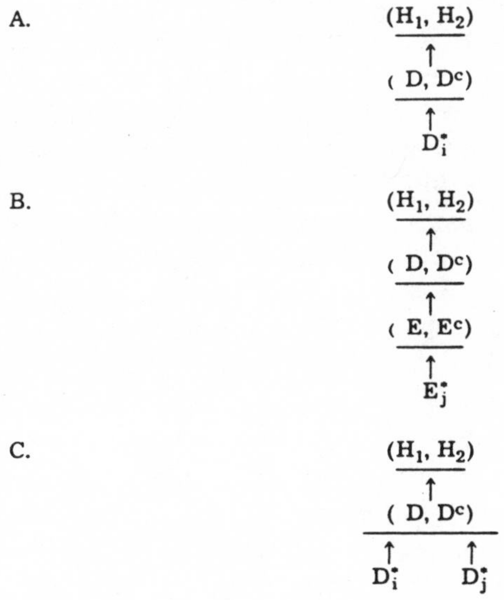

A.
$$(H_1, H_2)$$
$$\uparrow$$
$$(\,D, D^c)$$
$$\uparrow$$
$$D_i^*$$

B.
$$(H_1, H_2)$$
$$\uparrow$$
$$(\,D, D^c)$$
$$\uparrow$$
$$(\,E, E^c)$$
$$\uparrow$$
$$E_j^*$$

C.
$$(H_1, H_2)$$
$$\uparrow$$
$$(\,D, D^c)$$
$$\uparrow \qquad \uparrow$$
$$D_i^* \qquad D_j^*$$

importance of the defendant's being at the scene of the crime is
assessed. Equation 1 in the technical appendix shows the
expression for the likelihood ratio for testimony D_i^*.

Figure 1-B shows a "second-order cascaded inference."
Witness W_j asserts E_j^*, that event E occurred. Suppose E is the
event that the defendant's car was at the scene of the crime at
the time in question. The first stage of reasoning, from E_j^* to
events, E,E^c, is an assessment of the credibility of W_j. The next
stage involves circumstantial reasoning from E,E^c to events
D,D^c whether or not defendant was at the scene. The final
stage involves circumstantial reasoning from events D,D^c to
events H_1, H_2. Equation 2 in the technical appendix shows the
likelihood ratio for testimony E_j^*. Simple inference structures
like these two can have any number of reasoning stages or
"levels" of cascading or catenation.

In *complex* inference structures there is always foundation
testimony from more than one witness. Often there are
probabilistic linkages among events in the reasoning chains
based on each item of testimony. We have identified four basic
classes of complex inference structures: those representing
contradictory testimony, *corroboratively redundant* testimony,
cumulatively redundant testimony, and *nonredundant*
testimony. In contradictory testimony, one witness asserts that
event D occurred and another asserts that D did not occur.
Corroboratively redundant testimony concerns the assertions
of two or more witnesses that the (same) event D occurred.
Figure 1-C depicts a complex inference structure involving
corroboratively redundant testimony. In this structure, two
witnesses W_i and W_j assert that event D occurred; their
testimonies are D_i^* and D_j^*. That the testimony here is possibly
redundant is obvious, since they both testify to the same event.
If the first witness has perfect credibility, then testimony from
the second usually adds nothing. Suppose, however, we
thought that the first witness could not actually determine
whether or not D occurred. Then, testimony from the second
witness does have probative value depending, in part, on the
credibility of this second witness. This situation introduces the
important feature of *conditional nonindependence*. Two or
more items of evidence or events at reasoning stages suggested
by evidence are conditionally *non*independant if, considered
jointly, they mean something probatively different than they do
if considered separately. If not, then they are said to be

conditionally independent.[4] Equation 3 in the appendix shows the likelihood ratio for the second and possibly redundant testimony. There are terms in this expression which allow one to account, in a formally ideal way, for the degree of redundance involving these two witnesses.

In *cumulatively* redundant testimony, there is an assertion from one witness that event E occurred. A later assertion that a different event F occurred comes from either the same or a different witness. Suppose that event E, if it occurred, made event F highly probable in the nature of things (i.e. regardless of what else you know), and therefore testimony that F occurred yields little if any probative value if the first witness is believed. For example, the first witness asserts that defendant was at the scene/time of the crime. The second asserts that he/she found the defendant's coat at the scene/time. If the first witness is believed, testimony from the second adds little to our determination about whether or not the defendant was at the scene/time. The redundance of cumulative testimony of this sort can be represented, along with other subtleties, in an appropriate expression of conditional nonindependence.

If two or more items of testimony are redundant, earlier items tend to decrease the probative value of later items. Alternatively, testimony can be *facilitative* so that one item makes a later item seem more probatively valuable. In *nonredundant* testimony, either the assertion of one witness causes no change in the value of a later assertion, or it acts to enhance the value of a later assertion. For example, the first of

---

4 At various points we use the expression conditional independence or nonindependence of events, because with it we can represent a remarkable array of subtleties in evidence. Two events A and B are said to be unconditionally independent or simply *independent* if knowledge of one of the events does not cause you to change your mind about the probability of the other; if such knowledge does cause a change, then the events are said to be nonindependent. Suppose we have knowledge of a third event C. Events A and B are said to be *conditionally independent*, given event C, if knowledge of one of the events A or B does not cause you to change your mind about the probability of the other, provided that event C is true. If knowledge of event A causes you to change your mind about the probability of B, when event C is known or assumed, then A and B are said to be *conditionally nonindependent*, given event C. Very often, two or more evidence items or events at reasoning stages suggested by these items mean something probatively different when considered jointly than they do if considered separately. The concept of conditional independence/nonindependence allows you to express this probative difference. Unfortunately, the concepts of independence and conditional independence are often confused; they are related concepts, but they are not the same. Examples of subtleties which find expression via patterns of conditional nonindependence include a variety of credibility-related effects, redundance in testimony, the significance of weak links and rare events in reasoning stages, a reasoning stage relation called transitivity, and the locus of probative value in equivocal testimony or the nonproduction of testimony.

Evidence and Proof

two witnesses reports finding the defendant's revolver beside the victim's body in the defendant's apartment. The second witness reports the sound of a revolver shot coming (apparently) from the window of this apartment. On the issue of whether or not the defendant is guilty, the first testimony seems to have a facilitative effect upon the probativity of the second.

Finally, a *mixed* inference structure represents various combinations of the above structures. As an example, two witnesses testify that event E occurred; their testimony is corroboratively redundant. Then, three witnesses give joint corroborative testimony that event E did not occur, thus contradicting the testimony of the first two. The reader who is interested in a complete collection of the inference structures we have studied, including a derivation of likelihood ratio expressions for each structure, may refer to Schum and Martin (1980a; 1981).

Cases or collections of evidence can be thought of as collections of inference structures. Testimony or other evidence upon which these structures are based open up specific lines of reasoning which the structures indicate. Such evidence may be thought of as "main-frame" evidence, having direct probative value. Other evidence may be thought of as "ancillary" evidence in the sense that it allows the fact-finder to evaluate the strength of linkages among events at various stages in the reasoning suggested by an inference structure. Ancillary evidence may be said to have "acquired" or "derived" probative value. For example, Witness W_j asserts that the observational conditions were good on the day that a previous witness W_i observed E, an event linked circumstantially to major facts-in-issue. The testimony of W_j is not probative on these facts by itself; it does, however, acquire probative value since it bears on the credibility of W_i, whose testimony about E does have direct probative significance. Thus, all evidence at trial can be grossly categorized as "main-frame" or "ancillary" evidence. Had Wigmore realized this, he might have been able to simplify some of his very complex diagrammatic illustrations of case evidence, and he might also have been able to see how specific formalization of such evidence could be derived.

On Witness Credibility

The credibility of the source or sources of the evidence forms the foundation for cascaded reasoning from testimonial evidence. Likelihood ratio expressions for the process of assessing the probative value of testimonial evidence reveal several important logical characteristics of this process. First, established grounds for impeaching or supporting the credibility of witnesses find expression in these likelihood ratios (Schum and Kelley, 1973; Schum, 1977a). These grounds include observational capacity, bias, prior inconsistent statements, influence among witnesses, and character (Cleary, *et al.*, 1972). Second, our formal process makes clear the fact that the behavior of a witness, as revealed by the witness or by other evidence, is often a source of probative value in addition to that provided by the events reported by the witness. Finally, our studies show the precise nature of the important interaction between the credibility of a witness and the rarity of the event reported by the witness in determinations of the probative value of witness testimony (Schum, 1977a).

In studying the probative value of witness testimony we have found it useful to use two constructs from signal detection theory, a theory which has had great impact on sensory psychophysics and a variety of other research areas (e.g., see Swets, 1964; Egan, 1975). This theory provides the means for separating two basic dimensions of testimonial behavior. The first dimension, which concerns the observational sensitivity or capacity of a witness, is indexed by a measure labeled d'. The second dimension concerns motivational and other factors that influence the decisions by a witness about what event to report following an observation. This decision criterion, $L(x_0)$, can be determined from information about the observer's expectations, goals, and motives.

The hit and false-positive probabilities in our Λ formulations, together with other directly related probabilities called "misses" and "correct rejections" are key elements in signal detection theory; in fact, these labels come from this theory. For some observational task, if we know or assume the conditional probability of a report of an event, assuming that the event actually occurred (a 'hit' probability), and the conditional probability of a report of this event, assuming it did not occur (a 'false-positive' probability), we can then determine d' and $L(x_0)$. Moreover, we can vary d'-related information independently of $L(x_0)$-related information in the formal study of how such classes of information influence the probative value of testimonial evidence.

In our formal studies we first examined situations in which credibility-related hit and false-positive probabilities were not conditioned by other events in a reasoning chain. When this is true, straightforward trade-offs are possible between observational sensitivity and decision-related factors in determining the probative value of testimony. For example, testimony from a witness with low observational sensitivity but a strong bias against offering the testimony can have as much value as testimony from a highly sensitive witness who is biased in favor of giving such testimony. We also attempted to clarify the meaning of "biased" testimony in relation to testimony that lacks veracity. In our context, bias refers to a witness' apparent preferences for or against offering the testimony. Such preferences can sometimes be inferred from other evidence such as information about the relationship between witness and defendant. Suppose a witness is a close friend of defendant; this witness may have a distinct bias in favor of reporting an event favorable to the defendant's case. We may easily believe the witness to be biased without also believing that the witness is lying when he/she reports the occurrence of this event. Our formal process hows why biased testimony need not be untruthful, and how testimony which lacks veracity need not be biased. Generally, bias is a factor in the determination of the probative *strength* of testimony, while veracity determines the probative *direction* of testimony (i.e., which of the two rival facts-in-issue the testimony favors).

We also examined a variety of situations in which observational capacity and/or decision-related factors were made conditional upon events representing rival facts-in-issue. This is another way of saying that credibility-related factors for a witness provide probative value over and above the value of the event being reported. As an example of how factors underlying the observational and decision-related factors influence the value of testimonial evidence, we have examined a case in which a witness testifies against preference. In such a case one expects a "gain" in probative value over identical testimony from a witness who has no such preferential bias. Our formal studies show that this gain is jusitified and show the precise formal locus of such gain. In general, the observational and testimonial behaviors of a witness by themselves are important sources of probative value. These studies show just how important these sources are, since our formulations are remarkably sensitive to apparently minor alterations of credibility-related ingredients when they are made conditional upon one or the other facts-in-issue.

Redundance Issues

Redundance is among the most interesting but formally difficult evidentiary issues. Our interest in the formal study of the redundance of testimonial evidence was stimulated by Lempert's (1977) concern about the "double-counting" of such evidence. In our studies (Schum, 1979b) we distinguished between "cumulative" and "corroborative" redundance since we observed a formally necessary distinction between the instances in which two or more witnesses say the same thing and the instance in which two or more witnesses give different testimony but on obviously related matters. Our usage of the term *redundance* corresponds with the common interpretation that redundant evidence is superfluous and supplies little, if any, probative value in addition to previous evidence. We explored the various uses of the terms "corroborative" and "cumulative" and observed some confusion; some jurists make sharp distinctions between these terms, while others use them interchangeably. In our study we found it necessary to make a distinction since, formally, corroborative redundance is a special case of cumulative redundance. In our studies of the factors which influence the redundance of testimonial evidence, it is apparent that there are more factors influencing cumulative redundance than there are influencing corroborative redundancy.

In a strict sense *redundance* is a property of the *events* being reported and *not* the testimony of these events. To see that this must be so, consider the testimony of two witnesses who both report that event D occurred. The first witness, we are convinced, could not tell whether or not D occurred, and therefore we assign *no* probative value to this testimony. The second witness seems reasonably credible, and we are justified in assigning probativity to this second testimony to the extent that the second witness is credible and to the extent that event D is probatively valuable.[5] Equations 4 and 5 in the technical appendix express our measures of event redundance in the cumulative and corroborative cases.

The following six factors influence the *cumulative* redundance of testimony F_j^*, given prior testimony E_i^*: The strength of the redundance of *events* E and F (as measured by R_{cum} in Equation 4 in the technical appendix), the credibility of W_i and of W_j; the probative value of event F, given E^c (the first witness may be untruthful); the rarity of events E and F; and

---

[5] Concepts from *statistical communications theory*, often called *information theory*, allow us to measure the probative redundancy of events in well-defined reasoning chains. In this theory, measures of redundancy are crucial in assessing the efficiency of ideal and actual communications channels (e.g., Staniland, 1966). Our measure of *event* redundance has essentially the same properties as does the redundance measure in information theory.

the number of reasoning stages between E and F and major
facts-in-issue. Four factors determine the redundance of
corroborative tetimony E_i^* and E_j^*: the credibility of W_i and of
W_j; the rarity of event E; and the number of reasoning stages
between E and the major facts-in-issue. Careful study reveals
a large number of interesting consequences to probativity
assessment when redundancy is ignored. For example,
ignoring redundancy of E and F will sometimes, but not always
lead to the overvaluation of testimony F_j^*. Certain
combinations of credibility-related ingredients for witnesses W_i
and W_j cause one to *undervalue* testimony F_j^* even when
events E and F are strongly redundant. In the corroborative
case, ignoring the natural redundancy of such testimony is
most serious when the credibility of the prior witness W_i is
strong; i.e. "double-counting" of evidence in the corrobative
case is most serious because, when the prior witness is highly
credible, the value of testimony from the second witness is,
formally, nearly valueless. The rarity of events exerts an
interesting influence in the corroborative case. When the event
being reported is rare, a stronger level of credibility of the first
witness is required to make the value of the testimony of the
second witness vanish when natural corroborative redundance
is ignored.

Reasoning Chain Issues

In the analysis of inductive reasoning chains, a variety of
issues arouse considerable interest. Following are three issues
which we have examined using various analyses of likelihood
ratio formulations for simple inference structures based upon a
single item of foundation testimony (Schum, 1979c). The first
issue concerns a formal relation called *transitivity*. Suppose
foundation evidence A probatively favors B, and B probatively
favors C; this chain of reasoning is said to be *transitive* if A
probatively favors C. If A does not favor C, the relation in the
chain of reasoning is *intransitive*. We have examined a variety
of conditions under which such transitive relations are either
formally allowable or denied. The second issue concerns the
effects upon the probative value of foundation testimony of
locating a "weak link" at various points in an inferential
reasoning chain. The third issue concerns the effects upon the
probative value of foundation testimony of locating a "rare"
event at various points in a chain of inferential reasoning.
Transitivity and weak link issues and their analysis within the
conventional probability system were critically examined by

Cohen (1977). Our study of these issues was prompted, in part, by Cohen's analysis, since we did not believe that all problems raised were adequately posed.

Study of conditions favoring transitive relations among stages of inductive reasoning are particularly important in civil cases in which at least some courts enforce different proof standards at different stages of an inferential chain (Cohen, 1977: 69). For example, a foundation stage may require a more stringent standard of proof in order to support a subsequent stage whose proof standard is "on balance of probabilities" or "preponderance of the evidence." Our analysis shows that whether or not transitive relations occur formally in a chain of reasoning depends entirely upon the pattern of conditional independence/nonindependence relations among events in a reasoning stage. Suppose there is a complete pattern of conditional independence relations among events in a reasoning stage; this means that any event is conditioned only by events at the next higher stage of reasoning. When this is true, if foundation A probatively favors B, and B probatively favors C, then A will probatively favor C. However, under various patterns of conditional nonindependence in which an event at one stage may be linked with those at several higher stages, transitive relations, though intuitively expected, are frequently denied by appropriate formalization. Thus, it is not true in general that, if argument at each reasoning stage favors side A, then the overall argument favors A.

As an example, suppose testimony that the defendant was at the scene (D_i^*) favors the event that the defendant actually was at the scene (D) and, in turn, the defendant being at the scene (D) favors the event that the defendant is guilty as charged (H_1). Our formal process shows why it is not necessarily the case that testimony that defendant was at the scene (D_i^*) probatively favors defendant's guilt (H_1). This probative relation may be transitive or intransitive, depending on what we know about the witness.

Analysis of "weak links," "rare events," and their location in a reasoning chain also reveals the importance of conditional independence/nonindependence patterns among events in a reasoning chain. Some may expect that a weak link at the foundation stage of an argument is more damaging than one located at the "top" of a chain. Grounds for this expectation seem to be that a strong foundation for a weak argument is preferable to a weak foundation for a strong argument. Our formal analysis shows that neither is preferable provided that

120   LAW & SOCIETY / 17:1

there is a pattern of complete conditional independence among events in a reasoning chain. This says that the location of a weak link does not matter under these conditions and that the chain cannot be stronger than its weakest link wherever it is located. The location of "rare" events in a chain *does* matter. Rare events are more damaging to the probative value of foundation testimony if they occur at the top of the chain, whether or not there are conditional nonindependence patterns in the chain.

On Several Special Types of Evidence

Following is a brief account of formal issues encountered in our examination of three well-known types of evidence. Study of these types of evidence, all of which can involve cascaded inference, has required us to examine several issues of more general importance in the analysis of complex reasoning chains.

Hearsay Evidence One of the most difficult tasks in the formal study of evidence concerns a type of evidence that each one of us evaluates on a regular basis; in jurisprudence such evidence is termed "hearsay"; more generally it is called "second-hand" evidence. This latter designation is more general than it appears, since it is usually applied to instances in which one receives a report or testimony passed through several intermediate sources; often, the original source is unknown. In evidence law there is an abundant literature on the admissibility of various forms of hearsay but a sparse literature on the probative value of such evidence. Suppose a "simple" situation in which A, a witness at trial, reports testimony allegedly given by out-of-court assertor B. There are, of course, complex credibility-related issues concerning both A and B; so, at the very least, we have more than one foundation stage in reasoning from such evidence.

Our formal studies of hearsay (Martin, 1979) represent elaboration and extension of Tribe's model for the "triangulation" of hearsay in which only admissibility issues were of concern (Tribe, 1974). Likelihood ratio representations for the probative value of hearsay are made difficult by the fact that there are several possible different stages of reasoning involved. We may ask: did B actually observe the event in question; did B in fact report anything to A? (A may have "put words into B's mouth".) Derivation of Λ for alternative forms of reasoning from hearsay evidence led to the discovery of

some very important *recursive* algorithms which occur in all Λ
formulations. A recursive rule is one that is defined in terms of
itself. Such discovery led to the development of a *general*
algorithm for the analysis of inference structures of virtually
any degree of complexity and involving any pattern of
conditional independence assumptions involving events in the
structure (Martin, 1980). A computer program called CASPRO
has been developed which uses this algorithm and which
facilitates analysis of complex inference structures.

**Equivocal Testimony Or No Testimony On A Relevant Issue at
Trial** We now consider three species of "evidence" which some,
at least, would judge to be, by their very nature, probatively
vacuous regardless of the facts-in-issue (Schum, 1981b).
Formal study, however, convinces us that there is the
possibility of very strong probative value in each case. The first
concerns *equivocal testimony* given by a witness who, when
asked whether or not the event D occurred, replies "I don't
know," "I don't remember," "I couldn't tell," etc. In some
instances this may simply indicate a form of self-impeachment
by the witness who, in fact, is truthful in giving any of these
responses. Formally, such testimony is probatively valueless.
In other instances, depending upon what else we may know
about the witness, we may infer that the witness is
"sandbagging" and actually knows more than his/her
testimony indicates. In such instances, formal analysis shows
that the probative value of such equivocation can be even more
probative than *certain* knowledge of the occurrence of one of
the events about which the witness equivocates.

The second case concerns *silence* as evidence; queried
about whether or not event D occurred, the witness stands
mute or exercises privilege. In this case other facts brought to
light at trial can, under some conditions, formally justify
stronger opinion revision about facts-in-issue than would
specific testimony by the witness. The same also applies to a
third case involving the *nonproduction* of evidence (testimonial
or otherwise). Such nonproduction can be at least as probative
as specific evidence on the matter at issue given by a witness of
any level of credibility.

Opportunity And Alibi Testimony The array of subtleties in
evidence make the formal study of evidence rather like walking
through a mine-field; one wrong step, however minor, can cause
subsequent discomfort. We experienced such discomfort in
applying our formal processes to opportunity evidence and its

logical negation, alibi evidence. Probatively, opportunity evidence, even if given by a perfectly credible source, is inconclusive that the defendant committed the act as alleged. Alibi evidence, if given by a perfectly credible source, is conclusive evidence of defendant's nonparticipation in the act as alleged. We assume here that the act in question would, if performed by defendant, require his/her physical presence. Unless Λ equations are formulated with extreme care, certain embarrassing indeterminacies can arise in equations whose ingredients seem entirely plausible unless carefully examined (Schum, 1981c).

As a final word on formal issues we mention Wigmore's desire for "mental probative equations" (Wigmore, 1937: 8). Whether or not our Λ formulations bear any resemblance to the equations Wigmore had in mind, we can never tell. Our formal study reveals the intricacies of cascaded or catenated inference even for simple items of evidence. The process of "connecting up" the evidence is, formally, frightening to contemplate. We have done so, however, for small evidence sets. This process, we have noted, bears no small resemblance to the sensory-perceptual tasks of observing an object against a background. Prior evidence exerts a "contrast" effect on current evidence in the same way as the color of a background influences the perceived color of an object presented against this background (Schum, 1977b). Before considering empirical research issues we note our realization that formal study of evidence by itself can never prescribe what the "rules of evidence" ought to be. However, as one jurist (Keyser, 1929) remarked:

> An ensemble of experience-given propositions (like those constituting any existing branch of law) never gets so thoroughly examined and criticized and understood as when the ensemble is submitted to the severe processes of mathematicization.

IV. EMPIRICAL STUDIES: BACKGROUND, OBJECTIVES, AND METHODS

Our empirical research was designed to provide information about human capabilities and limitations in the task of assessing the probative or inferential value of evidence. In a series of related studies whose results are summarized below, research subjects provided specific numerical responses as indications of their assessments of the probative strength of individual items of evidence and of collections of evidence items. Examination of these responses in various ways is one means of studying certain characteristics of human behavior in the task of reasoning from inconclusive evidence. In actual court proceedings, however, fact finders are not encouraged to make public their judgments about the evidence. At the outset we note that no part of our study was designed to convince jurists that the fact finding process ought to require specific quantitative assessments of evidence strength or that forensic standards of proof ought to be specifically quantified. This disclaimer seems necessary in light of controversy among jurists about the use of various probabilistic representations in actual court trials (e.g., Tribe, 1971; Finkelstein and Fairley, 1970).

It is commonly believed that the quantitative reasoning skills of ordinary persons are not very strong and that quantitatively expressed human judgments are neither accurate nor reliable. In a variety of research contexts, psychologists and others have obtained useful results by relying heavily upon numerical judgments expressed by their research subjects; we do so here.[6]

Background and Specific Objectives

Our present studies of human capabilities and limitations in the task of assessing the probative weight of evidence have three major roots: Wigmore's work on the analysis of complex masses of mixed evidence, basic and applied research performed by psychologists and others concerning the design of more efficient ways to allocate tasks among persons and devices in various information-processing systems, and our recent work on the formal analysis of cascaded inference. We have already acknowledged our debt to Wigmore, who began the formidable task of decomposing complex inferences. Within psychology, study and analysis of complex inference tasks dates from the early 1960's with Ward Edwards' suggestions about how such inference tasks ought to be

---

[6] In the study of sensory and perceptual processes, for example, there is a large collection of *psychophysical* measurement procedures, many of which require numerical judgments from subjects. In sensory psychophysics, it is common practice to take seriously the numerical judgments individuals provide as indications of various attributes of their sensory experience. Such faith has not been unrewarded; a variety of useful metrics and measurement procedures based upon subjective quantitative assessments are employed on a regular basis in very practical applications related to vision and audition. Behaviorally useful measures of light and sound are all based upon psychophysical measures (e.g., Stevens, 1975). Our present studies are within the tradition of psychophysics in the sense that we take seriously the numerical judgments about evidence strength provided by our subjects. We do, in fact, construe these judgments as psychophysical judgments and, in so doing, are consistent with the philosopher Hume's assertion that all probabilistic reasoning is a species of sensation; the weight given to alternative arguments involves subjective feelings about the relative intensity or strength of the arguments (Hume, 1881).

decomposed so that a person, confronted with a mass of
evidence, could be relieved of the task of mentally aggregating
large amounts of probabilistic evidence (Edwards, 1962). As
Edwards discussed, Bayes' rule is suggestive of ways in which
such task decomposition ought to be performed. These ideas
generated a substantial amount of research on matters
concerning human performance on inductive or probabilistic
reasoning. Most of this research was performed in laboratory
settings involving tasks of varying complexity; excellent
reviews are to be found in papers by Slovic and Lichtenstein
(1971) and Rapoport and Wallsten (1972). Research on
inferential processes continues; recent research on various
attributes of human probabilistic judgments of concern to
jurists has been reviewed by Saks and Kidd (1981). Our own
formal research on cascaded or hierarchical inference was
designed to extend the applicability of Bayes' rule to complex
forms of evidence.

In planning our studies of cascaded inference in
jurisprudence we had a number of objectives. Three of these
objectives concern our basic interest in the task of assessing
the probative weight of evidence, and the results presented in
the next section bear upon these.

(1) In the study of many human tasks a natural question
is: how accurately or correctly can a person perform the task?
Unfortunately, as we recognize, we can *never* ask how correct
or accurate is a person's assessment of the probative weight
either of an item of evidence or a collection of evidence given at
trial. Such evidence involves unique or one-of-a-kind events,
and each fact finder evaluates the evidence according to
personal strategies based upon a unique matrix of prior
experience. In short, there is no "true" or "correct" probative
weight for any item or collection of evidence; still, even though
we cannot measure the accuracy of probativity assessment, we
can, under certain circumstances evaluate the consistency or
coherence of such assessments. One such circumstance occurs
when a person can be asked to perform the same task in
different but equivalent ways. As we shall see, a probativity
assessment task can be decomposed to varying degrees; we can
ask how consistent or coherent are assessments across various
levels of task decomposition. In a word, this objective concerns
the extent to which a person's assessment of the value of
"parts" of an evidence collection are consistent with this
person's assessment of the "whole" collection of the evidence.
Our formal process supplies the essential basis for showing

how probative value assessment tasks can be decomposed in formally equivalent ways; this process also, of course, shows us how the decomposed "parts" ought to be put back together again.

(2) The evidence items evaluated by our research subjects are classifiable into the logically distinct categories that we have termed "inference structures." Our second objective was to study characteristics of responses to these forms of evidence. One might expect that the consistency with which persons evaluate evidence would depend upon the logical form of the evidence.

(3) Study of the internal consistency of probativity assessment involves a focus on the performance of individual persons. We were concerned, however, about the extent of the agreement or concordance across subjects in probativity assessment for various forms and collections of evidence.[7]

Methodological Choices And Trade-Offs

At a fairly early stage in our empirical research planning, we abandoned hope of being able to present precise descriptions of our methodology in any journal-length account of our work. Our solution to this problem was to prepare a monograph in which we provided a detailed account of all aspects of our empirical studies, including precise descriptions of the subjects' tasks, the exact instructions that they were given in each part of the study, the evidence they evaluated, the formal basis for selecting the evidence, the nature of the subjects' responses to the evidence, and the means by which these responses were to be analyzed. The report is available to persons interested in these details (Schum and Martin, 1980a). The reader of this report may conclude that we over-reacted to criticism about the simplicity of "laboratory" studies of human inference (e.g., Winkler and Murphy, 1973), and that we sought

---

[7] Other objectives also guided some of our research. One objective concerned a test of the relative adequacy of Pascalian (mathematical) and Baconian (inductive) systems in charting the general course of probability revision based upon inconclusive trial evidence. A novel methodology is required for such a comparison, because the two competing systems have almost no comparable numerical properties. The reader interested in our approach to and results of such a comparison can refer to our recent preliminary report (Schum and Martin, 1980b).

Another objective of the research concerned how subjects' perceptions of the value of trial decision consequences for a defendant may influence their assessment of the probative value of evidence. Our analysis of results bearing upon this objective, though at this time incomplete, suggests that value influences are very slight. This should be good news to decision and inference theorists in general, since most decision theories assume an absence of interaction among inference-related and value-related judgments.

126   LAW & SOCIETY / 17:1

complexity for its own sake, but this assessment would be inaccurate. We sought to study, in a reasonably systematic way, human inferential reasoning processes in an evidentiary context which begins, at least, to approach the evidentiary complexity of actual court trials. Quite simply, there is a price to be paid for the incorporation in research on human inferential reasoning of the subtleties in evidence upon whose recognition and evaluation in actual trials so much depends.

Following is a brief account of the necessary trade-offs we were forced to consider in the design of our empirical research. If one wishes to study a person's evaluation of collections of formally identifiable classes of evidence, one must either find actual cases whose evidence fits into these classes, or one must contrive evidence which does fit in these classes. After an unsuccessful attempt at the former, we chose the latter. Our study of the consistency with which individuals evaluate evidence requires that a person evaluate the same evidence over again on several occasions; possible "carry-over" effects from one evaluation to another, though they cannot be eliminated, can be minimized. We were forced to rule out two ingredients which may have increased at least the "surface validity" of our studies. The first concerns the use of a "random" sample of juror-eligible persons. Our study demanded lengthy subject participation over a period of 5½ weeks, ability of subjects to understand fairly detailed instructions, and absolute subject commitment to participate in all parts of the study. We considered the use of actors in a video presentation of "trial testimony"; this was rejected for reasons of time and expense. Consequently, our subjects received written accounts of "testimony." Since our major purpose was to examine individual evaluations of evidence, our studies did not involve a group deliberation process similar to actual jury deliberation. Finally, to make certain evidentiary events occur "on cue," we were forced to take some liberties with the natural order of evidence presentation as it might occur at trial. Following is a brief account of the details of our method.

Research Subjects Twenty jury-eligible persons, ten males and ten females, from the undergraduate population at Rice University completed all phases of our study. None of these persons had taken a college-level course in probability theory (the only stated requirement), and all were paid at an hourly rate with a bonus for completion of all phases of the study. At the completion of our studies, we had compiled a data base of over 16,000 numerical assessments provided by the twenty subjects in response to the evidence they were asked to evaluate.

The Evidence Our subjects evaluated *testimonial* evidence in 12 separate *contrived* felony "cases." Evidence from each case was presented in written "transcripts," each of which consisted of a description of the defendant and the crime with which he/she was charged, followed by several separate blocks of evidence. Evidence presented in each case was not intended to represent a complete case; this is not a crucial issue, since our research subjects were never asked to make judgments about the guilt or innocence of the "defendant" in any case. In fact, their only task was to assess, in various ways, how strongly case evidence favored the guilt or the innocence of the "defendant" in each case.

Each block of evidence in a case consisted of two basic forms of information. The first, which we have called "main-frame" evidence, is a testimonial assertion by a witness whose assertion opens up a line of reasoning to major facts-in-issue. The second, which we referred to as "ancillary evidence," concerns other evidence which bears upon the task of evaluating the strength of linkages in the reasoning chains suggested by "main-frame" testimony. Such ancillary evidence included evidence regarding the credibility of the witness and other explanatory evidence such as that brought out in cross-examination or by other rebuttal witnesses. In Wigmore's terms, each block of evidence consisted of *proponent's assertion* followed by *opponent's explanation and/or denial*. Each of the twelve "cases" contained either four, five, or six blocks of evidence.

The most important characteristic of each block of evidence was that it was contrived to fit into one of 15 well-defined inference structures such as the ones shown above in Figure 1. Thus, the essential logic of each "case" was represented as a collection of inference structures; the substance of the evidence in a case was contrived to fit the logic of each case. These twelve cases, together with their "logic diagrams" and likelihood-ratio equations appropriate in each inference structure in the logic diagram, are also available upon request to the authors. Our formal research has provided the means for developing likelihood ratio expressions (Λ) for the evidence in each inference structure used. There were five

128   LAW & SOCIETY / 17:1

basic classes of inference structures, those representing:
"simple" inference structures, contradictory testimony,
corroboratively redundant testimony, cumulatively redundant
testimony, and nonredundant testimony. The substance of the
"main-frame" testimony concerned either means, motive, or
opportunity evidence relevant to each case. We drew heavily
upon Wigmore's examples in contriving the evidence in each
structure (Wigmore, 1937), especially his many examples of the
number of reasoning stages typically necessary for means,
motive, and opportunity evidence. Typically, for instance,
motive evidence requires more reasoning stages than does
opportunity evidence, since a motive is inferred from past
behavior. Finally, the likelihood ratios developed for each
inference structure show the necessary probabilistic
ingredients and the manner of their coherent combination in
the task of assessing the probative value of evidence in each
inference structure. As we now discuss, such formalizations,
together with other elements of Bayes' rule suggest three
equivalent formal means for assessing the probative value of
the evidence in each case.

Research Subjects' Tasks And Responses Subjects provided
assessments of the probative value of evidence in three
formally equivalent ways; these three response methods allow
us three ways of assessing the internal consistency of
evaluations of evidence for entire cases or collections of
evidence and one way of assessing the internal consistency of
evaluations of individual items of evidence. Two of these three
response methods involve the estimation by subjects of
likelihood ratios; the third involves the estimation of
conditional probabilities. Following are the three response
methods for probative value assessment used by every subject
for each "case."

Zero Task-Decomposition (ZTD) In this response method,
subjects estimated a single likelihood ratio for the *entire*
collection of evidence in a case. In giving such an estimate, a
subject is asked to assess the likelihood of case evidence
assuming defendant's guilt relative to the likelihood of this
same evidence assuming innocence. Subjects' actual responses
consisted of a letter-number pair which indicated both the
probative *direction*, i.e., whether the case evidence favored
guilt G or innocence I, and probative *force*. For example, the
pair G-10 indicates that the subject thinks the evidence 10
times more probable assuming guilt than assuming innocence;

the pair I-5 indicates that the subject believed the evidence 5 times more probable assuming innocence than assuming guilt. A response "N" meaning "neutral" was allowed if the subject believed the evidence was probatively neutral and favored neither fact-in-issue G nor I. Our computer converted these pairs to ratios according to the following definition of the likelihood ratio for case evidence C: $\Lambda_C = P(C \mid G)/P(C \mid I)$. For a G-10 response, for example, $\Lambda_C=10$; for an I-10 response $\Lambda_C=1/10$; for an N response $\Lambda_C=1.0$. This letter-number pair response was used to prevent subjects from being confused by the ratios involved where $\Lambda_C>1$ means C favors "G" and $\Lambda_C<1$ means C favors "I".

This ZTD response is the result of a subject's holistic or global assessment of the probative value of an entire collection of evidence. Subjects made these responses following the thorough reading of the entire collection of evidence in each case. In this ZTD condition of our study, subjects made one such judgment for each of the twelve cases. The condition is called "zero task-decomposition" since the subjects performed the entire process of aggregating the evidence mentally and provided a single judgment indicating the probative force and direction of the evidence.

Partial Task-Decomposition (PTD) In this condition, subjects made exactly the same kinds of likelihood ratio estimates as in the ZTD condition, except that they made one such judgment for each item of "main-frame" testimony in each case. Such judgments were supported by the ancillary evidence in each block of evidence. On occasion, subjects were asked to refer to previous items of main-frame testimony in a case when there was some linkage between the items; for example, if the second of two items were contradictory with the first, subjects were asked to recall the first testimony in assessing the likelihood ratio for the second. Thus, if there were K items of "main-frame" testimony in a case, each subject made K assessments, one for each item.

Consider Case Cj which has some number K of evidence items. Bayes' rule prescribes a multiplicative procedure for combining the probative value for individual items to find the probative value of the entire case Cj. Thus, for case Cj, $\Lambda_{Cj} = \prod_{k=1}^{K} \tilde{\Lambda}_{jk}$, where $\tilde{\Lambda}_{jk}$ is the estimated likelihood ratio for the kth item of main-frame testimony in case Cj. We can compare $\tilde{\Lambda}_{Cj}$ (ZTD), a person's estimated likelihood ratio in the zero task-decomposition condition, with Λ_{Cj}(PTD), a value calculated by simply multiplying together Λ_{jk} value for the individual testimonies in case Cj. Comparison between $\tilde{\Lambda}_{Cj}$(ZTD) and Λ_{Cj}(PTD) is one indication of internal consistency; are the probative value assessments of parts of a "case" consistent with the overall assessment of the entire case? This condition is called "partial task-decomposition," since the subject is now relieved of aggregating probativity assessments over the K evidence items in a case.

Complete Task Decomposition (CTD) In this condition, subjects' probativity-assessment tasks were decomposed to the "finest-grained" level of analysis allowed by our formal methods. This part of the study was conceptually the most difficult and required the most extensive instructions. As an illustration of the subjects' task in this condition, consider Equation 1 in the appendix. This shows the composition of a likelihood ratio, $\Lambda_{D_i^*}$, which describes the process of assessing the probative value of testimony D_i^* about event D, where D is circumstantial evidence of major facts-in-issue H_1 and H_2. Observe in Equation 1 that there are six conditional probability ingredients in $\Lambda_{D_i^*}$. Suppose D_i^*, from witness W_i, was an item of main-frame testimony in one of the cases the subjects evaluated. The subject's task was to estimate each of the six ingredient conditional probabilities required for a determination of $\Lambda_{D_i^*}$. For example, suppose that D represents the event that the defendant was at the scene/time of the crime. Subjects assessed the relative likelihood of this event under the assumption of guilt (H_1) and innocence (H_2) by means of the conditional probability ingredients $P(D|H_1)$ and $P(D|H_2)$. The remaining four ingredients in Equation 1 all concern the credibility of witness W_i, each of which the subject assessed. For example, $P(D_i^*|DH_1)$ asks: how probable is the witness testimony that defendant was at the scene/time, assuming that defendant was at the scene *and* guilty. The term $P(D_i^*|DH_2)$ asks: how probable is defendant's testimony, assuming defendant was at the scene *and* innocent. Subjects estimated such ingredient values on a probability scale [0,1] for Λ_{jk} values for each main-frame item of testimony in every case C_j.

In the actual estimation tasks in CTD, subjects responded to verbal descriptions of required conditional probabilities whose events corresponded to those in the case of concern. From these conditional probability estimates, we are able to calculate a value Λ_{jk} for any item of testimony in any case. These calculated values, for any subject, can be compared with that subject's estimate $\tilde{\Lambda}_{jk}$ for the same evidence item. In addition, for an entire case C_j we can determine Λ_{Cj} (CTD), a calculation of the probative value of entire case C_j based upon Λ_{ij} values calculated, in turn, from a subjects' conditional probability estimations.

In summary, our method allows three determinations of the probative value of each case for each subject; $\tilde{\Lambda}_{Cj}$ (ZTD), Λ_{Cj} (PTD), and Λ_{Cj} (CTD); these three values can be compared in consistency studies. In addition, our methods allow a comparison, for any subject and any evidence item k, between $\tilde{\Lambda}_{jk}$ (PTD) and calculated Λ_{jk} (CTD). Thus, we have consistency measures for whole-case probative value assessment and for individual evidence item assessment. As a final note, the three "levels" of task decomposition can be thought of as three sets of instructions of increasing specificity about the task or probativity assessment. The ZTD task leaves the entire aggregation and assessment burden on the subject. The PTD task requires holistic or global responses, but only to individual evidence items. The CTD task involves very specific instructions about the formally necessary linkages between events in reasoning chains established by foundation testimony. As we now relate, comparison of responses in these three conditions provides some interesting insight into human response characteristics in the task of weighing evidence.

V. EMPIRICAL STUDIES: RESULTS AND OBSERVATIONS

Following is a brief summary of major results obtained in those parts of our studies which concerned the assessment of the probative value of evidence. The accumulated data base is very large, and we have performed a variety of analyses on these data. A thorough account of the analyses and an extensive interpretation of the results are to be found in two recent research reports which, like others, are available to the reader interested in details (Schum and Martin, 1980c; 1981). Two types of results are presented here: those concerning the consistency of alternative ways of assessing the probative value of evidence for entire cases and for individual evidence items, and those bearing upon several interesting response patterns observed in the evaluation of several different species of evidence or inference structures. A few comments on our measurements and analyses are necessary before we begin.

Estimated or calculated values of likelihood ratio Λ are *vectors* having both probative *direction* and probative *force* properties. Probative direction specifies which major rival fact-in-issue (guilt or innocence) the evidence favors or "points toward" in an inferential sense. Probative force indicates the strength with which the evidence points toward the favored fact-in-issue. Some forms of statistical analyses are grossly misleading unless these two properties are examined separately. Consequently, we will talk about two "forms" of consistency. *Directional consistency* among two or more assessment methods means that the assessments in all methods agree in favoring the same fact-in-issue. *Force consistency* is measured by the degree to which two or more assessment methods assigned the same probative strength to the same evidence. For force consistency, we use a measure F, which indicates the factor by which two Λ values (estimated or calculated) differ. For example, if $\Lambda_1 = 10$ and $\Lambda_2 = 5$, then $F = 2$. All measures of directional and force consistency are within-subject measures; that is, they compare two or more responses made by the same subject. One useful measure of between-subject consistency or agreement in probativity assessment is the familiar *concordance coefficient*. Applied to whole-case Λ_C it measures the extent to which the 20 subjects agree in rank-ordering the 12 cases in terms of their aggregate probative value. Applied to individual evidence items, this coefficient shows the agreement among the 20 subjects in rank-ordering the evidence items in a particular case in terms of their probative value.

Consistency Among Alternative Methods For Assessing The Probative Value of Evidence

Table 1 below contains a summary of results bearing upon the consistency of the three alternative response methods (ZTD, PTD, and CTD) and two other results of interest. Blank cells in Parts A and B simply indicate that the ZTD procedure produces no results for individual evidence items, since it involves a single estimate for an entire case; F is a pairwise measure. Part A shows directional consistency results for the four possible types of comparisons among ZTD, PTD, and CTD for whole-case Λ_C (Row A-1), and for individual evidence items Λ_{jk} (Row A-2). For example, 183 of the 240 possible Λ_C comparisons involving PTD and CTD were directionally consistent. Part B, rows B-1 and B-2 show probative force consistency measures F for whole-case Λ_C comparisons in

Table 1. General Consistency Results Summary

	$\dfrac{ZTD}{PTD}$ CTD	$\dfrac{ZTD}{PTD}$	$\dfrac{ZTD}{CTD}$	$\dfrac{PTD}{CTD}$
A.				
1. Directional Consistency, Λ_C, 12 per subject	117/240 = 48.8%	132/240 = 55%	156/240 = 65%	183/240 = 76.3%
2. Directional Consistency, Λ_{jk}, 60 per subject	—	—	—	732/1200 = 61%
B.				
1. Force Consistency, Λ_C; Median F, directional agreement.	—	2.5* (132)	4.3 (156)	4.1 (183)
2. Force Consistency, Λ_C; Median F, directional disagreement.	—	10.0 (108)	30.0 (84)	20.0 (57)
3. Force Consistency, Λ_{jk}; Median F, directional agreement.	—	—	—	1.58 (729)
4. Force consistency, Λ_{jk}; Median F, directional disagreement.	—	—	—	2.30 (471)

C.	ZTD	PTD	CTD
1. Median Λ_C (G)	2.0 (183)	5.0 (163)	10.0 (207)
2. Median Λ_C (I)	4.0 (37)	5.0 (77)	8.0 (33)
3. Concordance: Ranking entire cases.	0.17	0.54	0.29

D. Concordance, individual items

Cases	1	2	3	4	5	6	7	8	9	10	11	12
PTD	.35	.25	.07	.18	.29	.60	.58	.24	.48	.32	.41	.56
CTD	.61	.60	.39	.55	.75	.61	.63	.53	.06	.61	.59	.39

* The lower the value, the greater the consistency.

which the assessments agreed directionally (B-1) and when they did not (B-2). Such separate analysis is necessary because F suppresses directionality. For example when Λ_C values in ZTD and PTD agreed in probative direction, they typically differed in probative force by a factor of 2.5. The number in parentheses under each F value indicates the number of comparisons over which a median F value was calculated. Rows B-3 and B-4 show median F for individual evidence item Λ_{jk} comparisons. For example, in the 729 instances in which PTD and CTD assessments of Λ_{jk} were directionally consistent, they differed typically by a factor of just 1.58.

Part C simply shows the typical (median) size of Λ_C estimated in ZTD or calculated in PTD or CTD; Row C-1 contains results when Λ_C favored guilt (G) and C-2 when Λ_C favored innocence I. Notice how Λ_C typically increases in size, whether it favors G or I, as the assessment task is decomposed to finer-grain levels. Row C-3 shows the concordance across the 20 subjects in rank-ordering the 12 cases in terms of Λ_C produced by each of the three methods; Λ_C in the PTD condition produces the greatest concordance among subjects. Finally, Part D shows the concordance or agreement among the 20 subjects in rank-ordering the evidence in each case using either PTD or CTD assessments. In all but two cases (9 and 12) the CTD procedure yielded Λ_{ij} values which were most in agreement across subjects.

ZTD In this response method, subjects had the task of assigning a single letter/number pair which indicated the probative strength and direction of the entire set of evidence in a "case." Though required to make only a simple response to each case, subjects had the complete burden of integrating or aggregating all of the evidence in a case. In determinations of the overall probative value of a case, ZTD fares worst in comparison with other methods. This method produces, pairwise, the weakest directional consistency with the other two methods, is most variable across subjects and across cases in directional comparisons, applies the weakest probative force, and has the lowest degree of concordance among subjects in ordering cases in terms of their probative value.

These results are not surprising. Similar results have been observed in other research on holistic assessments in comparison with other procedures (Edwards, *et al.*, 1968). There are several explanations for the typically weak force assessments provided by ZTD. The common explanation is the *misaggregation hypothesis*. This simply says that subjects, left to their own devices in combining large amounts of probabilistic evidence, use judgmental algorithms (or heuristics) which tend to let probative value inherent in evidence "leak out." By this hypothesis, we are all seen as "wasteful" processors of information. Another explanation is that the typically small Λ estimates used by subjects in ZTD simply reflects a *response bias* against using large numbers, particularly in situations in which there is ample evidence, even though conflicting, contradictory, and unreliable (Ducharme, 1970). Equally plausible is the notion that, in ZTD, subjects are free to discard any evidence for any reason. One could simply focus on a few "salient" features of evidence or only upon that evidence which agrees with prior expectations. This says that subjects are free to make the overall assessment task easier by reducing the number of items being considered. This strategy eliminates inconsistencies and reduces processing load; it may also yield weaker assessments if the subject is aware of the fact that evidence is being discarded.

PTD In this response method, subjects were forced to consider the probative value of the testimony of each major witness in a case. In this method Λ_C for an entire case is established by aggregating (multiplicatively) a subject's assessment of the probative value of each "main-frame" testimonial assertion. In such a method subjects are *partially* unburdened of aggregation, since they are never required to combine their assessments across other testimony. They do, however, have an increased response burden, being now required to provide one assessment for each of the "main-frame" items of testimony in a case. In directional consistency comparisons, PTD fares better than ZTD. There is a high directional consistency rate for PTD/CTD comparisons (A-1, A-2). These results are partially explainable by the fact that both use a common rule for aggregating probative value *across* the evidence items in a case (namely, multiplication). The closeness of these probative force results is also due to the apparent consistency of the ingredients subjects estimated in the CTD procedure, since a common between-item aggregation rule would not produce good agreement unless the ingredients in CTD were assessed in reasonable accordance with factors considered by subjects in the holistic PTD assessments. The PTD method produced the highest degree of concordance among subjects in ordering the 12 cases in terms of their probative value.

For individual evidence items, PTD agrees well with CTD in directional consistency and in force consistency (Part B). Concordance among subjects in ordering the evidence in individual cases is generally lower for PTD than for CTD. The PTD procedure, because it requires a focus on each individual witness, allows incorporation of factors which may be overlooked, discarded, or "integrated out" in the ZTD procedure. However, the PTD assessments for individual witnesses are holistic when compared to those assessments in CTD. Our results generally support the conjecture that additional features of probativity assessment required in CTD are overlooked, discarded, or "integrated out" in PTD.

CTD Most suprising to the authors was the overall consistency and adequacy of the many detailed probabilistic assessments made by subjects in the CTD procedure. Each subject made a total of 332 such assessments. In this response mode, subjects had a minimal aggregation burden but a maximal response or judgmental burden. In CTD, subjects were required to make judgments about the subtle linkages among events involved in the often-complex chains of reasoning from testimony to major facts-in-issue in each case. Judgments of the conditional probabilistic ingredients formally required in these chains, when aggregated by formally appropriate means, result in probativity assessments for entire cases and individual items which agree very well with assessments made by other, more holistic, means. This can only mean that the meticulous conditional probability assessments which CTD requires were performed in very reasonable and consistent ways by our subjects. As seen in Table 1-C, both directional and force consistency comparisons involving CTD are strongest for entire cases and for individual items. In addition, the degree of concordance among subjects in rank-ordering cases is second to PTD; in rank ordering individual items in a case, concordance among subjects is greatest using CTD procedures. CTD forces a person to look at the very fine-grained details of an inference task. Our study shows that persons required to bear the burden of such detailed analysis can perform the task in a manner very consistent with performance using other methods.

As the task of probativity assessment is decomposed into finer levels of analysis, a larger amount of the probative value latent in evidence is extracted and reflected in the assessment. This is explainable by at least two means. First, one locus of probative value in evidence is the possible conditional nonindependence of evidence items. Such nonindependence may easily be unrecognized or unaccounted for in ZTD. The PTD procedure alerts the subject to the existence of such nonindependence and simply tells the subject to account for it. In the CTD procedure, however, the method not only alerts the subject to such nonindependence, but also is instructive in how to reflect such nonindependence in assessments. Second and more obvious, as tasks are further decomposed, there is no chance that crucial evidence items, or factors concerning evidence items, will be overlooked, discarded, or "integrated out." For these reasons one expects more probative value in assessments in which more of the evidence in a collection is, in fact, incorporated and in which more of the subtle linkages among evidence items are reflected in the assessments.

We have also seen that there is greater concordance or agreement among individuals in probativity assessments as these tasks are further decomposed. The finer the level of decomposition, the more specific are the instructions required. It comes as no surprise to learn that agreement in judgment among persons is greater the more specific are the instructions about these judgments. We did, however, believe that the very specific conditional probabilistic judgments required in CTD would be difficult for our subjects to make. Results indicate that these judgments were made effectively, if not easily. The essence of task-decomposition in inference is that it forces consideration of finer-grained details of the task and ensures that such consideration is incorporated in overall assessments. Under procedures such as ZTD, where specific attention to these details is not enforced, entire evidence items or features of these items and their probabilistic linkages are easily discarded or overlooked by persons who may be unaware of their existence or who simply choose to ignore them.

Probative Assessment Characteristics For Different Inference Structures

Following is a collection of results obtained in a comparison of the PTD and CTD procedures for assessing the probative value of individual main-frame evidence items in each case. We first discuss results for evidence belonging to *simple* inference structures and then consider results for evidence in *complex* inference structures in which there were

138   LAW & SOCIETY / 17:1

patterns of contradictory, corroboratively redundant, cumulatively redundant, or nonredundant evidence.

Simple Inference Structures These structures are characterized by the number of intermediate reasoning stages separating a single item of main-frame testimony and the ultimate facts-in-issue. A direct testimonial assertion about a major fact has no intermediate reasoning stages; therefore, its "level" of cascading is *zero*. The value of such testimony depends only on the witness's credibility. In our simple inference structures there were three other "levels" of cascading representing either one, two, or three intermediate reasoning stages. Evidence of opportunity typically may have either one or two intermediate reasoning stages, while evidence of means or motive typically have more as Wigmore noted (1937). So our essential results concern the effects, upon probative value assessment in the PTD and CTD condition, of the degree of logical remoteness between testimony and major facts-in-issue. Table 2-A below summarizes probative directional and force consistency between assessments in PTD and CTD.

Table 2.   Directional and Force Consistency:
PTD and CTD Conditions

		Logical Remoteness			
		0	1	2	3
A.	Simple Inference Structures				
	1) Directional Consistency	65% 104/160	73% 146/200	79% 253/320	73% 88/120
	2) Force Consistency (Median F)	2.2	2.4	1.7	1.4
		CON	COR	CUR	NR
B.	Complex Inference Structures				
	1) Directional Consistency	41% 49/120	61% 49/80	65% 52/80	63% 76/120
	2) Force Consistency (Median F)	2.0	2.1	1.9	2.0

Row A-1 shows that logical remoteness has little effect upon the proportion of *directionally* consistent assessment in PTD and CTD. Row A-2, however, shows that logical remoteness does influence the force consistency of these assessments; such consistency typically improves as the remoteness of testimony and facts-in-issue increases. The reason is quite apparent; assessed values of Λ_{jk} in PTD and those based upon subject ingredient estimates in CTD both decreased in size as the remoteness of testimony and major facts-in-issue increased. Abraham Lincoln's assessment of inference-upon-inference thus applies formally as well behaviorally; he is quoted as saying that inference-upon-inference frequently has the same strength as "soup made by boiling the shadow of a pigeon that has been starved to death" (Maguire *et al.*, 1973).

Complex Inference Structures "Complex" inference structures feature the testimony of more than one witness and involve various probabilistic linkages among events in the reasoning stages suggested by the testimony. All complex inference structures in our study involved two items of testimony, and inference structures were defined for various instances in which the second testimony was either contradictory (CON), corroboratively redundant (COR), cumulatively redundant (CUR), or nonredundant (NR) with the first item of testimony. Part B of Table 2 above contains results bearing upon the directional and force consistency of assessments of Λ_{jk} in PTD and CTD; the Λ_{jk} of concern in each case is for the *second* testimony in each structure, the one which either corroborates or is redundant or nonredundant with the first. As shown in Table 2, Part B, there is little difference in probative force consistency across complex inference structures. Directional consistency, however, is lower for contradictory structures than for the others. The explanation of this result requires a more detailed analysis, which we now present for each inference structure.

(1) Contradictory Testimony: Subject's probative response patterns to contradictory testimony in the PTD and CTD conditions are among the most interesting in this study. In the evidence evaluated by subjects there were six instances of contradictory testimony from two witnesses of apparently equal credibility; across 20 subjects we thus observed 120 pairs of PTD/CTD assessments relative to contradictory testimony. Of these 120 assessment pairs, 57 (48 percent) exhibited the following pattern. In the holistic PTD assessments, subjects either ignored the second and conflicting testimony (i.e. they assigned it no probative value) *or* they gave it value but made it agree directionally with the first item with which it was contradictory. Thus, in nearly half the contradictory evidence occasions subjects either ignored contradictory testimony or

treated such testimony as if it were corroborative. However, on these *same* occasions, their assessed ingredients in CTD for the Λ_{jk} values for contradictory testimony resulted in calculated Λ_{jk} values which were directionally the opposite of those for the first item of testimony. In short, asked to examine the fine-grain details of the tasks, subjects' assessments "brought out" the contradictory nature of evidence either overlooked or suppressed in their holistic PTD assessments.

This result brings to mind the so-called "primacy" effects others have observed in human holistic reactions to conflicting or contradictory evidence (e.g., Peterson and Ducharme, 1967; Pitz, 1969). The mind is set in motion in one direction by early evidence and somehow resists being moved in the other direction following later contradictory or conflicting evidence. In our study two items of contradictory testimony were always temporally adjacent. We have labeled the suppression of contradiction in such instances a "local" primacy effect to distinguish it from more global primacy effects which may persist over longer periods of time and over much intervening testimony (Schum, 1980b). The interesting result in our present study is that such primacy or contradiction-suppression is removed when subjects assess fine-grain logical details of evidence. It is important to note that such removal is not due to the aggregation models themselves, since calculated Λ_{jk} values depend entirely upon values of assessed ingredients. A subject's assessed ingredients, when coherently aggregated, "brought out" contradictions that this same person ignored or suppressed in holistic assessments. In making holistic or global assessments of any kind, individuals obviously resort to simplification strategies. Unfortunately, one such strategy may be the removal of contradiction or, worse yet, the incorporation of contradiction as if it were corroboration.

(2) Redundant Evidence Structures: We now examine the subjects' PTD and CTD response patterns to corroboratively or cumulatively redundant testimony. We have mentioned Lempert's (1977) concern about the extent to which jurors "double count" redundant testimony. Our results, taken seriously, suggest that his concern is certainly well founded. The systematic holistic PTD tendency to "double count" testimony from the second of two corroborative witnesses is shown in Table 3-A, and the holistic PTD tendency to overvalue cumulatively redundant testimony is shown in Table 3-B. Also shown in these tables is that such double-counting and over-evaluation tendencies do not appear in the CTD procedure for

probativity assessment. These results are best illustrated and summarized using the correlational statistics which we now describe.

Table 3.   Subject Policies for Assessing Redundant Evidence in the PTD and CTD Conditions.

		PTD		CTD	
		r	b	r	b
A.	Corroborative				
	1. Instance 1	.96	.93	.72	.17
	2. Instance 2	.97	1.07	.72	.23
	3. Instance 3	.93	1.16	.65	.66
	4. Instance 4	.83	.84	.42	.42
B.	Cumulative				
	1. Instance 1	.93	1.11	.34	.26
	2. Instance 2	.79	.78	.25	.22
	3. Instance 3	.73	1.00	.33	.27
	4. Instance 4	.94	.99	.33	.19

In the case evidence subjects evaluated, there were four instances of testimony from two witnesses of nearly equal-appearing credibility who said the same thing. In Part A, for each of these four instances, are correlation coeffecients (r), and regression coefficients (b), in both PTD and CTD assessment conditions. To see how they were determined, take ZTD and instance 1 as an example. The value of r = 0.96 results from correlating, across all 20 subjects, the Λ_{jk} value assigned by a subject to the first testimony and the Λ_{jk} value assigned by the subject to the second (corroborating) testimony; values of b are found in the process. A value of r close to 1.0 means consistency across subjects in their policies for Λ assignment. The value b essentially tells what this policy was; if b = 1.0, this means that the subjects' values for the first and second items were identical; b < 1 means that Λ for the second item was smaller than Λ for the first; and b>1 means that Λ for the second item was greater than for the first.[8] So, for instance 1 in ZTD, the 20 subjects were nearly perfectly consistent in assigning the same probative weight to the second (corroborative) testimony as they assigned to the first. As can be seen, essentially the same thing happens in all four instances; in PTD (holistic assessment) subjects systematically double-counted corroboratively redundant testimony.

---

[8] These stated policies assume that the calculated intercepts are zero or near zero, which they were in all but one condition in Part A. An intercept of zero says that subject's Λ values have no initial bias toward guilt or innocence.

In the CTD condition the generally lower r values mean less consistency in policy; this is to be expected given the very large number of conditional probability ingredients involved in determining the Λ_{jk} value being correlated. Notice however that b is much less than 1.0 in every instance; this means that the probative weight assigned to the corroboratively redundant testimony was typically smaller than the weight assigned in the original testimony. In short, subjects' CTD estimates, when formally aggregated, "bring out" the redundance apparently overlooked in the holistic PTD assessments.

Part B of Table 3 shows the same analysis for the four instances of cumulatively redundant testimony in our evidence. Essentially the same results occur across subjects though it is evident that there is less consistency in estimating Λ_{jk} ingredients than there is in holistic estimates of Λ_{jk}. Cumulative redundance is a more subtle effect than is corroborative redundance, and Λ_{jk} models for cumulatively redundant testimony have many more ingredients than those for corroboratively redundant testimony. Nevertheless, cumulative redundancy overlooked in PTD is "brought out" in the fine-grained analysis in CTD. Once again we emphasize that the "bringing out" in CTD of subtleties due to contradiction or redundance are not necessarily due to the formal aggregation models for Λ_{jk}; it is the subject-assessed ingredients which allow these calculations to bring out these subtleties.

(3) Nonredundant Structures: In the evidence that subjects evaluated there were six instances in which the first of two testimonial assertions was contrived to be probatively facilitative on the second. Apparently, our contrived evidence failed to appear facilitative since, in both PTD and CTD, the second testimony was weighted essentially the same as the first. The formal distinction between redundant and nonredundant testimonial evidence is subtle and involves no sharply defined boundary. In fact, measures of the redundance of evidence suggest a continuum along which evidence may be placed in terms of whether it is redundant or facilitative (Schum, 1979b).

VI. CONCLUSION

The formal research summarized in this paper provides examples of the method whereby various identifiable forms of evidence can be subjected to a fine-grained analysis in which the subtleties in evidence can be identified and systematically examined. The stimulus and guidance for such research have come in large measure from existing evidence scholarship in jurisprudence, there being no similar body of scholarship to be found in other areas in which reasoning from inconclusive evidence is commonly encountered. Our formal research has concerned some matters of which jurists are already aware, such as the complex interplay between witness credibility and the value of what the witness says in a determination of the probative value of testimony by the witness. In fact, some of our specific formal studies on such areas as testimonial redundance have been enhanced by careful examination of evidentiary distinctions which jurists commonly recognize or, in a few instances, fail to recognize. It is generally the case that difficulty in the formal analysis of some forms of evidence (e.g. hearsay, cumulatively redundant evidence) parallels the difficulty jurists experience in formulating specific prescriptions concerning the relevance and admissibility of such evidence.

Our formal research also concerns matters about which there is only infrequent or oblique reference in evidence scholarship—event rarity and transitivity issues being examples. One distinct virtue of the formal analysis of various evidentiary patterns is that it allows one to observe the way in which a variety of evidence-related formal systems can be brought to bear in the study and analysis of evidence subtleties. Thus, we are able to show how the theory of "signal detection" provides very useful concepts and methods in the study of credibility-related ingredients in the analysis of the probative value of testimonial evidence. Similarly, concepts from "statistical communication theory" (or "information theory") allow one to be more precise in formulating problems relating to possible redundance in certain evidence.

How exciting or informative are the results of the empirical studies we summarize depends to some extent on the reader's expectations. Some of our results are very similar to those found in other, more abstract, laboratory studies; other results are unique because of the complexity of the tasks our research subjects performed. In these concluding comments about our empirical results we do *not* wish to leave the reader with the impression that these studies are simply further examples of psychological research demonstrating the inadequacy of human performance on inference-related tasks. In fact, our results show how well persons who are given adequate instructions about reasonably well-formulated problems can respond to a variety of subtle aspects of evidence and reflect these subtleties in their responses. Demonstrating human inadequacy at an inferential task presupposes uncontroversial performance standards, well-posed tasks, and adequate instructions. *No* empirical study of inference (including ours) has the first, and regrettably few have the other two.

A general result of our study is that individuals can capture in their probativity-assessment responses an assortment of subtle aspects of evidence provided that their probativity-assessment tasks are decomposed to a level at which these subtleties are exposed. Further, the concordance or agreement among the probativity assessors in our study was highest for decomposed assessment tasks. Finally, global, holistic, or nondecomposed assessments of the probative value in a collection of evidence are the most variable across persons and frequently disagree directionally with assessments made by other methods involving task decomposition. One suggestion is that individuals asked to mentally aggregate a large collection of evidence may ignore, discard, or integrate over contradictory evidence and otherwise overlook other subtleties in evidence. Our message to jurists cannot, for obvious reasons, be that fact finders' tasks ought to be decomposed in the manner in which they were in our study. Presumably, the deliberation process following a trial encourages a fact finder to consider factors which others have noted but which he/she has discarded or ignored; such mutual enlightenment, however, cannot be guaranteed.

Perhaps the most striking results of our study concern the manner in which our research subjects assessed the value of contradictory and of redundant testimony. Quite startling is the frequently-observed holistic tendency to make contradictory testimony either probatively valueless or, what seems worse, corroborative; such behavior, however, is certainly not unheard-of in more abstract studies of human inference. Our studies show the existence of local as well as global "primacy" effects in which, apparently, the mind resists changes in the direction of opinion revisions. The most systematic result in our study concerns the holistic tendency to "double count" corroboratively redundant testimony. Neither tendency is apparent when subjects are allowed to examine and respond to the fine-grained details of evidence having these characteristics.

If, as asserted earlier, the fact finder's task cannot be decomposed and the post-trial deliberation process cannot guarantee appropriate assessment of various forms of evidence, then it is left to the skill of one counsel in "decomposing" the arguments made by the other. Our formal research strongly suggests the essential formal adequacy of the rules and procedures for this process of "beating and boulting out the truth" (Hale, 1739). Our empirical studies suggest that attentive fact finders with reasonable intellectual skills can incorporate the many subtleties in evidence if, at least, they are alerted to the existence of these subtleties. Thus, the double-counting of redundant testimony and the "local primacy" of earlier testimony that is contradicted later are examples of common reasoning inconsistencies exhibited by many people which can, perhaps, be overcome by an equally attentive counsel.

TECHNICAL APPENDIX

A. THREE EXAMPLES OF LIKELIHOOD RATIO Λ DETERMINATION FOR THE THREE INFERENCE STRUCTURES SHOWN IN FIGURE 1 IN THE TEXT

Figure 1-A in the text shows the simplest possible case of cascaded inference. Witness W_i testifies that event D occurred; event D is circumstantial evidence bearing on major rival facts-in-issue H_1 and H_2. As a fact finder, what we have is W_i's testimonial assertion D_i^* that event D occurred. D_i^* and D are not the same events, and we shall be misled if we treat them so. The reason is that, unless we believe W_i to be perfectly credible, testimony D_i^* is consistent both with D, the actual occurrence of the event, and D^C, the nonoccurrence of this event. In this case, what can condition or change our opinion about the relative likelihood of H_1 and H_2 is the event D_i^* representing the testimony of W_i. In this inference structure the likelihood ratio for testimony D_i^* is as follows:

$$\Lambda D_i^* = \frac{P(D_i^*|H_1)}{P(D_i^*|H_2)} = \frac{P(D|H_1)[P(D_i^*|DH_1) - P(D_i^*|D^CH_1)] + P(D_i^*|D^CH_1)}{P(D|H_2)[P(D_i^*|DH_2) - P(D_i^*|D^CH_2)] + P(D_i^*|D^CH_2)} \quad (1)$$

In this expression the conditional probabilities $P(D|H_1)$ and $P(D|H_2)$ express the strength of the linkage between D and H_1 and H_2; in words, these probabilities prescribe how probatively valuable is event D. They indicate the strength of the linkage between D and H_1, H_2. All other terms concern the credibility of witness W_i and refer to the linkage between testimony D_i^* and D, the matter asserted. So far, intuition is supported by $\Lambda_{D_i^*}$; the value of an item of testimony depends upon the importance of what the source has to say and upon the credibility of the source.

There are two additional features of $\Lambda_{D_i^*}$ which we must also notice. Observe that the terms $P(D|H_1)$ and $P(D|H_2)$ occur separately in Equation 1 and not together as the ratio $P(D|H_1/P(D|H_2)$. This fact tells us that the probative value of testimony also depends upon the *rarity* of D, the event being reported. The reason is that the ratio of two numbers suppresses information about the precise values of the numbers; e.g., $4=0.40/0.10 = 0.04/0.01$. In $\Lambda_{D_i^*}$ we must have the precise values of $P(D|H_1)$ and $P(D|H_2)$ and not simply their ratio; such precision preserves the rarity of events, to which Λ is sensitive. In general, the rarer the event reported, the stronger credibility we may require from the source of information about the source.

The other feature concerns the four credibility-related ingredients of $\Lambda_{D_i^*}$ in Equation 1. Take $P(D_i^*|DH_1)$ for example. By itself, the conditional probability $P(D_i^*|D)$ is called a "hit" probability or a "true positive," and it expresses how likely testimony D_i^* is if event D actually occurred. The addition of the conditioning term H_1 in $P(D_i^*|DH_1)$ tells us essentially that W_i's "hit probability" may depend upon H_1. A similar process applies to another ingredient $P(D_i^*|D^CH_1)$, which is called "false positive," and also to these hit and false positives when H_2 is true. Here is the essential message; in assessing the probative value of testimony D_i^* we must consider whether or not the likelihood of testimony D_i^* depends upon factors other than the occurrence or nonoccurrence of the events being reported. Our formal process makes clear that the observational and reporting behavior of a witness may contain probative value over and above the probative value of the event being reported. In short, the witness' behavior can be probative in a number of ways. The manner in which credibility-related ingredients occur in Λ expressions allows us to incorporate a wide variety of subtleties associated with the behavior of witnesses including their observational sensitivity and many motivational considerations.

Figure 1-B represents a situation in which witness W_j offers testimony E_j^* that event E occurred; the occurrence of E is circumstantial on D which, in turn, is circumstantial on major facts-in-issue H_1 and H_2. Equation 2 shows $\Lambda_{E_j^*}$ in a special case which we shall identify:

$$\Lambda_{E_j^*} = \frac{P(E_j^*|H_1)}{P(E_j^*|H_2)}$$

$$= \frac{P(D|H_1)[P(E|DH_1) - P(E|D^CH_1)] + P(E|D^CH_1) + \left[\dfrac{P(E_j^*|E)}{P(E_j^*|E^C)}^{-1}\right]^{-1}}{P(D|H_2)[P(E|DH_2) - P(E|D^CH_2)] + P(E|D^CH_2) + \left[\dfrac{P(E_j^*|E)}{P(E_j^*|E^C)}^{-1}\right]^{-1}} \quad (2)$$

This structure reveals three reasoning stages: from testimony E_j^* to events E, E^C; from events E, E^C to events D, D^C; and from events D, D^C, to ultimate facts-in-issue H_1, H_2. Examination of Equation 2 shows probative ingredients for each stage of reasoning. The "special-case" nature of this expression concerns the foundation reasoning stage from testimony E_j^* to events E, E^C. In the more general expression for $\Lambda_{E_j^*}$, the hit and false-positive $P(E_j^*|E)$ and $P(E_j^*|E^C)$ have other conditioning terms, namely, the four possible combinations of one of D, D^C and H_1, H_2. The special case arises when one assumes that these hit and false positives do not depend upon any events "higher" in the chain of reasoning. The elimination of these higher-order conditioning events is accomplished by conditional independence assumptions. For example, $P(E_j^*|EDH_1) = P(E_j^*|E)$ is the assumption that testimony E_j^* is independent of D and H_1, given event E. In short, this is an assumption that the credibility-related hit probability $P(E_j^*|E)$ does not depend upon other events in the reasoning chain.

Figure 1-C shows a case in which two witnesses W_i and W_j both testify that event D occurred. Here is an instance in which the probative value of one item of testimony depends upon previous evidence; our Λ formulations account for such dependency, allowing us to represent a variety of subtle effects of one evidence item on another. This example allows us to show the degree to which testimony D_j^* is probatively redundant, since W_j reports the *same* event as did earlier Witness W_i.

The probative value of testimony from the first witness W_i is given by Equation 1. Now consider W_j who also testifies that D occurred. We must now examine testimony D_j^* *in light of* prior testimony D_i^*, since there is an obvious logical relationship—namely, both witnesses say the same thing. Formally, the likelihood ratio for D_j^*, given D_i^*, is prescribed by:

$$\Lambda D_j^* | D_i^* = \frac{P(D_j^* | H_1 D_i^*)}{P(D_j^* | H_2 D_i^*)}$$

$$= \frac{P(D | D_i^* H_1)[P(D_j^* | DD_i^* H_1) - P(D_j^* | D^C D_i^* H_1)] + P(D_j^* | D^C D_i^* H_1)}{P(D | D_i^* H_2)[P(D_j^* | DD_i^* H_2) - P(D_j^* | D^C D_i^* H_2)] + P(D_j^* | D^C D_i^* H_2)} \quad (3)$$

This formalization shows that there are two interesting factors in the relationship between D_i^* and D_j^*. The first concerns the terms $P(D|D_i^* H_1)$ and $P(D|D_i^* H_2)$. Basically, these terms prescribe the "residual" probative value in D remaining after W_i's testimony; how much is left depends upon W_i's credibility. If W_i is perfectly credible, then there is no probativity left for the testimony of W_j; if you believe W_i, then testimony by W_j should tell you nothing more in inference about H_1 and H_2. The other factor concerns the possible conditioning of testimony D_j^* by testimony D_i^*. Essentially, this allows for the incorporation of factors associated with possible influence of one witness on another. We may believe, for example, that W_i told W_j what to testify. If so, there is room in Equation 3 for incorporating such effects and adjusting probative values accordingly.

B. MEASURES OF EVENT REDUNDANCY

For the *cumulative* case, we define the redundancy of event F, knowing event E, as:

$$R_{cum} = 1 - \frac{Log^L F|E}{Log \, L_F},$$

where L_F is a likelihood ratio measure of the probativity of event F on facts-in-issue, and $L_{F|E}$ is a likelihood ratio measure of the probativity of event F in light of event E. If the occurrence of E makes F highly probable under both facts-in-issue, then $L_{F|E} = 1.0$. Since Log 1 = zero, this makes $R_{cum} = 1.0$, it maximum value. If knowing E causes no change in the probativity of F on facts-in-issue, then $L_{F|E} = L_F$ and so R_{cum} = zero; this means that F is not probatively redundant if you knew that E occurred. So, R_{cum} is a number between zero and one which indicates the extent of redundance in event F if you also knew that event E occurred.

In the *corroborative* case, we define:

$$R_{cor} = 1 - \frac{Log\ L_{E|E}}{Log\ L_E},\qquad(5)$$

and note immediately that R_{cor} *must always equal 1.0*. The reason, of course, is that the second discovery of the same event cannot be probative, $L_{E|E} = 1.0$. Since Log $1.0 = 0$, R_{cor} always equals one. In other words, event E is always perfectly redundant with itself. This is why we have said in the text that corroborative redundance is a special case of cumulative redundance.

REFERENCES

CLEARY, Edward (1972) *McCormick on Evidence*. St Paul.: West.

COHEN, L. Jonathan (1977) *The Probable and the Provable*. Oxford: Clarendon.

—— (1981) "Subjective Probability and the Paradox of the Gatecrasher," 1981 *Arizona State Law Journal* 627.

DUCHARME, Wesley M. (1970) "A Response Bias Explanation of Conservative Inference," 85 *Journal of Experimental Psychology* 66.

EDWARDS, Ward D. (1962) "Dynamic Decision Theory and Probabilistic Information Processing," 4(2) *Human Factors* 59.

EDWARDS, Ward D., William L. HAYS, and Barabara C. GOODMAN(1968) "Probabilistic Information Processing Systems: Design and Evaluation," 4 *IEEE Transactions on Systems Science and Cybernetics* 248.

EGAN, James P. (1975) *Signal Detection Theory and ROC Analysis*. N.Y.: Academic Press.

EGGLESTON, Richard (1978) *Evidence, Proof and Probability*. London: Weidenfeld and Nicolson.

EILS, I., David SEAVER, and Ward EDWARDS (1977) Developing a Technology of Probabilistic Inference: Aggregating by Averaging Reduces Conservation. 77 Social Science Research Institute, University of Southern California, Los Angeles.

FINKELSTEIN, Michael O. and William B. FAIRLEY (1970) "A Bayesian Approach to Identification Evidence," 83 *Harvard Law Review* 489.

HALE, Sir Matthew (1739) *The History of the Common Law of England*. Chicago: University of Chicago Press (1971 reprint).

HUME, David (1888) *Treatise of Human Nature*, Book 1, Part 3, Section 8. Oxford: Clarendon Press.

KAYE, David (1979) "The Paradox of the Gatecrasher and Other Stories," 1979 *Arizona State Law Journal* 101.

—— (1981) "Paradoxes, Gedanken Experiments and the Burden of Proof: A Response to Dr. Cohen's Reply," 1981 *Arizona State Law Journal* 635.

KEYSER, Cassius J. (1929) "On the Study of Legal Science," 1929 *Yale Law Journal* 38.

LEMPERT, Richard O. (1977) "Modeling Revelance," 75 *Michigan Law Review* 1021.

LEMPERT, Richard O. and Stephen A. SALTZBURG (1977) *A Modern Approach to Evidence*. St. Paul: West.

MAGUIRE, John M., J. WEINSTEIN, J. CHADBOURN, and J. MANSFIELD (1973) *Evidence: Cases and Materials on Evidence*. Mineola, N.Y.: Foundation Press.

MARTIN, Anne W. (1979) Cascaded Inference and Hearsay. Rice University Department of Psychology Research Report 79-03. Houston Texas.

—— (1980) A General Algorithm for Determining Likelihood Ratios in Cascaded Inference. Rice University Department of Psychology Research Report 80-03, Houston Texas.

PETERSON, Cameron R. and Wesley M. DUCHARME (1967) "A Primacy Effect in Subjective Probability Revision," 73 *Journal of Experimental Psychology* 61.

150   LAW & SOCIETY / 17:1

PITZ, Gordon F. (1969) "An Inertia Effect (Resistance to Change) in the Revision of Opinion," 23 *Canadian Journal of Psychology* 24.

RAPOPORT, Ammon and Thomas WALLSTEIN (1972) "Individual Decision Behavior," 23 *Annual Review of Psychology*, 131.

SAKS, Michael J., and Robert F. KIDD (1981) "Human Information Processing and Adjudication: Trial by Heuristics," 15 *Law & Society Review* 123.

SCHAFER, G. (1976) *A Mathematical Theory of Evidence*. Princeton N.J.: Princeton University Press.

SCHUM, David A. (1977a) "The Behavioral Richness of Cascaded Inference Models: Examples in Jurisprudence," in Castellan, Pisoni, and Potts (eds.), *Cognitive Theory* (Vol. II). Hillsdale, N.J.: L. Erlbaum Press.

—— (1977b) "Contrast Effects in Inference: On the Conditioning of Current Evidence by Prior Evidence," 18 *Organizational Behavior and Human Performance* 217.

—— (1979a) "A Review of a Case Against Blaise Pascal and his Heirs," 77 *University of Michigan Law Review* 446.

—— (1979b) On Factors Which Influence the Redundancy of Cumulative and Corroborative Testimonial Evidence. Rice University Psychology Dept. Research Report 79-02, Houston, Texas.

—— (1979c) A Bayesian Account of Transitivity and Other Order - Related Effects In Chains of Inferential Reasoning. Rice University Psychology Department Research Report 79-04, Houston, Texas.

—— (1980) "Current Developments in Research on Cascaded Inference," in Thomas S. Wallstein (ed.), *Cognitive Processes in Decision and Choice Behavior*. Hillsdale, N.J.: L. Erlbaum Press.

—— (1981a) "Sorting out the Effects of Witness Sensitivity and Response Criterion Placement Upon the Inferential Value of Testimonial Evidence," 27 *Organizational Behavior and Human Performance* 153.

—— (1981b) Assessing the Probative Value of Equivocal Testimony Or No Testimony on a Relevant Issue at Trial. Rice University Department of Psychology Research Report #81-04, Houston, Texas.

—— (1981c) Formalizing the Process of Assessing the Probative Value of Alibi Testimony. Rice University Psychology Dept. Research Report 81-05, Houston, Texas.

SCHUM, David A. and Wesley M. DUCHARME (1971) "Comments on the Relationship between the Impact and the Reliability of Evidence," 6 *Organizational Behavior and Human Performance* 111.

SCHUM, David A. and Clinton, W. KELLEY (1973) "A Problem in Cascaded Inference: Determining the Inferential Impact of Confirming and Conflicting Reports from Several Unreliable Sources," 10 *Organizational Behavior and Human Performance* 404.

SCHUM, David A. and Anne W. MARTIN (1980a) Empirical Studies of Cascaded Inference in Jurisprudence: Methodological Considerations. Rice University Department of Psychology Research Report 80-01, Houston, Texas.

—— (1980b) Probabilistic Opinion Revision on the Basis of Evidence at Trial: A Baconian or a Pascalian Process? Rice University Department of Psychology Research Report 80-02, Houston, Texas.

—— (1980c) On the Internal Consistency of Assessments of the Probative Value of Evidence. Rice University Dept. of Psychology Research Report 80-04, Houston, Texas.

—— (1981) Assessing the Probative Value of Evidence in Various Inference Structures. Rice University Dept. of Psychology Research Report 81-02, Houston, Texas.

SLOVIC, Paul and Sarah LICHTENSTEIN (1971) "Comparison of Bayesian and Regression Approaches to the Study of Information Processing in Judgment," 6 *Organizational Behavior and Human Performance* 649.

STANILAND, Alan C. (1966) *Patterns of Redundancy*. Cambridge: The University Press.

STEVENS, Stanley S. (1975) *Psychophysics: Introduction to Its Perceptual, Neural, and Social Prospects*. N.Y.: Wiley and Sons.

SWETS, John A. (1964) *Signal Detection and Recognition by Human Observers: Contemporary Readings*. N.Y.: Wiley and Sons.

TRIBE, Laurence (1971) "Precision and Ritual in the Legal Process," 84 *Harvard Law Review* 1810.

—— (1974) "Triangulating Hearsay," 87 *Harvard Law Review* 957.

SCHUM AND MARTIN   151

WIGMORE, John H. (1937) *The Science of Judicial Proof as Given by Logic, Psychology, and General Experience, and Illustrated in Judicial Trials* (3rd ed.). Boston: Little, Brown.

WINKLER, Robert and Allen MURPHY (1973) "Experiments in the Laboratory and the Real World," 10 *Organizational Behavior and Human Performance* 252.

ZADEH, Lofti (1978) "Fuzzy Sets As a Basis For a Theory of Possibility," 1 *Fuzzy Sets And Systems*.

Part II
Logic of Proof

General

[4]
ILLINOIS
LAW REVIEW

| Volume VIII | JUNE, 1913 | Number 2 |

THE PROBLEM OF PROOF[1]

By John H. Wigmore.[2]

This article aspires to propose, though in tentative form only, a *novum organum* for the study of Judicial Evidence.

The study of the principles of Evidence, for a lawyer, falls into two distinct parts. One is Proof in the general sense,—the part concerned with the ratiocinative process of contentious persuasion,—mind to mind, counsel to juror, each partisan seeking to move the mind of the tribunal. The other part is Admissibility,— the procedural rules devised by law, and based on litigious experience and tradition, to guard the tribunal (particularly the jury) against erroneous persuasion. Hitherto, the latter has loomed largest in our formal studies,—has, in fact, monopolized them; while the former, virtually ignored, has been left to the chances of later acquisition, casual and emphatic, in the course of practice. Here we have been wrong; and in two ways:

For one thing, there is, and there *must* be, a probative science— the principles of proof—independent of the artificial rules of procedure; hence, it can be and should be studied. This science, to be sure, may as yet be imperfectly formulated or even incapable of formulation. But all the more need is there to begin in earnest to investigate and develop it. Furthermore, this process of Proof

---

1. This is a chapter from a compilation shortly to appear, entitled *The Principles of Judicial Proof, as contained in Logic, Psychology and General Experience, and illustrated in Judicial Trials.*

The chapter here offered is the final one, and represents the objective to which the prior portions are directed. The author will be glad to receive comments on the method proposed. He adds that several other methods have been devised but rejected by him, and that this one, like Sir Frank Lockwood's celebrated but unsuccessful alibi, seems to be "the best of the lot," at any rate.

2. Professor of Law in Northwestern University; author of *A Treatise on Evidence; Pocket Code of Evidence, etc.*

Evidence and Proof

is the more important of the two,—indeed, is the ultimate purpose in every judicial investigation. The procedural rules for Admissibility are merely a preliminary aid to the main activity, viz. the persuasion of the tribunal's mind to a correct conclusion by safe materials. This main process is that for which the jury are there, and on which the counsel's duty is focused. Vital as it is, its principles surely demand study.

And, for another thing, the judicial rules of Admissibility are destined to lessen in relative importance during the next generation or later. Proof will assume the important place; and we must therefore prepare ourselves for this shifting of emphasis. We must seek to acquire a scientific understanding of the principles of what may be called "natural" proof,—the hitherto neglected process. If we do not do this, history will repeat itself, and we shall find ourselves in the present plight of Continental Europe. There, in the early 1800s the ancient worn-out numerical system of "legal proof" was abolished by fiat and the so-called "free proof"—namely, no system at all—was substituted. For centuries, lawyers and judges had evidenced and proved by the artificial numerical system; they had no training in any other,—no understanding of the living process of belief; in consequence, when "legal proof" was abolished, they were unready, and judicial trials have been carried on for a century past by uncomprehended, unguided, and therefore unsafe mental processes. Only in recent times, under the influences of modern science, are they beginning to develop a science of proof.

Such will be our own fate, when the time comes, if we do not lay foundations to prepare for the new stage of procedure. So far, there seems to be no attempt in English, since Bentham, to call attention to the principles of judicial Proof (distinguished from Admissibility) as a whole and as a system.[3]

---

3. Mr. Burrill's masterly work, two generations ago, covered only a part of the field, Circumstantial Evidence. Mr. Moore's recent treatise (a valuable arsenal of extensive research), on *Facts, or the Weight and Value of Evidence,* deals in substance to the Testimonial Evidence only. Mr. Justice Stephen's introduction to the Indian Evidence Act, entitled *The Principles of Judicial Evidence* (1872), contains a brief though thoroughly scientific survey of the subject; and perhaps his exposition should be classed as an attempt at a system. He seems to have believed that the logical Methods of Agreement and of Difference supplied the sufficient key to all such questions ("the principle is precisely the same in all cases, however simple or however complicated"). Inadequate though this may be deemed, certainly his point of view is so plausibly stated that it must be reckoned with in any future proposals of a system. The present exposition not being controversial, no attempt is made to note the objections to Mr. Justice Stephen's method.

The problem of collating a mass of evidence, so as to determine the net effect which it should have on one's belief, is an everyday problem in courts of justice. Nevertheless, no one hitherto seems to have published any logical scheme on a scale large enough to aid this purpose.[4] What is here offered is therefore only an attempt at a working method, which may suffice for lack of any other yet accessible.

Three questions naturally arise. What is the *object* of such a scheme? What are the necessary *conditions* to be satisfied? What is the *apparatus* therefor?

1. THE OBJECT. The object, of course, is to determine rationally the net persuasive effect of a mixed mass of evidence. Many data, perhaps multifarious, are thrust upon us as tending to produce belief or disbelief. Each of them (by hypothesis) has some probative bearing. Consequently, we should not permit ourselves to reach a conclusion without considering all of them and the relative value of each. Negatively, therefore, our object is (in part) to avoid being misled (it may be) through attending only to some fragments of the mass of data. We must assume that a conclusion reached upon such a fragment only will be more or less untrustworthy. And our moral duty (in court) is to reach a belief corresponding to the actual facts; hence it is repugnant to us to contemplate that our belief is not as trustworthy as it could be.

Why is there such a danger of untrustworthiness? Because *belief* is *purely mental*. It is distinct from the external reality, or actual fact. Hence the approximation of our belief of a correct representation of the actual fact will depend upon how fully the data for the fact have entered into the mental formation of our belief. But those data have entered into the formation of our belief *at successive times*; hence a danger of omission or of inferior attention. "Knowledge in the highest perfection would consist in the *simultaneous* possession of facts. To comprehend a science perfectly, we should have every fact present with every other fact.

On the Continent, the great pioneer work of Hans Gross, entitled (misleadingly) *Criminal Psychology* (translated in the Modern Criminal Science Series) is still the only systematic treatise on the psychology of testimony. However, not being written from the point of view of our law, its system is not directly useful.

Through the kind assistance of his colleague, Professor Horace C. Longwell, the present author has consulted the modern works on Logic, but must still avow that, for the purposes of judicial controversy, they do not afford the desired help.

4. Jevons, *The Principles of Science*, p. 34.

We are logically weak and imperfect in respect of the fact that we are obliged to think of one thing after another."[5] And in the court room or the office the multitude of evidential facts are originally apprehended one after another. Hence the final problem is to co-ordinate them. Logic ignores time; but the mind is more or less conditioned by it. The problem is to remove the handicap as far as possible.

It may be answered that psychologically each evidential detail, when originally apprehended, did have in due effect, and that subconsciously the total impression is meanwhile being gradually produced. For example, when a thousand bales of cotton are piled one by one in a warehouse, the whole original thousand will finally be found there, available for sale, even though they went in there piecemeal at different times. To rebut this argument, it is enough to say that we do not yet know by psychological science that this analogy is true of the mind in its successive apprehension of sundry facts; hence we cannot afford to assume it. But furthermore, even if it were true under certain abstract conditions, it is not the fact in the ordinary conduct of justice. So many interruptions and distractions occur, both to the lawyer in preparation to the jurors in the trial, that facts cannot be properly co-ordinated on their first apprehension. Hence our plain duty remains, to lift once more and finally into consciousness *all* the data, to attempt to co-ordinate them consciously, and to determine their net effect on belief.

Our object then, specifically, is in essence: *To perform the logical (or psychological) process of a conscious juxtaposition of detailed ideas, for the purpose of producing rationally a single final idea.* Hence, *to the extent that the mind is unable to juxtapose consciously a larger number of ideas, each coherent group of detailed constituent ideas must be reduced in consciousness to a single idea; until the mind can consciously juxtapose them with due attention to each, so as to produce its single final idea.*

2. THE NECESSARY CONDITIONS. Any scheme which will aid

---

5. They will perhaps some day be discovered. But the methods of observation and experiment in all inductive search for psychological laws involve inevitably a lengthy study of large masses of data. Moreover, the data available from judicial annals, though perhaps numerous enough, are almost always defective, in that the objective truth, necessary to test the correctness of any belief, can seldom be indubitably ascertained. *E. g.* if we were to study one hundred murder trials, so as to ascertain some law of thought lurking in certain combinations of evidence, the very basis of the study, viz. the actual guilt or innocence of the accused, cannot usually be known to us, and our study is useless without that fact.

THE PROBLEM OF PROOF   81

in the foregoing purpose must fulfill certain conditions, at least to a substantial degree.

(*a*)   It must employ *types* of evidence, suitable for representing all kinds of cases presented.   And these types must be based on some logical *system, i. e.* a system which includes all the fundamental logical processes.

(*b*)   It must be able with these types to include *all the evidential data* in a *given case*.   This requirement is mechanically the most exacting.   The types of evidence and the processes of logic are few; but the number of instances of each one of them in a given case varies infinitely.   *E. g.* there may be in one case fifteen witnesses to a specific circumstance and two each to two others; while in the next case there may be neither circumstances nor witness of that sort, but thirty separate groups of other sorts; and this would be a simple example.   Hence, the desired scheme must be capable mechanically of taking care of all possible varieties and the repeated instances of each.

(*c*)   It must be able to show the *relation* of each evidential fact to each and all others.   The process leading to belief is one of successive subsumings of single instances into groups of data and of the reduction of these groups into new single instances, and so on; hence the relations of the data to each other must be made apprehensible, and not merely the data per se.   By "relations" of data is here meant that each believed fact does or does not tend to produce in the mind a belief or disbelief in some other specific alleged fact.

(*d*)   It must be able to show the distinction between a *"fact"* *as alleged* and a *fact as believed* or disbelieved; *i. e.* between the evidential data as *first proffered* for a purpose, and the effect of those data for the purpose *after* the mind has passed on them.   *E. g.* the party offers a witness as proving that the defendant was on a near-by street corner at a certain hour; yet when the tribunal proceeds to reckon that alleged fact as an item towards the main issue, it must have had some way of noting for later use whether it does or does not believe the witness and accept that alleged fact as an actual fact.   Any scheme which fails to provide this would be like a bridge with the bolts left out of the truss angles; there would be nothing to show that it does not rest merely on an aggregation of hypotheses.

(*e*)   It must be able to represent all the data as potentially *present in time to the consciousness.*   The very aim of the scheme is to enable all the data to be lifted into consciousness at once. To be sure, the mind itself is not completely capable of this task, in other than the simplest cases. Numerous groups of subordinate data have to be first subsumed into other data by separate acts, until the number of these is small enough to be considered in a single continuous consciousness. Hence, the scheme in question *may* be so constructed that the records of these preliminary mental acts are not at all exhibited at once. Nevertheless, the mind will have to be sent back over these preliminary acts, from time to time, to verify, amplify, and correct them. And so (as first stated above) all of them must be at least *potentially* presentable to the consciousness, if the scheme is to be efficient.

(*f*) It must, finally, be *compendious* in bulk, and *not too complicated* in variety of symbols. These limitations are set by the practical facts of legal work. Nevertheless, men's aptitudes for the use of such schemes vary greatly. Experience alone can tell us whether a particular scheme is usable by the generality of able students and practitioners who need or care to attack the problem.

(*g*) But, negatively, the scheme need *not* show us what our belief *ought* to be. It can hope to show only what our belief actually *is*, and *how* we have actually reached it.

For example, assuming that the mind has accepted certain subordinate facts A, B, C, D, and E; and that A, B, and C point to X, the defendant's doing of an act, while D and E point to Not-X, *i. e.* his not doing it; there is no law (yet known) of logical thought which tells us that $(A + B + C) + (D + E)$ *must* equal X, or *must* equal Not-X. We know only that our mind, reflecting upon the five evidential data, *does* come to the conclusion X, or Not-X, as the case may be. All that the scheme can do for us is to make plain the entirety and details of our actual mental process. It cannot reveal laws which should be consciously obeyed in that process.

This is because no system of logic has yet discovered and established such laws. There are no known rules available to test the correctness of the infinite variety of inferences presentable in judicial trials. Much indeed has been done that is theoretically applicable to circumstantial evidence; *e. g.* the method of differences, in inductive logic, may enable us, with the help of a chemist, to say whether a stain was produced by a specific liquid. But these methods must be pursued by a comparison of observed or experimental instances, newly obtained for the very case in hand, and usually numerous; hence they are impracticable for the vast mass of judicial data. Morever, even so far as practicable in theory (so to speak), the required consumption of time would forbid their use in trials for any large masses of varied evidence. Hence, they do not serve our purpose. For testimonial evidence, also, those methods would be to some extent applicable in modern psychological experimentation. Yet merely to imagine two or three witnesses elaborately tested to determine their degree of trustworthiness as to memory or observation of sundry subjects of testimony, is to realize that such methods, by reason of the consumption of time alone, are not yet feasible in judicial trials. Finally, even so far as logic and psychology have gone with methods for estimating the probative force of individual inferences, they have apparently done nothing practical towards a method for measuring the *net effect* of a series or *mass of mixed data* bearing on a single alleged fact.

For these and other reasons, then, it must be understood that the desired scheme is not expected to tell us what *ought* logically to be our belief,—either as to individual subordinate data or as to the final net fact in issue.

What it *does* purport to achieve is to *show us explicitly* in a single compass how we *do reason and believe* for those individual facts and from them to the final fact. To achieve this much would be a substantial gain, in the direction of correctness of belief. Each separate proffered fact is tested in our consciousness, and the result is recorded. Perhaps we cannot explain *why* we reach that result, but we know at least that we *do* reach it. And thus step by step we set down the separate units of actual belief,—connecting, subsuming, and generalizing, until the subfinal grouping is reached; then dwelling in consciousness on that; until at last a belief (or disbelief) on the final fact evolves into our consciousness.

Hence, though we may not be able to demonstrate that we *ought* to reach that belief or disbelief, we have at least the satisfaction of having taken every precaution to reach it rationally. Our moral duty was to approximate, so far as capable, our belief to the fact. We have performed that duty, to the limits of our present rational capacity. And the scheme or method, if it has enlarged that capacity, will have achieved something worth while.

We now proceed to the third and final topic: an Apparatus suitable as a working method for attaining the foregoing purpose while fulfilling the necessary conditions just set forth.

3. Explanation of Apparatus for Charting and Listing the Details of a Mass of Evidence. The apparatus consists of a Chart for symbols and a List for their translation. The types of evidence and logical processes have already been set forth in former chapters.

1. *Symbols for Kinds of Evidence.* Each human assertion, offered to be credited, is conceived of as a testimonial fact; each fact of any other sort is a circumstantial fact.

□   Testimonial evidence affirmatory (M testifies that defendant had the knife).

⊓   Testimonial evidence negatory (M testifies that defendant did *not* have the knife).

○   Circumstantial evidence affirmatory (knife was picked up near where defendant was; hence, defendant had it).

∩   Circumstantial evidence negatory (knife was found in deceased's hand; hence, defendant did *not* have it).

⊟   Same four kinds of evidence, when offered by the *defendant* in a case. (These are the same four kinds of evidence; it is merely convenient to note which party offers them).

⊓

⊖   Any fact judicially admitted, or noticed as a matter of general knowledge or inference, without evidence introduced.

∩

¶   Any fact presented to the *tribunal's own senses, i. e.* a coat shown, or a witness' assertion made in court on the stand. Everything actually evidenced must end in this, except when judicially noticed or judicially admitted.

∞   *Explanatory evidence; i. e.* for *circumstantial* evidence, explaining away its effect (knife might have been dropped by a third person; for *testimonial* evidence, discrediting its trustworthiness (Witness was too excited to see who picked up the knife).

>   *Corroborative* evidence; *i. e.* for *circumstantial* evidence, strengthening the inference, closing up other possible explanations (No third person was near the parties when the knife was found); for *testimonial* evidence, supporting it by closing up possibilities of testimonial error (Witness stood close by, was not excited, was disinterested spectator).

◁

≫   Same two kinds of evidence, when offered by the *defendant* in a case.

◁

2. *Relation of Individual Pieces of Evidence, shown by position of Symbols.*

A supposed fact tending to prove the existence of another fact is placed *below* it.

A supposed explanatory or corroborative fact, tending to lessen or to strengthen the force of fact thus proved, is placed to *left* or *right* of it, respectively.

A single *straight* line (continued at a right angle, if necessary) indicates the supposed relation of one fact to another.

The symbol for a fact observed by the tribunal or judicially admitted or noticed (¶, ∞) is placed directly *below* the fact so learned.

3. *Probative Effect of an Evidential Fact.*

When a fact is offered or conceived as evidencing, explaining, or corroborating, it is noted by the appropriate symbol with a connecting line. But thus far it is merely *offered*. We do not yet know whether we believe it to be a fact, nor what probative force we are willing to give it, if a fact. As soon as our mind has come to the necessary *conclusion* on the subject, we symbolize as follows:

(1) *Provisional credit* given to *affirmatory* evidence, testimonial or circumstantial, is shown by adding an arrow-head.

Provisional credit given to *negatory* evidence, testimonial or circumstantial, is shown by adding an arrow-head above a small cipher.

Particularly *strong credit* given to those kinds of evidence respectively is shown by doubling the arrow-head; this is usually applicable where several testimonies or circumstances concur upon the same fact.

(2) A small interrogation mark, placed alongside the connecting line, signifies *doubt* as to the probative effect of the evidence.

Similarly, for each kind of symbol, a small interrogation mark within it signifies a mental balance, an uncertainty; the alleged fact may or may not be a fact.

(3) A dot within the symbol of any kind of *alleged fact* signifies that we now *believe* it to be a fact. Particularly strong belief may be signified by two dots;

thus (··).

A small cipher within the symbol of any kind of alleged fact signifies that we now *disbelieve* it to be a fact. Particularly strong disbelief may be signified by two such ciphers; thus ⊙⊙.

     (4) If a single supposed *explanatory* fact does, in our estimation after weighing it, detract from the force of the desired inference (in case of a witness, if it discredits his assertion), we signify this by an arrow-head pointing to the left, placed half way across the horizontal connecting line.

     If a single *corroborative* fact is given effect in our estimation, we signify this by a short Roman letter X, placed across the connecting line.

     Doubling the mark indicates particular strength in the effect, *i. e.* ⟨⟨—, or —✳—.

     Ultimately, when determining the total effect, in our estimation of *all* explanatory and corroborative facts upon the *net probative value* of the specific fact explained or corroborated, we place a short horizontal mark or small X, respectively, upon the upright connecting line of the latter fact.

Thus, for *net probative value*, several grades of probative effect may be symbolized: † signifies that the inference is a weak one; ╫ signifies that it has no force at all; ⚶ signifies that it is a strong one; ✳ signifies that it is conclusive. When the supposed inference is a *negatory* one, the same symbols are used, with the

addition of the negatory symbol, *i. e.* ⚶☐ (Witness asserts that defendant had *not* a knife in his hand; witness's credit is supported by the fact that he is a friend of the deceased).

     4. *Numbering the Symbols.*

     Each symbol receives a number, placed at the upper left outside margin. These numbers are then placed in the Evidence List; they are written down consecutively, and opposite each one in the list is written a brief note of the evidential fact represented by it.

     The List is thus the translation of the Chart.

     The separate pieces of evidence are given *consecutive* numbers in the List as they are being analyzed and noted in symbols, till all the evidence is charted. They need not run consecutively on the *Chart;* though naturally the numbers in any one chain of inferences will be consecutive. Should a further analysis of a particular piece of evidence develop new appurtenant evidence, the additional evidence can be given a decimal of the main number (so that on the Evidence List it will be found conveniently near to the main fact). *E. g.* if [27] ◯ is found later to have two new explanatory facts, one of them, with its appurtenant witnesses, may be numbered 27.1, 27.2, 27.3; the other may be numbered 27.4, 27.5, 27.6. N. B. that on the Chart it is immaterial whether the numbers are consecutive; the numbers serve merely to guide the eye quickly to the description of the fact on the Evidence List.

5. *Analyzing and Classifying the Evidence.*

a. Each supposed piece of evidence must be *analyzed,* so far as practicable and reasonably necessary, into all *its subordinate inferences.* Only in this way can the possibilities of explanation and corroborative facts be discovered. *E. g.,* the defendant's threats in *Com. v. Umilian;* the inference really is: threats show a plan to kill, and plan to kill shows actual killing. This enables us to chart separately the possible explanations weakening the inference from threats, and the testimony, if any, asserting those explanatory facts.

b. Where a *Human Act* is the issue, the classification in Part I of this work will be found convenient, *i. e.* Moral Character, Motive, Design, etc. Under Motive (Emotion) it is sounder to separate at the outset the distinct alleged motives, if any; *e. g.* desire for money, desire for revenge, etc., because they are in effect distinct and perhaps inconsistent probative facts.

c. In the same way, the *discrediting* (explanatory) *facts for a witness's assertion* should be separated into their component items. Thus, if bias is the general nature of the impeachment, let *e. g.* >[18] be the supposed general fact of actual bias and let [19]◯ and [20]◯ be the two circumstances tending to evidence it, 19 being the witness's relation to the defendant as a discharged employee, 21 being another witness who testifies to this, and 20 being the impeached witness's strong demeanor of bias while on the stand.

Thus the whole representation would be:

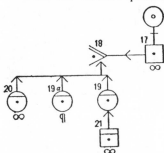

Here the added symbols of belief show that the probative effect has been that we refuse belief (if we do) to the fact asserted by this witness, because of his bias as shown by those facts.

Note that 19 is here supplemented by 19a, *i. e.* the supposed general truth that discharged em-

ployees are apt to have an emotion of hostility; the letter *a* added
to the main number will indicate the appurtenant relation of this
fact to 19.

In accordance with the analysis of impeaching evidence (as set
forth in prior chapters) it is usually desirable to note separately on
the Chart any supposed general truth implicitly or explicitly relied
upon. This is more commonly the case where a *mediate* or second
step of inference is involved, as in the above example. But even
there a general truth may not always be involved; *e. g.* in the above
example 20 ○ is the specific language or demeanor from which an
inference is made, without aid of a general truth, to the supposed
emotion. Where an *immediate* inference is involved, the only cases
where the supposed general truths need to be explicitly noted will
usually be those involving external conditions,—light, sound, etc.; in
such a case the first symbol can be
doubled, using the letter *a* with the main
number to indicate the appurtenant general truth. For example, if the location
of the witness is said to have obstructed
his vision and thus discredited his statement, it would be thus indicated:

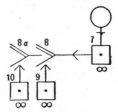

Here: 7 is the witness to be impeached; 8 is the facts of his location on the sidewalk, and 9 is a witness to those facts; 8 *a* is the
impossibility of correct vision from such location, and 10 is a witness to experiments showing such impossibility.

A special advantage in thus plotting separately the concrete
facts and the general truths is that the witnesses thereto may then
be plotted separately, and thus all the evidence thereon can be more
clearly distinguished and weighed.

6. *Plotting the Chart.*

Use an oblong sheet of unruled paper.

Allot the right-hand half to the plaintiff or prosecution, the
left-hand half to the defendant.

Allot the right-hand quarter to the plaintiff's testimonial evidence directly on the fact in issue; the next quarter (towards the
left) to his circumstantial evidence; and so on for the defendant.
If there are two or more distinct facts necessary in law to the issue,
use a separate chart sheet for each; unless the mass of evidence is
small enough for a single sheet (as in the annexed examples of
charts).

Since the quantity of each kind of evidence varies in each case, the above allotments of one quarter each are of course provisional only. In practice, a smaller or larger fraction will usually be needed. But by beginning at the right-hand end and disposing of all of each kind of evidence before proceeding to the next, the spacing will adjust itself. If desired, a line can be drawn perpendicularly to mark off the mass of one kind of evidence when charted.

When beginning on the next kind, allow a little extra space for later discoveries in the kind of evidence just finished.

Use right-angled continued lines freely in connecting the symbols, so as to economize space and to keep together the same kind of evidence.

Use a sharpened lead pencil.

If new inferences are later discovered and no space is left, erase some former symbols and rechart them, prolonging the lines so as to leave the new space needed.

Wherever a disbelief or doubt symbol is found, there ought to be some explanatory fact ($>$) to account for it. Hence, if such has been inadvertently omitted, analyze it into consciousness, chart it, and describe it in the Evidence List.

Where two or more witnesses, as to whose credit no question is raised, testify to the same fact, one symbol in the Chart may serve for all; but as many numbers should be given it as there are witnesses, bracketing these numbers to one description in the Evidence List.

A fact is to be classed as negatory or affirmatory in itself, and not according to the party offering it. Thus, as in Nos. 51, 52, 48, 49, of *Hackett v. Com.* (see Chart), the defendant may offer an affirmatory fact to prove another fact which is negatory of his guilt.

7. *Sundries.*

For clearness and quickness in studying the total effect of the mass of evidence when charted, colored pencils may be used.

Use a *blue* pencil for important facts favoring the plaintiff's or prosecution's contention, and a *green* one for those favoring the defendant's. Mark the arrow point of the belief symbol ($\blacktriangle$), or the cross of the disbelief symbol (†), respectively blue or green. Thus the subfinal facts can be conveniently concentrated in the mind, for the purpose of the net total effect on the mind. Varieties of detail in the use of the colored pencil can be invented as convenient; *e. g.* a simple arrow point ($\blacktriangle$), blue or green, can be used for the subordinate facts as the basis of a long line of inference, and a triangular arrow point for the subfinal facts when reached.

When ready to reach a final verdict, refresh the memory from the List, so that the tenor of the Chart symbols is as clear as possible in the mind. Then go over the whole Chart in the mind, force the subfinal facts into juxtaposition, and determine the net impression as to the ultimate fact in issue.

8. Finally, remember that

The logical (or psychological) process is essentially one of mental juxtaposition of detailed ideas for the purpose of producing rationally a single final idea. Hence, to the extent that the mind is unable to juxtapose consciously a larger number of ideas, each coherent group of detailed constituent ideas must be reduced successively to a single idea, until the number and kind is such that the mind can consciously juxtapose them with due attention to each. And the use of symbols has no other purpose than to facilitate this process. Hence, each person may contrive his own special ways of using these or other symbols.

As examples of the use of the Chart and List, the cases of *Com. v. Umilian (post)* and *Hatchett v. Com. (post)* are charted and listed in the following pages. Note that these Examples might have been charted with more economy of space, but in their present shape they show how the Chart develops in the actual making. The charter cannot know beforehand how many data will be found under each inference; hence he must allow space, which may not afterwards be needed.

THE PROBLEM OF PROOF 91

Commonwealth v. Umilian. (1901. SUPREME JUDICIAL COURT OF MASSACHUSETTS. 177 Mass. 582.)

Indictment for murder, returned June 12, 1900. At the trial in the Superior Court, before SHERMAN and STEVENS, JJ., the defendant at the close of the evidence asked the judges to rule and instruct the jury: first, that there was not sufficient evidence to warrant the jury in finding a verdict of guilty; and, second, that there was not sufficient evidence to warrant the jury in finding a verdict of guilty in the first degree. The judges declined to give either of these rulings. The jury found a verdict of guilty of murder in the first degree; and the defendant alleged exceptions.

J. B. O'Donnell, for the defendant. *J. C. Hammond,* District Attorney, for the Commonwealth.

KNOWLTON, J.—The defendant was found guilty of murder in the first degree, and the only question before us is whether there was any evidence to warrant the verdict. He and Casimir Jedrusik were working together as farm laborers for one Keith in Granby. On Sunday, December 31, 1899, Jedrusik disappeared, and was never afterwards seen alive. On April 10, 1900, his headless, mutilated body was found inclosed in a bran sack in an unused well between four hundred and five hundred feet from Keith's horse barn. His clothing was found inclosed in another sack in the same well. His skull was afterwards found buried in the cellar of the horse barn. The sacks were similar to those which Keith had in the horse barn. The stone, which was inclosed in the sack of clothing, exactly fitted a vacant place in a stone wall about in line between the old well and the north door of the horse barn. On the day of the disappearance there was no snow on the ground, and the surface of the ground was entirely frozen. In the cellar of the horse barn pigs were kept, and there was soft mud there. The clothing which was exhibited to the jury had mud upon it which the Commonwealth contended on the evidence was like that in the cellar. Mr. and Mrs. Keith drove away to church on December 31st, leaving the defendant and Jedrusik about the barn. The defendant's wife was in the house, where she was employed as a housemaid, and there was evidence tending to show that the only other person who came there during that day was a young woman who came to visit her. The defendant was outside of the house, about the premises, for some hours after Mr. and Mrs. Keith went to church, and when he came in he said that Jedrusik had gone to Granby. There were wounds on the head of Jedrusik, which the Commonwealth contented were made by a corn cutter that was in the horse barn, and was exhibited to the jury. The evidence tended to show that the defendant had ample opportunity to commit the murder, and that no other person had an opportunity to do it without discovery.

On November 18 the defendant went to Chicopee to the house of a Polish priest, to have the ceremony of marriage performed between him and a young woman who had been living as a maid at Keith's house, and he found that the priest had received a letter in a name which proved to be fictitious, charging him with having a wife and children in the old country, and with receiving letters from his wife asking for money for the support of himself and her children. The priest refused to marry him, and sent a trusted person with him to investigate. It turned out that Jedrusik wrote the letter, and that its contents did not appear to be true. The defendant was then married by the priest, and the evidence tended to show that he was very angry with Jedrusik, and that he made strong threats of vengeance against him. There was evidence from several witnesses that at different times between the defendant's marriage and Jedrusik's disappearance, the defendant manifested deeply hostile feelings towards him, and made threats against him. On the morning of December 31st, there was a new manifestation of this feeling in charges made to Mr. Keith that Jedrusik had stolen a plane and had stolen butter. There was evidence that, between the time of the disappearance and the discovery of the body, the defendant was seen to take up one of the planks covering the unused well, and also that when he was told in the daytime that Keith and one Olds had gone out of the house with a lantern, he said he "knew what they were going to do. Mr. Olds wants to buy the pump in the old well." There was evidence that nothing had ever been said by Olds about buying the pump. Immediately after being told this the defendant went into the horse barn, and was seen looking out of a window from which the well could be seen. When others went to the well after the body was found, he did not go. There was also evidence that about the middle of January he gave away Jedrusik's rubber boots, and said that he did not think Jedrusik would come back. There were many other things in his language and conduct after Jedrusik's disappearance which the Commonwealth relied on as tending to show guilty knowledge, and much of his testimony in explanation of facts was in direct contradiction of other witnesses.

Without going more at length into the evidence, which was voluminous, we are of opinion that it would have been error to take the case from the jury. So far as we can judge from the bill of exceptions the evidence well warranted the verdict. *Exceptions overruled.*

Plate Λ

ISSUE: DID U. KILL J.?

PROSECUTION'S CASE

Evidence Chart for COMMONWEALTH *v.* UMILIAN

EXAMPLE A.   COMMONWEALTH *v.* UMILIAN.

Evidence Chart.   [See Plate A.]

Evidence List (*Com. v. Umilian*).

1   Design to kill J.
2   Threats of unstated tenor, made on discovery of J.'s interfer-
    ence in prevention of marriage.
3   Anon.[6] witnesses thereto.
4   Threats might have meant merely some lesser harm.
5   Threats of revenge at later time.
6   Anon. witnesses thereto.
7   Threats might have meant merely some lesser harm.
8   Revengeful, murderous emotion towards J.
9   J. had charged him with intended bigamy Nov. 18., and had
    tried thereby to prevent his marriage.
10 Letter received by priest, stating that U. already had family in
    old country.
11 Anon. witnesses to this.
12 J. was author of letter, though it was in fictitious name.
13 Anon. witnesses to this.
14 Letter communicated by priest to U., with refusal to perform
    marriage; refusal later withdrawn.
15 Anon. witnesses to this.
16 Letter's statements were untrue.
17 Anon. witnesses to this.
18 U. being innocent, and marriage being finally performed, U.
    would not have had a strong feeling of revenge.
19 J. remaining in daily contact, wound must have rankled.
20 Wife remaining there, jealousy between U. and J. probably
    continued.
21 U. uttered threats and other hostile expressions between Nov.
    18 and Dec. 31.
22 Anon. witnesses to this.
23 U., on Dec. 31, charged J. to K. with stealing K.'s goods.
24 Anon. witnesses to this.
25 Does not appear that these charges were false, hence not ma-
    licious.
26 U.'s opportunity in time and place was almost exclusive.
27 On Dec. 31 U. was on premises.
27.1 Witnesses to this.
28 U. was only man so seen.

---

6.   Of course in an actual trial each witness is here named.   The opinion
of the court in this case does not name them.

29 U.'s wife and a woman visitor were there.

30 Anon. witnesses to this.

31 Passing tramp-villain might have been there.

32 In time between Dec. 31 and April others had access to J., if alive still.

33 U. had uneasy consciousness of guilt about J.'s disappearance.

34 U. lied about J.'s going to Granby.

35 U. said J. had gone there, though J. was dead.

36 Anon. witnesses to this.

37 J. might really have gone there, not being killed till later.

38 U. was conscious that the well was a place where damaging things would be discovered.

39 He watched those who searched there.

40 Anon. witnesses to this.

41 That might have been due to natural curiosity of a farm hand at strange doings.

42 U. lied about the reason for Olds and K. searching the well.

43 Anon. witnesses to this.

44 U. did not go to the well to see the body when found.

45 Anon. witnesses to this.

46 Several other reasons would explain this.

47 U. knew that J. was dead, though others did not.

48 He gave away J.'s boots and said that J. would not come back; this was about the middle of January.

49 Anon. witnesses thereto.

50 Like others, U. may merely have believed that J. had given up work at the farm.

51 Data of slayer on J.'s body were of a person having free and intimate access to horse barn of K.

52 Wound-marks were those of a horse-cutter from barn.

53 Anon. witnesses thereto.

54 Precise correspondence not stated; might have been a different weapon.

55 No other person but U. had at that time such access.

55.1 Anon. witnesses to 55; and see 26.

56 Sacks holding body and clothes came from horse barn.

57 Anon. witnesses thereto.

58 Stone in sack fitted wall near barn.

59 Anon. witnesses thereto.

60 Clothing in sack had marks of mud from barn cellar.

61 Anon. witnesses thereto.

62 Mud not specifically identified.

Hatchett v. Commonwealth. (1882. Court of Appeals of Virginia. 76 Va. 1026.)

Lewis, J., delivered the opinion of the Court. The plaintiff in error was indicted in the county court of Brunswick county for the murder of Moses Young, by administering to the said Young strychnine poison in whisky..... The facts proved, as certified in the record, are substantially these: That on the night of the 17th day of December, 1880, Moses Young died at his house in Brunswick county, and under such circumstances as created suspicions that he had been poisoned. He was an old man, 65 years of age, and was subject to the colic, and a short time previous to his death had been hurt in his side by a cart. In the afternoon of that day the father of Oliver Hatchett, the prisoner, gave him a small bottle of whisky, with instructions to take it to Moses Young; at the same time telling him not to drink it himself. The deceased lived about three miles from the prisoner's father, to whose house the prisoner at once proceeded. It seems that he was not acquainted with the deceased; or, if so, very slightly, and that he succeeded in finding the house only by inquiry of one of the neighbors. Soon after his arrival at the house of the deceased, he took supper with him, and a few minutes thereafter requested the deceased to go with him into the yard, and point out the path to him—it then being dark. After getting into the yard, the prisoner produced the bottle and invited the deceased to drink—telling him that it was a little whisky his father had sent him. The deceased drank and returned the bottle to the prisoner, who at once started on his return home. The deceased then returned into the house. In a short while thereafter he complained of a pain in his side, began to grow worse, and told his wife that the man (meaning the prisoner) had tricked him in a drink of whisky. He then got up, but fell immediately to the floor. Osborne and Charlotte Northington, two near neighbors, were then called in by his wife; and these three, whom the record described as ignorant negroes, were the only persons present with the deceased until his death, which occurred about three hours after he drank of the whisky from the bottle handed him by the prisoner. They described his symptoms as follows: The old man had the jerks, complained of great pain, and every now and then would draw up his arms and legs and complained of being cramped; that he put his finger in his mouth to make him vomit, and his teeth clinched on it so that one of his teeth was pulled out in getting out his finger. They also testified that his dying declaration was that the man had killed him in a drink of whisky. From the symptoms as thus described, two physicians, who were examined as witnesses in the case, testified that as far as they could judge from the statements of the ignorant witnesses, they would suppose that Moses Young died from strychnine poison. No post-mortem examination of the deceased's body was made or attempted; nor was any analysis made of the contents of the bottle, which was returned about one third full by the prisoner to his father, and was afterwards found.

After the arrest of the prisoner, and while under guard, he stated to the guard in charge of him that he would not be punished about the matter; that he intended to tell all about it; that his father, Littleton Hatchett, gave him that mess and told him he would give him something, to carry it and give it to Moses Young, and that it would fix him. He further stated that he went to Moses Young's house, called him out and gave him a drink, and returned the bottle and put it where his father had directed him to put it. The next day he made a statement on oath before the coroner's jury, and when asked by the foreman whether he was prepared, upon reflection, to say that what he had stated on the previous day was not true, he answered: "I am prepared to say that part of what I said yesterday was true." He then made a statement in which he said that he carried the whisky to the deceased by direction of his father, who told him not to drink of it; that he went to the house of the deceased and gave him a drink, and returned the bottle as directed by his father. But he did not state that his father told him that the whisky would "fix" the deceased, or that he (the prisoner) knew that it contained poison or other dangerous thing.

It also was proved that Henry Carroll, who was jointly indicted with the prisoner, gave to Sallie Young, wife of the deceased, about three weeks before his death, something in a bottle which he said was strychnine, and which he told her to put in the coffee or food of the deceased; and that Osborne and Charlotte Northington knew of the fact, but did not communicate it to the deceased. It was also proved that Henry Carroll was the paramour of Sallie Young, which fact was also known to Osborne and Charlotte Northington.

Such are the facts upon which the plaintiff in error was convicted and sentenced to death. Now, under the allegations in the indictment, it was incumbent upon the prosecution, to entitle the Commonwealth to a verdict, to establish clearly and beyond a reasonable doubt these three essential propositions: (1) That the deceased came to his death by poison. (2) That the poison was administered

by the prisoner. (3) That he administered it knowingly and feloniously. These propositions, we think, are not established by the evidence in this case.

In the first place, there is no sufficient proof that the deceased
died from the effects of poison at all. From the symptoms, as described by ignorant witnesses, one of whom at least was a party to
the conspiracy to poison the deceased, and who had been supplied
with the means to do so (a fact known to the others), the most that
the medical men who were examined in the case could say was that
they *supposed* he died from strychnine poison. Strange so say, there
was no post-mortem examination of the body of the deceased, nor
was there any analysis made of the contents of the bottle from which
he drank at the invitation of the prisoner, and which was returned
by the latter to his father and afterwards found—all of which, presumably, might easily have been done, and in a case of so serious
and striking a character as this ought to have been done........
Great strictness should be observed, and the clearest proof of the
crime required, to safely warrant the conviction of the accused and
the infliction of capital punishment. Such proof is wanting in this
case to establish the death of the deceased by the means alleged in
the indictment.

Equally insufficient are the facts proved to satisfactorily show
that if in fact the deceased died from the effects of poison, it was
administered by the prisoner; and if administered by him, that it
was done knowingly and feloniously. It is not shown that if the
whisky he conveyed to the deceased contained poison, he knew or
had reason to know the fact. It is almost incredible that a rational
being, in the absence of provocation of any sort, or the influence of
some strong and controlling motive, would deliberately take the life
of an unoffending fellow man. Yet in this case no provocation or
motive whatever on the part of either the prisoner or his father,
from whom he received the whisky of which the deceased drank,
to murder the deceased, is shown by the evidence. It is true that
the facts proved are sufficient to raise grave suspicions against the
prisoner; but they fall far short of establishing his guilt clearly and
satisfactorily, as required by the humane rules of the law, to warrant his conviction of the crime charged against him. On the other
hand, the facts proved show that the wife of the deceased, three
weeks before his death, had been supplied by her paramour with
strychnine to administer to her husband; and there is nothing in
the case to exclude the hypothesis that the death of the deceased may

THE PROBLEM OF PROOF   99

not have been occasioned by the felonious act of his own unfaithful
wife. It was not proven that the prisoner at any time procured, or
had in his possession, poison of any kind; nor was the attempt made
to connect him with, or to show knowledge on his part of, the poison
which was delivered by Henry Carroll to Sallie Young, to be administered to her husband.

In short, the facts proved are wholly insufficient to warrant the
conviction of the plaintiff in error for the crime for which he has
been sentenced to be hanged: and the judgment of the circuit court
bust, therefore, be reversed, the verdict of the jury set aside, and a
new trial awarded him.

Plate B

ISSUE A: DID Y. DIE OF POISON?

PROSECUTION'S CASE

ISSUE B: DID H. GIVE THE POISON?

PROSECUTION'S CASE

ISSUE C: DID H. KNOWINGLY GIVE IT?

PROSECUTION'S CASE

DEFENSE'S CASE

Evidence Chart for HATCHETT v. COMMONWEALTH

THE PROBLEM OF PROOF 101

EXAMPLE B. HATCHETT *v.* COMMONWEALTH.

Evidence Chart. [See Plate B.]

Evidence List (*Hatchett v. Com.*).

1   Y. himself, just before dying, declared that the drink of whisky was the source of his pains and illness.

2 3 4   His wife, O. N., and C. N. testified to this statement; but see 17-24, as discrediting them.

5   Y. might have had his colic cramps, and could not have had skill enough to *know* that the drink was the cause of the pain.

6   Same possibility for ptomaine or other poisoning in food at supper.

7   Y. died, being apparently in health, within three hours after the drink of whisky.

8 9 10   Same witnesses to this as 2, 3, 4.

11   Y. might have died by colic, from which he had often suffered.

11.1   Colic would not have had as symptoms the leg cramps and teeth clenching; only strychnine could produce these.

11.2   O. N., and C. N. and wife, witness to cramps, etc.

11.3   Expert witnesses to significance of symptoms.

11.4   No testimony as to strychnine traces in body by post mortem.

12   Anon. witnesses to his former attacks.

13   Y. might have died from the former injury in his side.

14   Anon. witnesses to that injury.

15   Y. himself declared when dying that the whisky drink was killing him.

16   Y.'s wife, Sallie, witness to this.

17   Sallie's bias to save herself at H.'s expense discredits her.

18 18*a*   Sallie had a paramour, and might herself intend the death of Y., hence might desire to fix crime on H.

18.1   Anon. witnesses to 18.

19   O. N. witness also to 15.

20   O. N.'s bias to save Sallie discredits him.

21 21*a*   O. N. knew of Sallie's paramour and of her probable wish to get rid of the old man; hence probably biased to support Sallie's story.

21.1   Anon. witnesses to 21.

22   C. N. witness also to 15.

23   C. N.'s bias to save Sallie discredits him.

24 ⎫
24a ⎬ Same as 21, 21a, 21.1.
24.1 ⎭

25   Y. died apparently in good health, within three hours after
        drinking deft.'s whisky.

26 ⎫
27 ⎬   Sallie Y., O. N. and C. N. witnesses to time of death.
28 ⎭

28.1   H. witness to time of drink.

29   Neither H. nor his father are shown to have possessed any
        strychnine to put in the drink.

30   Y. might have died by colic, from which he had often suf-
        fered.

31   Y. might have died from the former injury in his side.

32   Y. might have died of ptomaine poisoning in supper-food.

33   Y. might have died from poison put in his supper-food by
        third person; the only person having access being Sallie,
        his wife.

34   Sallie had desire for Y.'s death.

35   Her illicit relation with Henry Carroll points to 34.

36   Anon. witnesses to this relation with H. C.

37   Sallie possessed means of strychnine poisoning; see 38.

38   Sallie had a plan to kill Y.

39   Sallie had received strychnine from H. C. three weeks be-
        fore, with instructions to put it in Y.'s coffee or food.

39.1   Witness to 39.

40   Sallie's failure to use it during those three weeks' opportunity
        indicates abandonment of her design.

41   Secrecy of H.'s mode of giving drink indicated consciousness
        of something wrong.

42   Same witnesses as 26-29.

43   This perhaps due to desire not to waste whisky on Sallie.

43.1   Transaction was not really secret, for he knew Sallie and
        others were there when he summoned the old man.

44   His confession that his father had told him the whisky would
        fix Y. shows that he knew something was wrong.

45   Anon. witnesses to this confession.

46   H.'s second statement, retracting on that point, makes it
        doubtful whether he knew.

47 Anon. witnesses to this second statement.
48 Lack of any desire in H. to kill Y.
49 H. was even unacquainted with Y. up to this time.
50 Anon. witnesses to 49.
51 H. himself drank of whisky; hence did not know of strychnine in it.
52 This is shown by bottle being only one-third full on return.
53 Anon. witnesses to 52.
54 Y. might have drunk two-thirds of the bottle.
55 H. might have been deterred, by father's directions, from drinking any.

[5]

BOOKS AND PERIODICALS

NEW BOOKS.

A TREATISE ON FACTS, OR THE WEIGHT AND VALUE OF EVIDENCE   By Charles
C. Moore. Northport; Edward Thompson Co., 1908.   2 volumes, pp. 1612.

This treatise is in performance exhaustive, in scope novel, in utility large,
in avowed purpose it is partly good: partly it is what we should consider as bad
as possible.

The scope of the work includes all judicial utterances, English and American, touching "the causes of trustworthiness and untrustworthiness of evidence." Regarding the evidence as already before the tribunal, it seeks all the
guidance that has been given for estimating the elements affecting credibility
as found in the innumerable varieties of facts to be evidenced. Some of the
main words in the section-titles taken at random exhibit the range of topics:
Preponderance, suspicion, conjecture; Disinterested and biassed witnesses;
Improbable physical facts; Character and memory; Sound and hearing of gun-
shots, church-bells, train-noises, sleigh-bells, rain-storms, fog-horns; Light and
sight of highways, dark objects, lamps, trains, vessels; Taste of liquors; Distance
of people, vessels, cars, lights, Speed of cars, automobiles, wagons; Weather,
wind, fog; Non-production of evidence; Handwriting experts; Observation, attention; Memory, affected by time, age, intelligence, routine, association; Credibility of children, aged persons, women; Credibility of affidavits, depositions,
detectives; Perjury and mistake; Admissions and confessions. These scattered
terms will of themselves show the vast range of facts covered. In short, the comprehensive possibilities of proof are here represented. For argument upon the
weight of a piece of evidence, the counsel here finds all the aid that has ever been
furnished by the comments of hundreds of experienced judges, drawing from the
annals of thousands of trials. No counsel can expect in his own experience to
learn more than a small fraction of the possibilities of fallacy and untrustworthiness in the innumerable kinds of evidence; he will naturally profit by such generalizations as have been attempted (with more or less misguided confidence-
by his predecessors of greater experience. To profit by them at all, he must go
now to this book; for Wills' treatise on Circumstantial Evidence, and Ram on
Facts, its two forerunners, are of narrow scope and do not begin to compare
in the sources examined. As to the classification of topics, we can see numerous
inconsistencies; but the task of making a tenable classification is so nearly impossible that we do not pretend to pass judgment on the present one.

In the avowed purpose (one of them at least) and in the possible misuse of
the book, however, we see nothing but harm; and we are not going to be deterred
by our respect for the author form expressing our view. The preface speaks
of "the *rule* for measuring the probative force of testimony," and urges that
"judicial precedents" of the present sort will be "treated with the same consideration by courts in the determination of questions of fact as is accorded to the
reasoning or *ex cathedra* statements of judges on questions of law." In other
records, there are *rules of law which determine the weight or credibility of a piece
of evidence which has been duly admitted to consideration.* Now that proposition we deny. It is not known to the orthodox and traditional common law
So far as any Courts nowadays are tending to recognize it, it is a bad tendency,
and one that will wreck our whole system of proof. If there is one thing for
which the common law system of judge and jury stands, it is that the rules of
evidence, as determined and applied by the judge, are rules of admissibility
alone, and for the judge alone; the weight or credibility is for the jurors untram-
meled by any rules of law. "All the judge has to determine is whether a particular piece of evidence is at a particular period of the cause admissible to the
consideration of the jury."[1] "If the witness * * is incompetent under the
rules of law, the Court will not permit him to testify; but when the evidence of
the witness is before the jury, all questions of credibility are for them, and for
them alone."[2] If therefore any counsel attempts to get the judge to lay down

---

[1]Tindal. C. J., in *Wright v. Tatham*, 7 A. & E., 407.
[2]Beck, J., in *Callanan v. Shaw*, 24 Ia., 441, 444.

a *rule of law* for the jury in estimating credibility, he is undermining our system in a fateful manner. He is helping to introduce ten thousand more quibbles into the system—a system already loaded down to the breaking point by the quibbles of over-instruction on rules of substantive law. If our time-honored division of function between judge and jury is worth keeping at all, the serious problem of saving it from ruin by reversals based on erroneous instructions must not be further complicated by adding ten thousand more possibilities of error in instructions upon credibility. The counsel who uses the book to induce the judge to a ruling of law upon credibility is committing moral treason to our system. He may find great profit from its pages in preparing his case or in arguing to the jury as matter of experience and probability; but we are afraid (perhaps foolishly) that he will not stop at that. Hence our regret for the possibilities of misuse of this book.

Eliminating that misuse, we can find the appearance of it peculiarly timely. For in these days of the onslaughts of Professor Munsterberg on the imperfections of our methods of testing credibility, it is useful to be enabled to discover herein the fullest data which our profession has thus far recorded of its experience in that subject.

I. H. W.

[6]

THE decision rendered by the court in a lawsuit must always be based upon a rule of law, and that rule must be, as it were, an order directed *to the court*. Ordinary rules of civil law which, according to their tenor, are directed *to private parties,* can be translated into such rules. An example is the rule that, if a promise of payment has been made and the day of maturity has arrived, the debtor shall be *pronounced* obliged to pay. It is obvious, however, that in order to enable the court applying this rule to conclude that the action shall be sustained, two further premises are necessary: the existence of the alleged promise of payment and the maturity of the debt. Thus we could lay down the following pattern for the reasoning of the court:

> If a promise of payment has been made and the day of maturity has arrived, the debtor shall be pronounced obliged to pay.
> In this case a promise of payment has been made and the day of maturity has arrived.
> Consequently, the debtor shall be pronounced obliged to pay the debt.[1]

In this syllogism, the minor premise consists of an assertion of the *existence* of certain facts. But in what cases shall the court assume that a promise of payment has been made? This question may seem purely *theoretical* in character. On the basis of the evidence produced in the action, the court has to decide whether the minor premise of the syllogism is true or not.

However, the court must also make up its mind as to the question what amount of evidence is required for the assumption that a promise of payment has been made. The action is sustained

---

[1] A syllogism of this kind may be called *practical*, since the major premise and the conclusion have not a descriptive character (are not theoretical propositions) but are exhortations (practical propositions). Unlike theoretical propositions, these contain no element of truth, and the question whether they are true or false has no reasonable sense. It follows that in a practical syllogism the conclusion is not related to the premises as a consequence of these in the sense that, if they are true, this is also the case with the conclusion.

48   PER OLOF EKELÖF

only if the evidence produced in the case is *sufficiently* strong.
What measure is required is a *juridical question* which is not
accounted for in the syllogism set out above.

In this paper, we shall not give any attention to the last-
mentioned problem, which falls within the so-called doctrine of
the burden of proof. What will be treated is only the question in
what way the court obtains a knowledge of relevant facts. The
scope of the paper is further restricted to the methods of evaluating evidence and assessing its convincing force. The technical
methods of producing evidence fall wholly outside the discussion.
The author starts from the assumption that evaluation of evidence
as in Sweden is exclusively the task of the court and not a matter
decided by a jury of laymen.

The view which earlier prevailed in Sweden (the so-called doctrine of legal evidence) was that the convincing force of each
particular kind of evidence should be determined by statute. The
statement that nowadays the evaluation of evidence is "free"
means that legal rules of this kind are no longer in force. On
the other hand, it is obvious that evidence must not be evaluated
arbitrarily. Writers on evidence usually stress that this evaluation
is not a matter of discretion but must be based upon *objective*
considerations.[2] This view seems to presuppose that "free" evaluation of evidence is also subject to legal rules, though not in the
same manner as under the "doctrine of legal evidence". Precisely
in what way, then, is the evaluation of evidence bound by fixed
standards?[3]

The evaluation of evidence, it is usually stated, implies that the
judge concludes, on the strength of the existence of a *factum
probans* (evidentiary fact), that a *factum probandum* (theme of
proof) equally exists.[4] This, however, is an elliptical way of ex-

---

[2] See, e.g., Kallenberg, *Svensk civilprocessrätt*, vol. II, Lund 1931, p. 532.

[3] In Swedish legal writing, this problem has been most fully discussed by
Bolding in his treatise *Bevisbördan och den juridiska tekniken*, Uppsala 1951,
chap. II. American writers seem to have given most attention to the question.
See Ball, "Probability Theory and Standards of Proof", in *Essays on Procedure
and Evidence*, publ. by T. G. Roady *et al.*, 1961, p. 84, and works referred to
there.

[4] In the present paper, "*evidentiary fact*" ("fact relevant to the issue") means
a fact which is of importance for the outcome of the action through its *convincing force*. The fact which is to be proved is called *theme of proof* and
may be either an *ultimate fact*, i.e. a fact which is of importance because of
its *legal consequences*, or a fact which constitutes such *circumstantial evidence*
(*indicium*) from which the existence of an ultimate fact is conclusively assumed

pressing the matter, for as far as syllogisms are concerned, we are dealing with relations between *statements* and not between *facts*. On the other hand, it is justifiable to disregard this distinction for present purposes, for the truth of a proposition obviously presupposes the existence of the alleged fact. A more serious objection is that something must have been omitted when it is stated that the existence of one fact may be concluded from that of another fact.[5] Let us choose as an example the proving of identity through *fingerprints*. Suppose that such a print found upon a safe which has been forced with explosives presents nine features identical with corresponding elements in the accused's fingerprint. On the strength of this evidentiary fact it is concluded that, in one way or another, the first print also comes from the accused. This conclusion would obviously be arbitrary unless it were known that two fingerprints with nine identical features have never been found to have been made by different persons.

The lesson given by this case would obviously be that the evaluation of evidence is also based upon a proposition consisting of a piece of *general experience* (hereinafter called *laws of general experience*) according to which the existence of the evidentiary fact is a sufficient condition for assuming the existence of the theme of proof. If the former circumstance is denoted B and the theme of proof T, the evaluation of the convincing force of B should follow the pattern of this syllogism:

> If B exists, T also exists.
> In this case, B exists.
> It follows that T also exists in this case.

It may be of some interest to compare this syllogism with one of the kind which may be used where the doctrine of legal evidence is adopted.

in its turn. Where conclusions are thus made from one proof to another, we use the term *"chain of evidence"*. It should be observed, finally, that strictly speaking, the observation of the *factum probandum* made by a witness is in fact circumstantial evidence. For on the basis of the statement made by the witness in court, conclusions are made about the observation of the witness; on the strength of that observation, in its turn, the existence of the fact observed in concluded. Granted that the witness has described his observation correctly in court, this is no guarantee of the correctness of the observation as such, i.e. of its corresponding to actual facts. Indeed, the convincing force of the statement and that of the observation are dependent upon wholly different *"auxiliary facts"*. For with regard to the first, e.g., the memory of the witness may be decisive; in the case of the second, it may be his eyesight.

[5] Gulson, *The Philosophy of Proof*, 2nd ed. London 1923, p. 180.

50   PER OLOF EKELÖF

> The court shall base its decision upon what is testified by two
> witnesses who cannot be challenged.
>
> In this case, two witnesses who cannot be challenged testify T.
>
> It follows that the court must base its decision upon the ex-
> istence of T.

Thus under the doctrine of legal evidence also, the evaluation
of proof takes place by subsuming concrete cases under general
rules. It is true that when these rules are found in a statute, the
evaluation of evidence assumes the character of an ordinary
application of legal rules. However, the major premise of the last
syllogism is also to some extent based upon experience. What
characterizes the "free" evaluation of evidence, then, would be the
fact that the laws of general experience by which the judge is
bound have not been laid down as legal rules but consist of *our
knowledge of factual relations.*

Would this statement be true without any exceptions? Is *all*
"free" evaluation of evidence based upon laws of general experience?[6] It would seem, at least on a first view, that the evaluation of, e.g., the statement of a witness does not proceed along
the same lines as the evaluation of a fingerprint.

Before discussing this problem, however, there is another question which must be elucidated first. In legal writing it is usually
asserted that evidence in court does not admit the ascertainment
of actual truth but at most attains a high degree of probability.
The meaning of this assertion is not unambiguous.

"I admit that there is a considerable difference between *probatio juridica* and *logica,* and that *certitudo juridica,* in the *probatio facti,* cannot be held, without further ado, as a *philosophica
certitudo* but rather constitutes, in relation to such certitude, a
probabilitas": so wrote the Swedish writer Nehrman in his textbook on civil procedure from the middle of the 18th century.
Statements to the same effect are found in modern writing also.[7]
In the present writer's view, however, they tend to create a false
idea. The statements of logic and mathematics are true only in
the sense that their premises can be derived from certain axioms.

---

[6] It was in the first place Friedrich Stein, in his work *Das private Wissen
des Richters,* 1893, who attracted the attention of lawyers to the importance of
such laws ("*Erfahrungssätze*").

[7] As an example may be quoted the following statement by Kern (*Strafver-
fahrensrecht,* 1951, p. 50): "Zur Verurteilung ist nicht mathematische Gewissheit
notwendig, sondern nur eine hohe Wahrscheinlichkeit." See also Leo Rosenberg,
Lehrbuch des deutschen Zivilprozessrechts, 1961, § 111 I 2 a.

When evaluating evidence, on the other hand, it is not enough that the conclusion is a *consequence* of its premises: the premises must also be true in the sense that they *correspond to actual facts*. For what the evidence is intended to prove is the *existence* of the facts with which the conclusion deals.

But how can we know that the premises are true, e.g. in the example concerning fingerprints mentioned above? Let us assume that there is no reason to doubt the truth of the minor premise: any person can ascertain the identity between the two fingerprints as regards nine details.[8] What remains to be established, then, is the truth of the major premise. It is stated that it is founded upon experience. As we have already pointed out, all cases observed so far have confirmed that experience. The truth of the major premise would thus be based upon an *induction*.[9] It is concluded, from the fact that T follows upon B in all cases *observed*, that T *always* follows upon B. In such an "inductive syllogism", however, the truth of the conclusion does not constitute a necessary consequence of the truth of the premises. The generalization is founded upon limited material, and there is no certainty with regard to all the cases which have not been observed.[1] The history of science furnishes numerous illustrations of the necessity of revising traditional truth in accordance with new observations.

Thus it would be true that by evidence in court we can never obtain wholly reliable knowledge about relevant facts. On the other hand, it is evident that in actual practice we make a distinction between statements which are *certain* and statements which are only *probable*. It would be ridiculous to state that the mortality of man is only a probability! It may well be that the truth founded upon induction is no more than a marginal value, and that strictly speaking truth, in this connection, means only the highest degree of probability.[2] This distinction, however, is a subtlety which we may disregard. The relativity to which all human

---

[8] In this connection, we disregard the question of the criterion of identity of each detail, in other words the problem under what conditions the "same" detail shall be held to exist in two different fingerprints.

[9] On induction and probability, see A. Bennett and Ch. Baylis, *Formal Logic*, 1939, pp. 341 f.; Rudolf Carnap, *Logical Foundations of Probability*, 1951, and *Induktive Logik und Wahrscheinlichkeit*, 1959; S. R. Toulmin, *The Uses of Argument*, 1958, G. Polya, *Patterns of Plausible Inference* II, 1954, and John P. Day, *Inductive Probability*, 1961.

[1] Bennett, *op. cit.*, pp. 362 f., and Day, *op. cit.*, pp. 22 f. See also Gulson, *op. cit.*, p. 86.

[2] Day, *op. cit.*, p. 34.

knowledge is subject need not be taken into consideration in court.[3] Thus there are no reasons for denying that in certain cases the court is able to ascertain the "truth", provided that term is taken in the sense set out above.

However, in those cases where the "truth" may be found, the facts concerned are usually not disputed between the parties. If confronted by two incompatible assertions, the court will often be unable to decide which of them is true; it has to choose the more *probable* one. What does this mean, then, and how does the court proceed to determine which statement has the greater probability? Suppose that the court has to decide who is the father of a child. To simplify our example, we will make the un-realistic assumption that it has been made clear in the action that during the period of conception, the child's mother has had intercourse only with the defendant and another man, about whom there is no information, and that there is *no other evidence* about the former man's paternity than a genetic paternity test, which is based upon the fact that the child must have received from his father a feature found in only 5 per cent of the popula-tion and that the defendant also possesses this feature. The proba-bility that this is also the case with the unknown man obviously amounts to no more than 5 per cent. We assume that this admits the conclusion that there is a probability amounting to 95 per cent for the paternity of the defendant.[4]

In this case, the piece of experience in question concerns the *frequency* of a certain event; this means that the conclusion must be subject to a corresponding uncertainty. If the constellation of hereditary features found in the child and the two parties is called K and the alleged paternity is indicated by an F, the evaluation of evidence may be performed according to the following pattern:

> In 95 per cent of all those cases where K is found to exist, this is the case also with F.
> In this case, K has been found.

---

[3] Cf. Toulmin, *op. cit.*, p. 235.

[4] $\dfrac{1}{1 + 0,05} = 95,24\ \%$. See Eric Essen-Möller, *Die Beweiskraft der Ähnlichkeit im Vaterschaftsnachweis*, 1938, pp. 11 f., and I. J. Good, "Kinds of Probability" in *Science* 1959 (129), pp. 444 f. The course of reasoning above presupposes that the probability of the paternity of the defendant and the unknown man re-spectively, if the latter also possesses the feature concerned, cannot be calcu-lated on the evidence before the court.

It follows that the probability for F in the case amounts to 95 per cent.

The paternity of another person is not incompatible with this conclusion. This may be the case even if both the premises are true. In fact the conclusion should not be understood as a statement about the actual paternity but about our *knowledge* with regard to that relation.[5] Strictly speaking, all that this statement tells us is the convincing force of the constellation of hereditary features, considered as evidence.[6] This, however, is quite sufficient to enable the court to render a decision on the action, provided it knows what measure of convincing force the law requires from the evidence.

It is most unusual that in the evaluation of evidence the court can base its reasoning upon a law of general experience, the frequency of which may be expressed in figures. Normally, the degree of probability can only be expressed by a *vague* term, like *plausible, probable, certain* or *obvious;* in this connection, *probable* and *certain* also refer to different degrees of probability. This vagueness is due to the fact that no scientific inductions have been made which could give a more precise answer about the convincing force which may be claimed by various evidentiary facts.

As an example, we may quote *the observations of a witness* regarding the speed of a motorcar. If the circumstances are otherwise identical, it is more probable that the observation is correct if made by an experienced driver than if the witness is a person who has never been at the wheel of a car. And the degree of probability increases further if the observation is made by a policeman who has served in the traffic police and has often had occasion to notice and estimate the speed of passing vehicles. However, we possess no precise knowledge about these frequency relations, and consequently the same lack of precision is found in the conclusion which has to be drawn by the court about the probability that the car has been driven at the speed alleged by

[5] This also appears from the fact that the reality cannot be graduated: either the defendant is the child's father or he is not. Only our knowledge of that relation may be more or less certain. On the other hand, it is worth noticing that the major premise of the syllogism about fingerprints may be formulated as follows: If B exists, the probability of the existence of T amounts to 100 per cent; cf. Toulmin, *op. cit.,* p. 110.

[6] Carnap, *Logical Foundations of Probability,* p. 168, states that the conclusion implies "an estimate of relative frequency".

54   PER OLOF EKELÖF

the witness. On the other hand, the actual *procedure* of evaluating evidence seems to be the same as in the paternity suit.[7] What we call our "experience of life" is ultimately based upon inductions undertaken without scientific precision. And an objective graduation of the force of evidence does not seem possible by any other method than a calculation of frequency.[7a] Moreover, the existence of a degree of probability is obviously independent of the question whether it can be expressed in figures or not.[8] Thus, to take an example, if the strength of the evidence is held to be *obvious,* it must be greater than if the theme of proof has been proved with a probability of 60 per cent.

In fact, any evaluation of evidence is likely to be based, to a greater or smaller extent, upon the kind of *vague statements about frequency relations* now referred to. In those few cases where the strength of a proof can be expressed as a fixed percentage, there will always be other evidence in the action, and if there are two evidentiary facts and the convincing force of only one of them can be expressed by a percentage figure, it is nevertheless impossible to indicate their accumulated value as evidence in this exact way. *If the degree of probability is expressed, in some examples in the present paper, as a percentage or a fraction, this is solely because it is easier to make the reasoning comprehensible in this way.*

What makes the evaluation of evidence in courts of justice particularly difficult is the circumstance that the facts at issue usually belong to *the past.*[9] This is true especially of the most important group of ultimate facts: juristic acts and unlawful acts. When actually happening, they were not often observed with any particular care and at the time of the action they are no longer capable of being observed. What remains available for actual perception at that time does not often permit any safe conclusions about the theme of proof. Crimes are usually committed in secret, and the perpetrator tries to remove any traces if his doings.

---

[7] Bolding, *op. cit.,* chap. II, particularly at p. 75, and P. L. Kirk, *Crime Investigation,* 1953. pp. 22 and 24 f. See, on the other hand, W. Wundt, *Logik* II, 1920, p. 66.

[7a] Cf. F. P. Ramsay, *The Foundations of Mathematics,* 1954. pp. 187–198.

[8] Bolding in *Svensk juristtidning* 1953. p. 332.

[9] Hellwig in *Gerichtssaal* 1922, p. 430. In such cases it is customary to use the term "historical evidence". In the critical evaluation of sources made by the historian and in the evaluation of evidence which a court has to undertake the same methods are applied. (Cf. Gross in *Archiv für Kriminalanthropologie und Kriminalistik,* vol. 8, p. 84.)

Similarly, although it is true that evidence concerning, e.g., a contract may be secured by the drafting of a document, it is possible that the parties have forgotten to include some detail about which an action will later be brought;[1] moreover, it is a well-known fact that a great number of contracts are concluded by telephone. Thus courts are very largely obliged to rely on all kinds of hints and to people's memories of past events; the latter source of information is no less uncertain than the former.

In these circumstances, it is only natural that what the court has to evaluate is a *chain of evidence,* in which each link has a limited evidentiary value.[2] An example is furnished by evidence through witness, where the court infers from the statement of a witness to his observations of the fact observed and thereupon proceeds to this fact. The statement is indicated by A, the observation by B and the *factum probandum* by C, and we further make the unrealistic assumption that it has been possible to assess the convincing force of A and B at 75 per cent, each for *its own* theme of proof. This would imply that if the statement A is made in 16 similar cases, B exists in 12 of these, and C in 9 of the 12 cases. C has consequently been proved with a probability of not more than about 60 per cent. *Thus the convincing force of a certain circumstance depends also upon the degree of probability with which that circumstance has been proved.*[3] *The more links there are in a chain of evidence, the weaker is the evidence for the final link of the chain.*[4] If the court was in a position to observe a later link in the chain and thus make the chain shorter, this means that stronger evidence has been attained, unless the link concerned was proved with full certainty by the link preceding it. This fact has been held a sufficient reason for the inadmissibility of certain kinds of evidence; this, however, is a problem which cannot be discussed in the present paper.

In spite of the difficulties referred to above, courts often succeed in arriving at a fairly reliable idea of what has happened even in cases where the evidence at first appears to be meagre. The following pages are intended to show, at least in some respects, the course of reasoning followed in such cases. We shall discuss the

---

[1] It should be mentioned that the parol evidence rule is not part of Swedish law.

[2] On the meaning of chain of evidence, see p. 48 note 4.

[3] Ball, *op. cit.,* pp. 97 f.

[4] Day, *op. cit.,* p. 108.

question in relation first to cases where only one evidentiary fact is concerned and then to situations with several concurring facts.

It is generally admitted that if *the accused confesses,* this is an important evidentiary fact in criminal actions. Let us make the unrealistic assumption that in a case of this kind there was no other sign of the accused's guilt. The fact that the confession is to his prejudice obviously invests this proof with considerable value. But, at least if the action concerns a serious crime, a verdict against the accused presupposes very strong evidence of his guilt. At the same time, experience shows that, for various reasons, confessions may be more or less incorrect.[5] Let me give a few examples. The accused may have wanted to protect the actual perpetrator of the crime, he may have misunderstood the prosecution's statement of facts in some important respect, or he may find it advisable to stick to an incorrect statement which, for one reason or another, he has already made to the police. The purpose of a false confession may also be to bring an unpleasant action quickly to an end or to secure a reduction of a punishment which seems inevitable. Finally, there are persons suffering from a guilt complex of such strength that they have a tendency to admit the truth of accusations against them without giving much thought to the question whether these are true or not.

Suppose, now, that the act for which the defendant was prosecuted is a crime of such seriousness that the court does not consider itself entitled to condemn the accused upon his confession alone, without having established its truth scrupulously. In our example, this cannot be done in any other way than by examining possible reasons why the confession should be false and verifying that none of these can be found in the case at bar.[6] In this way, the degree of probability is increased, although full certainty cannot be obtained. Suppose that a thorough study of a great number of confessions in serious criminal actions would show that 1 per cent of these were incorrect, wholly or in some important respect. By means of the procedure described above, it seems possible to reduce the margin of error considerably.[7]

---

[5] von Hentig in *Schweizerische Zeitschrift für Strafprozess* 1929, pp. 23 f., and Hirschberg, *Das Fehlurteil im Strafprozess,* 1960, pp. 17 f.

[6] K. Hasler, *Die Feststellung des Tatbestandes im Zivilprozess,* Wädenswil 1926, pp. 38 f.

[7] This demonstrates an important difference between propositions about frequency relations of the kind now referred to and such where mere *chance* is decisive. The probability that the six will appear upon one particular throwing

The method now discussed may also be said to imply that the convincing force of a confession is strengthened by demonstrating that it has not been possible to produce counter-evidence based upon *auxiliary facts*,[8] which reduce or diminish the convincing force of the confession. Sometimes, however, it seems more natural to speak of auxiliary facts which are such as to increase the convincing force of the confession. Suppose for instance that, from what is known about the accused's character, the conclusion is drawn that certain reasons for the incorrectness of the confession must be wholly excluded. On the other hand, it can also be said that this implies making use of a law of general experience, which states how often confessions by persons with certain characteristic psychological features are correct. *To make use of auxiliary facts means the same as to apply a more specialized law of experience than would otherwise have been the case.*[9]

We now turn to the question how the degree of probability is increased by *several concurring evidentiary facts*, each of which is

---

of a dice can never amount to more than one out of six. This is due to the fact that the game of dice is constructed in such a manner that one cannot determine why this or that side is turned upwards. Moreover, the same percentage of probability will be obtained irrespective of the group of games examined, provided the number of games is great. Unlike this case, the degree of probability for the correctness of the confession depends upon the way in which the examined group is delimited. (See, on another case, *Svensk Jurist-tidning* 1961, p. 465.) If all cases concerning the same crime as the one in question are included, the percentage will be different from that obtained, if the material is limited to include only crimes committed by professional criminals. This, however, does not imply any objection against the use of statements on frequency for the purpose of evaluating evidence. For the choice of the group which is to be examined exercises an influence upon the question what *auxiliary facts* are of importance when applying the frequency proposition to actual cases, and what convincing force is to be ascribed to these facts. If the group examined consisted only of professional criminals, certain reasons for the incorrectness of confessions may be disregarded, whereas others are more frequent than in the population as a whole.

[8] As for the meaning of the term "auxiliary facts", see p. 48 note 4 *in fine*.

[9] This is also the case where the degree of probability of the more general law of experience could have been expressed by means of a percentage. Suppose that a blood test of all parents and children in the whole country shows that a certain constellation of blood groups exists only in one case out of 1000. As pointed out by the Danish scholar Professor Alf Ross in *Ugeskrift for Retsvæsen* 1955, p. 79, decisions in paternity suits cannot be based upon this experience without any modifications. For it is likely that a relatively considerable proportion of the cases deviating from the majority consists of those where *the mother claims* that a certain man is the child's father although the constellation of blood groups is that referred to above. At least in those cases where the mother gives an impression of reliability, the defendant must be the child's father much more often than in one case out of 1000. See also *California Law Review* 1941, p. 697.

in itself insufficient to prove the *factum probandum* concerned.[1]
Let us suppose that in an action concerning a highway accident
there are two facts tending to prove that one of the cars concerned
had a speed exceeding 60 miles per hour: the length of the braking
marks, and a witness who observed the collision. We further make
the unrealistic assumption that by examining a great number of
similar situations it has been possible to ascertain that each of
these evidentiary facts implies, in three cases out of four, a faithful description of reality, whereas in the fourth case it has no
value whatever as evidence of the speed of the car.[2] At least if
the value of each evidentiary fact is independent of that of the
other, their combined value must be greater than $3/4$. But how
much greater? The length of the braking marks proves that the
speed exceeded 60 miles per hour in 12 out of 16 similar cases;
at the same time, this is proved by the witness's statement in 3
of the 4 remaining cases. The convincing force of the combined
evidentiary facts would thus be $15/16$.[3]

If the convincing force of the tracks and of the statement of the
witness had been only 1 out of 10, the same method of calculation
would result in a combined force amounting to no more than 19
out of 100. And where there are 10 different facts, each with the
same small convincing force, the combined force only amounts to
$55/100$. *Thus the total value of several concurring proofs depends,
to a very great extent, upon the convincing force of each proof in
itself.*[4]

However, these arguments are not only unrealistic because they
express the convincing force of evidence in terms of percentages.
As has already been pointed out, they are based on the premise
that the force of one proof is entirely independent of that of the
other.[5] In actual practice it is frequent that one or several possible
sources of error are common to both proofs. Let us vary our first
example by assuming that the evidence consists of two witnesses
who have seen the collision. There may be several *unknown* rea-

---

[1] Gulson, *op. cit.*, pp. 104 f.; cf. Best on *Evidence*, London 1902, p. 77.
[2] Where the impression of the witness was not caused by what he observed
but is the result of, e.g., suggestion, his statement has no convincing force whatever, even if it happens to be true.
[3] Cf. Ch. O'Hara and J. W. Osterburg, *Criminalistics*, 1949, p. 671.
[4] Cf. Cohn in *Juridisk Tidsskrift* 1922, pp. 168 f.
[5] Cf. E. R. Bierling, *Juristische Prinzipienlehre* IV, 1911, pp. 120 f., and Gulson, *op. cit.*, pp. 115 f. Day, *op. cit.*, p. 56, makes use of the same expression
in a different, more restricted sense.

sons for error common to both witnesses. Both may have suffered a shock from the violent crash produced by the collision or from the sight of the seriously injured passengers and the wrecked cars. Or both have been influenced by a person who claimed that the speed of the car concerned was at least 60 miles an hour. The possibility of some such common influence implies that the combined value of the evidence is lower than would otherwise have been the case.

Finally, a few words will be devoted to what could be called "proving by elimination".[6] Suppose that the accused in an action concerning homicide denies that he has had anything to do with the crime. Certain facts seem to indicate that he has committed it, but their convincing force is not such as to admit a verdict against the accused. On the other hand, there is no other person who can be suspected, and any other hypothesis about the way in which the deceased person died seems highly improbable. These circumstances obviously strengthen the evidence against the accused. It is not permissible, however, to base one's conclusions only upon the absence of counter-evidence, for *the mere absence of knowledge has no value as evidence.*[7] Only an *investigation* which shows that other hypotheses are incorrect can furnish any support for the assumption that the accused is guilty. And if any of these hypotheses is strengthened by some evidence, this will reduce the degree of reliability which may be assigned to the hypothesis of the prosecution even if it still appears most probable.[8] However, it is difficult to know whether all possibilities have been taken into consideration. It appears from the history of those cases of miscarriages of justice that have later been unravelled that the true perpetrator of the crime may be a person against whom there was not even the faintest suspicion at the time of the action. Such cases

[6] Cf. Bierling, *op. cit.*, p. 122, note 38, and Wundt, *op. cit.*, II, p. 79; *vide* also p. 56 above.

[7] "If a hypothesis is initially very improbable but is the only one that explains the facts, then it must be accepted", says Sherlock Holmes. Expressed in this manner, the principle seems misleading.

[8] In scientific investigations it happens that less probable hypotheses are wholly disregarded, at least temporarily. Thus a historian may develop the most probable hypothesis as the final result of his study. And in the natural sciences, it may be used as a working hypothesis which the scientist tries to ascertain by further experiments. When evaluating evidence in courts of justice, on the other hand, the less probable hypotheses are used to determine the degree of probability with which the most probable one has been proved. Cf. above, the text at note 4, p. 52, and the Swedish case 1956 N.J.A. 713.

are instructive also from another point of view. The incorrectness
of a verdict in a criminal action does not necessarily mean that the
court has misinterpreted the evidence in the action. There may
be "sufficient evidence", although it would not have been considered sufficient if the court had known some other fact which
indicated that another version of the events was true.[9]

It follows from what has now been said that all evaluation of
evidence takes place by the subsuming of actual facts under laws
of general experience. Let us now return to the question why, at
least on a first view, this does not seem to be the case, when, e.g.,
oral evidence is evaluated. As we have found, the court has to
base its reasoning in these cases upon frequency relations which
have a very indefinite degree of probability. It is true that in some
cases it is possible to obtain greater certainty by having recourse
to experts in *witness psychology,* but this is so expensive and
demands so much time and labour that it is out of the question
except in actions concerning great economic values or very serious
crimes. As a rule, the court must try for itself to arrive at an
opinion based on greater certainty by using available *auxiliary
facts.* These, however, vary from one case to another, and their
convincing force is equally difficult to ascertain. Where there are
a great number of statements by witnesses and of other facts constituting evidence, the difficulties are increased. Under the principle of free evaluation of evidence, the force of the evidence as
to each particular theme of proof must be assessed on the basis of
the available material *as a whole.* But in a case of the kind now
discussed this material appears to be "unique" in the sense that
we possess no knowledge of any law of general experience concerning a complex of evidentiary facts of exactly that kind.

In these circumstances it appears inevitable that the judge will
make up his mind on the question of the force of evidence *intuitively.*[1] This implies a rapid survey of the whole complex of
evidentiary facts and of the general experience applicable to them;
the judge, arriving at his conclusion on the basis of this survey,

---

[9] "Probability is relative to evidence" (Bennett, *op. cit.,* p. 353, and Day,
op. cit., pp. 41 and 171). In the present writer's view, however, it seems to be
the *degree* of probability which is relative to the available evidence. Cf. Toulmin, *op. cit.,* p. 79.

[1] The word "intuitive" is used, in this connection, to denote the contrary
of "discursive". It is neither necessary nor permissible to resort to reflexion
governed by "sentiment".

will be unable to describe exactly how he so reached it.[2] On the other hand, intuition is influenced by our earlier experience, although our attention is not focused upon it at the moment of the intuitive judgment.[3] Therefore, there are good reasons for assuming that the result will be more reliable if the judge has previously undertaken a careful *discursive* analysis of the material available as evidence. In the present writer's view, such an analysis can only be performed in the manner discussed above. First, it is necessary to try to arrive at an evaluation of the convincing force of *each particular* evidentiary fact against the background of the general experience and of available auxiliary facts. In this process, the different links in the chains of evidence must be examined separately.[4] Thereafter, one proceeds to assess the *combined* convincing force of those facts which support the allegation that a certain ultimate fact exists. From the sum thus obtained, finally, one must subtract the combined force of such counter-evidence as supports the existence of facts incompatible with the allegation.[5] It is true that the evaluations obtained in this manner are usually quite vague, and sometimes the operation can be performed only partially. Nevertheless, the process may be of some use. A situation in which this is obviously the case is one where the judge in a criminal action in which the accused has pleaded not guilty arrives at the conclusion that among the numerous proofs invoked by the prosecution there is not one which has any particular force.[6]

It is also possible, however, that the order in which the judge proceeds to a discursive analysis of various elements of evidence and to an intuitive evaluation of the whole is reversed. The former part of the process then has the function of *checking* the results obtained through the latter. Further, the two methods may

[2] Nyman in *Theoria*, 1953, pp. 24 and 29 f., and Berne in *The Psychiatric Quarterly* 1949, p. 205.
[3] Cf. M. Bunge, *Intuition and Science*, 1962, pp. 84 and 98.
[4] See J. H. Wigmore, *The Principles of Judicial Proof*, Boston 1913, pp. 27 f.
[5] Day, *op. cit.*, pp. 57 f.—The subtraction of counterevidence which must be performed, where such evidence has been produced, seems to have been given little attention in writing on evidence. Let us vary the example on p. 58 and assume that whereas the braking marks retain their value as evidence for a higher speed than 60 miles an hour, the witness has stated that the speed of the car was *less* than 60 m.p.h., and further that the convincing force of this statement is only $1/4$. I venture to submit that under these premises the higher speed has been proved, but only with a force of $\frac{9}{16}\left[\frac{12}{16} - \left(\frac{1}{4} \times \frac{12}{16}\right)\right]$.

[6] Cf. above, the text at note 4, p. 58.

alternate several times. The final result, however, should always be based, in the present writer's view, upon an intuitive evaluation of the whole evidence.[7]

In treatises and papers on evidence there are many expressions of opinions which are in harmony with the views set out above. It seldom occurs, however, that the chosen method is maintained with any consistency. As an example of deviations, we may mention the fairly generally accepted distinction between *direct* and *indirect evidence*. Some writers use the term "indirect" to denote all evidence which does not put the court in a position to observe the fact at issue.[8] No objections can be raised against this terminology; but it is not very useful, for it is rare that the court is in a position to observe any ultimate facts. It is quite understandable, however, that as a rule the line between direct and indirect evidence is drawn according to other principles. The statement of a witness about his observation of an ultimate fact is considered to be direct evidence.[9] The course of reasoning which is at the bottom of this terminology appears from the statement of the Swedish scholar Kallenberg that "where a witness tells what he has observed of the *factum probandum*, the judge makes a conclusion which goes *immediately from the statement to this fact*".[1]

Thus it would be possible to disregard the fact that in all evaluation of oral evidence there is a chain of evidentiary facts.[2] If so, the discursive method recommended here cannot be applied, for the statement of the witness, on the one hand, and his observations, on the other, can be tested only against the background of quite different laws of general experience, and more-

---

[7] If this is correct, the part played by intuition in the evaluation of evidence would differ from its function in mathematics. A mathematician who has intuitively foreseen the solution of a complicated problem can subsequently verify the result by means of calculation. The evaluation of evidence cannot be subjected to any such reliable control. Besides the judge's intuitive gifts and his habit in evaluating evidence, there is no other check on the reliability of intuition than a discursive evaluation of the material as described in the text. On various kinds of intuitive judgments, see J. P. Guilford, *Personality*, 1959, pp. 25 f., and Pokorny in *Acta psychologica*, 1954, p. 251.

[8] See, e.g., E. Siegrist, *Grundfragen aus dem Beweisrecht des Zivilprozesses*, Bern 1938, p. 203, and G. Bohne, *Zur Psychologie der richterlichen Überzeugungsbildung*, Cologne 1948, p. 9.

[9] See, e.g., Gulson, *op. cit.*, pp. 123, 143 and 217.

[1] Kallenberg, *op. cit.* II, p. 569, note 29; see also p. 542.

[2] Cf. above, p. 55.

over different auxiliary facts must be used.[3] Consequently, the convincing force of the statement by the witness and of his observation of facts must be evaluated separately.[4]

The sense in which writers on evidence use the term *"ground of evidence"* is also significant.[5] Sometimes, it is taken to mean any circumstance with a value as a proof, i.e. what has been called in this paper "evidentiary fact".[6] As a rule, however, the term is used in a more specialized sense. When a place or an object is inspected by the court, it is said that the "ground of evidence" is the judge's perception of the theme of proof; where evidence consists of a statement by a witness, it is that person's observations which are the "ground of evidence".[7] Thus human observation is exalted as an evidentiary fact of particular importance for the evaluation of evidence. But whereas there is not often any ground to question the correctness of the judge's observation of what occurs in the course of the hearing, psychological investigations of statements by witnesses have shown that the contrary must be affirmed about the observations reported in such statements. The fact that the witness himself is convinced of the correctness of his observations cannot claim any decisive importance. What the decision must be based upon is the evaluation of the court, not of the witness, regarding the evidence produced.

One inconvenience attending the opinion now referred to is that it may create a temptation to overestimate the value of oral evidence in relation to proof by conclusive facts (indicia). In Sweden, there are probably still lawyers who consider that if evidence of the first kind is available, the decision should not be based upon such facts.[8] This view is wholly unfounded. In a criminal action for burglary, should a testimony to the effect that the accused and not another person who, has also been suspected is the per-

---

[3] Wundt (*op. cit.*, pp. 65 f.) holds that laws of general experience cannot be used in the evaluation of evidence.

[4] See Siegrist, *op. cit.*, pp. 196 f., and Johs. Andenaes, *Straffeprosessen*, Oslo 1962, p. 164.

[5] German: *"Beweisgrund."*

[6] R. Wrede, *Finlands gällande civilprocessrätt* II, Helsinki 1923, pp. 81 and 85; see, however, p. 90. This author uses the term "evidentiary fact" to denote the fact in issue. Cf. Rosenberg, *op. cit.*, § 111 II 1 b.

[7] See, e.g., H. Munch-Petersen, *Den danske Retspleje*, Copenhagen 1923, p. 193, and Hasler, *op. cit.*, pp. 42 f. Certain writers do not call the observation of the witness, but his statement, the "ground of evidence". Cf. the pertinent analysis of Siegrist, *op. cit.*, p. 24 note 1.

[8] Cf. Kallenberg, *op. cit.* II, p. 1019 note 36.

64   PER OLOF EKELÖF

petrator always be considered more reliable than the observation
on the safe of fingerprints belonging to the latter?[9] On the other
hand, it is equally incorrect to consider circumstantial evidence
preferable in principle to oral evidence ("facts cannot lie").
Generally speaking, it is impossible to make sweeping judgments
about the relation between oral and circumstantial evidence with
regard to their convincing force.[1] What is decisive are the qualities
of the witness, the conditions under which he made his observations, and, on the other hand, the kind of conclusive facts concerned and what they are intended to prove.

That one sometimes meets criticism of the ideas set forth above
may be explained, at least partly, by the fact that people have
not wholly got rid of a way of thinking which was natural at a
time when the law of evidence was characterized by the doctrine
of legal evidence. Under that doctrine, the court only had to
ascertain whether two witnesses, who could not be challenged,
made substantially identical statements about the theme of proof.
Under those circumstances, there was no reason to make any distinction between the statements of the witnesses and their observations. And as for circumstantial evidence, it was considered
with obvious distrust by the doctrine of legal evidence. It was
not permitted to condemn the accused upon the strength of such
evidence alone. This situation was partly due to the difficulty of
defining its convincing force by statute. As for oral evidence, it
was enough that the legislators made up their minds on the
question how many witnesses would be required for *plena probatio*.
When in Continental law, in the Middle Ages, similar rules were
laid down for the different kinds of circumstantial evidence, the
rules proved to be too complicated.[2]

The excessive belief in the convincing force of oral evidence
possibly also has some connection with the fact that human observation is an evidentiary fact of a very particular kind.[3] Where
the observation is in harmony with reality, there is no problem
about ascertaining what it actually proves. It is a different matter
in the case of circumstantial evidence, i.e. conclusive facts. These

[9] Illum, in *Ugeskrift for Retsvæsen* 1954, p. 143, contends that where oral
evidence is produced, courts often accept as sufficient proof evidence of less
convincing force than is obtained by blood tests in filiation actions.
[1] Day, *op. cit.*, p. 304, and Kenny's *Outlines of Criminal Law*, Cambridge
1952, pp. 374 f.
[2] J. W. Hedemann, *Die Vermutung*, 1904, pp. 64 f.
[3] Cf. Sebba in *Zeitschrift für deutschen Zivilprozess* 1908, pp. 86 f.

facts are seldom "photographs" which give clear information about the theme of proof. Once a fact of this kind has been verified, it is usually necessary to proceed to a laborious investigation of the question *what* can be proved by this fact. However, this is a fallacious habit of thought to indulge in, for the difficulty caused by circumstantial evidence in the respect now referred to has its counterpart when evaluating the convincing force of an observation by a witness. This is the question *whether the witness really registered the facts faithfully.*

It is frequently stated, particularly in German legal writing, that the decisive element in the evaluation of evidence should be the judge's *conviction*.[4] If the judge is convinced of the accused's guilt, he must condemn him. If, on the other hand, any doubt remains on this point after the evaluation of evidence, the action cannot be sustained.

It must be asked, however, what is the meaning of this statement. Obviously, the verdict must go against the prosecution if the judge is not convinced that the evidence has *sufficient convincing force*. What is meant, however, is that it is not enough that the judge finds it highly probable that the accused is guilty: he must have the personal conviction that this is the case.[5] What these German writers are really dealing with is in fact the *strength which must be required of the evidence* to justify a condemnation in a criminal action.[6] However, the requirement of conviction also seems to refer to the evaluation of evidence. It is stressed that the idea of the judge being convinced of the accused's guilt is compatible with the *theoretical possibility* that another version of the actual events is the true one, but is, nevertheless, incompatible with the existence of *actual facts* indicating that the latter version is correct.[7] The sense of these words is not altogether clear to me,

---

[4] The "Strafprozessordnung", sec. 261, has the following tenor: "Über das Ergebnis der Beweisaufnahme entscheidet das Gericht nach seiner freien, aus dem Inbegriff der Verhandlung geschöpften *Überzeugung*" (italics supplied); see also "Zivilprozessordnung", sec. 286.

[5] R. v. Hippel, *Der deutsche Strafprozess*, Marburg 1941, p. 388; H. Wassermeyer, *Der prima facie Beweis*, 1954, pp. 68 f.; Scanzoni in *Neue Juristische Wochenschrift* 1951, p. 222, and Mattill in *Goltdammers Archiv für Strafrecht* 1954, p. 338.

[6] Eb. Schmidt, *Lehrkommentar zur Strafprozessordnung* I, Göttingen 1952, p. 158.

[7] See Hartung in *Süddeutsche Juristenzeitung* 1948, pp. 582 f., Niese in *Goltdammers Archiv* 1954, p. 149, and Mattill in *Goltdammers Archiv* 1954, p. 340; see, *contra*, Hellwig in *Gerichtssaal*, 1922, p. 417.

66   PER OLOF EKELÖF

but I would insist upon the conclusion that the accused must
be acquitted where the evidence produced by the prosecution is
weak, even if there is no counter-evidence in favour of his innocence, whereas the verdict demanded by the prosecution should
be given where the evidence against the accused is strong, even
if there are one or two weak pieces of counter-evidence. *For what
is essential is the strength of the evidence after the substraction
of the convincing force of such counter-evidence as there may be
in the action.*[8]

Generally speaking, it does not seem wholly safe to state that
the judge must base his decision on the points of fact upon his
conviction. Suppose that a judge follows this course of reasoning:
"It is true that the evidence produced in the action is not of
sufficient strength, but nevertheless I am perfectly convinced of
the accused's guilt, and consequently I vote for condemnation."
What, really, is the content of this judge's conviction? Obviously,
it is not that the evidence has the required strength. But in that
case he ought to have thought: "Personally, I am convinced of
the accused's guilt, but since the evidence is not sufficient he
must be acquitted."[9]

---

[8] See above, p. 61.
[9] Cf. Bolding, *op. cit.*, pp. 67 f., and in *Sv.J.T.* 1953, pp. 311 f. Bohne in
op. cit., pp. 51 and 76, emphasizes that conviction is connected with a feeling
that the chosen solution is obvious ("Evidenzgefühl") and further that conviction presupposes a volition by the judge. See also Wimmer in *Deutsche Rechts-
zeitschrift* 1950, p. 392, and Hirschberg, *op. cit.*, pp. 93 f.

The Probability Debate

[7]

DEBATING PROBABILITIES

William Twining*

To start with a confession: as an innumerate I share with most lawyers some apprehension about the incursion of mathematics into law; as someone with no formal training in logic, I find it reassuring to be told that the standard model of reasoning employed by lawyers in dealing with evidentiary issues is a form of ordinary practical non-mathematical reasoning which is regularly and properly used in the conduct of everyday affairs. It may be comforting to find oneself classed with M. Jourdain here, even if it is daunting to discover the complexities of the arguments about what is involved in talking prose. At first sight lawyers who lack a basic grounding in mathematics may find comfort in the thesis of Jonathan Cohen in his book *The Probable and the Provable,* despite the complexity of the analysis on which this thesis is based.[1] They should also be grateful to Cohen and a number of other writers for drawing attention to some important but relatively neglected issues concerning reasoning about probabilities in forensic contexts. But they need to gird themselves to wrestle with complex questions which are likely to be the subject of protracted debate during the coming years. The purpose of this paper is to attempt to provide an introduction to one phase of this debate.

It is generally recognised that in dealing with questions of fact lawyers are concerned with judgments about "probabilities." For example, the standard of proof in civil cases is often expressed as "a preponderance of probabilities"; similarly it is a widely held view that the criminal standard of proof beyond

---

*Professor of Law, University of Warwick.

1. This paper deals with recent British and American writings on probabilities in legal reasoning. The main works under consideration are as follows: L. Jonathan Cohen *The Probable and the Provable,* Oxford University Press, 1977; R. Eggleston *Evidence, Proof and Probability,* Weidenfeld and Nicolson, 1978; M. O. Finkelstein and W. B. Fairley, "A Bayesian Approach to Identification Evidence" 83 *Harvard Law Review,* 489 (1970); L. Tribe "Trial by Mathematics: Precision and Ritual in the Legal Process" 84 *Harvard Law Review* 1329 (1971); (this debate was continued in 84 *Harvard Law Review* 1801 (1971), (Finkelstein and Fairley); 84 *Harvard Law Review* 1810 (1971), (Tribe); 2 *Journal of Legal Studies* (1973), 493 (Finkelstein) and in Finkelstein's *Quantitative Methods in Law,* Free Press, 1978. The latter work raises many issues which are beyond the scope of this paper. The exchange between Glanville Williams and Cohen is to be found in Glanville Williams "The Mathematics of Proof I" *Criminal Law Review* (1979), 297; II, id., 340; Cohen "The Logic of Proof" *Criminal Law Review* (1980), 91, Glanville Williams "A Short Rejoinder" id. 103; Sir Richard Eggleston intervened briefly in this debate in *Criminal Law Review* (1979), 682. Eggleston has discussed *The Probable and the Provable* in a number of papers, but since these were not available in published form at the time of writing they are not discussed in detail in this paper. A useful introduction to the mathematical approach is Alan D. Cullison "Identification by Probabilities and Trial by Arithmetic" 6 *Houston Law Review* (1969), 421. For references to classical discussions of probability see Cohen's *The Probable and the Provable,* and to the extensive American literature see Finkelstein's *Quantitative Methods in Law* and a review of the latter by David Kaye in 89 *Yale Law Journal* (1980), 601.

52   The Liverpool Law Review Vol. II [1980]

reasonable doubt falls short of absolute certainty and can be elucidated in terms of probability, although there is a general reluctance to express this in precise quantitive terms, even by those who think that it is possible to do so. Judicial decisions are typically decisions made in conditions of uncertainty; it is generally agreed that such decisions have to be made on the basis of estimates of probabilities, both in respect of the case taken as a whole and in respect of particular ultimate and intermediate probanda. There is, however, considerable doubt as to what kind(s) of probabilities are involved and the extent to which it is (a) theoretically possible, (b) feasible in practice and (c), when feasible, desirable as a matter of policy to express the criteria of correctness of such judgments in terms of a mathematical calculus of probability.

There are many different theories of probability, that is to say different criteria of correctness of judgments of probability.[2] For present purposes it is useful to distinguish at least four. Firstly, there is the *a priori* theory, otherwise known as the *classical doctrine of chances*. Here a probability is the ratio of favourable outcomes to all possible outcomes. This criterion only applies where all outcomes are equiprobable, for example estimating probabilities of particular throws with unweighted dice, dealing randomly shuffled cards or tossing 'true' coins. The calculations of *a priori* probabilities are, of course, mathematical.

Secondly, there are *statistical* or *actuarial* probabilities, based on determinations of relative frequency within a given class. For example, insurance premiums for life policies are based in part on life expectancies of members of particular classes of people.[3] Such probabilities are general judgments about frequencies within a class and, as Cohen puts it, "their application to inferences about particular facts is a rather tricky matter."[4] To use his example, we may know that Tom is a lorry-driver aged 30 and that members of that class have a 0.7 probability of survival until 70. But Tom may also be a rock-climber with a weak heart and relevant information about persons with these characteristics, singly or in combination, may not be available, in which case the conditions for the application of strict statistical analysis are not satisfied.[5] In the

---

2. The following account draws particularly on Cullison, *op. cit.*n.1 and A. J. Ayer *Probability and Evidence,* Macmillan, 1972. In distinguishing three classes of probability judgments Ayer says: "I take no side on the question whether there is one or more than one concept that goes under the name of 'probability,' because I am not sure what the criteria are for individuating concepts and suppose that they are rather arbitrary. I do, however, believe that what we normally characterise as judgments of probability can be divided into three distinct classes, and if anyone wishes to infer from this that the word 'probable' is used in at least three different senses, I shall not quarrel with him" (p.27). Ayer's account does not deal with probability in the psychological sense of expressions of intensity of belief, my third category.

3. On the limitations of the use of actuarial probabilities in fixing insurance premiums other than for life policies, see P. S. Atiyah, *Accidents, Compensation and the Law* Weidenfeld and Nicolson, 3rd ed., 1980, 605-6.

4. J. Cohen, *Criminal Law Review* (1980), 91, at 92.

5. *Ibid.*

notorious and rather over-used *Collins* case, the misuse of statistics by the prosecution started with crude estimates of the relative frequency of yellow automobiles, girls with blonde hair, girls with pony tails, men with moustaches, and blacks with beards — all in the Los Angeles area.[6] Sound estimates of actuarial probabilities require to be based on reliable empirical enquiries conducted according to valid statistical procedures. It is often hard or impossible in practice to satisfy rigorous statistical standards for want of sufficient data or because of methodological difficulties. In life many decisions have to be taken in reliance on estimates of frequencies based on more or less informed guesses.

Thirdly, some probability judgments are subjective expressions of *degrees of confidence* (intensity of belief) in some particular proposition, for example "I am .9 certain that it will rain today" or "I am confident that it was Y who murdered Z." These kinds of judgments may be based to a greater or lesser extent on evidence or experience or argument or intuition or irrational beliefs or pure guesswork or a combination of such factors. It is important not to confuse this kind of psychological probability as an expression of strength of belief with guesses or estimates of frequency in a situation where there is little or no empirical evidence on which to base a judgment. Both are sometimes confusingly referred to as "subjective probabilities"; they are often combined in a single judgment, but they are conceptually distinct. It is not paradoxical to say: "I think that there is a .8 likelihood of rain today, but I am not very confident of this, let me say .5 on a scale of 0 to 1." In ordinary language such expressions as "I know," "I am positive," "I am confident," "I think," "I would surmise" express different gradations of confidence in non-numerical terms; to translate such judgments into a numerical form of expression does not *ipso facto* convert them into statistical estimates of probability.[7] However, much has been written about whether, when and how "subjective probabilities" can be expressed in or constructed into Pascalian terms, for example in terms of the odds that a rational man would accept within a coherent system of betting odds. Thus subjective probabilities may or may not be Pascalian.

Fourthly, and more controversially, there are said to be *inductive* or *Baconian* probabilities, that is to say judgments of probability based on reasoning which, according to one view, is *in principle non-mathematical*. Typically such judgments are estimates of the likelihood of a particular event, past, present or future. For example, an estimate of the life expectancy of the class of 30 year

6. *People v. Collins* (1968) 438 P.2d 33, discussed *inter alios* by Cullison, op. cit. n.1. R. Eggleston *Evidence, Proof and Probability* (1978) at 142-3, and nearly all American writers on the subject.
7. Problems of quantifying "subjective probabilities" are extensively canvassed in the statistical literature, see *infra*. n. 12.

54   The Liverpool Law Review Vol. II [1980]

old lorry drivers is in principle statistical, but an estimate of the life expectancy of Tom (who is a lorry-driver, has a weak heart, is a mountain-climber and has a unique sense of humour) is in principle Baconian. So too is the typical mode of experimental reasoning in modern science in testing hypotheses about causal laws in the laboratory. This type of probability is the subject of the recent exchange between Jonathan Cohen and Glanville Williams and will be considered below.

At this stage my concern is merely to clarify the terminology. Baconian probabilities are, according to Cohen and others, *objective;* they are judgments which are susceptible to rational, though typically non-compelling, arguments; they are judgments of the weight or cogency of the evidence supporting a particular probandum or a case as a whole. Such probability judgments are not based solely on intuition or guesswork nor are they merely expressions of degrees of belief; accordingly they differ from both kinds of "subjective probabilities." Baconian and Pascalian probabilities are not rivals: "The two probability judgments differ substantially from one another. Nevertheless, neither implies the falsity of the other. Both judgments may be true, because each supplies us with a quite different kind of information from the other. The Pascalian judgement grades probability *on the assumption that* all relevant facts are specified in the evidence, while the Baconian one grades it *by the extent to which* all relevant facts are specified in the evidence."[8]

It would make no difference to Cohen's argument, and it may have some resonance with lawyers, if the term "credibility" were substituted for probability in respect of Baconian principles.[9] Cohen is concerned with the objective credibility of evidence and of competing versions of the truth about particular events, especially in adversary proceedings.[10] For some people the term "probability" has such strong associations with mathematical calculation that to talk of "non-mathematical" probabilities seems to them to be paradoxical. The disagreement between Cohen and others is not about the meanings of "probability," but about what constitute valid and appropriate modes of reasoning towards, or justifying, particular conclusions of fact in certain specific contexts. The central question at issue is which theory or theories of probability are applicable to such issues in forensic contexts?

---

8. L. Jonathan Cohen "On the psychology of prediction: Whose is the fallacy?" 7 *Cognition* (1979), 385, 393. In this article Cohen criticizes the "mathematicist" assumptions of two experimental psychologists, Kahneman and Tversky, along lines almost identical to his debate with Glanville Williams.

9. Ayer, *op. cit.* n. 2, refers to this class as "judgments of credibility," but seemingly confines this category to judgments about particular events. In such cases, according to Ayer, "the degree of probability cannot, or cannot in any obvious way, be given mathematical expression," (loc. cit. at 27-8).

10. One puzzle about Cohen's thesis is that he claims that Baconian probabilities provide criteria of merit for explanations of individual events in history (Ch. 20) as well as of Anglo-American judicial practice in adversary, as distinct from inquisitorial proceedings (120). It is widely believed that the judge in "inquisitorial" proceedings is closer to the historian than is the judge or jury in "adversary" proceedings. It is not clear what relevance the controversial adversary/inquisitorial distinction has to questions about the *logic* of proof in adjudicative processes.

Around each of these theories of probability an extensive body of learning has developed. Thus, according to Ayer, "the calculus of chances is a branch of pure mathematics";[11] frequency theory has been developed at both theoretical and applied levels as a part of statistics; both kinds of subjective probabilities are central, for instance, to game theory and decision theory, which are themselves meeting-grounds for several disciplines, including psychology and economics.[12] Baconian probabilities have been of particular concern to students of epistemology and inductive logic. Until recently little has been done systematically to map the connection between lawyers' concerns and various theories of probability. The lawyer who approaches recent writings about probabilities and the law needs to be aware that behind the debates lie several loosely connected bodies of specialized literature which have been developed with varying degrees of sophistication within and between a number of disciplines.[13] The subject is not only of practical and theoretical importance to the discipline of law, it is also a potentially fruitful point of contact with several other branches of learning.

It is useful to see Cohen's book *The Probable and the Provable* and the first reactions to it against this background. Cohen is a philosopher, whose primary concern here is with inductive logic; Sir Richard Eggleston and Glanville Williams are lawyers with a special interest in evidence and proof, as are leading American writers in the field such as Finkelstein, Cullison and Tribe. Although Cohen used judicial proof as his primary example, his general thesis is of very broad application. This thesis, as it applies to judicial proof, may be summarised as follows:[14] there have been three main theories about what concept of probability is appropriate to judicial proof at least within the Anglo-American system. Some writers, such as Boole, Laplace and Finkelstein and Fairley, have held that the probabilities involved should be mathematical (Pascalian) ones; some, such as Michael and Adler, Cowen and Carter, and Tribe have held or assumed that such probabilities are in principle mathematical, but are not normally in practice calculable.[15] Furthermore Tribe in particular has argued that the quantification of probabilities, though valid in principle, is socially and politically undesirable. A third view, exemplified by Bentham, Wigmore and Wills has suggested that the probabilities involved are not in principle mathematical ones. But these

---

11. *Op. cit.* no. 2, at 29.
12. See e.g., H. Raiffa *Decision Analysis: Introductory Lectures on Choices Under Uncertainty* Addison-Wesley, 1968, which contains a general guide to the literature up to 1968. A useful intellectual history is I. Hacking *The Emergence of Probability*, Cambridge University Press, 1975.
13. In addition to the fields already mentioned *The Probable and the Provable* is of direct relevance to historiography (see 284 ff.) and the philosophy of science (ch. 29).
14. The account in the text draws heavily on chapters 28 and 29 of *The Probable and the Provable*.
15. This appears to be the position of Glanville Williams and Sir Richard Eggleston.

56   The Liverpool Law Review Vol. II [1980]

writers were not always consistent nor has this view been properly argued or substantiated hitherto.[16] The object of Cohen's book is to show that the third view is correct and to explore why this is so and what are some of the practical and theoretical implications. This non-Pascalian, non-mathematical view is based on a polycriterial theory of probability which accommodates both mathematical and Baconian criteria of proof. Inductive probability fits better than mathematical probability characteristic examples of judicial proof, and historical explanations of past individual events, as well as certain statistical explanations, criteria of rational belief and dispositional statements.

Cohen's main argument in favour of his theory is that an inductive concept of probability does not encounter six difficulties facing a Pascalian account of judicial probability. Part II of the book, in which these arguments are explored, is of particular interest and importance to lawyers. First, the mathematicist encounters difficulties in civil cases in which the plaintiff's contention consists of several independent components each of which has to be proved on a preponderance of probabilities. The mathematical probability of a conjunction requires *multiplication* of each separate probability in order to establish the probability for the case as a whole. But in cases where there are several issues contested by the defendant in order to achieve a probability of .51, the plaintiff will have to establish some at a very high level of probability. This is not the way that Anglo-American law deals with this problem, nor would it be considered fair to plaintiffs if it did. The mathematicist cannot give an adequate explanation of the requirement that for the plaintiff to win he must establish each component point on a balance of probabilities *and* the outcome of the case as a whole. "[O]n the inductivist analysis, if the plaintiff gains each of his points on the balance of probability, he can be regarded as gaining his case as a whole on the balance . . . without any constraints being thereby imposed on the number of independent points in his case nor on the level of probability at which each must be won."[17]

The second difficulty of the mathematicist analysis relates to an inference upon an inference. At common law, according to Cohen — though he may state the principle more confidently than the authorities warrant[18] — the courts insist that in both civil and criminal cases, each tier of inference prior to the final one should rest on proof beyond reasonable doubt. The inductive theory of probability supports this, because the balance of proof cannot be assumed to be transitive: there may be incommensurable supports.

16. Notably Bentham, discussed by Cohen at 54-5.
17. *Ibid.*, 267.
18. *Ibid.*, 69-70, doubted by Sir Richard Eggleston in an unpublished paper.

"Inductive probability-functions evaluate the weight of relevant evidence, and what is relatively weighty for one type of conclusion may not be nearly so weighty for another . . . a judicial proof on the balance of probability sets out to show that the ultimately derived conclusion is probable on known facts, not to show that it is knowable from probable facts."[19] A mathematicist analysis, however, would permit inferences on inferences to go through, even though each tier was merely proved on a balance of probability. This, according to Cohen, neither conforms to legal practice nor explains the rule.

The third difficulty of the mathematical analysis makes the merit of the loser's case vary inversely with that of the winner's. Thus, to follow one of Cohen's favourite examples, if 1000 people have entered a rodeo but only 499 have paid at the turnstiles, the likelihood that any particular entrant has not paid is .501. But it would generally be considered unjust and a misapplication of law for such a person to be held civilly liable to pay the price of entry on this ground alone. Yet this appears to be the result indicated by the Pascalian theory. Similarly, if an innocent man accused of fraudulently entering a rodeo exhibited characteristics which tended to place him on the majority side of some critical statistical division (e.g. he had six prior convictions for this kind of fraud), even though in this case he belonged to the minority, the mathematical analysis would point to his conviction. This is because the mathematical principle for negation is complementational, that is to say that it chooses the most likely of the two sides. But inductive probability requires that there must be evidence against the particular individual; it is not enough that it merely be brought under some generalization. "On the inductivist interpretation litigants take part in a contest of *case weight* rather than in the division of a determinate quantity of *case merit.*"[20]

The fourth difficulty relates to proof beyond reasonable doubt. In inductive probability a conclusion falls short of certainty because of *specifiable reasons* for doubting it; it is not reasonable to doubt merely because the conclusion falls short of 100% certainty. A mathematical scale is otiose, because what is needed is a list of all the points which might give ground for doubt. A high statistical probability may be relevant when it enters into the proof of an interim probandum, i.e. a fact from which to argue (e.g. expert evidence that a letter was typed on a particular machine or fingerprint evidence pointing to the presence of the suspect at the scene of the crime)[21] rather than as a *measure*

---

19 *Ibid.*, 269.
20 *Ibid.*, 270 (emphasis added).
21 But fingerprint experts have traditionally been reluctant to attach numerical values to their findings, especially in relation to incomplete prints, perhaps for fear of abuse of statistics, see M. Houts, *From Evidence to Proof*, Springfield Ill., C.C. Thomas, 1956, 133.

58   The Liverpool Law Review Vol. II [1980]

of the extent to which the conclusions of the case as a whole have been established. The relevance of a fact and its significance for the outcome of the case have to be assessed in the light of other, typically non-mathematical, criteria.

The fifth difficulty is that, if it is assumed that the criterion of probability for jurors and judges is a mathematical one, it is not at all clear what that criterion is. Statistical criteria, Carnapian criteria (probability measured in terms of a ratio of ranges) and the acceptance of appropriate betting odds within a rational and coherent betting policy are all shown to be inapplicable. The mathematicist must propose some other criterion which satisfies two conditions: first, "it must not be excluded from application to judicial proof by any of the characteristic constraints on the latter";[22] secondly, it must invoke some definite criteria comparable to other mathematical criteria, such as those mentioned above. But the inductivist merely assumes that the decider brings to his task a vast range of commonplace generalizations about the human environment and about the conditions for applying those generalizations.[23]

The sixth difficulty is that the mathematicist view cannot be reconciled with the rule that cases are to be judged only on the facts before the court. For the mathematicist cannot give an account of corroboration and convergence of circumstantial evidence, where the corroborating and converging probabilities are themselves less than .5, unless some prior probability is assigned to the conclusion — e.g. that a person accused of crime is more likely than not to be guilty. The inductivist analysis readily explains convergence and corroboration without any need for recourse to prior probabilities: for example, independent evidence about opportunity and motive strengthen each other on the basis of the relevant variable, for one test of the truth of testimony is its *coherence* with other testimony.[24]

The Probable and the Provable has been welcomed as an important contribution to its subject, but it has already provoked some quite sharp responses from lawyers and it is likely that more will follow. In particular, two leading scholars, Professor Glanville Williams and Sir Richard Eggleston, have taken issue with Cohen, but on rather different grounds.[25] Perhaps four main potential lines of attack on Cohen's thesis should be distinguished:

  (i)   that the theory is erroneous that there are Baconian probabilities which are in principle non-mathematical;

---

22. Cohen *op. cit.* note 1, at 92.
23. *Ibid.*, 274.
24. *Ibid.*, 278.
25. For references, see n.1 *supra*.

(ii) that one or more of Cohen's arguments in support of (i) are erroneous;

(iii) that, whether or not there are legitimate non-Pascalian judgments of probability, Cohen's account of particular legal doctrines and practices (e.g. standards of proof) in Anglo-American law and his analysis of particular examples (e.g. the rodeo case) in terms of his theory are erroneous;

(iv) that Cohen's criticism of the views of Glanville Williams, Eggleston and some American lawyers as "misplaced mathematicisation" is itself misplaced.

From the first rounds of the debate it would appear that Glanville Williams' attack is directed against (i), i.e. Cohen's central thesis and all of its supports (ii), whereas Sir Richard Eggleston has, more cautiously, concentrated on some particular arguments under (ii) without clearly committing himself to a position on (i). Both take issue with Cohen on a number of specific issues in respect of (iii). As we shall see, the issues surrounding (iv) are rather murky, given that Cohen readily concedes some place to Pascalian probability in forensic contexts and both Eggleston and Glanville Williams clearly acknowledge the limited application in practice of mathematical reasoning — Glanville Williams going so far as to say that "[a]s every lawyer knows, established statistical probabilities are of little use in legal matters."[26]

Here, for reasons of space, I shall merely deal briefly with the Glanville Williams' attack on the main thesis. It is important to realize the precise nature of Cohen's claim: he is not merely suggesting that there is a weak form of inductive reasoning available in contexts where the conditions for precise mathematical analysis are not satisfied. Rather he maintains that, just as there is more than one kind of geometry, so there is more than one valid theory of probability:

> Nor am I arguing in favour of some popular, everyday conception of probability as against a professional or expert one. On the contrary, Baconian reasoning operates rigorously and professionally when concerned with the logic of controlled experiment in natural science . . . But in the enormously complex, and obfuscatingly untidy, affairs of everyday life, where nothing can be isolated, insulated or purified as in a laboratory, we can no more expect scientific rigour in our Baconian reasonings than we can expect quantitative accuracy in our Pascalian ones . . . On my view, a quite rich set of logically exact principles for conjunction, negation, priors etc. can be shown to be implicit in Baconian reasoning, and these principles admit of formal systematization

26. *Criminal Law Review* (1979), 298.

60   The Liverpool Law Review Vol. II [1980]

and axiomatisation just as do those of Pascalian reasoning. They merely happen to be different principles from those of Pascalian reasoning.[27]

Glanville Williams takes issue with each of Cohen's six arguments against a mathematicist interpretation of Anglo-American legal practices. In respect of each he argues either that the matter is theoretically susceptible to quantification, even if in practice it is not, or that it is to be explained by special considerations of law or policy or a combination of these. Most of his specific arguments are directed either to showing that Cohen's account of the legal position is incorrect or that the legal result is correct, but his explanation is untenable. Much of the interest of the critique lies in the details. However, what is significant in the present context is that Glanville Williams appears to reject completely the notion of an independent theory of Baconian probability. Although he has not sought to develop the philosophical arguments for this view, he is quite consistent in his attempt to explain away Cohen's examples on grounds other than that a Baconian logic of probability is both legitimate and appropriate. It is not unlikely that Glanville Williams' position will win support in other quarters, especially in the United States, and that a rather technical theoretical debate will proceed with judicial proof as one central example.

It would be easy to exaggerate the differences between the Baconians and the mathematicists. Indeed, if one looks at the concessions and *caveats* made by each, there appears to be a lot of common ground between them. Cohen is careful to emphasise some limitations of his thesis. In particular, it is clear that his main object is to show that the concept of inductive probability has *some regular* use in judicial proof, not that it gives a complete account of reasoning towards particular conclusions of fact. Moreover, Cohen does not claim that mathematical probabilities can play no part in judicial proof. He acknowledges that there are important applications for mathematical analysis in such areas as identification evidence, fingerprinting, issues about affiliation, actuarial risk, occupational disease, quality control (sampling), jury selection and so on.[28] His argument is not, therefore, that most of the recent American discussion about the use of mathematical probabilities in forensic contexts has been misconceived, but that typically such analysis is only logically appropriate to establishing some intermediate probanda (i.e. propositions of fact from which to argue to the ultimate result) and is typically not applicable to determining the standard of proof or the result of a case as a whole.

27. *Criminal Law Review* (1980), 95.
28. *Op. cit.* note 1, at 36-7, 83-6.

Thus, if we accept Cohen's general thesis, this still leaves open a number of important questions about the quantification of probabilities in judicial process, for example: in what contexts, with regard to what kinds of probanda, are mathematical probabilities applicable in principle? What conditions have to be satisfied in each context, for the application of mathematical criteria? Which mathematical criteria are appropriate? What are the practical constraints on calculation in such contexts? What kinds of misuses and abuses and errors in calculation need particularly to be guarded against? And, Tribe's question: in circumstances in which quantification is both theoretically applicable and practically feasible, are there policy reasons for or against presenting arguments in mathematical form — for example, that such arguments will not be intelligible to the relevant decision-makers or that they will be over-impressed by them? Even where, according to Cohen's arguments, some writers have been mistaken in assuming a mono-criterial, mathematicist account of probability, it does not follow that this invalidates what they have had to say on such questions as the above.

Similarly, the mathematicists make several important concessions. For example, nearly all are agreed that there is extremely limited scope in practice for the express invocation of Pascalian arguments in legal reasoning; while some writers, like Finkelstein, are concerned to extend the use of this kind of reasoning, others are at least as concerned with its dangers and abuses as with its practical value. Eggleston, in urging that statistical analysis should form part of legal education, emphasises the value of being able to spot fallacies and abuses.[29] All are agreed that only the most limited use should be made of such arguments where the decision-makers do not have the requisite mathematical background to understand them; at present this probably means nearly all judges and jurors. Tribe has advanced additional powerful arguments against "trial by mathematics." The mathematicists are not agreed among themselves about a number of important issues. Furthermore, it is by no means clear what some of them consider is involved in contexts where the conditions for Pascalian analysis are not satisfied or it is considered to be inappropriate expressly to invoke it. If Pascalian probabilities are the only legitimate, rational probabilities, as some appear to believe, does it follow that most of what passes in ordinary legal practice for reasoning about disputed issues of fact is not "reasoning" at all? Glanville Williams' position appears to be that it is typically a crude approximation to mathematical calculation, based on (typically unstated) guesses about frequencies. Others may take a more uncompromising stand on the position that, in this kind of context, mathematical reasoning is the only valid kind of reasoning.

---

29. *Evidence, Proof and Probability*, passim, esp. Ch. 11.

62   The Liverpool Law Review Vol. II [1980]

In approaching the current debates it is as well to bear these points in mind. For there is more common ground and a wider range of issues at stake than the recent sharp exchange between Glanville Williams and Cohen might suggest. Moreover, it is worth noting the history of these debates so far. Until the publication of Cohen's book and Sir Richard Eggleston's *Evidence, Proof and Probability* nearly all of the writing on probabilities in law published in English in recent years has been in the United States. The leading American writers, Finkelstein, Fairley, Tribe, Cullison and Kaplan have been concerned with the potential and actual use and abuse of explicitly mathematical analysis in legal argument; they have tended to proceed on the assumption that all relevant probabilities are in principle mathematical. The central concern of Eggleston's book is also with the uses, abuses and limits of mathematical reasoning in law; it does not deal directly with the notion of non-Pascalian probabilities and the extent of their application to disputed issues of fact in legal contexts. It is an accident of history that Cohen's and Eggleston's books were published almost simultaneously so that neither directly confronts the issues raised by the other. Subsequently in a series of published and unpublished papers Sir Richard Eggleston has criticised Cohen's thesis on a number of particular grounds, but it is not yet clear whether or not he is committed to an out-and-out rejection of the notion of non-Pascalian probabilities nor of Cohen's central thesis about its extensive application in legal argument. Conversely Cohen, perhaps prematurely, has lumped Eggleston together with Glanville Williams and American lawyers who are, in his view, guilty of "misplaced mathematicisation."[30] We are, it is to be hoped, at a relatively early stage in this debate and must wait to see whether Eggleston will join Glanville Williams in directly contesting Cohen's central theoretical position. Similarly, there has yet to be a sustained response to Cohen's thesis from American "mathematicists" interested in law and from the continent of Europe, where an extensive literature on theoretical aspects of evidence and proof in law had developed in almost complete and mutual isolation from Anglo-American writings.[31]

The purpose of this paper is to introduce an important debate rather than to contribute to it. But it may be appropriate to end by sketching some tentative conclusions.

First, the revival of interest in probabilities in law promises to help to adjust a glaring imbalance in legal theory. The equation of "legal reasoning" (and even "lawyers' reasonings")[32] with reasoning about disputed questions of law

---

30. *Criminal Law Review* (1980), 91.
31. See e.g. references cited in Tibor Király *Criminal Procedure: Truth and Probability*, 1979.
32. Julius Stone *Legal System and Lawyers' Reasonings*, Stanford University Press, 1964.

is symptomatic of the imbalances and distortions resulting from the dominance of the Expository Tradition within academic law.[33] One could read much of the literature of jurisprudence without realising that decisions on sentencing and other sanctions, on procedural issues, on disputed questions of fact, and many other decisions in legal processes also involve *reasoning* in rather specialized kinds of context. Evidentiary issues about disputed questions of fact clearly involve probabilities, but so do decisions about sentencing and, to a lesser extent, other examples of "lawyers' reasonings."

Secondly, in considering reasoning about disputed questions of fact, it would be dangerous to assume that only one type of reasoning is involved or that all phases of such arguments are necessarily concerned with probabilities. Even in a simple-seeming case, in which there is only one disputed issue of fact, the structure of the argument may involve complex series of relations between a large number of propositions, as can be seen by looking at Wigmore's attempts to present the logical relations of arguments about mixed masses of evidence in diagrammatic form.[34] The structure of the arguments may be correspondingly complex and may quite appropriately involve a combination of different types of reasoning. We should not rule out the possibility that all of the types of probability mentioned above, and possibly others, may be involved in a single case. Accordingly one should be suspicious of suggestions that there is one characteristic or typical or central form of reasoning about probabilities in forensic contexts. Moreover, if Cohen's theory of Baconian probability and of its application to evidentiary issues is correct, it does not follow from this that interest in the uses, abuses and limitations of mathematical reasoning in such contexts is misplaced.

Thirdly, I am persuaded that non-Pascalian probabilities appropriately play an important role in reasoning about issues of fact in forensic contexts. This is not to say that all Cohen's arguments in support of this view are correct or that he has given an entirely acceptable account of the operation of those arguments in Anglo-American "adversary" proceedings; for example, given time, I would wish to take issue with his treatment of standards of proof and his analysis of some particular examples, in which policy considerations may have a more important role to play than he allows for. But at this stage in the debate, I am at least provisionally persuaded that Cohen has provided a generally convincing and highly sophisticated theoretical justification for the views not only of many practising lawyers and judges, but also of leading writers on evidence such as Bentham, Stephen and Wigmore.

33   See W. Twining "Academic Law and Legal Philosophy" 95 *Law Quarterly Review* (1979). 557. 570 I.
34.   J. H. Wigmore *The Science of Judicial Proof*, 3rd ed . 1937

64   The Liverpool Law Review Vol. II [1980]

Finally, as was suggested above, the range of disagreement between Cohen and the mathematicists may not be as wide as at first sight appears. Cohen concedes some place in forensic reasoning to Pascalian probabilities; at least some mathematicists readily acknowledge the limitations and dangers of resorting to statistical analysis in litigation. Cohen and the mathematicists have severally opened up a wide range of issues of practical as well as theoretical interest to lawyers. Perhaps Holmes was only half-right. The life of the lawyer of the future will need to include logic as well as statistics.

[8]

Focusing on the Defendant

THE HONOURABLE SIR RICHARD EGGLESTON

Former Judge of the Commonwealth Industrial Court, and of the Supreme Court of the Australian Capital Territory

In 1979, in his review of Jonathan Cohen's *The Probable and the Provable*, Professor Glanville Williams discussed Cohen's "paradox of the gatecrasher". The facts postulated by Cohen are that 499 people have paid for admission to a rodeo, and 1,000 are counted on the seats, A being one of those present. No other testimony is available as to whether A paid for his seat. To quote Cohen:

"So by any plausible criterion of mathematical probability there is a 0.501 probability, on the admitted facts, that he did not pay."[1]

Cohen considered it absurdly unjust to hold the defendant liable when there was a 0.499 probability that he did pay. Glanville Williams agreed in the result, but not in the reasoning. In his view, even if only fifty people of the thousand had paid, raising the mathematical probability to 0.95 or 95 per cent, "[i]t would still be wrong to give judgment against A". He illustrated the problem by another example:

"For instance, if the Blue Bus Co. has far more buses on the road than the Red Bus Co., this is no reason in law for assuming that the plaintiff was knocked down by a blue bus rather than a red bus. Otherwise, the Blue Bus Co. would have to pay the damages in all cases where the sole issue is the ownership of the offending bus and it cannot be shown whether the bus was blue or red."[2]

Professor Williams's explanation for this conclusion is that statistics cannot make good a deficiency of evidence involving the particular defendant, and that the reason why the proof fails in these cases is that

"it does not sufficiently mark out the defendant from the others. . . . This requirement that evidence should focus on the defendant must be taken to be a rule of law relating to proof, distinct from the general rule governing quantum of proof."[3]

In my contribution to this debate[4] I pointed out that the practice of the courts was inconsistent with the requirement that the evidence should in some way mark out the defendant, since in a case where the plaintiff was in doubt as to the person from whom he was entitled to relief, he could join all the possible defendants, and the court would not dismiss his claim merely because at the end of his case he had not focused on any particular person. Professor Williams's suggested rule to this effect was not in my view supported by the authorities.[5] It may be observed that all these discussions proceed on the basis that *no other evidence is available*. Before we could accept the proposition that any spectator at the rodeo is as likely to be a gatecrasher as any other, which is an essential condition for the conclusion that A, chosen at random, is more likely than not to be a gatecrasher, we would need to be satisfied that there is in fact no evidence available as to the size of the hole in the fence (if any), how many of the spectators were small boys, and so on. Cohen eliminated these factors by his statement that "by any plausible criterion of mathematical probability there is a 0.501 probability, on the admitted facts, that he did not pay", but such a situation would of course be extremely rare in practice.

My attention has recently been drawn to a South Australian case in which reference was

---

[1] L. Jonathan Cohen, *The Probable and the Provable* (1977), p. 75.

[2] Glanville Williams, "The Mathematics of Proof" [1979] Crim. Law Rev. 297 at 304.

[3] Ibid., at 305.

[4] "The Probability Debate" [1980] Crim. Law Rev. 678.

[5] Ibid., at 681. See also Eggleston, *Evidence Proof and Probability* (2nd ed., 1983), pp. 40-42.

made to the disagreement between Professor Williams and myself. In *State Government Insurance Commission v. Laube*[6] the Full Court of the Supreme Court of South Australia had to consider a case in which the insured motorist was being sued by the State Government Insurance Commission for recoupment of damages paid to an injured pedestrian on the basis that, as he was proved to have had a blood alcohol reading of 0.155 seventy-five minutes after the accident, he was in breach of the warranty that the insured would not drive the vehicle while so much under the influence of intoxicating liquor as to be incapable of exercising effective control of the vehicle. The relevant Act, namely, the *Motor Vehicles Act 1959 (S.A.)*, provided that recovery of so much of the loss as "the court thinks just and reasonable in the circumstances" could be obtained

"if an insured person incurs any liability against which he is insured under this Part and he contravenes or fails to comply with . . . a term of the policy of insurance, and the insurer has been prejudiced thereby . . .".

The trial judge had declined to hold that the defendant was in breach of his warranty and his decision was upheld by the Full Court.

The defendant did not give evidence at the trial. His own version as given to the police was that he was at a party at the Lakes at Mt Gambier until after 1 a.m. When he left the party he was going uphill past a group of people on the left side on the road when he felt a bump, and noticed that the left front wheel was scraping something. After driving on he stopped and found the left front mudguard rubbing on the tyre. He pulled the metal away and after driving around for a while he went back and saw the lights of police vehicles and an ambulance. It dawned on him that the bump could have been a person hitting the vehicle, so he went to the police station.

The only evidence called at the trial consisted of the police brief including the defendant's statement and the evidence of a medical expert who testified that in his view "a level of the order of 0.15 implied that a particular person is most unlikely not to be impaired to a significant degree by the effects of alcohol".[7] He was asked whether he considered that *any* person with

blood alcohol level of 0.15 has an impairment in their ability to drive. His answer was:

"I would rather not agree to the suggestion when it includes any person. Strictly speaking I cannot guarantee that every person will be impaired up to a particular level on the grounds not every person has been tested."[8]

After referring briefly to the evidence, King C.J. said:[9]

"The most that can be said is that it is statistically more probable than not that any individual with such a blood alcohol level would be incapable of exercising effective control. [After referring to the *Criminal Law Review* debate, and to my book, he continued:] Professor Glanville Williams refers to a rule of law relating to proof 'that evidence should focus on the defendant'. Despite the Eggleston view ([1980] Crim. L.R. at 681) I am clearly of the opinion that the statistical fact that a particular proposition is true of the majority of persons cannot of itself amount to legal proof on the balance of probabilities that the proposition is true of any given individual. . . .

In my opinion it was not proved on the balance of probabilities that the respondent was under the influence of intoxicating liquor, still less that he was so much under the influence as to be incapable of effective control of a motor vehicle."

Millhouse J., agreeing that the appeal should be dismissed, said that the appellant had failed to show that the respondent was incapable of exercising effective control of his motor car, and had therefore failed to show a breach of the policy.

The third member of the Court, Prior J., appeared to be of opinion that the doctor's evidence would have been sufficient if only he had been asked the right questions:

"Dr James should have been asked whether the accident described may have indicated an impairment of Mr Laube's faculties. I think the answer would have been in the affirmative . . . ."[10]

Our concern is not with the approach of Prior J. but with the proposition of King C.J.,

---

[6] (1984) 37 S.A.S.R. 31.
[7] Ibid., at 38.

[8] Ibid., at 36.
[9] Ibid., at 33.
[10] Ibid., at 39.

supported as it is by the statement of Millhouse J. referred to above, that the statistical fact that a particular proposition is true of the majority of persons cannot of itself amount to legal proof on the balance of probabilities that the proposition is true of any given individual.

The subject is one on which there is little direct authority, but such as there is tends to refute the proposition. In *M'Donald v. M'Donald*[11] all three members of the House of Lords who took part in the case expressed the view that in assessing the expectation of life of a particular person, his expectation should prima facie be taken as that of an average person of that age, and it would be for those opposing that conclusion to bring evidence to show his actual state of health. The case was one in which the tenant in tail in possession of a Scottish estate sought to bar the entail. To do so he had to compensate those living persons who might succeed him as tenants in tail in possession. The first such person was his brother, Captain M'Donald, who supported his claim, and declined to be medically examined. Their Lordships said that his expectation of life should in the first instance be taken from the life tables, but that the other remaindermen, whose interest it was to reduce that figure, should be permitted to bring evidence as to his actual state of health.

Similarly, in *Rowley v. London and North Western Railway Co.*,[12] where the question was as to the damages to be paid in respect of the death of an attorney who had covenanted to pay his mother an annuity of 200 pounds a year during their joint lives, the majority of the Court said that the "jury might properly be directed to consider the lives in question as average lives, unless there was some evidence to the contrary".

These are cases of estimates of future events, in which the use of statistical tables is well recognised. In point of probability theory, however, there is no difference between the assessment of the probability of a future event and the assessment of the probability of a past event, the outcome of which is unknown. Whether we assess the likelihood of turning up a spade before we deal the card, or after we have dealt it and before we turn the card over, our estimate of the probability must be the same. That it is legitimate to use statistical frequencies in assessing the likelihood of *past* events was recognised by the High Court of Australia in *Luxton v. Vines*.[13] In that case the plaintiff had been struck from behind and was unable to say what had struck him. After pointing out that in order to succeed against the defendant (the Nominal Defendant) the plaintiff must prove that the injury arose out of the use of a motor car, the majority (Dixon, Fullagar and Kitto JJ.) said that in order to establish this

"he must primarily rely on the exclusion by the medical opinion, concerning his injuries, of any probability that they were caused by a mere fall. He must also rely on the existence nowadays of a higher a priori probability that if something on a highway runs a man down it will be a motor vehicle and not some other form of traffic. It may be conceded that these two considerations on which the plaintiff relies do suffice to raise a reasonable inference, in the absence of evidence to the contrary, that the plaintiff's injuries were the result of a motor vehicle coming into contact with him."[14]

An even more striking case of the reliance on mathematical calculations of probability is *The Brimnes*.[15] The question at issue was whether a payment had been received before a notice of withdrawal. The exact times were not known, but in each case the earlier and later limits of the time were known. Cairns L.J. reviewed the evidence and concluded: "A simple calculation will show that the mathematical probability was that there was only about one chance in seven of the payment being first."[16] Megaw L.J. agreed and Edmund Davies L.J. said: "My brethren have gone some distance towards satisfying me that the mathematical probabilities are in favour of the owners' contention . . . ."[17]

Another case in the Court of Appeal shows that where statistics are involved they need not be published statistics. In that case the accused was charged with robbery. It was alleged that with three others he had entered an office and demanded money. No doubt as a measure of intimidation, the leader of the party had broken an internal window. A scientist testified that he

---

[11] (1880) 5 App. Cas. 519 at 529, 532, 541.
[12] (1873) L.R. 8 Ex. 221 at 227.
[13] (1952) 85 C.L.R. 352.
[14] Ibid., at 359.
[15] *Tenax Steamship Co. Ltd v. The Brimnes (Owners)* [1975] Q.B. 929.
[16] Ibid., at 970.
[17] Ibid., at 951.

had analysed fragments of glass from the shoes of the accused (some from the soles and some on the upper part and inside the shoe itself) and had found that the refractive index of the glass was identical with that of glass from the broken window. All glass has a refractive index capable of being determined to five decimal places, and the Home Office had collected statistics of the refractive index of glass analysed in forensic laboratories over a number of years. Having consulted these statistics, the expert found that this refractive index only occurred in 4 per cent of all the analyses that had been made. He then expressed the view that

"considering that only 4 per cent of controlled glass samples actually have this refractive index I consider there is very strong evidence that the glass from the shoes is in fact the same as the glass from the window, in fact it originated from the window".[18]

The Court held that the expert was entitled to rely on the Home Office statistics, even though he had not himself done all the analyses, and even though the statistics did not appear in a textbook or other publication.

There are, it is true, some statements in the United States which reject mathematical probabilities as a basis for fact-finding. Thus in *Day v. Boston and Marine Railroad*[19] Emery J. said:

"That in one throw of dice there is a quantitative probability, or greater chance, that a less number of spots than sixes will fall uppermost is no evidence whatever that in a given throw such was the actual result. Without something more, the actual result of the throw would still be utterly unknown. The slightest real evidence that sixes did in fact fall uppermost would outweigh all the probability otherwise."

It will be observed that there is an internal inconsistency in this statement. The first sentence says that the mathematical probability affords no evidence whatever, but the last says that evidence, however slight, of the actual result will *outweigh* the mathematical probability, which implies that in the absence of such evidence the mathematical probability has

some weight. Underlying this distrust of mathematics is an attitude that was made manifest in another American case, *Sargent v. Massachusetts Accident Co.*,[20] where Lummus J. said:

"It has been held not enough that mathematically the chances somewhat favour a proposition to be proved ... After the evidence has been weighed, that proposition is proved by a preponderance of the evidence if it is made to appear more likely or probable in the sense that actual belief in its truth, derived from the evidence, exists in the mind or minds of the tribunal notwithstanding any doubts that may still linger there."

In *Smith v. Rapid Transit Inc.*[21] where the plaintiff, claiming to have been forced into a collision by a bus which she could not identify, sued the only operator licensed to ply on that route, the statement of Lummus J. was cited with approval, the Court accepting the view that the mathematical probabilities favoured the plaintiff's contention, but holding that that was not enough.

In the United States, writers on evidence have rejected the notion that "belief in the truth" of a proposition is required before a finding of fact can be made[22] and I have given my reasons elsewhere for taking a similar view.[23] But whatever attitude we take to the standard of proof, what is at issue in the present discussion is the general proposition that statistical data about the general population can never satisfy that standard in relation to an individual. But as appears from *Luxton v. Vines*, even Sir Owen Dixon, who was the leading exponent of the "actual belief in the truth" position in this country, was prepared to hold that it was possible that a statistical probability could be high enough to meet the standard.

In truth the argument against this view is a reversion to the argument that was rejected as

---

[18] *Reg. v. Abadom* [1983] 1 W.L.R. 126 at 128.
[19] *Day v. Boston and Marine Railroad* (1902) 96 Me. 207 at 217-218; 52 A. 771 at 774; 90 Am. St. Rep. 335 at 340.

[20] (1940) 29 N.E. 2d 825.
[21] *Smith v. Rapid Transit Inc.* (1945) 58 N.E. 2d 754.
[22] V. C. Ball, "The Moment of Truth" [1961] *Vanderbilt Law Review* 807 at 822; *McCormick on Evidence* (2nd ed., 1972), pp. 794-795; R. K. Winter, "The Jury and the Risk of Non-Persuasion" (1971) 5 *Law and Society Review* 335 at 337.
[23] R. M. Eggleston, *Evidence Proof and Probability* (2nd ed., 1983), pp. 129-137; see also my chapter "Subjective Probability and the Law" in *Uncertain Outcomes* (MTP Press, Lancaster, 1979), pp. 127-145.

long ago as *Byrne v. Boadle*.[24] In that case the defendant cited *Hammack v. White*[25] in which Erle C.J. had said that the plaintiff was not entitled to have his case left to the jury unless he gave some affirmative evidence that there had been negligence on the part of the defendant. Pollock C.B. said that Erle C.J. must have been referring to the nature of the accident in that particular case, and Bramwell B. added:

> "No doubt the presumption of negligence is not raised in every case of injury by accident, but in some it is . . . we know that these accidents do not take place without a cause, and *in general* that cause is negligence."[26]

Ever since *Byrne v. Boadle*, disguised under the tag, res ipsa loquitur, the view has been accepted that tribunals are entitled to apply generalisations derived from common human experience to the finding of facts involving the conduct of individuals, even though no specific act in breach of duty can be assigned. The refusal of the South Australian Full Court to make a finding against the defendant in the absence of evidence of some specific failure to control his vehicle is bad enough, but to say that the evidence of his blood alcohol level, coupled with that of the medical expert, could not even establish "on the balance of probabilities that he was under the influence of intoxicating liquor"[27] is in my view indefensible.

Before leaving *Laube's* case, reference should be made to the fact that two of the judges cited the decision of Bray C.J. in *Samuels v. Flavel*.[28] That was a criminal prosecution for driving a motor car "while he was so much under the influence of intoxicating liquor or a drug as to be incapable of exercising proper control over the vehicle". In fact, the defendant's blood alcohol level was 0.18 per cent. The police evidence was that although the defendant had driven the wrong way in a one-way street (being unfamiliar with the neighbourhood) he had parked his car correctly, was steady on his feet and neat in his appearance, and answered questions rationally and politely; moreover, the constable who tested him formed the opinion that he was sober. According to Bray C.J., the effect of the expert evidence was that at a level

of 0.180 per cent, 80 per cent of persons would show clinical impairment and 20 per cent would not. In the circumstances, it is not surprising that he found the evidence insufficient to sustain the charge. But his observations afford little support for the conclusions of King C.J. in the later case. He said that expert evidence of the kind tendered as to the effect of alcohol was of course admissible, and might afford confirmation of the evidence of observers

> "and no doubt there may be cases when it can be used to effect when there are no observers, and even possibly where a court could feel it safe to act on it in preference to the evidence of observers. There may also be cases when a court of appeal thinks that the rejection of expert evidence by the trial judge was so unreasonable as to compel its intervention . . . . But this it will do more readily when the issue only has to be proved on the balance of probabilities, and not beyond reasonable doubt."

In view of the expert evidence, there was clearly a gap capable of creating a reasonable doubt.[29]

If, as we have submitted above, the courts habitually use generalisations derived from common experience as a guide to the probabilities engendered by the evidence, surely where generalisations are established by statistical or other scientific research, or where common generalisations are supported or contradicted by such research, expert witnesses should be allowed to say so.[30]

The foregoing discussion illustrates the crying need for the legal profession to devote more attention to the underlying philosophy of the law of evidence and the fact-finding process. Another example, also involving a decision of the South Australian Full Court, can be found in the judgment of Gibbs C.J. and Mason J. in the High Court of Australia, in *Chamberlain v. The Queen*.[31] In *Reg. v. Van Beelen*[32] the South Australian Full Court had said that it was

---

[24] *Byrne v. Boadle* (1863) 2 H. & C. 722; 159 E.R. 299.
[25] (1862) 11 C.B.N.S. 588 at 594; 142 E.R. 926 at 929.
[26] 2 H.&C. at 726; 159 E.R. at 300 [emphasis added].
[27] See text above corresponding to n. 9, ante.
[28] (1970) 37 S.A.S.R. 256.

[29] Ibid., at 258-259.
[30] For a discussion of the role of generalisations in fact-finding see R. M. Eggleston, "Generalisations and Experts" in *Facts in Law* (Proceedings of the 9th Annual Conference of the Association for Legal and Social Philosophy, 1982) ARSP Beiheft No. 16, Wiesbaden (1983), pp. 22-36.
[31] *Chamberlain v. The Queen* (1984) 153 C.L.R. 521 at 538.
[32] *Reg. v. Van Beelen* (1973) 4 S.A.S.R. 353 at 379.

Evidence and Proof

"an obvious proposition in logic, that you cannot be satisfied beyond reasonable doubt of the truth of an inference drawn from facts about the existence of which you are in doubt".

In *Chamberlain v. The Queen* the judges mentioned expressed their agreement with this view, and their disagreement with the criticism I had voiced of that statement. In doing so, their Honours said that it must be taken that the Full Court was intending to say that inferences cannot be drawn from facts that remain doubtful at the end of the jury's consideration, and did not mean that facts which, viewed in isolation, seem doubtful must be disregarded. Although there are passages in *Van Beelen* which taken by themselves might suggest that the jury cannot "take into account" any material of which they are doubtful,[33] the interpretation put upon the decision by their Honours in the High Court means that the tribunal can retain consideration of doubtful evidence until all the evidence is in, but if it remains doubtful at that point the evidence must be discarded.[34]

This view does not accord with the dictates of probability theory, and may result in the rejection of inferences which are fully justified. If a coin is tossed ten times, the probability that at least one toss resulted in a head is one minus the probability that all tosses resulted in a tail. Assuming the coin is fair, that is to say, that the probability of a tail on each toss is 1/2, the probability that at least one head was tossed is $1 - (1/2)^{10}$, that is to say, 0.99902, or more than 99.9 per cent. So that although we do not know the outcome of any one toss, we can be reasonably certain that at least one head was tossed.

To illustrate how this principle might work in a trial, let us consider two cases. In the first, a murder takes place in the presence of a number of bystanders, all of whom knew the accused beforehand. All agree that the accused struck the fatal blow. Even if one feels that some of the witnesses are less than reliable, if the tribunal is satisfied beyond reasonable doubt that at least one is telling the truth, the accused will be found guilty. But if the tribunal is so satisfied, it

follows that all the witnesses are telling the truth. In this case it is true to say that the tribunal cannot convict unless it is satisfied that all the evidence on which it relies is true beyond reasonable doubt.

But suppose a case in which there is only one witness to the murder, but several other persons, who know the accused, say they saw him in the town where the crime occurred on that day. But as none of them were together when they saw him, no witness corroborates any other as to the particular identification. The defence of the accused is that he was many miles away and was never in the town on that day. In this case the jury may well have doubts as to each identification, but because they think it very highly improbable that all these witnesses could be lying or mistaken, they are satisfied beyond reasonable doubt that the alibi is false, and that the eyewitness is telling the truth.

This does not require them to decide that every witness who identified the accused is telling the truth, or which of them is truthful. Or, to take an example similar to the facts of the *Van Beelen* case itself, where identification of the accused depended on comparison of a number of different types of particles found in the clothes of the accused and the victim, a jury might well feel that there is a possibility of mistake in identifying any one particle with its opposite number from the other location, but might yet be satisfied beyond reasonable doubt that a sufficient number of matches would still remain after all the possibilities of error had been allowed for. Again, it would not be necessary to decide which identifications were free from error.[35]

Accordingly, it would in my submission be a misdirection to tell the jury that it should ignore any item of evidence if, at the close of the case, it was not satisfied beyond reasonable doubt that that evidence was true. In my view, Napier J. was correct in *Hinton v. Trotter*[36] when he said that

---

[33] E.g., at 374, 378-379.

[34] Brennan J. (at 599) seems to have gone even further: "First, the primary facts from which the inference of guilt is to be drawn must be proved beyond reasonable doubt. No greater cogency can be attributed to an inference based on particular facts than the cogency that can be attributed to each of those facts."

[35] In the coin-tossing example, we can multiply together the probabilities of a tail on each toss, since the outcomes are independent of each other. In the case of witnesses, however, even if we could assign a figure to the probability of error or deception, problems of independence would arise: see *Evidence Proof and Probability*, pp. 14-15, 204-205.

[36] [1931] S.A.S.R. 123 at 126, quoted in *Reg. v. Grant* [1964] S.A.S.R. 331, which was disapproved by Gibbs C.J. and Mason J. in *Chamberlain v. The Queen*, loc. cit., n. 31, ante at 538.

"facts which remain in doubt may be called in aid to fortify the inference from the other evidence, and it would be a misdirection to say that they cannot be considered at all".

By the same token, it is incorrect to say, as the South Australian Full Court said:[37]

"There is a clear distinction between drawing an inference of guilt from a combination of several proved facts, none of which by itself would support the inference, and drawing an inference of guilt from several facts whose existence is in doubt. In the first place the combination does what each fact taken in isolation could not do; in the second case the combination counts for nothing."

It is possible once more to make the point that probability theory can teach us lessons about fact-finding, even though we are quite unable to attach numerical values to the probabilities with which we are dealing.[38]

---

[37] (1973) 4 S.A.S.R. at 374.

[38] See, for example, *Evidence Proof and Probability*, at pp. xiii, 176, 207, and "The Mathematics of Corroboration" [1985] Crim. Law Rev. 640.

[9]

The Limits of the Preponderance of the Evidence Standard: Justifiably Naked Statistical Evidence and Multiple Causation

David Kaye

The preponderance-of-the-evidence standard usually is understood to mean that the plaintiff must show that the probability that the defendant is in fact liable exceeds 1/2. Several commentators and at least one court have suggested that in some situations it may be preferable to make each defendant pay plaintiff's damages discounted by the probability that the defendant in question is in fact liable. This article analyzes these and other decision rules from the standpoint of statistical decision theory. It argues that in most cases involving only one potential defendant, the conventional interpretation of the preponderance standard is appropriate, but it notes an important exception. The article also considers cases involving many defendants, only one of whom could have caused the injury to plaintiff. It argues that ordinarily the single defendant most likely to have been responsible should be liable for all the damages, even when the probability associated with this defendant is less than 1/2. At the same time, it identifies certain multiple-defendant cases in which the rule that weights each defendant's damages by the probability of that defendant's liability should apply.

I. INTRODUCTION

Quantitative or mathematical evidence typically has been a source of bewilderment to the legal profession.[1] Consider, for example, the following hypothetical case posed by Richard Lempert:

> [T]here are two taxicab companies in town who have identical cabs except that one has red cabs and the other green cabs. [S]ixty percent of all cabs in town are red. Plaintiff has been knocked down on a deserted street by a cab. He is color blind and cannot distinguish red from green. Shortly after the accident a taxicab driver said over the air, "I just hit someone at (the

David Kaye is Professor of Law, Arizona State University. S.B., 1968, M.I.T.; A.M., 1969, Harvard; J.D., 1972, Yale.

Preparation of this article was aided by the Faculty Grant-in-Aid Program of Arizona State University. I am also grateful to Richard Lempert for prodding me into thinking about some of the issues addressed here and to Richard Epstein, Dennis Karjala, Spencer Kimball, Glen Robinson, and Dennis Young for commenting on a draft of this article.

1. See, e.g., Ira M. Ellman & David Kaye, Probabilities and Proof: Can HLA and Blood Group Testing Prove Paternity? 54 N.Y.U. L. Rev. 1131 (1979); David Kaye, The Laws of Probability and the Law of the Land, 47 U. Chi. L. Rev. 34 n.1 (1979).

accident location). I should have seen him, but I was drinking and going too fast." The static was such that no identification of the voice was possible, but the frequency is used only by cabs from that town. Neither company keeps dispatch records, so [neither knows] what drivers were in what parts of town. And to make things complete, the garage in which all the cabs of the two companies [were] housed was burned down the night of the accident.[2]

If plaintiff could conclusively establish all these facts, should he be permitted to collect from the Red Company?

Lempert's illustration is but one of several cases, some hypothetical and some real, involving proof by what has been termed "naked statistical evidence."[3] In response to such cases courts have issued seemingly conflicting opinions often disapproving of this mode of proof.[4] Commentators, in their turn, have propounded a bewildering collection of explanations for this judicial reticence. Thus, it has been suggested that the cardinal structure of mathematical probability theory is incompatible with the law of evidence,[5] that courts seek to equalize the incidence of errors favoring plaintiffs and defendants even though this policy increases the number of mistaken verdicts,[6] and that the law governing the situation is essentially anomalous.[7] As I have argued elsewhere,[8] however, the legal issue created by naked statistical evidence can be resolved satisfactorily if it is granted that in most cases probative, nonquantitative evidence should also be readily available. In these circumstances, a rule requiring that at least some such evidence be brought to bear on the case is not so mysterious. It is merely a device calculated to enhance the accuracy of the fact-finding process in a manner that is fair to both parties and that is not overly burdensome to the proponent of the statistical evidence.[9]

2. Letter from Richard Lempert to David Kaye, Apr. 2, 1980, p. 1.
3. David Kaye, Naked Statistical Evidence (Book Review), 89 Yale L.J. 601 (1980) (*reviewing* Finkelstein), *infra* note 6.
4. E.g., Kaminsky v. Hertz Corp., 94 Mich. App. 356 (1979); David Kaye, Paradoxes, Gedanken Experiments and the Burden of Proof: A Response to Dr. Cohen's Reply, 1981 Ariz. St. L.J. 635.
5. L. Jonathan Cohen, The Probable and the Provable (London: Oxford University Press, Clarendon Press, 1977); Lea Brilmayer & Lewis Kornhauser, Review: Quantitative Methods and Legal Decisions, 46 U. Chi. L. Rev. 116, 135–48 (1978); L. Jonathan Cohen, Subjective Probability and the Paradox of the Gatecrasher, 1981 Ariz. St. L.J. 627.
6. Michael O. Finkelstein, Quantitative Methods in Law: Studies in the Application of Mathematical Probability and Statistics to Legal Problems 69 (New York: Free Press, 1978).
7. Michael J. Saks & Robert F. Kidd, Human Information Processing and Adjudication: Trial by Heuristics, 15 Law & Soc'y Rev. 123, 151 (1980–81) (decrying "the myth of particularistic proof"); Glanville Williams, The Mathematics of Proof I, 1979 Crim. L. Rev. 297, 305.
8. See Kaye, *supra* note 4, at 635 n.1.
9. A less procrustean rule might serve this same function. Where a party inexplicably fails to produce evidence under circumstances in which he would be expected to have favorable evidence, an inference that the evidence is in fact unfavorable could be drawn. See authorities cited, David Kaye, Probability Theory Meets Res Ipsa Loquitur, 77 Mich. L. Rev. 1456, 1475 n.59 (1979).
In a few situations a rule disfavoring naked statistical evidence can be defended on another

Still, this simple explanation does not supply a sufficient rationale for resolving all cases of naked statistical evidence. There may be instances in which useful, nonquantitative evidence is all but impossible to obtain. Lempert's taxicab case is one. The hypothetical facts are carefully crafted to ensure that the plaintiff could not be expected to adduce much more than the background statistics about red and green taxicabs. Nor, alas, can that case be dismissed as another manifestation of the well-known perversity of law professors. Although instances of "justifiably" naked statistical evidence may be rare, a few do find their way into the lawbooks. Thus, in *Sindell v. Abbott Laboratories*,[10] plaintiff brought a class action against 11 named drug companies that manufactured and marketed diethylstilbestrol. For a time, this compound, commonly referred to by its initials DES, had been prescribed to prevent miscarriage. Plaintiff alleged that the defendant companies knew or should have known that DES was ineffective in preventing miscarriage and that it would cause carcinomas in the daughters of the mothers who took it. The trial court dismissed the action because the plaintiff could not identify which company had manufactured the dosage responsible for her injuries. Plaintiff's difficulty in making this identification was not hard to explain. DES was often sold under a generic rather than a brand name, and in the two or three decades since the drug was prescribed, memories have faded and prescriptions have been lost or destroyed. Noting that DES victims can hardly be faulted for being unable to point to anything more individualized than statistics describing how much DES each company marketed for use in the prevention of miscarriages, the California Supreme Court reversed. It held that if plaintiff could prove her allegations of negligence and damages, then she should be entitled to recover from each defendant in proportion to that defendant's DES sales.[11] These figures, the court reasoned, could serve as an acceptable "measure of the

---

ground as well. Cohen's "paradox of the gatecrasher" (see note 5 *supra*) is a good illustration of a case in which the plaintiff has no evidence with which to distinguish any specific defendant from many other possible defendants who are equally likely to be liable. It can be argued that notwithstanding whatever probability theory may teach us, assuring the appearance of fairness precludes imposing liability in the absence of some evidence singling out particular defendants.

10. 26 Cal. 3d 588, 163 Cal. Rptr. 132, 607 P.2d 924 (1980).

11. The Supreme Court left open the possibility that a defendant could somehow demonstrate at trial that it did not market the quantity of DES that had caused plaintiff's cancer. 26 Cal. 3d at 612. It also indicated that plaintiff must join the manufacturers of a "substantial share" of the DES marketed for the prevention of miscarriages. *Id.* Commentary on these and other aspects of *Sindell* includes Glen O. Robinson, Multiple Causation in Tort Law: Reflections on the DES Cases, 68 Va. L. Rev. 713 (1982); Note, *Sindell v. Abbott Laboratories:* A Market Share Approach to DES Causation, 69 Calif. L. Rev. 1179 (1981) [hereinafter cited as A Market Share Approach]; Note, Market Share Liability: An Answer to the DES Causation Problem, 94 Harv. L. Rev. 668 (1981) [hereinafter cited as Market Share Liability]; Case Comment, Refining Market Share Liability: *Sindell v. Abbott Laboratories*, 33 Stan. L. Rev. 937 (1981) [hereinafter cited as Refining Market Share Liability].

490   AMERICAN BAR FOUNDATION RESEARCH JOURNAL   1982:487

likelihood that . . . the defendants supplied the product which allegedly injured plaintiff.''[12] The dissent tartly observed that under this rule ''a particular defendant may be held proportionately liable *even though mathematically it is much more likely than not that it played no role whatever in causing plaintiffs' injuries.*''[13]

Although *Sindell,* like the hypothetical taxicab case, involves naked statistical evidence as to the identity of a wrongdoer, the same type of evidence can arise in connection with very different factual questions. *Sindell* focuses on which defendant produced certain pills. No less important is the question of whether DES caused plaintiff's ailments. Presumably, the evidence that supports this allegation consists of a comparison of the incidence of adenosis and adenocarcinoma among ''DES daughters'' as opposed to otherwise similarly situated women.[14] If these conditions are sufficiently concentrated among the former group, the inference that DES is to blame in these cases seems warranted.[15] If we take the trouble to quantify the numbers involved, it becomes clear that we have another instance of proof by justifiably naked statistical evidence.[16]

Cases like *Sindell,* involving many defendants each of whom might have caused or contributed to a legally cognizable injury, also lead us into the tangled thicket of doctrines concerning multiple causation, joint tortfeasors, contribution, and apportionment of damages.[17] Did each of the *Sindell* defendants, for example, produce a share of the DES that affected the plaintiff, or did only one pharmaceutical house cause the individual plaintiff's injury? The answer to this question may determine which of several distinct legal doctrines comes into play.[18] Yet the *Sindell* court shifts unthinkingly from one perspective to the other.[19]

12. 26 Cal. 3d at 611, 163 Cal. Rptr. at 145, 607 P.2d at 937.

13. *Id.* at 616, 163 Cal. Rptr. at 147, 607 P.2d at 939.

14. It has been said that the particular form of cancer linked with DES, clear-cell adenocarcinoma, used to be rare. Comment, DES and a Proposed Theory of Enterprise Liability, 46 Fordham L. Rev. 963, 965 n.8 (1978) (*citing* Ulfelder, The Stilbestrol-Adenosis-Carcinoma Syndrome, 38 Cancer 426, 428 (1976)) [hereinafter cited as Comment, DES and a Proposed Theory].

15. It might be argued that DES is but one of several contributing causes. If such joint causation were present, the epidemiological data might be used to assess the relative magnitude of the contribution from DES. Whether it would then be appropriate to apportion damages in light of this figure is an interesting question. See, e.g., text and accompanying notes 70–73 *infra.* The apportionment issue, however, is distinct from the naked statistical evidence problem. It would arise even if the extent of relative contributions were quantified on the basis of ''individualized'' evidence.

16. See text accompanying notes 22–25 *infra.*

17. See generally, e.g., Frank H. Easterbrook, William M. Landes, & Richard A. Posner, Contribution Among Antitrust Defendants: A Legal and Economic Analysis, 23 J.L. & Econ. 331 (1980); William M. Landes & Richard A. Posner, Joint and Multiple Tortfeasors: An Economic Analysis, 9 J. Legal Stud. 517 (1980); A. Mitchell Polinsky & Steven Shavell, Contribution and Claim Reduction Among Antitrust Defendants: An Economic Analysis, 33 Stan. L. Rev. 447 (1981); Mario J. Rizzo & Frank S. Arnold, Causal Apportionment in the Law of Torts: An Economic Theory, 80 Colum. L. Rev. 1399 (1980); Robinson, *supra* note 11.

18. See note 15 *supra* and text accompanying notes 70–73 *infra.*

· 19. Compare 26 Cal. 3d at 612, 163 Cal. Rptr. at 145, 607 P.2d at 937 (''If plaintiff joins in the

In the hope of clarifying the issues arising in cases of naked statistical evidence and multiple causation, this article focuses on two recurring problems. The first is what to do when the only obstacle to recovery is plaintiff's justifiable inability to come forward with anything more than background statistics pointing to a single defendant (as opposed to natural forces or other factors that could not give rise to liability) as the cause of his injury. Part II treats this problem with the tools of statistical decision theory. It argues that ordinarily the traditional more-probable-than-not interpretation of the preponderance-of-the-evidence standard should be applied to the quantitifed probability. It contrasts this "maximum likelihood" rule with an "expected value" rule that would discount the damages by the probability involved, and it concludes that in one category of cases the maximum likelihood rule should yield to the expected value rule.

Part III enlarges the mathematical analysis to cope with the second problem—what to do when the only obstacle to recovery is plaintiff's justifiable inability to single out one of many possible causes to which liability might attach. Either the plaintiff must rely on background statistics to arrive at a probability figure greater than one-half, or, however the figure pertaining to the most probably liable defendant may be arrived at, it simply does not exceed one-half. It is shown that in these situations, the conventional understanding of the preponderance-of-the-evidence standard is in error. The maximum likelihood principle underlying this standard then demands only that liability be assigned to the single defendant who the evidence reveals was the most likely cause of the injury. Again, however, I argue that there are limited circumstances under which an expected value approach should substitute for the preponderance requirement.

Part IV illustrates how the framework constructed in parts II and III can be applied to some representative cases involving uncertainty in the identification of the one defendant who caused an injury. The now classic case of *Summers v. Tice*,[20] among others, is discussed. The distinct problem of allocating damages among concurrent causes is also mentioned but shown to be left unresolved by the analysis developed here. Finally, part V summarizes the argument, with particular attention to its assumptions and limitations.

---

action the manufacturers of a substantial share of the DES which her mother might have taken, the injustice of shifting the burden of proof to defendants . . . is significantly diminished") with *id.* at 612 n.28, 163 Cal. Rptr. at 145 n.28, 607 P.2d at 937 n.28 ("[i]f X [m]anufacturer sold one-fifth of all the DES prescribed for pregnancy and identification could be made in all cases, X would be the sole defendant in approximately one-fifth of all cases and liable for damages in those cases" (*quoting* Comment, DES and a Proposed Theory, *supra* note 14)).

20. 33 Cal. 2d 80, 199 P.2d 1 (1948).

492   **AMERICAN BAR FOUNDATION RESEARCH JOURNAL**   **1982:487**

II. Single Defendant Cases

A. Some Plausible Decision Rules

Analytically, the simplest cases of naked statistical evidence occur when only one person would be liable under plaintiff's allegations. Imagine, by way of illustration, that a worker in a chemical factory that produces phenoxy acids for herbicides develops stomach cancer. At issue is whether this is a work-related injury covered by a workers' compensation statute. Epidemiological studies, let us suppose, reveal that the incidence of stomach cancer among workers exposed to phenoxy acids is higher than the rate in the rest of the population.[21] Nevertheless, there is a nonzero rate (call it b, for base rate) outside the industry. Hence, when a particular worker develops stomach cancer, it is difficult to know whether it is the result of his working near the apparent carcinogens or whether he would have contracted the disease had he been otherwise employed. The evidence on this point is necessarily overtly statistical.[22] Assuming that the rest of the population constitutes an appropriate control group, the probability λ that the cancer was "caused" by working can be expressed in terms of the base rate b and the rate for workers (which we shall denote as a).[23] The increment in the probability of contracting liver cancer due to working is simply $a - b$. Roughly speaking, out of every a workers who develop stomach cancer, $a - b$ would not have been afflicted had they stayed away from employment near phenoxy acids. This is to say that $\lambda = (a - b)/a$.

For concreteness, suppose that the stomach cancer rate is three times higher among workers than among the rest of the population. Substituting $a = 3b$ into the equation for λ indicates that $\lambda = 2/3$. Should a court or agency conclude that the cancer in the case it is considering is work related? If all naked statistical evidence were disfavored, the answer would be no and recovery would be barred. Yet this "no recovery" rule seems inapt since this is a case of *justifiably* naked statistical evidence. The worker has stomach cancer, and there is no known way to tell a phenoxy acid–induced stomach cancer from other stomach cancers. Ex-

---

21. Although the probability figures that will be used here are merely illustrative, the possibility of some measurable discrepancy is real. See Defoliant, Cancer: Studies Show Link, 117 Sci. News 230 (1980).

22. In an important sense all empirical reasoning is statistical. The distinguishing feature of the naked statistical evidence cases is that reliance on a quantified probability is invited, to the exclusion of all nonquantified evidence. In justifiably naked statistical evidence cases this invitation seems appealing because the latter sort of evidence is impossible or impractical to obtain.

23. For simplicity, I am ignoring any latency period in carcinogenesis. The timing of disease onset in evaluating causation can be very important. See, e.g., Reyes v. Wyeth Laboratories, 498 F.2d 1264 (5th Cir.), *cert. denied*, 419 U.S. 1096 (1974).

cluding stomach cancers from coverage because there is a 1/3 chance that they would have occurred anyway would not serve the purposes of industrial accident insurance.

On the other hand, if we treat justifiably naked statistical evidence like any other form of evidence, we end up extending coverage to all workers with stomach cancers, including the $\frac{1}{3}$ whose conditions are not work related. Under the preponderance-of-the-evidence standard, all that is required is that the probability in question exceed $\frac{1}{2}$.[24] Since $\lambda = \frac{2}{3}$, this "$p > \frac{1}{2}$" standard is satisfied.[25]

However, there is a third solution that mediates between these two extremes. It is to give to the injured worker not the full amount of the damages but that sum multiplied by the probability that the costs are attributable to his employment. Let us denote the costs of the stomach cancer by D. Then this "expected value" rule would permit the injured worker to collect not D, as under the $p > \frac{1}{2}$ rule, but only $(\frac{2}{3})D$.[26] In this way we can avoid imposing "crushing liability"[27] on the enterprise. Conversely, in cases where $\lambda \leqslant \frac{1}{2}$, firms do not escape liability altogether, as they would under the $p > \frac{1}{2}$ rule. Instead, they are charged an amount λD, further promoting the goal of economic efficiency.[28]

Although the expected value rule may look attractive at first blush, to

24. See, e.g., Kaye, *supra* note 3; Richard Eggleston, The Probability Debate, 1980 Crim. L. Rev. 678, 680.

25. A little algebra shows that $\lambda > \frac{1}{2}$ if and only if $a/b < 2$. In other words, the "balance of the probabilities" (where λ completely captures the relevant probability) favors causation as long as the industry cancer rate is twice as large as the base rate.

26. Alternatively, one could allow the worker to recover D with a probability $\lambda = \frac{2}{3}$. The expected value of this gamble is simply $(\frac{2}{3})D$. A risk-averse employee would prefer the fixed sum $(\frac{2}{3})D$ to a $\frac{2}{3}$ chance of D and a $\frac{1}{3}$ chance of 0. A firm with the same degree of risk aversion would not be as concerned, however, because over a large number of cases it can be confident of paying an average figure very close to $(\frac{2}{3})D$.

27. The phrase is taken from Steven Shavell, An Analysis of Causation and the Scope of Liability in the Law of Torts, 9 J. Legal Stud. 463, 465 (1980). Shavell's explanation of the term may be instructive:

> Under strict liability it is not hard to imagine circumstances where a party decides against engaging in an activity when it would have been socially worthwhile for him to have gone ahead. Consider a firm that uses a carcinogenic substance in producing a good that we agree ought to be produced because the benefits to consumers of the good exceed the costs of production plus the costs of an increased incidence of cancer among the firm's employees. Were the firm liable for *all* cases of cancer among its employees, then it might well be forced out of business, for it would be paying not only for the increased incidence of cancer due to its activities, but also for the general incidence of cancer due to such factors as pollution from other sources and medical x-radiation. By appropriately restricting the scope of liability, this type of disadvantageous outcome, to be described as the result of *crushing* liability, can sometimes be avoided. [footnote omitted; emphasis in original].

28. Assume, for simplicity, that every case of employee stomach cancer has the same cost D and that N such cases arise in an appropriate time period. On efficiency grounds, it can be argued that the firm should pay λDN, since λ represents the increment in the stomach cancer rate due to the firm's activity. See *id*. The picture with regard to efficiency, however, is not as clear as Shavell seems to suggest. Whereas he treats the costs of production as fixed, it could be contended that even when the employer need not pay an explicit sum for the increment in stomach cancer due to employment, he pays this cost implicitly in the form of higher wages. If wage rates are subject to renegotiation in

494   AMERICAN BAR FOUNDATION RESEARCH JOURNAL   1982:487

suggest that it be used to cope with justifiably naked statistical evidence raises an intriguing question: why not use it all the time? Nothing precludes us from asking jurors to evaluate the strength of every plaintiff's case on a scale of, say, 0 to 100. The resulting figures can be taken as indicating subjective probabilities of liability given all the evidence.[29] If the damages are known, the calculation of the expected value is trivial.

Perhaps this proposal will seem fantastic. Still, some commentators have come close to endorsing it,[30] and identifying its defects is not so simple. This task, however, is worth performing because it helps expose the logical foundations of the traditional $p>\frac{1}{2}$ rule and thereby to indicate when that rule should—and should not—be applied.

B. The Expected Value Rule Versus the $p>\frac{1}{2}$ Rule

1. Some Unconvincing Arguments Against the Expected Value Rule

To begin with, one might oppose widespread application of the expected value rule on the ground that jurors are not used to thinking in numerical terms and are therefore unable to arrive at accurate or reliable estimates of the probability of liability.[31] If so, it is only in cases of justifiably naked statistical evidence, where the probability is already calculated "objectively," that the expected value rule can be confidently applied.

Yet, it is far from obvious that jurors and judges are so inept at characterizing the strength of evidence in a quantitative fashion. It is not unusual to hear people express their opinions about one thing or another "on a scale of 1 to 10." Numerical odds are quoted frequently in connection with sporting events. Nor has the inability-to-quantify argument stopped a strong movement toward comparative negligence and contribution[32]—with jury verdicts listing percentage figures[33] that are factored in-

---

an efficient labor market, then they will drop once the accident costs are imposed on the employer. E.g., Harold Demsetz, When Does the Rule of Liability Matter? 1 J. Legal Stud. 13 (1972).

Another complication arises if employer contributions are not tailored to the accident costs experienced by each employer. For the purpose of this article, I shall assume that each firm pays premiums calculated to provide the proper incentive to take cost-effective precautions.

29. See, e.g., Kaye, *supra* note 1; Anne Martin & David A. Schum, Quantifying Burdens of Proof: A Likelihood Ratio Approach, Rice University Report No. 78-02 (Dec. 15, 1978).

30. E.g., Joseph H. King, Jr., Causation, Valuation, and Chance in Personal Injury Torts Involving Preexisting Conditions and Future Consequences, 90 Yale L.J. 1353, 1396 (1981).

31. Cf. Laurence H. Tribe, Trial by Mathematics: Precision and Ritual in the Legal Process, 84 Harv. L. Rev. 1329 (1971) (arguing that most jurors cannot make reasonable quantitative estimates of the probability that a defendant is guilty).

32. See, e.g., Alvis v. Ribar, 85 Ill. 2d 1, 421 N.E.2d 886 (1981); Carroll R. Heft & C. James Heft, Comparative Negligence Manual (Mundelein, Ill.: Callaghan & Co., 1978, 1981 Cum. Supp.); Landes & Posner, *supra* note 17, at 551.

33. See, e.g., Garrison v. Funderburk, 262 Ark. 711, 561 S.W.2d 73 (1978); Downum v. Muskogee Stockyards & Livestock Auction, Inc., 565 P.2d 368 (Okla. 1977). Some fact-finders proffer such quantitative estimates even when not obliged to do so. See The Times (London) 60,948 (June 8, 1981, at 2, col. 8) (industrial tribunal finds employee 60 percent to blame for his dismissal).

to damage awards. One wonders whether there are not more compelling reasons to prefer the $p>1/2$ rule to the expected value approach.

An alternative (or perhaps supplemental) explanation emphasizes the costs that would arise in administering the latter rule. The expected value rule allows plaintiffs some recovery even when the factual case for liability is tenuous.[34] It might be thought that this feature would result in more suits being filed and tried. Naturally, this administrative cost argument also applies to justifiably naked statistical evidence cases, but such cases are, after all, infrequent. If they are easily identified and the application of the expected value rule is restricted to this class of cases, then the administrative costs should not be unduly high.

Concern with administrative costs is surely proper, but the problem is easily exaggerated. It is more difficult than it might first appear to assess the likely impact of an across-the-board expected value rule on the volume of litigation, threatened or actual. Indeed, if plaintiffs and defendants are all risk neutral, the rate at which suits are filed and settled should not change. Giving damages of pD with probability 1 instead of D with probability p does not affect the ex ante value of a case. Many suits are now instituted with full recognition that a favorable verdict is most unlikely. These cases have settlement value precisely because the defendant has a nonzero risk of losing a large sum.[35] And to the extent that the weakness in these cases is evidentiary, they are not now vulnerable to pretrial attack.

Of course, I am not suggesting that adopting the expected value rule could not conceivably increase administrative costs or affect settlements. If defendants are risk averse,[36] they would feel less pressure to settle before trial since the expected value rule exposes them to less risk. If the court could not keep a case from reaching a jury because plaintiff's evidence is very thin, plaintiffs might gain. Considering these and a number of other factors,[37] it seems fair to say that, on balance, the situation with respect to relative administrative costs is complex if not downright

---

34. To preclude this possibility, one might modify the expected value rule by insisting on some threshold level of p before permitting any recovery. The formal analysis of the expected value rule (to be developed shortly) applies, with obvious variations, to this modified expected value rule.

35. Plaintiffs may also be able to induce settlements by imposing heavy discovery and other trial preparation costs on defendants. A change in the evidentiary standard of the sort contemplated here should have no long-run effect on such matters.

36. For a discussion of the attitude of firms toward risk, see, e.g., Easterbrook, Landes, & Posner, *supra* note 17, at 351–53 n.50 (concluding that "the extent and intensity of risk aversion among firms is an unsettled empirical question").

37. See, e.g., Polinsky & Shavell, *supra* note 17, at 457–62; authorities cited, *id.* at 460 n.43 (considering the additional factors of litigation costs and differences of opinion about winning). See generally W. Craig Riddell, Bargaining Under Uncertainty, 71 Am. Econ. Rev. 579 (1981); Steven Shavell, Suit, Settlement, and Trial: A Theoretical Analysis Under Alternative Methods for the Allocation of Legal Costs, 11 J. Legal Stud. 55 (1982).

496   AMERICAN BAR FOUNDATION RESEARCH JOURNAL   1982:487

murky. It is hardly obvious that concern over these administrative costs adequately explains or defends the refusal to employ a generally applicable expected value rule.[38]

2. *The Expected Value Rule as the Error Equalizing Rule and the* $p > \frac{1}{2}$ *Rule as the Error Minimizing Rule*

A more satisfactory justification for the traditional $p > \frac{1}{2}$ rule does exist. It focuses on the costs of errors, and it starts from the premise that the best decision rule is one that, as far as is practical, imposes liability entirely on the party who would indeed be liable under the governing substantive law if only all the facts could be known with certainty. This premise leads to the following notion of errors in damage awards: (1) every dollar paid by a defendant who would not be found liable if the true state of affairs were known is a dollar erroneously paid, and (2) every one of D dollars not paid to a plaintiff who would be entitled to collect this sum if the true state of the world were known is a dollar erroneously "paid" by plaintiff. Plainly, these definitions do not correspond to the usual notion of *legal* error. A trial can be conducted flawlessly, but the jury's deductions and inferences as to the true state of affairs can still be mistaken. The two types of mistakes identified here, however, are real enough. They pertain to "factual" errors, and they are known in statistical theory as type I errors (or false positives) and type II errors (false negatives).

The $p > \frac{1}{2}$ rule emerges as optimal if two assumptions about these types of errors are granted. The first is that one type is neither more nor less costly than the other. A dollar mistakenly paid by defendant (a false positive) is just as onerous as a dollar erroneously paid by a plaintiff (a false negative).[39] The second assumption is that the best decision rule keeps the

---

38. One can say that to the extent that the expected value rule reduces the "risk premium" paid by parties who settle, it lowers social costs, enhancing the attractiveness of the rule from the standpoint of economic efficiency.

39. This equality is not intended to reflect the values held by jurors or judges in particular cases or to describe the costs to or utility functions of particular plaintiffs and defendants. It is a statement about institutional values, about the relative importance of these types of mistakes in the eyes of "the law."

This conception of "blindfolded" justice is, I believe, widely shared. Whether it can be motivated solely by an efficiency argument is a nice question. One such argument goes something like this: It would be best to look to the opportunity costs (willingness to pay to avoid errors) to each party in each case if these costs could be cheaply measured. Because this administrative cost is very high, however, it is more efficient to use average figures, and on average the cost of each type of error is the same.

This efficiency argument would not hold to the extent that there are easily identified classes of cases in which the costs of errors to each side diverge. If large businesses are risk neutral and individuals with small assets are risk averse, for example, the cost of a dollar erroneously "paid" by the latter exceeds that for the former. One suspects, however, that an instruction to consider the depth of a litigant's pocket would be superfluous. In cases where moral censure or other collateral effects would result from an award of damages, costs to plaintiffs and defendants clearly are not proportional to the dollars wrongfully páid, and the law requires plaintiffs to do more than adduce a preponderance of the evidence. See, e.g., John Kaplan, Decision Theory and the Factfinding Process, 20 Stan. L. Rev. 1065, 1072 (1968).

sum of the expected costs of each type of error to a minimum. In other words, the claim on behalf of the $p > \frac{1}{2}$ rule is that it does better than the expected value rule in minimizing the total expected number of dollars coming from the wrong pockets. In fact, I propose to prove an even stronger proposition—that the $p > \frac{1}{2}$ rule is optimal (in the sense defined above) with regard to all conceivable decision rules for cases involving a single defendant and a single plaintiff.[40]

To analyze the $p > \frac{1}{2}$ rule with the tools of decision theory, we begin by enumerating the possible outcomes under the various decision rules, given all the possible "states of nature." In our workers' compensation case, for instance, there are two relevant possibilities: s_1, that the cancer was caused by exposure to the work environment, and s_2, that it was not. Of course, we do not know which state of nature actually pertains, but the evidence (in this case the cancer rates a and b) enables us to estimate the probabilities of s_1 and s_2. The probability of s_1 is $p_1 = \lambda = \frac{2}{3}$. The probability of s_2 is $p_2 = 1 - \lambda = \frac{1}{3}$.

Now consider three decisions:

> d_1: claimant or plaintiff pays D; defendant pays 0
> d_2: plaintiff pays 0; defendant pays D
> d_3: plaintiff pays p_2D; defendant pays p_1D

In the hypothetical phenoxy acids case, we might decide that the worker should not recover at all; he or she must absorb all the damages D without compensation. This decision is symbolized by d_1. In contrast, d_2 imposes full liability on the firm, and d_3 is the expected value rule.

If s_1 is true, then the claimant should pay nothing, but d_1 forces him to bear all the costs D. A total of D dollars is "wrongfully" paid. If s_2 is true, the substantive law says that the plaintiff deserves compensation, so that under d_1 zero dollars are paid by the wrong party. Pursuing this reasoning, we construct the following table or matrix of "losses" (money wrongfully paid) for the three decisions under each possible state of nature:

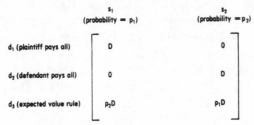

	s_1 (probability $= p_1$)	s_2 (probability $= p_2$)
d_1 (plaintiff pays all)	D	0
d_2 (defendant pays all)	0	D
d_3 (expected value rule)	p_2D	p_1D

Fig. 1. Matrix of losses for decisions d_1, d_2, and d_3

---

40. An essentially identical proposition was proved from a slightly different perspective in Kaye, *supra* note 3, at 605 n.19. The present development provides additional insights.

498   **AMERICAN BAR FOUNDATION RESEARCH JOURNAL**   **1982:487**

We now are in a position to state the "expected loss function" (f) for each decision. The expected value of a discrete random variable is the value of that variable multiplied by the probability that the variable will take on that value, calculated for each possible value and summed over all these values. Under d_1 there is a probability p_1 that D dollars will be wrongfully paid and a probability $p_2 = 1 - p_1$ that zero dollars will be wrongfully paid. Hence, the expected loss for d_1 is given by

$$f_1 = p_1 D + p_2 0 = p_1 D$$

In other words, making workers in the phenoxy acids illustration pay the costs of the illnesses means that on average a fraction p_1 of the costs will be borne by persons who would not have to pay in a world of perfect information. Likewise, the expected loss under d_2 is

$$f_2 = p_1 0 + p_2 D = p_2 D = (1 - p_1) D$$

Under d_3 the plaintiff recovers only a proportion of the damages D. There is a probability p_1 that $p_2 D$ dollars will be wrongfully paid and a probability p_2 that $p_1 D$ dollars will be wrongfully paid. The expected loss under d_3 is therefore

$$f_3 = p_1 p_2 D + p_2 p_1 D = 2 p_1 p_2 D = 2 p_1 (1 - p_1) D$$

To see the implications of these algebraic expressions, let us view the probability p_1 as varying from case to case. In other words, in some instances the justifiably naked statistical evidence will suggest a low value (near 0) for p_1 (e.g., hardly any stomach cancers are work related, relatively few taxicabs belong to the Green Company, etc.). In other situations, p_1 will be close to 1 (nearly all stomach cancers are work related, almost 100 percent of the taxicabs are red, etc.). Treating p_1 as a variable, we can draw a picture of the expected losses f_1, f_2, and f_3 as functions of p_1. The loss function f_1 increases in direct proportion to p_1, while f_2 decreases linearly as p_1 increases. The loss function f_3 is a curved line that rises to $D/2$, then falls back to 0. All this is depicted in figure 2.

Which way of deciding minimizes the expected losses? Over the interval $0 < p_1 < \frac{1}{2}$, figure 2 shows that $f_1 < f_3 < f_2$. Thus, as long as $p_1 < \frac{1}{2}$, d_1 is best. On the other hand, over the interval $\frac{1}{2} < p_1 < 1$, $f_2 < f_3 < f_1$; that is, for $p_1 > \frac{1}{2}$, d_2 works best. But the prescription to have the claimant pay all the damages (d_1) if $p_1 < \frac{1}{2}$ and to make the defendant pay (d_2) if $p_1 > \frac{1}{2}$ is essentially the $p > \frac{1}{2}$ rule.[41] The ordinary more-probable-than-not standard thus appears superior to the expected value rule.

Of course, d_1, d_2, and d_3 are not the only possible decisions. In fact,

---

41. Figure 2 shows that when $p_1 = p_2 = \frac{1}{2}$, all the decisions are equally effective in minimizing expected losses. To break these ties the $p > \frac{1}{2}$ rule awards the verdict to the defendant in those cases.

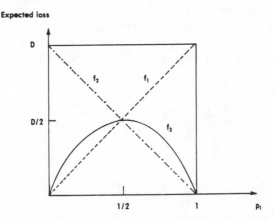

Fig. 2. Expected loss functions for decisions d_1, d_2, and d_3

each is a special case of the following, more general rule d: have defendant give the claimant xD dollars (or, D dollars with probability x). If $x = 0$, plaintiff recovers nothing, and d reduces to d_1. If $x = 1$, defendant pays all, and we have d_2. If $x = p_1$, damages are split according to the expected value rule d_3.

By selecting x to minimize the expected loss function f associated with this general decision rule, we specify the particular rule that is optimal with regard to all the possible decision rules—not merely d_1, d_2, and d_3. It should come as no surprise by now that this optimal rule is the $p > \frac{1}{2}$ rule.[42]

However, minimizing f has an interesting impact on the incidence of

42. The proof is straightforward, but worth stating, paying attention to the way the choice of the function $x(p_1)$ affects the rate of type I versus type II errors. The loss matrix is now given by figure A.

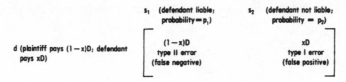

Fig. A. Matrix of losses for general decision rule d

If the costs of each type of error are the same, the expected loss function is just the sum of the expected number of false positive and false negative dollars:

$$f = n_I + n_{II} = p_2 x D + p_1 (1 - x) D = p_1 D + (p_2 - p_1) x D$$

500   AMERICAN BAR FOUNDATION RESEARCH JOURNAL   1982:487

false positives and false negatives. Figure 3 shows the expected number of each type of error when $p_1 > \frac{1}{2}$. It reveals two very important things. First, while the $p > \frac{1}{2}$ rule keeps expected losses to a minimum (of $(1 - p_1)D$), it does so in an extremely lopsided way. All the expected losses

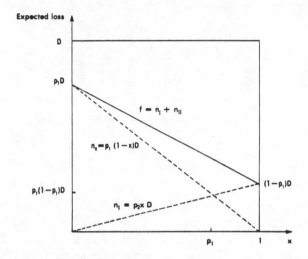

Fig. 3.   Expected type I and type II losses for rule d (drawn for $p_1 > p_2$)

are false positives when $p_1 > p_2$. (When the $p > \frac{1}{2}$ rule is used where $p_1 < p_2$, all the losses are false negatives.) Second, the expected value rule $x = p_1$ entails larger expected losses (totaling $2p_1(1 - p_1)D$), but these expected losses are equally divided among false positives and false negatives. In short, the $p > \frac{1}{2}$ rule is the error minimizing rule for each case, but the expected value rule is the error equalizing rule.[43]

3. Minimizing Total Expected Losses Versus Equalizing Expected False Positives and False Negatives

The criterion of minimizing the total expected losses, it will be recalled,

---

In a given case p_1, p_2, and D are fixed, and f is therefore minimized by choosing

$$x(p_1) = \begin{cases} 0 & \text{if } p_2 > p_1 \\ \\ 1 & \text{if } p_1 > p_2 \end{cases}$$

Since $p_1 > p_2$ is the same as $p_1 > \frac{1}{2}$, we have again arrived at the more-probable-than-not rule.

43. Finkelstein has spoken of raising the threshold of the $p > \frac{1}{2}$ rule to some figure larger than $\frac{1}{2}$ to make it an error equalizing rule. See Finkelstein, *supra* note 6. The expected value rule equalizes expected errors in the same sense as Finkelstein's modified $p > \frac{1}{2}$ rule, but it operates in a distinctive way.

incorporates the assumption that it is equally objectionable for either party to absorb or pay damages that the law would require the other side to bear if all the material facts were known with certainty. Yet, we have just seen that when the $p>\frac{1}{2}$ decision rule—which best meets this appealing criterion—is applied to a case in which p_1 exceeds $\frac{1}{2}$, the expected number of dollars that defendant must wrongly pay is p_2D, while the number that plaintiff must wrongly pay is 0. And we have seen that the expected value rule avoids this result.

Upon reflection, however, this feature of the $p>\frac{1}{2}$ rule should not prove paradoxical or troublesome; nor, as we shall see, does the error equalizing characteristic of the expected value rule provide a rationale for its unrestricted use. To borrow again from statistical terminology, the $p>\frac{1}{2}$ rule is a "maximum likelihood" rule. It tells us to act as if s_1 is true as long as s_1 is the most likely state of the world. In other words, if it is more probable that the defendant should pay D dollars $(p_1>p_2)$, we decide that plaintiff is entitled to collect these dollars. We than have a relatively small chance (of probability p_2) of making a mistake with all these D dollars; but we have a better chance (of probability p_1) of having *no* dollars wrongly paid. On average, we err with only p_2D dollars. In contrast, the expected value rule guarantees that we will make a mistake in every case. On average, in the proportion p_1 of the cases, p_2D dollars will be wrongly borne by the plaintiff, and in the remaining proportion p_2 of the cases, p_1D dollars will be wrongly paid by defendant. So the expected value rule equates the two expected dollar error rates (at p_1p_2D apiece) but only at the cost of making more errors ($2p_1p_2D$ instead of p_2D).[44]

An analogy may clarify the mathematical characteristics of the expected value rule and the $p>\frac{1}{2}$ rule. Returning to the stomach cancer case, let us visualize an urn filled with 300 marbles. Two-thirds of these marbles are red and one-third green. We pick a marble at random and must decide whether it is red or green. The red marbles correspond to the work-related stomach cancers and the green ones to the other stomach cancers among the workers. Ordinarily, we could tell green from red at a glance, so to make the analogy complete we must imagine that we are blindfolded or colorblind. As such, we must rely on probability theory to make the most accurate guess.

The maximum likelihood approach is to announce that the marble is red. It gives the right answer two-thirds of the time. Of course, this approach is "biased" in the statistical sense.[45] It leads us to announce that

---

44. Since $p_1>p_2$ and $p_1+p_2=1$, it follows that $2p_1p_2D>p_2D$.
45. Statistical inference consists of using sample data to reach conclusions about the population being sampled. Suppose we wish to estimate some numerical characteristic of a large group on the basis of a limited number of randomly drawn observations. For any particular sample, the estimate

502   AMERICAN BAR FOUNDATION RESEARCH JOURNAL   1982:487

every marble so selected is red, even though we know that in the long run one-third are green. The expected value approach is not "biased" toward red. It would have us say that each marble is two-thirds red.[46] We will be wrong in every instance, but *on average,* we will be exactly right. That is, we will correctly state what percentage of the color in the urn is red.

Similarly, the expected value rule gives each worker with stomach cancer $(\frac{2}{3})D$. But in $\frac{2}{3}$ of the 300 cases it gives $(\frac{1}{3})D$ too little, and in the other $\frac{1}{3}$ of the 300 cases, it gives $(\frac{2}{3})D$ too much. The total wrongly given is therefore $2(\frac{1}{3})(\frac{2}{3})D(300) = 133.33D$. The maximum likelihood $p > \frac{1}{2}$ rule gives full recovery D in all cases. In $\frac{1}{3}$ of the 300 cases, it gives D too much, making the total wrongly given $(\frac{1}{3})D(300) = 100D$, a distinctly smaller number. To summarize, the maximum likelihood rule makes a few expensive mistakes, but it does not err at all in most cases. The expected value rule errs in every case—a small amount in most and a larger amount in the rest, producing a larger weighted sum of errors.

In the example here, the "unbiased" nature of the expected value rule is appealing. It avoids overcharging the firm,[47] and the increment in the error rate does not seem extravagant at most values of p_1 and p_2. Where a single defendant faces the possibility of numerous suits from similarly situated plaintiffs and the probability that this defendant is liable is the same in each of these cases, the expected value rule seems superior to the $p > \frac{1}{2}$ rule. In general, however, we need not concern ourselves with equalizing error rates at a particular probability level because the values of p_1 and p_2 are not fixed in case after case. Most activities involve a group of potential plaintiffs and defendants for whom $p_1 > p_2$ sometimes and $p_1 < p_2$ at other times. In these situations, the maximum likelihood rule would also seem to be "unbiased." As long as the probabilities are distributed across cases and parties in a symmetric way, any discrepancies in the error rates tend to average out, and the enterprise as a whole is charged the appropriate gross amount for the injuries it causes. The expected value rule therefore rarely will emerge as the better evidentiary standard.[48] For example, in automobile accident cases the maximum like-

will not necessarily correspond precisely to the population value. Sometimes it may be on the high side, sometimes on the low side. If the errors systematically fall in one direction, the estimator is said to be "biased." If the errors are balanced, so that on average (in the limit) the estimator is accurate, it is said to be "unbiased."

"Unbiased" estimators can be a mixed blessing, however. For any sample, an unbiased estimator could be very inaccurate. In some applications a more accurate, albeit biased, estimator may be preferred. Selecting the "best" estimator is often a subtle matter, not amenable to rigid rules.

46. One could also randomize the guesses in such a way as to announce that a marble is red in two-thirds of the selections. See note 25 *supra.*

47. See note 27 *supra.*

48. It should be clear that the analysis is confined to the expected value rule that weights damages by the probability of liability. Another expected value rule is appropriate for measuring damages themselves in situations involving future contingencies and losses of valuable chances. See, e.g., King, *supra* note 30.

lihood rule falsely absolves some defendant drivers (when $p_1 < p_2$), while it falsely charges others (when $p_1 > p_2$) with the accident costs. On balance, no systematic unfairness is apparent despite the apparent "bias" for fixed values of p_1 and p_2. Since the rule promotes factually accurate decision making, it is superior to the expected value rule.

III. MULTIPLE DEFENDANT CASES

At this point, we have seen that in cases involving undisputed damages D caused by a single defendant with some quantifiable probability p_1, the traditional $p > \frac{1}{2}$ rule ordinarily is superior to the expected value rule. Except in special circumstances (which are sometimes present in cases of justifiably naked statistical evidence) it involves no systematic unfairness, and it is always superior in keeping the expected sum of the costs assigned to the wrong parties to a minimum. This provides a useful explanation of why the preponderance-of-the-evidence ($p > \frac{1}{2}$) standard is suitable for most cases but why it should nevertheless be replaced by an expected value rule in some instances of justifiably naked statistical evidence.

Strictly speaking, however, the formal analysis does not extend to cases like *Sindell* and the taxicab hypothetical, which involve more than one person who may have caused the injury. This section therefore extends the mathematical analysis to multiple defendant cases.[49] It generalizes the result of part II, initially to two-defendant cases like the taxicab problem, and then to cases involving any finite number of defendants. It proves what may at first seem an unlikely result—that the error minimizing rule calls for decisions assigning total liability to the single person most likely to have caused the injury, even if the probability pertaining to this person does not exceed one-half.

A. The Two-Defendant Case

We begin with the two-defendant case[50] because it illustrates the principles of the more general problem without requiring any complicated mathematics. For simplicity, we assume that the only disputed issue is the identity of the liable defendant. As in the taxicab hypothetical, one defendant, but not both, caused an injury of D dollars and would be fully liable under the prevailing law if the identity of this injurer could be spec-

---

49. It does this by solving the most elementary sort of problem in the branch of operations research known as linear programming. For a nontechnical introduction to the field, see Robert G. Bland, The Allocation of Resources by Linear Programming, 244 Sci. Am., June 1981, at 126.

50. I use the term "two-defendant" (and "n-defendant") rather loosely to indicate that more than one person might have independently caused the legally cognizable injury. Factual ambiguity prevents us from knowing which such person did so. Whether all such potential defendants are actually joined or impleaded is not crucial. Independence—that either defendant one *or* defendant two *or* defendant three, etc., caused the single injury—is critical. Persons acting in concert, concurrent causes producing indivisible injuries, and indemnity defendants all present "one-defendant" cases. See text accompanying notes 69–70 *infra*.

504 **AMERICAN BAR FOUNDATION RESEARCH JOURNAL** **1982:487**

ified.[51] The most general decision rule in this situation has one defendant Δ_1 paying x_1 dollars, the second defendant Δ_2 paying x_2 dollars, and the plaintiff absorbing the remainder, $D - x_1 - x_2$. As with the quantity x that we considered in the single-defendant case, the quantities x_1 and x_2 may depend explicitly on the probabilities p_1 and p_2 that Δ_1 and Δ_2, respectively, are indeed liable. If $x_1 = D$ and $x_2 = 0$, for instance, Δ_1 is liable for the entirety of the damages. If $x_1 = p_1 D$ and $x_2 = p_2 D$, then each defendant is liable for an expected quantity, as in the expected value approach discussed in part II. Note also that although $x_1 + x_2$ may equal D (in which case the plaintiff is fully compensated), they need not. Of course, $x_1 + x_2$ cannot exceed D, for D represents the full damages. More succinctly, the constraints on x_1 and x_2 can be expressed as follows:

$$x_1 + x_2 \leqslant D \tag{1}$$
$$x_1 \geqslant 0 \tag{2}$$
$$x_2 \geqslant 0 \tag{3}$$

Also, we should remember that $p_1 + p_2 = 1$.

The expected loss function f for this general decision rule is easily obtained. If the true state of the world is s_1, meaning that Δ_1 should be paying D to the plaintiff, then the amount paid by the wrong parties is everything that Δ_1 does not pay—namely, $D - x_1$. Likewise, under s_2, the loss as we have defined it is $D - x_2$. Hence, the expected loss function for the general division of damages is

$$f = p_1(D - x_1) + p_2(D - x_2) = D - p_1 x_1 - p_2 x_2 \tag{4}$$

Once again, our objective is to choose x_1 and x_2 so as to keep the expected loss f to a minimum. Attention to the geometry of the situation reveals that this is accomplished by letting $x_1 = 0$ and $x_2 = D$ (in other words by having Δ_2 pay for the full damages D) when $p_1 > p_2$, and by letting $x_1 = D$ and $x_2 = 0$ (i.e., having Δ_1 pay D) when $p_2 > p_1$. When both defendants are equally likely to have injured the plaintiff, any division of the damages D as between the two defendants ($x_1 + x_2 = D$) minimizes the expected losses.[52] Thus, the maximum likelihood $p > \frac{1}{2}$ rule is optimal with respect to all possible decision rules in cases involving two possible defendants. Again, it is optimal in the sense that this rule minimizes the expected sum of money paid by parties who should not be liable under the substantive law if the identity of the single wrongdoer were known.

Consequently, in the taxicab hypothetical the Red Company should be liable. Under the unusual circumstances of the case, the plaintiff's exclu-

---

51. Including the possibility that neither defendant is truly liable is straightforward. One need merely introduce an additional probabilty p, for the additional state s, (that plaintiff is liable). As far as the mathematics go, we have a three-defendant problem with the plaintiff playing the role of the third defendant.

sive reliance on background statistics is justifiable, so that the values for p_1 and p_2 may be taken from these background statistics. Letting Δ_1 stand for the Red Company, it follows that $p_1 > p_2$. The traditional preponderance-of-the-evidence standard thus selects the Red Company as

---

52. The inequalities (1)–(3) constrain x_1 and x_2 to the triangular region depicted in figure B.

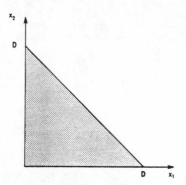

Fig. B. Feasible region for x_1 and x_2 (values for (x_1, x_2) outside the shaded area violate the constraints on x_1 and x_2)

The function f, being a linear combination of x_1 and x_2, is a portion of a plane lying above this feasible region. To sketch this plane, we need a third axis perpendicular to the x_1 and x_2 axes. From equation 4, we can readily find the height of f at the vertices of the feasible region. When $x_1 = D$ and $x_2 = 0$, then $f = p_2 D$. When $x_1 = 0$ and $x_2 = D$, then $f = p_1 D$. When $x_1 = x_2 = 0$, then $f = D$. Since three points determine a plane, we can now graph f. Suppose that $p_1 = \frac{1}{2}$. Then $p_1 D = p_2 D = D/2$, and the bottom edge of the portion of the plane projecting above the feasible region parallels the hypotenuse of that region, as shown in figure C.

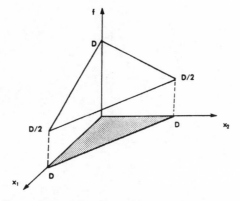

Fig. C. Expected loss function f for $p_1 = p_2 = \frac{1}{2}$
(expected losses are minimized by any choice of x_1 and x_2 as long as $x_1 + x_2 = D$)

506   **AMERICAN BAR FOUNDATION RESEARCH JOURNAL**   **1982:487**

the culprit. Furthermore, no good reason for departing from this maximum likelihood choice is apparent. The type of bias described in part II is not present. Unlike the workers' compensation case, it is difficult to

We can see that f is at its lowest as long as plaintiff is fully compensated, regardless of how much each defendant contributes. In other words, when each defendant is equally likely to be the liable party, the minimization criterion gives no guidance as to how Δ_1 and Δ_2 should share in the payment of D to the plaintiff. The criterion is met as long as the plaintiff recovers. Either Δ_1 and Δ_2 may be treated as jointly and severally liable, or equitable principles of contribution may be applied. For discussion of the merits of these alternatives, see, e.g., Landes & Posner, *supra* note 17; Robinson, *supra* note 11. Of greater interest are the more prevalent situations in which p_1 does not equal p_2. If $p_1 > p_2$, f drops to its lowest point when $x_1 = D$ and $x_2 = 0$. This is shown in figure D.

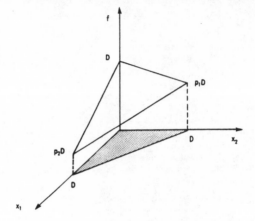

Fig. D.   Expected loss function for $p_1 > p_2$
(expected losses are minimized when $x_1 = D$ and $x_2 = 0$)

Finally, if $p_1 < p_2$, the lowest value of f lies above the point $x = 0$ and $x = D$, as revealed in figure E.

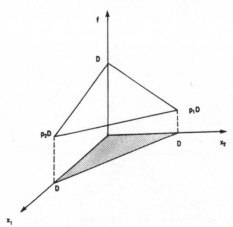

Fig. E.   Expected loss function for $p_2 > p_1$
(expected losses are minimized when $x_1 = 0$ and $x_2 = D$)

envision many repeated instances of litigation in which justifiably naked statistical evidence points to the Red Company. The concern that this company will be overcharged or suffer crushing liability seems far-fetched.

B. The *n*-defendant Case

To generalize the proof of the previous section to the *n*-defendant case, we follow the same procedure. We construct an expected loss function and examine its behavior over the feasible region. We discover that *f* is minimized by having the single defendant for whom the probability of liability is greatest pay all the damages D.[53]

It might be misleading to continue to call this a $p > \frac{1}{2}$ rule, however, for it may select a single defendant as fully liable even if the probability associated with that defendant's liability is less than $\frac{1}{2}$.[54] Nevertheless, this difference is largely superficial, since the $p > \frac{1}{2}$ rule is but a special case of the general maximum likelihood rule. When one must decide whether a disputed proposition of fact is true or false, the preponderance-of-the-evidence standard is adequately expressed by the more-probable-than-not ($p > \frac{1}{2}$) rule. This is nothing more than the maximum likelihood rule expressed for $n = 2$. When the decision involves more than two possible outcomes, as it does when a court or jury considers which one of several persons caused a result for which liability attaches, the maximum likelihood approach of selecting the single most likely outcome continues to minimize expected errors.[55] Instead of the more-probable-than-not

---

53. The expected loss function is now a portion of a plane extending over a feasible region in an *n*-dimensional space. Let x be a vector whose *n* components x_1 through x_n represent the money paid by Δ_1 through Δ_n, respectively. Similarly, let p be a vector whose *i*th component p_i stands for the probability that Δ_i caused the damage. Then the expected loss is just

$$f(p,x) = D - x \cdot p$$

where

$$\Sigma x_i \leqslant D, \ x_i \geqslant 0, \ \Sigma p_i = 1, \ \text{and} \ 0 \leqslant p_i \leqslant 1.$$

The function f is minimized by making $x \cdot p$ as large as possible for each p. Suppose that max $(p_i) = p_j$. In light of the constraints on the components of x and the meaning of the scalar product, $x \cdot p$ is then maximized by letting $x_j = D$ and $x_i = 0$ (where $i \neq j$)—by having the single most probably liable defendant pay all the damages. In the event that no single component of p is larger than all the others, several defendants emerge as the equally likely and most probably liable parties, and the minimization principle does not enable us to choose among them.

54. Where there are only two defendants, one of whom must be liable (or one plaintiff and one defendant), this cannot happen because the larger of the probabilities associated with the parties must exceed $\frac{1}{2}$. That is, the *n*-defendant solution reduces to the $p > \frac{1}{2}$ rule when $n = 2$, as indeed it must.

55. In deriving this result, we assumed that the only issue in dispute is the identity of the single, fully culpable party, so that the justifiably naked statistical evidence supplied the probabilities that each potential defendant is in fact liable. The same result also applies if the probablities p_n, $p_1, \ldots, p_n$ are subjective estimates of liability based on all the evidence in the case. How the prob-

508   **AMERICAN BAR FOUNDATION RESEARCH JOURNAL**   1982:487

test, perhaps we should speak of a "balance-of-the-probabilities" test (where the single largest probability tips the balance) or more succinctly, a "most probable" evidentiary standard in civil litigation.

IV. Applying the Maximum Likelihood Rule: Some Illustrations, Caveats, and Connections

Part III showed that the maximum likelihood rule is the expected error minimizing rule, even in cases involving many defendants. Nonetheless, as we saw in part II, there are circumstances in which an expected value approach may be more suitable. This section considers how the maximum likelihood standard might be used to resolve three perplexing cases. In the process, I shall comment on the connection between the maximum likelihood rule's most serious competitor—the expected value rule—and some recently proposed schemes for "causal apportionment."[56] Again, the emphasis is on the presence of factors that might make the use of the standard misleading or undesirable.

A. *Sindell v. Abbott Laboratories*

Initially, the maximum likelihood approach appears well suited to *Sindell.* Only one pharmaceutical company manufactured the quantity of the compound that injured Judith Sindell. Because of the time between the administration of the DES and the injury, her failure to adduce more than the background statistics seems justified. Taking market shares as a reasonable measure of the probabilities p_i, the maximum likelihood rule would make the dominant firm liable for all the damages.

The California Supreme Court did not consider this approach, perhaps because it conceived of the evidentiary standard in more traditional terms. It reasoned that as to each firm, the $p > \frac{1}{2}$ test was not met, and it thought it unfair to impose liability on a group of defendants for whom the aggregate probability was under $\frac{1}{2}$. Hence, it demanded the joinder of companies holding "a substantial share" of the relevant market in order to "significantly diminish" the "injustice."[57] Furthermore, it regarded the prospect of joint and several liability, which could result in the firm *least* likely to have caused the injury paying all the damages, as potentially being very unfair. At the same time, it perceived that holding none of the DES manufacturers liable had its drawbacks. Thus, it adopted an expected value approach on top of a "substantial share" requirement as, in effect, a compromise.

---

ablities pertaining to each element of the cause of action should be combined to obtain the overall probability of liability is beyond the scope of this article. This "problem of conjunction" is discussed in Cohen, The Probable and the Provable, *supra* note 5; Carl G. Wagner, Book Review, 1979 Duke L.J. 1071 (*reviewing* Cohen, The Probable and the Provable).

56. See Rizzo & Arnold, *supra* note 17; Robinson, *supra* note 11.
57. 26 Cal. 3d at 612, 163 Cal. Rptr. at 145, 607 P.2d at 937.

Although the court overlooked the maximum likelihood solution, its use of the expected value rule is defensible for the reasons stated in the simpler workers' compensation example. Both the evidentiary standard presupposed by the court—the $p>\frac{1}{2}$ rule—and its generalization—the maximum likelihood rule—produce biased results in this situation. In the long run, a minimum of errors occurs under the maximum likelihood approach, but these errors invariably are to the disadvantage of the "most probable" defendant. The $p>\frac{1}{2}$ rule fits even more awkwardly. If no defendant has more than half the market, it produces the maximum number of errors (100 percent assuming plaintiff would prevail on all other issues), all to the detriment of the DES victims. The probabilities, being market shares within the same geographic region and historical period, do not shift from case to case, reordering the manufacturers; hence, the bias inherent in the use of the maximum likelihood rule with a fixed set of probabilities persists throughout all DES cases. It is not as if the rule sometimes errs to the advantage of one company and sometimes to the benefit of another. Although this type of equalizing effect is typically present, as in automobile accident cases,[58] it does not occur here. As such, the expected value rule has the most merit. It increases the expected error rate relative to the maximum likelihood rule but not to the extent of the $p>\frac{1}{2}$ rule. It equalizes the expected incidence of errors affecting each firm and imposes, to the extent that we can measure it, the cost of the harm produced by each company on that firm.[59] From this perspective, *Sindell* is correctly decided.[60]

---

58. See text accompanying note 48 *supra*.

59. All this is a straightforward application of what was said in part II about the workers' compensation problem to the DES context. Yet, there is an intriguing distinction between the two cases. The point can be elucidated by recasting the DES situation slightly. Imagine that every DES victim joins in a class action against every DES producer. Although no single victim can prove which producer distributed the quantity that harmed her, such individualized proof would seem unnecessary and wasteful. If the probabilities used in dividing the damages among the producers are accurate, then the expected value approach quickly accomplishes what the individualized method of proof laboriously strives for: compensating each DES victim and charging each injurer for the cost of the injuries it caused. The fact that company A may pay part of company B's victim's costs while company B does the same for company A's victim is hardly a cause for alarm.

Seen in this light, the DES problem is better suited to the expected value rule than the phenoxy acids illustration. In the latter, only a fraction of the workers "deserve" compensation, but there is no way to match the employer only to these deserving workers, and we end up awarding every afflicted worker a reduced sum. In the DES situation, the causation problem amounts to matching the right firm with the right victim. See Refining Market Share Liability, *supra* note 11. There is no way to do this, but here the expected value approach does not reward any "undeserving" victims, and it awards the proper sum to each victim. For this reason, its use in *Sindell* is even more defensible than in the hypothesized phenoxy acids case. But see A Market Share Approach, *supra* note 11, at 1187–88 (administrative costs imposed on defendants may be excessive in cases involving many potential defendants).

60. If the expected value rule is used, however, it would seem that the "substantial share" requirement serves no meaningful function. See Robinson, *supra* note 11. But see A Market Share Approach, *supra* note 11, at 1197–99 (suggesting, among other things, that "[h]aving the major producers in court will facilitate the determination of the dimensions of the relevant market"). In addition, a more exacting measure of the probability than overall market share may be available. See Re-

B. *Summers v. Tice*

In essence, *Sindell* is but the mildly mutated and as yet poorly articulated offspring of the textbook case of *Summers v. Tice*,[61] decided by the California Supreme Court about 30 years earlier. Like *Sindell, Summers* involved a deficiency in the proof of causation. A shotgun blast from a fellow hunter struck the plaintiff in the eye and lip. The pellet in the eye was the major element of damages. It could have come only from a single gun. Plaintiff's two companions each negligently fired in plaintiff's direction at the same time. They were equidistant from plaintiff and used the same type of shotgun and birdshot. Each had an unobscured line of fire. Although plaintiff did not rely on any generalized background statistics to quantify the probability that each hunter was responsible for the injury, the case resembles the justifiably naked statistical evidence cases. Quantified probabilities leap to mind. A symmetry argument suggests that $p_1 = p_2 = \frac{1}{2}$, and the plaintiff's inability to single out either defendant seems understandable.

Proceeding with our usual analysis, then, we first consider what the generally applicable maximum likelihood rule dictates. If the probabilities are indeed equal, the expected loss function is the one pictured in figure C, and the maximum likelihood solution is "degenerate." It cannot distinguish between Δ_1 and Δ_2. Any division of damages between the two careless hunters minimizes the expected sum of dollars coming from persons who would not be held liable in a world of perfect information. Our analysis therefore merely requires that one defendant or the other, or both, compensate the victim.[62]

The court in *Summers v. Tice* reached this very result. Expressing discomfort with the reasoning of decisions holding defendants from the same hunting party jointly liable on a "concerted action" theory, the California court emphasized that the innocent plaintiff certainly should

---

fining Market Share Liability, *supra* note 11. It should also be clear that the expected value rule is tantamount to what some commentators have called "pro rata" liability. E.g., A Market Share Approach, *supra* note 11, at 1196. It does not permit 100 percent of the liability to be apportioned among defendants who collectively marketed less than 100 percent of the relevant DES—a point that troubled the sole dissenter in *Sindell*. See 26 Cal. 3d at 617, 163 Cal. Rptr. at 148, 607 P.2d at 940.

61. 33 Cal. 2d 80, 119 P.2d 1 (1948). For a perceptive comparison of the two cases developing this theme, see Robinson, *supra* note 11.

62. This much is required by the assumption that $p(s_a) = 0$, i.e., that the plaintiff would not be required to bear the cost of the accident if all the material facts were known with certainty. See note 51 *supra*. One might ask why the substantive law requires an injurer to compensate his innocent victims. See, e.g., George P. Fletcher, Fairness and Utility in Tort Theory, 85 Harv. L. Rev. 537 (1972); Richard A. Posner, The Concept of Corrective Justice in Recent Theories of Tort Law, 10 J. Legal Stud. 187 (1981); Robinson, *supra* note 11. The analytical tools constructed here can shed no light on such questions.

not bear any of the accident costs.[63] Hence, it upheld imposing joint and several liability on the two defendants unless one could somehow demonstrate that he was not responsible for the injury. This reasoning is often denominated an "alternative liability" theory,[64] presumably to distinguish it from the usual basis for joint liability.

The mathematical analysis presented here incorporates the operative premise of this alternative liability theory. We have assumed that $p_0 = 0$—that there is no chance that the facts are such that plaintiff should absorb any of the accident cost.[65] To fail to compensate the plaintiff under this condition is to ensure that the expected loss function will not be held to a minimum. Consequently, under both our analysis and the alternative liability theory of *Summers,* what matters is that only one person caused the injury and that this person was one of the defendants. Had the two defendant hunters come from unrelated hunting parties, the analysis would be identical. That our knowledge of the event is frustratingly incomplete means that we must make our best guess. As we have seen, the maximum likelihood guess—the one that satisfies the preponderance-of-the-evidence requirement, properly understood—is to hold at least one negligent hunter liable.

One might go one step further and suggest that the cost be apportioned between the careless hunters in accordance with the expected value rule. This refinement is exactly the innovation introduced in *Sindell,* which is why I have characterized *Sindell* as a mutated progeny of *Summers.* Our analysis neither requires nor precludes this. The maximum likelihood solution entails no bias in this type of case. There are no comprehensive class actions or repeated suits against the same defendants with the same recurring probabilities. Those who are plaintiffs and defendants as well as the probabilities pertaining to each defendant will vary across a spectrum of hunting accident cases. At the same time, the mathematical degeneracy resulting from the fact that $p_1 = p_2$ means that in *Summers* itself apportionment according to expected value fulfills the objective of reducing expected losses as well as (but no better than) any other method of contribution or apportionment. One may favor dividing damages according to the probabilties p_1 and p_2, but not on the basis of the logic presented here.

---

63. The court also relied on the more dubious proposition "[o]rdinarily defendants are in a far better position to offer evidence to determine which one caused the injury." 33 Cal. 2d 80, 86 (1948). As the California court recognized in *Sindell,* however, the principal concern of *Summers* is that "if one [defendant] can escape the other may also and plaintiff is remediless." 199 P.2d 1 (1948) at 4.
64. See, e.g., Market Share Liability, *supra* note 11, at 672.
65. See text accompanying note 51 *supra.*

C. *Michie v. Great Lakes Steel Division*

For a final illustration of the limitations on the usefulness of the maximum likelihood interpretation of the preponderance-of-the-evidence standard, we turn to a noted air pollution case, *Michie v. Great Lakes Steel Division*.[66] Thirty-seven persons living in Canada filed a federal diversity action, complaining that discharges from seven nearby plants in the United States operated by three corporations created a nuisance that damaged them and their property. They did not allege concerted action. The district court, construing Michigan law, denied the corporations' motion to dismiss. On interlocutory appeal, the Court of Appeals for the Sixth Circuit affirmed. It reasoned that under the developing law in Michigan, either the alleged injury is not theoretically divisible, or it is divisible but there is no feasible way to determine how much of the injury each defendant produced. Either way, the court surmised, Michigan courts would impose joint and several liability to avoid the "manifest unfairness in 'putting on the injured party the impossible burden of proving the specific shares of harm done by each.'"[67]

What does our analysis reveal about how this aspect of the case should be handled? The answer depends on whether the injury resulted from the conduct of exactly one defendant. We could say this about the injuries in each of the cases examined thus far.[68] If one company actually caused all the damages here, then employing certain meteorological and physical assumptions we would use the maximum likelihood rule to pick out the major polluter as the liable party, and we would pause only to see whether an expected value rule would be appropriate to avoid serious bias.

In *Michie,* however, it seems more likely that the quantum of damage resulted from the sum of the emissions of the seven factories. For example, had the total pollution from the factories been less, the market value of plaintiffs' properties might have been higher.[69] If so, the maximum

---

66. 495 F.2d 213 (6th Cir. 1974).

67. *Id.* at 216, *quoting* Maddux v. Donaldson, 362 Mich. 425, 108 N.W.2d 33 (1961).

68. See text accompanying notes 76–77 *infra.*

69. This is not to say that the damage from pollution is necessarily a continuous function of the quantity of the pollutants. On the contrary, if a certain threshold amount is required before a type of injury occurs, the cost function will be discontinuous. See, e.g., Bruce A. Ackerman, Susan Rose Ackerman, & Dale W. Henderson, The Uncertain Search for Environmental Quality: The Costs and Benefits of Controlling Pollution Along the Delaware River, 121 U. Pa. L. Rev. 1225 (1973). Where discontinuities exist, it may be possible to find that some defendants are "but for" causes. Had they not contributed, the threshold would not have been reached and the damage would not have occurred. There is a problem, of course, in deciding which defendants come within this category. If some of the defendants begin polluting earlier and have a prior right to pollute so that their conduct is not tortious, then the polluter whose emissions pushed the total above the threshold could be held liable (in the amount the cost curve jumps). This attention to marginal costs in apportioning damages in some concurrent cause cases seems promising, but the concept plainly needs more development. See Donald Wittman, Optimal Pricing of Sequential Inputs: Last Clear Chance, Mitigation of Damages, and Related Doctrines in the Law, 10 J. Legal Stud. 65 (1981).

likelihood rule does not apply as among the defendants. It is inapposite because all three defendants caused damages. It is therefore pointless to ask which *one* of the three defendants caused the total damages; yet that is the question that our appeal to statistical decision theory was intended to help answer.[70]

Of course, probabilistic reasoning is not irrelevant to the issues in *Michie*. The maximum likelihood rule still applies (in the form of the $p > \frac{1}{2}$ rule) as between each plaintiff and the defendants as a group. A finder of fact must evaluate the evidence at trial under this form of the preponderance-of-the-evidence standard to decide whether the aggregate emissions damaged each plaintiff. Moreover, a court or jury could try to disentangle each company's contribution to the fallout by treating diffusion and convective mixing as sufficient to randomize all the plants' emissions before they reached the plaintiffs, by examining the locations of each plant vis-à-vis each plaintiff, and by estimating the cost imposed by each plant's discharge. Suggestions for "causal apportionment,"[71] "culpability shares,"[72] and the like[73] are not lacking. There are many subtleties here,[74] but the key point is that these matters are beyond the ken of the mathematical analysis I have expounded. That analysis is essentially parasitic. It attaches itself to the governing substantive liability rule, which is exactly what one would expect of an evidentiary rule designed to guide decisions as to whether a plaintiff has proved the existence of circumstances that, if present, would generate liability.

V. Conclusion

This article has touched upon a potpourri of issues—the logical underpinnings of the preponderance-of-the-evidence standard, the treatment of justifiably naked statistical evidence, and multiple causation in tort cases. The analysis has been single-minded but rich enough to produce a lengthy

---

70. See note 50 *supra*.

71. Rizzo & Arnold, *supra* note 17.

72. Refining Market Share Liability, *supra* note 11.

73. Robinson, *supra* note 11.

74. Consider, e.g., Rizzo and Arnold's proposal to apportion damages among "simultaneous causes" according to a particular function of certain probabilities. Rizzo & Arnold, *supra* note 17, at 1410–11, 1415. When the causes act "simultaneously," they advocate dividing the aggregate damages in proportion to the probability that each defendant's conduct, acting alone, would have caused this amount of damage. When the causes interact, they offer a formula for measuring the "synergistic" contribution and dividing it equally among the defendants. There are serious difficulties with their formula (see David Kaye & Mikel Aickin, A Comment on a Proposed "Economic Method" of "Causal Apportionment" (1982) (unpublished article manuscript)), and there is reason to question the ability of "economic theory" to allocate jointly caused damages without resort to what are basically accounting conventions. See Armen Alchain & William R. Allen, Exchange and Production: Competition, Coordination, and Control 256 (2d ed. Belmont, Cal.: Wadsworth Publishing Co., 1977) (impossibility of apportioning the cost of a common input to two products).

argument. It may be well to recapitulate its essential points. Some elementary concepts of statistical decision theory were used to cope with some cases that seemed problematical under the preponderance-of-the-evidence standard. These cases all involved justifiably naked statistical evidence (or something quite close to it) and a variety of candidates for the role of the single culpable cause. From the standpoint of decision theory—and the law—the problem is to come to the "best" decision as to which actor or natural force was responsible. Because of limitations in the evidence at trial, we were obliged to speak of the probability p_0 that the plaintiff was responsible and the probabilities p_i associated with the other possible causes. Using these probabilities, we introduced the concept of an expected loss function, and we used one such function to discern the "best" decision rule in this situation. Specifically, we proved that the optimal decision rule is the "maximum likelihood" rule that selects the "most probable" cause (or causes). If this cause is such that liability does not attach, as with a "naturally occurring" cancer, a plaintiff who assumed the risk, or a legally immune defendant, then we argued that plaintiff should bear the costs of his injury. On the other hand, if the most likely cause is a legally responsible defendant, then we insisted that the defendant be fully liable.[75] This, we suggested, best implemented the function of the preponderance-of-the-evidence standard, and we criticized the *Sindell* court for assuming, in a case involving more than two possible causes, that this standard demanded a showing that an individual defendant was more probably than not responsible for the plaintiff's condition.

There was, however, a major qualification to these conclusions. We indicated that in situations where the probabilities never changed from case to case, the maximum likelihood approach would err systematically to the disadvantage of one person or group.[76] To avoid such bias, we advo-

---

75. If there are several equally likely causes, as in *Summers v. Tice*, the maximum likelihood rule leaves us indifferent as to how to allocate the damages among these causes.

76. The cases that seemed suitable candidates for the expected value rule involved the real possibility of repeated recovery from the same defendant. For example, under the maximum likelihood rule the pharmaceutical house that marketed the largest quantity of DES in California could be held liable for every DES-caused injury in California. The argument for the expected value approach also can apply when distinct defendants are implicated in different cases, yet certain probabilities remain fixed from one case to the next. Consider the scenario suggested by Glen Robinson: "Suppose [plaintiff] is exposed to carcinogen A that . . . creates a 20% probability of cancer. Carcinogen B enhances the risk of cancer by 10% (given a state of the world, which now includes A, the probability of cancer is now 30%). . . . Is it not possible that carcinogen B might *never* (or hardly ever) be the 'most likely' cause of cancer, albeit still a 'culpable' (unreasonable) contribution to the risk of cancer? Should we not therefore be concerned about the lost deterrence?" Letter from Glen O. Robinson to David Kaye, Feb. 25, 1982. The analysis developed in this article will apply if either A or B, but not both, caused the plaintiff's cancer. (If a single tumor could have resulted from the simultaneous action of the two carcinogens, the mathematical proofs are inapposite, and substantive doctrines of contribution must be considered.) If the risk due to A is independent of the risk due to

cated assigning expected damages to each potentially liable party. On this basis, we defended the most important facet of the *Sindell* case.

Finally, we turned to cases of true multiple causation primarily to make it clear that any use of probabilities to apportion damages had to rest on other principles. In every case to which we applied our analysis, only one defendant caused plaintiff's injury. In *Summers,* only one hunter fired the shot that wounded the plaintiff's eye. In *Sindell,* it is plausible to think that only one firm produced the particular DES that injured each individual plaintiff. In the taxicab hypothetical only one driver was at fault. And in the phenoxy acids hypothetical, we assumed that only those stomach cancers linked in the "but for" sense to the workplace were within the scope of workers' compensation. In all these cases, we saw that the maximum likelihood, or "most probable defendant" rule provided the best method for matching the injury with the true cause, but we also realized that in *Sindell* and the phenoxy acids case, the guess least likely to err would result in biased errors even in the long run.[77]

In sum, the recommended approach to the class of cases studied here can be cast as a two-fold injury. The court should ascertain whether the case at bar is of the type for which the maximum likelihood rule would achieve probable accuracy only at the cost of virtually certain bias. If so, it should apply rules of contribution or apportionment framed to assign expected damages to the liable parties. If, on the other hand, the case does not raise any serious, long-run bias problem, the preponderance-of-the-evidence standard should apply. The judge or jury should hold the single most likely defendant fully liable.[78]

Instances of naked statistical evidence represent hard cases for the preponderance-of-the-evidence standard, but I have attempted to show that even these cases are not inevitably beyond its reach and that the mathematical theory of probability can guide us in implementing this eviden-

---

B, then the maximum likelihood rule does make A liable (since A had a greater chance than the next most likely contender, B, of producing the cancer). If this is a recurring situation—if reasonable victims never confront the risk from B in the absence of that created by A—so that producers of B never would be found liable, then the maximum likelihood rule would yield biased results and "lost deterrence." This much follows from the fact that the probabilities associated with A and B are presumed to be fixed across a wide range of cases.

At the same time, we might hesitate before moving to an expected value rule in cases like these. In light of the vast number of carcinogens, manufacturers, and activities in which people engage, the cost of trying to apply expected value liability through the system of private tort litigation could well be prohibitive. Further discussion of the broad-based use of expected value liability can be found in Robinson, *supra* note 11.

77. As to *Sindell,* we also questioned the need for individualized matching in the first place.

78. Again, in cases of "ties" among defendants, other doctrines or theories about contribution and joint and several liability must be consulted.

516   **AMERICAN BAR FOUNDATION RESEARCH JOURNAL**   1982:487

tiary standard. I must confess that my treatment of these cases rests on certain assumptions, and I would not wish these to be obscured or buried. One such assumption is that the substantive law seeks to tailor the damages a culpable party must pay to the magnitude of the injury he has in fact caused and that the evidentiary standard should implement the substantive liability rules with a minimum of error or bias.[79] Another is that in the absence of any long-run bias, the law should be insensitive to the direction of errors. It is neither better nor worse for one defendant to pay damages that he would not be assessed if perfect knowledge of the facts were available than it is for a plaintiff or any other defendant to incur these costs. These sorts of value judgments are implicit in the mathematics. Although I have suggested that these assumptions are plausible, it should be plain that the mathematical aspects of this article do not guarantee the correctness or wisdom of its recommendations. Nevertheless, the formal reasoning does permit us to trace the implications of the assumptions in a careful and revealing way. To the extent this process enables us to appreciate the nature of the preponderance-of-the-evidence standard and to recognize its limitations in certain cases involving naked statistical evidence and multiple causes, the exercise will have been worth the effort.

79. In the situations of potential "bias," as I have defined them, one can say that the expected value approach reduces one sort of "error," since it imposes correctly estimated aggregate costs on the culpable parties. In addition, in a few such situations, the expected value approach is error minimizing, even as that term is used here. See text accompanying notes 53 and 59 *supra*.

[10]

LIABILITY AND INDIVIDUALIZED EVIDENCE

I

Cases like *Smith v. Rapid Transit, Inc.*[1] present a problem to students of tort law. Here is a typical hypothetical case—I will call it *Smith v. Red Cab*—which presents the problem more cleanly than the actual case does. Mrs. Smith was driving home late one night. A taxi came towards her, weaving wildly from side to side across the road. She had to swerve to avoid it; her swerve took her into a parked car; in the crash, she suffered two broken legs. Mrs. Smith therefore sued Red Cab Company. Her evidence is as follows: she could see that it was a cab which caused her accident by weaving wildly across the road, and there are only two cab companies in town, Red Cab (all of whose cabs are red) and Green Cab (all of whose cabs are green), and of the cabs in town that night, six out of ten were operated by Red Cab. Why is that the only evidence she can produce against Red Cab? She says that although she could see that it was a cab which came at her, she could not see its color, and as it was late, there were no other witnesses to the accident—other than the driver himself, of course, but he has not come forward to confess.

If we believe Mrs. Smith's story, and are aware of no further facts that bear on the case, then we shall think it .6 probable that her accident was caused by a cab operated by Red Cab. I think it pays to spell this reasoning out; what follows is one way of doing so. If we believe Mrs. Smith's story, then we believe that a cab, indeed exactly one cab, caused the accident, so that there is such a thing as *the* cab which caused the accident; and we believe that it was a cab in town that night. Thus we believe:

(1) The cab which caused the accident was a cab in town that night.

If we believe Mrs. Smith's story, we also believe:

(2) six out of ten of the cabs in town that night were operated by Red Cab.

Relative to the facts reported by (1) and (2), it is true that:

(3) The probability that the cab which caused the accident was operated by Red Cab is .6.

* Professor of Philosophy, Massachusetts Institute of Technology. A great many people made helpful criticisms of earlier drafts of this essay; I am particularly indebted to Jonathan Bennett, David Gauthier, Gilbert Harman, Paul Horwich, and Mary C. Potter.

1. 317 Mass. 469, 58 N.E.2d 754 (1945). Mrs. Smith's evidence against the defendant bus company consisted of evidence that she was caused harm by a negligently-driven bus on Main Street, and that the defendant bus company has the sole franchise for operating a bus line on Main Street.

200   LAW AND CONTEMPORARY PROBLEMS   [Vol. 49: No. 3

But those are the only facts such that we are both aware of them and aware of their bearing on the question who operated the cab which caused the accident. (Perhaps we are aware that the accident took place on, as it might be, a Tuesday. Even so, we are not aware of any reason to think that fact bears on the question whose cab caused the accident.) Other facts whose relevance is clear might come out later: for example, a Green Cab driver might later confess. But as things stand, we have no more reason (indeed we have less reason) to think that any facts which later come out would support the hypothesis that the cab which caused the accident was operated by Green Cab than we have to think they would support the hypothesis that the cab which caused the accident was operated by Red Cab. We are therefore entitled to conclude that (3) is true—in fact, rationality requires us to conclude that (3) is true, for .6 is the degree of belief that, situated as we are, we ought to have in the hypothesis that the cab which caused the accident was operated by Red Cab.[2]

Is it right that Mrs. Smith win her suit against Red Cab? The standard of proof in a tort suit is "more probable than not,"[3] which is plausibly interpretable as requiring only that the plaintiff establish a greater than .5 probability that the defendant (wrongfully) caused the harm. But most people feel uncomfortable at the idea of imposing liability on Red Cab on such evidence as Mrs. Smith here presents. Why? That is the problem.

II

People v. Collins[4] and its typical descendant hypotheticals raise an analogous problem for the student of criminal law, but less cleanly, so let us set them aside for the time being. Consider, instead, a hypothetical case which I shall call *People v. Tice.*[5] Two people, Tice and Simonson, both hated Summers and wished him dead. Summers went hunting one day. Tice followed with a shotgun loaded with ninety-five pellets. Quite independently, Simonson also followed, but *he* had loaded his shotgun with only five pellets, that being all he had on hand. Both caught sight of Summers at the same time, and both shot all their pellets at him. Independently: I stress that there

---

2. Some commentators on earlier versions of this essay have suggested that perhaps we ought not be entirely confident of the truth of (3), given only the truth of (1) and (2), on the ground that there just might have been more green cabs than red cabs in the part of town in which, and at the time at which, the accident took place. This suggestion seems to me to be a mistake—but one which is not worth going into here. Anyone who is similarly moved may suppose we are provided, in addition to (1) and (2), with an admission by Red Cab that there is good reason to think (and no reason not to think) that cab-distribution at the time, in the part of town south of the tracks (where the accident took place), was the same as overall cab-distribution in town that night.

3. *See generally* W. PROSSER & W.P. KEATON, PROSSER & KEATON ON THE LAW OF TORTS § 38 (5th ed. 1984).

4. 68 Cal. 2d 319, 438 P.2d 33, 66 Cal. Rptr. 497 (1968). Collins and his wife had been convicted of second degree robbery on evidence that the robbers, like the defendants, were an interrracial couple; the man black, with mustache and beard, who drove a yellow car, the woman white, with blond hair in a ponytail—the prosecution alleged on statistical grounds that there was only one chance in twelve million that a couple would possess all these features.

5. With apologies to Summers v. Tice, 33 Cal. 2d 80, 199 P.2d 1 (1948).

was no plot or plan. Only one pellet hit Summers, but that one was enough: it hit Summers in the head and caused his death. While it was possible to tell that the pellet which caused Summers' death came either from Tice's gun or from Simonson's gun, it was not possible to tell which. So what charges should be brought against Tice and Simonson? In the event, Simonson is charged with attempted murder, and in *People v. Tice*, Tice is charged with murder.

Well, why not? To win its case against Tice, the prosecution must show that it is beyond a reasonable doubt that the pellet which caused Summers' death was a pellet fired by Tice. But given the information in hand, that seems easy, for given the information in hand, we can say both:

(1') The pellet which caused Summers' death was a pellet fired at Summers

and

(2') Ninety-five out of the one hundred pellets fired at Summers were fired by Tice.

The facts these report are the only facts such that we are both aware of them and aware of their bearing on the question whose pellet caused Summers' death. We therefore may, indeed should, conclude that it is also true that:

(3') The probability that the pellet that caused Summers' death was fired by Tice is .95.

And isn't a proposition beyond a reasonable doubt if it is .95 probable?[6]

I hope you will feel at least as uncomfortable at the idea of convicting Tice of murder on such evidence as this that he caused the death as you feel at the idea of imposing liability on Red Cab in *Smith v. Red Cab*.

There are differences, of course. In *Smith v. Red Cab*, the information we have in hand gives no reason at all to think that both cab companies were at fault: it gives reason to think that one cab company was at fault, namely the one, whichever it was, that caused the accident. So if Mrs. Smith wins her suit, then Red Cab may be being held liable for her costs despite the fact that it not only did not cause her injury, but was entirely without fault.

By contrast, the information we have in hand in *People v. Tice* gives reason to think that both Tice and Simonson were at fault: it gives reason to think that both committed attempted murder. So if the people win their case against Tice, then while Tice may be being held liable for murder without having caused Summers' death, he was all the same gravely at fault, having at a minimum tried to bring that death about.

This difference brings in train yet another. If Tice did not cause Summers' death, then his failure to do so was—relative to the evidence we have in hand—just *luck*, good or bad luck according to the view you take of the matter. He did everything he could to cause the death, and if he did not cause it, well,

---

6. Rita James Simon invited a sample of judges to translate "beyond a reasonable doubt" into numerical probabilities. It is interesting to learn that almost a third of them translated it as a probability of one. Over two thirds, however, translated it as a probability of .95 or less. *See* Simon, *Judges' Translations of Burdens of Proof into Statements of Probability*, 13 TRIAL LAWYER'S GUIDE 103 (1969).

202   LAW AND CONTEMPORARY PROBLEMS   [Vol. 49: No. 3

that was certainly no credit to him. By contrast, if Red Cab did not cause Mrs. Smith's injury, that was a credit to Red Cab, for—relative to the evidence we have in hand—if Red Cab did not cause the accident, it was not at fault at all.

We could have eliminated these differences by altering the details of *People v. Tice* so as to make the evidence suggest only that one of the actors (Tice or Simonson) was at fault, the evidence that it was Tice who was at fault issuing from nothing other than the evidence that it was a pellet from Tice's gun which caused the death—just as the evidence that it was Red Cab that was at fault issues from nothing other than the evidence that it was one of Red Cab's cabs which caused Mrs. Smith's accident. It is not easy to alter the details in that way without introducing a measure of weirdness. But I think we ought to feel that there is no need to do so; that is, I think we ought not be moved by the differences I pointed to between *Smith v. Red Cab* and *People v. Tice*.

No doubt it was just luck for Tice if he did not cause Summers's death. But that does not justify convicting him of murder. Anyone who attempts murder, and goes about things as carefully and well as he can, is just lucky (or unlucky) if he does not cause the death he wishes to cause, but that does not warrant holding him for murder. So also for Simsonson. In fact, he too attempted murder, and it is also just luck for him if he did not cause Summers' death.

It is arguable that if a man attempts murder, and it is just luck for him that he does not cause the death he wishes to cause, then morally speaking he has acted as badly as he would have acted had he succeeded.[7] Many of those who take this view regard it as morally suspect that the penalty for murder should be heavier than the penalty for attempted murder. (Perhaps they view it as flatly unacceptable that there is such a difference in penalty. Perhaps they think the difference is just barely acceptable in light of the fact that imposing the same penalty might give unsuccessful attempters a motive to try again, or in light of some other, or additional, considerations.) At all events, the penalty for murder is everywhere heavier than the penalty for attempted murder. Or at least so I suppose; and we can anyway assume this true in the jurisdiction in which Tice is to be tried. So it is not enough to justify the charge of murder against Tice that it is just luck for him if he did not cause the death: to warrant imposition of the heavier penalty, the prosecution has positively to prove beyond a reasonable doubt *that* he caused it.

Well, isn't it beyond a reasonable doubt that Tice caused Summers' death? After all, it is .95 probable that he did.

III

It is often said that the kind of evidence available in *Smith v. Red Cab* and *People v. Tice* merely tells us the "mathematical chances"[8] or the "quantitative

---

7. Thomas Nagel denies this claim in a very interesting article, *Moral Luck*, in T. NAGEL, MORTAL QUESTIONS 24-38 (1979).

8. Smith v. Rapid Transit, Inc., 317 Mass. 469, 470, 58 N.E.2d 754, 755 (1945).

probability"[9] of the defendant's guilt. And it would be said that what is missing in those cases, the lack of which makes conviction suspect, is "real"[10] or "individualized"[11] evidence against the defendant.

I strongly suspect that what people feel the lack of, and call individualized evidence, is evidence which is in an appropriate way causally connected with the (putative) fact that the defendant caused the harm.[12]

Consider the evidence that it was a Red Cab which caused the accident in *Smith v. Red Cab:* it consists entirely of Mrs. Smith's testimony that a cab caused her accident, and that six out of ten of the cabs in town that night were operated by Red Cab. If we believe her, we believe there are such facts as that a cab caused her accident, and that six out of ten of the cabs in town that night were operated by Red Cab. But those facts lack an appropriate causal connection with the (putative) fact that Red Cab caused the accident.

What sort of causal connection would be appropriate? Well, if a witness came forward to say he saw the accident, and that the cab which caused the accident looked red to him, *then* we would have what would be called individualized evidence against Red Cab; and my suggestion is that that is because the accident-causing cab's actually being red (and therefore being Red Cab's) would causally explain its looking red to that witness. We might call this "backward-looking individualized evidence" of the defendant's guilt because the bit of evidence (the witness's believing the cab looked red to him) points back towards the (putative) fact that Red Cab caused the accident.

Or if it turned out that Red Cab had given a party for its drivers on the evening of the accident, a party which turned into a drunken brawl, then too we would have what would be called individualized evidence against Red Cab; and my suggestion is that that is because the party would causally explain its having been a Red Cab which caused the accident. We might call this "forward-looking individualized evidence" of the defendant's guilt because the bit of evidence (the party) points forward towards the (putative) fact that Red Cab caused the accident.

Or more complicated (since it involves a common cause), if a red cab crashed into a parked car shortly after Mrs. Smith's accident, and four blocks past the place of it, the driver giving all signs of being drunk, then that too would be called individualized evidence against Red Cab; and my suggestion is that that is because that driver's having been drunk would causally explain *both* his crashing into the parked car *and* his (and therefore Red Cab's) having caused Mrs. Smith's accident.

---

9. Day v. Boston & Me. R.R., 96 Me. 207, 217, 52 A. 771, 774 (1902).

10. *Id.* at 217, 52 A. at 774.

11. *See, e.g.,* Tribe, *Trial by Mathematics: Precision and Ritual in the Legal Process,* 84 HARV. L. REV. 1329 (1971).

12. An earlier version of these ideas appears in section 8 of Thomson, *Remarks on Causation and Liability,* 13 PHIL. & PUB. AFF. 101 (1984). What I here call "individualized evidence," in light of this term's frequency in the literature, I there called "internal evidence." Neither term strikes me as a particularly happy choice.

In the actual *Smith v. Red Cab*, no such further evidence came out. The facts available to us provide no forward-looking individualized evidence that Red Cab caused the accident, for they neither supply nor suggest any causal explanation of its having been a red cab which caused the accident. Moreover, the facts available to us neither supply nor suggest anything which might have been a common cause *both* of those facts available to us *and* of the (putative) fact that Red Cab caused the accident.

What is of interest is that we do have in the actual *Smith v. Red Cab a* piece of backward-looking individualized evidence for *a* hypothesis. Mrs. Smith says she could see it was a cab which came towards her, and its actually being a cab which came towards her would causally explain her believing this; so her saying she could see it was a cab which came towards her is backward-looking individualized evidence that it was a cab which caused her accident.

No one, of course, supposes that individualized evidence is (deductively valid) proof. In particular, our having backward-looking individualized evidence that a cab caused Mrs. Smith's accident is logically compatible with its not having been a cab which caused the accident.

Moreover, different bits of individualized evidence may differ in strength. For example, it is possible for a private car or bus or truck, or for all I know a gorilla, to be disguised as a cab, and the more non-cabs there are on the roads that are disguised as cabs, the less weight we are entitled to place on the causal hypothesis that Mrs. Smith's believing it was a cab which caused her accident was caused by its being a cab which caused her accident, and thus the less weight her believing it was a cab which caused her accident lends to the causal hypothesis that it was a cab which caused her accident. Still, her believing it was a cab which caused her accident is backward-looking individualized evidence that it was a cab which caused her accident, for her having that belief would be causally explained by its having been a cab which caused her accident.

Mrs. Smith's believing it was a cab which caused her accident would also be causally explained by its having been a red cab which caused her accident. (Again, her believing it was a cab which caused her accident would also be causally explained by its having been a cab once ridden in by a Presbyterian minister which caused her accident.) That does not mean that her believing it was a cab which caused her accident is backward-looking individualized evidence for the hypothesis that it was a red cab which caused her accident (or for the hypothesis that it was a cab once ridden in by a Presbyterian minister which caused her accident.) For there is no reason to think that the redness of a cab (or its past ridership) is causally relevant to its looking to a person like a cab. Mrs. Smith, of course, might be unusual in this respect: it might be that her retinas are so structured as to record "cabbiness" only when caused to do so by red-cabbiness. If we were given reason to think that that is true of her, we would thereby have been given reason to think her believing it was a cab which caused her accident *was* backward-looking individualized evidence that it was a red cab which caused her accident. But in the absence of a reason to think her odd in some such respect as that, what we have is backward-looking individualized evidence only for the hypothesis that it was a cab which caused her accident.

For Red Cab to be guilty, the cab that came at Mrs. Smith (supposing it was a cab that came at her, as we do suppose if we believe her story) has to have had the features which distinguish Red Cab's cabs from the other cabs in town that night. Redness is one such feature, and no doubt there are indefinitely many others. But we have in hand no facts about the accident in which the (putative) redness of the accident-causing cab, or its (putative) possession of some other feature which distinguishes Red Cab's cabs, can be assigned an appropriate causal role. The facts available to us, then, provide (backward-looking) individualized evidence that a cab caused Mrs. Smith's accident, but no individualized evidence that the cab that caused the accident was one of Red Cab's cabs.

The point, then, is not that the only evidence we actually have in hand in *Smith v. Red Cab* is numerical or statistical,[13] for we do have in that case a piece of individualized evidence for the hypothesis that it was a cab that caused the accident.

More important, numerical or statistical evidence too can be causally connected in an appropriate way with the (putative) fact it is presented to support. Suppose a plaintiff alleges that he was refused a job with a certain organization on grounds of race; in evidence, he presents statistics showing that the racial composition of the organization's work force diverges widely from that of the local population. Those data suggest a causal hypothesis, namely that the organization intends to discriminate in its hiring practices, and the organization's intending to discriminate in its hiring practices would causally explain *both* the existing divergence in racial composition, *and* the (putative) fact that it refused to hire the plaintiff on grounds of race. So that evidence too is individualized, although it is numerical or statistical.

If we had individualized evidence (and thus, on my hypothesis, appropriately causally connected evidence) against Red Cab, in addition to the evidence we already have in hand, then we would feel considerably less reluctant to impose liability on Red Cab. Why is that? That seems to me to be a very hard question to answer.

It cannot plausibly be said that the addition of individualized evidence against Red Cab would make us feel less reluctant to impose liability on it because the addition of individualized evidence against Red Cab would raise the probability that Red Cab caused the accident. Even in the absence of individualized evidence, the probability that Red Cab caused the accident is

---

13. It is of interest that although the court in *Smith v. Rapid Transit, Inc.* stated that "[t]he most that can be said of the evidence in the instant case is that perhaps the mathematical chances somewhat favor the proposition that a bus of the defendant caused the accident," 317 Mass. 469, 470, 58 N.E.2d 754, 755 (1945), the evidence in that case was entirely nonstatistical. I suggest that what the court felt the lack of was not nonstatistical evidence, but appropriately causally connected evidence.

already .6, which on a plausible interpretation of the requirements of tort law is higher than it need be.

Friends of the idea that individualized evidence is required for conviction have not really made it clear why this should be thought true. That has encouraged their enemies to suppose they have the idea because they think that individualized evidence is uniquely highly probabilifying.[14] The enemies have then found it easy to make mincemeat of the friends. The enemies draw attention to the fact (and it is a fact) that eyewitness testimony, for example, which is a paradigm of individualized evidence, may be quite unreliable, that is, may probabilify to a lower degree than would some pieces of purely numerical or statistical evidence. And they draw attention to the mistakes about probability (and they are mistakes) which have been studied by Tversky and Kahneman, in particular, those which issue from ignoring base rates.[15]

But I think that is at best an ungenerous diagnosis of what is at work in the friends of individualized evidence. What is at work in them is not the thought that individualized evidence is uniquely highly probabilifying, but rather the feeling that it supplies something which nonindividualized evidence does not supply, which further something is not of value because it raises the probability of the hypothesis in question.

IV

I think it is helpful at this point to look at an analogous problem faced by the student of the theory of knowledge. What is currently called the classical, or traditional, account of knowledge says that a person A knows that a proposition p is true if and only if three conditions are met. First, p actually is true. Second, A believes that p is true. And third, A has a reason, and indeed, not just any old reason, but a good enough reason, for believing that p is true.[16] (Some people prefer to express this third condition in the words "A is

---

14. Some friends of individualized evidence do seem to think it uniquely highly probabilifying. Consider, for example, the court's comment in *Day v. Boston & Me. R.R.*:

> Quantitative probability, however, is only the greater chance. It is not proof, nor even probative evidence, of the proposition to be proved. That in one throw of dice there is a quantitative probability, or greater chance, that a less number of spots than sixes will fall uppermost is no evidence whatever that in a given throw such was the actual result. Without something more, the actual result of the throw would still be utterly unknown. The slightest real evidence that sixes did in fact fall uppermost would outweigh all the probability otherwise.

96 Me. 207, 217, 52 A. 771, 774 (1902). But the passage is obscure, and perhaps not to be understood in the way that at first suggests itself. In any case, I take it that friends of individualized evidence who would express their view in words such as these are in a very small minority.

15. For a very helpful survey and further references, see Saks & Kidd, *Human Information Processing and Adjudication: Trial by Heuristics*, 15 Law and Soc'y Rev. 123 (1980-81). Judging from that article, I think that Saks and Kidd would say, not only that the friends of individualized evidence are mistaken in thinking it of any special interest, but also that it is a mistake to suppose there is a problem to be solved here—thus that it is a mistake to think it would be worrisome for Mrs. Smith to win her case in *Smith v. Red Cab* or for the people to win its case in *People v. Tice.*

16. It is arguable that we should add: "and it is because of having a good enough reason for believing that p is true that A does believe that p is true." (For it is arguable that a man might have a good enough reason for believing that p is true, and yet believe that p is true for no reason at all, or for a bad reason.)

justified in believing that p is true." Others express it in the words "A has adequate evidence for p.") Not surprisingly, it is this third condition which has generated the controversy. Nobody argues about the first or second conditions: it is plain enough that you know that the sun is shining only if it is shining and you believe it is. What is unclear is exactly what is required for A to have a reason which is good enough for it to be true that A satisfies the third condition.

But one thing is clear: if A's satisfaction of those three conditions is supposed to be sufficient for A's knowing that p is true, then A is not marked as satisfying the third condition by virtue of its being the case that in light of all of the facts available to A, he is entitled to conclude, indeed is rationally required to conclude, that p is highly probable. Suppose Alfred believes, truly, that Bert bought five tickets in a lottery, and that a hundred tickets were sold altogether. Suppose also that those are the only facts such that Alfred is both aware of them and aware of their bearing on the question whether Bert will win the lottery. (For example, Alfred is not aware of any reason to believe that the lottery is rigged, or, if he is aware of a reason to believe it rigged, there is no ticket such that he is aware of a reason to believe the lottery is rigged in favor of that ticket.) The following is therefore true:

> In light of all of the facts available to Alfred, he is entitled to conclude, indeed is rationally required to conclude, that it is .95 probable that Bert will lose the lottery.

Alfred is aware that he is so situated, and for that reason concludes that Bert will lose the lottery, so that it is also true that:

> Alfred believes that Bert will lose the lottery.

Suppose, lastly, that Bert will actually lose the lottery (though of course Alfred does not, and we may suppose we ourselves do not, find this out until later). Then it is also true that:

> Bert will lose the lottery.[17]

But it is plainly *not* true that:

> Alfred knows that Bert will lose the lottery.

It pays to stress: not merely is it not true to say now that Alfred knows that Bert will lose the lottery, it will also not be true to say later, after Bert has already lost the lottery, that Alfred then knew (that is, in advance) that Bert would lose the lottery.

There is something missing in Alfred, something the lack of which makes it false to say he knows that Bert will lose. The point obviously is not that .95 is not a sufficiently high probability. Pick any probability you like, as high as you like, and we need only suppose that the appropriate number of tickets were

---

17. Some people think that sentences which are contingent and in the future tense have as yet no truth-value. If that were true, then it would be wrong to say we speak truly if we say "Bert will lose the lottery," even if Bert does later lose the lottery. I say "if that were true" because I think it false. No matter. Anyone who holds this view is invited to substitute for the lottery a game in which Bert just drew five cards at random from a Superdeck (which contains 100 successively numbered cards), and then replaced them without looking. Alfred believes none of Bert's cards said "73." Let us suppose that is true; and so on, and so on.

sold to entitle Alfred to conclude it probable in that degree that Bert will lose the lottery. Still, even if in fact Bert will lose, Alfred does not know that he will.

Should we say that what is missing in Alfred is something which would make him satisfy a further, fourth, condition on knowledge? That is, it could be said that Alfred's reason for believing Bert will lose the lottery is good enough for him to satisfy the third condition, and that what the case shows is that knowledge requires something more than satisfaction of the three conditions laid out in the classical account. Or should we instead say that although Alfred has good reason for believing Bert will lose the lottery, what is missing is something which would make his reason be *good enough* for him to satisfy the third condition on knowledge? It makes no theoretical difference which choice we make, for the question what is missing in Alfred remains to be answered whichever choice is made. But I prefer the second, for the classical account of knowledge is so natural and intuitively plausible as to incline one to want to interpret it in such a way as to have it be immune to such cases as that of Alfred and Bert.

To get at exactly what is missing in Alfred, then, one would have (as I shall put it) to get at exactly what is required for A to have a reason which is good enough for it to be true that A satisfies the third condition on knowledge. That, alas, is a hard problem.

But it is easy enough to say very roughly what is missing in Alfred: what he lacks is something which would make it not be just luck for him that Bert will lose the lottery.

This is a helpful way of expressing what Alfred lacks[18] because it points towards anyway one of the things which is required for A to have a reason that is good enough for it to be true that A satisfies the third condition on knowledge. What I have in mind is this: it seems very plausible to think that A's reason for believing that p is true must ensure, or *guarantee,* that p is true. Alfred's reason for believing that Bert will lose the lottery does not in any way guarantee that Bert will lose it. By contrast, consider Alice. Alice believes that Bertha bought one ticket in a certain lottery, and that unbeknownst to Bertha, the ticket seller tore up her ticket stub directly after selling it to her, and that the drawing will be made from among the stubs. Suppose that belief of Alice's is true. Then Alice has good reason for believing that Bertha will lose the lottery, namely the fact that Bertha bought one ticket, the ticket seller tore up her stub, and the drawing will be made from among the stubs. Suppose Alice does therefore believe that Bertha will lose the lottery. Suppose, lastly, that time passes, and that it has now turned out that Bertha did lose the lottery, and that her losing it *was caused by* the ticket seller's tearing up her stub. Then the fact which was Alice's reason for believing that Bertha would lose the lottery caused, and thereby guaranteed, that Bertha would lose it. This makes it seem much less implausible to think Alice knew

---

18. It was suggested by Thomas Nagel's remarks on epistemology in T. NAGEL, *supra* note 7.

that Bertha would lose the lottery than it did to think Alfred knew that Bert would lose it.

Again, consider Arthur. Arthur believes he is having, and is in fact having, a visual impression as of a chicken in front of him, and his having that visual impression is his reason for believing there is a chicken in front of him. If it later turns out that there was then a chicken in front of him, and that there being a chicken in front of him *was causally necessary for* his having that visual impression, then his having that visual impression guaranteed that there was a chicken in front of him. This makes it seem much less implausible to think Arthur knew that there was a chicken in front of him than it does to think Alfred knew that Bert would lose his lottery. It is similarly so for more complicated cases, in which the guaranteeing proceeds via common causes.[19]

On most views about knowledge, even this is not enough. Suppose that A believes there is such a fact as q, and takes q to be reason for believing that p is true. On most views about knowledge, it is not enough to secure A's satisfying the third condition on knowledge that there actually is such a fact as q, and that q actually guarantees that p is true: in addition (on those views) A must have good reason for believing that there is such a fact as q, and A must believe, and have good reason for believing, that q does guarantee that p is true. Or perhaps, more strongly, that *these* good reasons must themselves contain guarantees. On some views about knowledge, if there is luck anywhere at all in A's route to his belief that p is true, then it is just luck for A if p is true, and A therefore does not know that p is true.

Those (most restrictive) views about knowledge had better be false, for down this road lies skepticism, that is, the thesis that nobody knows anything. (Only people who are excessively charmed by philosophy can regard it as a happy outcome that nobody so much as knows he has hands or feet.)

I think it helpful at this point to turn from knowledge itself to saying one has it. That in any case is what will matter for us.

If A says to B "I know that p is true," then A does something more than just assert something: he gives B his word that p is true, and in one of the strongest ways we have of doing this. Indeed, A positively invites B to take his word for the truth of p, and to rely on it. That being so, and because it is so, there are rather strong moral constraints governing the acceptability of saying "I know that p is true." Plainly A's saying this is not made acceptable by the mere fact that p turns out to be true. Suppose Boris will suffer a loss if he relies on the truth of p, where p is not true. He trusts Andrew; he tells Andrew he will suffer a loss if he relies on the truth of p where p is not true, and asks Andrew if Andrew knows whether p is true. Andrew says "Yes, I know that p is true," but he says this in awareness that he has not the slightest idea whether p is true—he does so because he decided to flip a coin, heads I

---

19. The guaranteeing required for knowledge need not proceed via causes at all. Compare mathematical knowledge: the truth of one statement may guarantee the truth of another via entailing it.

say it, tails I don't, and the coin came up heads. Then Andrew has acted improperly in saying what he said, even if, as it turns out, p is true.

One way, the weaker way, of explaining the impropriety in Andrew is to point to the fact that he said "I know that p is true" without having any reason at all, and a fortiori without having good reason, to think p true. Boris had said he would suffer a loss if he relied on the truth of p where p is not true; lacking good reason to think p true, Andrew could not be sure that p was true, and thus could not be sure that Boris would not suffer that loss if he relied on the truth of p—yet he all the same, and therefore wrongly, invited Boris to rely on it.

But that *is* weak. Consider Alfred again. Alfred has good reason to think Bert will lose the lottery he entered, for Alfred is entitled to believe it .95 probable that Bert will lose the lottery. Suppose the lottery works like this, and Alfred knows it does: the winner must prove he is the winner by producing his ticket, or he must wait six months for his prize, during which time the lottery organizers will assure themselves that he is who he says he is. Nevertheless Alfred says to Bert: "Look, it's silly of you to hang on to those five, by now grubby, lottery tickets. I *know* you are going to lose that lottery." Bert will suffer a loss (six months' interest on a large sum of money) if he accepts Alfred's invitation to rely on his losing the lottery, throwing out his tickets, and it then turns out that he wins the lottery; and Alfred knows this. The fact that Alfred is sure that Bert will lose the lottery, and thus that Bert will not suffer that loss, does not make it acceptable for Alfred to have said what he said.

Let us call the loss a person will suffer if he relies on the truth of p where it turns out that p is not true that person's "potential mistake-loss." Then we can say the fact that Alfred is sure that Bert will lose the lottery, and thus that Bert will not suffer his potential mistake-loss, does not justify Alfred's saying to Bert, "I know you will lose the lottery."

What Alfred implies by saying "I know you will lose" is not merely that he is sure that Bert will lose, and thus that Bert will not suffer his potential mistake-loss, but that Alfred has a certain kind of ground for being sure of this—"insider's information" (about rigging, perhaps) in the case of lotteries, stock markets, and other gambler's games. Alfred implies he has a guarantee of some kind that Bert will lose, so that not merely will Bert not suffer his potential mistake-loss if he relies on Alfred's word, but that Bert does not even risk suffering his potential mistake-loss if he relies on Alfred's word. (Think of Bert's reaction if he accepts Alfred's invitation to rely on his losing, and tears up his tickets, and then later learns that the ground on which Alfred issued his invitation was merely the large number of tickets sold, which made it highly probable that Bert would lose. Bert himself knew it was highly probable he would lose at the time of buying his tickets; and he will correctly view himself as having no less right to complain about Alfred's behavior if he loses the lottery than if he wins it.)

It is plausible to think, quite generally, then, that if A is aware that B will suffer a loss if he relies on the truth of p where p is not true, then A ought not say to B "I know that p is true" unless A is more or less sure that he has a guarantee that p is true[20]—so that B not only will not suffer, but does not even risk suffering, his potential mistake-loss. There are, after all, considerably weaker sentences than "I know that p is true" which the language makes available to A: he can say instead "I believe that p is true" or "It is highly probable that p is true" or "I believe that p is true because it is highly probable that p is true," and so on. To assert some such weaker sentence as this is not to do nothing: assertions of them are governed by moral constraints, too. But none of them is such that to assert it is to invite one's intended hearer to take one's word for the truth of p and rely on it. Doing *that* calls for being more or less sure that one has a guarantee of the truth of p—at any rate, it does where a potential mistake-loss is in the offing.

By way of making connection with what was said earlier, we could restate this point as follows: doing *that* calls for being more or less sure that it would not be just luck for one if p turns out to be true—at any rate, it does where a potential mistake-loss is in the offing.

This gives us a second, and stronger, way of explaining the impropriety in Andrew. He told Boris he knew that p was true because the coin he flipped came up heads. This was wrongful behavior on his part because he invited reliance without being in the slightest degree sure of having a guarantee, despite his awareness of Boris's potential mistake-loss.

A need only be, as I said, "more or less sure" that he has a guarantee, for circumstances differ. Suppose you ask me now, in the afternoon, if there's cold chicken in the icebox. I say, "Yes, I'm certain there is, in fact I know there is." Why do I say that? Because I believe I put some there this morning, and believe my putting some there this morning guarantees that there is some there now. In the normal course of events, my saying these words is acceptable, even if it turns out that there is no cold chicken in the icebox now, for example, because some burglars broke in at noon and ate it while burgling. That is because in the normal course of events I know your potential mistake-loss is small—you will merely waste a bit of energy on a trip to the icebox, and suffer a minor disappointment, if it is "chickenless." But we could imagine a series of cases in which your potential mistake-loss increases; that would be a series of cases in which the burden on me to make sure that I really do have a guarantee increases proportionately. Where I know your potential mistake-loss is truly terrible, then the burden on me is

---

20. Usage is slippery, and there are cases which suggest that this quite general claim may be overbroad. Suppose Alfred says to Bertha, "I know that Bert will not pay you the money he owes you," and says this on the ground that Bert has no money other than that which he will get if he wins the lottery, and that a large number of tickets were sold; wouldn't *that* be all right? (I owe this example to David Gauthier.) I strongly suspect, however, that this seems to us acceptable (if it does) only because we are not imagining the further details which would be required to make plain what Bertha's potential mistake-loss is; and I predict that the supplying of such further details would make Alfred's behavior seem unacceptable.

very heavy indeed. Did my putting cold chicken in the icebox this morning really guarantee that there is some there now? Your potential mistake-loss being so great, I ought not ignore the possibility that it did not. (Burglars are only one of many more or less weird possibilities.) I had better not invite you to run the risk of suffering that truly terrible loss unless I make *very* sure I have a guarantee—as, for example, by getting up out of my chair and going to have a look, and perhaps also a sniff and taste.

In light of these considerations it might well be wondered why we ever say anything so strong as "I know that p is true." Well, we do not normally say this unless we believe our hearer will gain something if he acts on the supposition that p is true where it is true, or suffer a loss if he fails to act on the supposition that p is true where it is true. (In the normal course of events, a person who asks whether there is cold chicken in the icebox wants to eat some, and thus has something to gain by acting on the supposition that there is some there if it turns out that there is). A foregone gain is what is sometimes called an "opportunity cost," and thus itself a kind of loss, so it could have been said, instead, more briefly: we do not normally say, "I know that p is true," unless we believe our hearer will suffer a loss (if only a loss which is an opportunity cost) if he fails to act on the supposition that p is true where it is true. What would be the point of inviting a hearer to rely on the truth of p if the hearer has nothing at all to lose by failing to rely on it even if p is true?

There might, then, be a case in which A believes both of the following about B. First, B will suffer a loss if he acts on the supposition that p is true where it is not true—that is B's potential mistake-loss. Second, B will suffer a loss if he fails to act on the supposition that p is true where it is true; I will call this B's "potential omission-loss." Here A has some more or less delicate balancing to do. But perhaps this much is clear enough: the greater the amount by which B's potential mistake-loss exceeds B's potential omission-loss, the more sure A must be that he has a guarantee that p is true before saying, "I know that p is true."

It is not knowledge itself, but rather saying one has knowledge, that will matter for us. But I think it is worth indicating, just briefly, why (as I said) I think it helps a student of knowledge to attend to what is required for acceptably saying one has it. According to the classical account of knowledge, A knows that p is true if and only if p is true, A believes that p is true, and A has good enough reason for believing that p is true. What marks A as having good enough reason for believing that p is true? I suggest it is enough if A takes himself to have a guarantee that p is true, and if, also, what he takes to guarantee this does guarantee it. Thus, for example, suppose (again) that I believe there is cold chicken in the icebox because I believe I put some there this morning, and believe my putting some there this morning guarantees that there is some there now. Suppose also that my believing I put some there this morning guarantees that I did put some there this morning, and that that guarantees that there is some there now. Then I do know that there is some there now. I could have been wrong: for example, my putting cold chicken in the icebox this morning could have failed to guarantee that there is some there now. (Perhaps burglars took the chicken.) I suggest we should take that fact to have a bearing, not on whether I know, but only on what I may acceptably say.

V

I fancy it may already be clear from this long digression on knowledge what, on my view of them, is at work in the friends of individualized evidence.

The jurors do not say, "we know that the defendant is guilty" at the close of the trial; they say only, "the defendant is guilty"; but in saying that they do something of great significance. It is not strong enough to say they declare the defendant guilty. If you and I have been watching the trial, I may say to you as we leave the courtroom, "the defendant is guilty." I have declared the defendant guilty, but have not done, because I am not so situated as to be able to do, what the jurors do when they say these words at the close of the trial. The institution in which they are participating is so structured that their saying these words then is their imposing liability on the defendant—for if they say these words at that time, appropriate others will act on the supposition that he is guilty, which includes imposing the relevant penalty on him. So they do not merely invite reliance, they act in awareness that reliance will follow.

Under what conditions is it acceptable for the jurors to agree to say those words at the close of the trial? One thing which is perfectly plain is that their agreeing to say those words is not made acceptable by the mere fact that the defendant actually is guilty of what he is charged with. That what the jurors declare true turns out to have in fact been true does not by itself make it acceptable for them to have declared it true.

This point is obvious, but it pays to make its source explicit. Suppose that a jury is puzzled by the evidence which has been presented to it, and cannot arrive at a consensus as to its weight. "I know," says one juror, "let's decide by flipping a coin—heads we impose liability, tails we don't." They agree; they flip a coin, which comes up heads; so they return and say, "the defendant is guilty." Their doing that is not made acceptable by the fact (supposing it a fact) that the defendant actually is guilty. If the defendant is guilty, then he deserves the penalty which this jury causes to be imposed on him; but that the defendant not suffer the relevant penalty unjustly is not all that matters to us. It matters to us, not just that a defendant not suffer a penalty unjustly, but also that the penalty not be imposed on him unjustly.

The defendant will suffer the penalty unjustly if he is not guilty, and so does not deserve the penalty; that means that it is unjust to impose liability on him, and thereby cause him to suffer the penalty, unless one believes one has good reason to believe that he is guilty, and therefore deserves the penalty. That being so, we can say, and we have an explanation of why we can say, that the jury I just described imposed liability unjustly: they imposed liability without believing they had good reason to believe that the defendant was guilty.

There is a second, and stronger, possible explanation of why we can say that that jury imposed liability unjustly: it was just luck for those jurors if what they declared true was true—just luck for them if it actually was the case that the defendant was guilty.

That *is* stronger. Consider the jury in the hypothetical case I called *People v. Tice* in section II above. Suppose it declares Tice guilty of murder, not on the ground that a coin was tossed and came up heads, but on the following two grounds. First, the evidence makes clear (perhaps Tice has even confessed) that he attempted to kill Summers. Second, Summers was killed by one of one hundred pellets fired at him, and ninty-five of the pellets fired at him were fired by Tice. Then the jury imposes liability on Tice on the ground of what is on any view good reason to believe Tice guilty. (Its situation in respect of Tice's being guilty is exactly like Alfred's situation in respect of Bert's losing the lottery: in both cases, rationality requires believing the conclusion highly probable.) If it is required of a jury only that it not impose liability without good reason to believe the defendant guilty, then this jury does not impose liability unjustly. All the same, it is just luck for the jury if it actually was Tice who killed Summers, and thus if Tice committed murder. So if it is required of a jury that it not impose liability unless it has, not merely good reason, but reason of a kind which would make it not be just luck for the jury if its verdict is true, then this jury imposes liability unjustly.

On my view of them, what is at work in the friends of individualized evidence is precisely the feeling that just imposition of liability requires that this stronger requirement be met.[21] They believe, as they say, that "mathematical chances" or "quantitative probability" is not by itself enough; on my view of them, that is because they feel, rightly, that if a jury declares a defendant guilty on the ground of nonindividualized evidence alone, then it is just luck for the jury if what it declares true is true—and they feel, not without reason, that it is unjust to impose liability where that is the case. I say "not without reason" because I feel in considerable sympathy with them.

What would make it not be just luck for the jury if what it declares true is true? A guarantee. I suggested that individualized evidence for a defendant's guilt is evidence which is in an appropriate way causally connected with the (putative) fact that the defendant is guilty, and hence (putatively) guarantees the defendant's guilt; so to require individualized evidence of guilt just is to be requiring a guarantee.

None of this is incompatible with the fact that there is a difference made in our law between the standard of proof required in criminal cases on the one

---

21. To say this is to rest the importance of individualized evidence on what the jurors do, rather than on something external to the trial. Compare Laurence H. Tribe, who rests it on the symbolic or expressive function of trials. *See* Tribe, *supra* note 11. Compare also Charles Nesson, who rests it on the messages communicated by trials. *See* Nesson, *The Evidence or the Event? On Judicial Proof and the Acceptability of Verdicts*, 98 Harv. L. Rev. 1357 (1985).

hand, and cases in tort on the other hand. Our law requires the jury in a criminal case to be sure beyond a reasonable doubt that the defendant is guilty before imposing liability on him; the friend of individualized evidence may be taken to say that the jury must be sure beyond a reasonable doubt that the defendant is guilty *because of* being sure beyond a reasonable doubt that there are facts available to it which guarantee that the defendant is guilty. Our law requires the jury in a case in tort to believe no more than that it is more probable than not that the defendant is guilty; the friend of individualized evidence may be taken to say that the jury must believe it is more probable than not that the defendant is guilty *because of* believing it more probable than not that there are facts available to it which guarantee that the defendant is guilty.

We met an analogous difference in section IV above, and the differences have analogous sources. Our society takes the view that, in a criminal case, the loss to society if the defendant suffers the penalty for a crime he did not commit is very much greater than the loss to society if the defendant does not suffer the penalty for a crime he did commit. (That is, in particular, we think it would be considerably worse that an innocent defendant be punished than that a guilty defendant go free.) This point might be reexpressed as follows: our society takes the view that in a criminal case, the society's potential mistake-loss is very much greater than the society's potential omission-loss. It would be no wonder, then, if our law imposed a heavy standard of proof on the jury in a criminal case; and according to the friend of individualized evidence, that means the jury must be very sure of having a guarantee before imposing liability for a crime. The fact that the standard of proof in a case in tort is more relaxed by itself suggests that our society takes the view that, in a case in tort, the society's potential mistake-loss is not much greater than the society's potential omission-loss. (Thus, in particular, we think it would be worse that an innocent defendant be forced to pay a plaintiff who either was not really harmed at all, or who anyway was not harmed by the defendant, than that a guilty defendant go free and the plaintiff he injured go uncompensated—but not by much.)

VI

The typical hypothetical cases which descend from *People v. Collins* raise the problem we are dealing with less cleanly than *People v. Tice*, and that in two ways.

Here is an example. Mrs. Smith testifies that she saw a man, indeed exactly one man, kill Bloggs, and that she could see he was one-legged, left-handed, entirely bald, and extremely tall. Mrs. Jones is a biologist-statistician, and she testifies that men with all four of those features are very rare: only one man in ten million has all four of them. There is the defendant Mullins, and we can see that *he* has all four of them. So we may be inclined to think we may conclude, on the basis of that evidence alone, and without hearing or seeing anything more, that it is highly probable that Mullins killed Bloggs.

As the commentators on this kind of case enjoy pointing out, however, this would be a mistake on our part. After all, there are a lot more than ten million men in the world. How many are there? Let us suppose there are a billion men in the world, thus 1,000 million. If, as Mrs. Jones' data suggest, one in ten million men have all four features, then 100 in 1,000 million have all four features; so we are entitled to conclude only that the probability that Mullins killed Bloggs is one in 100, thus .01—not at all a high probability.

I think it helps to see this point if we lay our information out in the way in which I laid our information out in *People v. Tice* and *Smith v. Red Cab.* Thus we believe, on the basis of what we can see on looking at the defendant Mullins:

> (1") Mullins is a man who is one-legged, left-handed, entirely bald, and extremely tall.

If we believe Mrs. Smith's story, we believe that exactly one man killed Bloggs, and that the man is one-legged, left-handed, completely bald, and extremely tall. If we also believe Mrs. Jones's story, we believe that one in ten million men have those four features. If we believe there are 1,000 million men, we are committed to believing that 100 men all told have those four features. So we are committed to believing:

> (2") One of the one hundred men who are one-legged, left-handed, entirely bald, and extremely tall killed Bloggs.

The conclusion we are entitled to draw is only:

> (3") The probability that Mullins killed Bloggs is .01.

Our problem is this: what should we think of the idea of convicting a defendant on the basis of evidence which makes it highly probable he is guilty, but which is nonindividualized evidence against him? So the first way in which the typical hypothetical descendant of *People v. Collins* is less clean than *People v. Tice* is this: in that kind of case, the available data do not even entitle us to conclude that it is highly probable that the defendant is guilty.

This may seem to be a relatively trivial difficulty, for there are a number of different ways in which the case against Mullins could be revised so as to raise the probability of his guilt, despite its anyway seeming to remain a case in which no individualized evidence is produced against him. We might suppose, for example, that Mrs. Smith testifies that the man she saw kill Bloggs had, not merely the four features I have mentioned, but in addition, only one eye—not one good eye and one bad eye, but exactly one eye, right in the middle of his forehead. Mullins, as we can see in the revised case, has not merely the four features, but exactly one eye, right in the middle of his forehead. Our biologist-statistician, Mrs. Jones, assures us that she would have said this was impossible if she had not seen Mullins: it is due to a freak genetic mutation which may be expected to occur no more often than once in 100 billion men. There being in existence only one billion men, it is highly probable that Mullins is the only existing man with all five features, and thus (if we believe Mrs. Smith's story) it is highly probable that Mullins did kill Bloggs.

This kind of move has to be watched, however, for once the probability is made high in this way, our problem does not come out more cleanly; it instead disappears. What I have in mind is this. In the original case against Mullins, Mrs. Smith believes she saw a one-legged, left-handed, entirely bald, and extremely tall man kill Bloggs. That is individualized evidence that a man with those four features killed Bloggs, for the (putative) fact that a man with those four features killed Bloggs would causally explain Mrs. Smith's believing she saw a man with those four features kill Bloggs. (Compare the fact that in *Smith v. Red Cab* Mrs. Smith's believing she saw a cab come towards her was individualized evidence that it was a cab that came towards her.) Our further evidence also suggests there are other men than Mullins, ninety-nine other men in fact, who have all four features, so getting individualized evidence against Mullins requires getting some fact in respect of which an appropriate causal role is played by a feature which distinguishes Mullins from the others. (Compare the need of a fact in respect of which an appropriate causal role is played by a feature which distinguishes Red Cab's cabs from the other cabs we believe were in town on the night of the accident in *Smith v. Red Cab*.)

In the revised version of the case, Mrs. Smith believes she saw a one-legged, left-handed, entirely bald, extremely tall, *and* one-eyed man kill Bloggs. That is individualized evidence that a man with those five features killed Bloggs, for the (putative) fact that a man with those five features killed Bloggs would causally explain Mrs. Smith's believing that she saw a man with those five features kill Bloggs. But *here* our further evidence suggests that only Mullins has all five features, and therefore that there is no such thing as a feature which distinguishes him from the other men who have all five features, and therefore that there is no possible fact in respect of which such a distinguishing feature so much as could play an appropriate causal role. To the extent to which we believe that further evidence, then, we shall take ourselves to have individualized evidence, not merely that a man with those five features killed Bloggs, but that Mullins did—he being the only available candidate with the five features.

There is more to be said here, but I bypass it, because whatever revisions might be made in the case against Mullins, there remains the second way in which the typical hypothetical descendant of *People v. Collins* raises our problem less cleanly than *People v. Tice:* in that kind of case, the sources of the statistical information are typically softer than the source of the piece of statistical information in *People v. Tice*. For example, that exactly one man in ten million has all four of the features which interested us in the original case against Mullins may be true; but we may well be pardoned if we do not feel much confidence in those figures. By contrast, I was inviting you to suppose that the evidence presented in court entitles us to feel entirely confident that exactly one hundred pellets were fired at Summers, and that exactly ninety-five of them were fired at him by Tice. (And compare *Smith v. Red Cab*. Perhaps we do not feel *entirely* confident that six out of ten of the cabs in town that night were operated by Red Cab, since we are so familiar with gypsy cabs. But we may have good reason to believe in the figures Mrs. Smith gives us, and no positive reason to disbelieve in them, perhaps in that Red Cab itself gives us no reason to think them wrong.)

On the other hand, I am not arguing that no hypothetical descendant of *People v. Collins* raises our problem cleanly. Quite to the contrary: *People v. Tice* itself descends from it.

VII

Commentators on this kind of case very commonly say that all evidence is "ultimately" statistical or probabilistic,[22] and that this itself means there is muddle in the friends of individualized evidence. Such comments are decidedly not transparent, and they can be interpreted in a number of different ways. The interpretation which makes them most plausible, however, seems to me to be one under which they do not really consitute a difficulty for the friends of individualized evidence.

Under that interpretation, to say all evidence is ultimately statistical says about causal hypotheses in particular that such evidence as we have for them is itself statistical (or anyway, is ultimately itself statistical), so that we can have no more confidence in the truth of a causal hypothesis than we have in the statistical data which (ultimately) support it. This does not strike me as obvious, but perhaps it is true. Perhaps it is true that I am entitled to place no more confidence in the hypothesis that my pressing the button marked "T" just now caused a "t" to appear on the page than I have in some set of statistical data. Alas, I do not know what exactly the members of the set are, but perhaps one member is not quite that every time I press the button marked "T" a "t" appears on the page, for sometimes I have previously pressed the button marked "SHIFT," so that a "T" appeared on the page instead, and sometimes the machine had not been turned on, so that nothing appeared on the page, and so on, but something *like* this.

Now why might it be thought that this should trouble the friend of individualized evidence? He is familiar with the idea that a causal hypothesis may be supported by statistical data. Compare, for example, the kind of race discrimination case mentioned in section III above, in which statistical data about the divergence between the racial composition of an organization's workforce and that of the local population suggests the causal hypothesis that the divergence was caused by an intention to discriminate in hiring.

Moreover, he is familiar with the fact that being presented with statistical data may entitle us to feel more or less confidence in the truth of a causal hypothesis. As I said in connection with *Smith v. Red Cab*, the more non-cabs there are on the roads that are disguised as cabs, the less confidence we are

---

22. Tribe himself says, "I am, of course, aware that *all* factual evidence is ultimately 'statistical,' and all legal proof ultimately 'probabilistic'." Tribe, *supra* note 11, at 1330 n.2. *See also* Saks & Kidd, *supra* note 15, at 153 ("Invariably, all information is really probability information.").

entitled to place in the hypothesis that its being a cab that came towards Mrs. Smith does causally explain her believing she saw a cab come towards her. Similarly for a surprise witness, who comes forward to say he saw the accident, and that the accident-causing cab looked red to him: the more often non-red things look red to that witness when he is placed in similar circumstances, the less confidence we are entitled to place in the hypothesis that the cab's being red does causally explain his believing that it looked red to him.

One can, after all, be more or less sure of having the kind of guarantee that, as I said, is what the friends of individualized evidence think some degree of assurance is necessary for just imposition of liability. That our assurance of having a guarantee of the appropriate kind rests (ultimately) on statistical data seems to me to be something he can in consistency agree to.

And it need not trouble the friend of individualized evidence that the particular causal hypothesis that this or that bit of individualized evidence points to may not be well supported by the available statistical data, and hence that the bit of individualized evidence may not lend much weight to the hypothesis that the defendant is guilty. As I said, it is an ungenerous diagnosis of what is at work in the friends of individualized evidence to take them to think it of value because of thinking it uniquely highly probabilifying. What interests them is something else—a something else that I have been trying to bring out, and to invite others to take an interest in.

Fact-scepticism

[11]

JEROME FRANK'S FACT-SKEPTICISM AND OUR FUTURE*

EDMOND CAHN†

I

W̲HEN̲ Dean Rostow asked me to describe the main features of Jerome Frank's legal philosophy, I resolved that—no matter how tentative my summary might be—I must speak in the perspective of the future. For one thing, this is the way he habitually faced and spoke and wrote; it is the way to be faithful to his thought. For another, his philosophy—which he called "fact-skepticism"[1]—is nothing more or less than a bold confrontation of the future and a flinging of gages at its feet. I believe that Jerome Frank's fact-skepticism represents an epoch-making contribution not only to legal theory and procedural reform, but also to the understanding of the entire human condition. The history of our time will record whether we profited by the challenges he bequeathed to us.

For about twenty-five years Jerome Frank's coruscating and marvelously restless mind planned and built and developed the meaning of fact-skepticism. Fully aware that his approach was novel, he deliberately repeated and reiterated his doctrines, phrased them first this way then that, and summoned analogies from every corner of the cultural world to make his ideas clearer. To justify the repetitions, he used the following story:

> "Mr. Smith of Denver was introduced to Mr. Jones at a dinner party in Chicago. 'Oh,' said Jones, 'do you know my friend Mr. Schnicklefritz, who lives in Denver?' 'No,' answered Smith. Later in the evening, when Smith referred to Denver, Jones again asked whether Smith was acquainted with Schnicklefritz, and again received a negative reply. As the dinner party broke up, Smith remarked that he was leaving that night for Denver, and Jones once more inquired whether Smith knew Schnicklefritz. 'Really,' came the answer, 'his name sounds quite familiar.' "[2]

Gradually, beneath the surface of the repetitions, the essential doctrine cumulated and moved forward. In 1930 when he wrote *Law and the Modern Mind*, the final chapter, filled with uncritical enthusiasm, was entitled "Mr. Justice Oliver Wendell Holmes, the Completely Adult Jurist." Holmes had originated the so-called "prediction theory" of law. He had declared that "the prophesies of what courts will do in fact, and nothing more pretentious are what I mean by the law. . . . The primary rights and duties with which juris-

---

*Address delivered at services conducted by Yale Law School in memory of Jerome Frank on April 12, 1957.

†Professor of Law, New York University School of Law.

1. As the title indicates, this paper does not purport to cover all of Jerome Frank's juristic views. It is restricted to "fact-skepticism," which he rightly considered his most characteristic and significant contribution.

2. F̲RANK, C̲OURTS ON T̲RIAL viii (1949).

prudence busies itself . . . are nothing but prophesies."[3] Such was the basis of Holmes' approach, which Jerome Frank accepted as unimpeachable in 1930. By 1949 when *Courts on Trial* was published, it began to be apparent that fact-skepticism either cancelled the value of Holmes' theory or at least required a drastic reformulation.[4]

Finally, in 1954 Jerome Frank acknowledged openly that he had traveled far from his initial discipleship. Here in a single passage we have an epitome of fact-skepticism and of its relation to Holmes' doctrine:

> "More than twenty years ago, I tried pragmatically to apply Holmes' prediction theory to future specific decisions of trial courts. If such decisions could not be prophesied, then usually lawyers' prophesies would be of comparatively little worth, since very few trial court decisions are appealed and the upper courts affirm most of those that are appealed. So I enquired whether, before suits commenced, lawyers usually could, with some high degree of accuracy, foretell the specific decisions of the trial courts in particular cases. . . .
>
> "I discovered that this sort of prophesying was markedly uncertain. Why? Briefly stated, these are the reasons: Most law suits are, in part at least, 'fact suits.' The facts are past events. . . . The trial judge or jury, endeavoring (as an historian) to learn those past events, must rely, usually, on the oral testimony of witnesses who say they observed those events. The several witnesses usually tell conflicting stories. This must mean that at least some of the witnesses are either lying or (a) were honestly mistaken in observing the past facts or (b) are honestly mistaken in recollecting their observations or (c) are honestly mistaken in narrating their recollections at the trial. . . . [T]he trial court (judge or jury) must select some part of the conflicting testimony to be treated as reliably reporting the past facts. In each law suit, that choice of what is deemed reliable testimony depends upon the unique reactions of a particular trial judge or a particular jury to the particular witnesses who testify in that particular suit. This choice is, consequently, discretionary: The trial court exercises 'fact-discretion.' . . . No one has ever contrived any rules (generalized statements) for making that choice, for exercising that fact-discretion. It therefore lies beyond—is uncapturable by—rules, and it is 'unruly.' Being unruly, it is usually unpredictable before the law suit commences.
>
> ". . . [T]he upper courts in most cases accept the trial courts' 'unruly' fact-findings, i.e., the trial court's exercise of its fact-discretion remains, ordinarily, unreviewable, final, undisturbed. . . . Lawyers can often (not always) make fairly accurate guesses as to what rules the courts will apply in uncommenced law suits. The difficulty lies in guessing to what facts the courts will apply those rules. Only in a modest minority of cases is that element of the decisions foreseeable. Therefore, seldom can a 'bad' man or a 'good' man obtain from his lawyer the sort of prophesy Holmes' theory envisioned. . . .
>
> "The foregoing represents but a sketch of a complex subject. However, it will suffice to show the shakiness of Holmes' prediction theory. For the most part, that theory succumbs to what I call 'fact-skepticism.' "[5]

3. Holmes, *The Path of the Law*, 10 HARV. L. REV. 457, 458 (1897), reprinted in COLLECTED LEGAL PAPERS 167 (1920).

4. Book Review, 59 YALE L.J. 809 (1950).

5. Frank, *A Conflict with Oblivion: Some Observations on the Founders of Legal Pragmatism*, 9 RUTGERS L. REV. 425, 447-49 (1954).

II

As we know, Jerome Frank had not set out to answer or criticize Holmes; in point of fact the outcome proved a surprise to him, a rather curious by-product of his enterprise. His chosen goal was quite different. He wished to dispel various popular myths about courts and trials so that truth might light the path to a more rational and humane judicial process. Fact-skepticism led him to advocate a number of procedural and administrative changes, which he hoped would be informed by special studies in comparative law. Though even fact-skeptics may dispute the desirability of this or that detailed proposal, no one can doubt that Jerome Frank's disclosures have helped make American judges and lawyers increasingly impatient—as they should be—with the wooden technicalities in traditional procedure. If you apply the goad often enough, even an ox may eventually move.

Nevertheless, the philosophy of fact-skepticism far transcends any question or program of procedural reform. It cannot be understood if one regards Jerome Frank merely as a penetrating, critical and imaginative jurist. "Merely," forsooth; there is an entire image of him implicit in that "merely." To know him at all was to be overwhelmed by the extraordinary scope, the opulent universality of his reading and thinking. Fortunately for fact-skepticism, it grew and developed in that phenomenally gifted mind of his. There it acquired depth and spaciousness, and became coordinate with the other main currents of his philosophy.

The first neighboring current was Jerome Frank's historiography.[6] From the 1920's until the very end of his days, he consistently defended the attitude called "historical relativism." Among the various relativists, he found particular clarity and candor in Carl Becker. It was Becker who told the American Historical Association in 1926:

> "The historian has to judge the significance of the series of events from the one single performance, never to be repeated, and never, since the records are incomplete and imperfect, capable of being fully known or fully affirmed. Thus into the imagined facts and their meaning there enters the personal equation. The history of any event is never precisely the same thing to two different persons; and it is well known that every generation writes the same history in a new way, and puts upon it a new construction. . . .
>
> "In this way the present influences our idea of the past, and our idea of the past influences the present. We are accustomed to say that 'the present is the product of all the past'; and this is what is ordinarily meant by the historian's doctrine of 'historical continuity.' But it is only a half truth. It is equally true, and no mere paradox, to say that the past (our imagined picture of it) is the product of all the present. . . ."[7]

---

6. See FRANK, FATE AND FREEDOM pt. 1 (1945).

7. Becker, *What Are Historical Facts?*, 8 WESTERN POL. Q. 327, 336-37 (1955). Professor Leo Gershoy, distinguished historian, has kindly supplied me with this archetypal statement of historical relativism.

This was the first of the persistent currents that fact-skepticism met and blended with in Jerome Frank's philosophy. The second was typified by William James and Horace Kallen. As Becker vitalized the dry records of the past, these philosophers humanized the dry notions of conceptual thinking. Concepts, though necessary and valuable, must be treated as implements and ministers, not as monarchs. Every human being is more than a member of the genus, he is also a unique individual. In fact, a human being's most generic characteristic is his very uniqueness. Many of the relations and transactions that make human experience are fortuitous, exuberant, filled with uncaptured residues, at best pluralistic, not to be domesticated completely by any of our abstract terms. To Jerome Frank's delight, William James used to refer to "wild facts,"[8] that is, those which furnish so much of the spirited element in our existence and which our logical propositions and scientific laws simply fail to net. It takes a more alert and compassionate nature than most men possess to sense the presence of "wild facts" and respect their worth and influence.

But it was in the juristic thought of Aristotle that fact-skepticism found its closest affinity. I mean, in Aristotle as Jerome Frank read and understood Aristotle. Not that I disagree with his interpretation of Aristotle; I find it completely valid. Nevertheless, since there are various and conflicting interpretations, and since I have just referred admiringly to William James' pluralism, I can hardly insist here that Jerome Frank was alone equipped to understand Aristotle.

What did he find in Aristotle? He found: that the general rules of any legal order, if applied automatically and impersonally, are often unfit to handle the "wild facts," the subtle, unexpected particulars and the infinite diversity of human affairs; that general rules must be continually adjusted, individualized and alloyed with considerations of equity to make them more malleable; and that the excellence of equity consists not in its following but in its refusing to follow established propositions of law.[9] Apparently Aristotle realized that if the rigid, abstract, impersonal norm is made our king and hero, our tale is liable to become a tragedy, for the hero suffers from a fatal flaw. In this view of things, what Carl Becker did to the inflexible past, what William James did to the abstract concept, Aristotle in his wisdom had done to the mechanical and impersonal rule of law.

These were the three currents of thought with which fact-skepticism merged, and among them Aristotle was foremost. On the only occasion I recall when Jerome Frank wrote as though he were speaking through the mouth of another, it was Aristotle whom he chose for his alter ego. This is what he suggested Aristotle would say if he were to return after 2300 years:

---

8. Frank, *Some Tame Reflections on Some Wild Facts*, in VISION AND ACTION: ESSAYS IN HONOR OF HORACE M. KALLEN 56 (Ratner ed. 1953). See also Frank, *Civil Law Influences on the Common Law—Some Reflections on "Comparative" and "Contrastive" Law*, 104 U. PA. L. REV. 887, 921-24 (1956).

9. Frank, *Modern and Ancient Legal Pragmatism—John Dewey & Co. v. Aristotle*, 25 NOTRE DAME LAW. 207, 460 (1950). For the criticism involved in Dewey's different approach to Aristotle see his EXPERIENCE AND NATURE c. 2 (1925).

"It is shocking, of course, to see how this personal element in justice has been shamefully exploited by totalitarian governments. They have put the best of things to the most evil uses. But that personal element, whether one likes it or not, is an inherent part of the decisional process, under any form of government. It is therefore folly to conceal its presence in the working of courts in a democracy. To conceal it, indeed, is to ensure that it operates at its worst, surreptitiously, without such intelligent ethical restraints as experience and wisdom show us both can be and should be imposed. Here, as elsewhere, we must distinguish the desirable and the possible. The wise course is openly to acknowledge the personal element, and then to do whatever can practically be done to get rid of its evils and to bring about its constructive uses. For the rest, we shall have to put up with it, however bad, as we do with ineradicable sickness and death."[10]

These, I believe, are the main attributes of Jerome Frank's skeptical philosophy—it is vitalistic, pluralistic, and above all, personalistic. Suppose now a lawyer is willing to say that everything in this exposition is true: will that make him an authentic fact-skeptic? No, it will not, for acquiescence is not enough. Even the naive lawyers who still live in the conceptualistic murk of the 1920's will acknowledge that past incidents may not always be reconstructed accurately in court. They will concede quite cheerfully that predictions are very uncertain before a controversy has developed—provided, of course, no one objects to their being paid, as all of us are, for making the predictions.

Acquiescence does not suffice. Too many who aver they have acquiesced are ready to rejoin their colleagues in the same old idolatry of concepts, where they chant the same old platitudes in praise of a wholly impersonal "government under law," "a government of laws and not of men." No wonder this sort of self-delusion provoked John Dewey to remark, "A government of lawyers and not of men!"[11]

Who then is a genuine fact-skeptic? I should say, only those who employ fact-skepticism among the constant postulates of their thinking, who use it as lenses to read the daily newspaper, and who endeavor to respond to its profound and manifold challenges. What are these challenges?

III

Before listing them (quite incompletely, of course), let me recall that fact-skepticism is a single doctrine with three associated prongs. It criticizes our capacity to ascertain the transactions of the past; it distrusts our capacity to predict the concrete fact-findings and value judgments of the future; and finally, it discloses the importance of the personal element in all processes of choice and decision. Now we can begin with:

---

10. Frank, *supra* note 9, at 491.
11. Private remark quoted in T. R. POWELL, VAGARIES AND VARIETIES IN CONSTITUTIONAL INTERPRETATION 24 (1956).

The challenge to the law

Wherever we look at the law, fact-skepticism has a leading role to perform. Consider, for example, the application of the Fourteenth Amendment. It would seem very curious if the fundamental human fabric of the world's most powerful nation were to be determined by what a few senators of varying intellectual caliber may have intended—or hinted they intended—during the remote and unattractive year of 1868. Curious it would be; curious enough to be insupportable, I should think. We were rescued from any such tyranny of the dead, at least in respect of desegregation, by the way the Supreme Court treated the strictly historical arguments in *Brown v. Board of Education*.[12] It was fact-skepticism that emancipated us. The Supreme Court declared that if 1868 aspired to rule the 1950's, 1868 ought to have been less ambiguous. With this profitable example to work with, the legal profession's next question may be: How many other despotisms of past over present can we undertake to subvert by the same technique; how many more historical bonds can fact-skepticism loosen, then dissolve?

Yet it is wise to remember that the shackles of the anticipated future can be tighter than those of the conceived past. Our entire juristic order—civil, criminal and administrative—is permeated with uncritical assumptions about future deterrence. The law takes property, liberty and even life under the supposed warrant of deterrence. What the judges call "public policy" they deduce in large part from inarticulate premises of deterrence. Deterrence shapes the rules of tort liability; deterrence attempts to vouch for censorship and sedition laws. In short, cool, self-possessed deterrence has its roster of victims no less than hot vindictiveness.

Fact-skepticism challenges us to make a detailed and radical re-examination of the entire rationale of deterrence. Does this or that assumed deterrent really deter? What other, uncalculated effects does it have? If in many instances it does deter, then how far dare the community go in penalizing one person to influence the behavior of others?

Let me mention a single practical application among many. Fact-skepticism, in and of itself, would provide two severally sufficient reasons for ending that national infamy of ours, capital punishment: First, because capital punishment is not demonstrated to deter in fact; second, because under our system there is substantial danger of convicting and executing the wrong person. Jerome Frank concurred that each of these reasons is more than sufficient for abolishing the death penalty.

The challenge to political theory and cultural anthropology

Here I suggest that fact-skepticism calls for a thoroughly candid review of what is taken for granted in phrases like "the rule of law," "representative

---

12. *Cf.* Order for Reargument, questions 1 and 2, 345 U.S. 972 (1953); Brown v. Board of Education, 347 U.S. 483, 489-90 (1954).

government," "popular mandate," and "the consent of the governed." Let the timorous have no misgivings: our fabric of government is so superior to Russia's that we can easily afford to turn the full force of fact-skepticism on it. For example, Cold War or no Cold War, no American needs to deny or disparage the important human and personal factors that animate every variety of so-called "constitutionalism," including our own. One of the best features of fact-skepticism is that it warns men away from false supports and treacherous comforts. In this way, it impels them toward truth, which remains their faithful ally.

The challenge to philosophy in general and pragmatism and analytic empiricism in particular

A few years before the publication of *Courts on Trial*, a professor of philosophy and historian of American pragmatism declared that Holmes' analysis was "the only systematic application of pragmatism that has yet been made."[13] If then fact-skepticism should edify the legal profession, how much more should it excite philosophers, ethicists and all who are concerned with the meaning of language and the foundations of moral responsibility! Surely they will wish to consider how deeply and how far fact-skepticism may affect Peirce's doctrine that the meaning of a concept is to be found in its conceived consequences and James' doctrine that "the true" is the long-run expedient in our way of thinking. In basic respects, are not these also prediction-theories? In so far as they are, it seems fair to analogize them to Holmes'. Since their subject matter is so very general, they may prove even more vulnerable to the prongs of fact-skepticism. Pragmatists and instrumentalists in every profession will appreciate the force and imminence of the challenge. . . .

Now we approach fact-skepticism's ultimate contribution. Let us suppose along with Jerome Frank and Carl Becker that accurate knowledge of the past is generally elusive. Let us suppose along with Jerome Frank and William James that our abstract concept is often like the iron claw of a toy crane in an amusement arcade: while it may succeed in grasping the ordinary, humdrum objects in the cage, it will continually miss the things that are interesting, deviant or eccentric. Further, let us grant—for grant we must—that though occasionally we may be able to foretell certain direct and immediate consequences of a proposed statute or decision, we cannot pretend to prophesy the spreading network of eventual, indirect, mediate, oblique consequences. As Judge Learned Hand has said, "Such prophesies infest law of every sort, the more deeply as it is far reaching; and it is an illusion to suppose that there are formulas or statistics that will help in making them."[14] No substitutes for critical judgment, no escapes from personal responsibility, no formulas? Yet

---

13. Fisch, *Justice Holmes, the Prediction Theory of Law and Pragmatism*, 39 J. PHIL. 85, 87 (1942).

14. Hand, *The Future of Wisdom in America*, The Saturday Review, Nov. 22, 1952, pp. 9, 10. See particularly Frank, *The Lawyer's Role in Modern Society*, 4 J. PUB. L. 8 (1955).

prophesies and the making of prophesies "infest" not only the law but the totality of human experience. Surely then our account has reached its climax, which is:

The challenge to American society

If fact-skepticism can accomplish its full work of emancipation, perhaps we shall at last be free to realize the pristine American dream. In the years when our nation began, there was a sort of axiomatic expectation that this "new order of the ages," this unprecedented experiment in republican government would develop a wholly superior breed of human beings. On American shores men would flourish as never before, and gain new personal stature. Here nature and society would invite them to unfold their individual talents, to discover themselves—as it were, to reach out and push back the cultural frontiers. Eventually this democratic republic of ours would exhibit a new kind of political community composed in large part of moral aristocrats.

Today most of us would acknowledge that what was then a charming vision has become a matter of arresting urgency. It is no longer merely desirable, it is virtually indispensable that American society produce a multitude of superior human beings, men and women of understanding judgment and moral rectitude, of expansive horizons and humane sensibilities, who can feel the full pathos of individual misfortunes and predicaments, yet venture to act on occasion as though the world were plastic.

By insisting on the personal element in all processes of decision, fact-skepticism underscores our state of need. It admonishes that the best and wisest propositions of social ethics, politics and law will not preserve us if the men who apply them to concrete transactions are themselves Philistines and mediocrities, even affable mediocrities. Nothing earthly can preserve us without sharply improved human qualities of leadership and citizenship.

Here, at this critical juncture, the fact-skeptic may be heard speaking a message of (perhaps) unexpected but entirely reasonable optimism. Once he has shown that the grip of the past is loose and the grip of the future even looser, he may fairly contend that we enjoy considerable new elbowroom in the realm of the present. He relishes the present with a special confidence. His very questionings and doubtings have earned him the right to declare that men possess an enormously wider and more diverse register of individual and social choices than they have ever exercised. He may go on to explain that fact-skepticism is as suspicious of alleged impossibilities as it is of pseudo-scientific nostrums. He may add—rather firmly—that one approved way to lift the heart is to exert the intellect. Who knows?—he will ask—while his congeners sit and fret in the darkness, some powerful source of enlightenment may be dangling there, within easy reach. This was the vital pattern of Jerome Frank's faith. He incessantly prodded and encouraged all our social institutions to produce *qualitative* men, and thus he paid a supreme tribute to the ideal of human dignity.

There—in the dignity of individual human beings—was the very core of Jerome Frank's religion. Though he counted himself as one of the "unchurched," he served and worshiped the divine through countless deeds of righteousness, charity and loving-kindness. Orthodox religions of every sort repelled him; by claiming despotic authority, they always prompted him to deny when he yearned to affirm. Then, not many years ago, in a novel by St. John Ervine, he happened upon something quite close to the belief he had been searching for. Here is the quotation:

> "It seemed to him that God was not a Being who miraculously made the world, but a Being who labored at it, suffered and failed, and rose again and achieved. He could hear God, stumbling through the Universe, full of the agony of desire, calling continually, 'Let there be light! Let there be light!'"

So it was with you, beloved friend, and so it must be with us. There will be many times when the vision grows dim, the judgment stumbles and the courage falters. Yet we will never give ourselves to despair. Guided and sustained by your example, we will never leave off calling, "Let there be light, let there be justice, and above all else let there be compassion!"

Part III
Law, Fact and Value

[12]

ON BRUTE FACTS

By G. E. M. Anscombe

FOLLOWING Hume I might say to my grocer: "Truth consists in agreement either to relations of ideas, as that twenty shillings make a pound, or to matters of fact, as that you have delivered me a quarter of potatoes; from this you can see that the term does not apply to such a proposition as that I owe you so much for the potatoes. You really must not jump from an ' is '—as, that it really is the case that I asked for the potatoes and that you delivered them and sent me a bill—to an ' owes ' ".

Does my owing the grocer in this case consist in any facts beyond the ones mentioned? No. Someone may want to say: it consists in these facts in the context of our institutions. This is correct in a way. But we must be careful, so to speak, to bracket that analysis correctly. That is, we must say, not: It consists in these-facts-holding-in-the-context-of-our-institutions, but: It consists in these facts—in the context of our institutions, or: In the context of our institutions it consists in these facts. For the statement that I owe the grocer does not contain a description of our institutions, any more than the statement that I gave someone a shilling contains a description of the institution of money and of the currency of this country. On the other hand, it requires these or very similar institutions as background in order so much as to be the *kind* of statement that it is.

Given this background, these facts do not necessarily amount to my owing the grocer such-and-such a sum. For the transaction might have been arranged as part of an amateur film production. Then perhaps I have said to the grocer " Send so many potatoes " and he has sent them, and he has sent a bill—but the whole procedure was not a real sale but a piece of acting;

even though it so happens that I then eat the potatoes (not as part of the film): for perhaps the grocer has said I can keep them; or has said nothing but doesn't care, and the question never comes up. Thus the fact that something is done in a society with certain institutions, in the context of which it ordinarily amounts to such-and-such a transaction, is not absolute proof that such-and-such a transaction has taken place.

Is it *intention* that makes the difference? Not if we think of intention as purely interior. What is true is this: what ordinarily amounts to such-and-such a transaction *is* such-and-such a transaction, unless a special context gives it a different character. But we should not include among special contexts the circumstance that I am suddenly deprived of all my goods and put in prison (through no fault of my own, if you like)—so that I can't pay the grocer. For in those circumstances it is still true to say that I owe him money. Nor is there ordinarily any need to look about for a special context so as to make sure there is none that makes a radical difference. Ordinarily there is not; or if there is it usually comes very readily to light, though not always: which is why it is true to say that deception is always possible. But it is not theoretically possible to make provision in advance for the exception of extraordinary cases; for one can theoretically always suppose a further special context for each special context, which puts *it* in a new light.

Let us return to the move of saying: " Owing the grocer consists in these facts, in the context of our institutions ". We ought to notice that exactly the same holds for the facts themselves as we described them. A set of events is the ordering and supplying of potatoes, and something is a bill, only in the context of our institutions.

Now if my owing the grocer on this occasion does not consist in any facts beyond the facts mentioned, it seems that we must say one of two things. Either (*a*) to say I owe the grocer is nothing but to say that *some such* facts hold, or (*b*) to say I owe the grocer adds something non-factual to the statement that some such facts hold.

But of course, if this is a valid point, it holds equally for the description of a set of events as: the grocer's supplying me with potatoes. And we should not wish to say either of these things about that.

The grocer supplies me with a quarter of potatoes: that is to say, he (1) brings that amount of potatoes to my house and (2) leaves them there. But not any action of taking a lot of potatoes to my house and leaving them there would be *supplying* me with them. If for example, by the grocer's own arrangement, someone else, who had nothing to do with me, came and took them away soon afterwards, the grocer could not be said to have supplied me.—*When*, one might ask, did he supply me? Obviously, when he left the potatoes; it would be absurd to add " and also when he did *not* send to take them away again ".

There can be no such thing as an exhaustive description of *all* the circumstances which theoretically could impair the description of an action of leaving a quarter of potatoes in my house as " supplying me with a quarter of potatoes ". If there were such an exhaustive description, one could say that " supplying me with a quarter of potatoes " *means* leaving them at my house, together with the absence of any of those circumstances. As things are, we could only say " It means leaving them . . . together with the absence of any of the circumstances which would impair the description of that action as an action of supplying me with potatoes "; which is hardly an explanation. But I can know perfectly well that the grocer has supplied me with potatoes; asked what this consisted in, I say there was nothing to it but that I had ordered them and he brought them to my house.

Every description presupposes a context of normal procedure, but that context is not even implicitly described by the description. Exceptional circumstances could always make a difference, but they do not come into consideration without reason.

As compared with supplying me with a quarter of potatoes we might call carting a quarter of potatoes to my house and leaving them there a " brute fact ". But as compared with the fact that I owe the grocer such-and-such a sum of money, that he supplied me with a quarter of potatoes is itself a brute fact. In relation to many descriptions of events or states of affairs which are asserted to hold, we can ask what the " brute facts " were; and this will mean the facts which held, and in virtue of which, in a proper context, such-and-such a description is true or false, and which are more " brute " than the alleged fact answering to that description. I will not ask here whether there are any facts that are, so to speak, " brute " in comparison with leaving a quarter of potatoes at my house. On the other hand, one could think of facts in relation to which my owing the grocer such-and-such a sum of money is " brute "—e.g. the fact that I am solvent.

We can now state some of the relations which at least sometimes hold between a description, say A, and descriptions, say
xyz, of facts which are brute in relation to the fact described by A.

(1) There is a *range* of sets of such descriptions xyz such that
some set of the range must be true if the description A is to be
true. But the range can only ever be roughly indicated, and the
way to indicate it is by giving a few diverse examples.

(2) The existence of the description A in the language in
which it occurs presupposes a context, which we will call " the
institution behind A "; this context may or may not be presupposed to elements in the descriptions xyz. For example,
the institution of buying and selling is presupposed to the
description " sending a bill ", as it is to " being owed for goods
received ", but not to the description " supplying potatoes ".

(3) A is not a description of the institution behind A.

(4) If some set holds out of the range of sets of descriptions
some of which must hold if A is to hold, and if the institution
behind A exists, then " in normal circumstances " A holds.
The meaning of " in normal circumstances " can only be indicated roughly, by giving examples of exceptional circumstances
in which A would not hold.

(5) To assert the truth of A is not to assert that the circumstances were " normal "; but if one is asked to justify A,
the truth of the description xyz is in normal circumstances an
adequate justification: A is not verified by any further facts.

(6) If A entails some other description B, then xyz cannot
generally be said to entail B, but xyz together with normality
of circumstances relatively to such descriptions as A can be said
to entail B. For example: " He supplied me with potatoes "
entails " The potatoes came into my possession ". Further, " He
had the potatoes brought to my house and left there " is in
normal circumstances an adequate justification for saying " He
supplied me with potatoes "; asked what his action of supplying
me with potatoes consisted in, one would normally have no
further facts to mention. (One *cannot* mention all the things
that were *not* the case, which would have made a difference if
they had been.) But " He had potatoes carted to my house and
left there " does *not* entail " The potatoes came into my possession ". On the other hand " He had potatoes carted to my house
and left there and the circumstances were just the normal
circumstances as far as concerns being supplied with goods "
does entail " The potatoes came into my possession ".

University of Oxford.

[13]

LAW, FACT OR JUSTICE?†

Adrian A.S. Zuckerman*

The distinction between law and fact is said to lie at the basis of adjudication and to have important implications. The law has to be applied to the facts of the case. The facts of the case are either admitted by the parties or ascertained by the court; either way they are not governed by the law. The law determines which types of facts give rise to rights and duties; the facts of the individual case are not themselves created by the law, but exist in the world that lies beyond the law. When the facts are disputed, the function of the legal process is to learn what these facts are so that the appropriate legal results may then follow. In other words, the judicial fact-finding process looks beyond the law into the world and ascertains what the facts look like out there. I shall refer to this as the assumption of objectivity in adjudication.

To distinguish between law and fact is to draw a distinction between the reasoning processes involved in drawing inferences of law and fact respectively. In legal reasoning we proceed according to normative rules laid down by the lawmaker or by morality, and we aim to determine what these rules require the citizen or court to do. By contrast, in factual reasoning, it is supposed, we are not concerned with what the rules of law or morality require but with what facts exist. To ascertain the facts, it is said, we only have to follow the forms of reasoning which are employed for this purpose in any form of factual inquiry.[1]

Much of the discussion of the role of probabilities in factfinding proceeds from the assumption of objectivity. Thus, it is supposed that since judicial factfinding is no different from any other fact-finding process, methods that lead to greater accuracy in other fields of investigation may be imported into the legal process to enhance its accuracy. It is suggested that greater use should be made of mathematical probabilities in deciding factual disputes. It is said that just as statistical assessments form the basis of social policy decisions, as where statistical patterns of road traffic determine resource

---

† © 1986 by Adrian A.S. Zuckerman.

* Fellow and Praelector in Jurisprudence, University College, Oxford.

[1] As Professor Thayer, the father of the modern law of evidence, put it, "The law furnishes no test of relevancy. For this, it tacitly refers to logic and general experience, assuming that the principles of reasoning are known to its judges and ministers, just as a vast multitude of other things are assumed as already sufficiently known to them." J. Thayer, A Preliminary Treatise on Evidence At Common Law 265 (1898).

allocation for road building, so should they guide factfinding in individual disputes.

Generalizations concerning distribution are, of course, in constant use in litigation as well as in many other areas where states of affairs are inferred from evidence. It is a generalization of this kind that gives rise to the venerable presumption that a person found in possession of recently stolen goods stole them himself. Similarly, when we hear that a suspect ran away from the scene of the crime after being accused of committing it, we tend to conclude that he was guilty, because experience has taught us that guilt is most frequently the reason for escape. The advocates of statistics in the law suggest that matters be taken a step further; they argue for allowing the rules of probabilities to actually dictate the results of litigation, and not just to operate as loose or semi-binding generalizations. Thus, to take a well-known example, if the plaintiff, who was injured in a road accident, proves that he was run down by an unidentified bus and that the defendant company operates eighty percent of the buses on the street in question, he should obtain judgment against the defendant company.[2] It is said that since there is a .8 probability that the bus that injured the plaintiff belonged to the defendant company, this evidence completely fulfills the requirement of proof on the balance of probabilities.

This kind of argument is based, as I have suggested, on the assumption of objectivity; the assumption that the sole function of the judicial process is to search for the objective truth that lies beyond, and is independent of, the law. However, as Hilary Putnam observed, "*truth is not the bottom line*: truth itself gets its life from our criteria of rational acceptability, and these are what we must look at if we wish to discover the values which are really implicit in science."[3] On examination we will find that the objective truth about litigated facts is not sharply detached from the rest of the legal system. The assumption of objectivity, in the form of the distinction between law and fact, is invoked at every important stage of the judicial process: the litigants must plead facts and not law; the jury decides questions of fact while questions of law are left to the judge; decisions on the law give rise to binding precedent, decisions on the facts do not; and legal determinations but not, generally, factual ones may be challenged on appeal. Yet the boundaries drawn between law and fact for these procedural and practical purposes do not conform to the theoretical distinction between law and fact. We will find that questions of law—namely, questions which are not concerned with the existence of facts outside the law—are frequently treated as questions of fact. Furthermore, we shall see that questions concerned with the process of ascertaining the facts sometimes receive the kind of treatment usually accorded to questions of law.

---

[2] *Cf.* Smith v. Rapid Transit Inc., 317 Mass. 469, 58 N.E.2d 754 (1945).

[3] H. PUTNAM, REASON, TRUTH AND HISTORY 130 (1981); *Cf.* Rorty, *The Contingency of Language*, 8 LONDON REV. BOOKS 3 (April 17, 1986).

I suggest that the law's designation as questions of fact of some of these questions that are theoretically questions of law is not merely a matter of haphazard convenience. On the contrary, the present procedural practices denote the existence of a meeting ground between factfinding and law application, where normative values shape the facts as well as the law. Many of the values and principles that are central in determining rights and duties also exert their influence on the fact-finding process and thereby affect the nature of the truth that emerges from the trial of the facts. I propose, first, to show how law application and factfinding converge in adjudication, and second, to discuss the implications of this convergence for the introduction of pure probabilistic methods into the trial procedure.

I. LAW, EVIDENTIAL FACTS, AND ULTIMATE FACTS

There is a great amount of literature on the distinction between law and fact. The discussion is entirely devoted, however, to the definition of law and to the question of how far the notion of law stretches, rather than to the notion of fact. Difficulties are supposed to exist only on the borderlines while the core meanings of law and fact are regarded as clear. Thus, identifying the elements of the offense of murder, for instance, is regarded as an obvious question of law, while the question whether the accused was present at the scene of the crime is seen as a clear question of fact. Uncertainty is thought to begin only when, in the course of applying rules, we encounter questions such as, "Was the accused's act proximate enough to the successful commission of the intended offense as to constitute a criminal attempt?"[4] or "Was the accused's conduct dishonest for the purpose of the offense of theft?"[5] While in theory the distinction between legal and factual reasoning is clear, in practice it is far from certain.

A. *Evidential Facts*

Evidential facts are facts presented to the tribunal for the purpose of establishing material facts (or facts from which the latter may be inferred). As Hohfeld put it, "An evidential fact is one which, on being ascertained, affords some logical basis—not conclusive—for inferring some other facts. The latter may be either a constitutive fact or an intermediate evidential fact."[6]

Hohfeld was careful to specify the kind of inference he had in mind. He emphasized that it was a mistake to suppose that the ultimate facts stated in the pleadings were proved by the real and specific facts established at the trial. Rather, he argued, the real and specific facts were the ultimate facts themselves. Thus, in a criminal trial where the accused is charged with

---

[4] Criminal Attempts Act, 1981, § 1.

[5] Theft Act, 1968, § 1.

[6] W. HOHFELD, FUNDAMENTAL LEGAL CONCEPTIONS 34 (1966).

490   *BOSTON UNIVERSITY LAW REVIEW*   [Vol. 66: 487

burglary by entering a building and stealing therein, the fact that he put his arms through the window is not proof of entry; it is itself the entry, the ultimate fact.[7] Yet the move from the statement "X put his hand through the window" to the conclusion "X entered the building" is also governed by some rules. Hohfeld implied that the rules pertinent to this move were different from the rules involved in inferring an ultimate fact from an evidential fact.

The first move, from putting an arm through the window to "entering," is governed by the law. The second move, from "The witness says he saw an arm appearing through the window" to the conclusion, "X put his arm through the window," is governed by what Thayer called "logic and common sense."[8] The relation of an evidential fact to the fact it tends to prove is referred to as relevance. One fact is relevant to another, to take Stephen's well-known definition, if "according to the common course of events one fact either taken by itself or in connection with other facts proves or renders probable the past, present, or future existence or non-existence of the other."[9]

Within this picture of adjudication the ascertainment of facts is carried out according to the rules of ordinary reasoning. Such rules are objective in that they do not vary fundamentally according to the nature of the inquiry, and are therefore distinguishable from legal rules. Thus, the factual inquiry is confined to drawing inferences about external facts according to the rules derived from our understanding of the world outside—Stephen's common course of events.[10] This process, it is assumed, is unaffected by legal rules, i.e., by the normative rules designed to direct conduct or to attach consequences to such conduct. We need to look now at the way in which legal rules are related to facts.

B. *Ultimate Facts*

The courts exist to adjudicate only factual disputes that are of concern to the legal system, disputes involving legal rights, duties or other legal consequences. Hence, the judicial process is only concerned with the ascertainment of a fact to which the legal system attaches some consequence. These facts are commonly referred to as ultimate, material, operative or dispositive facts.[11]

---

[7] *Id.*, ch. 33.

[8] J. THAYER, *supra* note 1, at 263.

[9] J. FITZJAMES, DIGEST OF THE LAW OF EVIDENCE art. 1 (12th ed. 1946).

[10] Interestingly, Thayer was aware that the mode of reasoning on matters of fact constituted as much a trial procedure as the old forms, such as ordeal and battle, but he did not attempt to develop a theory about the peculiarities of the modern procedure. Thayer, *"Law and Fact" in Jury Trials*, 4 HARV. L. REV. 147, 153 (1890).

[11] As Thayer put it, "When it is said that a fact is for the jury, the fact intended . . . is that which is in issue, the ultimate fact, that to which the law directly annexes consequences . . . ." *Id.* at 197.

From the very start of litigation the litigants are told to separate law and fact. Thus, in England, the pleadings initiating civil litigation must contain a statement of the material facts on which the party relies for his claim, but not the evidence with which he proposes to prove the facts.[12] Nor need a party state the law; the legal results that are to follow from the facts must be left to the tribunal to determine.[13] The rules concerning criminal indictments are somewhat different, but the distinction between law and fact is maintained there too.[14]

However, in practice, the distinction between law and fact in the pleadings cannot be completely sustained. For example, it is neither necessary nor sufficient for the plaintiff in a civil case to plead that the defendant owes him a sum of money; this is regarded as merely a statement of law and not of fact. But it is sufficient if the plaintiff pleads that the defendant had a contract with him under which he is liabie to pay the plaintiff that sum of money.[15] Yet in what sense is a contract any more a fact than a duty? Why may a plaintiff aver offer and acceptance but not aver the defendant's duty?

Writing fifty years ago, Professor Walter Cook drew upon a well-known philosophical discussion when he pointed out that while the brute facts of the external world exist independently of our will, we can only describe them by using language that makes distinctions among infinite patterns of color, sound, odor and the like.[16] Suppose one person asks another what he sees when looking out of the window. Since whatever the observer sees can be described at various levels of detail, the observer would be unable to answer the question unless he understood what his interrogator wished to know. Cook therefore concludes:

> [A] direction to "state the facts" of a situation or "describe the situation" is an inadequate guide without more. The matter will . . . be helped if I know for what purpose my answer is to be used; and of course that is the case in pleading: the pleader's statement is for the purpose of informing the court and the other party of the grounds upon which the pleader asks action in favor of his client.[17]

---

[12] SUPREME COURT PRACTICE 261 (1985).

[13] *Id.* at 261-62.

[14] An indictment in England contains two principal parts, the statement of the offense and the particulars of the offense. The former is "a statement of the offense with which the accused person is charged describing the offense shortly." ARCHBOLD, CRIMINAL PLEADING, EVIDENCE AND PRACTICE 36 (42d ed 1985). The latter consists of "such particulars as may be necessary for giving reasonable information as to the nature of the charge," and has to disclose the "essential elements of the offence." *Id.* The statement of the offense is designed to identify the law under which the accused is charged whereas the particulars of the offense are intended to identify the facts which, according to the prosecution, amount to the offense mentioned in the statement preceding the particulars.

[15] *Supra* note 12, at 262.

[16] Cook, *"Facts" and "Statements of Facts,"* 4 U. CHI. L. REV. 233, 238 (1936).

[17] *Id.* at 242.

492   *BOSTON UNIVERSITY LAW REVIEW*   [Vol. 66: 487

What a complaint must contain is determined by convention and by what is sufficient, in the circumstances of litigation, to give adequate notice to the opponent, rather than by a theoretical distinction. According to Cook, "[t]he time-honored distinction between 'statement of fact' and 'conclusions of law' is merely one of degree, comparable to the difference between saying: 'I see an object' and 'I see a sedan.' "[18]

We know what the ultimate facts are only because the law draws our attention to them by attaching legal consequences to their existence or nonexistence. For this reason the description of the ultimate facts would often contain references to the relevant rule in terms such as offer, acceptance, trespass and so on. The act of choosing certain facts, or combinations of facts, for the purpose of attaching legal consequences to them therefore involves an inevitable element of legal creativity. This explains why in describing the facts we often have recourse to legal notions. This explanation does not of itself challenge the theoretical distinction between law and fact; it only suggests that the law cannot be altogether kept out of the picture when the facts are described in judicial proceedings. However, we still need to consider the problem of definition: the question of how we can find out what counts as an ultimate fact for the purpose of legal consequences.

C. *Brute Facts and the Application of Law*

In litigation the tribunal has to ascertain what the ultimate facts are before it can attach legal consequences to them. The ultimate facts have their description and definition in the law, where they are stated in terms of ordinary usage or in technical nomenclature. Ordinary terminology consists of such terms as entering, setting fire, threatening, hitting, killing, injuring and the like. Supplying one with potatoes usually involves bringing the potatoes to one's house and leaving them there. But as Elizabeth Anscombe explained this is only generally the case, for there are exceptional circumstances where these actions do not amount to supplying the potatoes, for instance where the purported supplier sends somebody to remove them shortly after they have been left at the house in question.[19] She goes on:

> There can be no such thing as an exhaustive description of *all* the circumstances which theoretically could impair the description of an action of leaving a quarter of potatoes in my house as "supplying me with a quarter of potatoes." If there were such an exhaustive description, one would say that, "Supplying me with a quarter of potatoes *means* leaving them at my house, together with the absence of any of those circumstances." As things are, we could only say, "It means leaving them . . . together with the absence of any of the circumstances which would impair the description of that action as an action of supplying me with potatoes," which is hardly an explanation.[20]

---

[18] *Id.* at 244.
[19] Anscombe, *On Brute Facts*, 18 ANALYSIS 69, 70-71 (1958).
[20] *Id.* at 71.

Of what kind, then, are questions that are concerned with whether facts fit into a certain description employed by the law? Such questions take the following form: "Does a certain act amount to killing?" or "Is a certain injury grievous bodily harm?" It is difficult not to accept that these types of questions are concerned with the scope of the rule under consideration. If a certain act does not amount to "killing" then no offense of murder could have been committed. If the proven injury cannot be described as "grievous bodily harm" then the person who inflicted it cannot be convicted of the offense of inflicting such injury. The resolution of these questions depends on the aim of the laws in question, on the policy of the legislature, and on various other considerations that are typical of a legal, rather than factual, investigation.

It therefore follows that we must treat questions of this kind as posing legal problems and as presupposing an inferential process quite different from that process involved in the move from evidential facts to ultimate facts. We may conclude that while there may be a question as to whether in certain exceptional circumstances the facts that would ordinarily be regarded as "entering," "supplying," "injuring" or whatever should be so regarded, this kind of problem is different from the process of drawing factual inferences from evidence. It may be doubted, in the particular circumstances of an individual case, whether the leaving of the potatoes at the defendant's house should count as supplying them to him, but before we can resolve this doubt we must decide whether the potatoes were indeed left at the defendant's house. In other words, the question about "supplying" arises only once we have decided that the potatoes were left at the house.

However, when we examine the way in which the law-fact distinction is handled in practice we find a considerable divergence from theory. Despite the fact that questions of application of the kind I have been discussing involve legal rather than factual reasoning, both in England and the United States these questions of application are often considered to be questions of fact. It is supposed that one of the distinguishing marks of a question of fact is that it can be properly answered in a number of ways. By contrast, questions admitting of only one answer are characterized as questions of law. In an English tax case concerned with the construction of the word "trade" Lord Radcliffe said, "All these cases in which the facts warrant a determination either way can be described as questions of degree and, therefore, as questions of fact."[21]

This pronouncement is at odds with theory. For whether a certain activity is to be considered as "trade" cannot be free of legal considerations; it cannot be determined by the brute facts alone. Questions such as whether an activity is "trade," whether certain conduct is "dishonest,"[22] or amounts to

---

[21] Edwards v. Bairstow, [1955] 3 All E.R. 48, 56. The same view is expressed by Lord Hailsham, L.C. in Cole Bros. Ltd. v. Phillips, [1982] 2 All E.R. 247, 253.

[22] In R. v. Feely, [1973] 1 All E.R. 341, it was decided that dishonesty, for the purpose of the Theft Act of 1968, was a question of fact to be determined by the jury.

"insulting behavior"[23] cannot but give rise to problems of law because they are concerned with identifying what it is that the law forbids.[24] Since many of these questions of application are left to the jury it cannot be said that the jury is exclusively a trier of fact. As a result, it is sometimes argued that the designation of questions left to the jury as "questions of fact" exists only in order to provide a convenient and practical shorthand for referring to matters which are within the jury's province. In this view such a designation has no further significance.

Yet it seems to me that the matter cannot be left there, as if the assimilation of law application and factfinding in adjudication is determined merely by ad hoc considerations of semantic convenience. In order to appreciate how closely factfinding and law application are bound together we could try to imagine a procedure whereby the disputed facts are identified and isolated before they are brought before the jury. On a murder charge, for example, the prosecution's case may hinge on the presence of the accused in a certain place at a crucial time. The jury would then be kept ignorant of the nature of the charge and would be asked to pronounce only on the issue of the accused's presence. Yet I very much doubt whether this system of trial would appeal to many.

I suggest that this kind of procedure is counter-intuitive because our expectations of the trier of fact exceed mere mechanical factfinding. The divergence of the practice of adjudication from the theoretical fact-law dichotomy is not just a matter of convenience. The assimilation, for the purpose of adjudication, of factfinding and law application is vital for the role that we expect adjudication to fulfill. It indicates the existence of a meeting ground for the concerns involved in the two types of questions. This common ground becomes apparent when we examine the jury's function because, as we shall presently see, the system is designed to allow legal and moral values to be reflected in the fact-finding process as well as in the application of legal rules.

II. THE FUNCTION OF THE JURY IN ADJUDICATION

Under the common law tradition the jury is the trier of fact while the judge determines the law.[25] Since in the Anglo-American legal system many questions of application are considered to be questions of fact, the jury has wide

---

[23] Brutus v. Cozens, [1972] 2 All E.R. 1297, decides that this is also a question of fact for the jury.

[24] *See, e.g.*, Mureinik, *The Application of Rules: Law or Fact?*, 98 LAW Q. REV. 587 (1982).

[25] In England the jury has virtually disappeared from civil cases while in the United States trial by jury is still the standard method of adjudication in cases giving rise to issues of fact. However, the jury's disappearance from English cases does not affect my argument.

discretion in applying the law and is therefore a "trier" of law as well as of fact.[26] Yet modern champions of the jury system do not claim that the jury is peculiarly able to correctly apply the law. Nor do they argue that juries possess special qualities that make them a particularly accurate instrument for establishing the facts. Apparently, the existence of the jury system can be justified neither in terms of precise application of law nor in terms of accurate conclusions of fact. Therefore, a justification must be sought elsewhere.

When Lord Devlin, that indefatigable defender of the jury system, explains the advantage of jury trial, he mentions the ability of juries to do justice according to the "merits" and not just according to the law.[27] By this he means that the jury can determine the case according to extralegal considerations. "It is," explains Lord Devlin, "generally accepted that a jury will tend to favour a poor man against a rich man . . . because . . . there is a feeling that a rich man can afford to be less indifferent to the misfortune of others than a poor man can be."[28] The acceptance of this consideration is all the more telling since it runs counter to the law, according to which the relative wealth of the parties is irrelevant. It seems therefore that the jury has considerable freedom to disregard the law; it has discretion to regard as material to its decision facts that are not specified by the law as affecting the legal consequences in question.[29]

We need to distinguish between two closely related aspects of the jury's function of judging on the merits. The first, the substantive aspect, concerns the interpretation of the principle of judging on the merits. The second aspect is a functional one; it is concerned with the reason for putting the jury

---

[26] Not all questions of application are left to the jury. By and large, the jury determines the scope of words of common usage such as "grievous bodily harm," "insulting behavior," and "dishonesty," while the interpretation of technical terms and more general definitional questions are considered to be matters of law and are left to the judge. It is clear, therefore, that the jurisdictional divide does not follow the theoretical boundary between law and fact. There is no theoretical difference between questions of application that are left to the jury and questions of application that go to the judge. Thus, the division of jurisdiction is largely a matter of precedent. The reasons which prompt the courts to decide one way or the other will not be investigated here, but some of the considerations discussed in the following sections might turn out to be relevant in this respect. Even where a question of application is reserved for the judge, there will always be room for jury interpretation too, because, as we have seen, problems of interpretation can arise at lower levels of the factual description.

[27] P. DEVLIN, TRIAL BY JURY 151-58 (1956); *see also* Damaska, *Presentation of Evidence and Factfinding Precision*, 123 U. PA. L. REV. 1083, 1103-04 (1975).

[28] P. DEVLIN, *supra* note 27, at 155.

[29] The jury's possession of this power is inevitable in light of the fact that it has to apply the law, and that the list of exceptions to any description is not fully determinable in advance.

496   *BOSTON UNIVERSITY LAW REVIEW*   [Vol. 66: 487

in charge of implementing this principle and giving it the final word in the matter.[30]

The principle of adjudication on the merits, to which Lord Devlin draws attention, is concerned with doing justice in the particular circumstance of the case. It reflects the belief that neither legislative nor judge-made rules can, of themselves, provide a just solution to all the infinitely varying circumstances of individual litigants. Such rules can of course provide lists of material facts which, if found, would induce certain consequences. But these lists are bound to leave out factors which, when revealed in particular circumstances, may in justice require a different legal result. On the whole, it seems unjust to the individual litigant to prevent the possibility of an assessment of his claim that takes into account *all* the circumstances of his case, even those not listed in advance by the lawmaker.

Juries are suited to be put in charge of adjudicating on the merits because of the trust they command in the community. Since the efficacy of any judicial system depends on its ability to generate public confidence in its judgments, the element of trust in the tribunal is crucial.[31] Neither in respect to law application nor in respect to factfinding can we have an extra-judicial system for checking the accuracy of individual judgments.[32] Public trust in the fact-finding process cannot therefore be guaranteed by systematic testing of conformity between individual judgments and the facts. There is a mutual dependence between belief in the correctness of factual decisions and trust in the body making them. The substantive and the functional aspects of adjudication on the merits are inexorably interdependent. Trust in the jury is secured by the fact that it applies standards of adjudication which are both generally familiar and widely accepted.

Public acceptance of any principle or policy is a function of the extent to which the principle or policy is seen as morally valid and useful. In the criminal field there are present two central social needs which inevitably receive expression in adjudication: the need to protect innocent people from conviction and punishment,[33] and the need to protect the community from

---

[30] As a general rule there is no appeal on questions of fact and, as we have seen, all issues decided by the jury, whether of law application or factfinding, are regarded as questions of fact. In England, appellate courts have limited powers to quash jury convictions but, significantly, are not empowered to interfere with acquittals. *See* P. DEVLIN, *supra* note 27, at 83; M. KADISH, DISCRETION TO DISOBEY 162 (1973) (discussing the jury's "sovereign power to acquit"). This explains why, as every litigation lawyer would tell you, it is so important to enlist the jury's sympathy on your client's side.

[31] Hart & McNaughton, *Evidence and Inference in the Law,* in EVIDENCE AND INFERENCE 48, 52 (D. Lerner ed. 1958).

[32] "[E]ven in connection with the visible and tangible facts of a particular case, it is constructive truth, the verdict of the jury . . . that must pass as the unchallengeable truth." Issacs, *The Law and the Facts,* 22 COLUM. L. REV. 1, 6 (1922).

[33] Since we are fairly effectively guarded against the risk of conviction when

crime. What accounts for the strong public support for the jury system is the belief that the jury is well suited to give expression to these values in adjudication.

An example of the jury's ability to promote a public sense of security may be seen in the reaction of English juries to disturbing instances of unreliable police testimony. Recently, English juries have shown a marked reluctance to convict on the uncorroborated evidence of policemen.[34] Similarly, juries best express our need for protection from crime by adhering to, in the ascertainment and attribution of guilt, processes of reasoning and systems of values with which the public is familiar. Trust in the fact-finding process is, to a considerable extent, a function of confidence in the reasoning processes employed in factfinding.[35]

The twin social requirements of protection of the innocent from conviction and protection of the public from crime may weigh, in particular circumstances, in favor of different fact-finding standards. For instance, the more we protect innocence by increasing the standard of proof of guilt the fewer guilty people we are likely to convict, and the weaker will be our protection from crime. Of course, in this instance the decision about the required degree of proof has to be taken in advance of the individual trial and promulgated as a rule. Still, the factfinder will always be left with some scope for balancing competing considerations of this kind. An interesting instance is provided by the reluctance of English juries to convict policemen accused of committing offences in the course of their duties.[36] The explanation for this could well be that, since the police are regarded as protecting us from criminals, juries may tend to favor the police by refusing to convict on evidence emanating from the criminal classes.[37] If so, this tendency is not all that inconsistent with the mistrust of uncorroborated police evidence noted earlier.

---

innocent, it is easy to forget how easily one's personal security may be threatened by judicial injustice. Our law—in the form of the privilege against self-incrimination—still bears the scars imprinted by the objectionable practices of the courts of the Star Chamber and the High Commission in the seventeenth century.

[34] Especially when such evidence consisted of an alleged confession. Interestingly, neither judges nor lay magistrates have displayed mistrust to a similar extent.

[35] Thus, in cases where the evidence is entirely in the public domain, there may be a strong public expectation that the judicial result should conform with the public's own conclusion. After the killing of John F. Kennedy's assassin, Lee Harvey Oswald, by Jack Ruby in front of millions of television viewers there was some difficulty in finding an impartial jury to try Ruby. But is it conceivable that any verdict would have been acceptable other than one conforming to the general belief? *See*, Damaska, *supra* note 27, at 1105 n.45. For the influence of public expectations on decisions to prosecute see Williams, *Letting Off the Guilty and Prosecuting the Innocent*, CRIM. L. R. (Sweet & Maxwell) 115, 118 (1985).

[36] *See* Williams, *supra* note 35, at 118.

[37] Much of the evidence of deviant or corrupt policemen inevitably comes from the underworld.

By considering the difficulties involved in the use of naked statistical distribution as the sole basis for adjudication, it will be possible to see how some of the values involved in adjudication on the merits cut across the distinction between application of law and factfinding.

III.   INDIVIDUAL MERITS AND NAKED DISTRIBUTION AS THE GROUNDS FOR VERDICTS

In his book *The Probable and the Provable*, Professor Cohen gives an example which postulates a rodeo attended by 100 people of whom 10 paid and the rest were trespassers.[38] The management sues one of the spectators and, apart from the facts just mentioned, proves only that he attended the show. Would this suffice to justify a verdict for the management for the price of the ticket? To discharge his burden of proof in a civil case the plaintiff need only establish his claim on the balance of probabilities. Let us assume, for the sake of argument, that this means a probability over .5 in favor of the plaintiff's case. Looked at from a purely probabilistic point of view, therefore, the management should win because the probability that the defendant did not pay for his ticket is in fact .9. Yet most lawyers and laymen would think such a verdict unjust.

Before discussing whether naked distribution should justify a verdict for the management we need to remove a misconception regarding the nature of the requirement of proof "on the balance of probabilities." A decision in favor of the plaintiff would necessarily follow from the requirement of proof on the balance of probabilities if the value represented by this requirement is the maximization of correct decisions in the long run of cases. However, since a verdict for the plaintiff in the postulated circumstances is contrary to intuition, we should try to see whether the value inherent in the civil standard of proof may be found in a different direction.

It is clear that the heavier the burden of proof we impose on one party, say the plaintiff, the greater the probability that he would lose the case and that the judgment will be given for his opponent when the latter is in the wrong. Since, everything else being equal, plaintiff and defendant are equal before the law, there has to be some special reason why one party should be disadvantaged at the expense of another. In the absence of a good *a priori* reason for discrimination, the law must show its neutrality by not imposing a greater risk of losing the case on one party than it imposes on the other. A concession must be made, however, for the need to avoid paralysis in situations where the scales are finely balanced at the end of the day. Consequently, the law requires a small preponderance of evidence from the plaintiff in order to disturb the status quo. The requirement of proof on the balance of probabilities may therefore be taken to be an expression of the

---

[38] L. COHEN, THE PROBABLE AND THE PROVABLE 75 (1977). I am using different figures for the example.

law's neutrality between civil litigants and not an expression of the policy of maximizing correct conclusions. If this is so, we are not forced to accept that any preponderance in favor of the plaintiff, however small, must result in a verdict in his favor. It is open to us to give the civil standard of proof a different and, as we shall see, more flexible interpretation. Of course, this does not argue positively that the plaintiff in the rodeo case cannot meet such a burden. We still have to seek an explanation for our intuitive belief that this plaintiff cannot succeed.

We have seen that in applying the law the jury is expected to decide on the merits and not just according to the law. Judging on the merits expresses the importance we place upon being judged as individuals, according to our peculiar qualities and circumstances. In our aversion to a blind and unfeeling judicial process we have set up a system of trial in which the peculiarities of the individual litigant may be taken into account, even when they are not listed in advance among the list of circumstances affecting his legal position. This idea may also be seen to influence factfinding.

In the rodeo case, a decision against the defendant on the ground that ninety percent of the spectators did not pay would be analogous to corporate punishment, as the judgment will rest on nothing but the defendant's membership of a group most of whose members did not pay. As a principle for the imposition of responsibility, corporate punishment is characterized by the assumption that it is justified to hold an entire social group responsible for the transgressions of its individual members. Our moral and legal values strongly resist this principle because it fails to acknowledge that the individual is entitled to judgment on his own actions.[39]

The moral objection to corporate liability is of course underlined by our personal concern not to be held responsible for the actions of another.[40] Judgments based on naked statistical distributions openly acknowledge that the individual defendant may well belong to the innocent minority, and therefore undermine the citizen's confidence that the legal system will protect him from mistaken conviction of crime or mistaken imposition of liability. Yet such confidence is crucial to public respect for judicial adjudication. It seems to me that this consideration is more important in social terms than the objection, developed by Judge Posner, concerning the economic in-

---

[39] If judgment could in law be given for the management in the circumstances discussed here, then the management would be able to sue all one hundred spectators. However, once it obtained payment from the first ninety spectators it would not be allowed to seek judgment against the remaining ten, because a plaintiff is not allowed to recover more than his loss. If naked statistics were sufficient for judgment, it would be more just to make all one hundred spectators liable for 90% of the price of one ticket each. In this way the reasoning from naked statistics leads us to an explicit imposition of corporate liability.

[40] I am not dealing here with instances of vicarious liability, which in any event do not represent exceptions to the principle against corporate liability because vicarious liability is usually imposed due to some involvement by the person or body held vicariously liable in the activity giving rise to liability.

500   *BOSTON UNIVERSITY LAW REVIEW*   [Vol. 66: 487

efficiency of decisions of this kind.[41] Professor Nesson has criticized judgments based on naked statistical distributions on the ground that they do not project a judgment about what actually happened, but rather a judgment about the state of the proof. As such, Nesson maintains, these judgments do not encourage the citizen to comply with the law for its own sake but rather to act according to what might or might not be susceptible of being proved against him.[42] This line of argument works better in criminal cases than in civil ones, because in the latter the preponderance standard implicitly endorses as acceptable a considerable risk that the verdict against the defendant might be erroneous. For me, these explanations lack the central moral dimension provided by the principle against corporate liability. This principle holds equally well in criminal and civil cases and enables us to explain why, although we are prepared to accept a considerable risk of mistake in civil litigation, we object to a risk created by a decision on the basis of association only.

The means by which the facts are ascertained for the purpose of punishment or the imposition of responsibility are themselves of moral significance.[43] If naked statistical evidence were an acceptable means of proving liability, juries' freedom to express their view on the means of proof would be considerably restricted. In the rodeo case, for instance, a jury may well wish to demonstrate its disapproval of the management's tactics of attempting to place itself in a better position by relying solely on probabilities rather than taking the trouble to accumulate evidence about individual spectators.[44] Indeed, we may feel that when the management realized that only a minority had paid, they should not have held the show with the intention of later suing random spectators. It might be thought that since it was within the management's power either to obtain evidence about individuals or to avoid the loss, it would be unjust for the law to run a risk even as small as .1 of holding against an innocent spectator. Recent English case law openly acknowledges the freedom of the factfinder to chose a standard of proof appropriate to the nature of the dispute.[45]

---

[41] R. POSNER, ECONOMIC ANALYSIS OF THE LAW § 21.2 (1972).

[42] Nesson, *The Evidence or the Event? On Judicial Proof and the Acceptability of Verdicts*, 98 HARV. L. REV. 1357, 1357 (1985).

[43] After all, there are many practical measures that could lead to greater accuracy in the fact-finding process that we are prepared to forego on moral grounds, e.g., the questioning of an accused who would rather keep silent.

[44] This objection will, of course, not apply in all instances of pure distribution evidence. The widely discussed taxicab situation will serve as an example here. The plaintiff is injured by a taxicab in a hit and run accident. He cannot identify the cab, but he proves that 85% of cabs driven on the road on which the accident occurred are blue and 15% are green. Is he entitled then to a judgment against the blue taxicab company? Here the plaintiff cannot be blamed for relying on pure distribution. However, the principle against corporate liability still holds.

[45] Khawaja v. Secretary of State for the Home Office, [1983] 1 All E. R. 765; R. v. Hampshire County Council, [1985] 1 All E. R. 599.

If we accept the explanation I have put forward for the intuitive resistance to verdicts that are exclusively based on statistical distribution, a further question needs to be confronted, namely, whether naked statistical distribution is sufficient to make up a prima facie case so as to justify requiring the defendant to put forward his defense? Why should not the defendant in the rodeo case, it may be asked, be at least expected to justify himself, in light of the fact that the probabilities are so heavily against his innocence? Under present law, prima facie evidence sufficient to require the defendant to put forward his defense is defined as evidence that could justify a reasonable jury to decide in favor of the plaintiff. Since the naked statistical evidence cannot justify a verdict in the plaintiff's favor, it cannot be sufficient to put the defendant to his defense either. The question arises, however, of whether we should change the law in this respect.

I do not wish to pursue this question here except to make two points. First, it is clearly desirable to require some evidence before we trouble a defendant, whether in a criminal or civil case, to come forward with evidence, defend himself and run the risk of a judgment being given against him. Second, there are situations where statistical distributions will go a long way towards meeting this threshold test, as we shall see later. Still, making pure statistical distributions sufficient prima facie evidence may not provide a complete solution to our problem. Suppose that, after the plaintiff has proved that ninety percent of the spectators did not pay, the defendant in the rodeo case is called upon to put forward his defense and he declines to do so. We will again be facing the question whether the distribution should be sufficient to establish liability. A change in the prima facie rule may therefore involve changes in other rules. For example, presumptions regarding the shifting of the burden of proof may need to be altered. Changes of this kind involve value choices which cannot be made simply by reference to the assumption of objectivity.

If I am right in assuming that the fact-finding process is impregnated with moral and legal choices, then we have an explanation of why, in settling the jurisdictional divide between judge and jury, the law does not follow the theoretical distinction between law and fact. The principle against corporate liability, for example, cuts across both substantive and evidential matters. In setting out this principle as antagonistic to decisions based on pure distributions, it is not suggested that the law never allows pure distributions to influence liability. When a plaintiff proves that two independent defendants were guilty of negligence towards him but he cannot prove which of them caused his injury he may, under the law in some states in the United States, obtain judgment against both of them, each being held liable for a share of the damage.[46] It is suggested, however, that problems of this kind cannot be

---

[46] *See* Nesson, *supra* note 42, at 1384. This sort of situation should be distinguished from situations of overdetermination, as where two assassins shoot their victim, both hit him and both inflict injury that is bound to kill, but it is not known

solved by strictly adhering to the assumption of objectivity, by restricting oneself to ascertaining what is out there in the world.

IV. ADJUDICATION ON THE MERITS AND OTHER USES OF STATISTICS

It is useful to consider now how statistical evidence is used while accomodating the values I have mentioned. There is no problem with the generalizations that the factfinder brings with him to the adjudication. By applying the beliefs held by members of the community to the resolution of disputes, the jury is unlikely to create a credibility gap between its verdict and the community's beliefs. Moreover, the jury's function of judging on the merits is preserved, since these generalizations are capable of being overridden by other considerations that the trier of fact may find pertinent. It remains, then, to consider how statistical distributions which do not represent general knowledge are used in adjudication.

There are many circumstances in which statistical evidence is admissible quite apart from instances where the statistical values themselves are in issue. Evidence that a palm print found at the scene of the crime matches that of the accused and that such print would be left by the palm of one person in a thousand is admissible. This type of evidence does not pose any problem to the jury's jurisdiction to adjudicate on the merits, since it is not by itself enough to produce persuasion beyond reasonable doubt. Consequently, the jury still has considerable scope for assessing other pertinent evidence and judging the accused according to his circumstances.

Yet there are situations where the evidence produces such probability values as to leave little scope for the jury to do much further assessment. Suppose that what is found at the scene of the crime is a fingerprint which is probabilistically unique, so that the probability of more than one person displaying such a print is one in hundreds of millions. It might be thought that in these circumstances the jury must accept that the fingerprint at the scene of the crime was that of the accused. However, there is still a difference between this case and the rodeo case. In the latter we know for certain that there are innocent people with the defendant's characteristics, i.e., those who have attended the show. However, in the former case there is no evidence that another person with the same fingerprint exists.[47] The probabilities themselves help dismiss the hypothesis that another such person exists. A recent English case illustrates this point.

In *Regina v. Abadom*[48] the accused was charged with robbery. According

---

which assassin fired the fatal bullet. This is different from the situation where a person uses drug X produced by company A, but we do not know whether, had he not done so, he would have used the similar drug produced by company B.

[47] *See* L. Cohen, Is There a Base-Rate Fallacy? (unpublished manuscript).

[48] [1983] 1 All E. R. 364.

to the evidence four masked men broke into an office, whereupon their leader smashed an internal window and the men robbed the occupants. The prosecution alleged that the accused was the leader who broke the window. To prove this it called evidence that the police had removed from the accused's home a pair of his shoes in which fragments of glass were found. In order to establish that these fragments came from the window broken by the robbers, the prosecution called an expert witness who testified on two points: 1) the refractive index of the glass in the shoes and the glass from the broken window was the same, and 2) only four percent of the glass used in the entire country had that particular index. Thus, it was shown to be highly likely that the glass in the shoes came from the broken window.

But this evidence by itself would have been insufficient because four percent of the glass used represented a considerable quantity of glass in use (twenty to forty thousand tons). Consequently, there would have been nothing in the evidence to exclude the possibility that the fragments became attached to the accused's shoes not because he broke the window in question, but for some other reason. To exclude this hypothesis the prosecution showed that some of the fragments were found on the upper part of the shoes, some were inside the shoes, and others were imbedded in the soles. This suggested that the fragments had fallen from above in the accused's presence and he had then trod on them, a suggestion consistent with the prosecution's version of the event. The accused was convicted.

Yet as far as the probabilities themselves are concerned, it could be argued that they fall short of proof beyond reasonable doubt because there was still a considerable chance that the glass in the accused's shoes did not originate from the robbery. It may be difficult to put a figure on the incidence of breakage in the glass of the relevant refractive index and the likelihood of it appearing in a man's shoes in that position, but we cannot dismiss it as insignificant.

The factfinder remained unimpressed by this factor, I suggest, for three related reasons: first, the low probability of the discovery of that type of glass in the shoes of a man picked at random; second, the jury's disbelief that the accused was chosen at random to have his shoes examined; and third, the absence of evidence of any other known instance of glass being found in a man's shoes in the same way.

It is this combination of inferences which separates this case from instances such as the rodeo case. The latter involved a group of people, some of whose members were innocent and some who were not; and there was no way of telling to which group the defendant belonged. This, as we have seen, gave rise to the feeling that to hold the defendant liable would be tantamount to holding him liable by association and not because of something he had done to set him apart from the rest of the spectators. Of course, the evidence does not have to show something the accused or the defendant has done to indicate involvement. It is enough that he has some peculiarly individual characteristics—such as fingerprints, or shoes full of glass—that single him out from other potential wrongdoers.

Several objections may be raised against the factors that impressed the jury in the *Abadom* case. The jury must have surmised that the accused was not picked at random, and it could not have avoided wondering how the police came to look for the accused's shoes and examine them for glass traces.[49] Nor could it have avoided concluding that the reason for searching the accused had to do with some information the police had about the robbery or about the accused's character. Once they have reached that conclusion, the jury is no longer concerned with the incidence of shoes with that particular type of glass in them, but with the incidence of this combination among persons about whom there is this particular information. It might be said that to allow this kind of consideration to play a part in the fact-finding process is inconsistent with the presumption of innocence. That presumption requires that the accused be treated as innocent until proven guilty, and that the jury approach its task without any assumption that the accused is other than innocent. The presumption does not, however, require that the jury ignore the common-sense implications of the evidence. If the evidence at the trial draws attention to generalizations that support a conclusion of guilt, it is inevitable that the jury will be more inclined towards guilt.

Sometimes it is the policy of the law to suppress generalizations of this kind, as is the case with previous convictions or other derogatory information about the accused's past. But even then the prohibition is rarely absolute and admissibility depends on whether the influence of the discreditable evidence on the trier of fact is considered justifiable. Thus, evidence of prior convictions of the accused is admissible in England if its probative value outweighs its prejudicial effect.[50] Exclusion of evidence of this kind requires a calculation of the cost of the exclusion.[51] In the *Abadom* case there was only one way of preventing the jury from drawing the inevitable conclusion from the finding of the glass in the accused's shoes: exclusion of the evidence altogether. This would not be any more justifiable than excluding

---

[49] Since naked probabilities are unacceptable, the jury could not have supposed that the prosecution conducted random checks among the population and brought to trial the first person to be found with the relevant glass in his shoes.

[50] D.P.P. v. Boardman, [1974] 3 All E.R. 887.

[51] The topic of similar factual and character evidence throws an interesting light on adjudication on the merits. The general tendency of the law to restrict evidence of this kind rests on the belief that juries attach far greater probative weight to evidence of similar offenses than is probabilistically justified. I do not think, however, that this is a correct explanation of the jury's inclination to be swayed by this kind of evidence. I do not believe that the phenomenon is explicable in terms of a pervasive mistake about the probabilistic significance of past incidents of misbehavior. Rather, it expresses a moral judgment, held by the public, that persons with previous offenses do not deserve the same benefit of doubt as persons without such a record. This is, therefore, another instance where factfinding is influenced by moral considerations. In excluding such evidence, the law signifies its disapproval of this particular moral judgment.

evidence about the commission of a prior offense when such evidence is of high probative value.

There is a further objection that may be interposed at this point. In dismissing the possibility of there being another person with the same glass in his shoes, the jury must have reasoned that, had there been an innocent explanation for the presence of the glass in the accused's shoes, it would have been forthcoming.[52] I pointed out earlier that naked probabilities are not sufficient in the law to found a prima facie case such as to require a defendant or an accused to be put to his defense. Could it not be said that *Abadom* is inconsistent with this rule because the accused's lack of explanation in fact clinched the case against him? This case shows that sometimes lack of explanation does count. It counts at the point at which we have no reason to believe, on the evidence presented, in the existence of such an explanation. There is a further aspect to this. It concerns the special significance attached to the jury's decision to believe or disbelieve an accused person or any other litigant. I shall return to this shortly.

V. Justice as a System of Immeasurable Merits

I have tried to show that the use of pure statistical methods in judicial factfinding meets resistance where it threatens other values that are believed to be pertinent to adjudication. Some of these values cut across the distinction between law and fact in ways which have yet to be satisfactorily worked out. It might be possible to separate factfinding from law application by insulating factfinding from moral and legal influences, thereby sparing the trier of fact many difficult and complex choices. However, I very much doubt whether such a system would appeal to the public even if it were statistically provable that in a long run of cases we would obtain more factually correct decisions by such a method of trial.

The values present in adjudication are naturally connected to social and moral expectations. If we expect adjudication to protect us from being convicted, or from being incorrectly found liable in civil law, then it is to be expected that a verdict should be required to reflect the individual's guilt or liability. Verdicts based purely on the ratio of the guilty to the innocent are unacceptable as long as there is an innocent person in view. The reverse side of the right to be judged on the merits of one's case is that one may suffer from one's demerits. In a civil case the tribunal is expected to consider the relative merits of the opposing parties. If merits are relevant to the decision of whether to accept this or that risk of mistake, then it is difficult to see how an a priori probability figure could be attached to the civil standard.

The importance of individual merits in judical proceedings is very old. The medieval forms of trial were as much based on this idea as the modern trial.

---

[52] I assume for the sake of argument that no explanation was given, though the report is silent on the point.

506   *BOSTON UNIVERSITY LAW REVIEW*   [Vol. 66: 487

When people believed in divine intervention they also believed that true innocence would prevail. In some respects the jury trial still provides a test of innocence in a way that a statistically geared trial cannot. The trial of Dr. John Bodkin Adams in 1957 illustrates this point. At his trial Dr. Adams, a medical practitioner, stood accused of the murder of a Mrs. Morrell who had been his patient. In preliminary proceedings two other murder charges were leveled against the accused, but were later dropped. In addition, rumors prevailed that the accused had murdered many other patients for personal gain.

In his memoirs of the trial Lord Devlin, who tried the case, draws an analogy between the conduct of this case and the old forms of trial.[53] For the trial by battle the Crown selected one champion in the form of a charge related to the death of Mrs. Morrell. This champion was defeated because the accused was acquitted. Lord Devlin points out, however, that the accused was not altogether cleared because he declined to enter the witness box, which Lord Devlin compares to the trial by ordeal. He explains the effect of the accused's failure to testify as follows:

> As for the ordeal, the accused declined it. The only way in which he could have challenged his invisible foes [the public rumors] was by going into the witness-box and submitting to cross-examination. He could not, of course, have been cross-examined on anything except the Morrell case. The result of the test would have depended not so much upon the content of his answers as upon his demeanour and what he showed of himself to the public. Certainly he had something to explain in the Morrell case and his explanations would have had to have been plausible. If they were and if he had been acquitted, the British public would have acquitted him of all else because he had faced the music. Refusal of the ordeal left him with a verdict of Non-Proven on all that was rumoured or alleged and untried as well as in the trial.[54]

To be believed by a jury seems tantamount to receiving a special moral dispensation.[55] I very much doubt that the force of this arises, as Professor Nesson suggests, from the fact that the jury but not the public saw the accused, and that therefore the latter is bound to accept the judgment of the former.[56] To base a verdict on the accused's credibility, or lack thereof, is to come to a conclusion that is both factual and evaluative. The force of this dispensation rests, I suggest, on the supposition that in exposing one's entire character to a jury's examination, the jury is furnished with the fullest information to enable it to reach a decision on the merits.

One may object to my thesis by arguing that while it explains why it is

---

[53] P. DEVLIN, EASING THE PASSING 197 (1985).

[54] *Id.*

[55] I am not suggesting that jury verdicts always have this effect, only that they usually do.

[56] Nesson, *supra* note 42, at 1370.

important that the judicial system should allow scope for judgment on the merits, it does not explain what these merits are or how they are to be identified and weighed. To this charge I do not have a complete defense. I have outlined one principle, that against being judged purely by association, but there are many others. To identify more of the values that affect factfinding we have to reconsider the distinction between law and fact, and accept that what facts we find may well depend on what we want to achieve in any particular field of the law. This may be a difficult task, for the fact-finding procedure is devised so as to disguise the reasons that lead the factfinder to its conclusion. The jury does not give reasons for its verdict, and its deliberations are secret. This paucity of information is not an exclusive mark of the jury. Even judges couch their reasons for arriving at factual conclusions in language that conceals many of the more profound reasons for preferring this party rather than that. Expressions to the effect that the judge believes this witness, or that he finds the case of that party on the whole more compelling, often disguise as much as they reveal. Moreover, appellate courts have steadfastly refused to penetrate deeply into the reasoning processes of the factfinder. However, I am not sure that a complete defense to the charge that I have neglected substance at the expense of function is possible without first understanding what would count as a complete explanation of the fact-finding process. It could well be the case that the present system is inherently incapable of a complete explanation.

Bentham thought that greater accuracy would be introduced in judicial factfinding if witnesses expressed the strength of their persuasion in the facts they deposed by reference to a fixed scale ranging from 0 to 100. That, he believed, would enable the trier of fact to arrive at a sharper assessment of the sum total of the testimonies given on any particular point.[57] Bentham's proposal was rejected not so much because it was unsophisticated but, I believe, because it was foreign to the nature of adjudication. It is this alien quality that mathematical methods of proof have to overcome.

The adjudication of issues of fact has to be carried out against the background of two somewhat inconsistent but deeply held attitudes, which are so marvelously depicted in the story of Solomon's judgment. The first part of this story is often neglected in favor of the spectacular outcome of the judgment. But it is important to remember that at the beginning the Lord appeared to Solomon in a dream and said to him, "Ask what I shall give thee."[58] Solomon's reply was, "Give therefore thy servant an understanding heart to judge thy people. That I may discern between good and bad: for who is able to judge this thy so great a people?"[59]

This reflects the ever present awareness of the shortcoming of human judgment. We cannot get away from the realization that, try as we may, we

---

[57] 1 J. BENTHAM, RATIONALE OF JUDICIAL EVIDENCE 58 (London 1827).

[58] I *Kings* 3:5.

[59] I *Kings* 3:9.

cannot be sure of getting the facts as they really happened. And yet we cannot help hoping that this may not be so. This is the point of the second part of the story which expresses our deep yearning for a procedure whereby one's merits will emerge triumphant regardless of the difficulties and the ambiguities involved in the evidence. I say that this part of the story express-es hope rather than fulfillment for there is no way of checking whether the king was right in his factfinding. The claims of the litigants were inconsistent: "The one saith 'This is my son that liveth, and thy son is the dead' and the other saith, 'Nay; but thy son is the dead, and my son is the living.' "[60] The king decided in favor of the litigant that would rather forego the child than see it being divided in two, but what reason have we for being so sure that he got it right? It is not impossible that the mother whose child was dead balked at seeing the live child killed too, whereas the mother of the living child felt so antagonistic to the woman who stole her child that she would have rather seen the child dead than let him go. Immediately after recounting the king's command to divide the child in two, the text goes on: "Then spake the woman whose the living child was unto the king, for her bowels yearned upon her son, and she said, 'O my lord, give her the living child, and in no wise slay it.' "[61] It is not without significance that the Bible directly iden-tifies as the mother of the living child that woman whose action conforms to the moral perception concerning the kind of sacrifice that a mother should be prepared to make for her child.[62]

The debate about the introduction of probabilistic assessment into the judicial process reflects much of this age old conflict between our deeply rooted attitudes concerning factfinding. On the one hand, the doubts that we entertain regarding our ability to arrive at the truth would seem to argue for the adoption of mathematical methods which would at least maximize the number of correct decisions in the long run. On the other hand, such a step would involve us in giving up, to a considerable extent, the hope of seeing justice supervene in individual trials.

---

[60] I *Kings* 3:22.

[61] I *Kings* 3:23.

[62] Professors Green and Nesson suggest that the judgment on the fact of moth-erhood may have been used as a cloak for deciding according to a different test altogether, e.g., which of the litigants would be best suited to look after the child. TEACHER'S MANUAL FOR PROBLEMS, CASES, AND MATERIALS 2 (E. Green & C. Nesson eds. 1983).

Part IV
The Law of Evidence: Its Nature and Scope

[14]

THE MODERN LAW OF EVIDENCE AND ITS PURPOSE.—It is a pleasure and a privilege to be asked to speak a word or two to the profession through the highly esteemed AMERICAN LAW REVIEW. It would be pleasanter to do this were the theme less distinctly personal. One hardly speaks of himself with much

[1] Hon. Thomas I. Chatfield, U. S. District Judge, E. Dist. N. Y.

grace, and there is always the familiar truth of psychology that in all subjective conditions lurks the danger of self deception. Still, it is always comforting to realize that when compared with the importance of proper administration of speedy and complete justice, the claims of any individual to personal attention are so insignificant that one may reasonably hope to drop out of sight through the reader's interest in the subject itself.

If I am asked to furnish to my profession an *apologia pro vita mea,* I shall unhesitatingly and with deepest respect and affection place whatever I have been privileged to accomplish, and that which I still seek to do, as a sort of votive offering at the feet of the late Professor James Bradley Thayer, of the Harvard Law School. It all takes its rise in the old class-room of the long out-grown Dane Hall, and the dominating influence of that commanding personality which from that time on has never ceased to be a determining force. The legal world—and this, in reality, means the world at large—is under great obligation to the broad-minded, keen-sighted, humanity-loving American protagonist of the modern law of Evidence—the Royall professor of law at Harvard University. His name has been graven indelibly into the very heart of the subject. But the man, it seems to me, was great, not only because of what he himself directly did, but for the enthusiasm which he has aroused in others. In connection with the future development of the law of Evidence, the impression which he created in the minds of some of his pupils was profound and lasting. The then present situation of that branch of the law was laid bare before us, as with the remorseless scalpel of a demonstrator of morbid pathology. Listen to him, for example, as he states one phase of the matter in his "Preliminary Treatise":[1]

> "In part the precepts of evidence consist of many classes of exceptions to the main rules—exceptions that are refined upon, discriminated, and run down into a nice and difficult attenuation of detail, so that the courts become lost, and forget that they are dealing with exceptions; or perhaps are at a loss to say whether the controlling principle is to be found in the exception or in the general rule, or whether the exception has not come to be erected into a rule by itself.

[1] Thayer, Prelim. Treat., 512.

NOTES OF CURRENT TOPICS. 759

In part, our rules are a body of confused doctrines, expressed in ambiguous phrases, Latin or English, half understood, but glibly used, without perceiving that ideas pertinent and just in their proper places are being misconstrued and misapplied."

Or, again :[2]

"The chief defects in this body of law, as it now stands, are that motley and undiscriminated character of its contents which has been already commented on; the ambiguity of its terminology; the multiplicity and rigor of its rules and exceptions to rules; the difficulty of grasping these and perceiving their true place and relation in the system, and of determining, in the decision of new questions, whether to give scope and extension to the rational principles that lie at the bottom of all modern theories of evidence, or to those checks and qualifications of these principles which have grown out of the machinery through which our system is applied, namely, the jury. These defects discourage and make difficult any thorough and scientific knowledge of this part of the law and its peculiarities. Strange to say, such a knowledge is very unusual, even among the judges."

And to those of us who realized, even faintly, the social dangers which such a situation involved—the contempt for the impotency and uncertainty of judicial administration; the delays which sicken the heart of honest suitors vainly seeking justice; the expense which compels unconscionable compromises; the ability of the well-paid criminal lawyer to outwit the efforts of society to punish its law-breakers, of high or low degree or position, by laying traps for overworked judges on points of evidence, almost too fine for statement, and springing them in an appellate court, until outraged society sees its only hope for safety in the convenient branch of a tree, the duty of seeking a more rational and flexible system grew heavy and impressive. The time seemed propitious for reform in this direction. The hope of it was, as it were, in the air of that class-room. Mr. Justice Stephen, in the "Digest of the Law of Evidence," had blazed a broad path into the tangled thicket of ambiguity and contradic-

[2] Thayer, Prelim. Treat., 527.

tion by his doctrine of Relevancy. The modern law of Evidence had hopefully been inaugurated. The instant popularity of the "Digest" showed a general professional appreciation of the need for a change, and a readiness to welcome any well directed attempt at improvement. The "Digest," however, had defects which even its warmest admirers were forced to admit; and Professor Thayer, while enthusiastically recognizing the advance made, found himself unable to assent to many of Stephen's conclusions. He sought for himself, and urged upon his pupils to find, if possible, a "more excellent way."

My own continuous writing, for a series of years, on this topic has, as appears from my published work, been devoted to the single purpose of finding this more excellent way, through the preparation of a helpful treatise on the law of Evidence along lines which, while furnishing needed assistance to the practitioner in finding, within the limited time at his command, the law, good or bad, which he needs for his purpose, may yet constitute a formative force for the more speedy attainment of truth and more complete doing of justice.

It has always been a serious purpose of mine not to bewilder or impede the reader, in his search for a case in point, with evidence of any didactic or philosophical purpose in writing the treatise. I have deemed it the untransgressible right of a reader to find the topic he is looking for at the place where he reasonably expects to find it, and stated in language with the meaning of which he is, or may readily become, familiar. I have sought, however, to the extent of my ability, to serve the more scientific ends which I have had in mind, by the arrangement of these familiar rules of evidence as illustrations of the employment of some fundamental principle, or as violations of that principle.

I have not found myself able to agree with Professor Thayer as to the constructive value of the historical method of inquiry and treatment when applied to the field of evidence. I have differed with reluctance, with diffidence. But the "more excellent way," in Evidence at least, lay, as it seemed to me, in another direction.

With regard to the historical method and the critical study of cases used as precedents, when applied to the rights and duties of citizens, either in relation to the State or to each other, I offer no possible criticism. As such rights and duties grow in complexity, these valuable methods of handling the substantive law will, I think, increasingly demonstrate their usefulness. But it appears to me that in the field of Evidence much of the good expected from them has not been realized. There is a reason for this; and the reason seems to me to be that a more constructive treatment is needed to afford suitable relief. The historical method of inquiry and treatment, in view of the present situation of the law of Evidence, and especially since the death, in 1902, of Professor Thayer, appear to me, if I may be perfectly frank, *instructive* rather than *constructive*. What might have happened had Professor Thayer himself have been able to finish his long—alas! too long—delayed complete treatise on the law of Evidence, it is idle to conjecture. The call and lure of the past was, indeed, powerful upon him. Possibly, the master hand might, nevertheless, have been strong and skillful enough to have so arranged the historical data collected by his industry as to have moulded the entire law of Evidence into a scientific and flexible body of rules, which should force general adoption. But the work actually done by the great professor, though highly instructive, was essentially preliminary to the constructive task of making a more adequate working system for Evidence. To show the historical development of a rule of exclusion, or of a legal institution like the jury; to show at what precise time an anomolous digression took place, or by what specific act a new and wrong meaning was given to a familiar term; who first attempted to add a novel rule to the substantive law of a given subject by telling the jury that there was a "presumption of law" to that effect, is undoubtedly valuable; but such facts are merely, at is seems to me, a necessary preliminary to more constructive work. To reform an abuse, and prevent its recurrence, it is helpful to know how it originated. But this knowledge does not constitute reform. The wise physician does not fail to study the disease with which he is dealing; but he does not mistake diagnosis for cure. Light on the road over which a traveler has passed may, to a certain extent, light him forward; but it cannot supply the objective of the journey, or determine accurately the best method for reaching it.

Except in some such preliminary and subordinate capacity, the historical method, as ordinarily applied, contains, so far, at least, as relates to legal procedure, an inherent element of weakness when used as an agency for reforming errors and abuses. It affirms the value of precedent as a formative power in legal growth, and demands for it a controlling influence. It brings out into clear relief the strength and importance of the ligatures which bind the present to the past. It is always looking instinctively toward the west for light, rather than to the dawn of the coming day. It vitalizes the forces of conservatism, already sufficiently dominant in legal professional life; forces which have always proved the nucleus of resistance to all legal reform. To apotheosize precedent as part of an effort to draw the profession away from existing precedent, in order that it may follow principle, or an earlier precedent, since overruled or modified, is apparently circuitous, to say the least.

It would seem that in the death of Professor Thayer the historical method of treatment lost its great opportunity of achieving reform in the law of Evidence. Whether his great personal power and widely recognized authority would have enabled him, had his life been spared, to formulate a complete statement of the modern law of Evidence, along the lines to which his "Preliminary Treatise on Evidence at the Common Law," and the two editions of his "Cases on Evidence" furnish our only guides, can never be determined. The golden bowl was broken before it had fulfilled its measure of usefulness. His life work, so far as this subject of evidence is concerned, must be completed by his pupils.

If I may venture to compare, from my own point of view, my work with the learned and admirable treatise of Dean Wigmore, a gentleman to whom I am under great obligation, and for whom I have a feeling of deep admiration, I may at once frankly confess that his work follows more closely upon the lines which Professor Thayer—our common teacher—laid down in his preliminary work, than does my own. Indeed, it is obvious but well-merited praise to say of Dean Wigmore's work that he has written very much such a treatise as Professor Thayer has led us reasonably to believe he might have written had he lived to finish his work in this respect. With the aid of the most commendable industry and painstaking research, he has carried forward Professor Thayer's habits of historical investigation into fields not publicly considered by the latter; and has amplified and enriched, in the field entered by Professor Thayer, the results obtained by him. To the force of this historical method of inquiry, arranged in a more scientific method of classification than is at present employed by the court, Dean Wigmore is trusting, in his effort to commend Professor Thayer's views to the acceptance of the profession, which is already so much indebted to him. If the result can be reached in this way, it has already been done.

In my opinion, however, the effectiveness of this method, in this connection, is greatly limited by the very nature of the subject. The path by which I am seeking the same end is sharply divergent from that pursued by Professor Thayer and Dean Wigmore. Naturally, I believe in it. I beg to point out certain essential differences, and indicate, very briefly, the reasons for holding to them in the face of such eminent authority.

Perhaps the most fundamental difference is that I cannot concede the scientific propriety of applying the doctrine of *stare decisis* to the rules regulating the admissibility of evidence. I at once agree that there is a large element of substantive or positive law which is covertly or openly within the scope of the rules of evidence; and, as to this, I make no question as to the right of an aggrieved party to carry an adverse ruling up to a higher court. But I feel convinced that the control of precedent should extend only to matters of the substantive rights or duties of the parties; and that the admissibility of evidence is not a question of substantive right, but an incident in the administration by the court of its judicial function for the doing of justice. In my view, the presiding judge has the administrative duty of protecting and enforcing the substantive rights of the parties; but that in connection with the trial of a disputed proposition of fact the substantive right of the party is practically limited to insisting upon the opportunity of trying to establish, by the most probative evidence at his command, the truth of his contention, and that the evidence in the case shall be received and weighed according to the rules prescribed by reason. So long as reason is followed, it is not, according to my view, part of the substantive right of a litigant to insist that it should be exercised in a particular way, merely because in the most closely analogous case such a ruling was made. In other words, the admissibility of evidence, so long as reason is applied, is a matter of administration. I confess that nothing could well be more fundamentally subversive of the present situation in Evidence than this contention. Should it be adopted, many, if not most, of the present difficulties in the law of Evidence would automatically drop from sight, and the procedure of an American trial more closely approximate that of an English one.

From a scientific point of view, the correctness of my contention would seem to depend upon whether the rules of evidence were part of the substantive rights of the parties, or were a means or method of enforcing these substantive rights. It would appear to me that the original and proper administrative function of the presiding judge is shown in his unquestioned power to deal with witnesses, subject only to the use of reason; including, as part of the basis of the reasoning, previous action of the court on similar facts or any established practice or custom. To me, at least, it seems clear that a party should have no more right to insist upon asking a particular question because it was admitted in a similar case, than he would have to insist upon putting in his evidence in a particular *order* because that order had been allowed in another case.

As I have elsewhere said: "The law of Evidence is, properly considered, not so much a thing in itself as a *mode* or method of doing something else. It is a tool, not a product; a form, not its content. In other words, it is a perfectly practical method of getting at results. Its utility is its only test. If this fails to demonstrate itself, change is easy. If the law of Evidence is not practical, it is nothing which jurisprudence should keep or need keep." ("How Should Evidence Be Taught?"—Green Bag, vol. 18, p. 679.)

So treated, the rules of Evidence regarding admissibility, as those regarding examination, may properly, in all cases, be regulated by local practice, subject to administrative control and modification under exceptional circumstances; or be changed from time to time, as in England, through the adoption by the judges of rules of court.

Second in importance only to this fundamental conception that the administration of evidence is a part of procedure, and, as such, is divorced from the controlling power of precedent, are certain distinctive propositions which commend themselves to me as sound and proper canons for the judicial administration itself. Certain of these may be formulated, with fair approximation to accuracy, thus:

NOTES OF CURRENT TOPICS. 765

(1) The social objects of litigation are vastly more important than the personal.

(2) The transcendently important end which the community seeks to accomplish by litigation is not that the dispute between A and B should be settled by the use of reason and without violence; but that truth should be discovered and justice done as accurately and speedily as possible.

(3) While old terminology is best retained, the connotation of terms should, so far as practicable, be restricted to a single meaning.

(4) - Substantive law, including the determinate probative force of any given inference of fact, should be eliminated from the field of evidence.

(5) The parol evidence rule and presumptions of law should not be treated as a part of the law of evidence.

(6) Any rule which excludes probative or constituent facts actually necessary to proof of the proponent's case is scientifically wrong.

(7) Any privilege accorded a witness which prevents the ascertainment of truth is scientifically wrong.

(8) The presiding judge should be strengthened in the exercise of the administrative function, and not subordinated to the prestige of the jury.

The first of these propositions—that the social objects of litigation are vastly more important than the personal—constitutes the underlying thought on which the others rest. It seems to me important to notice that the litigation between A and B is not conducted primarily for the benefit of A or B, but by society, acting through judges, juries, witnesses and counsel, whose supreme loyalty is to the State itself, i. e., to the cause of justice. This proposition is one for which it is easy to secure intellectual assent. It is also one for which it is difficult to secure practical obedience. In a sense, the cause for this is part of the nature of things. Certain ideas of our ordinary thinking—such as that we are, after all, very much like other people; that there is a general similarity between all world religions; that the way to serve a party is to serve the country; that a life of social service is a finer thing than one employed in the successful acquirement of material possessions, and the like,—seem automatically, as it were, to sink below the threshold of our consciousness as soon as we cease to give them our immediate attention. Confronted with them, we assent, indeed, to their truth; and straightway proceed to forget it. The trouble is, that such facts do not gear in without regular trains of thought. We cannot keep them there except by an effort of the will. Relax this, and the mental machinery goes on as if nothing of the kind existed. We customarily think in terms of *self*, and such ideas as these, how-ever true, are in conflict with the supreme importance of the individual selfhood. The mind shies away. It accepts, but does not assimilate. It is not hard to see how this fact bears in this connection. The natural man understands fighting. He loves its self-assertiveness, its excitement, its triumphs. The long past of an aggressive race has woven this into the very fibre of his being. He understands this, he craves it. In the slow evolu-tion of his legal institutions, the Englishman, native or trans-planted, has gotten beyond fighting out the question of right by force of arms. He has reached the point where he is prepared to fight with mental weapons—the use of reason. But still, it is a fight, and the ethics are those of war. These new weapons of the intellect are peculiar; special training and experience are needed to handle them. He must engage a suitable person to counsel and direct his fighting. He must have a band of assist-ants in his camp, in the form of witnesses, expert or ordinary. But he still is fighting his own battle, though under new rules, and the ethics are still those of war. He dominates and directs the skill of his professional adviser; who, in turn, recognizes that in his loyalty to his employer lies his highest allegiance. Whatever else may be questionable, he prides and justifies him-self by the feeling that he has been true to him by whom he was employed. The witnesses around the campfire of the consulta-tion room refresh each other's memory, and develop a fine spirit of "loyalty" to the party, which deeply colors the facts produced by the memory thus refreshed. Meantime the man of scientific skill is estimating what precise measure of expression and sup-pression of the truth will best win for his employer such a result as will justify him in securing the largest financial return to himself. This is war. All is permissible that the rules do not forbid. It is even pitifully true that much which the rules do forbid, but do not in themselves detect, is also deemed justified, on the general theory that "the other side will do it if we don't." This is the train of legal thinking to which the mind of the practitioner is apt to revert, and in which it rests with the greatest satisfaction. Back of it is a long legal heredity; the heredity of the blood feud, the ordeal, the wager of battle, the *combat a l'outrance*, the duel—all the efforts of stalwart, self-assertive men to vindicate their rights or keep their booty by the force of arms, or by the cunning that enabled them to gain it. Naturally, all that this individualistic conception of the proper purposes of litigation has ever demanded of society is that it should stake out and maintain the lists, enforce the rules, and make the victory effective to the victor. To this view, it is of but little consequence that the rules of evidence should be so understood or misunderstood as to lead to constant reversal and retrial, and so administered as to prevent the discovery of truth and to enable a skillful advocate unscrupulously to baffle and confound an inexperienced practitioner in presenting his case. To such a feeling, it is nothing that the court should be clothed only with such powers as would be necessary to the moderator of a New England town meeting, and that the real appeal of the parties should be to the emotions of an untrained and easily over-persuaded jury. It may well be regarded, from such a standpoint, merely as making litigation a game with a high percentage of risk, and so the more interesting to those who play it. If one can delay the progress of the game itself, why not? Were not the carefully planned delays of Fabius Maximus, the Cunctator, generally admired as having caused the defeat of Hannibal? From the view point of the parties, it is deemed the right of the litigant to take every advantage which any natural or acquired ability enables him, under the rules, to gain over an opponent. The more technical, therefore, these rules, the better for the purpose of litigation when viewed as a game of skill or endurance. The strength of the strong shall thus be made his shield; the wealth of the rich, his protection; in the fraud of the crafty shall lie the guaranty of his success. Power, in any form, may thus be made to press remorselessly upon weakness; though there should be as little of justice in its exercise as when Clovis settled the dispute as to the vase of Soissons with a blow of the battle-ax well planted in the skull of the offending tribesman.

There is, however, a different, and, it seems to me, more ethical conception of the functions of judicial administration. I have tried to state it thus:

> "American civilization, like that of any other free people, rests, in the ultimate analysis, upon doing speedy and complete justice between man and man. Confidence in the best human discharge of this God-like function is, as it were, the very cement of society, which holds its varied classes together. Confessedly, the highest obligation which the legal profession owes to the community is to see to it that this confidence is justified and increased. And yet, a very general feeling is to the effect that the administration of law is uncertain, to say the least; an imperfect and inadequate means for the attainment of justice. This feeling, in civil matters, results in the jettison of part of one's just rights by way of compromise, in order to obtain any rights whatever without inordinate expense, and within a reasonable time. In dealing with crime, its effect is shown in general lawlessness, in the emotionalism of juries, or the savagery of lynching.
>
> "It cannot well be asserted that this situation, this general disrespect for law, not as for something which is corrupt, but as for something which is impotent to give justice or punish crime, is due entirely to the degradation of the law of Evidence from a scientific system for reaching truth, to a bundle of empirical rules with which, as with cords, courts have been content to tie the hands of Justice, so that she cannot properly use either her scales or her sword. What may with confidence be said is, that no single step could be so quickly and so helpfully taken as to place the subject of Evidence and its practical administration on a proper scientific basis; to define correctly its field, and maintain the landmarks so established."[*]

Serious as is the conflict, as I view it, in civil cases, between the personal interests of the litigant and the general interests

[*] "Best's Principles of Evidence," 3d Am. Ed. Preface viii ix.

of society, I regard that conflict as being still more sharp and impressive in the administration of criminal law. Typically, the criminal is an Ishmael. His hand is against every man. He is fond of looking upon himself as carrying on a war with Society. Is it not, when one thinks of it, strange that Society should unreservedly accept the criminal at his own valuation, and accord him the full rights of a belligerent? Is it not still more remarkable that Society, in waging this extraordinary warfare, should impose upon itself a heavy handicap; fight, as it were, with one hand tied behind its back? We accord the criminal the valuable privilege of silence. He cannot be asked to incriminate himself; his wife cannot be required to incriminate him. If he confesses, we feel that great care must be exercised to see that the statement is "voluntary," we insist on knowing that a statutory warning was given, and so forth. Has Society any interest in the administration of criminal procedure superior to that of ascertaining the exact truth? If not, why attempt to wink the facts out of sight or to block the path to justice with hurdles, behind each of which may lurk pitfalls for the representative of the State? Admit the claims of mercy, the purpose of ultimate reformation. How can any of these important considerations be aided or otherwise than injured by attempting to deal with them upon the basis of a lie?

At the root of this indulgence is undoubtedly a rather creditable sentiment inherent in the English nature;—creditable, at least, to our hearts if not to our brains. It is the curiously mixed instinct of the sportsman; to even up the chance, make the game exciting; and all with a touch of pity and a sense of fairness. It is the same spirit which gives the fox a start before the hounds are loosed; that holds back the terrier until the rat has fairly started; that declines to shoot a sitting bird. If a criminal is fighting for his life or liberty, it is not "fair" to use his own mouth out of which to convict him, or to force his wife to be the instrument of his downfall. Give the poor chap a chance! He has but one hope. Do not foreclose it. But this is not generosity; it is more nearly suicide. How gravely this natural, if misapplied, feeling was, in earlier days, deepened by the bloody rigor of the criminal code of Sixteenth century England is a familiar matter of history. But, while the rigor has passed away, the counterbalancing indulgence remains.

Nor do I find it possible to admit the scientific propriety of excluding from the court or jury any evidence from which a logical inference, necessary to the case of the proponent, could reasonably be drawn; or for according to any witness, or class of witnesses, a right to conceal material facts. No social gain from such exclusion or privilege is adequate compensation for the loss incurred by Society where anything less than the entire truth is placed before its courts. Intentionally to disregard any light on the path to truth is wrong. Stephen's postulate that all relevant evidence should be received seems to me sound; —viewed as a canon of administration. Undoubtedly, it is true that certain species of probative facts are of such a nature as to present danger that a jury will be misled. Others tend to the production of confusion, by introducing collateral issues. Still others suggest important considerations of public policy. All these infirmative suggestions are, without doubt, sound. They afford ground for careful thinking by the court in discharging its judicial function of administration. They suggest the need of caution to the jury from the court; or impeachment in the argument of counsel. But, in my view, it is crude, unscientific, and unjust to impose an unconditional exclusion on probative evidence merely because it may be abused. The same argument was relied on, with much greater cogency, for excluding parties and privies from the witness stand on account of interest. Why not apply to the present exclusions of relevant evidence under the rules relating to hearsay, character, *res inter alios,* confessions, or the like, and to all privileges of silence at present accorded to witnesses, the same rule which Bentham applied to the exclusion of witnesses on the ground of interest? One cannot doubt that on the ground of interest a party is apt to be biased in his own favor. But should truth, on that account, suffer by absolutely closing his mouth? It is equally clear that the most probative hearsay statement is dangerous from an administrative point of view because the jury may mistake gossip for evidence; it is necessarily weak because untested by cross-examination and because every remove from the percipient witness means a chance for error. But because light is faint along the path to the truth, is it wisdom to shut off what little light there is? In an age of formal, sacramental judicial procedure, where results followed automatically as certain things were done or not done, a single fortuitous circumstance, such as oath or no oath, might well be selected as a ground for determining the fate of a species of evidence under all conditions. Such is not, I respectfully submit, the proper method of treating the subject in a system where reason is accepted as the guide to truth. As Bentham said: "Receive the evidence and determine by your mental scales how much of probative weight should be deducted from the evidence on account of the considerations on which you have been excluding it." It may well happen that this process will eliminate all probative force; in the same way that a jury may decline to believe a plaintiff's story although the law allows them to receive it. In fact, many exclusionary rules are used as specific assignments of irrelevancy. But the case is sure to arise where there will be a residuum of probative force; and this residuum will constitute a clear gain to the tribunal in its search for the truth. The introduction of this principle of administration was, perhaps, the crowning value of Bentham's work. Are we quite sure that the limits of its helpful application have been reached?

The attainments of the objects which the modern law of evidence, as I conceive it, was intended to serve, seems to me incompatible with the inverted relation of the court and jury which forms so unique a feature in American jurisprudence. The interests of society for the doing of justice under such laws as the legislature may enact or the courts may formulate are in the keeping of the judicial branch of the government. If these interests are to be well served, it is essential that the judiciary be clothed with adequate powers and in no sense subordinated in importance to a casual tribunal like the jury, which is without continuous traditions, but, on the contrary, feels entirely irresponsible for the wider consequences of litigation; and is, therefore, very apt to overlook the great concern of Society in uniform and accurate administration by looking exclusively at the more human and dramatic facts of a particular case. The American elevation of the jury at the expense of the court is demonstrably a direct result of the conscious rebellion of the Democracy of England against the power of the Crown as rep-

resented by the royal judges. The more strongly did the Stuarts
insist upon the power of the court, the more stoutly did the
people resist in the interest of the jury. The reason is obvious.
Their sole hope of escape from punishment lay in the exaltation
of the only judicial body in full sympathy with themselves. The
reason, I imagine, is much the same as that which leads labor
agitators of our day to demand a jury trial on contempt proceedings arising out of the violation of injunctions passed for the protection of property or the personal liberty of non-union workmen.
But, happily, the battles of Democracy have been won;—completely and forever. That issue is finally closed. All danger of oppression of the citizen from the superior force of an alien power is
completely over. Would it not then be wise to recognize the
fact, and cease incessantly looking, in alarm, over our shoulders
for the now phantom danger of three centuries ago? The present problem is not whether Democracy shall be safe from the
assaults of centralized power acting through the courts; but
whether Democracy, when in full control of all branches of
government, shall have sufficient self-restraint to impose upon
itself that obedience for the law which alone is true liberty.

The Democracy of the future will be found to possess and
able to exercise this power. But it cannot, in my opinion, best
be done by minimizing the legitimate power of the court.

Such are certain of the more salient features of the way in
which I have been, and am still, seeking to do constructive work
in the field of Evidence. That the rules of Evidence are canons
of judicial administration and not properly within the real scope
of the doctrine of *stare decisis;* that the social objects of litigation outweigh in importance the personal; that Society has
a transcendent interest in the ascertainment of truth and should
remove all barriers across the path of its tribunals in reaching
it; that the interests of justice should be intrusted to the Court
rather than to the jury;—these are the fundamental propositions which I venture to commend to the favorable attention of
the profession.

A satisfactory solution of the difficulties at present in the
law of Evidence must and undoubtedly will be found. When
the need is suitably recognized, and the attention of the profession properly focused upon it, no problem in jurisprudence

has, as yet, proved unsolvable, and the law of Evidence will not constitute an exception.

It may be doubted, however, whether in the quarter of a century since the coming out of Stephen's Digest any large measure of relief has been furnished to the cause of judicial administration in this particular. Time has apparently but intensified the situation to which Professor Thayer was then calling the attention of his pupils. The multiplicity of connotations for a single term has increased; the admixture of substantive law has grown more pronounced; the attenuated lines of hair-splitting decisions have become yearly more numerous; the percentage of reversal to trial has crept steadily higher; the length of time required for final adjudication against an alert opponent with adequate financial resources has extended; the average expense of litigation has increased. In fact, the administration of justice, especially of criminal justice, is, in many parts of the country, obviously breaking down; the courts have necessarily lost much in popular respect. Indeed, they are the object of open, grave and continued political attack. And the end is not yet reached. "The more excellent way," for which Professor Thayer sought, still remains to be discovered and applied.

No apology is needed for frankly seeking to impress upon the profession the value of the methods which some reflection on the subject has convinced me are best adapted for reaching this end. Nor, I trust, is apology needed for insisting upon this value at some length. I am insisting upon these views not because they are mine, but because they are true. They are not only mine. They are the views of many. I am simply privileged to speak for them in a particular way and on this occasion. If what I have said, in doing so, seems unduly dogmatic or self-assertive, may I hope that the transcendent social importance of the subject may prove the justification as it assuredly will have been the cause for any such transgression?

CHARLES FREDERIC CHAMBERLAYNE.

No. 21 STRONG PL., BROOKLYN, N. Y.

[15]

Philip McNamara*

THE CANONS OF EVIDENCE — RULES OF
EXCLUSION OR RULES OF USE?

> In a very real sense the entire structure of the modern law of evidence rests on the specialised and limited use of evidence.
>
> 1 Wigmore, *Evidence*, (Tillers Rev 1983) 695.

The common law principles of evidence are commonly expounded on the footing that they are dominated by rules of exclusion of evidence. One reads in the most respectable contemporary texts on evidence[1] that the common law rules embody four great canons of exclusion along with a disorderly miscellany of minor principles predicating the rejection of evidence to which they apply. The four "great canons" referred to are the hearsay rule, the opinion evidence rule, the rule against prior consistent statements and the rule expounded in *Makin* v *Attorney-General (NSW)*.[2] The characterisation of these canons as rules of exclusion of evidence is probably the source of the conceptual difficulty which most students feel in grasping, and the subsequent discomfort which many practitioners confess to in applying,[3] the common law rules of evidence. Their description as principles of exclusion is as illogical and inaccurate as it is confusing. The confusion is exacerbated by the fact that the so-called canons of exclusion are themselves subject to exceptions. The conceptual disorder is compounded by resort in practice by some judges to an overriding "res gestae" principle to justify the admission of evidence which would otherwise be required, by a strict and literal application of the "canons of exclusion," to be rejected, where rejection would be an affront to common sense.

If the common law rules of evidence are dominated by a single principle or set of principles, they are dominated not by canons of exclusion but by the inclusionary principle that all information sufficiently relevant to the facts in issue at a trial is not only admissible but positively required to be admitted if elicited in proper form from a competent witness and for a proper purpose. All other rules of evidence are both conceptually subordinate to and in practical terms dwarfed by this single principle.

Modern perceptions of the inter-relation of the common law principles of evidence are unquestionably clouded by the historical truth that the law has developed without a pre-ordained structure and has, from period to period, appeared to treat one particular rule as ascendant over all others. Some 800 years ago, the common law courts abandoned the primitive, irrational modes of trial by test and ordeal and began to insist that the tribunal of fact determine disputes on the basis of its own

---

* Barrister (SA); Senior Lecturer in Law, University of Adelaide.

1 See, for example, 1 Wigmore, *Evidence* (Tillers Rev 1983) par 8c; Buzzard et al, *Phipson on Evidence,* (13th ed 1982) 74; Cross, *Evidence* (5th ed 1979) 19; Gobbo et al, *Cross on Evidence* (2nd Aust ed 1979) 18; Thayer, *A Preliminary Treatise on Evidence* (1898) 264-270; Nokes, *An Introduction to Evidence* (3rd ed 1962); Eggleston, *Evidence, Proof and Probability* (2nd ed 1983) chapter 5.

2 [1984] AC 57, 65.

3 Cf Wigmore, supra n 1, 631.

collective reasoning powers. That step was the most fundamental to be taken by judges in connection with the system of dispute-resolution in the King's Courts. But, even when that step was taken, there emerged a blend of new rules and old. Certain vestiges of the old scheme of things lingered on with no justification other than a purely historical one.[4] Then, in the 16th century, came the second revolutionary step: the tribunal of fact ceased to be entitled and required to determine cases on the basis of its collective personal knowledge and was instead required to decide issues on the basis of the admitted evidence only. This step threw the concept of admissibility of evidence to the forefront. The competence and compellability of witnesses and the rules of privilege assumed paramount practical importance and began to be conceptually entangled with the notion of admissibility of information. For approximately 200 years, advocates and judges were obsessed with rules disqualifying witnesses or certain aspects of their evidence. The law of evidence was still developing unsystematically.

The first treatise on the law of evidence was Gilbert's work, published posthumously in 1754.[5] Perhaps because, in a then recent era, the courts had been agonising over whether to adopt the numerical system of proof in preference to a rational system based on an assessment of the credibility of witnesses and on the inherent cogency of information, Gilbert almost entirely devoted his efforts to laying down rules as to the weight of evidence and to ranking evidence by degrees of acceptability. There was born the "best evidence" rule, which dominated the law to its detriment until the middle of the 19th century.[6]

After the advent of the 19th century, "rules" of evidence began to emerge in unprecedented quantities. To some extent, this was a by-product of the growing number of law reports. And cases whose sole importance to practitioners was a ruling on evidence came frequently to be reported. The right of cross-examination of witnesses called by one's opponent became entrenched and nurtured the hearsay rule and numerous exceptions to it. Cases could be won or lost according to the advocate's knowledge of the fine points of recent rulings; consequently, a large number of treatises on evidence were published early in the 19th century,[7] largely to serve as practitioners' handbooks. Like all loyal common lawyers, advocates in 19th century England became slaves to precedents. Rulings which were no more than the application of a settled rule to a new fact situation were elevated to the status of independent principles of evidence. Exceptions to accepted principles multiplied when earlier rulings were qualified which, if literally applied to the information presented in the case at bar, would have served no good purpose. The policies of the law of evidence and the objectives of the trial system went unarticulated and were submerged in the maze of particular rulings. The works of Stephen (1876), who emphasised the paramountcy of the concept of relevance, and of Evans and Bentham, had their beneficial effects. But, nevertheless, the law of evidence continued to be haunted

---

4 Ibid 607.

5 Gilbert, *The Law of Evidence* (1754).

6 Wigmore, supra n 1, 609; Twining, "The Rationalist Tradition of Evidence Scholarship" in Campbell & Waller, *Well & Truly Tried* (1981) 211, 212-218. In the intervening years, the best evidence rule has come to be confined to documents: *Garton* v *Hunter* [1969] 2 QB 37,44.

7 Wigmore, supra n 1, 610; Twining, supra n 6, 222-234.

by the disorderly maze conceived before the law adopted rational fact-finding as its goal. The common law rules of evidence are now relatively static and it is perhaps opportune to re-examine this strange creature of the past for the purpose of assessing whether the rules of evidence can be reduced to a coherent and internally consistent set of principles.

1. Framework of Rules of Evidence

Since the beginning of the 20th century, it has been true to say that, judged by their practical effect, the common law rules of evidence fall in to the following framework:

1. There is *one principle of inclusion:* evidence is admissible and required to be admitted if sufficiently relevant to the facts in issue between the parties to be capable of assisting a rational tribunal of fact to determine the issues. This rule determines whether, as a matter of substance, information can lawfully be admitted by the tribunal of law and used by the tribunal of fact.

2. There is *one principle of exclusion:* information is not admissible in any form from any witness for any purpose if its reception is contrary to the public interest. This is the only principle which predicates that, as a matter of substance, information cannot be received by the tribunal of law or acted on by the tribunal of fact.

3. There are four principle[8] rules which, to the extent to which they are independent of the inclusionary rule, restrict the *use of relevant evidence* once admitted:

   (a) Evidence of an out-of-court assertion cannot in general be tendered to be used for the sole purpose of supporting the credibility of a witness;

   (b) Evidence of an out-of-court statement cannot in general be tendered to be used for the sole purpose of proving the truth of matters asserted by the statement;

   (c) Evidence that an actor or witness formed, expressed or holds a particular opinion cannot in general be tendered to be used for the sole purpose of proving the existence of the matter opined;

   (d) In a criminal case evidence of the misdeeds of a defendant not connected with the events charged cannot in general be tendered to be used for the sole purpose of authorising the inference that the defendant has a bad character and is therefore guilty of the crime presently charged.

It will be suggested that all but the second of these "great canons of exclusion" are merely facets of the inclusionary rule.

4. There are rules as to the *competence and compellability of witnesses:* at common law, the parties and their spouses, children, lunatics, convicts and atheists were incompetent as witnesses.[9] The

---

8 This list is not intended to be exhaustive. There are other rules which are characterised as rules of exclusion of evidence but which, in their practical operation, immediately restrict the use which can be made of evidence of relevant facts. For example, the parol evidence rule forbids the use of material extrinsic to a contract as an aid in the construction of the contract and the interpretation of words used by the contracting parties.

9 *Phipson on Evidence*, supra n 1, 691-693.

competence and compellability of witnesses is now regulated by statute.

5. There are rules conferring *privileges* on competent and compellable witnesses to withhold relevant information: into this category falls the privilege against self-discrimination and the rules regulating legal professional privilege.[10]

6. There are rules as to the *form* of evidence: for example, evidence of the contents of a document must, in general, be given in the form of the original document itself.[11]

7. There are rules regulating *the manner of giving evidence:* for example, in general, a witness must give evidence on oath from memory[12] and, in general, examination in chief cannot be conducted by the use of leading questions.[13]

8. There are rules qualifying or restricting *the powers of the tribunal of fact:* into this category fall the rules as to presumptions, the rules as to burden and standard of proof, and rules of law requiring corroboration as a condition of conviction in certain criminal cases.[14] In addition, there is the fundamental rule that the tribunal of fact must act on the evidence alone and not on its own knowledge.[15]

9. There are rules of law and of practice conferring powers or imposing obligations on trial judges: for instance, the judge presiding over a criminal trial by jury has a duty to warn the jury as to its assessment of the credibility of the evidence of certain witnesses (complainants in sexual cases, children, and accomplices),[16] and as to the manner in which it uses evidence which lends itself to a proper use and to an improper use.[17] In addition, the judge in a criminal trial has the power to reject relevant evidence pursuant to the judge's obligation to ensure that the trial is fair to the defendant.[18]

---

10 The decision of the majority of the High Court of Australia in *Baker* v *Campbell* (1983) 57 ALJR 749 may, if taken to its logical conclusion, transform legal professional privilege from a genuine privilege to a substantive rule of law of uncertain status and effect. Legal professional privilege is treated as a rule of exclusion of evidence in Pieris, "Legal Professional Privilege" (1982) 31 ICLQ 609.

11 *Phipson on Evidence*, supra n 1, 884.

12 J.H. Wigmore, *A Treatise on Evidence* (3rd ed 1940) para 725, 734.

13 *Phipson on Evidence*, supra n 1, 775.

14 Eg at common law, a defendant could not be convicted of perjury solely upon the evidence of a single witness, as far as concerned the falsehood of the perjured evidence: *Muscott* (1713) 10 Mod Rep 192.

15 *Phipson on Evidence* supra n 1, 26-27; *Swarbrick* v *Swarbrick* [1964] WAR 106.

16 See eg, *The People* v *Casey (No 2)* [1963] Ir R 33, 38; *Beck* (1982) 74 Cr App R 221; *Knowlden* (1983) 77 Cr App R 94; contrast *Vetrovec* v *The Queen* (1982) 67 CCC (2d) 1, 17-18; *R* v *James* (1983) 111 LSJS 422,446-448. And see *Phipson on Evidence*, supra n 1, para 32-02.

17 Eg *R* v *Gunewardene* [1951] 2 KB 600; *R* v *Golder* (1960) 45 Cr App R 5; *Corak and Palmer* v *The Queen* (1982) 101 LSJS 1, 10, 22-23; *Donnini* v *The Queen* (1972) 128 CLR 114; *Pemble* v *The Queen* (1971) 124 CLR 107, 117-118; Phipson, supra n 1, 76; *Barca* v *The Queen* (1975) 133 CLR 82, 107.

18 *R* v *Christie* [1914] AC 544; *Noor Mohammed* v *The Queen* (1949) AC 182, 192.

2. The Inclusionary Rule

It is now well established that the cardinal rule of evidence which regulated trials in common law systems is the rule that evidence is admissible and required to be admitted if and only if it is sufficiently relevant to a fact in issue to be capable of assisting the tribunal of fact rationally to resolve the issues between the parties.[19] As Professor Cross has demonstrated, this rule has both a positive and a negative aspect.[20] In its negative aspect, it requires the exclusion by the tribunal of law (the judge) of information which is incapable, as a matter of law, logic or experience, of assisting a properly instructed and rational decision-maker or which is too remote from the facts in issue to deserve any place in the deliberations of a rational tribunal of fact. Its negative aspect is subject to no genuine exceptions whatsoever, at common law.[21] In its positive aspect, the cardinal rule requires the tribunal of law — the judge — to admit relevant evidence elicited from a competent witness in proper form for a proper use. In its positive aspect, the rule is subject to the single exclusionary principle referred to in section four of this article, and it is also subject to the qualification that where, in a criminal trial, the judge forms the view that there is a substantial danger that the jury will put particular information to an irrational use (to the exclusion of its proper use) the judge should exclude. This positive aspect of the cardinal rule has been obscured by the "great canons of exclusion". Nevertheless, it must be remembered that it is as much an error of law for a trial judge to reject admissible evidence as it is for the judge to admit inadmissible information.[22] The inclusionary rule does not merely confer a power on the trial judge to admit relevant information as a matter of discretion. It confers on parties the right to require the judge to accept relevant material which is elicited from a competent witness in proper form for a proper purpose.

It has often been, and it continues to be, stated or implied that this fundamental rule is supplemented by an inclusionary principle styled "res gestae".[23] This is incorrect. The phrase "res gestae" or "res gesta pars rei

---

19 *Kuruma* v *The Queen* (1955) AC 197; *Wilson* v *The Queen* (1970) 123 CLR 334; *Markby* v *The Queen* (1978) 52 ALJR 626; *Blake* v *Albion Life Assurance Society* (1878) 4 CPD 94, 109; *Thompson and Wran* v *The Queen* (1968) 117 CLR 313, 317; *Gregory* v *The Queen* (1983) 57 ALJR 629, 631; Eggleston, "The Relationship between Relevance and Admissibility in the Law of Evidence" in Glass (ed) *Seminars on Evidence* (1970) 53,61.

20 Cross, supra n 1, 17.

21 One apparent exception is the anachronistic rule which permits a defendant to adduce evidence of good character to be used by the jury as material relevant to the defendant's innocence. This rule stems from *Rowton* v *The Queen* (1985) Le & Ca 520; [1861-1873] All ER 549. The practice of adducing good character evidence is now being discouraged and this apparent exception will probably wither. Cf *Manwaring* [1983] 2 NSWLR 82.

22 Wigmore, supra n 1, 226; *Curneen* v *Sweeney* (1969) 103 ILTR 29; *Piddington* v *Bennett & Wood Pty Ltd* (1940) 63 CLR 533; *Hally* v *Starkey* [1962] Qd R 474; *Stokes* v *The Queen* (1960) 105 CLR 279; *In re van Beelan* (1974) 9 SASR 163, 193; *Woodhouse* v *Hall* (1981) 72 Cr App R 39; *R* v *Collins* (1976) 12 SASR 501; *R* v *Toohey* [1965] AC 595; *Commissioner of Railways* v *Young* (1962) 106 CLR 535, 546, 553, 559.

23 Cross, supra n 1, 43-44, 575; *Phipson*, supra n 1, 77; *Corak and Palmer* v *The Queen*, supra n 12, 16; *R* v *Manh* (1983) 107 LSJS 241, 247, 256; Aronson, Reaburn, Weinberg, *Litigation: Evidence and Procedure*, (3rd ed 1982) 803; Waight and Williams, *Cases and Materials on Evidence* (2nd ed 1985) 812, 822-823; *R* v *Nye* (1977) 66 Cr App R 252.

gestae" was coined as a linguistic alternative to the phrase "relevant facts". It was not coined to describe a substantive alternative to the principle that only relevant facts can be proved in evidence.[24] The "principle" continues to find acceptance only because it is in Latin.[25] It probably continues to be used as an inclusionary principle by virtue of a combination of misconceptions, namely, a misconception as to the width of the genuine inclusionary rule; the misconception that evidence must be said to be "positively probative" in order to be relevant;[26] and a misconception of the true effect of the rules discussed in the next section of this article. The "res gestae" principle is a substitute for analysis and a symptom of superficial thinking. No amount of exegesis of the tenor of "the rule" can predicate whether it is applicable or not in a given fact situation, because it has no tenor or purport and it cannot, therefore, be a rule of law. When invoked in a practical setting, it relies on artificial concepts and fine distinctions.[27] But the real objection to it is the disorder which it wreaks on an otherwise coherent set of rules. What proponents of the "res gestae" approach are attempting to state is that particular information is admissible because it is relevant (even if not positively probative of a centrally material fact) and because it is tendered for a lawful and rational purpose, and that the information can be received in evidence despite that its admission apparently flies in the face of a "canon of exclusion".

The use of the cryptic Latin phrase to justify the reception of probative information has three unfortunate consequences. First, it obscures the distinction (which is both forensically and logically clear and wide) between *admitting* evidence (which is the function of the judge) and *acting on evidence* (which is the function of the tribunal of fact). Secondly, it fails to acknowledge that a single item of information more usually than not lends itself to more than one application in the mind of

---

24 *The Trial of John Tooke* (1794) 25 Howard St Tr 1,440; *Robson v Kemp* (1802) 4 Esp 234; *R v Hardy* (1794) 24 How St Tr 19,453; Manetta, "The Admissibility of Spontaneous Statements in Exception to the Hearsay Rule" (1984) 8 Crim LJ 69, 91, 95.

25 A Latin phrase that cannot be translated into an intelligible English clause can hardly merit acceptance as a rule of law. Unlike the "res acta" maxim, it has never been set in a clause or sentence, even in Latin. The apotheosis of this phrase to a rule of law has been deprecated by so many authoritative jurists that, given its vagueness and weak jurisprudential foundation, one wonders why its use is persevered with. For criticisms, see *Homes v Newman* [1931] 2 Ch 112, 120; Morgan, "Res Gestae" (1922) 31 Yale LJ 229; Stone, "Res Gesta Reagitata" (1939) 55 LQR 66; Wigmore, *A Treatise on Evidence* (3rd ed 1940) vol 6, s 1745, 1757. (The maxim "res acta inter alios alteri nocere non debet" is in substance merely an illustration of the operation of the genuine inclusionary rule.)

26 See *R v Rance* (1976) 62 Cr App R 119,121. Note in this respect the discussion in Eggleston, supra n 19, 55-64, especially 61, & Eggleston, supra n 1, ch 6.

27 This was frankly admitted by the Privy Council in *Ratten v The Queen* [1972] A.C. 378. The fact that the *res gestae* principle has never been authoritatively characterised as a rule of a particular kind is reason enough to doubt its validity. It is variously treated as an aspect of the cardinal rule, as an overriding and independent inclusionary principle and merely as an exception to the hearsay rule. The first approach is exemplified by what appears to be the general purport of *Phipson*, although there are passages where this approach is departed from. See, in particular, chapter 7; see also Kelly and Sulan, *Wells's Introduction to the Law of Evidence* (3rd ed 1979) 37, 133-146. The second approach is that adopted by Cross: see *Cross on Evidence* (Aust ed) supra n 1, ch 19; Cross, supra n 1, ch 21. The third approach is taken by *Archbold*: Mitchell et al, *Archbold: Pleading, Evidence & Practice in Criminal Cases* (41st ed 1982), 867-870; see also Eggleston, supra n 19, 63.

the tribunal of fact. And thirdly, to the extent that it wears the guise of an overriding inclusionary principle, its employment wrongly creates the impression that the law of evidence imposes no restrictions on the use which can be made, by the tribunal of fact, of information which, because relevant and tendered for a proper use, was required to be admitted by the judge.

3. Rules Restrictive of the Use of Admitted Evidence

Evidence is never tendered or elicited by competent counsel without an end in view. Evidence is adduced by a party intending that it will be put to one or more uses in favour of that party by the tribunal of fact. While admitted information can, in theory, be used by the tribunal of fact in a way unintended by the party tendering it, the law does not permit the unrestricted use of information which is relevant. The modern jury is required to discharge its duties according to the dictates of reason. And, beyond that, some restrictions are imposed by law on the use of received evidence, both to satisfy various policy objectives and to reinforce the adversarial system of dispute-resolution adopted by the common law.

To the extent that they are rules of law independent of the cardinal inclusionary rule, the four principle "canons of exclusion" of the common law of evidence are, in their practical operation, rules restricting the use to which admissible evidence may be put by the tribunal of fact. These rules operate only indirectly to exclude evidence. They so operate solely where relevant evidence is tendered to be used for a purpose prohibited by law, and for that purpose only. Where, on the other hand, evidence is tendered to be used for more purposes than one and where one of the intended uses is a proper use, then the evidence is admissible, and required to be admitted, to be used for that proper purpose. That is, the trial judge is required to admit it. The tribunal of fact — the jury, if there be one, or the judge — is permitted to put the material to its proper use but is prohibited from putting it to an improper use.

These simple propositions have, somewhat unhelpfully, been elevated by text writers to the status of "the principle of multiple relevancy".[28] A principle of law has thus been created for the sole purpose of resolving a dilemma created only by lawyers' choice of terminology. This approach can perhaps be explained as symptomatic of a reluctance to accept that the rules of evidence embody principles which are neither rules of admission nor rules of exclusion of evidence, or exceptions to such rules, and to accept that there are rules which, in their practical effect, impose fetters on the tribunal of fact and not merely on the judge. Each of the so called "exclusionary rules" is, in its practical effect, a rule restricting the deliberative freedom of the tribunal of fact.

---

28 Wigmore, supra n 1, vol 1, para 13; Cross, supra n 1, 20-21; *Phipson*, supra n 1, 76. Cross describes this "principle" as a "rule" and "doctrine". Cross's characterisation of the proposition as a rule is accompanied by the following statement of dissatisfaction:
> "It is, however, difficult to suggest anything better, and, although the term [multiple relevancy] is not employed by English judges, the doctrine it embodies is mentioned in numerous dicta. The application of the doctrine is fraught with danger, but the total exclusion of the evidence could be productive of even greater injustice."(p 21)

(a) The Rule Against Prior Consistent Statements:

At common law, witnesses are not permitted to narrate out-of-court assertions by themselves or by another witness for the purpose of supporting their own credibility or the credibility of the other.[29] This rule applies both to express assertions and to assertions which may be implicit in conduct.[30] There are two common law exceptions to this rule: an out-of-court assertion can in limited classes of cases be tendered to be used for the sole purpose of supporting the credibility of a complainant of a sexual assault[31] and of a person alleged to have recently invented evidence.[32]

The rule applies only to conduct, verbal or otherwise, which bespeaks or asserts something. It does not apply to conduct, verbal or non-verbal, which does not assert or imply a fact. Conversely, it is quite clear that this rule does not preclude the admission of out-of-court assertions which are themselves relevant facts. For example, an out-of-court complaint by an injured person (who subsequently gives evidence as a plaintiff) as to contemporaneous pain, suffering and distress can be received in evidence; an out-of-court complaint by a worker to an employer that a system of work is unsafe can be received in evidence if the system results in injury to a worker and the question at the trial is whether the employer should have foreseen a particular risk of injury in the system; a pre-contractual statement by one party to a contract as to that person's post-contractual statement intentions (relative to the subject-matter of the contract) can be received in evidence on the issue of quantum of damages; in an action by a tenant against a landlord for breach of the latter's covenant to repair, the tenant's out-of-court complaint of disrepair and notice to repair, which gives rise to the right to sue for damages, can be proved;[33] and out-of-court statements which assist in fixing the time, place and circumstances of relevant conduct can be proved.[34] To the extent that the out-of-court assertions are made relevant facts in the assessment of damages or on the issue of liability, by the substantive law, they are required to be admitted by the judge. They must not, however, be used as supporting the credibility of a witness. If the sole purpose of the tender were the proscribed purpose, the information is excluded by the negative aspect of the cardinal rule: the information is unhelpful because it is tendered to be used solely for a purpose to which it cannot lawfully be applied by the tribunal of fact and it must be rejected by the judge.

---

29 *Jones v S E and Chatham Ry* (1918) 87 LJKB 775, 779; *Gillie v Posho* [1939] 2 All ER 196,201; *Corke v Corke and Cooke* [1958] P 93; *R v Roberts* [1942] 1 All ER 187; *R v Oyesiku* (1972) 56 Cr App R 240, 245-247; and see the cases cited in *Phipson* supra n 1, 788 and Cross, supra n 1, 236-238.
30 Nokes, supra n 1, 100.
31 *Kilby v The Queen* (1973) 129 CLR 460; see the numerous authorities collected in Waight and Williams, supra n 23, 286-300; *Phipson*, supra n 1, 149-152; Cross, supra n 1, 238-244.
32 See, in particular, *Nominal Defendant v Clements* (1960) 104 CLR 476 and *Fox v General Medical Council* [1960] 3 All ER 225.
33 See eg *Wills on Evidence* (3rd ed 1938) 209; *Ramsay v Watson* (1961) 108 CLR 642, 647-649; *Aruna Mills Ltd v Dhanrajmal Gubindram* [1968] 1 QB 655; *Koufos v Czarnikow Ltd* [1969] 1 AC 350; *Hewitt v Rowlands* (1924) 93 LJKB 1080. The conventional analysis of this process, both in England and Australia, would involve the characterisation of B's assertion as "part of the *res gestae*": See Cross, supra n 1, 244, 463; *Phipson* supra n 1, 83, 789.
34 *R v Kooyman and Brydson* (1979) 22 SASR 376.

In *R* v *Roberts,*[35] Humphreys J said of the rule and of a prior statement relevant only to the credibility of the speaker as a witness:

> "[T]he reason for the rule appears to us to be that such testimony has no evidential value. It is because it does not assist in the eludicating of matters in dispute that the evidence is said to be inadmissible on the ground that it is irrelevant. It would not help the jury in this case in the least to be told that the appellant said to a number of persons [before he gave evidence]...that his defence was this, that or the other."

On this analysis of the rule, it is not an independent rule of evidence at all. That is, it is neither a rule of exclusion nor a rule of use. On this view, the two exceptions referred to earlier can be supported as operating in instances where the credibility of the witness concerned has become a live issue in the trial and is of such importance that no rational tribunal of fact would decide the case without the benefit of the prior consistent statement. However, it is more likely that the foundation of the rule is pragmatism rather than relevance. In some cases, it operates indirectly to exclude evidence which could reasonably be regarded by a lay person as "relevant",[36] because the credibility of the witness was immediately at stake even if that witness's evidence was not alleged to be concocted.

(b) The Hearsay Rule

The hearsay rule is probably the most difficult rule of the common law of evidence to explain, justify and defend, because it clearly can operate to prevent the use of reliable, relevant information. It is not merely an aspect of the cardinal rule. Because it excludes evidence irrespective of its reliability and relevance, the hearsay rule has some of the trappings of an absolute rule of exclusion. It is, however, important to bear in mind that the modern formulation of the hearsay rule emphasises that the rule operates only on out-of-court assertions and then only where such an assertion is tendered for a particular purpose. As the Privy Council said in *Subramaniam* v *Public Prosecutor:*[37]

> "Evidence of a statement [made out of court] may or may not be hearsay. It is hearsay and inadmissible when the object of the evidence is to establish the truth of what is contained in the statement. It is not hearsay and is admissible when it is proposed to establish by the evidence, not the truth of the statement, but the fact that it was made. The fact that the statement was made, quite apart from its truth, is frequently relevant..."

The point was made even more clearly by the Privy Council in *Ratten* v *The Queen:*[38]

---

35 Supra n 29, 191. This view is supported by Sir W.D. Evans in his notes to *Pothier on Obligations* (1806 ed) vol 2, 189 and by the speech of Lord Radcliffe in *Fox* v *General Medical Council,* supra n 32, 230, and Cross, supra n 1, 236.

36 See Fox, "Expediency and Truth-Finding in the Modern Law of Evidence," in Campbell and Waller, *Well & Truly Tried* (1982) 140, 146-147.

37 [1956] 1 WLR 965, 969. This decision was applied by the Supreme Court of Canada in *Phillion* v *The Queen* [1978] 1 SCR 18,24.

38 Supra n 27, 387. The matter was put most clearly by Lord Reid in argument at 380-381. In *In re Van Beelen* (1974) 9 SASR 163, 200, the Full Court of the Supreme Court of South Australia expressed the position as follows:

> "1. Subject to certain exceptions established under the general law or by

"The mere fact that evidence of a witness includes evidence as to words spoken by another person who is not called, is no objection to its admissibility. Words spoken are facts just as much as any other action by a human being. If the speaking of words is a relevant fact, a witness may give evidence that they were spoken. A question of hearsay only arises when the words spoken are relied on "testimonially", i.e. as establishing some fact narrated by the words..."

The hearsay rule operates as a complement to the rule limiting the use of prior consistent statements. Both rules operate on statements made out-of-court and on non-verbal conduct in which statements are implicit. The hearsay rule precludes the use of out-of-court assertions as a *medium of proof* of relevant facts, unless an exception applies. The other rule precludes the use of out-of-court assertions as a *medium of proof* of the witness's credibility. Statements which are themselves relevant facts are proper *objectives of proof* and can as such be proved. They are not excluded by either rule, but their use may be restricted.

In the context of the hearsay rule, it has become acceptable to describe out-of-court assertions which are relevant facts (rather than means of proof of relevant facts) as "original evidence" or part of the *res gestae*.[39] The first label tells us nothing about the practical operation of the hearsay rule. It does not emphasise, as terminology should, that the hearsay rule applies only to out-of-court assertions of fact; that is, to out-of-court words or conduct by which the actor sought to assert a fact expressly or impliedly. The rule does not apply at all to non-assertive conduct. The unhelpful phrase "original evidence" is used to direct the mind indiscriminately both to conduct not intended to be assertive and to evidence of out of court assertions not tendered to be used assertively. It confuses the field of operation of the hearsay rule with its forensic effect. There is an important conceptual distinction between these two phenomena. Conduct not intended to be assertive lies entirely outside the field of operation of the hearsay rule. Out of court utterances not tendered to be used assertively would lie within the reach of the rule but for the fact that the rule is a purposive and not an absolute "rule of exclusion". The relevant distinction is between statements whose tenor is relied upon and those whose truth is relied upon by the party tendering. (By "tenor" is meant "contents" or "purport".)

---

38 *continued. . .*

statute, evidence of an extra-judicial statement (oral or written), even where its subject matter is relative to the issue, is inadmissible as hearsay if the sole purpose of introducing the statement is to use the assertions of fact contained in it as proof of the truth of those assertions.

"2. Evidence of such an extra-judicial statement is admissible where it is sought to prove, not the truth of the assertions contained in it, but that they were, in fact, made, and either the making of the statement is the, or one of the, facts in issue, or it is open to the tribunal of fact, in all the circumstances, to draw an inference from the character of the statement and the making of it that connects both with, and renders them relevant to the issues."

39 Both *Phipson* and Professor Cross use both labels: see Cross, supra n 1, 437; *Phipson on Evidence,* supra n 1, 331, 335. In Carter, *Cases and Statutes on Evidence* (1981) 7, the use of the former phrase is defended. *Wells,* supra n 27, 134 uses the classification of "primary" and "secondary" statements.

Within the field of operation of the rule, two further distinctions must be drawn, namely between genuine assertions and apparent assertions, and secondly between assertions and operative words. Operative words often wear the trappings of assertions. Operative words are utterances which directly operate on or affect legal rights, such as words of formation of contract, words of libel or slander, words of consent or authority to do what would otherwise be unlawful, words of threat or menace, and words of assignment, disposition or assurance. These are not intended by the speaker to assert facts although they may often appear to be assertions. ("You can have my car for the day", "I want to buy this painting", "I want to place $10 on Nag in the third at Rosehill").[40] Such utterances are entirely outside the reach of the hearsay rule, and in any event they are not in practice tendered to be used assertively.

When dealing with genuine out-of-court assertions, it is more useful to adopt the language of Lord Wilberforce in *Ratten,* where his Lordship drew a distinction between the testimonial (or assertive) use of an out-of-court assertion — the proscribed use — and the non-testimonial (eg inferential) use of an out-of-court assertion — a proper use. This terminology emphasises the qualified nature of the prohibition in the hearsay rule, as stressed by the Privy Council in the advices referred to earlier. It is the intended use (not the potential use) of the evidence of the out-of-court assertion which attracts the hearsay rule. The hearsay rule operates on out-of-court assertions according to the purpose of the party tendering, not the purpose of the original speaker. Even out-of-court statements which, when uttered, had purely an assertive function can in theory be tendered to be used non-assertively and if tendered to be so used are not caught by the hearsay rule. If and only if the out-of-court assertion is tendered *solely* to be used testimonially, that is as a means of proof of what is asserted, is the tender objectionable. Evidence of the assertion is, in those circumstances, precluded by the cardinal rule, in its negative aspect, because the evidence is not tendered for a use to which the tribunal of fact can lawfully put it. If the out-of-court statement is tendered to be used as the basis for an inference to which it rationally gives rise whether it is true or false,[41] or if it is tendered merely to be used as a step in the unfolding of the drama which gave rise to the litigation,[42] or if it is tendered merely because it is part of the background necessary to set the stage, and so add life and colour to the narrative given by the witness, its tender cannot be objected to on the basis of the hearsay rule. Where the out-of-court statement lends itself to both a testimonial and a non-testimonial use, it is still required to be admitted. The judge may have to warn the jury (if there be one) not to put the statement to the proscribed use.[43]

---

40 Contrast the reasoning in *McGregor* v *Stokes* [1952] VLR 347; *Fingleton* v *Lowen* (1979) 20 SASR 312.
41 See the examples given in *Phipson,* supra n 1, 331, and Cross, supra n 1, 473-478, and *Shone* (1983) 76 Cr App R 72.
42 *Ladlow* v *Hayes* (1983) 8 A Crim R 377, 382-383.
43 *Wilson* v *The Queen,* supra n 19, 340, 345; *Willis* v *Bernard* (1832) 8 Bing 376, 383; 131 ER 439, 441; *People* v *Heiss* 186 NW 2d 63 (1971). Spontaneous utterances have proved problematic because they often have both an assertive and a non-assertive aspect and also an inferential aspect: strictly speaking, such statements should be admissible to be used merely either as a step in the narrative or inferentially. There is, however, in Australia and Canada some authority to the effect that spontaneous

To label as "part of the *res gestae*" material which is inherently not assertive or material which is not tendered to be used testimonially is for reasons already given jurisprudentially indefensible. It is also potentially harmful at a practical level, particularly in criminal cases. For, when an out-of-court utterance is admitted by a judge as "part of the *res gestae*" (or, indeed, as "original evidence") and for as long as the hearsay rule is treated as an exclusionary rule, the hearsay rule is set aside completely on the reception of the information into evidence and such protections as the rule may rightly confer on a party are lost. The consequence is that there are no longer any perceived safeguards on the forensic use of the utterance. This can be counterproductive, unjust and, as Professor Cross has noted, dangerous in particular instances.[44]

If, however, the hearsay rule is treated as a rule restricting, not the admission, but rather the use of *relevant* utterances, the admission of an out-of-court assertion is not the end of the matter. The question of the intended and lawful use of the assertion remains to be the subject of argument or concession, ruling by the judge and, if there is a jury, a direction by the judge to the jury. If, consistently with general principle, the assertion can be used testimonially (because it is, say, an admission by the party against whom it is tendered), the jury should be so directed. If, on the other hand, no relevant exception to the hearsay rule applies so that the assertion can lawfully be used only non-testimonially, then the jury should be given a negative warning not to use the utterance testimonially. Further, in a criminal trial, where the judge is satisfied that there is a substantial danger that, despite a warning, the jury will put the assertion to the proscribed use, and that danger outweighs the tendering party's legitimate need for the evidence, the judge would be

---

43 continued. . .

statements forming part of or accompanying a relevant fact can be used assertively in exception to the hearsay rule. See the conflicting judgments in *Adelaide Chemical & Fertiliser Co Ltd* v *Carlyle* (1940) 64 CLR 515; and compare *Ratten* v *The Queen,* supra n 27, 391; *Hissey* v *The Queen* (1973) 6 SASR 280, 293. See also Manetta, supra n 24, 85, 101. In *R* v *Mahoney* (1979) 50 CCC (2d) 197, the defendant stood trial charged with the murder of a woman. At the trial, the Crown elicited evidence from a person who testified that he saw the defendant banging on the door of the house in which the victim was murdered, shortly before the murder, and then heard the sound of a window smashing. The witness then testified that he saw the defendant through the broken window smashing at the door of the house with an object in his hand and that, at that time, he heard the deceased utter words to the effect of "Jack, what are you doing" or "no, Jack". The defendant was known as Jack. The witness did not see the murder. The trial judge directed the jury as follows:

"However. if you find that [the deceased] spoke those words, if you find from that, that she believed that the person who was at the door was the accused then you may treat her belief as corroborative of the evidence of the other ones who identify him, *but her evidence as to the person who was at the door may not be used as direct evidence of the identity of that person.*"(Emphasis added).

Both the Ontario Court of Appeal (50 CCC (2d), 392) and the Supreme Court of Canada (67 CCC (2d), 216) regarded this direction as wrong and held that the deceased's utterances could have been used by the jury as evidence of the facts asserted or implied in them. With respect, while the first part of the summing up is incorrect, the second (the underlined portion) is fully consistent with general principle. The case is on all fours with *R* v *Fowkes* (1856) Steph Dig Art 3 illustration a; cf 9th edition, Part 1, Ch II, 4-5.

44 Cross, supra n 1, 21.

empowered to reject the evidence of the assertion at least when it is tendered by the Crown.[45]

In *Hughes* v *National Trustees Executors and Agency Co (A/Asia) Ltd*[46], several members of the High Court of Australia expressed concern at the breakdown of the often justifiable safeguards inherent in the hearsay rule which is caused, on the admission of a relevant assertion for a proper purpose, by treating the hearsay rule as an exclusionary rule whose effect is spent once relevant evidence is admitted. Unfortunately, the members of the Court, by treating the hearsay rule as a rule of exclusion of relevant assertions, did not offer a conceptually satisfactory solution to the problems which they perceived. In that case, the Court was required to determine the proper use in evidence of statements of fact made by a testatrix both in a will and verbally which reflected adversely on the character and conduct of the applicant. The will gave rise to an application under the testator's family maintenance legislation of Victoria, which provided that the application might be refused by the Court "if the character or conduct of the applicant" were such as should, in the opinion of the court, disentitle him or her to relief. The executor contended that the testatrix's statements could be used as evidence of the facts asserted. The applicant contended that, at most, the assertions were evidence of the reasons motivating the testatrix, those reasons being, in themselves, a relevant fact. The High Court upheld the latter contention.

Barwick CJ said:[47]

"In the view I take of this appeal, it is not really necessary for me to discuss the admissibility of such statements or the use to which, being admitted, they may properly be used (sic). But as others have expressed a view on these matters, I shall briefly state my own opinion.

"Evidence of the reasons given by a testator or testatrix for making or not making a provision by will are, in my opinion, admissible as evidence of those reasons. Such statements are not evidence of the facts they assert: they provide evidence only of the subjective attitude or beliefs of the testator or testatrix. Of these other facts, the evidence is technically classed as hearsay...What matters, however, it seems to me, is not so much the admissibility of the statements as the use to which they may judicially be put.

"But however that may be, I must concede that, in any case, such statements do not afford any proof of the objective facts they assert."

Gibbs J, (as he then was) with whom Mason and Aickin JJ agreed said:[48]

"In my opinion consistently with principle it is impossible to treat a statement of this kind as evidence of the truth of the matters stated. Unless the statement is admissible to prove that

---

45 This is one aspect of the exclusionary discretion recognised in the line of cases stemming from *R* v *Christie* [1914] AC 545; see especially the speech of Lord Atkinson at 554-556. See Wigmore, supra n 1, 701.

46 (1979) 23 ALR 321. And see Note: "The status of Hearsay and Other Evidence Admitted Without Objection" (1985) 1 *Aust Bar Rev* 155.

47 Ibid 325-326.

48 Ibid 336-337. Emphasis added.

what was said was true, it cannot shift the onus of proof. It is admissible only to prove the reasons which actuated the testatrix in making her will. There are no doubt some cases in which inadmissible evidence, having been admitted, may be treated as evidence for all purposes; for example, where one party by his conduct at the trial has led the other to believe the evidence, although hearsay, may be treated as evidence of the facts stated, and the other in reliance on the belief has refrained from adducing proper evidence, the former party is precluded from objecting to the use of the evidence to prove the facts stated. However, in general it is the duty of a judge to reach his decision on evidence that is legally admissible, *and to put evidence only to those uses which the law allows.* When a statement is admitted, not as evidence of its truth but simply as original evidence, *the mere fact of its admission cannot enable it to be given an additional probative value which the law denies it.*"

If the Court had characterised the hearsay rule as a rule restrictive of the use of received relevant evidence rather than as a rule of exclusion, the result of the proper application of the hearsay rule would have been somewhat easier to state — the testatrix's assertions could be proved in evidence becasue they were relevant facts (being evidence of the reasons which actuated the tenor of the will) but, by virtue of the hearsay rule, could not be used as evidence of the facts asserted.[49] This method of characterisation has the advantage of conceptual clarity and, in the context of the hearsay rule in particular, tends to preserve the effectiveness of the principle underlying that rule despite the admission of an out-of-court assertion which is a relevant fact.

(c) The Opinion Evidence Rule

"I understand the general rule to be that it is for the court and not the witness to draw inferences of fact from the primary, observed facts; but the difficulty is that this cannot, in the nature of things, be treated as a strict or hard and fast rule without getting in the way of reasonable proof and thus impairing the judicial process."[50]

The hesitation evident in this leading formulation of the "opinion evidence rule" is understandable. It is agreed on all sides that the common law of evidence embodies a canon of exclusion known as the opinion evidence rule. But expressions of the rule reflect no uniformity. Professor Cross states the rule as follows:

"A witness may not give his opinion on matters which the court considers call for the special skill or knowledge of an expert unless he is an expert in such matters, and he may not give his opinion on other matters if the facts upon which it is based can be stated without reference to it in a manner equally conducive to the ascertainment of the truth."[51]

---

49 Emphasis on the impact which the hearsay rule has on the use of evidence can also be found in the judgments in *Trotter* (1982) 7 A Crim R 8, 19, 21; and *Buck* (1982) 8 A Crim R 208, 212-213; see, generally, Eggleston, "Evidence Admitted for a Limited Purpose", in *Judicial Essays*, (Law Foundations of NSW and Victoria) 85.

50 *Sherrard v Jacob* [1965] NI 151, 156 per Lord MacDermott LCJ.

51 Cross, supra n 1, 442.

Phipson asserts quite concisely that "the opinion, inferences or beliefs of individuals (whether witnesses or not) are inadmissible *in proof of material facts*".[52] Other texts insist that the rule is that, in general, witnesses must give evidence of their own perceptions and not of their inferences.[53] With respect, *Phipson* is more accurate because the formulation in that text draws attention to the fact that what is prohibited is the use of witness's opinion to prove facts opined, inferred or believed. At common law, information to the effect that an actor or witness formed the opinion or drew the inference or held the belief that fact X obtained at a material time cannot in general be used to prove that X did obtain at that time.

Functionally, two crucial distinctions must be drawn in this context. First, between the expression and formation of opinion in court and the expression and formation of opinion out of court; and secondly, between opinions *about* relevant facts and opinions which *are* relevant facts.

The expression, *in court,* of an opinion, inference or belief that X obtained at a material time can be admitted to be used as evidence that X obtains only if (a) the opinion, inference or belief is one which the tribunal of fact could not rationally hold, or draw from the factual material before it, *without assistance* and (b) the witness is qualified to give that assistance. In other words, like all other evidence, the evidence is admissible only where it is needed and would, if admitted, assist the jury.[54] If it is not needed or if it would not assist the jury, the negative aspect of the cardinal rule excludes it. Lay opinion, inference or belief is excluded by the cardinal rule either because no rational jury conscientiously discharging its consititutional function as tribunal of fact would seek assistance from it or because (which is the same thing in substance) a rational jury is as capable as the lay witness of drawing inferences from the known facts.

It is entirely otherwise with expert opinion. In so far as it concerns the opinions of experts, it is historically and functionally wrong to regard the "opinion evidence rule" as an exclusionary rule. The reception of qualified opinion evidence represents, in effect, an expansion of the inclusionary rule,[55] not a qualification on it. Expert evidence is adduced in order to assist the tribunal of fact to draw rational and correct inferences from facts proved by the narrated observations of the witnesses. The reason for the admission of the evidence is that, without it, a lay tribunal of fact (including a judge sitting as tribunal of fact) may be thwarted in the discharge of its constitutional functions or unable to form a correct judgment on the observational material before it.[56]

The *out-of-court expression* of an opinion, inference or belief that X obtained at a material time cannot, in general, be used as evidence that

---

52   Supra n 1, 553. Emphasis added.
53   See, eg Waight and Williams, supra n 23, 549; Aronson, Reaburn and Weinberg, supra n 23, 783. The imprecise nature of the "rule" is demonstrated in Cowen and Carter, "Some Observations On The Opinion Rule", in *Essays on the Law of Evidence* (1956) ch V.
54   See *R v Turner* [1975] QB 834; *Chard* (1972) 56 Cr App R 268; *Schultz* (1981) 5 A Crim R 234, 239-240; *R v Barry* [1984] Qd R 74.
55   See Eggleston, supra n 11, 59, 73-74, 145; Wigmore, supra n 1, Vol 7, s 1917; *Folkes v Chadd* (1782) 3 Doug KB 157; *Beckwith v Sydebotham* (1807) 1 Camp 116.
56   *Carter v Boehm* 1 Smith LC 7th ed (1876) 577; *Clark v Ryan* (1960) 103 CLR 486, 491; *R v Camm* (1883) 1 QLJ 136; *Phipson* supra n 1, 556;

X obtained at that time; this is a consequence of the operation of the hearsay rule and not of the "opinion evidence rule". The out-of-court *formation* of an opinion or belief that X obtains cannot be given in evidence unless the relevant fact in issue is the formation of the opinion that X obtains[57] rather than X itself. This consequence flows not from the opinion evidence rule, but from the cardinal rule: the formation by an actor of an opinion out of court that X does not tend objectively to prove that X obtains; because the information has no probative tendency, and would not be acted on by a rational and conscientious tribunal of fact, it is excluded by the negative aspect of the cardinal rule.

(d) Evidence of bad character

No branch of the law of evidence has become so conceptually obscure in recent times as the rules relating to the admission of evidence of character, and particularly of bad character in criminal cases. This is perhaps due to a movement, late in the 19th century, away from the solid, pragmatic foundations laid in earlier times, a movement stabilised by recent appellate decisions at the highest level.[58]

For most practical purposes, in order to decide whether character and reputation can be proved, one simply applies the cardinal inclusionary rule. That requires that a distinction be drawn between cases where character (or reputation) is in issue and cases where it is not. Reputation is a relevant fact in civil defamation actions and can therefore be the subject of evidence. Character and reputation may be made relevant facts in a criminal trial by operation of statute.[59] But, in general, neither the characters nor the reputations of the parties are in issue in proceedings, before verdict or conviction. That being so, the cardinal rule of evidence, in its negative aspect, operates in the general run of cases to exclude information the sole rational use of which is to assist the tribunal of fact to form a judgment as to a party's character or reputation. Information cannot be tendered for the sole purpose of assisting a decision as to the existence or non-existence of an immaterial fact.

At common law, however, a defendant in criminal proceedings was entitled, in the defendant's case in chief, to adduce evidence of the defendant's good reputation to be used by the jury as material bearing on the likelihood of the defendant's innocence.[60] When the accused was made a competent witness by statute, it became accepted that such

---

57 For example, in a case revolving around a fraudulent misstatement, the victim's belief in the truth of the misstatement when the statement was acted upon (by the victim) is a relevant fact and can as such be proved. A statement by way of identification, that is an out-of-court statement whereby a witness to a crime (or to some other relevant fact) objectively manifests the mental process of identifying a person in a line-up with the criminal (or other involved actor), is an outcome of the drawing by the speaker of a conclusion and can, if it becomes relevant at a particular trial, be proved by the speaker or by direct observation evidence of the making of the statement. Finally, on a charge of larceny, the defendant can give evidence of his state of belief at the moment of asportation of the goods where the defence is claim of right.

58 See the plea for clarification in *Phipson*, supra n 1, 238.

59 See, eg Atomic Energy Act 1953 (Cth) s 47; Summary Offences Act 1953 (SA) s 21; Criminal Law Consolidation Act 1936 (SA) s 200.

60 *Stannard* (1837) 7 C & P 673, 173 ER 296; *Rowton* (1865) Le and Ca 520; 169 ER 1497; *Attwood v The Queen* (1960) 102 CLR 353, 359; *R v Simic* (1980) 54 ALJR 406; *Williams* (1981) 4 A Crim R 441; *Andrews* [1982] 2 NSWLR 116.

evidence could also be used to support the defendant's credibility as a witness.[61] The converse was not true. The prosecution was not entitled, in its case in chief, to adduce evidence of the bad reputation of the accused. However, where, in the course of the defendant's defence, the defendant set up a good character, the prosecution was entitled to adduce evidence (including evidence of convictions) in rebuttal of the defendant's pretended good character.[62] (The proper use of such evidence from the prosecution is a matter of conjecture at present.[63]) Thus, good reputation was an acceptable means of proof of innocence, while bad reputation was not an acceptable means of proof of guilt. And while the common law permits evidence to be adduced of the defendant's good reputation, it does not permit good character or innocence to be proved by way of specific good acts not connected with the event giving rise to the charge.[64]

The straightforward approach, outlined above, based on the cardinal rule, is workable only if one accepts four related propositions: first, that character cannot, in any real sense, be "proved": secondly, that even if it can be proved, character is not a logical basis for drawing inferences as to the conduct of an actor on a specific occasion; thirdly that (except where character is a material fact) a rational system of fact-finding requires that the tribunal of fact be forbidden from acting on its estimation of the character of a party as it is forbidden reliance on the party's reputation, and on rumour and suspicion; fourthly, that in our criminal justice system, it is the constitutional function of the judge, as sentencing tribunal, to form a view as to the moral culpability of the defendant's conduct, and that of the jury merely to determine guilt or innocence as a matter of law, not as a matter of morals. If, by way of contrast, one accepts that character can be proved to such a degree of certainty that it can satisfactorily be used as a premise in a chain of reasoning and that a proven character is a secure and rational basis for an inference as to conduct on a particular occasion,[65] then a more complicated approach is required in order to prevent the reception of information which might subvert the deliberations of a jury. The more complicated approach is manifested by the dictum of Lord Herschell in *Makin* v *Attorney-General* (NSW).[66]

The writer has sought elsewhere[67] to demonstrate that "the rule in *Makin*" is neither more nor less than an illustration of the negative aspect of the cardinal rule of evidence and that the rule articulated in *Makin* was brought about by confusion between means of proof and objectives of proof. It was a premise of the reasoning expressed in that article that "character", as an abstract concept, was not a logical basis for drawing inferences as to conduct on a specific occasion. The decision

---

61 *Cheatley* (1981) 5 A Crim R 114, 115, 117; *Nilon* (1981) 5 A Crim R 385; *R* v *Trimboli* (1979) 1 A Crim R 73. The English authorities are collected in *Phipson*, supra n 1, 239-240.
62 *R* v *Carrol* unreported, SA Supreme Court (1971); *R* v *Vere* [1981] 75 Cr App R 354; *Gibson* (1930) 30 SR (NSW) 282; *Redd* [1923] 1 KB 104; *Rowton*, supra n 60; *Campbell* (1979) 69 Cr App R 221; *Stalder* [1981] 2 NSWLR 9, 13.
63 *Phipson* supra n 1, 224; Archbold, supra n 27, par 4-436.
64 *Rowton*, supra n 60.
65 See, eg the remarks of Gibbs CJ in *Perry* v *The Queen* (1983) 57 ALJR 110, 112, and Eggleston, supra n 1, 101-102.
66 [1894] AC 57, 65.
67 "Dissimilar Judgments on Similar Facts" (1984) 58 ALJ 74, and especially at 83-84.

in *Rowton,*[68] that specific good acts, not connected with the charge, cannot be tendered to prove innocence, appears to be based on that premise. Aggregating *Rowton* with the cardinal rule, the following cumulative rules were accepted as applying to criminal trials governed by the common law in the decades before *Makin:*

(a) Good character (in the sense of reputation) is a proper objective of proof on the part of a defendant, because good reputation was deemed to be a logical means of proof of innocence.

(b) Specific good acts are not a proper objective of proof unless connected with the instant charge nor are specific good acts a proper means of proof of good reputation.

(c) The defendant's bad character (ie bad reputation) is not a proper objective of proof on the part of the Crown except in rebuttal. Whether or not bad reputation is, when proved in rebuttal, a proper means of proof of guilt is not clear.

(d) Specific bad acts are not a proper objective of proof unless connected with the present charge. Nor are specific bad acts a proper means of proof of bad reputation.

To this, *Makin* added the supererogatory gloss:

(e) Specific bad acts are not a proper means of proof of guilt where the chain of reasoning underlying the intended use in evidence of those bad acts necessarily includes, as an inevitable intermediate step, a conclusion that the defendant has a bad character and is therefore guilty or more likely to be guilty of the crime charged.

It is contended that this last proposition is unnecessary as an independent proposition of law because it proscribes a chain of reasoning which is inconsistent with a rational system of fact-finding. Proposition (e) is a corollary of our very system of trials.

In any event, specific bad acts not directly connected with the charge are neither in themselves a proper objective of proof nor a means of proof of guilt. Specific bad acts cannot be used in evidence except so far as they are indirectly connected with material facts. They are a proper means of proof when — not their "badness" or criminality — but their objective details, ingredients and constituents assist the tribunal of fact to come to a rational conclusion in the present trial. In other words, where evidence of "bad" acts is tendered which substantially connects D with the crime charged and the evidence merely incidentally *invites* (as opposed to inevitably and exclusively requiring) the conclusion that D is a bad person, at the same time rationally authorising the inference that D is the culprit on the occasion charged (without any considered judgment as to D's "character"), the evidence is, as a matter of law and basic principle, admissible. If it is to be excluded, it is excluded by the exercise of the power of exclusion of relevant evidence which is an incident of the judge's duty to secure a fair trial to the defendant in a criminal case.[69] This analysis demonstrates that *Makin,* so far as it may

---

68 Supra n 60.
69 This articulation of principle coincides in substance with the views of the Court of Criminal Appeal of South Australia in *Sutton* v *The Queen* (1983) 8 A Crim R 276, which must now be considered to be heretical, in the light of the reasons for judgement of the High Court in that case: (1984) 58 ALJR 60. Only the course of decisions will indicate whether the hearsay is formal or material (cf the remarks of Windeyer J in *Iannella* v *French* (1967-1968) 119 CLR 84, 106).

lay down a rule independent of the cardinal rule, merely proscribes a certain use of admissible information: it proscribes the use of admissible information as a means of proof of bad character which, strictly speaking, is an irrelevant matter.

This approach permits one to reconcile the practical effect of the decisions in the criminal "similar fact" cases with the approach taken in civil cases in which evidence of similar conduct by an involved actor on other occasions is tendered as the basis of an inference as to what was done on the occasion giving rise to the present litigation. Although there has recently been some wavering,[70] the hallowed approach in civil cases, in reference to evidence of conduct not immediately connected with material facts, is merely to examine its probative force and the *procedural* fairness and convenience of permitting it to be adduced.[71]

To sum up: as a matter of fundamental general principle, both in civil cases and criminal, evidence of conduct (good, bad or neutral) of an actor (including a party) on an occasion other than the material occasion is inadmissible unless sufficiently connected with some material fact to assist the jury to resolve the issues in the case. This is one illustration of the cardinal rule in operation. Evidence of conduct on other occasions cannot be tendered to be used for the sole purpose of inviting or compelling an inference as to the character or reputation of an actor (including a party), unless that character or reputation is material. If (character not being in issue) evidence of conduct on other occasions logically invites or supports an inference as to a material fact, it is admissible and *prima facie* required to be admitted even if incidentally it invites the formation of an opinion (favourable or otherwise) as to the actor's character. Prima facie, the judge must admit it. The jury must be instructed, and the judge in a civil case should direct himself or herself, to use the evidence only for its proper use.[72] The fact that the evidence lends itself to an irrational use does not require its exclusion. In a criminal trial, however, this circumstance authorises the rejection of the evidence where a warning to the jury might be ineffective. Thus, the "rule in *Makin*" is not a rule of exclusion of evidence but rather a rule as to the proper use of evidence which is admissible because it is relevant.

4. The Exclusionary Rule

Relevant evidence is required to be rejected as a matter of law if and only if it is contrary to public policy that it be received. Public policy is rightly described as an "unruly horse",[73] because its demands appeal to one's moral values, political instincts and prejudices and meet a different response from period to period. This holds true in the realm of adjectival law as in the domain of substantive law. One consequence of

---

70 *Sattin* v *National Union Bank* (1978) 122 Sol J 367; contrast the reasoning in *Thompson* v *Allen* (1983) 48 ALR 675; *Mister Figgins* v *Centrepoint Freeholds Pty Ltd* (1980) 36 ALR 23; *Gates* v *City Mutual Life Assurance Society Ltd* (1982) 43 ALR 313; *Berger* v *Raymond Sun Ltd* [1984] 1 WLR 625.

71 *Mood Music Publishing Co Ltd* v *de Wolfe Ltd* [1976] 2 WLR 451; *Hollingham* v *Head (1858)* 4 CBNS 388; 140 ER 1135; *Thompson* v *Allen* supra n 70.

72 See Wigmore, supra n 1, 695, 697; *Thompson and Wran* v *The Queen*, supra n 19, 317; the authorities collected in McNamara, supra n 67, n 69; *Conley* (1982) 6 A Crim R 51; *Schlaefer* (1984) 12 A Crim R 345.

73 *Richardson* v *Mellish* (1824) 2 Bing 229, 252, 130 ER 294, 303 per Burroughs J.

this is that there can be no closed list of categories of evidence whose rejection may be required in the public interest. However, the cases demonstrate that there are three established classes of evidence whose rejection is, in general, required irrespective of the purpose of the tender (or intended use) of the evidence, irrespective of its form and irrespective of the qualifications of the witness. These three classes of evidence comprise documents protected by Crown privilege (or "public interest immunity", as it is now known);[74] information tending to disclose the identity of police informers;[75] and information as to the tenor of communications between estranged spouses aimed at achieving a reconciliation of their marital differences.[76] There is a fourth[77] class of information (evidence of the tenor of communications made "without prejudice") whose rejection is required by the public interest only if tendered for a certain purpose.

---

74 Eg *Rogers* v *Secretary of State for the Home Department* [1973] AC 388; *Sankey* v *Whitlam* (1978) 53 ALJR 11; *Burmah Oil Co* v *Bank of England* [1980] AC 1090; *Australian National Airlines Commission* v *Commonwealth* (1975) 132 CLR 582; *Hughes* v *Vargas* (1893) 9 TLR 471, 551 (CA); *Chatterton* v *Secretary of State* [1895] 2 QB 189; *Smith* v *Johnston* (1957) 75 WN (NSW) 313; *Bercove* v *Hermes* (3) (1984) 51 ALR 109, 115; Cross, supra n 1, ch 12; *Phipson*, supra n 1, ch 14. In so far as it attaches to documents, the "privilege" extends to prevent forensic uses other than the tendering of the document, eg its use to refresh memory: *Gain* v *Gain* [1961] 1 WLR 1469. A further distinctive feature of this "privilege" is that, if it is not asserted by the Crown or by either party, it must be asserted by the judge.

75 *Marks* v *Beyfus* (1980) 25 QBD 494; *R* v *Watson*, (1817) 2 Stark 115, 135-136, 171 ER 591, 600; *Phipson*, supra n 1, 278-279; *R* v *Hardy* (1794) 24 St Tr 199; *A G* v *Briant* (1846) 15 M and W 169, 153 ER 808. This category extends to the names of persons who set in motion State machinery for the care, custody or protection of children: *D* v *NSPCC* [1978] AC 171. It has been suggested that the public interest puts this rule in abeyance where disclosure of the informer's name is necessary to making out a defence in a criminal case: *Marks* v *Beyfus*, supra 498; *Rogers*, supra n 74, 407; see, too, *Hennessey* (1979) 68 Cr App R 419, 425-426. The rule also protects the names of persons to whom information pertinent to crime was given, the nature of the information, the channel of communication of the information, and official action on the basis of the information: *R* v *Carpenter* (1911) 156 Sess Pap CCC 298; *Auten* v *Rayner* [1958] 3 All ER 566; *R* v *Herlihy* (1898) 321 LT 38. Again, like the Crown Privilege head, this rule of protection must be enforced by the judge if not asserted by either party.

76 *McTaggart* v *McTaggart* [1949] P 94; *Mole* v *Mole* [1951] P 21; *Bell* v *Bell* [1970] SASR 310; *Theodoropoulas* v *Theodoropoulas* [1964] P 311; see also Family Law Act 1975 (Cth) s 18(2); Phipson, ante n 1, 375; Cross, ante n 1, 301; *Henley* v *Henley* [1955] P 202; *Constable* v *Constable* [1964] 5 FLR 278. Evidence of communications otherwise protected by this head can be adduced with the consent of both parties to the marriage: *McTaggart* v *McTaggart*.

77 There are perhaps two additional categories of public policy privilege which are usually formally characterised as rules regulating the competence of witnesses. These are the rules: first, that a judge may not be compelled to give evidence as to matters arising during a trial over which he presided: *R* v *Gazard* (1838) 8 C & P 595; *Hennessey* v *Broken Hill Pty Ltd* (1926) 38 CLR 329, 342; and secondly, that a juror may not give evidence as to the deliberations of a jury in the jury room: *McKay* v *Elias* (1928) 28 SR (NSW) 340; see too NSW Law Reform Commission, *Competence and Compellability*, (Discussion Paper) 74, where it is suggested that the relevant rule is properly characterised as a privilege. Edwards, *Cases on Evidence in Australia* (3rd ed 1981) 248-250; Aronson, Reaburn and Weinberg, supra n 23, 460; Cross, supra n 1, 317 treat these as rules of competence and compellability. *Phipson*, supra n 1, 279 and *Archibold*, supra n 27, 12-15 aggregate the categories under the heading "Judicial Disclosures". These rules permit secondary evidence of the information to which they apply, and accordingly (even though they may arise from a perceived public interest) they are rightly characterised as rules restricting the competence and compellability of witnesses.

The rule excluding information within each of these categories is fundamentally different in effect from the rules discussed in the preceding section. The rules which fall within the rubric of the genuine exclusionary principle have five characteristics which distinguish them from the other so-called exclusionary rules of evidence: first, they operate to prevent the proof of certain evidentiary facts irrespective of the purpose underlying the attempt to tender the evidence;[78] secondly, they prevent the tender of what is known as "secondary evidence" of the protected facts.[79] Thirdly, they have no connection with any principle of substantive law; fourthly, their application in a particular case depends on the judge's balancing of competing public interests, not on any hard and fast rule; and, finally they are not dictated by the adoption of either an adversarial or a rational system of dispute-resolution.

The fourth category of communication protected by the public interest, that is, without prejudice communications, has some of the features of a rule merely restricting the use to which evidence can be put. This category protects admissions made for the purpose of enabling a dispute to be resolved or litigation to be settled by agreement before trial or before judgment. Admissions actuated by that purpose cannot be used (in the litigation which generated it) as a means of proof of the admitted fact without the consent of the parties to that litigation.[80] It matters not whether the communication was made orally or in writing or whether it was expressly declared to have been made "without prejudice".[81] In other words, evidence cannot be given of a communication (by which a fact was conceded or admitted with the objective of facilitating the settlement of litigation) for the purpose of proving the conceded fact, unless the parties to the communication consent to that use of the communication.[82] It is contrary to public policy to permit such a use of the concession. Public policy favours the negotiated settlement of disputes. But the fact conceded by protected communications continues to be provable, as a matter of substance, by proper means, if it is material. Equally the otherwise protected communication can be used for any other material purpose compatible with the public interest.[83]

These four heads of exclusion protective of information or communications are often referred to as "privileges". The use of this

---

78 Eg *R v Watson* supra n 75, 148; 171 ER 604. This proposition is subject to a qualification in the case of "without prejudice" communications.
79 *Williams v Star Newspaper Co Ltd* (1908) 24 TLR 297; *Anthony v Anthony* (1919) 35 TLR 559.
80 *Walker v Wilshen* (1889) 23 QBD 335; *Rogers v Rogers* (1964) 114 CLR 608; *Field v Commissioner for Railways (NSW)* (1955) 99 CLR 285; *Davies v Nyland* (1974) 10 SASR 76; *Re Turf Enterprises Pty Ltd* [1975] QD R 266.
81 See the authorities cited in n 80 and *Bentley v Nelson* [1963] WAR 89.
82 *Re Turf Enterprises Pty Ltd* [1975] Qd R 266; *Blow v Norfold C C* [1967] 1 WLR 1280; *Walker v Wilsher* (1889) 23 QBD 335.
83 Eg, on the question of costs, after judgement (where the offer is "without prejudice" except as to costs): see *Computer Machinery v Drescher* [1983] 3 All ER 156; *McDonnell v McDonnell* [1977] 1 All ER 766; *Cutts v Head* [1984] 2 WLR 349 or to prove a compromise of the action *Tomlin v Standard Telephones & Cables Ltd* [1969] 1 WLR 1378. There is a basis for characterising this rule as one aspect of the rules regulating the proof of informal admissions. This is the approach in *Phipson*, supra n 1, 19-10, 19-11. The true status and effect of this head of immunity is left outstanding by the decided cases: see the discussion in Australian Law Reform Commission, *Privilege*, (Evidence Reference, Research Paper no 16) 246, 247 and the decisions discussed in *Phipson*, supra n 1, 322-328, 374.

terminology is confusing.[84] It is of the very essence of a privilege that it can be waived and that it confers only defensive rights on persons. The common law of evidence acknowledges only two genuine privileges which may be invoked in the course of a trial itself, namely legal professional privilege and the privilege against self-incrimination. Each of these privileges confers advantages on specific persons: in the one case, on the citizen who has retained a lawyer; in the second case, on witnesses generally. Each of these privileges can be waived, expressly or by conduct. They each confer purely defensive rights and, in particular, the right to prevent the eliciting of relevant evidence from a particular source. Legal professional privilege involves the right in each litigant not to be compelled, while giving evidence at the trial, to disclose communications made to their legal adviser for advice or for use in litigation, and the right to object to attempts, by the opponent, to elicit evidence from the legal adviser (and the advdiser's agents) as to communications made professionally by or to the legal adviser incidental to giving advice or conducting litigation for the litigant concerned.[85] The privilege against self-incrimination has two forensic aspects: it entitles the defendant at a criminal trial to insist that the tribunal of fact be directed to draw no inference adverse to the defendant from the fact that, when questioned by persons in authority before the trial, the defendant maintained silence;[86] and secondly it entitles witnesses generally to withhold information (and litigants to withhold documents) whose publication might result in their exposure to a charge, penalty or forfeiture.[87] Where a genuine privilege is concerned, secondary evidence of the privileged information or communication is admissible.[88] By contrast, the public policy exclusion rule attaches to information and not merely to communications, and secondary evidence of the information is in general inadmissible.[89]

5. Conclusion

Confronted with an item of information which may be of potential use at a trial, the first question which many practitioners and, indeed, some judges, ask of themselves is: does the information come within any of the exceptions to the exclusionary rules of evidence, with the result that it is admissible. This reaction to evidence is one result of labouring

---

84 Tapper, "Privilege and Policy" (1974) 37 Mod L Rev 92.
85 *Wilson* v *Rastall* (1972) 4 TR 753; *Bursill* v *Tanner* (1885) 16 QBD 1. The propositions in the text on the status of legal professional provision will be incorrect in Australia if the High Court adopts the views of Brennan J in *Baker* v *Campbell*, supra n 10, 773. There, indicating disapproval of *Calcraft* v *Guest* [1898] 1 QB 759 and *Lloyd* v *Mostyn* (1842) 10 M and W 478, 481-482, 152 ER 558, 560, his Honour held that secondary evidence of certain privileged communications is not admissible. If this view prevails, legal professional privilege has ceased to be a genuine privilege and is properly characterised as an aspect of public interest immunity.
86 *Gilbert* v *The Queen* (1977) 66 CR App R 237; *Sadaraka* [1981] 2 NSWLR 459.
87 *Blunt* v *Park Lane Hotel Ltd* [1942] 2 KB 253. The second limb of the privilege does not prevent the cross-examination of an accused who gives evidence in his or her own defence, as to facts relevant to the accused's guilt of the offence charged: this is the effect of Criminal Evidence Act 1898 (UK) s 1(e) and its equivalents in Australia.
88 As far as concerns the privilege against self-incrimination, see *Tomkins* (1978) 67 Cr App R 181. As far as concerns legal professional privilege, see *Coates* v *Birch* (1841) 2 QB 252 and the authorities cited in n 85 and in Heydon, "Legal Professional Privilege and Third Parties" (1974) 37 Mod L Rev 601, nn 3-7.
89 See the authorities referred to in n 79, and *Foran* v *Derrick* (1892) 18 VLR 408; *King* v *Bryant* (No 2) [1956] QSR 570; *Honeychurch* v *Honeychurch* [1943] SASR 31.

under the misconception that the common law of evidence is dominated by rules of exclusion. This is the very reverse of the truth. The first question to be asked of any item of information of potential use at a trial is, is it relevant? That question logically leads the mind to ask the related question, what is the intended use of the evidence? In other words, how is the information relevant? If the information is relevant and its intended use is rational then prima facie it is both admissible and required to be admitted and if it is elicited in proper form from a competent witness, in practice its rejection would be quite exceptional.

The common law has developed certain rules as to the form of evidence particularly in relation to documents. Legislation and the common law regulate the competence and compellability of witnesses. But these are not substantive rules as to what information may or may not be received by the judge. The common law also clearly lays down one general rule restricting the use to which relevant information may be put, once admitted: evidence of out-of-court assertions cannot in general be used as evidence of the facts thereby asserted. In addition to this rule (the hearsay rule), there are three other canons, namely the prior consistent statement rule, the opinion evidence rule and the rule laid down in *Makin* v *Attorney-General*[90] (widely accepted as rules of exclusion) which in their real operation merely restrict the use to which admitted evidence may be put. It has been sought to demonstrate that not only are these three rules not rules of exclusion of evidence, but that, properly analysed, they are but illustrations of the practical operation of aspects of the cardinal rule of evidence, namely that evidence is admissible if and only if it is needed to assist, and capable of assisting, a rational and properly instructed tribunal of fact to determine the issues between the parties. Strictly speaking, at common law, the exclusion of evidence from a competent witness in proper form is always worked either by the negative aspect of the cardinal rule or by one facet of public policy. Substantively speaking, there is only one common law rule of exclusion of evidence, namely that information is required to be rejected by the trial judge if its reception would be contrary to the public interest.

The conceptual structure advanced in this article has a number of advantages. First, it will tend to eliminate the unthinking use of jargon, labels, stereotypes and precedents. Secondly, it better serves the policy of the law encapsulated in the hearsay rule (and the other "canons of exclusion") by attracting attention to the two crucial stages in the impact of evidence in the courtroom: its reception by the tribunal of law and its use by the tribunal of fact. The characterisation of these canons as "use" rules rather than "exclusion" rules has this latter advantage because it emphasises that these rules are not a spent force once relevant information which is subject to them is admitted by the judge. The use of that information by the tribunal of fact continues to be controllable by the parties. Where there is a jury, the jury should be instructed as to the proper use of relevant information admitted by the judge.[91] The

---

90 Supra n 2.
91 The United States Federal Rules of Evidence provide:
       105. When evidence which is admissible as to one party or for one purpose but not admissible as to another party or for another purpose is admitted, the

third advantage pertains to the effect of the undoubted exceptions to the prior consistent statement rule and to the hearsay rule. If these rules are characterised as rules of exclusion, it would follow that evidence falling within an exception to them is, once admitted, "at large" and uncontrolled by legal rule. However, if these rules are viewed as rules of use, the exceptions merely predicate that the relevant information which is subject to the exception can, contrary to the general run of things, be used for the purpose normally proscribed by the rule. But that information continues to be governed, as far as concerns its application by the tribunal of fact, by such other of the use rules as may apply to it.

The distinction between controlling admission of relevant evidence and controlling its use is one well known to common lawyers. It permeates the law of evidence in contexts beyond those of the "canons of exclusion" treated in this article. It often happens, for example, that information relevant only to the credibility of a witness is adduced at a trial; such information can be used by the tribunal of fact only in assessing the credibility of the witness concerned. Its use for any other purpose would be wrongful. Equally, in trials involving more than one defendant, evidence is often adduced which can lawfully be used only against one defendant. In the interests of clarity of thinking and proper application of the policy underlying the "canons of exclusion", the distinction is one which should be explicitly applied to the four "great canons". It is of the highest importance that lawyers' use of terminology corresponds with lawyers' perception of the practical operation of legal rules.

Continued . . . .

Court, upon request, shall restrict the evidence to its proper scope and instruct the jury accordingly.
But contrast the dissenting judgment of Spence and Laskin JJ in *Perras* v *The Queen* (1973) 11 CCC (2d) 449, 460.

[16]

An Approach to Rules of Evidence

for Nonjury Cases

Since five out of six trials in courts of general jurisdiction are without juries, and 97 per cent of all trials in all tribunals, including administrative, are nonjury, Professor Davis argues that it is time to reshape the law of evidence to fit these proceedings. He contends that it is wrong for our legal system to apply rules of evidence designed for the jury system to nonjury adjudications.

by Kenneth Culp Davis • *Professor of Law at the University of Chicago Law School*

THIS ARTICLE elaborates four simple propositions.

1. Five out of six trials in courts of general jurisdiction are without juries. If trials in lesser courts are added, jury trials may be about 5 per cent of all trials in all courts. If trials before administrative officers and arbitrators are also added, jury trials are probably not more than 3 per cent of all trials in all tribunals.

2. We have no rules of evidence designed for nonjury trials. Our only rules of evidence are designed for jury trials. We need rules of evidence or standards of evidence for the 97 per cent of trials without juries.

3. Although reform of evidence law is long overdue. the reforms proposed by the Model Code of the American Law Institute and by the Uniform Rules of Evidence, both heavily weighted with jury thinking, have failed for want of adoption. A new approach is needed.

4. The new push for evidence reform should be (a) focused primarily on nonjury trials, (b) toward enlarged discretion guided by broad standards and away from precise and rigid refinements, and (c) stimulated by experience with American administrative processes and by court systems in other parts of the world.

The Proportion of Nonjury Trials

Official statistics from federal courts and from sixteen states having more than half the national population provide the basis for an estimate that only one sixth of all trials in courts of general jurisdiction are jury trials and five sixths are without juries. (See the state-by-state list, page 726, *infra.*)

Figures from some of the same sources show that the proportion of nonjury trials is much higher in municipal, police, traffic, and small claims courts. These figures provide the basis for a guess, as distinguished from an estimate, that only about 5 per cent of all trials in all courts are before juries, although statistics are not available to support a close estimate. The number of trials before administrative officers (federal, state and local) and before arbitrators is unknown, and figures are lacking even for a guided guess. A meaningful figure brought out by the Administrative Conference of the United States is that 80,140 proceedings were commenced in federal agencies in one year (involving oral hearings with verbatim transcripts) to determine private rights, privileges or obligations, compared with fewer than 10,000 trials in all federal courts in one year. If jury trials are about 5 per cent of all trials in all courts, the guess seems to be a safe one that jury trials are not more than 3 per cent of all trials in all tribunals, that is, courts of all levels, administrative agencies and arbitrators.

Lack of Evidence Rules for Nonjury Trials

Our evidence system is indeed queer: We have rules of evidence for the 3 per cent of trials that use juries but we have no rules of evidence for the 97 per cent that are without juries.

Evidence Rules for Nonjury Cases

Today's law of evidence is focused almost entirely on jury trials and almost completely ignores nonjury trials. Thayer regarded our law of evidence as "a product of the jury system".[1] Wigmore asserted his agreement with Sir Henry Maine's statement that "the system of technical rules . . . fails . . . whenever the arbiter of facts . . . has special qualifications for deciding on them".[2] Chief Justice Vanderbilt wrote: "It is well known that the extensive and highly refined rules of evidence have developed largely as methods of controlling juries".[3] The American Bar Association's Committee on Improvements in the Law of Evidence reported in 1938: "The rules of evidence are designed primarily to meet the necessities of trial by jury."[4] The strongest statement of all, but one that seems fully justified, is that of McCormick: "As rules they are absurdly inappropriate to any tribunal or proceeding where there is no jury."[5] The only rules of evidence we have are "absurdly inappropriate" for 97 per cent of our trials in all tribunals and for 83 per cent in courts of general jurisdiction!

We sometimes pretend to have rules of evidence designed for nonjury trials, even though we have developed no such rules. For instance, Rule 43(a) of the Federal Rules of Civil Procedure refers to "rules of evidence heretofore applied in the courts of the United States on the hearing of suits in equity". One might suppose from this that somewhere some rules of evidence for equity cases could be found. But the supposition would be false. No such rules have ever existed. Wigmore asks: "Where are we to look for those [equity] rules?"[6] And he answers that he has no idea. Professor Moore in his treatise indulges in a delightful bit of understatement: "One who goes to the former federal equity cases expecting to find a body of evidence law which will inform him whether particular evidence is admissible is likely to encounter some difficulty."[7]

The fact is, as most practitioners know, that judges sitting without juries follow or depart from the jury-trial rules as they see fit, and the variations from one judge to another cover all parts of the spectrum. The only principle for nonjury cases is what the Special Committee on Evidence of the Judicial Conference of the United States in a 1962 report called "the general principle that the law of evidence is relaxed in cases tried without a jury".[8]

Not only is our law of evidence geared to the jury system, but so is our legal literature and nearly all our thinking about evidence problems. The courses in evidence in the law schools are devoted almost entirely to jury-trial rules. Many students who have completed the courses know nothing of evidence practices in nonjury cases. Of the two leading casebooks on evidence, one seems to say nothing of nonjury trials and the other devotes only ten pages to them.

Thinking within the legal profession about problems of evidence is so much distorted by the false assumption that all evidence problems pertain to juries that even such a subject as judicial notice is dominated by ideas about judge-jury relationships. Even in jury cases, judicial notice problems arise in pretrial consideration of pleadings, disposition of motions and the like, and arise in post-trial opinion writing and other determinations, as well as appellate consideration of cases. Perhaps two thirds of the occasions for judicial notice even in a jury case have nothing to do with the jury. If jury trials are 3 per cent of all trials, this means only about one per cent of judicial notice questions have any relation to juries. But the judicial notice provisions of the Model Code of Evidence and the Uniform Rules of Evidence are dominated by jury thinking, especially the utterly unsound idea that judicially noticed facts may never be subject to rebuttal.

An amusing incident in New Jersey illustrates how far the usual assumption goes that all evidence problems pertain to juries. The *1963 Report of the New Jersey Supreme Court Committee on Evidence,* a generally admirable study, proposes evidence rules to apply to all courts and also to "formal hearings before administrative agencies and tribunals".[9] The committee rejected a proposal of a commentator (the writer) about judicial notice with the remark that the commentator's "orientation is toward administrative law and nonjury adjudications".[10]

Thinking oriented to 99 per cent of the occasions for judicial notice or official notice was rejected in favor of thinking oriented to one per cent of the occasions! Jury thinking must dominate, even for administrative proceedings! The small incident is significant because the attitude is typical of almost any group in the American legal profession of the present generation.

Need for New Approach To Evidence Reform

Reform of basic evidence law is long overdue. The American Law Institute quickly decided that the present law of evidence was not worth restating, and the remark was made in the introduction to the Model Code that "the law of evidence is now where the law of forms of action and common law pleading was in the early part of the nineteenth century".[11] Professor Morgan explained that the American Law Institute "did not attempt a restatement of the law of evidence because its members were convinced that no restatement could eliminate the obstructions to intelligent investigation which currently accepted doctrines have erected".[12] Wigmore says that "the

---

1. THAYER, EVIDENCE 509 (1898).
2. 1 WIGMORE, EVIDENCE § 4b (3d ed. 1940). See also, Wigmore, *Administrative Boards and Commissions: Are the Jury-Trial Rules of Evidence in Force for Their Inquiries?* 17 ILL. L. REV. 263 (1922): "Historically, the rules of evidence familiar to Anglo-American lawyers were a direct growth out of trial by jury."
3. Vanderbilt, *The Technique of Proof before Administrative Bodies,* 24 IOWA L. REV. 464, 467 (1939).
4. 63 A.B.A. REP. 570, 594 (1938).
5. 5 ENCYC. SOC. SCI. 637, 644 (1931).
6. 1 WIGMORE, EVIDENCE 201 (3d ed. 1940).
7. 5 MOORE'S FEDERAL PRACTICE 1328 (1951).
8. REPORT, SPECIAL COMMITTEE ON EVIDENCE OF

THE JUDICIAL CONFERENCE OF THE UNITED STATES 4 (1962).
9. Page 9, Rule 2(3).
10. Page 40, rejecting the idea that noticed facts should be subject to rebuttal—an idea embodied in Section 7(d) of the Federal Administrative Procedure Act and giving general satisfaction. The New Jersey committee earlier had adopted the more important proposal of the same commentator in its Rule 9(3): "Judicial notice may be taken of any matter which would be of aid in deciding what the law should be."
11. MODEL CODE OF EVIDENCE 5 (1942).
12. Practising Law Institute, SIGNIFICANT DEVELOPMENTS IN THE LAW DURING THE WAR YEARS, EVIDENCE 1 (1946).

rules to a large extent fail of their professed purpose. They serve, not as needful tools for helping the truth at trials, but as game-rules, afterwards, for setting aside the verdict."[13]

For the past twenty years or more the hopes for evidence reform have gone into the Model Code of Evidence and the Uniform Rules of Evidence. But these proposals have been rejected. The Model Code and the Uniform Rules are unsatisfactory in that they rest so heavily on the jury system, and they go much too far in providing precise and rigid requirements. During more than twenty years, they have won only a single adoption—Kansas. The time has come for a new approach.

Suggested New Approach Escapes Jury Thinking

The most important aspect of a new approach should be escape from the deep-seated habit of allowing all thinking about evidence law to be dominated by the needs of the 3 per cent of trials that involve juries. The thinking should reflect primarily the needs of the 97 per cent of trials that are without juries. We should undertake *for the first time* to prepare a set of rules or standards for nonjury trials. Then the main set of rules or standards can be qualified or modified to fit the peculiar needs of the small minority of cases that are tried before juries.

An outstanding characteristic of the Model Code and the Uniform Rules is their treatment of refinements in precise and rigid detail. This characteristic runs counter to the strong trend of the law during the past half century toward replacing detailed rules with discretion. For instance, the Supreme Court generalized in 1952: "The trend of the law in recent years has been to turn away from rigid rules of incompetence, in favor of admitting testimony and allowing the trier of fact to judge the weight to be given it."[14] A year earlier the Supreme Court had said: "However halting its progress, the trend in litigation is toward a rational inquiry into truth, in which the tribunal considers everything 'logically probative of some matter requiring to be proved'."[15] The new rules of evidence should go with this trend, not against it.

Precise and rigid rules of evidence should give way to discretion to be exercised under broad legal standards. For instance, instead of a rigid hearsay rule with numerous precise exceptions leaving little or no room for taking into account special circumstances, what is needed is a broad standard that reliable hearsay is admissible and may support a finding, and that in appraising hearsay a tribunal may be influenced by availability or unavailability of the declarant.

When our minds are released from jury thinking, we shall see the obvious soundness of McCormick's observation that "The trustworthiness of hearsay ranges from the highest reliability to utter worthlessness",[16] and we shall see that the hearsay rule and its exceptions fail to fit this basic observation.

When our minds are released from jury thinking, we shall see the merit of building on our valuable experience under the satisfactory provisions of the Administrative Procedure Act that "Any oral or documentary evidence may be received . . ." and that a finding may be supported by "reliable, probative, and substantial evidence" without regard to the question whether the evidence is "competent".[17]

When our minds are released from jury thinking, we shall see that when the only available alternative to giving the hearsay as much weight as it seems to deserve is to decide without evidence, our belief that direct evidence is usually better than hearsay is unhelpful because it is irrelevant.

When our minds are released from jury thinking, we shall see the nonsense of a hearsay rule that operates in the same way irrespective of the reliability or unreliability of the hearsay and irrespective of the availability or unavailability of the declarant. We shall see that even somewhat unreliable hearsay may for some purposes in some circumstances be better than no evidence.

When our minds are released from jury thinking, we shall see that the hearsay rule, which was designed to govern *admissibility* of evidence before a jury, should not be allowed to

Kenneth Culp Davis, John P. Wilson Professor of Law at the University of Chicago, was educated at Whitman College (A.B. 1931) and the Harvard Law School (LL.B. 1934). He has been a law teacher since 1935 and is the author of *Administrative Law Treatise* and other books.

govern *evaluation* of evidence by judges or officers, and we shall agree with Judge Learned Hand that the test of sufficient evidence to support a finding should not be jury-trial rules of admissibility but should be "the kind of evidence on which responsible persons are accustomed to rely in serious affairs".[18]

The proposal here made that precise and rigid rules of evidence should give way to discretion to be exercised under broad legal standards does not mean increasing practitioners' difficulties in preparing for trial by reason of lack of definite rules. On the contrary, the proposal is that practitioners should have better advance knowledge than

13. 1 WIGMORE, EVIDENCE § 8c (3d ed. 1940).
14. On *Lee v. United States*, 343 U. S. 747, 757 (1952).
15. *Universal Camera Corporation v. National Labor Relations Board*, 340 U. S. 474, 497 (1951). See other examples of the trend in 2 DAVIS, ADMINISTRATIVE LAW TREATISE § 14.01 (1958).
16. MCCORMICK, EVIDENCE 627 (1954).
17. The quoted provisions are in Section 7(c), 60 Stat. 237 (1946), 5 U.S.C.A. § 1006(c). Earlier drafts of the bill provided that findings must be supported by "competent" evidence, but the draft that was adopted imposed no requirement that a finding be supported by "competent" evidence. For full discussion of the legislative history on this point, see 2 DAVIS, ADMINISTRATIVE LAW TREATISE § 14.05 (1958).
18. *National Labor Relations Board v. Remington Rand*, 94 F. 2d 862, 873 (2d Cir. 1938), cert. denied, 304 U. S. 576 (1938).

Evidence Rules for Nonjury Cases

they now have of the evidence practices that will be followed in the 97 per cent of all trials, in the five sixths of trials in courts of general jurisdiction. Under the present system practitioners have no means of knowing how much the jury-trial rules will be relaxed in nonjury trials. Under the proposal discretionary power of the judge or other presiding officer will not be as large as it is now; it will be confined by broad but meaningful standards.

Evidence Rules Need a Thorough Examination

Anglo-American exclusionary rules of evidence are unique in the world. Lawyers of other lands are unable to understand why relevant evidence that has probative force should be barred from consideration. Our only excuse is that we use juries and don't trust the juries to consider all relevant and probative evidence. But our only excuse does not even purport to reach the 97 per cent of trials without juries.

Our sick body of evidence law will get well sooner if our American evidence doctors will consult with some European evidence doctors.

That the views of European lawyers largely coincide with practices emerging from our American administrative process is not accidental.

APPENDIX
Number of Jury and Non-jury Trials in Sixteen States

The figures do not allow a precise count because categories and counting systems differ from state to state, and some categories are missing or combined with other categories. The most serious infirmities are pointed out in parentheses with respect to eight of the sixteen states in the following tabulation. Estimates based on adding the figures about trials in courts of general jurisdiction are: jury trials, 40,274; nonjury trials, 210,232.

ARIZONA, *Second Report of the Administrative Director of the Supreme Court of Arizona* (1962), superior courts only (half-year figures doubled). Civil cases terminated: after court trial, 663; after jury trial, 32. Criminal cases: jury trials, 46; court trials, 45. Totals: jury trials, 78; court trials, 708.

CALIFORNIA, *Judicial Council of California, Administrative Office of the*

Courts (February, 1962), for fiscal year 1960-1961, pages 26, 28, 30. Superior courts, dispositions after trial, contested matters, 35,641. Juries sworn, 6,792. (The report says: "Figures cited for 'juries sworn' are not the equivalent of jury trials. On the one hand a jury may be sworn to try a matter which is settled prior to completion of trial. On the other hand a single jury may try several cases consolidated for trial." Of the juries sworn, 3,381 were "in personal injury, wrongful death and property damage cases", and 2,634 were in criminal cases.)

FLORIDA, *Judicial Council, Sixth Annual Report* (1960), Exhibit VI, cases disposed of in the circuit courts in 1959. Law dispositions: jury trials, 1,371; nonjury trials, 1,069. Criminal dispositions: jury trials, 149; nonjury trials, 234. Totals: jury, 1,510; nonjury, 1,303. (Equity cases apparently are not included. The table shows 2,420 "contested divorces", but does not show the number that went to trial.)

ILLINOIS, printed report by Albert J. Harno, Court Administrator, and John C. Fitzgerald, Deputy Court Administrator for Cook County, pages 5-16, 32, 38-39, for superior and circuit courts (figures for partial year adjusted to annual basis). Civil cases: Cook County, jury, 1,044; nonjury, 18,074. Twenty circuits outside Cook County: jury, 672; nonjury, 10,901. Totals: jury, 1,716; nonjury, 28,975. Criminal cases: jury, 369; nonjury, 1,932. Total: jury, 2,085; nonjury, 30,907.

IOWA, *1961 Annual Report Relating to the Trial Courts of the State of Iowa*, by the Judicial Department Statistician. Civil cases disposed of in district court: tried to jury, 528; tried to court, 1,924. Criminal cases disposed of in district court: tried to jury, 308; tried to court, 191. Totals: tried to jury, 836; tried to court, 2,115.

KANSAS, *Judicial Council Bulletin* (October, 1958), district courts, civil cases, contested trials: to court, 3,852; to jury, 351. (No figures given on jury and nonjury criminal cases.)

MARYLAND, *Administrative Office of the Courts, Annual Report (1961-1962)* pages 32, 33, 36. Circuit courts only. Law cases tried: motor tort, jury, 838; nonjury, 510. Other tort: jury, 184; nonjury, 102. Condemnation: jury, 137; nonjury, 6. Contract: jury, 107; nonjury, 534. Other law: jury, 242; nonjury, 784. "Equity hearings" (here assumed to be nonjury, but not so indicated in the report), 3,194. Criminal cases tried: jury, 480; nonjury, 9,516. Totals: jury, 1,988; nonjury, 14,646. (Not included are 2,901 bastardy and nonsupport cases "tried" in Baltimore; all but six "were tried before the court". Some

of the "equity hearings" may not be trials.)

MICHIGAN, *Supreme Court, Office of the Court Administrator, Annual Report and Judicial Statistics for 1961*, page 26. Circuit courts: jury trials, 1,760; nonjury trials, 4,185.

NEW HAMPSHIRE, *Eighth Biennial Report of the Judicial Council* (1960), pages 59, 62. Statistics on work of the superior court, criminal cases: tried by jury, 51; heard by court, 11. Civil cases: jury trials at law, 210; jury trials in other actions, 20; actions at law tried by court, 430. Totals: jury cases, 281; nonjury cases, 441. (In addition, contested marital cases heard, 97; other equity cases heard, 397. Cases "heard" are not necessarily trials but may include many trials.)

NEW JERSEY, *Annual Report of the Administrative Director of the Courts* (1960-1961). Table F, proceedings in superior court, law division, trials and appeals: jury, 958; nonjury, 1,207. Table J, proceedings in the superior court, chancery division, general equity: jury trials, 15; nonjury trials, 966. Table M, proceedings in the superior court, chancery division, matrimonial: (total trials, 6,130); (uncontested trials, 4,698); contested trials, 1,432 (presumably nonjury). Table U, law divisions of superior and county courts, dispositions of indictments and accusations: jury trial, 1,076; nonjury trial, 276. Totals (omitting figures in parentheses): jury trials, 2,049; nonjury trials, 3,881. (These figures are weighted in favor of jury trials because of the lack of separation of county court criminal trials.)

NEW YORK, *Sixth Annual Report of Judicial Conference* (1961), Table 12 (after page 214). Supreme Court, civil cases, summary of dispositions, after trial: verdict of jury, 2,344; decision of court or reserved decision, 7,481. (Table 32 at page 260 shows, for supreme court and county courts, felonies and misdemeanors: 618 convictions by verdict, 290 acquitted by jury. These figures are excluded because (1) the proportion from county courts is not indicated, and (2) the number of nonjury trials are not indicated.)

NORTH CAROLINA, *Annual Report of the Administrative Assistant to the Chief Justice (1961-1962)*. Page 20, civil cases disposed of in superior courts (excluding 4,395 uncontested divorce actions "tried by jury"): jury, 2,383; judge, 4,330. Page 32, criminal cases disposed of in superior courts: jury, 3,589; judge, 12,119. Total civil and criminal: jury, 5,972; judge, 16,449.

TEXAS, *Civil Judicial Council, Judicial Statistics* (for the year 1961, dated May, 1962). Total of all civil suits: tried with a jury, 3,186; tried without a jury,

58,550. Criminal cases: tried with jury, 2,018; tried without jury, 17,918. Total civil and criminal: tried with jury, 5,204; tried without jury, 76,468.

WASHINGTON, letter of March 21, 1963, from Albert C. Bise, Administrator for the Courts, State of Washington. Superior courts only: civil jury, 1,096; civil nonjury, 3,901; criminal jury, 448; criminal nonjury, 161. Totals: jury, 1,544; nonjury, 4,062.

WEST VIRGINIA, Reports of Judicial Council, for two six-months' periods ending June 1, 1962 (figures found by adding figures from each of two reports). Civil cases: tried by jury, 707; heard and determined by court, 7,911. Criminal cases: tried by jury, 554; heard and determined by court, 2,258. Totals: jury,

1,361; court, 8,958. (Not clear whether "heard and determined by court" may include cases not tried.)

WISCONSIN, *Judicial Council, Biennial Report* (1961), page 17. Total contested trials in circuit courts: disposed of after jury trial begun, 752; after nonjury trial begun, 1,600. (Of the 752 jury trials, 518 involved auto accidents.) (Not included are 12,894 trials by the court and 278 jury trials in "criminal and ordinance violations", because the bulk may be traffic cases.)

FEDERAL, *Annual Report of the Director of the Administrative Office of the United States Courts* (1961) 162. Civil trials: nonjury, 3,245; jury, 2,911. Criminal trials: nonjury, 982; jury, 2,456. Total trials: jury, 5,367; nonjury, 4,327.

In the foregoing tabulation, the variations from one state to another are large. In New York supreme courts the ratio of nonjury to jury trials is three to one; in Illinois superior and circuit courts and in Texas district courts the ratio is about fifteen to one.

Juries are used much more, of course, in criminal cases than in civil cases, much more in accident cases than in commercial cases, and much more in law than in equity. In California (which may or may not be typical, but for which figures are readily available) 89 per cent of juries sworn are in two categories of cases—"personal injury, wrongful death and property damage" (50 per cent) and criminal cases (39 per cent).

[17]

COLUMBIA LAW REVIEW

| Vol. 66 | FEBRUARY 1966 | No. 2 |

SOME DIFFICULTIES IN DEVISING RULES FOR DETERMINING TRUTH IN JUDICIAL TRIALS

JACK B. WEINSTEIN*

Pressure for reform of the American law of evidence has been increasing. Among the major indicia of the strong forces at work in the last quarter century are the 1942 American Law Institute's *Model Code of Evidence*, and the *Uniform Rules of Evidence* approved by the Commissioners on Uniform State Laws and the American Bar Association in 1953. Recently there have been a number of important state revisions: the Kansas rules, adopted in 1962 and based on the *Uniform Rules*;[1] the New Jersey Rules, following the *Uniform Rules* to a large extent, adopted in 1964;[2] and the 1965 California Evidence Code which is based on a prior code, extensive original research and the *Uniform Rules*.[3] The prospect for additional revisions has recently been greatly enhanced by the support for change in the federal system which preceded Chief Justice Warren's appointment of a committee to draft Rules of Evidence for the Federal District Courts.[4]

Fundamental changes in our society and modifications in judicial procedure have created an atmosphere—far different from that of the era when the rules were developed—particularly conducive to revision. For example, the complexity of modern business, with its increased reliance on records, man-

---

* Professor of Law, Columbia University. B.A., Brooklyn College, 1943; LL.B., Columbia, 1948.

1. See KAN. GEN. STAT. ANN. §§ 60-401 to 60-470 (1964). See also C.Z. CODE tit. 5, ch. 109, §§ 2731-2996 (1962); V.I. CODE tit. 5, §§ 771-956 (1965) (adopting the *Uniform Rules*).

2. See SUPREME COURT OF NEW JERSEY RULES OF EVIDENCE (effective July 1, 1965); REPORT OF THE NEW JERSEY SUPREME COURT COMMITTEE ON EVIDENCE (March, 1963). See also N.J. Laws of 1960, ch. 52 (authorizing rules and conforming statutes).

3. See CALIFORNIA LAW REVISION COMMISSION, TENTATIVE RECOMMENDATION AND A STUDY RELATING TO THE UNIFORM RULES OF EVIDENCE (1964); CALIFORNIA LAW REVISION COMMISSION, RECOMMENDATION PROPOSING AN EVIDENCE CODE (1965); CAL. EVIDENCE CODE §§ 600-68 (effective Jan. 1, 1967).

4. See SPECIAL COMMITTEE ON EVIDENCE OF COMMITTEE ON RULES OF PRACTICE AND PROCEDURE OF THE JUDICIAL CONFERENCE OF THE UNITED STATES, A PRELIMINARY REPORT ON THE ADVISABILITY OF DEVELOPING UNIFORM RULES OF EVIDENCE FOR THE UNITED STATES DISTRICT COURTS (1962). See also Degnan, *The Law of Federal Evidence Reform*, 76 HARV. L. REV. 275 (1962); Green, *Federal Civil Procedure Rule 43(a)*, 5 VAND. L. REV. 560 (1952); Joiner, *Uniform Rules of Evidence for Federal Courts*, 20 F.R.D. 429 (1957).

Simultaneously, in England the Criminal Law Revision Committee, for criminal cases, and the Law Reform Committee, for civil cases, is considering a revision of the law of evidence as a whole. Griew, *What the Butler Said He Saw*, [1965] Crim. L. Rev. 91.

dated expansion of the business entry exception to the hearsay rule. This expansion, coupled with increased pretrial discovery and more extensive use of depositions has undermined our traditional preference for oral testimony and thus has accelerated a general weakening of the rationale for exclusion of hearsay.

The trend toward specialization of knowledge has necessitated an increased reliance on expert witnesses; the correlative changes in the evidentiary rules on the form of expert testimony have had the secondary effect of decreasing the impact of rules on opinion and hearsay. Simultaneously, the need for rules designed to control the untrained trier has been reduced by more extensive use of judicial notice, bench trials of special issues, and the use of "impartial" experts where scientific issues are involved.[5]

Developments which have had a primary impact on the court itself have also had repercussions upon the evidentiary rules. Calendar congestion has forced courts to deemphasize or circumvent rules which may delay the trial— for example, by pressuring attorneys to waive the right to insist on time-consuming strict proof.[6] Widespread acquaintance with administrative hearings is producing a greater inclination on the part of judges to assume an affirmative responsibility for obtaining information, particularly when, as in an antitrust, civil rights or family law case, a major public interest is involved.[7] The exercise of such judicial discretion may be expected to increase in the future as the emphasis on improved methods of selecting and training judges[8] (with some slippage from time to time) increases the bench's prestige. As a result, more states are likely to permit the court, on its own motion, to rule on the admissibility of evidence, examine witnesses, call its own experts, regulate argument and comment on the evidence. Detailed and rigid exclusionary rules are somewhat incongruous where extensive judicial discretion is accepted.

Extensive liberalization of pretrial procedures has affected both the philosophy and the practice in a litigation to a degree bound to liberalize evidence rules. Increased use of discovery, authentication of documents by stipulation and notice to admit procedure, notice of intention to use hearsay with opportunity for depositions, and use of summary judgment and pretrial conferences[9] to reveal contentions and evidence have limited somewhat the

---

5. Korn, Law and the Determination of Facts Involving Science and Technology 34-40 (Mimeo. 1965).

6. Note, *Judicial Admissions*, 64 COLUM. L. REV. 1121, 1122 (1964).

7. See, *e.g.*, United States v. United Shoe Mach. Corp., 89 F. Supp. 349, 355 (D. Mass. 1950) (Wyzanski, J.); *cf.* Shuttlesworth v. City of Birmingham, 86 S. Ct. 211, 219 (1965) (concurring opinion of Fortas, J.) (judicial notice that defendant was a Negro leader and that a civil rights dispute was at the center of the prosecution); Matter of Ekstrom, 24 App. Div. 2d 276, 265 N.Y.S.2d 727 (3d Dep't 1965) (court will not grant custody by reason of burden-of-proof rules where neither party submits evidence).

8. See, *e.g.*, Institute of Judicial Administration, *Judicial Education in the United States: A Survey*, in N.Y.L.J., Nov. 5, 1965, p. 4, col. 1; Friesen, Jr., *The Judicial Seminar: Foundation for Judicial Education*, 46 J. AM. JUD. SOC'Y 22.

9. See ROSENBERG, THE PRETRIAL CONFERENCE AND EFFECTIVE JUSTICE 37 (1964) (suggestion that pretrial did have a "positive impact on the quality of trial evidence"); *id.* at 39-40 (pretrial reduced surprises at trial); ROSENBERG & WEINSTEIN, ELEMENTS

gamesmanship and surprise aspects of trial and, accordingly, have increased restiveness with technical exclusionary rules.[10] Indeed, the better judges are more and more describing themselves with pride as "letter-iners" rather than "keeper-outers" of evidence.

Many rules of evidence can be understood only in terms of the judge's need to rigidly control a group of ignorant illiterates—the jury. But change is also apparent here: the present day juror is much more sophisticated and educated than was the juror sitting when the rules of evidence solidified in the last century.[11] This factor, when coupled with extensive use of bench trials or judicially supervised negotiations, makes possible the elimination of at least some of the exclusionary rules.

Tendencies which have eroded the original bases for numerous evidentiary rules have, however, failed to sap two pillars of American procedure—the civil jury and the lawyer controlled adversarial system. Direct attacks on the jury are violently repulsed. Explicit extensions of the judge's functions have been treated warily by both the bench and bar.[12] The task of the draftsman is to devise evidentiary rules which recognize and capitalize upon the changes in climate yet remain faithful to these two fundamentals of our litigation system.[13]

Despite a few statutory modifications,[14] the American law of evidence

OF CIVIL PROCEDURE 629-34 (1962) (pretrial and supervision of entire litigation by single judge useful in complex cases).

10. See, *e.g.*, Degnan, *The Evidence Law of Discovery: Exclusion of Evidence Because of Fear of Perjury*, 43 TEXAS L. REV. 435 (1965) (liberal use of discovery helps overcome objectionable application of exclusionary rules). See also Louisell, *Criminal Discovery and Self-Incrimination: Roger Traynor Confronts the Dilemma*, 53 CALIF. L. REV. 89 (1965).

11.

School year	Number students graduated from high school per 100 persons 17 years of age	Undergraduate residents degree-credit students in institutions of higher education to 100 of population 18-21
1869-70	2.0	b
1889-90	3.5	2.99
1919-20	16.8	7.88
1929-30	29.0	11.89
1939-40	50.8	14.49
1949-50	59.0	26.94
1959-60	65.1	31.15
1961-62	69.7	32.48
1962-63	70.7[a]	b

a preliminary data
b data not available
Source: U.S. DEP'T OF HEALTH, EDUCATION & WELFARE, DIGEST OF EDUCATIONAL STATISTICS 56 (table 37), 76 (table 54) (1964).

12. *Cf.* BREITEL, ETHICAL PROBLEMS IN THE PERFORMANCE OF THE JUDICIAL FUNCTION 65 (U. of Chi. L. School Conference on Judicial Ethics, No. 19) ("Consciously or unconsciously, the most important decision that the judge makes for himself is whether he will play an affirmative or quiescent role in the performance of his function").

13. *Cf.* Ramble, Jr., *American Legal Realism and the Reduction of Uncertainty*, 13 J. PUB. L. 45, 47 (1964) (the legal realists contended that "the best way to reduce fact-uncertainty—that is, the uncertainty which stems from an inability to predict what will be regarded as the facts of a case—is to reform its two major sources, the adversarial mode of trial and trial by jury").

14. See, *e.g.*, COMMONWEALTH FUND, PROPOSED BUSINESS ENTRIES STATUTE (1927);

has heretofore been peculiarly immune to legislative reform. The New York
Court of Appeals' recent summary of one state's history is typical of the
situation in the United States:

> New York, like most Anglo-American jurisdictions, has never
> adopted a comprehensive scheme of evidence. Field's proposal for a
> New York Code of Evidence was ignored. . . . Neither the Model
> Code of Evidence nor the Uniform Rules of Evidence have been
> considered for adoption by this State's Legislature, although the Ad-
> visory Committee on Practice and Procedure urged that a code of
> evidence, somewhat similar to those proposed in New Jersey, Kansas
> and Utah, be adopted. . . . Our statutory provisions cover only a
> few of the hearsay exceptions developed by the courts and recog-
> nized in New York.[15]

Abortive attempts to modify such rules as the dead man statute are illustrative
of the strong resistance to legislative change.[16] The progress of reform in the
law of evidence has been accurately characterized by Professor Morgan as
"glacier-like."[17]

Partly because of legislative inertia and partly because the rules of evidence were developed by the courts for control of their own procedures, some
courts have begun to recognize a greater responsibility for reform. As Judge
Fuld recently noted in *Fleury v. Edwards*:[18]

> The common law of evidence is constantly being refashioned by the
> courts of this and other jurisdictions to meet the demands of modern
> litigation. Exceptions to the hearsay rules are being broadened and
> created where necessary. . . . Absent some strong public policy or a
> clear act of pre-emption by the Legislature, rules of evidence should
> be fashioned to further, not frustrate, the truth-finding function of the
> courts in civil cases.

But, as Professor Morgan has pointed out, "our adversary system makes entirely impracticable the process of comprehensive procedural reform by judicial
decision in contested cases."[19] Most modern appellate courts have been reluctant to assay even minor attempts at establishing "a rational edifice."[20]
In fact, only a relatively small number of evidence issues are ever accepted

---

UNIFORM BUSINESS RECORDS AS EVIDENCE ACT (1936) ; Note, *Revised Business Entry
Statutes: Theory and Practice*, 48 COLUM. L. REV. 920 (1948).
  15. Fleury v. Edwards, 14 N.Y.2d 334, 340, 200 N.E.2d 550, 553, 251 N.Y.S.2d 647,
652 (1964).
  16. See, *e.g.*, 5 WEINSTEIN, KORN & MILLER, NEW YORK CIVIL PRACTICE ¶¶ 4519.01-
.03 (1964) ; Morgan, *Practical Difficulties Impeding Reform in the Law of Evidence*, 14
VAND. L. REV. 725, 728-32 (1961).
  17. Morgan, *supra* note 16, at 725.
  18. 14 N.Y.2d 334, 341, 200 N.E.2d 550, 554, 251 N.Y.S.2d 647, 653 (1964). The
opinion cites Dallas County v. Commercial Union Assur. Co., 286 F.2d 388 (5th Cir.
1961), as illustrating the tendency toward reform. See MAGUIRE, WEINSTEIN, CHAD-
BOURNE & MANSFIELD, *op. cit. supra* note 7, at 536, 544. *But see* Griew, *supra* note 4, at 93
(Myers v. Director of Pub. Prosecutions, [1964] 3 Weekly L.R. 145, "has established
that no new exceptions to the hearsay rule can be judicially created," in England).
  19. Morgan, *supra* note 16, at 725.
  20. Michelson v. United States, 335 U.S. 469, 486 (1948) ("To pull one misshapen
stone out of the grotesque structure is more likely simply to upset its present balance
between adverse interests than to establish a rational edifice").

for review by the highest appellate courts. The paucity of modern decisions has caused some text writers and trial judges to accept old evidence opinions as current authority even though it is fairly clear that the controlling appellate court would overrule these earlier opinions were a proper case presented. Moreover, there is often a self-selective process at work which prevents many of the new, more liberal, rulings on admissibility from appearing in published opinions: the trial court does not indicate its reasons for admitting except, occasionally, in the trial record, and the appellate court will not discuss the point when there is no ground for reversal. The large spate of exclusionary opinions of the last century seem, therefore, to be unassailable if opinions only are relied upon to decide what are the present rules.

Some observers fear that codification may cause new and unnecessary rigidities in interpretations by the courts and that trial judges may conclude that their discretion to ameliorate the effect of a rule in the special circumstances of an individual case has been reduced. Such unfortunate results of revision are unnecessary. Justice Traynor, in discussing the effect of codification on California's rules, has pointed out that the legislature did not "freeze the law of evidence" but permitted the courts to liberalize the rules "in the light of common-law principles and . . . basic objectives."[21] To prevent stultification through codification, Rule 5 of the New Jersey Rules of Evidence declares:

> The adoption of these rules shall not bar the growth and development of the law of evidence in accordance with fundamental principles to the end that the truth may be fairly ascertained.

Extensive and systematic revision of rules of evidence by statute and rule in the United States is a development which should, and probably will, be welcomed rather than resisted by the legal profession. Such resistance as exists should be a minor factor to be weighed in the revision process. Certainly lawyers and judges need to be satisfied by new rules of evidence. Conceivably, the novelty of a new rule, such as one abolishing the dead man provision, might be so disquieting to lawyers that its possible advantages in truth finding would not be enough to warrant adoption. But we ought not be strongly influenced by the factor of satisfaction of the bar arising solely from preservation of the status quo. Practitioners and judges tend to accept procedural rules, including rules of evidence, uncritically and to resist change by closing their minds to its advantages. Although the pressures of society tend to keep substantive law improving, this tendency is muted in adjective law since laymen have only intermittent interest in its problems. This explains, perhaps, the reason procedural law "petrifies," while substantive law is, according to one commentator of the last century, "in its budding growth."[22]

---

21. People v. Spriggs, 60 Cal. 2d 868, 871, 389 P.2d 377, 379, 36 Cal. Rptr. 841, 843 (1964).

22. HEPBURN, THE HISTORICAL DEVELOPMENT OF CODE PLEADING IN AMERICA AND ENGLAND 31, 37 (1897).

It is important, however, to bear in mind that extensive reform of the evidentiary rules does not promise a panacea for our courts. Indeed, even the most extensive revision will have but a relatively limited influence on the effectiveness of trials. For example, recent decisions guaranteeing indigents the right to counsel and statutes providing resources for investigations on behalf of poor defendants have a far more beneficial effect on the truth-finding capacity of the courts than could variants of the rules on cross-examination and hearsay.[23]

While draftsmen may make substantial improvements, they face difficulties which are not appreciably reduced when they are drafting court rules rather than legislative statutes.[24] Only the fundamental difficulties of the draftsmen of rules of evidence are discussed in this article: the truth-finding capability of the trier is limited by numerous human and administrative obstacles which

---

23. In analyzing the impact of the right to counsel cases—which do improve the truth-finding capacity of the courts by permitting early investigation and the like—it must be conceded that there is merit in the contentions of prosecutors that they have, in some respects, resulted in increasing the difficulty of arriving at the truth in criminal cases. The paradox is more apparent than real. For reasons of extrinsic policy, society has adopted rules, such as "self-incrimination" and exclusion of evidence obtained in violation of "search and seizure" protections, which permit defendants to withhold evidence from prosecutors and tribunals. Though written into our constitutions they have been moribund for most defendants. What the Supreme Court and many state courts have recently done is to make possible their equal and full application in accordance with the spirit of our constitutions by ensuring the presence of counsel. Attention of legislators, courts, law enforcement officials, and the public may now be properly focused on whether the public policy served by such "truth-hiding" rules can be served by means less corrosive of the judicial system's ability to ascertain the truth.

In determining retroactive effect, there is a difference between "truth-finding" constitutional rules, such as the right to counsel upon arrest, which are important to a correct determination of the facts, and those "truth-hiding" rules based upon extrinsic policy. See, *e.g.,* Mishkin, *Foreword: The High Court, The Great Writ, and the Due Process of Time and Law, The Supreme Court, 1964 Term,* 79 HARV. L. REV. 56, 97-101 (1965). The latter need not be given retroactive effect by the state. See, *e.g.,* Tehan v. State, 34 U.S.L. WEEK 4095 (U.S. Jan. 19, 1966) (self-incrimination).

24. See American Bar Association, *Report of Committee on Federal Rules of Procedure,* 38 F.R.D. 95, 102-03 (1965):

> The recent case of Hanna v. Plumer, 380 U.S. 460, 85 S. Ct. 1136, 14 L. Ed. 2d 8 (1965), has, in our opinion, failed to eliminate the difficulties. Indeed, they have, if anything, added to the burdens of draftsmen of amended federal rules. The majority opinion in the Hanna Case states fairly clearly that the rule making power is as broad as Congress' legislative power. As it noted, a Federal rule is valid unless:
> "the Advisory Committee, this Court, and Congress erred in their prima facie judgment that the Rule in question transgresses neither the terms of the Enabling Act nor constitutional restrictions." Id. 380 U.S. at 471, 85 S. Ct. at 1144, 14 L. Ed.2d at 17.

The Court used the normal legislative test for determining validity declaring:

> "a federal court system (augmented by the Necessary and Proper Clause) carries with it congressional power to make rules governing the practice and pleading in those courts, which in turn includes a power to regulate matters which, though falling within the uncertain area between substance and procedure, are rationally capable of classification as either." Id. 380 U.S. at 472, 85 S. Ct. at 1144, 14 L. Ed.2d at 17.

Rulemakers must, therefore, weigh in much the same way as Congress might, the desirability of uniformity and efficiency in federal litigation against the desirability of permitting the states, wherever possible, to exercise power and enforce their own policy in areas normally regulated by the states."

Draftsmen of the new California Evidence Code were aided by the fact that they could modify statutes which, as in the case of burdens of proof, have an important substantive impact. See, *e.g.,* CAL. EVIDENCE CODE §§ 600-68 (effective Jan. 1, 1967).

can be but partially ameliorated; and truth-finding is but one of several goals which must be satisfied, as far as possible, by the draftsmen's rules. The painful choices between the "particular justice policy" and the "procedural justice policy"[25] are particularly significant to draftsmen of rules of evidence since these rules, unlike most, must often be applied by the court without substantial time for reflection.[26] Not dealt with are the more common difficulties of procedural rule makers—how, for example, to devise specific rules which will be general, understandable, efficient and enforceable and will simultaneously assure a sound result in the individual cases.

I. The Difficulties Inherent in Ascertaining Truth

In developing any set of rules of evidence designed to assist a judicial trier in determining the facts, certain fundamental limitations must be faced. In the first place, it is necessary to rely upon incomplete sources of information. Secondly, knowledge of the real world is subjective, and often unreliable. Thirdly, societal assumptions substantially affect the trier's (as well as the witness's) conclusions. And, finally, factual findings are based, not upon a description of the real world, but upon a modified or constructive world of the law.

A. *Incomplete Sources Must Be Relied Upon by the Trier*

Despite some interesting suggestions of science fiction authors, time still remains irreversible. The trier-of-fact's resultant inability to re-view past events has led Max Radin to describe the determination of facts as one of the permanent and insoluble problems of the law. For "events are unique, and no imagined or imitative reconstruction will precisely reproduce them"; yet "every act or event is necessarily a past act when it comes before the judge."[27] Even when designed to affect future conduct, judicial determinations must be based upon assumptions with respect to past events. The court is required to assume the role of historian[28]—without the historian's opportunity to reserve decision. It is saved embarrassment by its acknowledgment that it is finding only "operative facts," for the purpose of the litigation. Aided by rules of presumptions and burdens of proof, it must affect the legal relations of the parties on the basis of current probabilities.

The necessity of basing decisions upon an evaluation of probabilities exists even if the sources of evidence are full and reliable. It is compounded in most litigation situations where the evidence is limited. A collision with no surviving

25. Gausewitz, *Presumptions in a One-Rule World*, 5 Vand. L. Rev. 324, 331 (1952).
26. See Chandler, *The Role of the Trial Judge in the Anglo-American Legal System*, 50 A.B.A.J. 125, 128 (1964) ("[the judge] should not only know the laws of procedure and evidence, but he must be able to use them functionally in making adroit and incisive rulings").
27. Radin, *The Permanent Problems of the Law*, in Jurisprudence in Action 415, 419 (1953).
28. See, comparing the two disciplines, Rescher, *Evidence in History and in the Law*, 56 J. Philosophy 561, 577 (1959).

eye-witnesses or a homicide committed in private furnish extreme examples, but even in run-of-the-mill litigation, substantial gaps in evidence are common.

There are only a few situations in which the trier can put himself in almost the identical position of an observer of a legally significant event. For example, a judge deciding whether a film is obscene may view the film. But even in the obscenity case, the judge must attempt to measure the effect of viewing the movie on someone in the social setting of a movie house rather than its effect on himself in a private room; hence he is not in the identical position of the observer whose supposed reactions are at issue. In some instances, the documentation is full and the trier can place himself in very nearly the position of the parties, as in some contract cases based wholly on papers; but this condition exists only because the law ignores verbal and other forms of communication not integrated in the controlling documents.

Views, experiments and pictures or sound recordings purporting to record or reconstruct the event may sometimes create the illusion of presence by the trier. But danger of error by the trier may be enhanced rather than diminished by a failure to recognize that the object or event being observed cannot be identical with the original event and that its probative force may depend upon the credibility of one or more persons responsible for creating the illusion.

Although it is necessary to decide cases on the basis of probabilities,[29] many courts still insist that mere "mathematical chances are not enough to support a finding" and "a proposition is proved by a preponderance of the evidence [only] if it is made to appear . . . that actual belief in its truth derived from the evidence exists in the minds . . . of the tribunal."[30] The evidentiary rules establishing such more-than-probable standards need rethinking.[31] Apart from their deleterious effect in many routine litigations, they deny courts the assistance that will be increasingly available from statistical analysis and expert testimony. Recognition of the fundamental inadequacies of proof should also lead to a reevaluation of some of our more extreme standards with respect to opinions of laymen and experts which have the effect of denying much evidence that an intelligent trier would consider useful.[32] It should also permit

---

29. See, *e.g.*, Ball, *The Moment of Truth: Probability Theory and the Standards of Proof*, 14 VAND. L. REV. 807 (1961).

30. Smith v. Rapid Transit, Inc., 317 Mass. 469, 470, 58 N.E.2d 754, 755 (1954). See also MAGUIRE, WEINSTEIN, CHADBOURNE & MANSFIELD, *op. cit. supra* note 7, at 547-61, 682-97.

31. This problem will be discussed in greater detail in a future article by the author. The issues in this area have substantive as well as procedural implications. See MAGUIRE, WEINSTEIN, CHADBOURNE & MANSFIELD, *op. cit. supra* note 7, at 682-85, 688-92. Their complete resolution requires modifications of many of each jurisdiction's statutes. See, *e.g.*, the treatment of presumptions in CALIFORNIA LAW REVISION COMM'N, TENTATIVE RECOMMENDATION AND A STUDY RELATING TO THE UNIFORM RULES OF EVIDENCE 1087, 1093-1102 (1964).

32. *Cf.* MAGUIRE, WEINSTEIN, CHADBOURNE & MANSFIELD, *op. cit. supra* note 7, at 245-52, 255-75.
Two important conclusions, in this connection, are furnished in Diamond & Louisell, *The Psychiatrist as an Expert Witness: Some Ruminations and Speculations*, 63 MICH. L. REV. 1335 (1965). They are, first, that the "usefulness of psychiatric evidence is not

the trier greater freedom to rely upon a broadened doctrine of spoliation conclude that a party, who fails to supply evidence which he could be expected to produce, has not met his burden of persuasion.[33]

B. *The Subjective Nature of Our Knowledge About the Existential World*

Berkeley's questioning of the very existence of a physical outside world —a world visualized from what man believes are sense impressions—may be extreme. But assuming that there does exist a real world which can be known, the limitations on man's ability to "know" are of critical importance to the court.[34] For its determination is based primarily upon a world of the past—a world reconstructed with the aid of sense impressions, of varying reliability, of witnesses who usually are strangers to the trier. The necessity of reconstructing past events on the basis of such subjective knowledge involves difficulties comparable to those of Plato's image of the cave: we deal not with the facts, but with shadows and reflections of the real world.

Ideally, the world visualized by the court would be limited only by the sensory capacities of the witness. But the witness is incapable of reporting his raw sense impressions. "Some witnesses lie, and some (though blessed few) perhaps observe, remember and recount with a high degree of fidelity to what 'really happened,' but by far the greater number do neither. Witnesses (like plumbers, lawyers, psychiatrists and even judges) filter what they perceive through a complex maze of ego-preserving defense mechanisms . . . , which have the effect of deluding themselves most of all into believing that they are telling the truth, the whole truth and a great deal of it."[35]

For the moment, it is sufficient to note that the testimony of any witness describes the combination of himself and the event. As Santayana put it, "every perception . . . involves an act of judgment, nay is an act of judgment. Our mind is governed by a system of checks; every perception left to itself is an

---

determined by the exactness or infallibility" of the witness, but rather "it is measured by the probability that what he has to say offers more information and better comprehension of the human behavior which the law wishes to understand." *Id.* at 1342. Second, "the remedy [for supposed impartiality of the psychiatrist-expert] must lie in the full disclosure to the jury of the psychiatrist's role and function in the particular case." *Id.* at 1345. See also Roberts, *Some Observations on the Problems of the Forensic Psychiatrist,* 1965 WISC. L. REV. 240, 244 (lack of certainty in psychiatric findings).

33. See, *e.g.,* Hofstadter & Richter, *Effect of Failure to Call a Witness—New Rule Proposed,* N.Y.L.J., June 4-7, 1956, p. 4; MAGUIRE, WEINSTEIN, CHADBOURNE & MANSFIELD, *op. cit. supra* note 7, at 653-60. The matter will be discussed in a subsequent article.

The jury will tend to speculate with respect to any evidence which it expects to see introduced and which is not introduced. See, *e.g.,* Hinds v. John Hancock Mut. Life Ins. Co., 155 Me. 349, 370-76, 155 A.2d 721, 733-36 (1959). It is therefore normally best to expose the evidence and to instruct the jury on how to use it to avoid prejudice, if such an instruction is sought.

34. "Naive or Natural Realism" provides a satisfactory system for the trier of fact even though its philosophical underpinnings are shaky. See, *e.g.,* HIRST, PERCEPTION AND THE EXTERNAL WORLD 1 (1965).

35. Allen, *The Dynamics of Interpersonal Communications and the Law,* 3 WASHBURN L.J. 135, 137 (1964).

hallucination."[36] "What we see is apparently a function of some sort of weighted average of our past experience."[37]

The problem becomes more complex when the witness is not an objective spectator, but an observer involved in the event and subject to the distortions of his own heightened emotional and intellectual expectations and needs. The possibility of error in the trier's reconstruction of the event is compounded by the necessity of discounting what the trier believes to be the effect of such involvement on the witness's observation, memory and relation.[38]

The effort to know or to reconstruct the real world is inhibited by the deficiencies inherent in reliance on subjective knowledge. Yet our survival as individuals and as a species must be attributed to fairly accurate, albeit subjective, observation and comprehension of events in the world around us. In spite of the remarkable success of our own reliance on such knowledge, we often deny lay triers the opportunity to evaluate such evidence. A more reliable result might often be achieved were the trier candidly warned of the inherent difficulties and then permitted to evaluate the evidence as rationally as possible. There may well be a need to require minimum standards. But this would seem to be a matter best left for the discretion of the judge who is in a favorable position to predict whether the probative value of the evidence is substantially outweighed by the problems—such as prejudice, surprise, and undue consumption of time—created by its admission.[39]

C. *The Effect of Societal Assumptions and Values on the Trier's View of the Existential World*

The effort to reconstruct the past accurately is also inhibited by the effect which societal expectations and assumptions have on the trier. In analyzing these influences, it is helpful to distinguish between "unconscious distortion," which occurs even when the trier carefully evaluates the evidence, and "conscious distortion," the product of a deliberate effort to view the facts in a manner likely to increase the possibility of error. Conscious distortions are, for the purposes of this analysis, further subdivided into "mandatory" and

---

36. SANTAYANA, THE IDLER AND HIS WORKS 77 (1957).
37. KILPATRICK, EXPLORATIONS IN TRANSACTIONAL PSYCHOLOGY 49 (1961).
38. The "abnormal" witness presents additional problems. See, *e.g.*, Weihofen, *Testimonial Competence and Credibility*, 34 GEO. WASH. L. REV. 53, 81-90 (1965).
39. UNIFORM RULE 45 sets a useful tone. It reads in part as follows:
     The judge may in his discretion exclude evidence if he finds that its probative value is *substantially outweighed* by the risk that its admission will (a) necessitate undue consumption of time, or (b) create substantial danger of undue prejudice or of confusing the issues or of misleading the jury, or (c) unfairly and harmfully surprise a party who has not had reasonable opportunity to anticipate that such evidence would be offered.
(Emphasis added.) Use of the words "substantially outweighed" suggests a great reliance on the jurors' good sense. Coupled with a substantial power in the court of explication, it may be a rule as precise as it is desirable to draft.

"unauthorized" types—though this pedantic terminology should not suggest a comprehensive treatment.

1. *Unconscious Distortions.* In coming to any conclusions, a trier considers the specific evidence produced in the case before him, utilizes hypotheses which he has previously absorbed to draw inferences from that evidence, and, as a result of his conscious reasoning and subconscious emotional-cognital processes, arrives at conclusions with respect to the existence or non-existence of the facts which are material under the applicable rule of law.

Limited experience and preconceptions derived from communal attitudes may lead the most conscientious trier to apply an unsound hypothesis to reliable and specific evidence and thereby to reach a conclusion which is completely inaccurate. He may, for example, be firmly convinced that Indians have extraordinary powers of observation and he will therefore give great credence to an Indian's testimony; or he may conclude that the Chinese witness must be telling the truth because Chinese never lie when money is involved; or he may believe that a prosecutrix was unlikely to have had intercourse with the defendant voluntarily because she was a "lady" and he a member of the working class.[40]

Even when a party is aware that the trier accepts an unsound hypothesis, he will find it difficult to rectify the false assumption by exposing it in argument. Expert testimony and statistical and other evidence to meet an unsound hypothesis head-on may be available, albeit in relatively few cases. Judicial notice can be used more frequently than it has been in the past to allow the judge to instruct the jury on the facts as revealed by current research in the social and physical sciences.[41] Expansion of the power of the court to comment on the evidence and to warn the jury of possible prejudice is, in this connection, vital; too many courts in this country are still required to give mere abstract charges on the law.[42] Judges, by virtue of their education and office, are apt to take a broader view of matters than jurors of the vicinage; where they do not, review by higher courts and criticisms in legal literature and the press can have a useful effect.

It is important to bear in mind that misconceptions of the trier are not eliminated by the usual evidentiary protections such as excluding hearsay. If,

---

40. *Cf.* N.Y. Herald Tribune, Oct. 20, 1965, p. 11, col. 1:
When the trial began Monday, Mr. Flowers [the Attorney General] startled the courtroom, and all the people of Lowndes County and Alabama, by asking prospective white jurors if they believe Negroes are inferior to whites. When virtually every prospective white juror answered yes, Mr. Flowers then asked him if he also believed that a white woman, by associating with Negroes, renders herself inferior. Most every prospective white juror gave some sort of affirmative answer.
In such a setting, the defense of consent by a white woman to alleged rape by a Negro would present difficulties to his attorney.
41. See Korn, *op. cit. supra* note 5, at 17-19.
42. See, *e.g.*, MAGUIRE, WEINSTEIN, CHADBOURNE & MANSFIELD, *op. cit. supra* note 7, at 737-40; VANDERBILT, MINIMUM STANDARDS OF JUDICIAL ADMINISTRATION 224-29 (1949).

for example, the tribunal accepts society's assumption that there are witches and that certain observable manifestations are reliable indicia of witchcraft, procedures for a "fair" trial result in more rather than less assurance that the trier will properly adjudicate the defendant a witch. The standard medieval treatise on witchcraft—*Malleus Maleficarum*[43]—contains extensive procedural protections. The third part of that treatise relating to the "judicial proceedings in both the ecclesiastical and civil courts against witches" sets out in detail "the formal rules for initiating a process of justice, [and] how it should be conducted."[44] The trier is repeatedly put on notice of the need for care. For example, it is stated that, "although two witnesses seem to be enough to satisfy the rigour of the law (for the rule is that that which is sworn to by two or three is taken for the truth) : yet in a charge of this kind two witnesses do not seem sufficient to ensure an equitable judgment, on account of the heinousness of the crime in question. For the proof of an accusation ought to be clearer than daylight."[45] Yet it was these very "protections" which helped to convert ancient fears of sorcery into the dangerous conspiracy and high treason of witchcraft.[46] The furnishing of an authoritative text and procedures "explains the enormous influence which the Malleus exercised in extending and intensifying the persecution, for it was in its numerous editions circulated everywhere throughout the Continent as a practical handbook, confirming belief and teaching pitiless procedure."[47]

The recent exculpation of the Jews of Trent in the alleged "ritual murder" of a boy in 1475 seems anachronistic because of changed attitudes

---

43. MALLEUS MALEFICARUM (Rodker ed. 1928) (transl. by Rev. Montague Summers). Summers' introduction is a highly favorable apology for the inquisition and witch trials. Speaking of the inquisition, he notes :

There can be no doubt that had this most excellent tribunal [the Inquisition] continued to enjoy its full prerogatives and the full exercise of its salutory powers, the world at large would be in a far happier and far more orderly position today [1928]. . . . [T] Waldenses, the Albigenses, the Henricians, the Poor Men of Lyons, the Cathari, the Vaudois, the Bogomiles and the Manichees . . . were in reality branches . . . of the same dark fraternity . . . as the Third International, the Anarchists, the Nihilists, and the Bolsheviks.

Id. at xviii.

44. In practice, however, deceit and torture were approved and relied upon. See 2 LEA, MATERIALS TOWARDS A HISTORY OF WITCHCRAFT 894-904 (Howland ed. 1957).

45. MALLEUS MALEFICARUM, *op. cit. supra* note 43, at 208.

46. See Burr, *Introduction to* LEA, *op. cit. supra* note 44, at xli (criticizing Kittredge's studies of New England witchcraft because they failed to make clear that "they who developed the new conception were the theologians of the Inquisition . . . the leaders of state and church").

47. 1 LEA, *op. cit. supra* note 44, at 336. See also The Bull of Innocent VIII, at xxxviii, xliii (December 9, 1484), approving the work of Fr. Henry Kramer and Fr. James Sprenger, authors of *Malleus Maleficarum.* Lea suggests, relying on Hansen's work, that the approbation of the University of Koln was obtained, partly by fraud, to give an air of respectability to the witch trials, which were looked down upon by many of the educated. 1 LEA, *op. cit. supra* note 44, at 336-43.

When the hypothesis of witchcraft became official and important to policy, "a few men . . . had the courage to express their views more or less openly . . . but most . . . opposition was under the surface and its utterance suppressed by fear of prosecution on the charge of aiding and abetting the works of the devil." *Id.* at vii. Eventually, official rejection was conducive to a decline in popular belief. *Cf. id.* at vii.

in some parts of our society. Reporting the matter, the *New York Times*[48] stated:

> For the record, and despite the obvious implausibility of the charge in 20th-century eyes, Father Echert made a careful examination of the "evidence" in archives in Trent, Rome and Vienna and concluded that the trial of Trent had led to a judicial assassination.

The term "judicial assassination" is not properly used if the Trent result was due to good faith evaluation of evidence by triers with distorted hypotheses. It is properly used where the conviction results from a policy determination requiring mandatory skewing of the facts as in the cases of Nazi and Soviet trials discussed below.

Often it is not possible to clearly differentiate the inadvertent from the deliberate miscarriages of justice. A deliberate policy to convict certain groups wrongfully may lead to public hysteria or so misinform society that it generates a deeply rooted incorrect hypothesis.[49] The Trent incident, for example, has been laid to local prejudice, generated in particular by one church official; higher church and secular officials apparently sought to stop the extended torture which led to "confessions"; but Rome's ultimate approval of the result gave the matter an official standing that undoubtedly encouraged subsequent horrors.[50] (The Nazi genocide and concentration camp policy cannot, of course,

---

48. N.Y. Times, Nov. 1, 1965, p. 1, col. 1.

49. *Cf.* Frankel, *The Alabama Lawyer, 1954-1964, Has the Official Organ Atrophied?*, 64 COLUM. L. REV. 1243 (1964) (suggesting that the publication policy of that bar journal has had the effect of foreclosing any reevaluation of the separation of races policy and its hypothesis of racial inferiority).

The organized persecution of witches was in part designed to stamp out widespread heresy and relapses into paganism. *Cf.* MALLEUS MALEFICARUM, *op. cit. supra* note 45, at xvi, xviii, xix. Summers properly reflects the attitude of medieval authority in stating "it seems plain that the witches were a vast political movement, an organized society which was anti-social and anarchical, a world wide plot against civilization." *Id.* at xviii. See also HOLE, A MIRROR OF WITCHCRAFT 18 (1957) ("It was not until witchcraft had been identified with heresy that the Church's earlier skepticism was replaced by thorough-going faith."); MURRAY, THE WITCH-CULT IN WESTERN EUROPE 11-12, 18, 19 (1921) (many witches' customs are remnants of pagan worship [still said to be extant in England]; this "ritual witchcraft," the "Dianic cult," was sought to be stamped out by the church through the Inquisition).

Burr, in his introduction to LEA, *op. cit. supra* note 45, at xxxix-xl, warns that Lea probably would not have regarded either Murray or Summers as useful authorities—Murray because she accepted the "confessions" as true without considering that they resulted from torture, and Summers as a "wholly credulous" relict of the past; Summers' cruel books are meant "to help bring the witch-panic."

50. See 11 THE JEWISH ENCYCLOPEDIA 374-75 (1964) (The Pope's commissary, Bishop Grambattista, attempted to stop the proceedings, but Bishop Hinderbach interfered since he planned to enrich himself by confiscating the estates of those executed. Although Bishop Ventimiglia reported the Jews innocent, the church approved the proceedings "since the whole Catholic Church would have been involved in the condemnation of the Bishop of Trent"); 4 HISTORY OF THE JEWS 296-99 (1894) (attributing prosecution to the Franciscan Bernardinus of Fettre who utilized the superstitions of the lower classes as a device to sever the close relations between the aristocracy and the Jews); CARDINAL LORENZO GANGANELLI (later Pope Clement XIV), THE RITUAL MURDER LIBEL AND THE JEW 66 (Roth ed. 1935) ("In the populations of all countries are prevalent certain preconceptions which are called prejudices by the enlightened people of the age . . . . I will confine myself simply to pointing out the grave peril which is brought about for many innocent people, should they be judged by anyone under the influence of such prejudices.").

be analyzed in juridical terms.)[51] Similarly, there is substantial evidence that attacks on witches had substantial genesis in official policy designed to stamp out remnants of paganism and heresy.[52]

On the issue of witchcraft or ritual murder, evidence which a medieval jurist might have found conclusive would likely be viewed by a modern American trier as inadequate because of his different assumptions about the nature of the world. Similarly, a contemporary American trier's view of relevant but inherently ambiguous evidence would be influenced by his assumptions about the existence of the Cosa Nostra or a communist conspiracy.[53] And a Soviet trier, influenced by long-held common views of a capitalist conspiracy, might make a finding of espionage on evidence that a contemporary Italian trier might find unconvincing. The rejection in times past of newly proffered conclusions with respect to such matters as the nature of the solar system was not merely perverse, but resulted in part from beliefs and assumptions strongly imbedded in contemporary society.

Since the acute intelligence of the hindsighter is absent at a current trial, guarding against unconscious distortions is extremely difficult. Skepticism furnishes no guarantee against error because the skeptic may too readily reject the possibility of witches that in fact exist.

2. Conscious Mandatory Distortions. The law mandates many conscious distortions in the fact-finding process in order to gain some supposed social advantage. For example, we require a very high degree of probability—proof beyond a reasonable doubt—as a prerequisite to a finding of fact necessary to establish guilt of a crime. The result is to ensure more errors in the findings of fact than would exist were we merely to require a bare preponderance of probabilities.[54] But we deliberately choose to allow some criminals to escape because we believe fact-finding errors favoring defendants are less harmful than errors which result in conviction of the innocent. This deliberate choice is based upon deeply held moral values and ethical judgments. Given a particularly dangerous crime indulged in by relatively small numbers of the population and a relatively small number of suspects, a perfectly rational argument could be developed for conviction on the least shadow of a doubt. Essentially this was the position recently taken with respect to security risks in the government service of the United States.[55]

---

51. See ARENDT, ORIGINS OF TOTALITARIANISM 426 (1951) (policy of destruction of individuality by Nazis).

52. See notes 47, 49 *supra*.

53. *Cf.* PACKER, EX-COMMUNIST WITNESSES 6 (1962) ("On the basis of the public record, the reality of a Communist conspiracy cannot be doubted." Much less firm conclusions can be reached as to who participated and who "knowingly cooperated."). Firmness of belief as to the existence of the conspiracy may well affect the degree of proof required to convince the trier that a particular individual participated.

54. Ball, *supra* note 29, at 807.

55. This is not to suggest that this position of the Federal authorities was sound under the circumstances. It was in this author's opinion wrong not only on moral grounds but on the practical ground that it weakened rather than strengthened our

Deliberate impediments to the truth-finding ability of the trier have been created for a variety of other reasons. For example, Rule 37(b) of the Federal Rules of Civil Procedure permits an order prohibiting a party "from introducing in evidence designated documents or things or items of testimony" as punishment for violating procedural rules. The danger of an improper answer to a question of fact is clearly increased when such relevant evidence is excluded.[56] The risk is justified on the ground that such punishment strengthens the operation of the system of procedural rules as a whole and increases the likelihood of better answers to factual questions in other cases.

It would seem strange, in view of our usual generous treatment of criminal defendants, to see the risk of conviction of the innocent deliberately proposed as a matter of policy. Yet, the *Second Preliminary Draft of Proposed Amendments to Rules of Criminal Procedure for the United States District Courts*[57] contained, in proposed Rule 16(g), a provision permitting the court to "prohibit" the defendant "from introducing in evidence material not disclosed," which should have been disclosed to the Government under the Rule. Whether such a criminal rule is sound or not (and putting aside possible constitutional objections), at the very least it would constitute a conscious mandatory distortion of the fact-finding process whenever applied.

The incremental erosion of the truth-finding capability of triers in general is, to be sure, relatively small as each such rule of exclusion is created. But the truth-finding criterion for rules of evidence is so important that even minor mandatory distortions need to be viewed very critically. It is necessary to constantly bear in mind Wigmore's warning that only the clearest and most over-riding necessity warrants interfering with the fact-finding ability of the courts because of extrinsic social policy.[58] In most instances in the past, when the issue has been posed, primary attention has been given to the importance of the extrinsic policy rather than to the policy's effect on the system of litigation. Draftsmen of new rules have an opportunity to provide a needed shift in perspective.

3. *Conscious Unauthorized Distortions.* On first view, there would appear to be a contradiction in terms were the law to countenance unauthorized deliberate errors in fact finding by triers. The thought, for example, that a white jury may deliberately find a white man not guilty where its own analysis points clearly to guilt or that it might find a black man guilty where it doubts

---

resistance by eliminating valuable public servants unnecessarily and by causing others to take safe positions rather than those they believed would most benefit the nation.

56. *Cf.* Societe Internationale v. Rogers, 357 U.S. 197, 209 (1958) (sanctions must be considered in the context of "constitutional limitations upon the power of courts, even in aid of their own valid processes, to dismiss an action without affording a party the opportunity for a hearing on the merit.") ; Rosenberg, *Sanctions to Effectuate Pretrial Discovery*, 58 COLUM. L. REV. 480, 495-96 (1958) (reluctance of courts to utilize harsh sanctions).

57. March, 1964. The same effect is obtained in many of the alibi statutes, requiring advance notice by the defendant. See, *e.g.*, N.Y. CODE CRIM. PROC. § 295-e.

58. 8 WIGMORE, EVIDENCE § 2175 (3d ed. 1940).

guilt, is revolting to men trained in the law. But the allegations that such distortion occurs on a wide scale find substantial support in current events.[59] A trier's view that society is better off with white killers out of jail and innocent black men in jail[60] is, most of us believe, no justification for flouting the law, and most lawyers are deeply grieved by such a perversion of legal process.

Yet the assumption that such deliberate and unauthorized distortions of the fact-finding process take place is integrated into our procedural system. "The power of a jury in a criminal case to reject, though unreasonably, evidence which is uncontradicted and unimpeached, and to extend mercy to an accused . . . cannot be challenged."[61] The jury has almost unlimited power to find the defendant in a criminal case guilty of a lesser included crime.[62] Indeed, one of the chief justifications of the jury system is that it can ignore and ameliorate the law by distorting the fact-finding process to reach a result acceptable to the community. Many who cringe at the phrase "white justice" as applied by some juries today, would have found little difficulty some years ago in ignoring the evidence to protect a runaway slave by an appropriate finding of fact or, perhaps, to find lack of miscegenation in a modern case.[63]

That the jury is "permitted" to and "may" consciously distort the evidence to achieve a result palatable to it does not mean that the judicial system should accept these distortions as proper. In so perverting the truth, the jury flouts and ignores the substantive law; to this extent its distortions must be considered as "unauthorized."

The rules of evidence can do little, by themselves, to prevent conscious distortions by the trier. They should, however, permit all possible relevant evidence and argument to be brought to bear on the trier so that he will at least be forced to bare his soul to himself and to consciously, though silently, justify his actions. There is, for example, considerable difference between the situation where the juror is confused over whether the plaintiff was contributorily negligent and yet finds for him and the situation where the evidence and charge are clear, yet the juror decides to ignore them because the result is, in his view, unjust. If a rule which is now relatively unimportant in its impact—such as contributory negligence—proves to be unenforceable, it should be changed; continuous circumventing of the rule by triers cannot help but decrease respect for, and the efficiency of, the judicial system. When more

---

59. See, *e.g.*, Broeder, *The Negro In Court*, 1965 DUKE L.J. 19, 23 ("The juror summed up his views in this manner: Niggers have to be taught to behave. I felt that if he hadn't done that, he'd done something else probably even worse and that he should be put out of the way for a good long while.").

60. *Cf.* Broeder, *supra* note 59, at 24 ("a reflection of the attitude, said to be prevalent in many quarters, that a Negro stealing from a Negro should be dealt with more leniently than one who steals from a white, and there are some laws which no Negro can ever, 'in justice' be expected to obey.").

61. People v. Rytel, 284 N.Y. 242, 245, 30 N.E.2d 578, 580 (1940).

62. See People v. Mussenden, 308 N.Y. 558, 127 N.E.2d 551 (1955).

63. *Cf.* Black, Jr., *The Problem of the Compatibility of Civil Disobedience With American Institutions of Government*, 43 TEXAS L. REV. 492 (1965).

fundamental rules, such as those providing for equality before the law of members of different races, are flouted by juries, the substantive law obviously cannot be changed. There is some indication that insistent and consistent action by legislative, judicial and executive branches will lead to eventual acceptance of these fundamental substantive rules by juries.

Conscious distortions may be a partially unavoidable consequence of the jury system. But they are totally unacceptable when, as occurred in Nazi Germany, judges or government officials are involved. There is substantial reason to believe that the German courts themselves, acting in furtherance of Nazi policy, made factual determinations and abused "legal authority for the purpose of intimidation and suppression of opposition views."[64] Recent "rehabilitations" of the dead in Soviet Russia indicate that the communists were also guilty of such large scale perversions. Deliberate distortion of the fact-finding process by officials charged with law enforcement has also apparently taken place recently in the South in connection with prosecution of those accused of attacking civil rights workers.[65] This, it has been reported, occurred in the *Coleman* case, in which state police officials, local prosecutors and the judge were alleged to have cooperated to achieve an acquittal of a person charged with murdering a minister.[66] Such a gross abuse of legal process is intolerable. But, obviously, rules of evidence are useless in revealing truth when confronted by a lawless conspiracy of officials. Rules which encourage rather than discourage introduction of relevant data probably do have some tendency to discourage such conspiracies, since the press will be in a position to reveal what took place in the courtroom. And federal prohibitions against conspiracies designed to deprive individuals and groups of the equal protection of the laws are becoming more effective.[67]

---

64. Pappe, *On the Validity of Judicial Decisions in the Nazi Era*, 23 MODERN L. REV. 260, 267 (1960) (the author suggests that court officials went beyond what a jury reflecting popular attitudes would have countenanced).

65. *Cf.* Recommendations of United States Civil Rights Commission, N.Y. Times, Nov. 14, 1965, p. 87, col. 2 ("failures of state and local law enforcement officials to prevent or punish crimes of racial violence"); SOUTHERN JUSTICE 43-56, 76-79, 103-06, 112-26, 136-64 (Friedman ed. 1965).

66. See N.Y. Herald Tribune, Sept. 28, 1965, p. 1, col. 1 (case brought to trial by judge despite illness of chief prosecution witness; refusal of state police chief to reveal evidence to State Attorney General and substantial indication of perjury being procured by state officials on behalf of defendant); N.Y. Herald Tribune, Sept. 29, 1965, p. 1, col. 5 (State Attorney General who protested action of state officials ousted by trial judge); N.Y. Herald Tribune, Oct. 1, 1965, p. 1, col. 1 (acquittal); N.Y. Herald Tribune, Oct. 1965, p. 16, col. 1 (Attorney General of United States: "It is difficult to get convictions in some areas. This is the price you have to pay for the jury system, but I don't think it is too high a price to pay. The situation has changed a great deal already."). Compare the proper conduct of Alabama Attorney General Richmond Flowers in attempting to obtain an unbiased jury in the Wilkins case, involving the killing of another civil rights worker. See N.Y. Times, Oct. 20, 1965, p. 1, col. 8 (Liuzzo Prosecutor Asks Juror Purge); N.Y. Herald Tribune, Oct. 20, 1965, p. 11, col. 1 ("Strange Questions at Trial in Alabama").

67. See, *e.g.*, N.Y. Times, Dec. 4, 1965, p. 1, cols. 3-4 (federal jury convicts three Klansmen of conspiracy to deprive citizens of civil rights). Where local police and judicial authorities participate, the violation would seem more clearly amenable to federal prosecution.

D. *The Constructive World of the Law*

Carl Sandburg's famous lines from *The People, Yes*[68] poignantly state man's inability to comprehend the real world:

> "Do you solemnly swear before the ever-living God that the testimony you are about to give in this cause shall be the truth, the whole truth, and nothing but the truth?"
> "No, I don't. I can tell you what I saw and what I heard and I'll swear to that by the everliving God but the more I study about it the more sure I am that nobody but the everliving God knows the whole truth and if you summoned Christ as a witness in this case what He would tell you would burn your insides with the pity and the mystery of it."

But the court, as a legal institution, is not even curious about much of what the witness could tell; if his knowledge is not relevant to a "material" proposition the court will properly cut him off. What factors in the real world are material in a law suit depends upon the substantive aims of the law. For example, it will be material in a criminal case that a fire was set at "night" only when it is an element of the crime of arson in a higher degree. Such a definition of arson is based on our assumption that fires at night are more dangerous to society, that the criminal law has some deterrent value, and that setting a higher penalty for nocturnal arson will somewhat reduce the incidence of such fires. Even in the document-based contract case, we can speak of an identity of situation because the law accepts a bloodless and ghost-like substitute for the real world. It will be of no significance to the trier—or ought not be—that at the time of a "revocation," the barometric pressure was low, the defendant's wife had snapped at him or a colleague had just received an unjustified bonus, and that but for such conditions there would have been no revocation.

That the parameters of the law mark out an artificial world is not necessarily a valid basis for objection, for somewhat the same reason that it is not a telling criticism of the artistic quality of a painting by Chagall that it distorts a scene; nor is it a proper objection to Sandburg's biography of Lincoln that not everything then known about Lincoln is in the book. The trier's as well as the artist's success in re-creating a world must be tested within the frame of reference being used. The law is not interested in the "whole truth" but only in the evidence on the propositions of fact it deems material. This simplification of the issues is, in most instances, a great convenience to the trier, enormously reducing his burdens since so many possible factual issues are immaterial and so much evidence is irrelevant.

Nevertheless, the lack of congruence between the artificial world of the law and that seen by laymen or experts sometimes creates severe problems at a trial. For example, a great part of the debate between doctors and lawyers about the legal definition of insanity and its use by doctors has its source in this incongruity. The frame of reference for the doctor is diagnosis for purpose

---

68. Sandburg, The People, Yes 193 (1936).

of treatment while that of the law is judgment for the purpose, among others, of deterrence. Similarly, the lawyer or judge often must struggle with the witness to get to the "facts in the case," by which is meant what the law thinks important, not what the witness cares about.[69]

When fact-finding problems result from the creation of an artificial world which is too far removed from reality, one remedy is to reform the substantive law. For example, the concepts of "fault" or "cause" in automobile collision cases and "insanity" in criminal cases result in problems of proof which might be avoided by rules providing for universal compensation or treatment instead of punishment in civil and criminal cases, respectively. Where the clash is not resolved substantively, the courts attempt to deal with it by relaxing perfectly logical rules of admissibility, thereby permitting the trier to bridge the gap by forcing the law, the facts, or both.[70] Such problems can hardly be solved by general rules of evidence.

II. THE VARIETY OF ENDS SERVED BY OUR RULES OF EVIDENCE

Even were it theoretically possible to ascertain truth with a fair degree of certainty, it is doubtful whether the judicial system and rules of evidence would be designed to do so. Trials in our judicial system are intended to do more than merely determine what happened. Adjudication is a practical enterprise serving a variety of functions. Among the goals—in addition to truth finding—which the rules of procedure and evidence in this country have sought to satisfy are economizing of resources, inspiring confidence, supporting independent social policies, permitting ease in prediction and application, adding to the efficiency of the entire legal system, and tranquilizing disputants.

The draftsman of evidentiary or other procedural rules is constantly obliged to strike a balance between these often competing goals with the inevitable result that some will be compromised. As James has noted:

> The full pursuit of the . . . facts and applicable law in any dispute may . . . be limited by the need for efficiency and finality. The hardest and most important job of a procedural system is to keep striking a wise balance throughout the various points of conflict.[71]

Indeed, any set of rules, viewed as a whole, will probably serve no one end completely. Even the merit-minded Federal Rules of Civil Procedure provide that the rules "shall be construed to secure the just, speedy and inexpensive determination of every action."[72] "Speedy" and "inexpensive" are coupled with "just" as equal ends with the result that the court may need to forego a

---

69. See Korn, Law and the Determination of Facts Involving Science and Technology 23-24 (Mimeo 1965) (disparity between legal and scientific concepts; value and policy ingredients).

70. *Id.* at 25-30. See also MODEL PENAL CODE, at 32-33, 198 (Tent. Draft No. 4, 1955) (problem of insanity dealt with in large measure by encouraging broader admission of expert testimony).

71. JAMES, CIVIL PROCEDURE 2 (1965).

72. FED. R. CIV. P. 1.

"just" decision in an individual case to preserve and enforce a rule designed to provide "speed" in other cases.

A system for determining issues of fact very accurately in all tribunals might permit a few adjudications a year of almost impeccable precision. But the resulting inability of the courts to have time to adjudicate the thousands of other pending litigations would mean that justice would be frustrated; people could flout the substantive law with relative impunity, knowing that the likelihood of being brought to trial was remote; and plaintiffs would be forced to avoid litigation because of its extraordinary expense and delay. A cheap and swift, rough and ready, approximation of the facts with increased risks of error would be much more effective in carrying out social policy as embodied in the substantive law.

The balance may well vary depending upon the nature of the tribunal. It may differ in a criminal as against a civil court or a small-claims court as contrasted with a court of major civil jurisdiction or a legislative committee as compared to an administrative agency.[73] The Warren Commission on the Assassination of President Kennedy had a superb group of triers, a large staff of skilled lawyers, all the investigative resources of the United States at its command, and ample time. As Professor Goodhart pointed out, "no other inquiry in the whole of legal history ever approached the Warren Commission in the extent and detail of its researches."[74] Yet even this enormous fact-finding machine left some lingering doubts.[75] While it is true that there were special difficulties in the Oswald case, few litigations are without complications.

Although this article is concerned primarily with litigations involving individual defendants and relatively narrow issues, and not with "official fact-

---

73. See MAGUIRE, WEINSTEIN, CHADBOURNE & MANSFIELD, CASES ON EVIDENCE 769-74 (1965).

74. Goodhart, *The Warren Commission from the Procedural Standpoint*, 40 N.Y.U.L. REV. 404, 422 (1965).

75. See, *e.g.*, FOX, THE UNANSWERED QUESTIONS ABOUT PRESIDENT KENNEDY'S ASSASSINATION (1965); Crawford, *20 Questions For the Warren Report*, in CRITICAL REFLECTIONS TO THE WARREN REPORT 1 (1965); Delvin, *Death of a President: The Established Facts*, Atlantic Monthly, March, 1965, pp. 112, 116-18 (refuting critics); Freese, *The Warren Commission and the Fourth Shot: A Reflection on the Fundamentals of Forensic Fact-Finding*, 40 N.Y.U.L. REV. 424, 459 (1965); MacDonald, *A Critique of the Warren Report*, Esquire, March, 1965, pp. 59, 61 (noting critical comments and adding some); Nash & Nash, *The Other Witnesses*, The New Leader, Oct. 12, 1964, p. 6; Packer, *The Warren Report: A Measure of the Achievement*, The Nation, Nov. 2, 1964, p. 295; Saturday Review, Nov. 7, 1964, pp. 35-37 (summary of reactions from newspapers abroad).

There were, in addition, a good many comments by those with a professional stake in criticising the Warren Report. See, *e.g.*, treating some of these: Ludwig, *"Who Killed Kennedy,"* Partisan Review, Winter, 1965, p. 63 (describing public "demonstration" by Mark Lane); Sauvage, *As I Was Saying*, The New Leader, Nov. 9, 1964, p. 11 (discussing Buchanan); Sparrow, *Making Mysteries About Oswald*, Atlas, March 1965, p. 173 (dealing with Trevor-Roper). The most deft disposal of the conspiracy-to-suppress-crowd is in MacDonald, *A Critique of the Warren Report*, Esquire, March, 1965, p. 59.

finding as a basis for public enlightenment," to use Professor Packer's phrase,[76] it is worth noting that the Warren Commission probably reached a more satisfactory conclusion[77] than would have been achieved in a criminal court.[78] It is clear that we must be satisfied with a far more niggardly use of our judicial resources except in cases involving major public issues.[79]

Once the judicial framework has been established, the draftsman must strike a balance among the goals desirable and achievable within that framework. Truth finding must be a central purpose whatever the tribunal. Unless we are to assume that the substantive law is perverse or irrelevant to the public welfare, then its enforcement is properly the primary aim of litigation; and the substantive law can be best enforced if litigation results in accurate determinations of facts made material by the applicable rule of law. Unless reasonably accurate fact finding is assumed, there does not appear to be any sound basis for our judicial system. The "last-ditch" dispute settling function could be served more cheaply by a machine granting judgments by operation of chance. The fundamental condition for enhancing the possibility of accurate fact finding is that as much of the available relevant information as possible be placed before the trier.

In most instances, the impact of a rule making evidence available or unavailable is clear, but sometimes this impact may be quite indirect. For example, witnesses or prospective witnesses may hold back information because of fear of abuse on the witness stand unless the rules protect them; yet intensive cross-examination may be essential to get at the truth even though it

---

76. PACKER, EX-COMMUNIST WITNESSES 226 (1962).

77. *But compare* Fox, *op. cit. supra* note 75 (strongly urging a dissenting voice or a devil's advocate within the Commission), *and* Freese, *supra* note 75, at 458 (suggesting a "critical examiner" or "Devil's Advocate" as a necessity), *and* Rosenberg, *The Warren Commission*, The Nation, September 14, 1964, pp. 110, 111 (approving the shift from a purely investigative body to a hearing body with "both sides" represented when the Commission appointed an "independent lawyer" to protect Oswald's interest), *with* Packer, *The Warren Report, A Measure of the Achievement*, The Nation, Nov. 2, 1964, pp. 295, 298 ("the commission compromised the integrity of the distinctive fact-finding process for which it was constituted by making the appointment" of an independent lawyer).

Hindsight suggests that it would have been better if the Commission had appointed one of our many aggressive, skilled and ethical criminal defense attorneys to act as a devil's advocate. An alternative device would have been to publish the record, issue a tentative report, wait for criticism, and then conduct such additional investigations as seemed warranted. A revised report could then have been issued. While theoretically possible, it is unlikely that the Commission's members would have been able to review their own work with complete objectivity or, if they could, that their critics would have been willing to concede them that ability.

78. See PACKER, EX-COMMUNIST WITNESSES 227-31 (1962) for a discussion of advantages and disadvantages of congressional investigations, administrative hearings and court trials for discovering facts about American communism. See also Scobey, *A Lawyer's Notes on the Warren Commission Report*, 51 A.B.A.J. 39 (1965) (pointing out how much useful evidence would have been excluded in a criminal trial of Oswald in Texas).

79. See, *e.g.*, PACKER, EX-COMMUNIST WITNESSES 236-39 (1962); Freese, *supra* note 75, at 453-58. See also Goodhart, *supra* note 74, at 412-19.

makes the witness unhappy. An examination in camera may overcome some objections of the nervous or youthful witness or the thin-skinned expert, but it may cause doubts in the public mind about the fairness of the system and disserve the confidence-inspiring aim of litigation. Moreover, the retributive, deterrent and educative effects of the law require that the courts operate "in due form, conspicuously, so that justice may be seen to be done."[80] While prejudice may result from a prejudging of the issues based upon press reports,[81] witnesses sometimes are led to come forward as a result of the publicity. In any event, except for limited special situations such as those involving infants or lurid testimony, the draftsmen of rules of evidence probably must accept public trials as an incident of the judicial system in the same way as they must assume the continuation of the jury system.

Even the hearsay rule, which seems designed only to serve a truth-finding function, requires the consideration of a variety of ends by anyone reconsidering the rules of evidence. With its numerous exceptions, it represents a series of somewhat inconsistent compromises between free admissibility of relevant information and exclusion of information dangerous because it may be overvalued by the trier.[82]

One proposal, acted on in part by New Jersey,[83] has been to admit hearsay more freely provided the opponent is given advance notice that it will be used[84] so that he can be prepared to attack the credibility of the out-of-court declarant and can produce contradictory evidence.[85] The proponents of this device argue that much hearsay evidence may be overvalued, unless the system permits the trier and adversary to check effectively on the accuracy of information adduced, to attack it by other proof and to explain it away. By making

---

80. Slater, *The Judicial Process and the Ascertainment of Fact: Impressions of a Psychiatrist*, N.Y.L.J., Feb. 6, 1962, p. 4, col. 2. See also the discussion of the Warren Commission's reception of testimony in secret in Goodhart, *supra* note 74, at 405-07.

81. See, *e.g.*, Estes v. Texas, 381 U.S. 532 (1965) (conviction reversed because of televised courtroom proceedings); Le Wine, *What Constitutes Prejudicial Publicity in Pending Cases?*, 51 A.B.A.J. 942 (1965).

82. MORGAN, SOME PROBLEMS OF PROOF UNDER THE ANGLO-AMERICAN SYSTEM OF LITIGATION 141-43 (1956).

83. Rule 64 of the New Jersey Rules of Evidence provides that "whenever a statement . . . is in the form of writing, the judge may exclude it at the trial if it appears that the proponents' intention to offer the writing in evidence was not made known to the adverse party at such a time as to provide him with a fair opportunity to prepare to meet it." The hearsay exceptions made subject to the rule are 63(3) (depositions and prior testimony), 63(15) (reports and findings of public officials), 63(16) (filed reports), 63(17) (official records), 63(18) (certificates of marriage), 63(19) (records affecting interest in property), 63(21) (judgments), 63(29) (recitals in documents affecting property), 63(32) (trustworthy statements made in good faith by declarants unavailable because of death). Uniform Rule 64, developed some time earlier, refers to fewer hearsay exceptions.

84. This technique of advance notice may also be useful in other areas, such as authentication of documents. See, *e.g.*, State v. Spreigl, 34 U.S.L.W. 2335 (Minn. S.C. Dec. 17, 1965) (proof of similar crimes shall not be received unless within a reasonable time before trial the state furnishes the defendant a statement of the offenses it intends to show he committed, described with the particularity required of an indictment, with certain exceptions); UNIFORM COMMERCIAL CODE § 2-723(3) (notice of intention to prove relevant prevailing price).

85. See Meyer, *Trial Observations*, Nassau Law., June 1965, pp. 3, 10-12; Weinstein, *Probative Force of Hearsay*, 46 IOWA L. REV. 331, 340 (1961).

more effective the possibility of searching cross-examination and the ferreting out of contradictory evidence, rules for advance warning increase protections against unreliability.

But there is a price to be paid for such warning devices—sanctions when the requisite notice is not given, extension of trials as more hearsay and rebutting evidence is admitted, and added wrangling and possible repeated trials when it is claimed that inadequate notice was given. Resources may be used less economically because of the increased length of trials and new trials resulting from inadequate notice. If the sanction for failure to notify is exclusion of the hearsay, truth finding may be disserved. If continuances are granted, trials may be lengthened or new trials required since the jury cannot be detained for any substantial period. Even if the rule works well, the burden on the opponent of gathering more evidence before trial will add to the expense of litigation.

Although the hearsay rule has its main justification in truth finding, some of its vitality is due to its psychic value to litigants, who feel that those giving evidence against them should do it publicly and face to face. This rationale seems to justify, in part, the constitutional analogue of the hearsay rule, the right to confrontation.[86] Constitutional limitations permitting a defendant to refuse to assist the state in convicting him may also inhibit the use of a rule on advance notice, unless, as should be the case, some separate rules in criminal and civil cases are acceptable to the draftsmen. To some extent—minor though it be—even extrinsic social policy is therefore involved in a restructuring of the hearsay rule.[87]

Another proposal for dealing with the hearsay problem is to grant the court a great deal of discretion to exclude or admit depending on the probative value of the evidence in the individual case. A contemporaneous affidavit from a disinterested minister who is an acute observer may be more useful than a dying declaration from a confused and vindictive deceased. If the desirability of introducing as much relevant evidence as may reasonably affect the trier's decision is accepted as an overriding guide, a general rule, incorporating a substantial element of judicial discretion, may be desirable and practicable.

Discretion does not, however, necessarily lead to greater admissibility— the individual judge may use his discretion to exclude. Moreover, discretion is often at war with predictability. Ease in prediction and application of rules is desirable in the case of any procedural rule. A rule successful in this respect assists in economizing resources since the lawyer will know what he must be

---

86. See Douglas v. Alabama, 380 U.S. 415 (1965); Note, *Preserving the Right to Confrontation—A New Approach to Hearsay Evidence in Criminal Trials*, 113 U. Pa. L. Rev. 741 (1965).
87. See Richardson, *Law and Policy: Emphasis on Exclusionary Rules of Evidence*, 53 Ky. L. Rev. 663, 664 (1965).

prepared to do at the trial. It also assists in inspiring confidence by insuring impartiality and can be easily applied without a great deal of thought.

An important function of litigation is to encourage repose among the litigants so that, once decided, disputes can be forgotten.[88] Generally, it would seem that most litigants feel more assurance with rules that allow free admissibility—and, therefore, with a less restrictive hearsay rule. A litigant who has been prevented from supporting his case, whatever the technical reason, is bound to feel dissatisfied. Allowing the introduction of evidence provides an opponent with little reason for feeling abused so long as he can tell his side of the story. As a general rule, then, allowing litigants to introduce hearsay relatively freely and to rely on hearsay, provided the opponent can call the declarant and otherwise attack him with a minimum of barriers, tends to tranquilize them. This truism is demonstrated repeatedly in magistrates' courts where a complaining witness pours out his heart to an attentive judge and then, having had his day in court, withdraws his complaint.

CONCLUSION

Draftsmen of new rules of evidence undertake a stimulating and challenging task. It is not possible to produce a system permitting facts to be found with any certitude. Nor is it possible to satisfy fully all the purposes served by our law of evidence since, in particular instances, a rule which aids one end will disserve another. In case of conflict, the court's truth-finding function should receive primary emphasis except when a constitutional limitation requires subservience to some extrinsic public policy. Pretrial discovery and notice provisions reduce the need for some of the exclusionary rules. These and other procedures, in addition to generally better educated juries, make possible the abandonment of some of the rules designed to prevent prejudice and misapprehension of probative value by triers.

That particular rules of evidence have only a marginal effect on the truth-finding ability of the courts ought not discourage draftsmen of new rules. Indeed, this knowledge allows some relaxation on their part. Since it is unlikely that the judicial system will crumble because of any decision they make about a rule, they may feel free to risk changes on the basis of less than complete certainty about how well the new rule will perform.

---

88. See Chafee, Book Review, 37 HARV. L. REV. 513, 519 (1924) ("a trial is not an abstract search for truth, but an attempt to settle a controversy between two persons without physical conflict") ; Hart & McNaughton, *Evidence and Inference in the Law*, in EVIDENCE AND INFERENCE 48, 53 (Lerner ed. 1959) ("this is a last ditch process in which something more is at stake than the truth").

Part V
Basic Concepts of the Law of Evidence

[18]

BASIC CONCEPTS OF THE LAW OF EVIDENCE

Part I—Historical Introduction

It may be said to be traditional for commentators on the English law of evidence to complain about its unsatisfactory character. Lord Mansfield's thesis that precedents do but serve to illustrate principles is said to be particularly inapplicable to this branch of the law, where it is alleged that there are multitudes of cases but few clearly enunciated principles.[1] It is submitted that perhaps the principal cause for this state of affairs is the failure to give adequate attention to the basic concepts which are required for the satisfactory elaboration and exposition of the rules of evidence. It is submitted, moreover, that there are but a few concepts underlying the law, and that their characteristics have already been discerned by writers on the subject : in particular they are described by Wigmore in his monumental treatise on *The Law of Evidence*.[2] It is the strange neglect in this country of American literature on the subject which justifies this article. In it an attempt is made to state the presuppositions for rational discussion of the law of evidence. This, it is considered, involves a scheme of four basic concepts. The scheme is the outcome of the work of many jurists, among whom Thayer and Wigmore are predominant, and its general adoption would help to eliminate much of the confusion which now exists.

Sketch of the Historical Development of Doctrine

A presupposition of discussion of the law of evidence is that courts of law are seeking to determine " facts " by means of " rational " processes. Early forms of procedure, such as trial by battle, by ordeal, by compurgation, in so far as they involved the determination of facts did so by divine guidance or in some arbitrary manner. These procedures were replaced by newer methods in which courts sought to apply laws to facts, and there was gradually developed a set of principles for the finding of facts. The rules of evidence which were thus brought into operation, like other rules of common law, were elaborated by busy judges in the course of deciding the issues brought forward by litigants. Indeed it

---

[1] A recent number of the L.Q.R. contains two repetitions of the complaint: Carter, 69 L.Q.R. at p. 80; Megarry, 69 L.Q.R. at p. 141.
[2] All subsequent references to Wigmore are to the third edition of his work; the first edition was published in 1904.

is reasonable to conjecture that judges have given much less time
to consideration of points of evidence than to questions of substantive law. The law of evidence has been in greater need of
systematisation by juristic commentary, and the need has not gone
entirely unsatisfied. The system of evidence has been derived from
judicial good sense and practical understanding,[3] but the judicial
work has been supplemented by juristic exposition of the principles
implicit in it.

The first substantial exposition of the law of evidence was by
Gilbert.[4] Though he prefaced his work with some considerations
derived from Locke's *Essay Concerning Human Understanding,*
they do not form the basis of his treatment [5] which, valuable as it
is, is largely a digest of case law. The one rule which is advanced
as a general principle of the law of evidence is the best evidence
rule. It is necessary to turn next to Bentham, whose *Rationale
of Evidence* was published in 1827. It is not concerned with the
principles of the English law of evidence, which he criticised as
being irrational,[6] but with the principles on which any law of
evidence ought to be based.[7] He did, however, use terms and
concepts which were subsequently adopted by Best in his treatment
of the English law. According to Bentham, the law of evidence
deals with " persuasion concerning the existence of . . . matter of
fact." He defines " facts " as " events or states of things," and
classifies them as either " primary " or " evidentiary." Evidence
is not conceived by Bentham as a concept employed only in courts
of law : on the contrary, he considers that we rely on evidence

---

[3] " A system of evidence like this, thus worked out at the forge of daily
experience in the trial of causes, not created, or greatly changed, until lately,
by legislation, not the fruit of any man's systematic reflections or forecast,
is sure to exhibit at every step the mark of its origin. It is not concerned
with nice definitions, or the exact academic operations of the logical faculty.
Its rules originate in the instinctive suggestions of good sense, legal experience,
and a sound, practical understanding."

Thayer, *Preliminary Treatise on the Law of Evidence*, p. 3. All subsequent references to Thayer are to this work.

Cf. p. 509: " Our law of evidence is a piece of illogical, but by no
means irrational, patchwork; not at all to be admired, nor easily to be
found intelligible, except as a product of the jury system, as the outcome
of a quantity of rulings by sagacious lawyers, whilst settling practical
questions, in presiding over courts where ordinary, untrained citizens are
acting as judges of fact."

[4] The first edition of Lord Chief Baron Gilbert's *The Law of Evidence* was
published in 1756. Morgan (62 Harvard L.R. p. 182, n. 5) says it was
written before 1726.

[5] *Cf.* Stephen who said " Gilbert's work . . . is founded on Locke's ' Essay '
much as my work is founded on Mill's ' Logic.' " *Digest of the Law of
Evidence* xii.

[6] " In the map of science, the department of judicial science remains to this
hour a perfect blank. Power has hitherto kept it in a state of wilderness;
reason has never visited it." *Works* (ed. Bowring) Vol. VI, p. 209.

[7] Accordingly he says " The species of reader for whose use this book is really
designed is the legislator." *Ibid.*, p. 209.

in all human activities, scientific and non-scientific. He defines " evidence " as " a word of relation " meaning " any matter of fact the effect, tendency or design of which, when presented to the mind, is to produce a persuasion concerning the existence of some other matter of fact." [8] In this definition " evidence " is equated with " evidentiary fact ": the " other matter of fact " evidenced by the " evidentiary fact " is, in Bentham's language, the primary fact. Bentham's distinction between " primary fact " and " evidentiary fact " is more generally expressed as the distinction between *factum probandum* and *factum probans*. The relation between the two has subsequently been called that of relevance. [9]

While Best adopted Bentham's basic notions, he rightly pointed out that Bentham was wrong in assuming that some unitary view of evidence, applicable " in all human activities, scientific and non-scientific," was capable of dealing with all problems of evidence in courts of law. He affirmed that there was a distinction between the approach required for any determination of facts by any human being—historian, scientist, judge, business man or ordinary citizen —and the qualified approach which courts of law must also adopt because of the conditions of litigation and the policies which courts of law carry out. This distinction gives rise to the concepts which he called " natural evidence " and " judicial evidence." He criticised Bentham for failing to consider the problem of " judicial evidence." He said that Bentham's work " embodies several essentially mistaken views relative to the nature of judicial evidence, and which may be traced to overlooking the characteristic features whereby it is distinguished from other kinds of evidence." [10] Best does not assert, however, that courts of law are concerned solely with " judicial evidence." In his view they have to take account of both " natural evidence " *and* " judicial evidence." He discusses the general problem of establishing facts by what he calls " historical proof ": this is the function of " natural evidence." Courts of law, however, have to take into account also many factors which give rise to " judicial evidence." The relation between the two is stated in a proposition which expresses the basic distinction from which the framework of concepts for the law of evidence is derived. " Judicial evidence is, for the most part, nothing else more than natural evidence, restrained or modified by rules of positive law." [11]

---

[8] *Ibid.*, p. 208.

[9] For a criticism of Bentham's introduction of psychological factors into the concept of relevance see *post*, p. 539.

[10] *Principles of the Law of Evidence*, Art. 34. The first edition was published in 1849. In the preface Best asserts that previous writers on evidence had produced but digests of case law: he was seeking to set out the principles behind the cases.

[11] *Ibid.*, Art. 34. There is no need for the qualification " for the most part."

Best did not make the distinction between natural evidence and judicial evidence the basis of his treatment of the law of evidence. The distinction, though not completely ignored, is little stressed in his subsequent exposition. The principle which he uses as the framework for the exposition is the one to which Gilbert had already attached importance, *viz.*, the best evidence rule. It is in the later work of Stephen and Thayer that basic importance is attached to the distinction; in their writings it is discussed in the language of " relevance " and " admissibility."

Stephen first published a theory about the nature of the law of evidence in 1872 in his *Introduction to the Indian Evidence Act*. But his views are best known from his very influential *Digest of the Law of Evidence*, which first appeared in 1876, and has been through many editions. In the *Digest* Stephen modified his first theory : and it is his revised theory which is stated here.[12] Stephen introduces the language and concept of " relevancy " by considering the various meanings of the word " evidence." He speaks of " the ambiguity of the word evidence (a word which sometimes means testimony and at other times relevancy)."[13] The ambiguity can be illustrated by sentences like " similar fact evidence is not generally evidence," " hearsay evidence is not evidence," but the concept of " relevancy " as used by Stephen is not sufficient to explain both those sentences. For Stephen " relevancy " is the principle of " natural evidence " of Best. Proffered testimony, he says, may not be given of facts which are not relevant to " facts in issue." This is a reference to the relation between the " evidentiary facts " and the " primary facts " of Bentham, a relationship not determined by law, but by " the common course

---

[12] All subsequent references to Stephen are to the 5th edition. The pagination of the introduction is, however, the same in subsequent editions. (The latest edition is the 12th revised, reprinted with additions, 1948. Thayer and Wigmore, in my submission, misinterpret Stephen's later thesis.

[13] p. xi. Four different meanings of the word " evidence " are listed by Stephen in *The Indian Evidence Act*. A distinction exists between testimony, the utterances of a witness, and the facts asserted in the testimony. The process of accepting a fact, (a), because it has been asserted by a witness merits examination, but discussion about evidence may not be concerned with this subject. Discussion is often concerned with the relation between (a), the fact asserted, and some other fact (b) which the proponent of the testimony is seeking to establish. Such discussion is concerned with the relevance of (a) to (b); it considers whether (b) can be inferred from (a) and assumes the inference of (a) from the testimony. The distinction between testimony and fact asserted by testimony is not considered, and the word evidence may be used to refer to both. Stephen says (p. 3) " It sometimes means the words uttered and things exhibited before a Court of Justice. At other times it means the facts proved to exist by those words or things, and regarded as the framework of inferences as to other facts not so proved."

of events," by science and "inductive logic."[14] Certain classes of facts, however, "which in common life would usually be regarded as falling within this definition of relevancy, are excluded from it by the Law of Evidence."[15] The four classes are similar facts, hearsay, opinion and character. The principle asserted by Stephen, though his formulation is not felicitously worded, is that evidence is generally receivable by courts if relevant, but that relevant evidence may not be received by virtue of " exclusive rules " of law. Unfortunately, Stephen adopted a terminology which has produced considerable confusion, and has obscured the nature of relevance and its relation to receivability. Where relevant evidence is excluded by a rule of law, he says that such evidence is " deemed to be irrelevant." We must turn to the United States for a clearer statement of the basic concepts of the law of evidence.

It was Thayer[16] who demonstrated most fully the basic distinction between the rejection of evidence by a court of law because of want of relevance, and the rejection of evidence, even though relevant, because of some specific policy of the law. He introduced the language which stresses the distinction by the use of the words " relevance " and " admissibility," language, which though widely used in England is not yet universally adopted here.[17] To indicate that the concept denoted by the term " relevance " was an extra-legal concept, the " natural evidence " and " historical proof " of Best, Thayer often employed as a synonym for " relevant " the phrase " logically probative." This phrase does carry out the purpose of its author, but may be misleading, and the term " relevant " is by itself adequate.[18] In Thayer's view, though the concept of relevance was a presupposition of a rational system of evidence, it was not the function of the law of evidence to determine

---

[14] " When the inquiry is pushed further and the nature of relevancy has to be considered in itself, and apart from legal rules about it, we are led to inductive logic, which shows that judicial evidence is only one case of the general problem of science." p. xii.

[15] p. xiv.

[16] Most of Thayer's work was originally published as separate essays in the *Harvard Law Review*: see Vols. 3–7 (1889–1893) and Vol. 12 (1898). The chapter in the *Preliminary Treatise* from which the majority of my quotations are taken is Chapter VI, which is entitled " The Law of Evidence and Legal Reasoning as Applied to the Ascertainment of Facts." This chapter had not been previously published in the *Harvard Law Review*.

[17] See for example Hammelman's criticism of the terminology employed by Nokes in " *An Introduction to Evidence* ": B.R. 16 M.L.R. at 256.

[18] " Logically probative " may indicate that relevance is an affair of deductive logic, which Thayer certainly did not think was the case. Wigmore substitutes the phrase " rationally probative." Either phrase is preferable to the misleading uses of the phrases " legally relevant " and " legally irrelevant." In *Noor Mohamed* [1949] A.C. at 194, Lord du Parcq ventured on some unhappy criticisms of the phrase " logically probative." These criticisms, and much subsequent juristic and judicial comment on them, appear to have been uttered in ignorance of the source and original significance of the phrase.

whether particular kinds of evidence were relevant or irrelevant. He characterised the function of the English law of evidence as being the formulation of rules for the exclusion of relevant evidence. However, he stated two principles connected with relevance which lie at the basis of the law of evidence. The first is the principle " which forbids receiving anything irrelevant, not logically probative." [19] The second is : " Unless excluded by some principle or rule of law all that is logically probative is admissible." [20]

Thayer excluded from the scope of the law of evidence some topics which other writers classified as belonging to it. Thus for Stephen " the most important of all questions that can be asked about the law of evidence " is " what facts are relevant? " [21] But for Thayer that question was for science, not for the *law* of evidence. He examined the nature of " admissibility " not " relevance," though, of course, it was one of his fundamental tenets that on the answer to Stephen's question depended the receivability of evidence. In a similar manner he considered the question " what are the facts in issue? " as lying outside the scope of the law of evidence, and depending on " substantive law or the law of pleading," though again he realised that on the answer to the question depended the receivability of evidence. [22] Wigmore, however, rightly considers it necessary to emphasise the distinction between (a) the rejection of evidence because it is not relevant to facts sought to be established thereby and (b) the rejection of evidence because it is not relevant to a fact in issue, two matters which were often confused. He distinguished the two by employing the name " materiality " in relation to the latter, reserving " relevancy " strictly for the former. [23] This is not the place to review Wigmore's many contributions to the law of evidence. In relation to basic concepts all that has to be added is that he differed from Thayer by asserting that judicial decisions on questions of relevance were as binding as other decisions of courts, so that for him " relevancy " was within the scope of the law of evidence.

The scheme of concepts that thus emerges in Wigmore is, at any rate so far as names go, a threefold one: the names used being relevancy, materiality and admissibility. The scheme

---

[19] It is this principle which he describes as being " not so much a rule of evidence as a presupposition involved in the very conception of a rational system of evidence." *Preliminary Treatise*, p. 265.

[20] *Preliminary Treatise*, p. 265.

[21] *Indian Evidence Act*, p. 4.

[22] " The greater part of statements denying admissibility to evidence are not related to these basic problems of relevance, but are really reducible to mere propositions of sound reason as applied to points of substantive law or pleading." *Preliminary Treatise*, p. 269.

[23] Vol. I, p. 7.

proposed in this article is a fourfold one, the extra term being
" receivability."

PART II—THE FOUR CONCEPTS

The logical derivation of the four concepts : Receivability

The brief historical sketch has indicated the evolution in juristic
writing of the basic concepts of the law of evidence. It is now
proposed, despite the repetition involved, to approach the question
of basic concepts in a synchronistic manner, amplifying somewhat
the examination of the concepts, though not attempting a complete
treatment of each. All that it is sought to do is to explain the
character of each concept; it is not sought to demonstrate the
various theorems concerning the matters to which these concepts
apply. It is hoped to show what " materiality " and " relevance "
are, not to propound theorems involving " materiality " and
" relevance," still less to establish rules for saying what particular
facts are material or relevant.[24] In this examination the " admissibility " of Thayer and Wigmore is resolved into two elements,
for one of which the term " admissibility " is retained, while the
other receives the name " receivability."

Writers are agreed that the law of evidence is concerned with
the procedure whereby courts of law determine the " facts " which
are in dispute. The term " facts " is in ordinary language possessed
of multiple meanings [25]: *e.g.,* Cohen and Nagel in their *Introduction
to Logic* list four different meanings.[26] Within the context of the
law of evidence the word is generally employed with the meaning
of discriminated parts of the totality of existence, sections of
history, empirical phenomena. Bentham's "events or states of
things " has been considered a satisfactory definition; it doubtless
is adequate if it be taken broadly to include properties of events
and things, such as shapes and colours, and relations between diverse
events and things, such as comparative size and spatial or temporal
order.[27] But even within the context of the law of evidence

---

[24] Compare Carnap's distinction between the classification of an *explicandum*
and the formulation of an *explicatum. Logical Foundations of Probability,*
arts. 2 and 3.

[25] " A word of universal use, carrying such different meanings, cannot be used
in rational thinking and argument without causing immense confusion. That
is why all who hope to use reason fruitfully must make it their first duty
to agree upon a clear definition of ' fact.' " Brown: 28 *Philosophy* 154.

[26] (1934), p. 217.

[27] The fourth category of Cohen and Nagel. is " those things existing in space
or time, together with the relations between them, in nature of which a
proposition is true. Facts in this sense are neither true nor false; they
simply are: they can be apprehended by us in part through the senses."
Epistemological questions are raised when this meaning of " fact " is compared with their first meaning which is " discriminated elements in sense

ambiguity exists, and it is important to distinguish between the use
of the term " fact " in Bentham's sense, and the use of the term
to denote a " proposition "; for example, a true proposition such
as " twice two are four " or " beer as a beverage is not necessarily
harmful." [28]   " Brute facts " must be distinguished from propositions of fact; and it is, moreover, necessary to distinguish between
a particular proposition of fact, one which asserts the past or
present existence of *a* fact,[29] and a general proposition of fact such
as a scientific law.[30]   The subjects of dispute between parties are
particular propositions of fact.   They are the issues : one party
asserts the truth of one or more particular propositions of fact, the
other enters a denial.   General propositions are the means which
may be invoked, explicitly or implicitly, in argument about particular propositions : they may be in issue, but they do not state
the facts in issue.   They determine whether evidence is relevant.

For a law of evidence to be " rational " the proof of the
particular proposition of fact containing the *factum probandum*
must be rational.   It is considered to be so if there is a rational
connection between the proposition containing the *factum probandum* and another proposition containing the *factum probans*, which
latter proposition is made self-evident by " evidence."   There is,
however, duality of meaning of the word " evidence," arising from
this rational character of litigation.   Parties who seek to establish
or deny facts in issue ask the court to receive " evidence " which
they tender : for example, they may proffer the testimony of a
witness.   It is, however, an important judicial function, performed
in English judicial administration by the judge, to say what tendered
evidence is to be received and relied on in the proof of facts in
issue.   The judge may say " You must not tell us what the soldier
said . . . it's not evidence."   The word " evidence " is sometimes
used to mean (a) " tendered evidence," statements of witnesses

---

perception." Lawyers do not usually distinguish between sense data and
things-in-themselves, between the "references" and "referents" of the
scheme of Ogden and Richards. But they are often concerned with the problem of discriminating between the totalities involved in sense perception.
The difficulty of defining "res gesta" is that of drawing boundaries between
"facts."

[28] The latter example is cited by Thayer as a "fact" of which a U.S. court
held it could take judicial notice. His thesis was that "judicial notice" was
often not concerned with the proof of "facts" but with judicial reasoning.

[29] Propositions asserting the future existence of a fact are in a separate category:
and their character is complex.

[30] Cohen and Nagel give as their second and third meanings of "fact":—
(2), "propositions which interpret what is given to us in sense experience.
This is a mirror." (3), "propositions which truly assert an invariable
sequence or conjunction of characters. *All gold is malleable.*"

or documents,[31] proffered by the parties and sometimes to mean (b) " received evidence," statements of facts which the courts receive in proof of facts in issue as being in accordance with the law of evidence.

Thus arises the basic concept of " receivability," which is that of tendered evidence being in accordance with the law of evidence. It follows, moreover, that " receivability " is a complex concept depending on the principles under which the rules of the law of evidence can be classified. The law of evidence is composed of various rules, and by virtue of its character of being a rational method of determining facts for the purpose of settling disputes and of being part of the legal system maintaining various public policies, the rules do not necessarily fall under a single principle. There are, it is submitted, three broad principles involving three further basic concepts. In the first place evidence is only received in proof of facts to which it is " rationally " related : this gives rise to the concept of " relevance." Secondly, evidence must be related to facts in issue before the court. Hence arises the concept of materiality. Furthermore, evidence may be excluded by reason of a rule of law taking note of the conditions of litigation or some specific policy of the law : there is, in other words, also the concept of admissibility. While it is possible to conceive of a system of law ignoring some of these concepts, English law does employ all three concepts. Before evidence is receivable it must in English law satisfy the conditions of each of these concepts : it must be relevant *and* material *and* admissible.

In Wigmore's scheme the word " admissible " has to perform the dual function of signifying both the specific concept denoted by admissibility in the present scheme, and the general concept of being in accordance with the law of evidence, which I call " receivability." In his terminology evidence is inadmissible if it is irrelevant. It is, however, important to distinguish the general concept from the specific elements of which it is composed, and to specify why evidence is not received. It is important to distinguish rejection of evidence for irrelevance from rejection for inadmissibility. This requires four terms. With this terminology it is possible to construct sentences such as the following which have significance and clarity. " Evidence, though relevant, is not receivable because it is not admissible." " Evidence, though

---

[31] It is not necessary for the present purpose to consider the nature of " real evidence," nor to comment on the difference between Bentham's definition of " evidence " as being " matter of fact " and Stephen's definition as being " statements made by witnesses in court " and " documents produced for the inspection of the court." This difference is referred to above in note 13.

admissible, is not receivable because it is not relevant to a material fact."

The significance of such sentences depends, of course, on the meaning of the terms used for the three concepts. The nature of these three concepts is now discussed.

Materiality

As has been stated, the concept of materiality was considered by Thayer as falling outside the scope of the law of evidence. This is, however, largely a matter of terminology and classification; as he admitted, questions of receivability do involve what is here called the concept of materiality. Other writers, such as Taylor,[32] have included it within the scope of evidence, and have applied the name " relevance " solely to it. Still others use the word " relevance " to apply to the two distinct concepts which Wigmore rightly separates by means of the terms " materiality " and " relevance." " The two problems," he says, " are wholly distinct, and yet the inaccuracy of our usage tends constantly to confuse them." [33]

Materiality of evidence signifies that the evidence is concerned with an issue before the court. The question of materiality is not whether the evidence is adequately related to the facts sought to be established thereby, but whether those facts are adequately related to the case made by the party. As Wigmore says, materiality defines " the status of the proposition " sought to be proved " to the case at large." [34] A court is not concerned with the entirety of history, but only with that section of it which is being litigated. An important branch of legal procedure is concerned with provisions requiring the parties to specify issues to be decided by the court. Such requirements may be detailed or general, rigid or flexible.

---

[32] See the index for the references to relevance, and note pp. 211 *et seq.*, particularly p. 222 (12th ed.).

[33] Vol. I, p. 7.

[34] The relativity of the concepts makes the difference between materiality and relevance less clear cut than might appear at first. Let fact T be the subject of tendered evidence, and let M be the fact it is sought thereby to establish. If, in the opinion of the court, T does not tend to establish M then the evidence is rejected as irrelevant, (i). If, however, T does tend to establish M the evidence may still be rejected. For M may be neither a fact in issue nor related to a fact in issue. If no one contends that M is related to a fact in issue then the rejection of T is classified without difficulty as an instance of immateriality, (ii). But it may be contended that M does tend to establish a fact in issue, I; in such a case the rejection of T where the contention is not accepted by the court presents difficulties of classification. It may be said to be an instance of immateriality, as in (ii) above. On the other hand, it may be said to be an instance of irrelevance; for though tendered to prove M directly it was tendered to prove I indirectly through M. The concept of relevance is usually applied to take note of the contentions of the proponents, so that the case is one of irrelevance. But this reduces considerably the area of materiality in practice.

In the course of the development of English law its requirements have varied considerably in character, and today they are more elaborate in civil cases than in criminal cases. These requirements determine what facts may properly be proved by the party who wishes to succeed in his claim or by the party who wishes to succeed in his defence. Unless evidence is concerned with establishing such facts it is not received: and the reason for rejection is usefully termed want of materiality.

Relevance

I propose in this section to attempt an elucidation of the concept designated by the use of the word " relevance " here proposed, and also to state a number of propositions about facts and litigation which embody the concept of relevance.

It is essential for the theoretical construction of possible systems of evidential rules, and for the critical evaluation of any actual legal system, to conceive of the relationship which facts have to each other in history itself, in the actual stream of events, aware, of course, of the limitations of man's knowledge of such matters. It is to such a conception that it is suggested the word " relevance " be limited. The concept of materiality derives from the division of history by the litigants into sections for investigation by the court, a division which takes note of the facts required by law to be established for a legal remedy to be granted or denied. It is concerned with the relation borne by the facts that those tendering evidence seek to establish " *facta probanda* " to the section of history thus constructed by the litigants, or, as Wigmore states, with their character in relation to the case as a whole. The concept of relevance is concerned with the relationship which the tendered evidence has to the fact it is sought thereby to prove because of the order of nature : it posits a " natural " connection between *factum probans* and *factum probandum*. Evidence is rejected as immaterial because the fact it is sought to establish is not by reason of the choice of the parties, and man-made rules of substantive law, an issue before the court. Evidence is rejected as irrelevant because it does not " prove " the fact it is sought to establish by reason of its natural, " historical," connection with that fact.

The determination of whether a particular fact is relevant, in the sense in which the word is here employed, is dependent on man's knowledge of historical relationships, a knowledge which includes the primitive science of inarticulate common sense as well as the formulated propositions of organised sciences. In order to

538   *The Law Quarterly Review*   [VOL. 70

make clear that the concept denoted by relevance was an extra-
legal (pre-legal might be a better term) notion of natural connection,
Thayer often used as a synonym the phrase " logically probative "
and Wigmore used the phrase " rationally probative." Stephen [35]
qualifies " proof " by the more empirical phrase " common course
of events " in his definition of relevance, but it is the same concept
that he designates. He says [36] : " The word ' relevant ' means that
any two facts are so related to each other that according to the
common course of events one, either taken by itself or in connection
with other facts, proves or renders probable the past, present or
future existence or non-existence of the other."

While enough has been said to explain the nature of relevance,
it is nevertheless desirable to state some propositions concerning
the application of the concept, if only to challenge a number of
misconceptions which are still often held. It is, however, not
possible here to do more than present a number of dogmatic
assertions. A much fuller exposition of the nature and operation
of relevance is required. It is also necessary to point out that no
examination, however full, of the nature of relevance, can ever
provide " practical help " to enable anyone to determine whether
one fact is relevant to another. Such an examination can only
indicate the nature of the factual inquiry which has to be conducted
in order to answer a problem of relevance. A definition propounded
by Stephen earlier than the one set out above has been wrongly
criticised for using terms which are not mechanically determinative
of a problem of relevance.[37] Such criticism is indicative of a lack
of understanding of the nature of both relevance and definitions.
No definition of relevance can set out the infinite number of
empirical propositions on whose existence the relevance of facts
depend.

The following theorems are, it is believed, true. (1) The relevance of facts depends on objective order, not on subjective beliefs.
(2) Relevance is an affair of science not of logic. (3) Relevance
involves probability not certainty. (4) Relevance is relative; there
is no relevance in the air. (5) The categories of relevance are
never closed : it is impossible to say *a priori* that fact A is not
relevant to fact B.

(1) Bentham employs the concept of relevance in his use of
the word " evidence." [38] In effect he says that one fact is relevant
to another if the effect or tendency of the former " when presented

---

[35] *Digest of the Law of Evidence, ante*, n. 12.
[36] p. 2.
[37] See Phipson's *Law of Evidence*, 9th ed., p. 48.
[38] See above, pp. 528, 529, and footnote 8.

to the mind, is to produce a persuasion concerning the existence of some other matter of fact." This is to base relevance on subjective attitudes, not on the objective order of things. It is true, of course, that the objective order of things is only known to us through subjective constructs, but, in so far as we are rational, we endeavour to relate our beliefs to a natural reality. The ordinary usage of the word " evidence " indeed provides often the touchstone to distinguish between the myths and illusions of men and the objective reality of history. Relevance is based on objective order not on psychological effect.[39] It is because the subjective attitudes of juries often incorrectly reflect the actual relationships between facts that much relevant evidence is excluded in law, and that judges withdraw from juries evidence which is not relevant.

(2) The connection between facts which gives rise to relevance is neither psychological nor logical. Of course, if the word " logical " is used in the wide sense of " valid thought " then no objection can be raised to statements such as " relevance is an affair of logic and not of law." But " logic " often refers to deductive logic, to logical entailment, and connotes certainty of relations between propositions. But relevance is concerned with relations between facts : and what mediates between the facts is an empirical proposition. The " logic " which is involved is inductive logic, the reasoning being the inference of science not the implication of logic.[40]

While relevance is an affair of science the matters of fact which come before courts of law range far beyond the boundaries of the organised sciences. The empirical propositions which are involved are rarely established in the recognised scientific departments : they are asserted by the primitive science of common sense, and, indeed, have only infrequently been made articulate outside courts of law. The presumptions of fact on which courts rely, and the generalisations about facts of which they take judicial notice, represent formulations based on common sense.

(3) Inasmuch as relevance is concerned with empirical facts the relation is one of contingency. Moreover, the common sense generalisations often resemble statistical " laws " of many of the

---

[39] Carnap has some valuable comments on psychologism in logic: see Arts. 11 and 12 *Logical Foundations of Probability.*

[40] The text incorporates, of course, Hume's theory, dealing with knowledge of facts, that " all the laws of nature . . . are known only by experience." The simplest statement by Hume of his theory is to be found in section IV of his *Enquiry.* It has been summarised by Ayer. " There can be no possibility of *deducing* the occurrence of one event from another. That the events are connected is a matter of fact, which is in no way necessary *a priori* . . . logical necessity is eliminated ": *British Empirical Philosophers,* p. 25. A Holmesian summary is that relevance is an affair not of logic but of experience.

sciences. There is no complete assurance that observed uniformities can be extended, and what is frequently observed is not uniformities but frequencies. A *factum probandum* cannot be established with absolute certainty. In order for *factum probans* to be relevant to *factum probandum* it is not necessary that the former should conclusively prove the latter.[41] Relevance is an affair of probability not of certainty.

(4) Though Bentham was wrong in introducing psychological factors into his treatment of " evidence," he was right in stressing the relativity of " evidence." " Evidence," *factum probans*, is always relevant to some *factum probandum*; there is no relevance " in the air." Evidence may be relevant to one fact and irrelevant to another; it may be relevant to many facts.

Where there are different issues evidence which is relevant to one issue may be irrelevant to others. It is a question of policy for each legal system whether to reject evidence which is relevant to one issue because it is irrelevant to a different issue. The English law of evidence does not reject evidence for such a reason; evidence is received if it be relevant to any issue irrespective of its relation to other issues.[42]

(5) The parallel with negligence can be taken one stage further. Just as it is true that there is no relevance in the air, so it is true that the categories of relevance are never closed. The relations between facts may be intricate and indirect. It cannot be laid down *a priori* that members of one class of facts are never relevant to members of another class of facts, or are only relevant in a limited number of ways. Everything depends on the circumstances. An instance of one kind of facts may be irrelevant in one set of circumstances to an instance of another kind of facts, and in different circumstances a similar instance of the former kind may be relevant to a similar instance of the latter kind. Another reason for the difficulty surrounding similar fact evidence has been a failure to realise the validity of the proposition that similar conduct

---

[41] Stephen's definition does suggest that *factum probans* may sometimes " prove " *factum probandum*. But what is often regarded as proof is only a high degree of probability.

[42] The topic of multiple issues though neglected by English writers is dealt with fully by Wigmore: see Vol. I, pp. 712 *et seq.* Evidence may be relevant to more than one *factum probandum* and on grounds of policy it may be irreceivable in respect of a particular *factum probandum*. It will, nevertheless, be received in proof of another *factum probandum*. Failure to appreciate the existence of this rule has given rise to much of the confusion about evidence of similar conduct. The rule was the basis of the decision in *Sims*, and was expressly affirmed in *Noor Mohamed* (see [1949] 1 All E.R. at 372A). Yet commentators said *Sims* was upset by *Noor Mohamed*!

may be relevant to *factum probandum* not only through disposition, but in an unlimited number of other ways.[43]

Admissibility

The concept of admissibility is essentially negative and exclusively legal. It implies the existence of " canons of exclusion," rules of law which say that evidence is not to be received even though it be both material and relevant. In the terminology here proposed, evidence is inadmissible if it be rejected for some reason other than immateriality or irrelevance : it is admissible if there is no rule for its rejection other than one dealing with materiality or relevance. It may be admissible and yet irreceivable, for it may be rejected because it is either immaterial or irrelevant. While the historian, for example, may take into account any evidence that is relevant a court of law must consider the public policy of the society of which it is an organ and the actual circumstances of its investigation. The possibility must be considered that a court of law may exclude material and relevant evidence. Thus state documents may be excluded on grounds of public policy, and evidence of only slight weight may be excluded because of the need for some measure of speed in litigation. The broad concept under which rules for such exclusion may be grouped is that to which I give the name " inadmissibility." I employ the word " admissibility " for the concept of the absence of an applicable rule of exclusion.[44]

---

[43] Just what the other ways may be has only recently been the subject of investigation: and needs further examination. In *Harris* Viscount Simon, commenting on the proposition 'of Lord Herschell in *Makin's* case that similar fact evidence may be relevant otherwise than through disposition, said " It is, I think, an error to attempt to draw up a closed list of the sort of cases in which the principle operates " ([1952] 1 All E.R. 1046G). But though the list must remain open there is no need for absence of distinction between the various kinds of relevance. In *Sims, Hall,* and *Straffen* different kinds of relevance have been confused with the specific kind of relevance through identification which occurred in *Thompson.* Carter in 69 L.Q.R. 80 adequately distinguishes relevance via disposition from relevance depending on some other factor. But in my view he has not adequately dealt with *Thompson.* The " correct explanation " is not that the disputed evidence was relevant " to establish identity "; this is much too vague and comprehensive a phrase, and indeed is little more specific than " to establish guilt," which provides no explanation at all: the correct explanation is that the evidence was relevant in corroboration of an act of identification, as stated by Lord Finlay [1918] A.C. at p. 225. The correct explanation of *Sims, Hall,* and *Harris* is that the evidence was relevant to indicate the single causal factor responsible for the pattern exhibited by diverse events, an explanation which requires further elucidation, some of which is provided by Russell in *Human Knowledge* at p. 482. The correct explanation of *Straffen* is that the evidence was relevant to establish a technique of action characteristic of one individual: this explanation is rightly suggested by Treitel in 16 M.L.R. at 74, but he is wrong in saying that the case involves a new departure.

[44] It is the existence of the concept of " admissibility " which makes " receivability " an instance of the class of " defeasible concepts " examined by Hart in *The Ascription of Responsibility and Rights* (being Chap. VIII of *Logic and Language* ed. Flew), see p. 148.

Thus, while the concept of relevance is one of fact, the concept of admissibility is one of law. For Thayer the distinction is not only fundamental, it has the result of confining the law of evidence to the concept of admissibility. He says : " The excluding function is the characteristic one in our law of evidence " : the laws of evidence are not, in his view, concerned with what is relevant, but what " among really probative matters shall for this or that reason be excluded." [45] Wigmore provides a corporeal demonstration of the distinction. He has written two separate works. *The Science of Judicial Proof* embraces the topic of relevancy and is largely a work of science, referring to few legal authorities. His multi-volumed *Treatise on the Law of Evidence* deals mainly with canons of exclusion, and abounds with citations of cases and statutes.

It is not the province of an explanation of the concept of admissibility to indicate the nature of "this or that practical reason," which is the basis of a rule of inadmissibility. Thayer was prepared to make a sweeping generalisation, and to say that the main reason for rules of exclusion was the existence of the jury. Experience had suggested to the judges that juries placed so much more weight on certain kinds of relevant evidence than they really merited that it was politic to exclude those kinds.[46] Hearsay evidence and character evidence were examples of such kinds. The rule recently laid down in *Harris* is a striking illustration of the operation of a principle of exclusion based on the reaction of a jury to evidence.[47] Wigmore considered that Thayer's generalisation was an over-simplification. It is submitted that the exclusion of character evidence, for example, is not solely due to a belief that juries give too much weight to such evidence—hang a dog because of a bad name—but is due in part to an appreciation

[45] This thesis cannot be sustained in its entirety. Even after separating from the mass of so-called presumptions those which are not " true " presumptions, but rules of substantive law or rules concerned with burden of proof, there remain those which are propositions concerned with the relevance of the facts they deal with. One aspect of this question is dealt with below, see p. 554.

[46] In *Doe* d. *Wright* v. *Tatham* Bosanquet J. said: " By the rules of evidence established in the courts of law, circumstances of great moral weight are often excluded, from which much assistance might be afforded in coming to a fast conclusion, but which are, nevertheless, withheld from a consideration of the jury upon general principles lest they should produce an undue influence upon the minds of persons unaccustomed to consider the limitations and restrictions which legal views upon the subject would impose " (1838) 7 A. & E., at 375.

[47] For the rule laid down in *Harris* see *per* Viscount Simon [1952] 1 All E.R. at 1048A. The following dictum supports the view of Thayer in relation to hearsay evidence. " In England where the jury are the sole judges of the fact, hearsay evidence is properly excluded because no man can tell what effect it might have upon their minds ": *per* Mansfield C.J., *Berkeley Peerage Case* (1811) 4 Camp. at 415.

by judges that Englishmen consider it a principle of justice to ignore character. Each rule of exclusion must be carefully related to the policy on which it is based, and such policies are in need of continuous examination. While definition of the concept of admissibility cannot provide a statement of such policies it does draw attention to their existence and emphasises the importance of the tasks just formulated. Much of the valuable work accomplished by American jurists dealing with the character and efficacy of the various rules of exclusion can be fairly said to derive from realisation of the distinctive character of the concept of admissibility.

Realisation of the policy behind a rule of exclusion helps to bring out the truth that while evidence may be inadmissible when tendered for one purpose it may, nevertheless, be receivable when tendered for another purpose in respect of which the policy of exclusion does not apply. Of course, in order that it should be receivable it would have to be relevant for the second purpose as well as for the first, but, as already seen, multiple relevance is not impossible. Similar conduct evidence furnishes many examples of the above proposition. An instance of such conduct may be relevant for many purposes, for example, to show disposition, to establish knowledge or intention, to corroborate identification, to establish a characteristic technique of action, to suggest the causal factor producing a sequence of similarly patterned events. Exclusion of such evidence for the purpose of proving disposition does not entail the consequence of exclusion also for the proof of other facts to which it may be relevant.

It is theoretically possible for a rule to make a particular kind of evidence inadmissible irrespective of the purpose for which it is tendered. Where the policy of a rule of exclusion is based on the effect produced on the jury then it may be reasonable to ignore such purpose. Whatever be the purpose for which the evidence is tendered, the effect may be of a kind it is desired to prevent. An example of such a general rule of exclusion is that affirmed in *Harris, viz.,* evidence may not be received, irrespective of purpose, if its effect in prejudicing the jury against the prisoner is considered as far outweighing the probative value of the evidence.[48]

---

[48] Authority for this rule is to be found in *Makin* as well as in *Christie* and *Noor Mohamed,* which were referred to by Viscount Simon. Twenty years ago Stone stressed the importance of excluding similar conduct evidence, even though relevant otherwise than via disposition, where its effect was too prejudicial:—his words were "where the peg is so small and the linen so bulky and dirty that a jury will never see the peg, but merely yield to indignation at the dirt." *Exclusion of Similar Fact Evidence,* 46 H.L.R. at 984.

PART III—THE UTILITY OF THE SCHEME OF CONCEPTS

It is believed that the existence and nature of the four concepts
have been made clear and an adequate terminology proposed. The
utility of the scheme of concepts has perhaps also appeared, but
further comment may be useful. In this comment attention is
drawn to the manner in which in past literature the concepts have
been confused and an inadequate terminology employed. It would,
perhaps, be more orderly to consider terminology and concepts in
the order hitherto followed, *viz.*, receivability, materiality, relevance,
admissibility. But the confusion between relevance and admissibility has in many ways been the most dramatic, despite the fact
that it was to the distinction between the two that Thayer directed
so much of his energy. I begin, therefore, with the importance of
distinguishing between relevance and admissibility.

Relevance and Admissibility

Failure to appreciate the distinct character of the two concepts
of relevance and admissibility has been the main reason for the
confusion surrounding the subject of similar fact evidence, and for
the many misinterpretations of *Makin* which have been entertained
for more than fifty years. The subject has been conceived in terms
of a general rule of undifferentiated irreceivability of similar fact
evidence irrespective of the purpose for which it is tendered,
subject to exceptions in specified cases. Considerable controversy
has surrounded the nature and principles of the exceptions. In
terms which distinguish between relevance and admissibility the
doctrine of similar fact evidence is clear. To be receivable similar
fact evidence must be relevant. Mere similarity does not result in
relevance, but similar conduct *may* be relevant in unlimited ways,
examples of which are given by Lord Herschell in *Makin*, *viz.*, to
show design or accident or to rebut a defence otherwise open to
the accused. Similar conduct is relevant where it shows disposition
or propensity,[49] but there is a rule of admissibility which denies
receivability to similar conduct tendered to show such disposition.
Thus, in criminal cases, in the words of Lord Herschell, similar
fact evidence is inadmissible where it is tendered to show " that

---

[49] I regard disposition and propensity as synonymous. For Carter " ' Disposition ' is assumed to differ in meaning from ' propensity ' in degree only "
(69 L.Q.R. at p. 83). I regard " character " as largely identical in meaning
with disposition, though it is often used to mean the totality of different
dispositions an individual has. Huxley gives to it a meaning equivalent to
disposition when he says " character is the sum of the tendencies to act
in a particular way " (*Evolution and Ethics*, p. 61). A reason why mere
similarity does not establish relevance is that a single act does not establish
disposition. A driver is not " accident-prone " because he has been involved
in a single accident.

the accused is a person likely from his criminal conduct or character to have committed the offence for which he is being tried." The rule of inadmissibility does not extend beyond evidence tendered to show disposition; evidence is receivable even though its *effect* is to establish disposition if tendered to prove some relevant fact other than disposition. Where, however, the effect of such evidence is to create prejudice out of proportion to the weight to be attached to the proof of relevant facts, it is a rule of practice not to receive it. These principles are implicit, and to a large extent explicit, in Lord Herschell's speech in *Makin*. The *locus classicus* for the analysis of that speech is Stone's article on the " Exclusion of Similar Fact Evidence." [50] The principles are implicitly affirmed by Lord du Parcq in *Noor Mohamed*,[51] and are authoritatively stated by Viscount Simon in *Harris*. However, it is not certain that there may not be fifty years of misunderstanding of that speech. The dust of controversy still surrounds the subject of similar fact evidence, and the air will not be cleared until clarifying concepts are more widely employed. It will then be seen that various tasks remain to be done : the policy of inadmissibility calls for investigation and elaboration ; the manner in which similar fact evidence may be relevant has to be considered, and the nature of the various modes of relevance stated.

Perhaps the most striking illustration in the realm of similar fact evidence of the confusion which has followed from the absence of recognition of distinguishing concepts is the misunderstanding which has surrounded *Sims*. In *Noor Mohamed* [52] Lord du Parcq, confronted apparently for the first time with Thayer's language in the judgment of *Sims*, subjected the passage containing that language to a criticism in which he committed the " entire misconception "

---

[50] 46 H.L.R. 975. The conclusion of his analysis is: " Here is no broad rule of exclusion with exceptions, but a broad rule of [receivability], except where the only relevance is via disposition ": p. 984.

[51] Attention is directed to one dictum : " If all that the court in *R.* v. *Sims* meant to say was that evidence of the kind specified in the first of the principles stated in *Makin's* case may be admitted if it is relevant for other reasons, then the dictum has no novelty " ([1949] 1 All E.R. at 372A). The court had indeed said this in *Sims*: " Evidence is not to be excluded merely because it tends to show the accused to be of bad character, but only if it shows nothing more " ([1946] K.B. at 537). Wigmore states the proposition in these terms: " The fact that a defendant's act of misconduct could be inadmissible as showing his bad character does not in the slightest stand in the way of receiving the same acts in evidence if they are evidential for some other purpose " (Vol. I, p. 712). The view that evidence relevant otherwise than through disposition is not to be received because its effect may be to show disposition is called by him a fallacy, and he adds: " No fallacy has been more frequently or more distinctly struck at by denial, by argument, by explanation on part of the courts. It has been rebuffed, rebuked, repudiated, discredited, denounced so often that it ought by this time to be abandoned forever."

[52] [1949] A.C. at 194; [1949] 1 All E.R. at 371.

against which Wigmore had warned.[53] This misled one writer
into saying that *Sims* had been disturbed [54]; another writer implied
that the judgment in *Sims* was nonsensical.[55] *Sims* has been
approved in *Hall* and *Harris*: but misunderstanding still exists and
appears in the textbooks. In Nokes' admirable *Introduction to
the Law of Evidence* he says that the dicta in *Sims* " reverted to
the older law, reversing the approach to this subject of the last
hundred years, by laying down that evidence of similar fact was
relevant and admissible unless there was some ground for
exclusion." [56] This is erroneous. *Sims* does not lay down the
principle that all similar fact evidence is relevant : this is the entire
misconception of Lord du Parcq. It expressly affirms the hundred-
year-old rule that evidence to show disposition is inadmissible.
It is made clear that similar fact evidence must be relevant before
it can be received. The principle on which *Sims* proceeds is that
there is no rule of exclusion of similar fact evidence which is relevant
otherwise than through disposition; there is here " no novelty,"
no new approach.[57]

The value of the distinction between relevance and admissibility
is by no means confined to the topic of similar fact evidence. One
general value is that it keeps a concept of fact distinct from a
concept of law. One of the great sources of fallacious reasoning
in the law is the use of concepts which confuse law and fact, so
that policies are not clearly revealed. A principle of legal policy
that certain kinds of evidence should not be received by the courts
may be concealed by statements which suggest that the evidence
is not being received because it has no worth measured by extra-
legal standards. The policy behind the exclusion of hearsay evidence is not discussed so long as hearsay is thought of only by
means of notions which do not ask whether it is relevant and why
it is inadmissible.

---

[53] " This principle does not mean that everything which has probative value
is admissible: this would be an entire misconception " (Vol. I, p. 293). The
principle referred to is that evidence must be relevant before it can be
received.
[54] Hammelman, 12 M.L.R. 232.
[55] Seaborne Davies: 1951 J.S.P.T.L. at 432.
[56] p. 89.
[57] The pessimistic statement in the text that *Harris* may be misunderstood for
the same length of time as *Makin* is confirmed by a review of Nokes'
Evidence, which not only accepts Nokes' statement about *Sims* but says that
Harris rejected the approach approved in *Sims*: see Armitage, B.R. 1952,
J.S.P.T.L. p. 58. Lord Oaksey in *Harris* expressly approved of the approach
in *Sims* (expressly disagreeing with Lord du Parcq): see [1952] 1 All E.R.
at 1052D. Viscount Simon makes express reference to the " approach," but
does not disapprove. He merely refers to the possibility of misunderstanding
the language: see [1952] 1 All E.R. at 1049 F and H. He fails to distinguish the questions of materiality and relevance which were confused in
Sims (see below, p. 549). He expressly approves of the conclusion of *Sims*.

Current Terminology : Relevance and Admissibility

One of the reasons for the lack of recognition of the distinct concepts of relevance and admissibility is to be found in current terminology.   Powell states that relevancy is concerned with " what facts a party will be allowed to prove at the trial of any legal proceeding," [58] and Cockle likewise uses the term in a manner which fails to make any distinction between materiality, relevancy and admissibility.[59]   Taylor uses the word " relevancy " to denote " materiality," and Roscoe ignores both the word and the concept.[60]

Stephen was aware of the distinction between the concepts of relevance and admissibility, but, unfortunately, he used a terminology which blurred the distinction.   For the concepts of admissibility and inadmissibility he used the phrases " deemed to be relevant " and " deemed to be irrelevant."   These do not clearly manifest his intention : for Stephen " deemed to be irrelevant " meant " though relevant, nevertheless to be rejected as if it were irrelevant."   Isolated from a context, however, the phrase " deemed to be irrelevant " may well be taken to mean " adjudged to be irrelevant," so that the phrase " evidence is deemed to be irrelevant " may be taken to assert that evidence is rejected because of want of relevance.[61]   Nor did Stephen always supply an adequate context.   Moreover, the phrases are sometimes abbreviated in Stephen's own *Digest* to the words " relevant " and " irrelevant." The texts which contain the propositions hearsay and character are " deemed to be irrelevant " appear under the headings " Hearsay irrelevant except in certain cases "; " Character generally irrelevant." [62]   It is not surprising that law students and others have taken their language and ideas from the headings and not from the text.[63]

---

[58] *Law of Evidence*, 10th ed., p. 3.

[59] *Cases and Statutes on Evidence*, 5th ed., p. 58.

[60] *Digest of the Law of Evidence*.

[61] Lord du Parcq, when he used the phrase " deems to be irrelevant," meant thereby " considers to be irrelevant." The dictum in which he uses the phrase is this " The expression ' logically probative ' may be understood to include much evidence which English law deems to be irrelevant." The passage in *Sims*, criticised in this dictum of Lord du Parcq, stated that " logically probative evidence might be excluded." His dictum would have been pointless if all he meant by " deems to be irrelevant " was " may be rejected."

[62] Headings (i) to Chap. IV (ii) to article 55.

[63] Nokes, like Stephen, is aware of the distinction between relevance and admissibility, but adopts a terminology which does not adequately bring out the distinction. Hammelman rightly criticises him for such phrases as " irrelevant facts may be admissible " (B.R. 16 M.L.R. 256). See also *post*, note 77.

Receivability and Admissibility

According to Hammelman [64] the term "admissible" has a "strictly technical sense." I do not agree. Current terminology uses "admissible" and "inadmissible" sometimes as general terms denoting receivability and non-receivability, and sometimes as specific terms, opposed to relevant and irrelevant, denoting absence and existence of rules of exclusion of relevant evidence. In current terminology, whether evidence is rejected on the ground of irrelevance, or whether it be rejected on the ground that it offends a canon of exclusion, it is said to be inadmissible. Both what the soldier said about battles long ago which are like the flowers that bloom in the spring, and what he said about the fight which is subject of the proceedings for assault, are classified as inadmissible. It is true that the context often makes it clear how the term is used, but the adoption of a terminology of "receivability" and "admissibility" avoids ambiguity. Appreciation of the distinction between the concepts makes it clear that rules exist for the exclusion of evidence which is material and relevant, and emphasises the need for examination of the policy of exclusion of such evidence.

Materiality and Relevance

The distinction between the two concepts is not always clearly stated and confusion is sometimes the source of error. *Sims* provides an illustration of such an error. The question of joinder before the court depended on the receivability on a charge of sodomy of evidence of other acts of sodomy. The court held that the evidence was relevant otherwise than through disposition, and was, accordingly, receivable. In giving judgment the court said: "If one starts with the general proposition that all evidence that is logically probative is admissible unless excluded, then evidence of this kind does not have to seek a justification, but is admissible irrespective of the issues raised by the defence." [65] (In my discussion of this dictum I translate the court's language into my terminology. I substitute "relevant" for "logically probative" and "receivable" for "admissible.") The argument of the dictum is as follows. (i) All evidence that is relevant is receivable unless there is a specific rule of exclusion. (ii) As a consequence, since the evidence of the other acts of sodomy is relevant, it is receivable irrespective of the issues raised by the defence. Lord du Parcq singled out the first proposition for attack. In my opinion, the target he selected was not vulnerable to the weapons he employed.

---

[64] 16 M.L.R. 257.
[65] [1946] K.B. at 539. The judgment was read by Lord Goddard C.J., but was largely prepared by Denning J.: see p. 535.

The dictum as a whole, however, is vulnerable, for it contains a *non sequitur*, and the first proposition, moreover, can be criticised for failure to take note of the necessity of materiality. Relevancy is a relative term; evidence is not just relevant " in the air," it is relevant to some fact, and if the evidence is to be receivable the *factum probandum* must be a fact in issue, or the evidence will be rejected as immaterial. What is in issue depends on principles other than those of relevance : it may well depend in a criminal trial on the issues raised by the defence. The question depends on consideration of rules relating to materiality not relevance. It is true that Viscount Simon has said that where the accused has pleaded " Not Guilty " in a criminal trial issues exist irrespective of the particular issues raised by the defence, and that the evidence in *Sims* was relevant to an issue of this kind, and so was receivable irrespective of the issues raised by the defence.[66] But the agreement with the conclusion does not establish the validity of the reasoning in the passage quoted from *Sims*. Viscount Simon supplied the missing premiss dealing with materiality. His judgment confirms the importance of careful attention to the distinction between the concepts of materiality and relevance.[67]

Part IV—The Actuality of the Concepts

Theoretical Exclusion of Concepts

The scheme of concepts displayed in this article has been suggested by English law, just as concepts of straightness, lines and angles may be suggested by a roughly drawn triangle. The scheme has been presented as an ideal scheme, as a theoretical framework for any " rational " system of law. It has not been fully established that the concepts do actually lie behind the rules of English law, though it has been claimed that they may be employed in the juristic exposition and criticism of English law. In the section dealing with the utility of the concepts it has indeed been assumed that they are embodied in English law. It is worth while, however, considering the scheme as one of possibilities and not as realised actualities, and to consider the nature of a system of evidence which did not exemplify all the concepts.

It is possible for a legal system not to make use of the concept

---

[66] [1952] 1 All E.R. at 1049H and 1050B.
[67] The fallacy pointed out in the text exists only if the " condemned " passage be read in isolation. The passage is followed by one treating of relevance in relation to facts in issue, and the court itself supplied the missing premiss by asserting that the evidence was relevant to an issue with which the court had to deal irrespective of the nature of the defence. Nevertheless, there is a fallacy in the passage which it is believed would have been avoided had the distinction between materiality and relevance been more generally recognised.

of materiality. That concept would have no actuality in a system which permitted litigants once they were before the court to range over every topic that occurred to them. Such a system might also require the court to remedy all grievances which were established, irrespective of whether they formed part of the original complaint. The efficiency of a society where such a system existed might well be doubted.

It is possible for a legal system to ignore the concept of relevance. It might do so completely by providing for the proof of facts by arbitrary rules. It might do so partly by the use of a " tariff " of evidence, requiring specified modes of proof for various kinds of fact. In such systems the time spent in litigating each case might be reduced, but there might well be lack of confidence in the judicial process, producing harmful social consequences outweighing the social gain of reducing unproductive energy-consumption. Such legal systems would not be termed " rational."

Finally, it is possible for a legal system to ignore the concept of admissibility. This would be the case if it were provided that all evidence that was material and relevant was *ipso facto* receivable. This indeed was the situation at Nuremberg, where the Tribunal was directed " to admit any evidence which it deems to have probative value." It is clearly debatable whether under such a system the time spent in litigation would be increased or decreased.[68]

English Law : Materiality and Admissibility

It is unnecessary to cite authority to show that in English law litigation is confined to particular issues. The Judicature Act has widened the number of issues that may be brought before courts, and simplified the manner in which they may be presented. Issues, however, have still to be specified. The case of the general issue which survives in the plea of " Not Guilty " in criminal trials may, however, still require clarification.

It is equally unnecessary to cite authority to show that there are rules for the exclusion of material and relevant evidence. The topic of privilege embodies the notion of admissibility. It is perhaps necessary to reiterate that the exclusion of hearsay and character evidence depends on the concept of admissibility, for there are still some who regard such evidence as irrelevant. Viscount

---

[68] Art. 19 of the Charter of the International Military Tribunal reads in full: " The Tribunal shall not be bound by any technical rules of evidence. It shall adopt and apply to the greatest possible extent expeditious and non-technical procedure, and shall admit any evidence which it deems to have probative value." It is not surprising to find that Lord Oaksey, who was a member of the Tribunal, found nothing wrong with the language of the judgment in *Sims*.

Simon has said that they are relevant,[69] but subsequent to his judgment Devlin J. has repeated the view that character evidence is irrelevant.[70]

English Law : Relevance

It is submitted that Thayer's two basic principles are principles of English law. The first is the negative principle, that no evidence is receivable unless it is relevant; the second is the positive principle, that all evidence that is relevant is receivable unless excluded by a rule of admissibility.

The negative principle

A particular instance of the general principle is stated by Viscount Simon in *Harris* : " Evidence of ' similar facts ' cannot in any case be admissible to support an accusation against the accused unless they are connected in some relevant way with the accused and with his participation in the crime." [71] An excellent illustration is afforded by the case of *Maxwell*.[72] The case was concerned with the application of the statutory provision in the Criminal Evidence Act, 1898, that a prisoner " shall not be asked any question . . . unless . . ." [73] It was held that this provision was not the equivalent of a provision that " a prisoner may be asked questions . . . if . . ." Consequently the fact that the statutory conditions had been fulfilled did not result in absolute

---

[69] *Harris* [1952] 1 All E.R. at 1049G. The relevance of hearsay evidence is discussed by Baker, *Hearsay Evidence*, p. 13: see also the dicta of Bosanquet J. and Mansfield C.J. cited in notes 46 and 47.

[70] " It is not normally relevant to inquire into a man's previous character, and particularly, to ask questions which tend to show that he has previously committed some criminal offence. It is not relevant because the fact that he has committed an offence on one occasion does not in any way show that he is likely to commit an offence on a subsequent occasion. Accordingly, such questions are in general inadmissible, not primarily for the reason that they are prejudicial, but because they are irrelevant " (*Miller* [1952] 2 All E.R. at p. 668H). There is *non sequitur* in this argument. An isolated previous offence may be irrelevant, but " character " depends on more than a mere isolated act. The strongest dictum asserting the irrelevance of character evidence is that by Lord Summer in *Thompson* (13 Cr.App.R. at p. 78): " No one doubts that it does not tend to prove a man guilty of a particular crime to show that he is the kind of man who would commit a crime, or that he is generally disposed to crime or even to a particular crime." It is submitted that this is contrary to the commonsense view that character is a reliable test of conduct.

[71] [1952] 1 All E.R. at 1048E: see also *per* Lord Oaksey at 1052D.

[72] [1935] A.C. 317.

[73] " A person charged and called as a witness . . . shall not be asked, and if asked shall not be required to answer, any question tending to show that he has committed or been convicted of or been charged with any offence . . . unless : —

    (i) the proof that he has committed . . . such other offence is admissible evidence . . .

    (ii) he has . . . asked questions of the witnesses for the prosecution . .

    (iii) he has given evidence against any other person . . ."

—s. 1 (6) Criminal Evidence Act, 1898.

permission to ask the questions; there might be common law conditions which had to be fulfilled. The question whose validity was challenged was whether the prisoner had been previously charged with a similar offence. This was one of the questions which the statute said could not be asked unless certain conditions were fulfilled. Those statutory conditions had been fulfilled in this case. It was clear, as a matter of statutory interpretation, that the effect of the statute was that if those conditions were fulfilled the common law rule of exclusion of character evidence did not apply. But the overriding rule that evidence must be relevant before it can be received was not affected by the statute. In the circumstances of the case it was considered that the fact that the prisoner had previously been charged with a similar offence and acquitted could have no bearing on the issue of the commission of the offence on which he was arraigned.[74] Such evidence was irrelevant, and the question accordingly improper. Thus the court in effect interpreted the statute as dealing with the problem of admissibility, and affirmed the negative principle that no evidence can be received unless it is relevant.

The positive principle

As has already been seen, the positive principle, that all evidence that is relevant is receivable unless excluded, was expressly accepted by the court in *Sims*. There it was stated in these terms : " All evidence that is logically probative is admissible unless excluded." The manner in which this dictum has been criticised would appear to demonstrate that the positive principle is no self-evident and universally recognised principle of English law. That it is not self-evident is confirmed by Stephen's account in the introduction to his *Digest*[75] of his discovery of the principle. In effect he claims to have been the first to have realised that such a principle was the " unexpressed principle which forms the centre and gives unity to . . . the great bulk of the Law of Evidence." How far the principle has been recognised in England since Stephen wrote is doubtful, though there has been no adverse reaction to Stephen. Criticism in England has been directed to his definition of relevance in terms of cause. In America the positive principle has, of course,

---

[74] In accordance with the doctrine of relativity of relevance, it does not follow that evidence of a previous charge that resulted in acquittal is always irrelevant. In *Waldman* (24 Cr.App.R. 204) the prisoner was charged with receiving stolen goods from X. Evidence that he had previously been charged with receiving stolen goods from X was held receivable, even though he had been acquitted. The evidence was relevant to the fact of the prisoner's knowledge that X was a thief, and that fact was relevant to knowledge of the goods being stolen goods.

[75] pp. xi and xii.

been approved, and Stephen is criticised for failure to state it
clearly, and to distinguish between relevance and admissibility.

The popularity of Stephen's *Digest* suggests that the principle
is accepted in England. In the two works on Evidence written in
England since Stephen, the principle, though far from being emphasised, is adopted. Phipson does so expressly,[76] and Nokes does so
implicitly.[77] If the principle is accepted, why the criticism of its
statement in *Sims*? It may be that Viscount Simon is correct
and that criticism is concerned with the language of the formulation
of the principle, *viz.*, with the phrase "logically probative." [78]
Further explanations reconciling criticisms with acceptance of the
principle are these : (i) The context in *Sims* appears to suggest
there is a denial of the rule that evidence tendered to show disposition is inadmissible. The criticism says this denial is wrongful.
(ii) The context appears to suggest that there is a denial of Lord
Sumner's doctrine, laid down in *Thompson*,[79] that the prosecution
has no right " to credit the accused with fancy defences " in order
to adduce evidence that would otherwise be irreceivable. The
criticism considers such denial wrongful. If these explanations be
correct then the criticism is directed not at the particular dictum
setting out the principle but at the fallacy in the passage as a
whole,[80] and does not impugn Thayer's positive principle.

However, as already explained in Part III, an important factor
in the misunderstanding of *Sims*, one which may have affected the
general acceptance of the positive principle, is the lack of clear
recognition of the distinction between the concepts of relevance and
admissibility, which lack has been aided by the want of adequate
terminology. If these deficiencies are overcome no citation of
specific judicial authority is required for the positive principle,
which has been asserted to be a principle of English law by Best
and Stephen, by Thayer and Wigmore. Nevertheless, *Harris* and
Makin should perhaps be cited.

Harris contains a dismissal of the criticism to which the dictum
in *Sims* was subjected. Viscount Simon reduces the criticism to a
comment on the phrase "logically probative." Lord Oaksey's
judgment approves of the " approach " in *Sims* and of the " general

---

[76] English ed., p. 94.
[77] Chap. V *passim*: and in particular at p. 69. Nokes' qualifications are
basically terminological. In my view, when he says " irrelevant facts may
be admissible " (p. 70) he means facts indirectly relevant. He elsewhere
specifically accepts Thayer's negative principle that evidence must be relevant:
see pp. 15 and 68. It is unfortunate that he conceives of " logic " solely in
terms of deduction.
[78] [1952] 1 All E.R. at 1049F.
[79] [1918] A.C. at p. 232.
[80] See above, pp. 548, 549.

rule of admissibility " [81] stated in *Sims*. It is to be noted that his dissent is not from the general principles of evidence approved by the other members of the House of Lords but only with their application to the facts of *Harris*.[82]

Makin is an application of the general principle of relevance to the specific instance of similar fact evidence. The crucial passage in Lord Herschell's opinion is : " The mere fact that the evidence adduced tends to show the commission of other crimes does not render it inadmissible if it be relevant to an issue before the jury." [83] This is followed by a passage, giving some examples of relevant evidence. It is preceded by a passage stating that evidence tendered *for the purpose* of showing disposition is inadmissible. The major premiss behind the paragraph as a whole is that where any evidence is relevant it is receivable except where there is a specific rule asserting inadmissibility. This is the positive principle of Thayer.

PART V—LEGAL RELEVANCE AND LEGAL IRRELEVANCE

Though the concept of relevance is an extra-legal one, what is relevant being dependent on the order of nature not on the policy of lawyers, it is, nevertheless, necessary for courts to judge whether tendered evidence is relevant or irrelevant. Since courts of law are human institutions, it is possible for them to err. Judges may find that tendered evidence is relevant when the better judgment is that it is irrelevant, and, vice versa, they may find that such evidence is irrelevant when the better judgment is that it is relevant. The problem that arises for consideration is whether decisions of courts of law on questions of relevance are binding on subsequent courts of law.

On this matter Thayer and Wigmore differ. Wigmore maintains that the area of the doctrine of precedent includes the field of relevance.[84] According to this view, if a court holds that fact x

---

[81] [1952] 1 All E.R. at 1052D.

[82] Lord Oaksey thought that the evidence was relevant otherwise than through disposition, and important enough not to be excluded by the rule of practice excluding evidence over-prejudicial in relation to its weight. He thought that the other members of the Lords also considered the evidence relevant otherwise than through disposition, but slight enough to be caught by the rule of practice. His words were " As I understand it your Lordships are of opinion that the evidence . . . was relevant, but so slightly relevant that it should have been excluded " ([1952] 1 All E.R. at 1052E). Unfortunately, it is not absolutely clear that this is the correct view of the majority speeches. There was, however, no dissent from his statement.

[83] [1894] A.C. at p. 65.

[84] Vol. I, p. 298. " So long as courts continue to declare in judicial rulings what their notions of logic are, just so long must there be rules of law which must be observed. For these rules the only appropriate place is the law of evidence." He cites in support of his view the dictum of Cushing C.J. in *State* v. *Lapage*, 57 N.H. 288, that " the subject of the relevancy of testimony has become . . . matter of precedent and authority."

is relevant to fact y, and x is an instance of class X, while y is an instance of class Y, then the proposition " facts of class X are relevant to facts of class Y " is a proposition of law. If in a later case counsel tender fact x, to prove fact y, the court is bound to hold that it is relevant. According to Thayer, the doctrine of precedent is inapplicable since relevance is not an affair of law. " The law has no orders for the reasoning faculty, any more than for the perceiving faculty—for the eyes and ears." [85]

In my opinion, the teaching of Thayer is the sounder : *ex facto non oritur jus*. Courts of law ought not to stand committed to theories about natural happenings and human behaviour that have been discarded by science and common sense. But the possibility of courts considering themselves bound by decisions as to relevance or irrelevance cannot be ignored : and indeed courts do, in fact, consider themselves bound. Thus arise concepts of general legal propositions of relevance and irrelevance. These can be distinguished by the names " legal relevance " and " legal irrelevance." These names, however, suffer from the defect that they may suggest that there is a different concept of relevance employed in courts of law from that employed outside courts of law. Thayer has warned against " the common but uninstructive distinction between legal and logical relevance." Those who make that distinction mean by " logical relevance " nothing but relevance, and by " legal relevance " reference is made to admissibility. By " legal relevance " in the terminology here proposed is indicated a combination of precedent and relevance—a concept that a court of law is bound by a finding of an earlier court law about a question of relevance.

J. L. Montrose.

---

[85] 14 H.L.R. 139. This sentence occurs in a reply made by Thayer to a criticism expressed by Fox of Thayer's doctrine that relevance is not an affair of law. Thayer makes a half-concession to his critic. He says that decisions as to relevance " may stand as a precedent to half-settle other cases."

[19]

Relevancy, Probability and the Law

*George F. James**

SINCE scholars first attempted to treat the common law of evidence as a rational system, relevancy has been recognized as a basic concept underlying all further discussion. Thayer gave this recognition its classic form:

> "There is a principle—not so much a rule of evidence as a presupposition involved in the very conception of a rational system of evidence, as contrasted with the old formal and mechanical systems —which forbids receiving anything irrelevant, not logically probative."[1]
>
> "The two leading principles should be brought into conspicuous relief, (1) that nothing is to be received which is not logically probative of some matter requiring to be proved; and (2) that everything which is thus probative should come in, unless a clear ground of policy or law excludes it."[2]

The proposed *Code of Evidence* of the American Law Institute (hereinafter referred to as the Code) substantially follows Thayer.[3]

Early attempts to state the requirements of relevancy were confused and fragmentary, but in the suggested rules, and even more in the suggestive illustrations, the germ of modern doctrine—both sound and fallacious—may be found. Thus Phillipps, writing in 1814, stated five primary general rules governing the testimony of witnesses, of which the first was that "Evidence must be confined to the points in issue".[4] The author then expanded and illustrated this general rule, saying in part

> "And, first, as the intent of evidence is to ascertain the truth of the several disputed facts or points in issue, either on one side or the other, no evidence ought to be admitted to any other point. Thus,

*Associate Professor of Law and Assistant Dean, University of Chicago Law School; Ph.B., J.D., University of Chicago; LL.M., Columbia University. Author of articles in various legal periodicals.

[1] THAYER, A PRELIMINARY TREATISE ON EVIDENCE AT THE COMMON LAW (1898) 264.

[2] *Ibid.* at 530.

[3] " 'Relevant evidence' means evidence having probative value upon any material matter and includes opinion evidence and hearsay evidence." " 'Material matter' means a matter the existence or non-existence of which is provable in the action." "...all relevant evidence is admissable." CODE OF EVIDENCE T. No. 2 (Am. L. Inst. 1941) Rules 1(10), 1(7), 9(f).

[4] PHILLIPPS, EVIDENCE (1814) 69.

for example, in an action of debt upon a bond, if the defendant pleads non est factum, (which puts in issue whether it be the defendant's deed or not), he cannot give a release in evidence. Nor, in an action of trespass for an assault and battery, will the defendant be allowed to prove, under the general issue, that he was first assaulted by the plaintiff. For the same reason, it would not be allowable to shew, on the trial of an indictment, that the prisoner has a general disposition to commit the same kind of offence as that charged against him. Thus, in a prosecution for an infamous crime, an admission by the prisoner that he had committed such an offence at another time and with another person, and that he had a tendency to such practices, ought not to be admitted. So, when a right is claimed by custom in a parish, proof of a similar usage in an adjoining parish, is not evidence of the custom. But where all the manors within a certain district are held by the same peculiar tenure, and a question arises, in any one of the manors, upon an incident to the tenure, evidence may be given of the usage which prevails in any of the other manors within the district."[5]

Phillipps' illustrations bring out a double meaning in the requirement of relevancy which continues in the modern statements and tends to produce confusion in the cases. Relevancy, as the word itself indicates, is not an inherent characteristic of any item of evidence but exists as a relation between an item of evidence and a proposition sought to be proved. If an item of evidence tends to prove or to disprove any proposition, it is relevant to that proposition. If the proposition itself is one provable in the case at bar, or if it in turn forms a further link in a chain of proof the final proposition of which is provable in the case at bar, then the offered item of evidence has probative value in the case. Whether the immediate or ultimate proposition sought to be proved is provable in the case at bar is determined by the pleadings, by the procedural rules applicable thereto, and by the substantive law governing the case. Whether the offered item of evidence tends to prove the proposition at which it is ultimately aimed depends upon other factors, shortly to be considered. But because relevancy, as used by Thayer and in the Code, means tendency to prove a proposition properly provable in the case, an offered item of

---

[5] *Ibid.* Peake, on whose text Phillipps greatly relied, had said in 1801, "Another rule is, that the evidence must be applied to the particular fact in dispute; and therefore no evidence not relating to the issue, or in some manner connected with it, can be received; nor can the character of either party to a civil cause be called in question, unless put in issue by the very proceeding itself, for every cause is to be decided on its own circumstances, and not to be prejudiced by any matter foreign to it." PEAKE, A COMPENDIUM OF THE LAW OF EVIDENCE (4th ed. 1813) 7.

evidence may be excluded as "irrelevant" for either of these two quite distinct reasons: because it is not probative of the proposition at which it is directed, or because that proposition is not provable in the case.[6]

The distinction between these two senses of irrelevance seems not to have been observed by the early authors. Thus Phillips combines in a single paragraph a rule against evidence of a release under a plea of *non est factum* with a rule against proving the customs of one parish by evidence of the customs in an adjoining one, and even states that rules against proof of self defense under the general issue in an assault and against showing the general criminal disposition of an accused exist "for the same reason".

Only lack of careful analysis—an easy satisfaction with surface similarities—can explain such statements as Phillipps'. A little consideration shows that in the bond case, for example, no one would suppose or urge that proof of a release is in any sense probative of the proposition that the defendant never executed the bond sued upon. This evidence must have been offered in the erroneous belief that it constituted an ultimate material fact available as a defense. On the other hand, it is equally clear that proof or disproof of the custom of parish *B* would not be material—in the sense of involving an ultimate material fact—in a suit brought or defended on the custom of parish *A*. In such a case the custom in *B* could be useful only if relevant, as giving the basis for a permissible inference as to the custom in *A*. Phillipps' appreciation of the form of the argument in the second case, together with a basic understanding of the "methods of agreement and difference",[7] appears from his approval of a third case, ruling that usage in one manor may be proved to show the incidents of tenure in another manor in the district *provided the two are held by the same peculiar tenure*. Nevertheless, he places these three cases together without noting that in the first we are dealing with a problem of pleading, while genuine questions of evidence arise in the second and third.

The same confusion can exist between questions of evidence and

---

[6] Henceforth, for brevity, propositions of ultimate fact properly provable in a case under the pleadings and substantive law will be referred to as "material propositions"; the characterization "relevant" will be reserved for propositions of evidence which, whether or not material themselves, tend to prove other propositions which are material. "Irrelevant" and "immaterial" are of course the contraries of the two first terms, as defined.

[7] See 1 WIGMORE, EVIDENCE (3d ed. 1940) § 12.

692   *CALIFORNIA LAW REVIEW*   [Vol. 29

of substantive law, as Phillipps proceeds to demonstrate by according uniform and consolidated treatment to cases holding that a civil defendant cannot prove his good character, even to rebut imputations of fraud, that in an action for criminal conversation the defendant may prove the light character of the plaintiff's wife (in mitigation of damages), and that in an action for malicious prosecution the defendant, after circumstances of suspicion, may show the plaintiff's generally bad character as evidence of reasonable suspicion.

Under modern codes the substantive law confusion is more common than the one based on rules of pleading, and may appear in very subtle forms. Let us analyze a single interesting case, *Union Paint & Varnish Co. v. Dean,*[8] an action of assumpsit to recover the purchase price of waterproof roof paint. The defendant relied upon the plaintiff's warranty that the paint would wear for ten years, breach of which he sought to show by proof that another drum of paint of the same brand, which he had purchased six months earlier, not only had failed to prevent leaks but had ruined the shingles to which it had been applied. The drum of paint in issue, purchased just before leaks developed in the first roof painted, had never been opened. Reversing the trial court, the Supreme Court of Rhode Island held that the defendant's offer of proof (apparently almost the only evidence offered in defense) should have been received, saying:

> "If paint of the same brand, sold by the same concern under the same warranty within six months, had proved within that time to be not in conformity with the warranty, in that it was not only not suitable for stopping and preventing leaks but was actually injurious to a roof, a person might well hesitate before using more paint of the same brand when he had no reason to expect the second lot to be any better than the first."[9]

Considered as evidence of the condition of the second drum of paint, proof of the results of use of the first is not very impressive. Waiving any doubts whether the leaks in the first roof were traceable to defects in paint in the first drum, there is no showing whether the defects in the first drum of paint were due to poor ingredients, to a poor formula, or to some error in preparation. If poor ingredients had been used, there is no showing that use of poor ingredients was a policy of, rather than an error of, the plaintiff company. It is easier to believe that one lot of defective paint went out than it is to believe

---

[8] (1927) 48 R. I. 288, 137 Atl. 469; MORGAN and MAGUIRE, CASES ON EVIDENCE (1937 reprint) 289.

[9] *Ibid.* at 291, 137 Atl. at 470.

that plaintiff customarily sold, under a ten-year guaranty, waterproof roof paint which would rot out shingles and cause leaks in six months. And the two drums of paint were probably not out of one lot; certainly there was no showing that they were. Proof of the condition of the paint in the first drum was of negligible value in judging the probable character of the paint in the second, unopened drum. It merely showed that plaintiff company sometimes sold bad paint. If the issue was whether the paint in the second drum *was* bad, an issue on which the defendant had the burden, the trial judge's ruling seems sound. At worst, the issue is close enough so that an appellate court should not reverse. Yet there is still a ring of reason to the supreme court's statement that "a person might well hesitate before using more paint of the same brand". He would hesitate to risk ruining a second roof even if he only feared that the second drum of paint might be no better than the first. And if he was reasonable in his hesitation, should the plaintiff be allowed to recover even if it could show at trial that the paint in the second drum was perfectly good? The defendant, reasonably hesitant to use the doubtful paint, by now has probably painted all of his roofs with some other paint and has no further use for the drum which he is tendering back to the vendor. If the customer is to be protected, even against proof that the second drum of paint was in fact satisfactory (as the writer should like to do in such a case[10]), a novel rule of substantive law stands revealed behind a somewhat doubtful ruling on evidence.

But after excluding all cases which turn upon the materiality or immateriality under the pleadings and substantive law of ultimate propositions sought to be proved, there remain many cases in which there is no question of the materiality of the proposition sought to be proved and the probative value of the offered evidence is the real issue. These cases, and these alone, raise the problem of relevancy as a problem in the law of evidence. How should they be handled?

Thayer, after stating the principle which forbids receiving anything not "logically probative", excluded legal criteria from further operation, saying

> "How are we to know what these forbidden things are? Not by any rule of law. The law furnishes no test of relevancy. For this, it tacitly refers to logic and general experience,—assuming that the

---

[10] Professor Malcolm Sharp, my colleague who deals with contracts, expressed his offhand opinion that the bad quality of the paint in the first drum should serve the buyer as an excuse for non-acceptance of a second drum of the "same paint"—*i.e.*, paint sold under the same brand.

principles of reasoning are known to its judges and ministers, just as a vast multitude of other things are assumed as already sufficiently known to them."[11]

Wigmore, agreeing with Thayer in much, questions the conclusion that the law furnishes no test of relevancy,[12] citing in opposition a well-known passage by Chief Justice Cushing of New Hampshire:

> "... although undoubtedly the relevancy of testimony is originally a matter of logic and common sense, still there are many instances in which the evidence of particular facts as bearing on particular issues has been so often the subject of discussion in courts of law, and so often ruled upon, that the united logic of a great many judges and lawyers may be said to furnish evidence of the sense common to a great many individuals, and, therefore, the best evidence of what may be properly called *common*-sense, and thus to acquire the authority of law. It is for this reason that the subject of the relevancy of testimony has become, to so great an extent, matter of precedent and authority, and that we may with entire propriety speak of its legal relevancy."[13]

This question of the propriety of speaking of "legal relevancy", of the expediency of framing rules with the authority of law to govern offers of evidence of particular facts as bearing on particular issues, is the central one in circumstantial proof. But since it is agreed on all sides that relevancy is at least originally a matter of logic and common sense rather than a matter of law, let us first see whither logic and common sense lead us, and by what means.

Dean Wigmore, recognizing this priority of logic, discusses the form of argument involved in the use of circumstantial evidence. His views deserve extended quotation and criticism. After stating that proof reduces to two great forms, inductive and deductive, and quoting Professor Sidgwick's description of the two, Wigmore states:

> "A brief examination will show that in the offering of evidence in Court the form of argument is always *inductive*. Suppose, to prove a charge of murder, evidence is offered of the defendant's fixed design to kill the deceased. The form of the argument is: 'A planned to kill B; therefore, A probably did kill B.' It is clear that we have here no semblance of a syllogism. The form of argument is exactly the same when we argue: 'Yesterday, Dec. 31, A slipped on the sidewalk and fell; therefore, the sidewalk was probably coated with ice'; or, 'To-

---

[11] THAYER, *op. cit. supra* note 1, at 265.

[12] 1 WIGMORE, *loc. cit. supra* note 7.

[13] State v. LaPage (1876) 57 N. H. 245, 288. Wigmore suggests that the difference between Thayer and Cushing is "one of nomenclature only", a very fundamental error as should appear hereinafter.

day A, who was bitten by a dog yesterday, died in convulsions; therefore, the dog probably had hydrophobia.' So with all other legal evidentiary facts. We may argue: 'Last week the witness A had a quarrel with the defendant B; therefore, A is probably biassed against B'; 'A was found with a bloody knife in B's house; therefore, A is probably the murderer of B'; After B's injury at A's machinery, A repaired the machinery; therefore, A probably acknowledged that the machinery was negligently defective'; 'A, an adult of sound mind and senses, and apparently impartial, was present at an affray between B and C, and testifies that B struck first; therefore, it is probably true that B did strike first.' In all these cases, we take a single or isolated fact, and upon it base immediately an inference as to the proposition in question.

"It may be replied, however, that in all the above instances, the argument is implicitly based upon an understood law or generalization, and is thus capable of being expressed in the *deductive* or syllogistic form. Thus, in the first instance above, is not the true form: 'Men's fixed designs are probably carried out; A had a fixed design to kill B; therefore, A probably carried out his design and did kill B'?

"There are two answers to this. (1) It has just been seen that every inductive argument is at least capable of being transmuted into and stated in the deductive form, by forcing into prominence the implied law or generalization on which it rests more or less obscurely. Thus it is nothing peculiar to litigious argument that this possibility of turning it into deductive form exists here also. It is not a question of what the form might be—for all inductive may be turned into deductive forms—, but of what it is, as actually employed; and it *is* actually put forward in inductive form. (2) Even supposing this transmutation to be a possibility, it would still be undesirable to make the transmutation for the purpose of testing probative value; because it would be useless. We should ultimately come to the same situation as before. Thus, in one of the instances above: 'A repaired machinery after the accident; therefore, A was conscious of a negligent defect in it'; suppose we turn this into deductive form: 'People who make such repairs show a consciousness of negligence; A made such repairs; therefore, A was conscious of negligence.' We now have an argument perfectly sound deductively, *i.e.* if the premises be conceded. But it remains for the Court to declare whether it accepts the major premise, and so the Court must now take it up for examination, and the proponent of the evidence appears as its champion and his argument becomes: 'The fact that people make such repairs indicates (shows, proves, probably shows, etc.) that they are conscious of negligence.' But here we come again, after all, to an inductive form of argument. The consciousness of negligence is to be inferred from the fact of repairs,—just as the presence of electricity in the clouds was inferred by Franklin from the shock through the kite-string, *i.e.* by a purely inductive form of reasoning. So with all other evidence when resolved into the deductive form; the transmutation is useless, because the Court's attention is merely transferred from the syllogism as a whole to the validity of the inference contained in the major premise; which presents itself again in inductive form.

"For practical purposes, then, it is sufficient to treat the use of litigious evidentiary facts as *inductive* in form."[14]

Note, Wigmore does not deny that in every instance proof must be based upon a generalization connecting the evidentiary proposition with the proposition to be proved.[15] Conceding this, he argues that the generalization may as well be tacitly understood as expressed, that "the transmutation [from the inductive to the deductive form] is useless, because the Court's attention is merely transferred from the syllogism as a whole to the validity of the inference contained in the major premise".[16] Yet it is precisely in this transfer of attention that the value of the transmutation lies. The author's own examples illustrate the point. In the case of the repaired machinery we are told: " 'People who make such repairs [after an accident] show a consciousness of negligence; A made such repairs; therefore, A was conscious of negligence.' "[17] Before this deductive proof can be evalu-

---

[14] 1 WIGMORE, *op. cit. supra* note 7, at 416. Compare Starkie's equally surprising observation: "Circumstantial, or, as it is frequently termed, presumptive evidence, is any which is not direct and positive.

"An inference or conclusion from circumstantial or presumptive evidence may be either the pure result of previous experience of the ordinary or necessary connection between the known or admitted facts, and the fact inferred, or of reason exercised upon the facts, or of both reason and experience conjointly. And hence such an inference or conclusion differs from a presumption, although the latter term has sometimes, yet not with strict propriety, been used in the same extended sense. For a presumption in strictness is an inference as to the existence of one fact, from a knowledge of the existence of some other fact, made solely by virtue of previous experience of the ordinary connection between the known and inferred facts, and independently of any process of reason in the particular instance." STARKIE, EVIDENCE *478.

[15] The argument thus far may be summarized as follows: Relevancy is formal relation between two propositions. To determine the relevancy of an offered item of evidence one must first discover to what proposition it is supposed to be relevant. This requires analysis of the express or tacit argument of counsel. Then, since evidence is admissible only if relevant to a *material* proposition, analysis of the pleadings and applicable substantive law is required to determine whether the proposition ultimately sought to be proved is material. Having isolated the material proposition sought to be proved, we still must determine whether the evidentiary proposition is relevant to it—does tend to prove it. This tendency to prove can be demonstrated only in terms of some general proposition, based most often on the practical experience of the judge and jurors as men, sometimes upon generalizations of science introduced into the trial to act as connecting links. If the evidentiary proposition itself is material, there is no problem of relevancy.

[16] 1 WIGMORE, *op. cit. supra* note 7, at 417.

[17] *Ibid.*

ated, ambiguity must be eliminated from the major premise. By "people" shall we understand "some people" or "all people"? If the argument is intended to read, "Some people who make such repairs show consciousness of neglience; *A* made such repairs; therefore, *A* was conscious of negligence," it contains an obvious logical fallacy. If intended to read, "All people who make such repairs show consciousness of negligence; *A* made such repairs; therefore, *A* was conscious of negligence," it is logically valid. However, few could be found to accept the premise that *all* persons who repair machinery after an accident show consciousness of guilt; that is, that no single case could be found of one who, confident of his care in the past, nevertheless made repairs to guard against repetition of an unforeseeable casualty or to preserve future fools against the consequence of their future folly. Here the result of transmuting a proposed direct inference into deductive form is discovery that it is invalid—at least in the terms suggested.

The other proposed argument is equally interesting: "'Men's fixed designs are probably carried out; A had a fixed design to kill B; therefore, A probably did kill B.'"[18] Once one attempts to deal, in a quasi-syllogistic form, not with certainties but with probabilities, additional opportunities for fallacy are presented. Suppose that it is argued: "Most *A*s are *X*, *B* is an *A*, therefore *B* is probably *X*"; or "Nine-tenths of all *A*s are *X*, *B* is an *A*, therefore the chances are nine to one that *B* is *X*." Neither of these arguments is logically valid except upon the assumption that *A*s may be treated as a uniform class with respect to the probability of their being *X*. This can be because there really is no way of sub-dividing the class, finding more *X*s in one sub-class than in another, or because no subdivision can be made in terms of available data. Suppose that nine-tenths of all people in the world have dark eyes. If absolutely all one knew about *B* was that he was a person, it would be an apparent nine-to-one chance that *B* had dark eyes. But if one knew *B* to be a Swede, the percentage of dark eyes in the total population of the world would no longer be important. One would want to know about the proportion of dark-eyed Swedes, which might differ from the ratio among humans generally.[19] Similarly in Wigmore's example. We know that we are inter-

---

[18] *Ibid.*

[19] The form of the invalid argument would be as follows: Nine-tenths of men have dark eyes. *B* is a Swede. All Swedes are men. Therefore nine chances to one *B* has dark eyes.

ested in the probability of execution of a fixed design of a particular kind: to commit murder. There may be variation in the probability of execution of fixed designs on various subjects. As an initial criticism, therefore, the primary generalization should be "Men's fixed designs to kill are probably carried out." In this form we have a valid, quasi-syllogistic argument based upon the limited data available.[20] Still, is the premise sound?

"Men's fixed designs to kill are probably carried out," as a major premise in this argument, must mean that they are carried out more often than not. While the word "probable" can be used in other senses, its meaning here is clear. Hence one would conclude from the single datum that *A* had a fixed design to kill *B*, no other evidence being offered, that more likely than not *A* actually did kill *B*. But when this argument was presented to a group of law students and teachers, only one was willing to accept the indicated conclusion. Several would accept it if supported by adequate evidence that *B* had been intentionally killed by some one. Others refused to accept it without still further evidence connecting *A* with *B's* death, or at the very least evidence that *B* had no other enemies. Moreover, there was less hesitancy in accepting the argument in its "inductive" form. Once the generalization was made explicit, and particularly after discussion of the meaning of "probably" as there used, doubts as to the propriety of the inference arose or sharpened. The demonstration, however "valid", is no better than its major premise, and the more one considers this premise the less reliable it looks. Certainly a permitted inference should rest upon some more easily acceptable law.

Of course, it does not follow that a proposed inference is improper because it can be shown not to follow on the basis of one possible generalization, or because another—which by the rules of logic would validate the inference—is unacceptable. There may be a third law, as yet unexpressed, which would justify the inference and at the same time be commonly accepted as true. And it may be very important to find the valid and accurate link, since the form of the link will control the form of the conclusion.

Persons who are unwilling to agree that men's fixed designs (at least in case of murder) are "probably" carried out—or, even con-

---

[20] Probability is not an actual state. Nothing really *is* probable. It is true or false. Probability is a matter of appearance. Apparently probability is always relative to the data available at the time judgment is exercised. If all possible data were available we should be dealing not with probability in an ordinary sense but with the approximation of certainty.

ceding the fact of murder, that proof of *A's* fixed design to kill *B* establishes *A*, more likely than not, as *B's* killer—still agree that somehow this bit of evidence does have some tendency to indicate *A's* guilt. What form of general statement can reconcile these views? Perhaps something like this: "Men having such a fixed design are more likely to kill than are men not having such a fixed design." Those who contend that even fixed designs to kill are more often abandoned or thwarted than carried out can and doubtless will still concede that enough such designs are carried to execution so that the percentage of murderers is higher among persons entertaining such a fixed design than among the general public. Obviously this proposed generalization does not lead us from *A's* fixed design to kill *B* to the conclusion that *A* probably did kill *B*. There is nothing disturbing in this. This conclusion simply does not follow from the evidence of design. The error was in the original "direct induction". In fact, no useful conclusion about *A's* guilt can be drawn from design or intent alone. On the basis of an acceptable generalization we are able only to place *A* in a class of persons in which the incidence of murder is greater than among the general public. We cannot now say that *A* is probably guilty, but we can say that *the apparent probability of his guilt is now greater than before the evidence of design was received.*[21] This is logical relevancy—the only logical relevancy we can expect in dealing with practical affairs where strict demonstration is never possible.[22] The advantage of the transmutation into deductive (though not strictly syllogistic) form is that we know to what degree of proof we have attained, and do not overstate our results.[23]

Before leaving the subject of induction and deduction, consider

---

[21] Or, the apparent probability of his innocence is now less. The two statements mean the same.

[22] It should be unnecessary to point out the fundamental distinction between relevancy of evidence and the degree of probability necessary to establish a *prima facie* case. Almost every careful writer has discussed it. See, for example, 1 WIGMORE, *op. cit. supra* note 7, §§ 28, 29. If the sum total of evidence received falls short of satisfying the burden of persuasion, the jury is there for the express purpose of finding against the party who must bear that burden. If the sum total of evidence received is so slight that the jury as reasonable men could not be persuaded, the trial judge may enter a non-suit or direct a verdict. There is no reason for worrying about such issues while passing upon an offer of evidence. The one exception might be an item of evidence which, although logically relevant in a very remote sense, is so slight that in the opinion of the trial judge it could not sway an even balance.

[23] In some cases we may be able to discover no acceptable generalization to connect the offered evidence to any material proposition. Such cases will be very rare, unless they involve errors of pleading or substantive law.

one more example. Wigmore asserts: "There is just as much probative value in the argument 'A is quarrelsome, therefore he probably committed this assault,' as in the argument, 'B is peaceable, therefore he probably did not commit the assault . . . .' "[24] So it may appear when the two arguments are stated as direct inductions. But transmutation of the two arguments shows a different result. In the second case we say: "Peaceable men are not likely to commit assaults. *B* is a peaceable man. Therefore he was not likely to commit (this or any) assault." In the first case the most we can say is: "Quarrelsome men are more likely than others to commit assaults. *A* is quarrelsome. Therefore he is more likely than others to commit assaults." This may be equally good if there is no doubt of an affray between *A* and *B*, one of them surely being the aggressor. But suppose that we know someone assaulted *C* and are attempting to decide whether *A* or *B* or some third person was the culprit. We know that *B*, the peaceable man, was unlikely to commit any assault, hence unlikely to have committed the one in issue. All we know of *A*, the quarrelsome fellow, is that he has a general predilection for trouble. While it is some help, it does not show an affirmative probability of his guilt in any particular case. There is a definite difference in the probative value of the two offers of proof.

Nevertheless, both offers of proof are logically relevant; the apparent probability of guilt in each case would be changed, though not in the same degree, by the evidence of character. Why then is the evidence rejected in the weaker case? A possible answer would be simply because it is weaker—too weak. Although logically relevant, it falls short of the minimum requirement of legal relevancy.[25] Such an answer merely raises a further query. Why should there be a standard of "legal relevancy" more strict than, or in any respect different from, the standards of logic? Why exclude any data which if admitted would change the apparent probabilities and hence serve, even to a slight degree, to aid the search for truth? Justice Holmes suggested one answer, it is "a concession to the shortness of life"[26]

---

[24] 1 WIGMORE, *op. cit. supra* note 7, at 454.

[25] Bouvier, after defining "relevancy in a logical sense" goes on to say "Legal relevancy requires a higher standard of evidentiary force. It includes logical relevancy and demands a close connection between the fact to be proved and the fact offered to prove it. The fact, however, that it is logically relevant does not insure admissibility; it must also be legally relevant." 3 BOUVIER, DICTIONARY (Rawle's 3d ed. 1914). BLACK, LAW DICTIONARY (3d ed. 1933), is to the same effect.

[26] Reeve v. Dennett (1887) 145 Mass. 23, 28, 11 N. E. 938, 944.

—and perhaps to the shortness of purse of harassed litigants. If any and all evidence may be admissible which—in terms of some commonly accepted generalization about human conduct or natural events—would operate to any extent to alter the apparent probability of some material proposition, the field of judicial inquiry in most cases would be almost unlimited. Trials could come to an end only by the exhaustion of lawyers' ingenuity or clients' money, and the trial judge or jury might be overwhelmed and bewildered by the multiplicity of collateral issues. Such a rule would result in the apparent justice and the practical injustice characteristic of English Chancery practice a century and a half ago. Hence the requirement, in many cases, of something more than bare logical relevancy.

In addition to the simple factors of time, confusion and expense, other practical considerations may justify the exclusion of relevant evidence of but slight probative weight.[27] As noted above, evidence is irrelevant in the clearest sense if its tendency is to prove some proposition not properly provable in the action. Sometimes the same evidence may be remotely relevant to a material proposition and directly relevant to an immaterial one; in such a case its exclusion could be justified lest the jury be misled into deciding the case on the immaterial issue. Or evidence might be excluded because under the issues as framed in the pleadings such evidence would unreasonably surprise the opponent.[28]

Probably the greatest part of judicial rulings excluding evidence as irrelevant go primarily on the first principle—that the evidence is relevant, but its probative value is so slight as not to justify the time and expense involved in receiving it and the confusion of issues which might result in the mind of the trier of fact. Does this sound practical policy justify creation of the concept of "legal relevancy" —higher and more strict than logical relevancy, to which offers of proof must be referred? On the contrary, the concept can only be a nuisance. In the first place, it defies definition.[29] No statement of a

---

[27] All of these factors are listed as permissible grounds for the exclusion of evidence in the proposed Code, *op. cit. supra* note 3, Rule 403, which Rule is expressly made a qualification of most other rules, but is then followed by several specific and somewhat confusing rules on proof of character, habit, etc.

[28] A similar policy is expressed by pleading rules which require the affirmative allegation of defenses likely to surprise the opposing party, whether or not the defense is affirmative as a matter of analysis. See, *e.g.*, ILLINOIS CIVIL PRACTICE ACT (1933) § 43(4).

[29] See *supra* note 25. Such a definition is sufficient to raise doubts in every case and to satisfy them in none.

standard of probative value higher than logical relevancy can be made precise enough for use without excluding much evidence which is used daily, without argument and to good effect. And there is a definite reason for this. When a judge must decide whether a particular item of evidence, logically relevant, is of sufficient force to justify the time and expense necessary to establish it, he should not confine his attention to the effect of the offered evidence alone. He should consider how difficult it will be to establish the evidentiary fact—whether there is any real contest about it and whether confusing side issues must be explored. He should consider how the offered evidence may fit in with other evidence. It may form a small but useful part of a pattern of proof. It may stand alone, lending its negligible aid to unconnected lines of proof. It may be merely cumulative, so that the trouble of establishing it will result in little of practical value. He may even want to consider the importance to the parties of the issues being tried, in the light of mounting trial expense. Such considerations cannot usefully be reduced to a simple formula for relevancy of particular items of evidence.[30]

The method suggested by Chief Justice Cushing,[31] that of building up a body of rulings on the bearing of particular facts upon particular issues, is no better—for the same reason. The ruling in each case will seldom if ever be that the offered fact has *no* bearing upon the issue. It will be that it has no sufficient bearing to justify its use in view of all the circumstances of the case in which it is offered. Such a precedent, rightly understood, is of no value save in another case substantially identical in all of its particulars. Treated more broadly, its tendency will be to mislead subsequent judges.

Take, as an example, *State v. LaPage*[32] where Chief Justice Cushing enunciated his theories on legal relevancy. The state, in a prosecution for murder of one Josie L. in which there was some evidence of murder during an attempted rape, was permitted to show that the defendant had raped one Julienne R. The evidence was offered not

---

[30] As good an attempt as any was that of Justice Cooley in Stewart v. People (1871) 23 Mich. 63, 75: "The proper test for the admissibility of evidence ought to be, we think, whether it has a tendency to affect belief in the mind of a reasonably cautious person, who should receive and weigh it with judicial fairness." This is practically a definition of logical relevancy applied to important issues depending on indeterminate probabilities.

[31] *Supra* note 13.

[32] *Ibid.*

to show that the defendant had killed Josie, but to show that if he had done so it was in the course of an attempted rape and therefore first degree murder under the New Hampshire statute. A conviction was reversed, the court holding that evidence of another crime, not relevant *save as showing the character or disposition of the accused,* could not be presented by the prosecution when the accused had not "put his character in issue". The reasons for this ruling are clear on principle and from the opinion itself. First, the offered evidence, while it had some probative value, was not particularly cogent. Second, by attacking the character of the accused, it raised the danger that he might be "overwhelmed by prejudice, instead of being convicted on that affirmative evidence which the law of this country requires".[33] Third, by using specific instances of misconduct to demonstrate bad character, it confronted the accused with a dangerous issue which he might have been entirely unprepared to meet. These are substantial arguments for exclusion, which are in no way aided by saying that the defendant's bad character is not "legally relevant", or that specific instances of misconduct are not "legally relevant" to prove bad character.

On the contrary, there is real danger that talk of legal relevancy in such cases may mislead other judges. Thus in a prosecution for murder the character of the decedent as quarrelsome and violent should be admissible in aid of a plea of self-defense. Most courts admit it,[34] but those who do not often seem confused by the inadmissibility of the violent character of the accused. If the ruling excluding the bad character of criminal defendants were always expressly made on the ground that such evidence is relevant but inadmissible because unduly prejudicial, without reference to "legal irrelevancy", such confusion would be unlikely.

Similarly the argument of undue surprise is less likely to lead courts into error if stated as such. Specific immoral acts clearly are not irrelevant as evidence of lack of the corresponding virtue. If not actually conclusive they are certainly much more cogent than reputation. If they are really excluded because of the danger of surprise, it would be better to say so. Then courts might in time discover in pre-trial practice a method of obviating unfair surprise in the use of the specific instance whenever its value is sufficiently great to justify the time and expense of trying a collateral issue.

---

[33] Regina v. Rowton (1865) Leigh & C. 520, 540, 169 Eng. Rep. 1497, 1506.
[34] 1 WIGMORE, *op. cit. supra* note 7, § 63.

Such considerations, whether taken singly or together, afford most unsuitable materials for the construction of a body of case law. Like the simpler problem of time and expense, all involve a balance of competing considerations—the value of the evidence, the importance of the point sought to be established, the availability of other evidence, the precise degree of inconvenience or prejudice— never likely to be duplicated in different cases. "The evidence of particular facts as bearing on particular issues" does not repeat its pattern closely enough to permit its petrifaction into rules having "the authority of law" without over simplification. The history of evidence has been in the development of sound principles into arbitrary and unworkable rubrics, a development not to be encouraged in case law or by code.

The remedy lies in Thayer's advice in holding to logic and general experience, assuming that the principles of reasoning are known to the judges and ministers of the law. In this analysis evidence is relevant if it can be demonstrated, in terms of some generalization acceptable to the court, to alter the apparent probability of any material proposition in the case. The generalization may rest either upon the general experience of the court or upon expert testimony, but it should be susceptible of expression.

Because of the wide range of relevant evidence under such a test, the trial judge must have discretion to exclude it, and may well be furnished with general criteria to aid, but not to control, the exercise of this discretion. Although it is rather brief, Rule 403 of the proposed Code is a step in this direction. Attempts at further specification, either by code or by decision, should then be discouraged. Limiting the review of trial court rulings on circumstantial proof will do much to check the proliferation of precedent. Virtually never would an appellate court be justified in reversing a trial judge for the admission of remote but non-prejudicial evidence. Time thus wasted cannot be recovered by requiring a second trial. Where remote evidence was excluded, an upper court should refuse to reverse unless it appears that a contrary ruling would actually have altered the result. To the extent that this rule allows somewhat more control than the one on erroneous admission, its tendency would be to liberalize rulings on evidence where the only objection is remoteness.

Finally no judgment should be reversed because evidence was prejudicial, or caught the opponent by surprise, unless the objection was made on this express ground. If problems of surprise or prejudice were necessarily designated as such and not lumped under the heading of irrelevancy, the bench and bar might learn, instead of regarding them primarily as ammunition of appeal, to handle them at the trial stage by instructions to the jury, by continuances, and above all by discussion of the problems of proof at pre-trial conferences. The domination of the appellate court, the printed report and the misleading precedent might be ended, the largely unrelated principles making up the concept of "legal relevancy" be disentangled, and that ambiguous phrase returned to the grave wherein the great Professor Thayer laid it almost fifty years ago.

Part VI
Burdens of Proof and Presumptions

Burdens and Standards of Proof

[20]

HARVARD

LAW REVIEW

VOL. IV.   MAY 15, 1890.   NO. 2.

THE BURDEN OF PROOF.

IF we conceive to ourselves a legal system in which the pleadings,
if any there be, admit of only one defence, that of mere negation, — that is to say, where not merely the pleading is negative
in form, but where no other than a purely negative defence is
open under it, and all other defences, as if they were cross actions,
require a separate trial; we can see that the phrase Burden of
Proof (*Onus probandi, Beweislast, Fardeau de la preuve*)
may have a very simple meaning. Under such a system the
defendant has nothing to prove; it is the plaintiff, the *actor*, who
has the duty of proving, while the defendant, the *reus*, has only
the negative function of baffling the plaintiff.

If, on the other hand, we picture a system in which any defence
whatever may be open upon a plea of general denial, in which a
defendant who stands upon the record as merely denying, may,
at the trial, turn himself into a plaintiff by setting up an affirmative
defence, and the original plaintiff may become a defendant by
merely denying this new case of his adversary; then we observe
that so simple a conception of the proof and the duty of proving,
is no longer possible. Either party may have it, and it may
shift back and forth during the trial, because each party in turn
may set up, in the course of the trial, an affirmative ground of
fact, which, if he would win, he must, of course, make good by
proof. We can no longer say when the pleading is over and

before the trial begins, "the proof belongs here and cannot belong elsewhere ; the *onus probandi* is on the plaintiff and it cannot shift."

If now we further conceive that under this last system the action of the tribunal passing upon questions of fact is subject to review, so that an appellate court may have to consider whether such a body as a jury has acted reasonably in weighing evidence and counter-evidence, and whether the judge who has presided over a trial by jury has rightly ordered the trial, and rightly instructed the jury as to comparing and weighing evidence, we may see that questions will be introduced into legal discussion as to the respective duties of the parties in producing evidence at different points of the trial, and in meeting evidence produced against them, which may be wholly absent from another system where there is no such judicial revision of the method of using and estimating the evidence.   The conception is brought to light of producing evidence to meet the pressure of an adversary's case, a duty which may belong to either party, and to both parties in turn ; and this conception now takes its place in legal discussion and requires its own terminology.

Let us further suppose that this new topic,— new in the sense of requiring now to be discriminated and discussed,— the mere duty of producing evidence, belonging thus to neither party exclusively, and to each by turns, gets also called the burden of proof ; it becomes plain that, as regards the meaning of this term, we have advanced from a region of simple and clear ideas to one which is likely to be full of confusion.   We have, in fact, proceeded from conceptions which we may roughly describe as those of the Roman law and of some later systems founded upon it, to those which fill and perplex the books of our common law to-day.

If now, furthermore, recognizing that there are these two wholly distinct notions of the burden of proof, both called by the same name, we then observe that, as regards one of them, the duty of establishing, it is often a very difficult thing to determine whether a given defence be an affirmative one or not, and so to decide which party has the burden of the proof in this sense, and that the common-law judges have fallen into the way of giving as the test,[1] as the regular professional " rule of thumb," for tell-

---

[1] "The proper test is, which party would be successful if no evidence at all were given."   Alderson, B., in Amos *v.* Hughes, 1 Moo. & Rob. 464.

ing who has this burden of proof, a precept which selects a circumstance common to both meanings of the term, and, indeed,
generally characteristic of the other one, namely, the duty of
going forward with evidence,— we shall see how the confusion is
likely to be heightened.

Finally, if we go on to remark the way in which this topic is
mixed up with that of presumptions, as when it is said that "presumptions of law and strong presumptions of fact shift the burden
of proof," we have a glimpse of another fruitful source of confusion ; and in fact these two subjects of presumption and the
burden of proof have intercommunicated their respective ambiguities and reflected them back and forth upon each other in a
manner which it is wellnigh hopeless to follow out.[1]

If all this or the half of it be true, it will be admitted that he
would do a great service to our law who should thoroughly discriminate, explore, and set forth the legal doctrine of the burden
of proof. But that would be a large undertaking. The fit
performance of it would require a deep historical and critical
examination of pleading and procedure, a careful consideration of
legal presumptions and the principles of legal reasoning, and a
just analysis of the fundamental conceptions of substantive law.[2]
Such a discussion would have to take a wide range, for the subject belongs to universal jurisprudence, and the phrase and the
things it stands for have a long descent. The leading maxims
about it (often ill understood) are from the Roman law. During
the Dark Ages and among our Germanic ancestors it had a very
peculiar application. Conceptions coming from these periods
still linger in our law, as will easily seem probable when we reflect that not only do our early judicial records show the ordeal
and other mediæval modes of proof in full operation, but that
wager of law and wager of battle were legally resorted to in
England in the second and third decades of this century.[3] With

---

[1] " Look to the books," says Bentham, in speaking of the burden of proof (Works,
vi. 139), " and . . . instead of clear rules, such as the nature of things forbids to be established by anything but statute law, you have darkness palpable and visible."

[2] It may be assumed, I suppose, that this phrase of the "substantive law," and Bentham's discrimination between this part of the law and that which is merely auxiliary to
it, are already familiar. See *e. g.*, Bentham's Works, vi. 7. " The adjective branch of
law, or law of procedure, and therein the law of evidence, has everywhere for its object,
at least ought to have, the giving effect . . . to the several regulations and arrangements
of which the substantive branch or main body of the law is composed."

[3] For the mediæval conception of the burden, or, as it generally was in those times,

the use of the jury came a new set of ideas and a new system
of pleading, very different from those of Rome and modern
continental Europe ; and gradually, with the slow and strange
development of the jury system, and the irregular working
out of common-law pleading, there has arisen and come into
prominence a new set of discriminations. Much that never,
in other times and countries, was the subject of legal discussion, and never passed out from the mass of the unrecorded
details of forensic usage, now, through the working of our
double tribunal of judge and jury, and the constant necessity
which it brings of marking their respective boundaries, and reviewing in a higher court the instructions given by the judge to
the jury, comes into the region of law and judicial precedent.
Of all these things will the writer of that careful statement of
which I speak find it necessary to treat. It is probable that he
will have abundant occasion to remark in this region that obscure
operation of obsolete conceptions to which Sir Henry Maine referred in saying, "It may almost be laid down that in England
nothing wholly perishes."[1]

At present I am concerned with no such task as this, but only
with an attempt to help rid this phrase, the burden of proof, of
some of the distressing ambiguity that attends it, (*a*) by pointing
out the different conceptions for which it stands, and bringing to
view some important discriminations ; (*b*) by considering the
possibility of a better terminology for the subject ; and (*c*) by indicating its proper place in our law.

I. In legal discussion this phrase is used in two ways : —

(1.) To indicate the duty of bringing forward argument or evidence in support of a proposition, whether at the beginning or later.

(2.) To mark that of establishing a proposition as against all
counter-argument or evidence.

It should be added that there is a third indiscriminate usage,

---

the *privilege* of proof, see Von Bar's " Beweisurtheil " and Brunner's " Entstehung der
Schwurgerichte," *passim*. See also Professor Laughlin's paper on " Legal Procedure"
in " Essays on Anglo-Saxon Law," and Bigelow's " Hist. Proc. in England," ch. viii. In
citing German books I should confess at once that I have to depend upon my friends for
a knowledge of them, and should express my thanks to Mr. Gamaliel Bradford for the
most generous kindness in reading to me not only the whole of the two books above
named, but others. I am also very much indebted to the accurate learning of a younger
friend, Mr. Fletcher Ladd, of the Boston bar, for a knowledge of the contents of several
German treatises relating more exclusively to the subject of this article.

[1] Early Law and Custom, 187.

far more common than either of the others, in which the term may mean both or either of the first two. The last is very common; the first or second, that is to say, any meaning which makes a clear discrimination, is much less usual.

II.   It will be convenient at this point to illustrate the different uses of the term by some citations.

(1.)   The use of it in ordinary, untechnical speech, as indicating the effect of a natural probability or presumption, of the pressure of evidence or argument previously introduced, and of what is called a mere "preoccupation of the ground," may be seen in a passage from Bishop Whately's "Elements of Rhetoric:"[1] "It is a point of great importance . . . to point out . . . on which side the presumption lies, and to which belongs the (*onus probandi*) burden of proof. . . . According to the most correct use of the term, a 'presumption' in favor of any supposition means . . . in short that the burden of proof lies on the side of him who would dispute it."

Of the same use of it in our law books, the following are instances: (*a.*) "The burden of proof is shifted by those presumptions of law which are rebuttable; by presumptions of fact of the stronger kind; and by every species of evidence strong enough to establish a *prima facie* case against a party." (Best, Evidence, s. 273.) And again: "As . . . the question of the burden of proof may present itself at any moment during a trial, the test ought in strict accuracy to be expressed thus, viz.: 'Which party would be successful if no evidence at all, or no more evidence, as the case may be, were given.'" (*b.*) A very clear expression of this sense of the term is found in Lord Justice Bowen's opinion in Abrath *v.* No. East. Ry. Co.[2] "In order to make my opinion clear, I should like to say shortly how I understand the term 'burden of proof.' In every lawsuit somebody must go on with it; the plaintiff is the first to begin, and if he does nothing he fails. If he makes a *prima facie* case, and nothing is done by the other side to answer it, the defendant fails. The test, therefore, as to burden of proof is simply to consider which party would be successful if no evidence at all was given, or if no more evidence was given than is given at this particular

---

[1] Part I. c. 3, s. 2.

[2] 32 W. R. 50, 53.   In the regular report (11 Q. B. D. 440, 455–6) the phraseology is slightly, but not materially, different.

point of the case, because it is obvious that during the controversy in the litigation there are points at which the onus of proof shifts, and at which the tribunal must say, if the case stopped there, that it must be decided in a particular way. Such being the test, it is not a burden which rests forever on the person on whom it is first cast, but as soon as he, in his turn, finds evidence which, *prima facie*, rebuts the evidence against which he is contending, the burden shifts until again there is evidence which satisfies the demand. Now, that being so, the question as to onus of proof is only a rule for deciding on whom the obligation rests of going further, if he wishes to win." (*c.*) From Mr. Justice Stephen's Digest of Evidence [1] we may gather that he understands this to be the established usage in England. And the like is laid down for Scotland.[2]

(2.) As to the second sense of the term, expressing the duty of the *actor* to establish the grounds upon which he rests his demand that the court shall move in his behalf,— that is the sense to which, since the year 1832,[3] the Supreme Court of Massachusetts has sought to limit the expression. (*a.*) In 1854[4] it was put thus: "The burden of proof and the weight of evidence are two very different things. The former remains on the party affirming a fact in support of his case, and does not change in any aspect of the cause; the latter shifts from side to side in the progress of a trial, according to the nature and strength of the proofs offered in support or denial of the main fact to be established. In the case at bar, the averment which the plaintiff was bound to maintain was that the defendant was legally liable for the payment of tolls. In answer to this the defendant did not aver any new and distinct fact, such as payment, accord and satisfaction, or release; but offered evidence to rebut this alleged legal liability. By so doing he did not assume the burden of proof, which still rested on the plaintiff; but only sought to rebut the *prima facie* case which the plaintiff had proved." (*b.*) In the following passage may be seen an instance of what is not uncommon now-a-days, a recognition of this as one sense of the term, and also of the other. In 1878,[5] Lord Justice

---

[1] Articles 95 and 96 and the illustrations.
[2] Dickson, Evidence in Scotland (2 ed.), ss. 12–16.
[3] Powers *v.* Russell, 13 Pick. 69.
[4] Central Bridge Co. *v.* Butler, 2 Gray, 130.
[5] Pickup *v.* Thames Ins. Co., 3 Q. B. D. p. 600.

THE BURDEN OF PROOF. 51

Brett remarked, with valuable comments on the case of Watson *v.* Clark (1 Dow, 336), that "The burden of proof upon a plea of unseaworthiness to an action on a policy of marine insurance lies upon the defendant, and so far as the pleadings go it never shifts. . . . But when facts are given in evidence, it is often said that certain presumptions, which are really inferences of fact, arise and cause the burden of proof to shift ; and so they do as a matter of reasoning, and as a matter of fact. " [1] (*c.*) In New York, [2] Church, C. J., for the court, expresses himself thus : "The burden of maintaining the affirmative of the issue, and properly speaking, the burden of proof remained upon the plaintiff throughout the trial ; but the burden or necessity was cast upon the defendant, to relieve itself from the presumption of negligence raised by the plaintiff's evidence. "

(3.) A few cases may be added which illustrate the common confusion in the use of the term. (*a.*) A doctrine was formerly laid down in England that in prosecutions under the game laws, the defendant had the burden of establishing that he was qualified. This really rested in part upon the construction of the statutes. [3] But it came to be laid down generally, as we read in Greenleaf to-day, [4] that "where the subject-matter of a negative averment lies peculiarly within the knowledge of the other party, the averment is taken as true unless disproved by that party. " There is great sense in such a doctrine as indicating a duty of producing evidence, but little or none as marking a general duty of establishing ; but by reason of the ambiguity of this phrase, the doctrine is afloat in both senses. That it should be limited, as a statement of the common law, to the sense of a duty of giving evidence, is plainly shown by the remarks of Holroyd, J. : " In every case the *onus probandi* lies on the person who wishes to support his case by a particular fact which lies more peculiarly within his own

---

[1] Compare the same judge in Anderson *v.* Morice, L. R. 10 C. P. 58 (1874), Abrath *v.* No. East. Ry. Co., 11 Q. B. D. 440 (1883), and Davey *v.* Lond. & S. W. Ry. Co., 12 Q. B. D. 70.

[2] Caldwell *v.* New Jersey Co., 47 N. Y. 282, 290.

[3] The King *v.* Turner, 5 M. & S. 206, 210 (1816): "There are, I think, about ten different heads of qualification enumerated in the statutes. . . . The argument really comes to this : that there would be a moral impossibility of ever convicting upon such an information. " *Per* Lord Ellenborough. See King *v.* Stone, 1 East, 639 (1801), where the court was divided.

[4] Ev. i. s. 79.

knowledge. . . . This indeed is not allowed to supply the want of necessary proof," etc. [1] (*b.*) A striking instance, at once of the common English sense of the term, and of the perplexing way in which this is mixed up with the other sense of it, is found in a recent opinion of so great a judge as Lord Blackburn. In an Irish negligence case [2] a very interesting discussion arose as to the relation between the court and the jury, and the circumstances under which a judge can direct a verdict ; incidentally it touched the burden of proof. Lord Blackburn, who held, in this case, that a verdict should be entered for the defendants, put his view thus : To justify this, " it is not enough that the balance of testimony should be overwhelmingly on one side, " so that a verdict the other way ought to be set aside, but " the onus must be one way, and no reasonable evidence to rebut it. " By "onus" and " onus of proof, " Lord Blackburn does not mean the duty of ultimately establishing a proposition ; but his use of the term is so connected with that meaning, and with the doctrine that the general issue does not necessarily mean a negative case, that it will be instructive to quote his words : " It is of great importance to see on whom the onus of proof lies, for if the state of the case is such that on the admissions on the record, and the undisputed facts given in evidence on the trial, the onus lies on either side, the judge ought to give the direction, first, that if there are no additional facts to alter this, the jury ought to find

---

[1] King *v.* Burdett, 4 B. & Ald. p. 140 (1820). See also Steph. Dig. Ev. art. 96 : " In considering the amount of evidence necessary to shift the burden of proof, the court has regard to the opportunities of knowledge with respect to the fact to be proved which may be possessed by the parties respectively. " Compare Best, Ev. ss. 275, 276. Bonnier, Traité des Preuves (4 ed.), i. 33 : " La difficulté de la preuve . . . n'est point un motif suffisant pour intervertir les rôles. " And again, 49 : " C'est toujours au demandeur à prouver, et qu'il peut le faire, même lorsqu'il s'agit d'un fait negatif ; il le pourra bien plus facilement si on admet cette sage restriction que, pour rendre la négative définie, il est permis d'obliger la partie adverse à préciser ses prétentions. " The sound common-law doctrine, together with a reference to statutes that change it, is found in Wilson *v.* Melvin, 13 Gray, 73, and Com. *v.* Lahy, 8 Gray, 459. The question arising under the English Game Laws was afterwards regulated by statute. (1 Tayl. Ev., 8 ed., s. 377, note). Such statutes, exempting a party from the duty of giving evidence in certain cases, or imposing the " burden of proof " on the other, are common enough both here and in England. They might easily give rise to questions of construction as to the meaning of the phrase now under discussion. In dealing with one of these statutes (which had not, however, used the very phrase), it was said by the court in Mugler *v.* Kansas, 123 U. S. p. 674, that it simply determined what was a *prima facie* case for the government.

[2] Dublin, etc. Ry. Co. *v.* Slattery, 3 App. Cas. 1155.

against that party on whom the onus now lies " (p. 1201). " I think the recent decision of your Lordship's House in Metropolitan Railway Company *v.* Jackson conclusively establishes this doctrine in cases in which the onus was, on the issue, as joined on the record, on the party against whom the verdict was directed. I am of opinion that it is equally so when a fact found, or undisputed at the trial, has shifted that onus" (p. 1202). " The cases in which the principle that the onus may shift from time to time has been most frequently applied, are those of bills of exchange. At the beginning of a trial under the old system of pleading . . . the onus was on the plaintiff to prove that he was holder, and that the defendant signed the bill. If he proved that, the onus was on the defendant ; for the bill imports consideration. If the defendant proved that the bill was stolen, or that there was fraud, the onus was shifted, and the plaintiff had to prove that he gave value for it. This . . . depends not on the allegation, under the new system, on the record, that there was fraud, but on the proof of it at the trial " (p. 1203). " It was laid down in Ryder *v.* Wombwell that 'there is in every case a preliminary question, which is one of law, viz., whether there is any evidence on which the jury could properly find the question for the party on whom the onus of proof lies ; if there is not, the judge ought to withdraw the question from the jury, and direct a nonsuit if the onus is on the plaintiff, or direct a verdict for the plaintiff if the onus is on the defendant,' and this was approved of and adopted in this House in the recent case of Metropolitan Railway Company *v.* Jackson. I have already given my reasons for thinking that the expression, 'the party on whom the onus of proof lies,' must mean, not the party on whom it lay at the beginning of the trial, but the party on whom, on the undisputed facts, it lay at the time the direction was given " (p. 1208). (*c.*) Baron Parke's statement in Barry *v.* Butlin [1] is well known : " The strict meaning of the term *onus probandi* is this, that if no evidence is given by the party on whom the burden is cast, the issue must be found against him " This might seem to point to the duty of establishing. Does it ? It describes only the duty of one, whoever he may be, having the *onus probandi*, whatever that may be, to produce evidence. Now, the common English conception is

---

[1] 2 Moore, P. C. 484 ; s. c. 1 Curteis, p. 640 ; and so Metcalf, J., in 6 Cush. p. 319.

that when he does have this and makes a prima facie case, the other party, and not he, is the one who then has the *onus probandi ;* so that then Baron Parke's remark will apply to him.[1] Baron Parke's expression appears to be consistent with either view, since the duty of beginning and that of finally establishing, *may* rest upon different persons.[2] (*d.*) A recent case in the Supreme Court of Connecticut[3] is a striking illustration of the perplexity that attends many attempts to deal with this subject in criminal cases. The defendant was prosecuted under a statute, for neglecting and refusing to support his wife. At the trial, under the usual plea of not guilty, he set up her adultery. The jury were charged that the defendant had the burden of proof to sustain the adultery beyond a reasonable doubt. A verdict for the State was set aside, and a new trial granted for misdirection. It was laid down by the court (Andrews, C. J.) that the burden of proof is on the government to prove its case in all its parts; that the issue is but one, the defendant's guilt, and that whenever a defence is so proved that a reasonable doubt is caused as to any part of the case, the jury should acquit. But in setting this forth, the court at the same time says : " If the defendant relies upon some distinct substantive ground of defence not necessarily connected with the transaction, . . . as insanity or self-defence, or an *alibi*, or, as in the case at bar, the adultery of the wife, he must prove it as an independent fact. . . . It is incumbent upon the defendant to establish the fact. . . . All authorities agree that the burden is upon the State to make out its accusation . . . beyond all reasonable doubt. . . . When a defendant desires to set up a distinct defence, . . . he must bring it to the attention of the court ; in other words, he must prove it, . . . that is, he must produce more evidence in support of it than there is against it. When he has done this by a preponderance of the evidence, the defence becomes a fact in the case of which the jury must take notice . . . and dispose of it according to the rule before stated, that the burden is upon the State to

---

[1] Such is Baron Parke's own use of the term in Elkin *v.* Janson, 13 M. & W. pp. 662–3, and Lord Halsbury's and Lord Watson's in Wakelin *v.* London, etc. Ry. Co., 12 App. Cas. 41 ; where also Lord Blackburn, having read Lord Watson's opinion, remarks: "In it I perfectly agree. " See also Stephen, Dig. Ev. arts. 95 and 96, and L. J. Bowen,. *ante*, p. 49.

[2] See *infra*, p. 66.

[3] State *v.* Schweitzer, 57 Conn. 532 (1889).

prove every part of the case against the prisoner beyond a reasonable doubt."[1] The court here avoid saying in terms that the defendant has any "burden of proof," but they say it in substance. If the defendant must establish the insanity or *alibi* by the preponderance of the evidence, he has the burden of proving it. It would seem that the true theory of this case is that the defence has nothing to "prove,"[2] but has only to do what the court intimated in Com. *v.* Choate (105 Mass. 451), when it said : "The evidence which tended to prove the *alibi*, even if it failed to establish it, was left to have its full effect in bringing into doubt the evidence tending to prove the defendant's presence at the fire." So here, defendant need not establish the adultery; he need only bring the jury to a reasonable doubt about it ; for, according to the theory of the case, *that* is a reasonable doubt of the defendant's guilt.[3]

III. The subject is, of course, very intimately connected with that of pleading.

(1.) It is important to notice further one or two peculiarities of the Roman law, already alluded to ; for that body of law has given us the term *onus probandi* and a variety of often-quoted maxims about it. Under the system which prevailed in classical times, and for two or three centuries after the Christian Era, — a period which includes the great jurists whose responses are preserved in the Digest, — the Prætor sent to the judex a formula containing a brief indication of the plaintiff's claim, of the affirmative defence, if any, of the affirmative replication, if any, and so on, — with instructions to hear the parties and their witnesses, and then decide the case. No denials were mentioned in the formula, but each affirmative case was understood to be denied. Then followed a trial of each of these cases separately, — first, the plaintiff's ; then, unless that failed, the defendant's ; and then, unless that failed, the plaintiff's replication ; and so on. What, in our

---

[1] For this exposition the court cite, among other cases, Brotherton *v.* The People, 75 N. Y. 159, and the charge in Com. *v.* Choate, 105 Mass. 451; and they remark that this last charge was "held to be correct." But surely this is misleading. The Massachusetts court held in effect that the charge was inconsistent and in part bad, but that it contained its own antidote, and therefore the verdict might stand.

[2] "It is a prisoner's burden, the only burden ever put upon him by the law, that of satisfying the jury that there is a reasonable doubt of his guilt." R. H. Dana, *arguendo*, York's Case, 9 Met. p. 98.

[3] See the clear statements in State *v.* Crawford, 11 Kans. p. 44-5 (1873), and in Scott *v.* Wood, 81 Cal. 398 (1889).

system, is a plea in confession and avoidance, was, in the Roman
system, merely a supposition of the truth of the opposite case,
an anticipation of a possible proof of it, and an avoidance of it ;
nothing was really admitted. As illustrating this, I quote in a
note from Professor Langdell's clear account of a procedure which
is thought to have " differed but slightly in principle " from that
of the period to which I now refer.[1]

Now, under such a method, where every case presents, at the
trial, a clear and unchangeable affirmation and denial, the phrase
onus probandi (and so the leading Latin maxims about it) may
have a very simple meaning. The proof, the burden of proving,
belongs to the *actor;* it cannot shift, and cannot belong to the
reus, whose function is not that of proving, but the purely
negative one of repelling or making ineffective the adversary's
attempts to prove.[2]

(2.) It would be possible to conduct legal controversies, as
well as others, without any written or recorded pleadings, or in
disregard of them. It has often been done. The convenient
practice of trying cases upon agreed facts, whether resting on a
statute[3] or on the practice of the courts, will readily come to mind.
As regards everything following the declaration in civil cases and
the indictment in criminal cases, we are familiar in modern times
with that state of things, — indeed the common law has always
known it.[4] An oral plea of not guilty and a written general

---

[1] Equity Pleading (2 ed.), ss. 4–14. "There were . . . as many stages in the
trial as there were pleadings. The first stage consisted of the trial of the plaintiff's case
as stated in the libel. For this purpose the plaintiff would first put in his evidence in
support of his case, and the defendant would then put in his evidence, if he had any, in
contradiction. The evidence bearing upon the libel being exhausted, the next stage was
the trial of the exception, which proceeded in the same manner as the trial of the libel,
except that the defendant began, he having the burden of proof as to his exception. In
this manner the trial proceeded, until all the evidence bearing upon each of the pleas in
succession was exhausted, each party being required in turn to prove his own pleading,
if he would avail himself of it (s. 8). . . . Finally it will be found that all the essential differences between a trial at common law and by the civil law, arise from this,
namely, that by the common law a cause goes to trial with everything alleged in the
pleadings on either side admitted, except the single point upon which issue is joined,
while by the civil law it goes to trial with nothing admitted " (s. 12). This system has
largely survived on the continent of Europe, in Scotland, and in our equity procedure.

[2] This is equally plain in any simple case under our system, such as Hingeston *v.* Kelly,
18 L. J. N. S. Ex. 360 (a neat case), and Phipps *v.* Mahon, 141 Mass. 471, a like instance, where the thing is well expounded.

[3] *E.g.,* St. 15 & 16 Vic. c. 76, s. 46.

[4] Co. Lit. 283.

denial are very common answers, whatever may be the real nature of the defence. It may be remembered that within a few
years it was formally recommended by a committee of the leading judicial and legal personages in England, appointed by the
Lord Chancellor, that litigation should thereafter be conducted in
the High Court of Justice without any pleadings. " The committee is of opinion that, as a general rule, the questions in controversy between litigants may be ascertained without pleadings. "
The recommendation followed of a rule that " No pleadings
shall be allowed unless by order of a judge."[1] The substitute
for pleadings which these propositions contemplated was a brief
endorsement upon a writ of summons, indicating the nature of the
plaintiff's claim, and a brief notice from the defendant of any
special defence, such as the Statute of Limitations or payment.
Although these suggestions were not in form adopted, yet English
common-law pleading has come down to a very simple basis
indeed ; and so generally in this country.

But whether there be pleadings or not, and whether they be
simple or not, you come down, at some stage of the controversy, just
as they did at Rome, upon a proposition, or more than one, on
which the parties are at issue, one party asserting and the other
denying. It may be that this issue is not stated in the pleadings and
that it is left to come out at the trial, in the giving of evidence.
An admission may, of course, end the controversy ; but such an
admission may be, and yet not end it ; and if that be so it is
because the party making the admission sets up something that
avoids the apparent effect of his adversary's facts ; as subsequent
payment avoids the effect of facts which show a claim in contract.
When this happens the party defending becomes, in so far, the
actor or plaintiff. In general, he who seeks to move a court to
take action in his favor, whether as an original plaintiff whose
facts are merely denied, or as a defendant, who, in setting up an
affirmative defence, has the rôle of *actor* (*reus excipiendo fit actor*),
— must satisfy the court of the truth and adequacy of the grounds
of his claim, both in point of fact and law.[2] But he, in every case,
who is the true *reus* or defendant holds a very different place in

---

[1] This interesting report may be found in the London Times for Oct. 8, 1881. It is
signed by Lord Coleridge, Lord Justice James, Justices Hannen and Bowen, the Attorney-
General (James), the Solicitor General Herschell, and others.

[2] Bonnier, Preuves, i. 30 (4 ed.) : "Celui qui doit innover doit démontrer que sa préten-
tion est fondée."

the procedure. He awaits the action of his adversary; and it is enough if he simply repel him. The *reus* has no duty of satisfying the court; it may be doubtful, indeed extremely doubtful, whether he be not legally in the wrong and his adversary legally in the right, and yet he may gain and his adversary lose, simply because the inertia of the court has not been overcome, or, to use the more familiar figure, because the *actor* has not carried his case beyond the point of an equilibrium of proof, or, as the case may be, of all reasonable doubt.[1] Whatever the standard be, it is always the *actor* and never the *reus* who has to carry his proof to the required height; for, truly speaking, it is only the *actor* that has any duty of proving at all. Whoever has the duty does not even make out a prima facie case till he comes up to the requirement, and, of course, he has not, at the end of the debate, accomplished his task unless he has held good his case, and held it at the legal height, as against all counter proof. This duty, in the nature of things, here, as well as at Rome, cannot shift, except as the position of *actor* shifts; it is always the duty of one party and never of the other. But as the *actor*, if he would win, must begin by making out a case, and must end by keeping it good, so the *reus*, if he would not lose, must bestir himself when his adversary has once made out a case, and must repel it. And then, again, the *actor* may move and restore his case, and so on. This shifting of the duty of going forward with argument or evidence may go on through the trial. Of course, the thing that thus shifts and changes is not the peculiar duty of each party, — for that remains peculiar, *i.e.*, the duty, on the one hand, of making out and holding good a case which will move the court, and, on the other, the purely negative duty of preventing this; but it is the common and interchangeable duty of going forward with argument or evidence.

(3.) The question of how it shall be determined whether a particular claim or defence be an affirmative one might seem very

---

[1] Bracton, fol. 239 *b*; Bonnier, Preuves, i. 51 (4 ed.), remarks: "Nos anciens auteurs, de leur côté, ont proposé divers expédients pour résoudre les questions douteuses. Les uns veulent qu'on tranche le différend par la moitié, ce que Cujas appelle avec raison *anile judicium*. D'autres proposent l'emploi du sort, emploi qui a été réalisé effectivement en 1644 dans la fameuse *sentence des bûchettes*." He adds in a note : "Par un juge de Melle qui avait fait tirer aux plaideurs deux pailles ou *bûchettes*, qu'il tenait entre les doigts. Heureusement pour l'honneur de la justice, elle a été reformée par le parlement de Paris."

simple, but often, in fact, it is not. It is far from being a mere question of the form in which a party phrases his claim or his defence, whether that be affirmative or negative. The general question might be answered on various principles. It might turn on the mere form of the pleadings, and in some instances it does.[1] In civil cases, and, in some jurisdictions, in criminal cases, matters are often in no such simple condition. "Undoubtedly," says Mr. Justice Holmes, "many matters which, if true, would show that the plaintiff never had a cause of action, or even that he never had a valid contract, must be pleaded and proved by the defendant; for instance, infancy, coverture, or, probably, illegality. Where the line should be drawn might differ, conceivably, in different jurisdictions." (Starratt *v.* Mullen, 148 Mass. p. 571.) In general, the considerations of detail which affect this matter are those of precedent and of mere practical convenience, tempered by logic. Whatever they be, it is not my purpose to deal with them; it is, as I have indicated before, too large a matter. If there were space, I should insert here the substance of Professor Langdell's very valuable statement upon this subject;[2] but as there is not, I beg to commend it to the perusal of the reader. Bentham recognized the difficulties attending this subject, and offered as his chief and indispensable remedy "the restoration of that feature of primitive justice, — confrontation of the parties at the outset *coram judice*," and the application of the maxim that he should have the burden "on whom it would sit lightest," *i.e.*, who could fulfil the requirements with the least "vexation, delay, and expense."[3]

(4.) But now, keeping all this in mind, it is very important to remark certain sources of ambiguity.

(*a.*) He who has to move the court and establish his case, has also, as we see, to go forward with the proof of it; the other may rest until then, and will win without a stroke if the first remain idle. This duty is generally given as the distinctive test of an affirmative case, — "Which party would be successful if no evidence at all were given."[4] But when the *actor* has gone forward and made his prima facie case, he has brought a pressure to bear

---

[1] See Professor McClain's valuable article on "The Burden of Proof in Criminal Prosecutions," 17 Am. Law Review, 892.

[2] Equity Pleading (2 ed.), ss. 108 *et seq.* See also Pomeroy, Remedies, c. 4.

[3] Bentham, Works, vi. 139, 136. [4] Amos *v.* Hughes, 1 Moo. & Rob. 464.

upon the *reus*, which will compel him to come forward; and he again may bring a pressure to bear upon the *actor* that will call him out. This duty of going forward in response to the pressure of a prima facie case, or of a natural or legal presumption, — a duty belonging to either party, — is, in its nature, the same as that which rests upon the *actor* at the beginning, and which is put as the distinctive test of an *actor;* it is merely a duty of going forward. This fact was perceived, and it led to a use of the test, which imperceptibly draws the mind away from the notion of an affirmative case, to something quite different. "As, however," says Best,[1] "the question of the burden of proof may present itself at any moment during a trial, the test ought, in strict accuracy, to be expressed thus, viz. : Which party would be successful if no evidence at all, or no more evidence, as the case may be, were given?" Now, when this has been said and accepted, all notion of a duty that is limited to the beginning of a case is thrown away, and so every circumstance that discriminates the *actor* and the *reus.* We are told that we may know him who has the burden of proof by considering whether, *at any given moment*, a party would lose if the case stopped then and there. But that is a test that may apply to either party, for it points to a situation in which either may find himself, that of having the duty of going forward. In short, the test for the burden of establishing has become a test which is good only for the burden of producing evidence. This duty now comes prominently forward, and the other is lost sight of. Meantime, this change is unobserved. And, as we have but one term for the two ideas, it gets used now for one and now for the other ; and, again, in a way which makes it impossible to say what is the meaning ; and so there is no end of confusion.

(*b.*) Another source of ambiguity relates to the "shifting" of the burden of proof. We see that the burden of going forward with evidence shifts from side to side, while the duty of establishing his proposition is always with the *actor*, and never shifts. But as we have only one phrase for the two ideas, we say, alternately, that the burden of proof does and does not shift. And then still another ambiguity. The burden of establishing is sometimes called "the burden of proof upon the record," and it is assumed that the record shows the full allegations of the parties.

---

[1] Evid. s. 268, and so Bowen, L. J., in Abrath *v.* N. E. Ry. Co., 11 Q. B. D. 440.

But in fact, as we have seen, the record very often indeed fails to do that, and when the general issue is pleaded the denying party is often allowed in his evidence to set up affirmative defences.[1] So far as the record shows us anything in such a case, the plaintiff is the *actor*, and the burden of establishing the proposition of the case appears to be upon him. And yet, since his adversary may offer evidence of an affirmative case, and when he does, becomes the *actor*, and has, with his affirmation, the burden of establishing it, this burden of establishing has shifted, because a new proposition has been introduced. The real fact is, that under this mode of pleading the point of time required for setting up the affirmative case is different from that fixed where the pleading is scientific; instead of requiring that it be disclosed before the pleadings are ended, it is allowed to be made known during the progress of the trial, and the sense in which we say that the burden of proof has shifted is that sense in which, under a strict rule of pleading, it would be said to shift while the pleadings are going forward, being first upon the plaintiff, "shifting" to the defendant when he pleads in confession and avoidance, and remaining fixed at the end where the last purely negative plea leaves it. In both cases the burden of establishing is said to "shift," in the sense that a new affirmative case has been disclosed, which carries with it the duty of making it out. It remains just as true as ever that the burden of establishing a given proposition in issue never shifts, *i.e.*, it is always upon the *actor;* but since new issues may be developed at the trial, we say that the burden of establishing shifts during the trial. Accordingly we find that Chief Justice Shaw, in the very act of starting the peculiar practice which has since existed in Massachusetts of limiting the meaning of the term "burden of proof" to the one meaning of the *actor's* duty of establishing his proposition, lays it down that, "Where the party having the burden of proof gives competent and *prima facie* evidence of a fact, and the adverse party, instead of producing proof which would go to negative the same proposition of fact, proposes to show another and a distinct proposition which avoids the effect of

---

[1] Such is a very common doctrine about the defence of contributory negligence. Ind. R.R. Co. *v.* Horst, 93 U. S. 291; Wakelin *v.* Ry. Co., 12 App. Cas. 41. In Missouri (Stone *v.* Hunt, 94 Mo. 475), as in Ireland (Dublin, etc. Ry. Co. *v.* Slattery, 3 App. Cas. 1155), the defendant must plead contributory negligence specially. See Hubbard *v.* Harden Exp. Co., 10 R. I. p. 254; and compare Hutch. Carriers, § 766-8.

it, there the burden of proof shifts, and rests upon the party proposing to show the latter fact." [1]

It is common now, in Massachusetts, to say that "the burden
of proof never shifts." [2]

(*c.*) Another source of ambiguity lies in the relation between
legal presumptions or rules of presumption, and the burden of
proof. What is true of these phrases in one sense may not be true
in another. When it is said that the burden of establishing lies
upon the *actor*, this refers to the total proposition or series of
propositions which constitute his disputed case. As when in an
action for malicious prosecution [3] the Master of the Rolls said:
" The burden of proof of satisfying a jury that there was a want of
reasonable care lies upon the plaintiff, because the proof of that . . .
is a necessary part of the larger question, of which the burden of
proof lies upon him." Suppose, then, that it be settled in any
case, upon the principles, whatever they be, which govern the
question, that the burden of establishing a given issue is upon A,
and that upon some detail of this issue a rule of presumption
makes in favor of A, *e.g.*, that he has to establish a will, and that
the presumption of sanity helps him as to this one element of his
proposition; [4] or that he has to establish the heirship of a child,
including its birth of certain parents, in wedlock, and legitimately,
and that the presumption applying in such cases helps him as to
the last point; [5] on the supposition, I say, that in any given case
the burden of establishing is thus fixed, and that the presumption

---

[1] Powers *v.* Russell, 13 Pick. 69, 77 (1832).

[2] As in 142 Mass. p. 360; but this, even under the existing practice in Massachusetts,
is not quite true, for after the answer there need be no replication; while anything is open
to the plaintiff at this stage. By the St. 1836, c. 273, special pleas in bar in Massachusetts were abolished in all civil actions, and the general issue substituted. This had
been the law as to certain sorts of action before. Of the condition of the law as it stood
after this change Mr. B. R. Curtis, afterwards Mr. Justice Curtis, said (Report of Commissioners on the Massachusetts Practice Act, Hall, p. 139): " He who now surveys
what remains sees every plaintiff left to inhabit the old building, while all others are
turned out of doors." The "Practice Act" of 1851, prepared by these Commissioners,
abolished the general issue in all but real and mixed actions and substituted a stricter
system. But this strictness was in part done away the next year, when the first Practice
Act was repealed, and a new one enacted. Under this one, now in force, no pleadings
are required after the defendant's answer (compare St. 1851, c. 233, s. 28, with St.
1852, c. 312, s. 19), and the old looseness still exists from this point on.

[3] Abrath *v.* The N. E. Ry. Co., 11 Q. B. D. p. 451.

[4] Sutton *v.* Sadler, 3 C. B. N. s. 87.

[5] Such a case may easily be constructed out of Gardner *v.* Gardner, 2 App. Cas. 723.

THE BURDEN OF PROOF. 63

thus operates as touching a part only of the total proposition, how does this affect the duty of the *actor*? Of course it does not touch the burden as regards the whole issue, which covers not only the presumed thing, but more. Does it then transfer to the other the duty of establishing a part of the issue? If so, we may easily suppose a variety of presumptions, which would split up the issue in a manner very confusing to a jury or even a judge. What happens in such a case seems rather to be what the Romans called a *levamen probationis*, *i.e.*, the presumption has done the office, as regards a particular fact, of prima facie proof, so that the *actor* need not in the first instance go forward as to this matter; his case is proved by this, without evidence, just as it would have been by such an amount of evidence as makes a prima facie case. Of course his case may not be finally proved thus, for he must meet the defendant's counter proof, and must make good his total proposition not merely at the beginning but at the end of the trial.

Such is the import of the case of Sutton *v.* Sadler,[1] where, in an action of ejectment by an heir-at-law against a devisee, the court held it a misdirection to instruct the jury that the heir-at-law was entitled to recover unless the will was proved; but when the execution of the will was proved the law presumed sanity, and, therefore, the burden of proof shifted and the devisee must pre-

---

[1] 3 C. B. N. s. 87, and so Symes *v.* Green, 1 Sw. & Tr. 401. So Baxter *v.* Abbott, 7 Gray, 71 (1856), where a decision on an appeal from a degree of a court of probate allowing a will, sustained the ruling (p. 74) that "the burden of proof was on the appellee to show to their [the jury's] reasonable satisfaction that the testator was of sound mind when he executed the instrument in question; that the legal presumption, in the absence of evidence to the contrary, was in favor of the testator's sanity, and that the appellee was entitled to the benefit of this presumption, in sustaining the burden of proof which the law put upon him." "We all agree [p. 83] that it ['the legal presumption'] does not change the burden of proof, and that this always rests upon those seeking the probate of the will." And so Brotherton *v.* The People, 75 N. Y. 159(1878, Church, C. J.), and People *v.* Garbutt, 17 Mich. 9 (1868, Cooley, C. J.); Dacey *v.* The People, 116 Ill. 555; and a great number of criminal cases in this country holding the like; to the effect that the burden of establishing sanity in an indictment for murder is upon the government, that the presumption of sanity puts upon the defendant the burden of going forward with evidence upon this question, but does not affect the duty of ultimately sustaining sanity,— a fact, which, upon the theory of these cases, is none the less a part of the government's case because it is impliedly and not in terms alleged. This doctrine was adopted in Massachusetts as regards the defence of idiocy, an original absence of natural capacity, in Com. *v.* Heath, 11 Gray, 303 (1858), and by Chief Justice Gray and Morton, J., as to insanity in general, in Com. *v.* Pomeroy (Wharton, Homicide, (2d ed.), Appendix, 753, 754, 756); and it is understood to be now the law in that State.

vail unless the heir-at-law established the incompetency of the
testator, and, if the evidence made it a measuring cast and left
them in doubt, they ought to find for the defendant.   The court
held, on the contrary, that while the presumption of sanity freed
the defendant from the need of proof in the first instance, it did
not relieve him of the fixed, unshifting burden of making out his
case of a valid will.   In this case there is much talk about whether
the presumption of sanity be a presumption of law or of fact.
Is not this an idle discussion ?   There is no rule of legal reasoning
which is more commonly called a presumption of law than this,
which, prima facie, attributes sanity to human beings.   That it is
a rule of presumption and a legal rule there is no doubt. The
important question in any particular instance is what is the effect
and operation of the rule, not what its name is.   And in Sutton
v. Sadler the result is that where the case is an affirmative one,
the effect of this legal rule of presumption, on a part of the *actor's*
case, is that of making out a prima facie case on this part, and
not that of shifting or otherwise affecting the burden of establishing this part of the case.

It is true then that " presumptions shift the burden of proof,"
in the sense of the duty or going forward with evidence.   And in
this sense they relieve at the outset, as touching the thing presumed, him who has the duty of establishing ; they are always
levamen probationis.   It is also true that rules of presumption
may fix the duty of establishing, because they are rules of law ;
and a rule of law which determines who has the affirmative case
may be cast in the form of a presumption ; this is a very common
form of expressing all sorts of rules of law. But it is not the nature
of rules of presumption, simply as such, to determine the duty of
establishing the thing presumed, while it is their nature to fix the
duty of meeting the presumption, *i.e.,* of coming forward with argument or evidence.   When, therefore, if ever, a rule of presumption
does fix the duty of establishing, it is because of what may be called
an outside reason, *e. g.,* the existence of a statute or a rule of the
substantive law which imparts to the presumption this quality of
determining the affirmative side ; or, to speak exactly, it is the
statute or the substantive law that determines it, and not the
rule of presumption.[1]   It must be firmly held in mind that rules

---

[1] To illustrate what is meant by this, let me refer to a passage in Professor Langdell's
powerful and remarkable book on Equity Pleading (2 ed.), ss. 117 and 118.   In actions

of presumption are adopted for a variety of reasons; that they are not fixed merely with reference to litigation and procedure, but are a part of the machinery for the general administration of justice. They are propositions which, for any purpose, fix the legal equivalence of one set of facts with another. The need of them comes up very often in considering whether a given fact, as death, or life, or title, has been sufficiently proved, but often, also, in determining merely what the substantive law of property or persons may be.[1] The validity, then, of this proposition that a presumption of law fixes the burden of proof (in the sense of establishing), depends on the question whether in any given instances it fixes the affirmative or the negative character of a case for purposes of procedure ; and since that question has to be first determined, there seems to be no need of introducing the notion of presumption at all.

IV. As regards a proper terminology for the conceptions now indicated by the "burden of proof." It seems impossible to approve a continuation of the present state of things, under which ideas of great practical importance, and of very frequent application, are so imperfectly and dubiously intimated. What can be done ? Of courses that are theoretically possible there are three ; to abandon the use of this phrase and choose other terms, or to

---

to recover property, he says, the foundation of them is the plaintiff's present ownership; it will not, therefore, be enough to allege that he or his ancestor once had a good title unless on proof of that " the law will raise a presumption that the plaintiff owns the *res* now," or, as it is again put, "that he continues to own it until his death ;" but there is such a presumption ; had the right of alienation been coeval with the right of property, this would probably have been otherwise; but under the feudal system, as regards land, there was no such right of alienation. "When alienation came to be allowed, the presumption, of course, ceased to be conclusive, but it remained until rebutted; and, as there has been nothing to destroy it, it doubtless continues to exist to this day," etc., etc.

The conception here appears to be that the former rule of real property was a conclusive " presumption of law," that the statute made it a rebuttable presumption of law, and that this presumption of law fixes the "burden of proof" and so determines who holds the affirmative case (see s. 108). But why bring in the term or the notion of "presumption"? Does it not all come down to this that a former rule of the substantive law has been changed by statute, and that he who would avail himself of the statute novelty must set up and prove the matter that entitles him to it,— according to the principle of the rule (Stephen, Pleading (Tyler's ed.), 295, note *y*) that " regulations introduced by statute do not alter the forms of pleading at common law." The rule, in this instance, which determines the affirmative case, seems to have nothing to do with any notion of presuming the continuance of a state of things which is notoriously obsolete, and the "presumption" appears to be a mere form of expression.

[1] On this subject the writer begs to refer to an article on " Presumptions and the Law of Evidence " in 3 Harv. Law Rev. 141.

fix upon it one of the two meanings now in use, and find another phrase for the other. In favor of the first course, there are the obvious reasons of clearness and precision. But it would be a mere dream to imagine that the phrase could ever be wholly banished from legal usage. We might as reasonably expect to exclude it from the common speech of men. Use it we must.

It remains only to choose in what sense it shall be used. Or shall we say here also, that it is hopeless to make a change ? No doubt it is difficult, but it cannot be hopeless. A change is simply necessary to accurate legal speech and sound legal reasoning ; and we may justly expect that those who have exact thoughts, and wish to express them with precision, will avail themselves of some discrimination in terminology which will secure their end. Particular courts, or judges, or writers, may adopt the course of discarding this phrase altogether and substituting other terms ; that is an intelligible plan. But if any one prefers to follow the course which seems certain to be taken by the current of legal usage, that of retaining the phrase in some sense or other, he will be driven, if he would speak accurately, to tie up the term to a single meaning. Which then shall it be, that of going forward with proof, or that of establishing a given proposition in the upshot ?

(*a.*) In favor of the former there seem to be these considerations : (1.) It is the meaning that the term has in common speech. Whoever, men say, asserts a paradoxical proposition, has the burden of proof. But equally, they say, whoever supports his paradoxical proposition by sufficient evidence to make it probable, shifts the burden of proof, and now his adversary has it upon him[1]. (2.) This is also a common legal usage.[1] (3.) It is a very comprehensive sense, for it includes not merely the duty of meeting a prima facie case against you, but also that of meeting a presumption, and that of going forward at the beginning. This last may be fixed upon the plaintiff by a mere rule of practice, as in Massachusetts,[2] irrespective of his true place in the procedure ; or by the same considerations which determine whether a case is affirmative or negative ; but, however fixed, the duty itself is in its nature merely the duty of going forward with the argument or the evidence, a duty wholly separable from that of finally establishing.

---

[1] See *ante,* p. 49.
[2] Dorr *v.* Bank, 128 Mass. p. 358; Page *v.* Osgood, 2 Gray, 260.

(*b.*) In favor of the other meaning it may be said (1) that it is the one which is prominent in the Roman law and in countries which have the Roman system of pleading ; and (2) that for this exclusive sense there is a certain body of legal authority, *e. g.*, that it has been formerly adopted as the only proper usage by one of our best courts, the Supreme Court of Massachusetts, and, in particular opinions, has been approved by other tribunals and judges. [1] But (1) as to its use in the Roman system, although it would be desirable to harmonize our use of the term *onus probandi* with theirs, that cannot well take place so long as our conceptions, our methods of legal procedure, and the questions which enter into our legal discussions are so unlike theirs. [2] It may be observed also that the immediate intuitus of the phrase, as used in that system, was rather to the duty, at the beginning, of going forward with evidence, than to the duty at the end, of holding the case made out ; these two things, as I have said, are quite separable. According to the Roman conception he who had furnished evidence at the outset had furnished *probatio*. If counter evidence were offered, he must, indeed, keep up his *probatio ;* but the notion of *probare* and *probatio* was answered by a prima facie case. (2) As regards the fact, that there is high authority for fixing upon the phrase the single meaning of a burden of establishing, it may be doubted whether experience favors a continuance of this experiment. Chief Justice Shaw began it in 1832, [3] and not, as I venture to think, with a sufficient recognition of the fact that the other use of the phrase was also perfectly well fixed in legal usage. During the following twenty-eight years of his most valuable judicial life, he was able to hold the terminology of his court with fair success to the new rule, and to establish it in that State. But the example of this strictness has not, I believe, been followed. The discrimination thus boldly marked has been recognized often in other courts, and this meaning allowed and even preferred, or suggested as the only proper one, in particular opinions ; but, so far as I know, no other court has undertaken to distinctly and steadily reject the other meaning.

Let me illustrate the difficulties that have attended the Massachusetts experiment. In 1840 [4] Chief Justice Shaw restates his view, and calls the other use of the word "a common misapprehension of

---

[1] See *ante*, p. 50.
[3] Powers *v.* Russell, 13 Pick. 69, 76.

[2] See *ante*, pp. 46, 55.
[4] Sperry *v.* Wilcox, 1 Met. 267.

the law on the subject. " But in 1842 [1] the opinion of the court distinctly lays down the other doctrine : " The [auditor's] report being made evidence by the statute, it necessarily shifted the burden of proof ; for being *prima facie* evidence, it becomes conclusive where it is not contradicted or controlled." In 1844 (Taunton Iron Co. *v.* Richmond, 8 Met. 434) the reporter, afterwards Mr. Justice Metcalf, gives a decision of the court (Shaw, C. J.) that an auditor's report is prima facie evidence for the party in whose favor it is made, and adds in his head-note the expression, " and changes the burden of proof. " In 1848 [2] the court (Metcalf, J.) state that, in a suit by the payee of a promissory note against the maker, " the burden of proof is on the maker " to establish want of consideration. But two years later, [3] they say that the burden of proof is on the plaintiff, and remark (Fletcher, J.) of the previous case that " there is a sentence in this opinion which may be misunderstood ; . . . [quoting it]. This must be understood to mean that the burden of proof is on the maker to rebut the *prima facie* case made by producing the note, otherwise the *prima facie* evidence will be conclusive. " In this same year, 1850, [4] the court (Metcalf, J.), while distinguishing, in the case of an alteration in a writing, between " the burden of proof " and the " burden of explanation, " define the burden of proof in terms borrowed from Baron Parke, but not understood by him or in English legal usage to be limited to the duty of establishing : [5] " The effect . . . would be that if no evidence is given by a party claiming under such an instrument, the issue must always be found against him ; this being the meaning of the ' burden of proof.' 1 Curteis, 640. " In 1858 [6] the court (Dewey, J.) remark upon the fact that the Chief Justice of the lower court had used the phrase in another than " the more precisely accurate use of the term . . . as now held by the court, " but they conclude that it did not mislead the jury. In 1859 [7] the judge below ruled

---

[1] Jones *v.* Stevens, 5 Met. 373, 378, Hubbard, J.

[2] Jennison *v.* Stafford, 1 Cush. 168.

[3] Delano *v.* Bartlett, 6 Cush. 364, 368. It may well be doubted whether this case rests upon the true analysis of the substantive law ; but it is still followed in Massachusetts, *e. g.*, in Perley *v.* Perley, 144 Mass. 104 (1887), and, to some extent, elsewhere.

[4] Wilde *v.* Armsby, 6 Cush. 314, 319.

[5] See *ante*, p. 53.

[6] Noxon *v.* DeWolf, 10 Gray, 343, 348.

[7] Morgan *v.* Morse, 13 Gray, 150.

that "the burden of proof was upon the defendant to . . . control the auditor's report," and the court (Bigelow, J.) is obliged again to set forth the discrimination between "the technical sense" of the burden of proof and the other; and then follows what looks like a confession that their exclusive use of the word had not gained any firm hold in the seven and twenty years since Judge Shaw had begun it. "This mode of using the phrase, though somewhat loose and inaccurate, *is quite common*, and where not improperly applied to a case, so as to confuse or mislead the jury, cannot be held to be a misdirection."[1]

Considering, therefore, that the widest legal usage, both in England and here, applies the term "burden of proof" in a sense which is satisfied by making out a prima facie case; that this sense covers the greater variety of situations, viz., not merely the case of one who has a prima facie case, or a presumption against him, but also that of him upon whom rests the duty of going forward with evidence at the beginning; and that it corresponds with the use of the phrase in ordinary discourse, — it would seem wise to fix upon it this meaning only, and to employ for the duty of making out a given proposition, some term, like that, already widely used, of the burden of establishing; in other words, to adopt the meaning which is so carefully stated by the Lord Justice Bowen in Abrath *v.* North-Eastern Railway Co.[2]

V. Whereabout in the law shall we place the subject of the burden of proof? It is common in our system to treat of it, when treated at all, in books on evidence; and the result is that it is little discussed, for it does not belong there.[3] It belongs, as the law of evidence does, to the auxiliary, secondary, "adjective" part of the law; but it is by no means limited to the situation

---

[1] The opinion goes on: "In this sense it was manifestly used in this case. The attention of the court was not called to the distinction between that evidence which was sufficient to impeach and overcome a *prima facie* case, and that which was necessary to sustain the issue on the part of the plaintiff. . . . It would have been more correct for the court to have instructed the jury that the report of the auditor in favor of the plaintiff was *prima facie* evidence, and sufficient to entitle him to a verdict, unless it was impeached and controlled by the evidence offered by the defendant. But we see no reason to believe that the instruction given was not properly understood, or that the defendant was in any way aggrieved thereby." See also the difficult exposition in Wilder *v.* Cowles, 100 Mass. 487 (1868).

[2] See *ante*, p. 49.

[3] Bentham, Works, vi. 214. "This topic [the *onus probandi*] . . . seems to belong rather to Procedure than to Evidence."

where parties are putting in "evidence"; it applies equally where the "evidence" is all in. It covers the topic of argument, of legal reasoning; and equally of reasoning about law and about fact; while the law of evidence relates merely to matter of fact offered to a judicial tribunal as the basis of inference to another matter of fact. To undertake to crowd within the limits proper to the law of evidence the considerations necessary for the determination of matters of a far wider scope, like those questions of logic and general experience and substantive law involved in the subjects of Presumption and Judicial Notice,[1] and that compound of considerations of the same character, coupled with others relating to the history and technicalities of pleading and mere forensic procedure, which lie at the bottom of what is called by this name of the "Burden of Proof," — to attempt this is to burst the sides of the smaller subject and to bring obscurity over the whole of it. And, moreover, it is to condemn this topic, so important in the daily conduct of legal affairs, and so much needing a clear exposition, to a continuance of that neglect, and that slight and merely incidental treatment which it has so long suffered.

James B. Thayer.

CAMBRIDGE, May, 1890.

Presumptions

[21]

THE JOURNAL OF PHILOSOPHY

VOLUME LXXX, NO. 3, MARCH 1983

ON PRESUMPTION*

Presumptions have to do with assumptions made ahead of time, in advance. The concept is suggestive, I think, of a supposition not fully justified, yet not quite rash either. There is in presumption a sense of an unquestioned taking for granted, but at the same time of some tentativeness, overturnability. Given this fertile soil of gently contrasting connotations, it is hardly surprising that philosophers have not altogether shunned the use of this notion.[1] But their employment of it is neither systematic nor critical, and the notion itself has not so far been the focus of proper philosophical attention. I shall in this paper give it the attention I think it deserves.

The clarification of the epistemic claims that presumptions have on us—or rather on our set of beliefs—is undoubtedly part of any adequate account of the notion of presumption. But this will not be the orientation of the explication I shall offer. I shall look, rather, to the role that the notion of presumption can be made to play within the theory of action. That is to say: rather than treat a presumption as an assumption made in advance of some theoretical venture, I shall treat it as an assumption made in advance of practical deliberation. Furthermore, rather than view presumption as a logical prerequisite for the launching of a theoretical inquiry,

---

* Sidney Morgenbesser saw the earliest draft of this paper, and his incisive comments helped me redirect my thinking on the subject. A subsequent version was read to members of the philosophy department at Princeton University in January, 1979. I wish to thank L. Jonathan Cohen, Derek Parfit, Isaac Levi, J. R. Lucas, Avishai Margalit, and Joseph Raz for helpful conversations, and P. F. Strawson and J. L. Mackie for their comments in writing. Part of the research for this work was done during a sabbatical year at Oxford which was made possible by a Rothchild Foundation grant.

[1] Among the articles using 'presumption' in their *titles*: James W. Lamb, "Knowledge and Justified Presumption," this JOURNAL, LXIX, 5 (Mar. 9, 1972): 123-127; Louis I. Katzner, "Presumptions of Reason and Presumptions of Justice," *ibid.*, LXX, (Feb. 22, 1973): 89-100; J. E. Llewelyn, "Presuppositions, Assumptions and Presumptions," *Theoria*, XXVIII (1962): 158-172.

144   THE JOURNAL OF PHILOSOPHY

I shall view it as a rational prerequisite for arrival at a variety of decisions about action.[2]

I. PRESUMPTIONS IN THE LAW

Explication is usually guided by the pre-systematic, everyday usages of the notion under consideration. In the present instance, however, it seems to me that the ordinary-language analysis of the notion of presumption (or such cognates as 'presumably', 'a presumptive such-and-such') will not get us very far. Guidance in the present case is to be sought rather in the realm of the law. Within the framework of the law and, more specifically, within the law of evidence presumptions are both extensively used and made the center of much theorizing.[3] It will be rewarding, therefore, to devote some space to unraveling the nature of legal presumptions, in spite of the fact that theoretical discussions about their status are not free from controversy and that there is no unanimity of opinion among lawyers even about their mode of functioning. It is not my intention to try to arrive at an exhaustive summary of the issue of presumptions in the law, nor to scrutinize all the uses of this notion in the legal literature. My intention is different: to locate the hard core of the use of presumptions within the law, in order that this may serve as a starting point for the task of philosophical explication. Accordingly, at various stages along the way, the explication will be halted momentarily and a point will be checked in the legal realm so as to clarify the direction in which the explication is to proceed. It should be stressed, then, that the reference to the law is for purposes of guidance and illustration only. My aim is to import the notion of presumption from the law into philosophy, not to export philosophical advice for the use of lawyers.

Here, first, is a sample list of legal presumptions: that a child born during lawful wedlock is legitimate; that a person who, without reasonable explanation, has not been heard from for at least seven years is dead; that a marriage regularly solemnized is valid;

---

[2] This might be contrasted with Nicholas Rescher's treatment of presumptions in his *Methodological Pragmatism* (New York: NYU Press, 1977). His framework is not practical deliberation, but what he refers to as the "cognitive venture," where presumptions are conceived of, roughly, as working hypotheses.

[3] Every text on the Law of Evidence contains a chapter on presumptions. Among the eminent authors of such texts are Phipson (1892, 8th edition 1942), Jones (1896, 5th edition 1958), Wigmore (1904, 3rd edition 1940) and Stephen (1925).

The *locus classicus* of theorizing on presumptions is the chapter devoted to them in James Bradley Thayer's *A Preliminary Treatise on Evidence at Common Law*, Boston, 1898. Also of special significance are two articles by Edmund M. Morgan: "Some Observations concerning Presumptions," Harvard Law Review, LXIV (1931): 906–934, and "Instructing the Jury upon Presumptions and Burden of Proof," *ibid.*, XLVII (1933): 59–83.

that a child under fourteen years of age has no criminal intention; that if *A* buys property from *B* and directs it to *C*, *C* was intended to be a trustee for *A*; that when in a common disaster the death occurs of two or more persons related as to inheritance, the younger (or healthier) person survived longer. Also: that a person accused of crime is innocent; that every person is sane; that a person intends the natural consequences of his or her actions.

Consider the first presumption cited above. "There is a presumption that a child born in wedlock is legitimate (i.e., that its father is the mother's husband)." In stating this, what is the law actually saying? Let us consider what consequences follow, if any, from these two premises:

(1) There is a presumption that a child born in wedlock is legitimate.

(2) Adam (a particular child) was born in wedlock.

More specifically, are there conditions under which the conclusion:

(3) Adam is legitimate (i.e., Adam's father is his mother's husband).

can be validly drawn from (1) and (2)? Or perhaps the conclusion should be

(4) There is a presumption that Adam is legitimate.

But then we shall want to know what it is that (4) is saying, and how it is related to (3). Does it actually say anything about Adam? It may perhaps be felt that (4) is not *asserting* anything at all, or at any rate not primarily, but that its import lies elsewhere.

The law itself has some things to say about what it is saying, or perhaps doing, by means of its presumption statements. Here are just two authoritative passages from the law of evidence:

> A presumption means a rule of law that courts and judges shall draw a particular inference from a particular fact, or from particular evidence, unless and until the truth of such inference is disproved (Stephen).

> A presumption may be defined to be an inference *required* by a rule of law drawn as to the existence of one fact from the existence of some other established basic facts.—It is a true presumption of fact in the sense that another fact is assumed from established basic facts. It is a presumption of law in the sense that a rule of law requires the assumption to be made (Jones).[4]

---

[4] There are also several further distinctions in the law concerning presumptions, notably (a) between presumptions of law and presumptions of fact; (b) between rebuttable presumptions and irrebuttable, or conclusive, presumptions. The first is commonly taken to be rather confused and confusing, a presumption of fact being perhaps an altogether redundant notion (see Thayer's attack on this distinction, *op. cit.*, pp. 339-342). The second is interesting, but will not occupy us here.

The way a specific presumption, that of death upon the expira-
tion of seven years of unexplained absence, is put to work is illustrated thus:

> . . . *if* they [the jury] find the fact of absence for seven years unheard
> from, and find no explanatory facts to account for it, then *by a rule of
> law they are to take for true the fact of death,* and are to reckon upon
> it accordingly in making up their verdict upon the whole issue
> (Wigmore, §2490).

Above all, it is the notions of *taking something for true* and of
"reckoning upon it" which interest me in this explicative venture.

The picture that begins to emerge is this. Suppose the descent of
a certain man's estate is at stake. The fact in issue before the triers
of fact (judge or jury) may be whether or not Adam is this man's
legitimate heir (or, *mutatis mutandis,* whether or not this man,
long absent, is still alive, or whether or not this man died before
his wife in the airplane crash that killed them both). In the absence
of evidence on this issue, or in case of conflicting evidence, how are
the fact triers to proceed? Considerations of statistical, or of "prior"
probability, even where they can be appealed to, will clearly not do
as substitutes for particular evidence in each particular case. However, the law sometimes intervenes by laying down rules, in the
form of presumptions, which effect the inference (or "inference")
from certain basic facts already established to the existence of the
fact in issue, as long as no evidence (or no sufficient evidence; see
below) to the contrary is produced. These rules supply, where they
apply and pending rebuttal, a ready-made answer, prescribed rather
than ascertained, to the factual question involved. "When an inference derives from the law some arbitrary or artificial effect and is
obligatory upon judges and juries, that inference is a true presumption" (Jones §11). I would go one step further and claim that
there is not only an element of arbitrariness or artificiality in presumptions, but also an element of bias. Given that there are two
possible answers to the factual question under consideration, either
"yes" or "no", the presumption rule is partial toward one of them
and favors it in advance over the other. What we have here is not
the proverbial situation of gauging, preferably blindfold, which
side of an evenly balanced scale turns out to tip the balance. Rather,
we are deliberately putting the thumb on one side of the scale to
begin with.[5]

---

[5] See Barbara D. Underwood's paper under the suggestive title "The Thumb on
the Scales of Justice: Burdens of Persuasion in Criminal Cases," *Yale Law Journal,*
LXXXVI, 7 (1977): 1299–1348.

Before we are ready to move on from the law, then, a rough preliminary answer to our question concerning the import of sentence (4) suggests itself: for purposes of coming to a verdict and provided that no (sufficiently strong) evidence to the contrary is in, the trier of fact is (instructed by the law) to take Adam's legitimacy for true.

II. THE EXPLICATION

Sentences like (1) will be referred to as *presumption formulas*. The presumption formula will be represented by the string 'pres (P,Q)'. 'P' stands for the *presumption-raising fact* (the lawyers call it the *basic fact*)—in our example, being born in wedlock. 'Q' stands for the *presumed fact*—in our example, being fathered by the mother's husband. Capital letters indicate that generic descriptions of states of affairs are involved; lower-case letters will stand for particular descriptions.

The presumption formula is read, then, as 'P raises the presumption that Q',[6] or, alternatively, as 'There is a presumption from P that Q'. When it is said that it *applies* in a certain concrete instance, this should be taken to mean that the presumption-raising (generic) fact is instantiated in that concrete instance.

I proceed now to interpret the presumption formula in terms of a *presumption rule*. The presumption rule expressed by the formula 'pres (P,Q)' is directed to any person who is engaged in a process of practical deliberation whose resolution materially depends, among other things, on an answer to the factual question of whether q is or is not the case. Such persons may be referred to as the *rule subjects*. The rule is this:

> Given that p is the case, you (= the rule subject) shall proceed as if q were true, unless or until you have (sufficient) reason to believe that q is not the case.

(a) "Proceed . . .": the nature of the rule

What sort of a rule is a presumption rule? What does it actually instruct its subjects to do?

Note first that the presumption formula is propositional in nature ("P raises the presumption *that Q*"); it is ostensibly about facts. However, I submit that it is concerned not so much with *ascertaining* the facts as with *proceeding* on them, as its rule interpretation brings out. Presumption rules belong in the realm of praxis, not theory. Their point is to enable us to get on smoothly with business of all sorts, to cut through impasses, to facilitate and expedite action. But there is no specific action that a presumption

---

[6] Note: 'raises' not in the sense of "increases" but of "creates," "brings about."

rule charges its subjects with. It instructs its subjects to hold a certain proposition as true so as to have a foothold (as it were) for action. Put somewhat differently, the instruction is this: given p, make q a premise in the rest of the pertinent piece of your practical reasoning.

What are we to make of the quasi-jussive mode ("you shall proceed as if . . .") in which the presumption rule is cast: is it, or is it not, a mandatory rule?

In the law it is: the triers of fact are *required* to draw the inference from the P-fact to the Q-fact. Outside the law, with respect to the rather looser and more amorphous framework of practical deliberation in general, the answer is less clear-cut. I tend to think of presumption rules as offering *a way out* and, therefore, tend to regard the question of their status—i.e., whether they prescribe or permit, license, or enjoin—as slightly beside the point. What matters, in my view, is that they *entitle* the deliberators to make—and to ground their subsequent course of action in—an assumption they are otherwise not justified in making.

At the same time, as with many rights and norms, waiving such entitlements or failing to exercise them may be censurable. The very offer of a way out creates the expectation that it will be resorted to in the appropriate circumstances. Thwarting such expectations may well count as violation of a norm and be subject to disapprobation.

(b) ". . . as if q": an inference?

Are presumption rules concerned with inference? Is it their point that the presumed fact is inferred, in some sense or under certain conditions, from the presumption-raising fact?

To avoid confusion, let me draw attention to a distinction. Quite apart from whether or not presumption rules are *about* inference, there is associated with them a rule *of* inference. It is the formal rule governing the operation of the 'pres' operator: from (i) pres (P,Q) and (ii) p, it follows that (iii) pres q [compare sentences (1), (2), and (4) above].

This underscores the following feature of the operator: that it functions either as a two-place operator, its two variables standing for generic descriptions of states of affairs (the presumption formula), or as a one-place operator, its single variable standing for a particular description of a state of affairs (the presumed fact). The connection between these two functions is at the same time understood as well. Note, too, that a 'pres q' formula in effect presupposes a 'pres (P,Q)' formula. That is, if it is the case that, for some

q, pres q, then there is a state of affairs represented by 'p' such that both p and the appropriate presumption rule expressed by the formula 'pres (P,Q)' obtain.

So, the conclusion of the rule of inference associated with presumption rules is to the effect *that a certain fact is presumed*. But this is not to be confused with an inference *to the presumed fact*. And the question with which we started was whether or not what presumption rules are about is inference to the presumed fact(s). In answer to this question I submit that the presumption rule involves no commitment to, nor guarantee of, the truth value of the presumed fact q. It makes no claims upon its subjects' cognitive or epistemic systems. The rule entitles one to hold q as true for the purpose of concluding one's practical deliberation on the impending issue; it neither requires nor entitles one to believe that q.

In light of these considerations I shall avoid talking of presumption rules as being about, or prescribing, inference. Rather, I shall say of the presumption rule expressed by 'pres (P,Q)' that, with a view to its subjects' pertinent practical purposes, it sanctions for them the passage from p to q. Somewhat more succinctly, the phrase to be adopted is that a presumption rule *sanctions the practical passage* from p to q.

(c) *"Unless or until . . .": the rebuttal clause*

The ordinary-language word 'presumption' is suggestive of something tentative, contestible, reversible. There are various terms used, or usable, in this connection: a presumption may be said to be rebutted, overcome, overridden, reversed, defeated, displaced, nullified, and more. I shall single out the first of these and speak of the "unless or until" clause of the presumption rule as *the rebuttal clause*.

The question before us now is, What is it for a presumption to be rebutted? More specifically, we shall want to know what the rebuttal consists in and what it takes to bring it about.

Recall the rule: given that p, you shall proceed as if q unless or until you have (sufficient) reason to believe that q is not the case. This rule sanctions the practical passage from p to q while at the same time acknowledging the possible falsity of q. The rule should be understood as setting some sort of mechanism in motion. It sets its subjects on a certain course of action, namely, that of proceeding to act on the assumption that q. This course can be blocked only *if* (this is the perfective sense conveyed by the 'unless') or *once* (this is the continuate sense conveyed by the 'until') the rule subject has (sufficient) reason to believe that q is not the case. When this happens, the presumption is rebutted; so long as it doesn't, the presumption stands and is operative.

Note: it is the presumption-that-q which is rebutted, not the presumption rule itself. Given a presumption rule expressed by the formula 'pres (P,Q)' and a certain rule subject A, the presumption that q is rebutted for A if the circumstances are such that p is the case and A has (sufficient) reason to believe that not-q: the "unless" clause having been fulfilled, the proceed-as-if-q injunction lapses. (The presumption rule, though strictly speaking not rebuttable, is nevertheless revisable.[7])

The question of what it takes to bring about the rebuttal of a presumption concerns the allocation of duties, and corresponding benefits, by the presumption rule. It has to do with the twin notions of the *burden of proof* and the *benefit of the doubt*. Let us once again take our cue from the law. In litigation, where a presumption rule applies, if and as long as no (sufficient) evidence-that-not-q is in, the triers of fact are to proceed as if q were established to be the case. With legal presumptions, then, it is *evidence* that rebuts them, and it takes the production of evidence to bring the rebuttal about. Now since in an adversary system evidence can be produced only by one or the other of the litigants, the law has to be clear about who is charged with the task of producing such rebutting evidence. The answer is indeed straightforward. To the extent that the unrebutted presumption serves to further the case of one of the parties, referred to as the "presumption proponent," it is up to the other party, referred to as the "presumption opponent," to attempt to rebut it. This is so regardless of who it was who established the presumption-raising fact to begin with, or, for that matter, regardless of where the over-all burden of persuasion lies. (The law distinguishes further between the so-called "persuasive burden" and the evidential burden, but this need not detain us here.)

So, in addition to the substantive aspect of the presumption rules, viz. the sanctioning of the practical passage from p to q, these rules also have a procedural aspect, that of casting a burden of producing counterevidence upon the presumption opponent. The presumption proponent becomes entitled to something: to the

---

[7] Any presumption rule is revisable, even those relating to so-called "conclusive," or irrebuttable presumptions. In "Analyticity by Way of Presumption" (Edna Ullmann-Margalit and Avishai Margalit, *Canadian Journal of Philosophy*, XII, 3 (1982): 435–452) the distinction between revisability and rebuttability, as well as the notion of conclusive presumption, are used to shed some new light on the notion of analyticity.

fact-triers' proceeding on q; the presumption opponent is charged with something: with the burden of showing that not-q. And the entitlement holds as long as the burden has not been discharged.

How can this be related to the wider and looser framework of practical deliberation, where no procedures for "going forward with evidence", and no pair of disputing parties, are part of the picture?

In the foregoing discussion it was already suggested that rebuttal in this framework consists in the deliberator's having (sufficient) reason to believe that q is not the case. That is, it is reasons for belief which rebut a presumption, and it takes the deliberator's coming to have them to bring the rebuttal about. It may not be idle to note at this point that it is not the *existence* of reasons for believing that not-q, but rather the deliberator's *having* them, which counts so far as rebuttal is concerned. Otherwise, the plain and "objective" fact that q is not the case would by itself rebut the presumption.

It follows that here, in contrast with the legal context, the presumption rule's procedural aspect of casting a certain duty on some specified person or party is rather diffuse. Anyone or anything that provides the deliberating agent with the appropriate reason for belief rebuts the presumption for him (or for her). It may, but it needn't be, another person who convinces the deliberator that q is not the case. It is in general just up to the deliberator to check that no available counterindication has been overlooked before he or she is both entitled and enjoined to proceed as if q; and any such (sufficiently weighty) counterindication that turns up may rebut the presumption, thereby halting the mechanism that was set in motion by the presumption rule. There is, then, some mild version of the principle of total evidence at work here. But there is still the question of the length to which one is to go in active search of such counterindication, how far away from the region of the immediately at hand and into the regions of the reasonably accessible or potentially obtainable. This question, however, cannot be given a general answer. It can be answered only relative to the pressures and constraints, notably time constraints, that the deliberator is under. (Another factor here is the strength of the presumption, to be taken up presently.) Indeed, it may turn out that the very point of some presumption rules (e.g., the conversational) is not that of coming to the aid of a person whose process of deliberation gets stuck, but rather to anticipate and preclude the deliberation process altogether, by providing the agent with a baseline for action which is to be abandoned just in case some counterindication is more or less thrust upon him.

Be that as it may, it is important to note the asymmetry that goes to the heart of the matter: whereas the presumption (that q) and the injunction corresponding to it (to proceed as if q) are triggered *in the absence of* certain reasons for belief, it is only *the possession of* certain reasons for belief which rebuts the presumption and annuls the injunction. Where one has reasons for belief sufficient for the grounding of action, there is no deliberation problem; it is to pave the way to action in default of such reasons that presumption rules come about.

(d) *The strength of the presumption*[8]

The presumption that q is rebutted for A when A has *sufficient* reasons to believe that not-q. How much is sufficient?

The "sufficient" qualifier is, I contend, a place holder. It should be replaced by an indication of the weight of the reasons for belief required for the rebuttal. Correlated with this measure will be an index of the strength of the presumption. Thus, a presumption rule relating to a strong presumption will be expressed by the formula 'pres$_s$ (P,Q)', read as "P raises a *strong* presumption that Q." Spelled out, it will say, "Given that p, you shall proceed as if q unless or until you have a *conclusive* reason to believe that not-q." Similarly, the presumption rule relating to a presumption of an intermediate strength will be worded in terms of *good* or *prima facie* reasons for belief, and the rule relating to a weak presumption in terms of *some* reason for belief.[9]

The situation underlying the working of a presumption rule relating to a weak presumption is this. Take a rule subject who is constrained to act and whose choice of course of action depends on whether or not he believes q to be the case. Suppose now that he has no reason for belief either way, i.e., he is in a state of ignorance regarding the answer to the factual question q or not q. Such persons cannot act on the balance of reasons since the proverbial scales are for them empty and in equipoise. But, given that a (weak) presumption rule applies to their deliberation situation, they are to proceed on q. One may think, for example, of the variety of interpretative presumptions that come to our aid in resolv-

---

[8] I am indebted to Ronald Dworkin for illumination on the topic of this section.

[9] This is an extension of the grading of legal presumptions according to their strength. The presumptions of legitimacy and of innocence are strong presumptions in Anglo-American jurisdictions, requiring conclusive counterevidence for their rebuttal. The presumption of sanity is sometimes considered weak in the sense that it lapses as soon as *some* counterevidence is in [see Durham *v.* United States, 214 f. 2d 862 (D.C. Cir. 1954), 741-749]. Most legal presumptions, however, are intermediate in degree of strength.

ing practical deliberations which turn on the ascription of intentions and motivations in the case of a piece of human behavior, either verbal or nonverbal. Prominent among them is the Interpretative Presumption of Cooperation, which enjoins the hearer to interpret his converser's utterance as if it is an appropriate contribution to the accepted purpose or direction of the talk exchange between them, unless or until he has some reason to believe it is an *inappropriate* contribution thereto.[10]

No such lack of reasons for belief underlies the working of presumption rules relating to the stronger presumptions. The situation in which the rule subjects find themselves may broadly be characterized as one of doubt regarding the factual question of whether q is or is not the case. They may well have some reasons to believe q not to be the case, and these reasons may even be weightier than the reasons they have, if any, to believe the opposite. So there *is* in principle a possibility of acting on the balance of reasons here. Yet if these reasons are perceived as not sufficiently weighty for the person concerned to proceed to act on them, if there isn't sufficient conviction, there remains a deliberation problem. Now insofar as a presumption rule applies to this situation, it may operate so as to sway the deliberator toward acting on q. The situation here may be pictured not as one of evenly balanced scales, the presumption rule operating so as to tip the balance, but rather as one where the presumption rule operates so as to tilt the *un*evenly balanced scales toward the other side.

As a case in point, consider the situation where the future academic employment of a junior faculty member is to be decided upon at the end of a certain probationary period. If the person either excels or obviously fails there is no deliberation problem. But if the person succeeds somewhat, there may well remain a deliberation problem. It can be resolved, however, if the institution adopts a clear presumptive tenure policy, e.g., a policy that treats the academic job as belonging to the person hired as qualified for it, unless he or she proves *in*capable of meeting the professional standards of the university within the specified probationary period.[11]

---

[10] Implicit in this is the proposal, which I develop elsewhere (see note 23 below), to recast Grice's well-known Cooperative Principle (in H. P. Grice, William James Lectures, Harvard 1968, 2nd lecture) as a principle governing the *interpretation* of utterances rather than as a principle governing the *production* of utterances; as such it becomes a Presumption of Cooperation.

[11] See Margaret Atherton, Sidney Morgenbesser and Robert Schwartz, "On Tenure," *Philosophical Forum*, x, 2-4 (Winter–Summer 1978-79): 341-352.

But this is not quite accurate enough. If a presumption rule applies in a certain instance, it is there prior to the deliberation process and may at times preempt it altogether. The situation is more correctly to be pictured, then, as involving scales which, because of the presumption rule and the bias inherent in it, are tilted (toward the q side) *to begin with,* and where the balance can be reversed only when a certain weight is put on the other side: when one has some reason to believe not-q in the case of a weak presumption, good (prima facie) reasons to believe not-q in the case of a presumption of intermediate strength, or downright conclusive reason to believe not-q in the case of strong presumptions.

It is this image of some fancied scales being atilt prior to any weighing which is conveyed by the 'pre-' of 'presumption'. And it is the strength of the presumption which determines the weight required for reversing the balance. As for the question of the factors that determine the differential strength of presumptions, these have to do with the relative strength of the considerations in which the justification of each presumption is grounded, as well as with the "work" it is expected to do. There are no generalizations that can be made here, except perhaps for the tentative observation that strong presumptions can hardly be expected to be encountered outside of the framework of the law. We turn now to the issue of justification.

III. THE JUSTIFICATION OF PRESUMPTIONS

The central question up to now was, What are presumptions (or presumption rules)? The question to be taken up now is, *Why* presumptions?

There are in point of fact two justificatory tasks involved. The first concerns the justification for there being a presumption rule, some presumption rule, rather than none: Why are there, or why should there be, presumption rules? The second concerns the justification of the specific presumption espoused by a presumption rule: Why this presumption rather than some alternative?

These two tasks are obviously connected. Only if the first can be met satisfactorily is there any point in embarking upon the second. And also this: the fact that the second can, in certain cases, be answered constitutes part of the answer to the first.

(a) *Why presumption rules?*

A presumption rule, we recall, comes to the aid of a deliberating agent when he or she is called upon to act, when the choice of the course of action to be taken hinges in a material way on whether a certain state of affairs obtains, and when the agent is in a state of ignorance or doubt concerning the answer to the question. The significant factor in the description of the situation is that the person concerned is constrained to take action, *some* action, before his or her deliberation can be terminated: the time to act precedes the rational resolution of the deliberation process.[12] (Note that this may comprise cases where one is constrained to act, or perhaps to react, not just before concluding one's deliberations but even without having started to deliberate.) In particular, the wait-and-see option allowing for suspended judgment is supposed to be ruled out in this type of situation on either logical or practical grounds.

This is a description of a deliberation process which, whether because inconclusive, aborted, or altogether preempted, is unresolved. Unresolved deliberations, to be sure, need not be unresolvable. But from the standpoint of the deliberating agents, constrained as we imagine them to be by time pressure as well as by such "extraneous" factors as emotional stress, distraction, and languor, resolvability-in-principle is all but beside the point. The agents may be in need of some means of extrication. Now a variety of rules, or strategies, or second-order reasons for action, have been suggested and explored by writers on the subject. I cannot here, however, delve into that.[13] The pertinent point I wish to make as a starter on the justification issue is that presumption rules should be regarded as coming to satisfy just such a need: they function as a method of extrication, one among several, from unresolved deliberation processes. What they do is supply a procedure for decision by default.

In order to grasp the rationale of presumption rules qua means of extrication, I suggest that we revert once again to the law and look at the working of the presumption of innocence, which in more ways than one forms a class of its own.

A criminal trial is a process at the end of which the triers of fact must reach an unambiguous verdict for or against the defendant, however inconclusive the evidence before them may be. There is a point beyond which no more evidence is, or can be, introduced,

[12] In his "Reasons for Action, Decisions and Norms," in Joseph Raz, ed., *Practical Reasoning* (New York: Oxford, 1978), pp. 128–143, Raz says: "It should be remembered that a decision is reached only when the agent (1) reaches a conclusion as to what he ought to do and (2) forms the belief that it is time to terminate his deliberations" (134). He is there concerned to emphasize that the first condition is not enough. What I wish to point out is that often the second condition is met but the first is not; it is in this context that various means of extrication have a role to play.

[13] I would just like to mention in this connection the treatment of the notion of *picking* as a means of extrication from unresolved deliberation problems of a rather special and restricted nature, in Edna Ullmann-Margalit and Sidney Morgenbesser, "Picking and Choosing," *Social Research*, XLIV, 4 (Winter 1977): 757–785.

and there is a time at which the fact triers' deliberations must terminate. If the evidence is conclusive and leaves no doubt in their minds as to the defendant's guilt or innocence, there is no problem. But where doubt persists, should they decide by mere preponderance of evidence, however slight? And what if the scales are evenly balanced?

This situation paradigmatically calls for a generic means of extrication. It is not to function as a surrogate for the deliberation process in each particular case. It is, rather, to provide a general direction for solution for the unresolved deliberation processes. The defendant—any defendant—is either to be acquitted for lack of proof of guilt or else is to be found guilty for lack of proof of innocence. Structurally speaking, either of these two counterpresumptions will do; both supply a procedure for decision by default. (Indeed, the old modes of trial—by ordeal, by wager of law, or by battle—were controlled by a presumption of guilt: a man charged with a criminal offense would be punished unless he managed to clear, or rather to "clear" himself.) The question whether to adopt one of these two counterpresumptions—and, if so, which—already slides us into the second justificatory task.

Taking stock: presumption rules function as, and are thus justified qua, means of extrication from unresolved deliberation processes. They are called for in situations which, when described generically, present a recurrent pattern inherent to which is a decision problem such that those required to act can be anticipated to be stuck with an inconclusive or an aborted deliberation process. They are thus called for where arbitrary or haphazard decisions are otherwise likely to be made.

But the mere need for extrication does not in itself suffice to justify the institution of a presumption rule. What such a rule in effect offers is a policy of extrication based on a systematic bias favoring one of the available alternative-types over the other(s). And it is the independent justifiability of such a biased solution which is crucial for the institution of a rule espousing it to be justified.

A presumption rule may be seen, then, as replacing arbitrariness with something like rational prejudgment; although plainly prejudging an issue, it may nevertheless be defended as rational[14] in the following twofold sense: (i) in any particular instance the pre-

---

[14] An altogether different approach to the question of the rationality of presumptions is offered by Louis I. Katzner (*op. cit.*), who addresses himself to the question whether the presumptivist principle of formal justice is rational in the specific sense of whether or not it is necessarily true.

sumption it relates to is open to rebuttal; (ii) the bias it promotes is independently justifiable.

There remain to be discussed the grounds on which a specific presumption, i.e., the biased solution promoted by a presumption rule, may be justified, once the need for some presumption rule in the pertinent type of situation has been established.

(b) *Why the specific presumption?*

The justification of a specific, though generic, presumption-that-Q is, I suggest, a blend of two major types of consideration, sometimes supplemented by a third ancillary one.[15] They are these:

   (i) inductive-probabilistic considerations

  (ii) value-related considerations

 (iii) procedural considerations

Considerations of inductive logic and probability, in a broad sense, have to do with the likelihood of Q, given P. Broadly speaking, they underlie most presumptions. Most people unexplainably absent for upward of seven years are in fact dead; most people living together as man and wife are in fact man and wife; most people mean what they say (most of the time); the evidence of our senses is trustworthy in most cases; a descriptive word is mostly correctly applied to an object displaying certain antecedently specified features;[16] and so on. When the presumed fact-type Q is routinely a concomitant of the presumption-raising fact-type P, it would seem to be a waste of time and energy—sometimes even to the point where the very purpose of the action to be taken is defeated—to begin an investigation as to whether q is indeed the case in any instance of the occurrence of p. It would seem to make good practical sense to proceed on the assumption that q so long as no indications to the contrary crop up.

So with presumption rules relating to presumptions that accord with the normal balance of probability the chance of an error (i.e., proceeding on q while in fact q is not the case) is reduced. The nature and function of the inductive-probabilistic considerations in justifying a specific presumption vis-à-vis its counterpresumption is thus straightforward enough. The point to be emphasized about these considerations, however, is this: they cannot by themselves provide the ground on which a presumption is justified and, hence, on which the institution of a presumption rule is justified.

---

[15] On the interplay of these considerations with regard to legal presumptions see Thayer (1898) and Morgan (1931), *op. cit.*

[16] For more on the issue of presumptions of reference see Ullmann-Margalit and Margalit *op. cit.*

If the sole rationale of the proceed-as-if-q injunction of a presumption rule expressed by the formula 'pres (P,Q)' were the fact that P probabilizes Q, then we would have on our hands just a piece of practical advice in accordance with some canons of inductive reasoning, not a presumption rule properly so called. Indeed, to the extent that pre-systematic or nontechnical uses of the term 'presumption' merely convey the notion of some probability connection, I consider the term to be devoid of its special significance. For a presumption rule to count as such, its justifying considerations from the realm of inductive logic and probability, to the extent that they exist, have to combine with *other* justifying considerations.

Moreover, considerations of the second, normative type may even outweigh those of the first and lead to the espousal of a presumption-that-q in spite of the fact that the odds may possibly favor not-q. Thus, consider the presumption of innocence: it is not even clear in that case whether the relevant probabilistic consideration relates to the entire class of human beings or to the much narrower class of persons charged with criminal offenses. This is a tricky question. But the point is that, even if the relevant class is taken to be that of persons charged and even if it turns out that most of the people in this class are actually guilty of the crimes attributed to them, the presumption in favor of proceeding as if the person charged is innocent may nevertheless be retained and defended; it may fly in the face of the probabilistic consideration. Or take the case of the presumptive principle of equality, in situations falling under the broad heading of the administration of distributive justice.[17] The proponent of this presumption will hold on to its injunction, i.e, to proceed as if the people to be treated were similar in all relevant respects unless or until relevant differences among them are shown, regardless of whether people are in fact likely or unlikely to be thus similar.

So the justification of presumptions may, and perhaps commonly is, couched in inductive-probabilistic terms; but such considerations are neither necessary nor sufficient to justify the presumption rules relating to them.[18]

[17] For discussions of the presumptivist principle of equality (or of justice) see, e.g., S. I. Benn and R. S. Peters, *Social Principles and the Democratic State* (London: Allen & Unwin, 1959), p. 111, and *The Principles of Political Thought* (Glencoe, Ill.: The Free Press, 1965), pp. 127/8; Joel Feinberg, *Social Philosophy* (Englewood Cliffs, N.J.: Prentice-Hall, 1965), pp. 100–102; Katzner, *op. cit.*

[18] Consider this statement by David Lyons [*Forms and Limits of Utilitarianism* (New York: Oxford, 1965), p. 124], who joins issue with Marcus Singer and claims: "A presumption against lying, for example, is fully compatible with most instances of lying, or lying in most kinds of cases, not being wrong. We might say that presumptions as such have no qualitative implications."

It is the justification of presumptions in normative terms which touches what I take to be the core of the concept of presumption. If the first type of consideration had to do with the *chance* of error, this normative type of consideration has to do with the *acceptability* of error. Presumption rules operate in situations where actions have to be decided upon in the light of insufficient information and often under external pressures and constraints. Errors (i.e., proceeding on q when not-q is in fact the case and vice versa) are bound to occur. There is no question of avoiding errors; at best there is the question of reducing their number. But a different sort of question is whether one type of error is to be preferred, on grounds of moral values or social goals, over the other(s). Evaluative considerations may exist which justify a systematic and generic bias in favor of erroneously proceeding on Q rather than erroneously proceeding on not-Q, given that P and given lack of sufficient reasons in the circumstances to believe either q or not-q to be the case.

Thus, in his *Treatise on Judicial Evidence* Jeremy Bentham[19] says that "in doubtful cases [the judge should] consider the error which acquits as more justifiable, or less injurious to the good of society, than the error which condemns." Hence the presumption of innocence. It is, then, as a corrective device that this presumption, as well as others, may be thought of: as regulating in advance the direction of errors, where errors are believed to be inevitable.

Similarly, take Louis Katzner's view with regard to the two rival presumptions, against treating people differently/similarly in any respect until grounds for distinction/similarity have been shown:

> The only possible basis for opting for one of them rather than the other is which state of affairs one would rather see—that in which some of those who are similar are treated differently or that in which some of those who are different are treated similarly.—[*I*]*t comes down to a question of goals or values* (*cf*, note 1; emphasis added).[20]

Consider now the case of the various so-called "conversational" presumptions, like the presumption of truthfulness, or sincerity, or Grice's Cooperative Principle (see fn 10 above). It is easily realized that spending time and effort, in each and every instance in which

---

[19] Extracted from the manuscript by M. Dumont (London: J. W. Paget, 1825), pp. 197/8.

[20] Joel Feinberg argues that to presume equal treatment "would be to make a presumption every bit as arbitrary as the presumption in favor of *unequal* treatment in the absence of knowledge of the relevant similarities and differences of the persons involved" (*Social Philosophy*, p. 102). He concludes that neither of the two opposing presumptions is independently justifiable, on moral grounds (he ignores all other considerations altogether).

one's interlocutor has uttered something, to find out to one's satisfaction whether or not it is indeed true or sincere or whether or not
it indeed contributes appropriately to the purpose of the talk exchange in which one is engaged, before one proceeds to respond to
that utterance is quite likely tantamount to undermining the particular piece of conversation under consideration, if not interpersonal
communication in general. It is along such lines, then, of the general interest in the smoothness of talk exchanges, that the justifying
considerations for there being conversational presumption rules
(*some* presumption rules, rather than none) are to be couched. But
which presumptions shall they be? Can a specific presumption in
this area be independently justified?

It may or may not be true that most utterances of indicative sentences by most human speakers in situations of communication are
true, or are uttered in sincerity. Again, it may or may not be true
that most utterances of most speakers constitute appropriate contributions to the (accepted, mutually recognized) goal or direction
of the talk exchange in which they are engaged. To the extent that
these things *are* true, there will be inductive-probabilistic considerations in favor of the presumptions in question. But regardless of
the question whether or not a given utterance is likely to be true
(etc.), there is the further question of which—if any—of the following alternatives is morally or socially "better": to proceed (respond,
react) erroneously on the assumption of truth (sincerity, appropriateness of contribution), or to proceed erroneously on the assumption of falsity (insincerity, inappropriateness of contribution). Now
it is my contention that if there is no commitment to some value
according to which one type (or "zone") of errors is judged as preferable to the other, then talk of presumption in this area is inappropriate.[21] And it is further my contention that such a value judgment is indeed congenial to anyone who accords primacy to such
notions as the dignity of persons in one's thinking about the fundamentals of ethics. This evaluative consideration comes, of course,
on top of the factor of social desirability, if not necessity, of main-

---

[21] Quine's Principle of Charity, the way he formulates it, is in this sense not a
presumptive principle: "Assertions startlingly false on the face of them are *likely* to
turn on hidden differences of language" [*Word and Object* (Cambridge, Mass.: The
MIT Press, 1960), p. 59, my emphasis]; "One's interlocutor's silliness, beyond a
certain point, is *less likely* than bad translation" (*ibid.*). It seems to me, however,
that this principle can be viewed as a presumptive principle to the extent that the
charitable interpretations it calls for are perceived not just as more likely to be true
but also as conforming better with one's moral conception of one's fellow men and
women; to the extent, that is, that giving credit where credit is not due is judged
more pardonable, and of a higher moral order, than denying credit where it is in
fact due.

taining and sustaining interpersonal communication, which is furthered by the conversational presumptions of truth, sincerity, and appropriateness of contribution and not by any of their contrary presumptions. The normative consideration we are dealing with, in sum, can be viewed as two-tiered: it has to do (i) with the question of which sort of error is morally or socially more acceptable, and (ii) with the moral or social evaluation of the regulative effect on people's behavior of the presumption rule's being instituted and operative.

There is yet another consideration intermingled here, which ought nevertheless to be kept analytically separate. It may perhaps be labeled the *determinateness consideration*.[22] Sometimes it is the case that, once the need for *some* presumption rule has been recognized, there is little real choice in the matter of *which* presumption it should espouse. For example, the presumption in favor of equal treatment even where there is ignorance as to the characteristics of the persons to be treated is determinate, whereas the counterpresumption, in favor of *un*equal treatment in the absence of knowledge of the relevant similarities and differences among the persons involved is so indeterminate (or, as one might say, merely determinable) as to be quite useless. The same might seem to apply to the presumption of sincerity (or that fluent speakers mean what they say): any contrary presumption would be determinable rather than determinate, and as such could hardly be of use as a guide for action.

In such cases, where it is primarily the determinateness consideration that decides which specific presumption shall be espoused by the presumption rule, regardless of whether or not it is supported by inductive-probabilistic considerations, the following stipulation needs to be made: where no separate normative argument is available according to which erroneously proceeding on *q* is judged morally or socially superior to erroneously proceeding on not-*q*, it ought at least to be the case that no such normative argument is available to justify any *contrary* presumption.

A consideration distinct from those dealt with thus far, and often appealed to in the law, is that of procedural convenience. In the case of a railway passenger who is injured by wreck or derailment, the presumption is that the railway company was negligent. Morgan (1931, p. 931, cf. note 3) conjectures that this presumption is grounded in a combination of all three types of justifying considerations: in the normal balance of probability, in a normative judi-

---

[22] I am indebted to the late John Mackie for this point.

cial policy directed toward protecting the public, *and* in the procedural consideration of the comparative convenience with which the parties can be expected to produce pertinent evidence. In general, the procedural consideration has to do with the question of what presumption will be the most useful to adopt as an initial step in the process of deliberation, what will "help the game along best"—quite apart from the question whether the conclusion to which the adoption of this rule points is likely to be true, as well as from the question whether there exists a standard by which one sort of error is judged as more acceptable than the other.

Obviously, if the answer given to the procedural question conflicts with the answer given to the other two questions, the procedural consideration will be outweighed. But in those cases where there is no conflict, where it is in line with the answers to the other questions, or indeed where it is the only clear and solid answer available, it counts.

I would like, finally, to return to the discussion raised above (section IIb) about the nature of the inference involved in presumption rules and to offer the following observation. Underlying the notion of presumption rules there lies a conception of reasoning peculiar to the practical sphere and different both from deductive and from inductive reasoning. In deductive reasoning, once the premises are specified, arrival at the conclusion is a matter of *derivation*, in accordance with some rules. In inductive reasoning, once the premises are specified, the arrival at the conclusion is, roughly speaking, a matter of *calculation*, in accordance with some canons. With presumption rules, once the premises (presumption-raising facts) are specified and provided the context is practical rather than theoretical, arrival at the conclusion (the presumed fact) is in principle a matter of a prior, generic *decision*. It is the decision to sanction the practical passage from P to Q. This decision may be motivated, to a lesser or to a greater degree, by the canons governing inductive reasoning, but not exclusively by them. As we have seen, it must be motivated also by certain evaluative considerations which are primarily concerned with the differential acceptability of the relevant sorts of expected errors: the fact that one sort of error is judged to be, in the long run and all things considered, preferred on grounds of moral values or social goals to the alternative sort(s) constitutes an overriding reason for the decision underlying the presumption rule. The presumption rule itself, which such a (generic) decision underlies, then enables the deliberating agents to arrive, when necessary, at a (specific) decision by default in each concrete instance to which it applies.

This concludes my systematic presentation. Clearly, this is but a bare skeleton. The question whether these dry bones can live will be answered only when some flesh and sinews—in the form of detailed illustrations and case studies—are brought upon them. This, however, is a task for another time.[23]

EDNA ULLMANN-MARGALIT

The Hebrew University of Jerusalem

Part VII
Auxiliary Probative Policy

[22]

"STICKPERSON HEARSAY": A SIMPLIFIED APPROACH TO UNDERSTANDING THE RULE AGAINST HEARSAY

Michael H. Graham *

I. INTRODUCTION

Determining whether a statement is hearsay generally poses little difficulty, provided the basic definition of hearsay has been mastered. Occasionally, however, a statement objected to as hearsay presents an extremely difficult determination for the court. Part of this problem stems from confusion, misunderstanding, and outright disagreement among courts and commentators concerning the proper definition of hearsay. Part of this difficulty also stems from a desire to admit the statement if it is highly probative, highly necessary, and highly trustworthy when the statement, if found to be hearsay, would be inadmissible due to the lack of an applicable common law "pigeonhole" hearsay exception. Under such circumstances, it is not surprising that courts and commentators have squeezed and consequently distorted the definition of hearsay to justify admission of the disputed evidence.

The pressure felt by common law judges to creatively "alter" the hearsay definition to ensure admissibility of a highly probative, necessary, and trustworthy statement no longer exists under the Federal Rules of Evidence. Such a hearsay statement, not meeting the requirements of a traditional hearsay exception, may now be admitted under the other hearsay exceptions of rules 803(24) and 804(b)(5).[1] Thus, the

---

* *Professor of Law, University of Illinois. B.S.E. 1964, University of Pennsylvania; J.D. 1967, Columbia University.*

1. FED. R. EVID. 803(24) provides:

The following [is] not excluded by the hearsay rule, even though the declarant is available as a witness:

. . . .

A statement not specifically covered by any of the foregoing exceptions but having equivalent circumstantial guarantees of trustworthiness, if the court determines that (A) the statement is offered as evidence of a material fact; (B) the statement is more probative on the point for which it is offered than any other evidence which the proponent can procure through reasonable efforts; and (C) the general purposes of these rules and the interests of justice will best be served by admission of the statement into evidence. However, a statement may not be admitted under this exception unless the proponent of it makes known to the adverse party sufficiently in advance of the trial or hearing to provide the adverse party with a fair opportunity to prepare to meet it, his intention to offer the statement and the particulars of it, including the name and address of the declarant.

federal courts and those states which have adopted provisions identical to rules 803(24) and 804(b)(5) can avoid the confusion, misunderstanding, and distortion caused by common law courts' creative twisting of the hearsay definition.

Through use of the heuristic device known as "Stickperson Hearsay" analysis, this article presents a change in the form, but not the substance, of the definition of hearsay. Together the diagrams provide a simplified approach to understanding the hearsay rule, an approach free of the pitfalls of its common law predecessors.

II. THE RULE AGAINST HEARSAY

The common law definition of hearsay is "testimony in court, or written evidence, of a statement made out of court, the statement being offered as an assertion to show the truth of matters asserted therein, and thus resting for its value upon the credibility of the out-of-court asserter."[2]

When the statement is hearsay, the trier of fact is not in a position to assess the proper weight to be accorded the out-of-court statement; the hearsay statement was not made under oath and in the presence of the trier of fact, subject to contemporaneous cross-examination.[3] Un-

---

FED. R. EVID. 804(b)(5) is identical to rule 803(24), except that rule 804(b)(5) also requires that the declarant be unavailable.

2.   C. McCORMICK, EVIDENCE § 246, at 584 (E. Cleary 2d ed. 1972).

The term "assertion" includes both matters directly expressed and matters necessarily expressed by implication. *See infra* notes 50 & 75.

3.   CROSS ON EVIDENCE 1-2, 6-7 (5th ed. 1979) (emphasis in original):

Although some of the modern rules of evidence can be traced to the middle ages, the story of their development really begins with the decisions of the common law judges in the 17th and 18th centuries. Those decisions were responsible for a complex and now almost defunct body of law concerning the competency of witnesses together with other far from defunct rules such as the rule against hearsay with its numerous exceptions, the rule excluding evidence of opinion and the rudiments of the modern law of character evidence. The 19th and 20th centuries have witnessed a number of statutory reforms, but it is the older decisions of the common law judges which dictate the form in which much of the law of evidence must be stated for this law still consists to a large extent of exclusionary rules, rules declaring that certain matters which might well be accepted as evidence of a fact by other responsible inquirers will not be accepted by the courts, rules declaring, in other words, what is not judicial evidence.

For instance, a careful non-judicial inquirer into the question whether A. had been unfit through drink to drive a car on the particular occasion might well attach some importance to the following: (i) the fact that X., since deceased, told a police officer that he had seen A. consume 6 large whiskies before getting into the car; (ii) the fact that Y., a publican who tells him hesitantly a year after the event that he served A. with 6 large whiskies, signed a statement to that effect the morning after the occasion in question; (iii) . . . Yet [both] of the above items of evidence are inadmissible at common law. . . .

Three factors that have contributed to the exclusionary nature of the law of evidence are the jury, the oath and the English adversary system of procedure. . . . [O]ne reason why Y.'s signed statement is excluded is that it was not made on oath; X.'s statement is excluded partly for this reason, partly because the jury might attach undue weight to it, but mainly because the statement has never been subject to cross-examination by A.'s counsel.

. . . . .

The following will suffice as a succinct statement of the rule: "a statement other than one made by a person while giving oral evidence in the proceedings is inadmissible as *evidence of any fact stated*." Examples of the exclusionary effect of the rule at a trial for driving when

less the statement falls within one of the exceptions to the hearsay rule, it is inadmissible. If the statement is not hearsay, or if it falls within a hearsay exception, it still must meet other requirements for admissibility. These requirements include relevancy, authenticity, and when the contents of a document are in issue, the best evidence (original writing) rule.

The Federal Rules of Evidence approach hearsay in the traditional manner. Hearsay, as defined in rule 801(c), is a statement, other than one made by a declarant while testifying at the trial or hearing, offered in evidence to prove the truth of the matter asserted. Rule 801(b) provides that a declarant is a person who makes an out-of-court statement.[4] According to rule 801(a), a "statement" may be an oral or written assertion, or nonverbal conduct if the declarant intends such conduct to be an assertion.[5] Thus, documentary evidence as well as the oral statement of a witness may fall within the definition of hearsay. Whether the declarant subsequently testifies at trial is irrelevant, as is whether the statement was self-serving. A declarant's actions, referred to as non-verbal conduct in rule 801(a)(2), may constitute hearsay when the action of the individual was intended by him as an assertion.

A statement falling within the definition of hearsay is inadmissible unless the statement is defined as "not hearsay" or falls within an exception to the hearsay rule.[6] Acts of Congress, other Federal Rules of Evidence, and rules prescribed by the U.S. Supreme Court create these exceptions. Acts of Congress which provide for admissibility of hearsay statements, however, are narrow in their scope.[7] Non-evidence

---

unfit through drink have already been given . . . . X. deceased's statement to the police officer that he had seen A consume 6 large whiskies was not made by a person while giving oral evidence, and it would have been tendered as evidence of the fact stated—the consumption of the whisky. Y. would have been giving evidence at A.'s trial, but his signed statement to the effect that he served A. with 6 whiskies was not made while he was testifying, and it would have been rejected, although many people might think it was more cogent evidence of the fact stated than Y.'s testimony given at the trial a year later. The words in italics in the above formulation of the hearsay rule are crucial. If the question had been whether the police officer had reason to believe that A. had drunk 6 whiskies X.'s statement would have been admissible because it would not have been tendered to prove the fact stated, but in order to justify the officer's belief. Similarly, if it were suggested to Y. when cross-examined on behalf of A. that his testimony was a recent invention, Y.'s signed statement could be proved in re-examination, not as evidence of the fact stated, but in order to rebut the suggestion of recent fabrication.

4. FED. R. EVID. 801(b).

5. Rules 801(a), (b) & (c) provide the following definitions:

(a) Statement. A "statement" is (1) an oral or written assertion or (2) nonverbal conduct of a person, if it is intended by him as an assertion.

(b) Declarant. A "declarant" is a person who makes a statement.

(c) Hearsay. "Hearsay" is a statement, other than one made by the declarant while testifying at the trial or hearing, offered in evidence to prove the truth of the matter asserted.

FED. R. EVID. 801(a), (b), (c).

6. FED. R. EVID. 802.

7. See, e.g., 7 U.S.C. § 94 (1976) (certificate by Secretary of Agriculture classifying naval stores is prima facie evidence of analysis, classification, or grade of such stores, and of contents of any package, as well as correctness of such analysis, classification, or grade); 8 U.S.C. § 1441(a)(1) (1976) (service on a vessel operated by the United States may be proved by the records of execu-

rules of the Supreme Court which admit hearsay statements are rules such as Federal Rule of Civil Procedure 56, which deals with affidavits in support of a summary judgment motion, and Federal Rule of Criminal Procedure 4(a), which deals with affidavits that show grounds for issuing warrants.[8]

The federal rules employ a number of methods to admit statements which qualify as hearsay. The operation of some exceptions depends on the unavailability of the declarant as a witness.[9] Other exceptions, however, disregard the declarant's availability.[10] Rule 805 admits hearsay within hearsay so long as each component part of the statement satisfies the requirements of a hearsay exception. The federal rules also provide that a party may attack the credibility of a hearsay declarant.[11] Further, the federal rules depart from the common law by treating certain prior statements falling within the definition of hearsay contained in rules 801(a)-(c) as "not hearsay" and also by treating party admissions as "not hearsay."[12]

III. "Stickperson Hearsay" Analysis Described

When a witness testifies in court, four risks must be considered in evaluating the trustworthiness of the witness' testimony. These risks are: (1) perception (the witness' ability to observe what actually oc-

---

tive departments or agencies having custody of the records of such service); 8 U.S.C. § 1440(c) (1976) (separation from military service or under other than honorable conditions, when used as grounds for revoking citizenship, shall be proven by an authenticated certification from the executive department in which the defendant was serving at the time of his separation); 21 U.S.C. § 371(g) (1976) (certified copy of transcript of the record and proceedings of an administrative hearing under the Food and Drug Act which concerns regulations is admissible in any other proceeding under the Act); 49 U.S.C. § 16(13) (1976) (copies of schedules and classifications and tariffs of rates, fares, and charges, and contracts and agreements filed with the Interstate Commerce Commission are admissible in all judicial proceedings as prima facie evidence of what they purport to be).

    8. Fed. R. Civ. P. 32(b) and Fed. R. Crim. P. 15 govern, in part, the admissibility of depositions.

    9. Fed. R. Evid. 804.

    10. Fed. R. Evid. 803.

    11. Fed. R. Evid. 806.

    12. Rule 801(d)(1) provides that a prior statement by a witness is not hearsay if:

    The declarant testifies at the trial or hearing and is subject to cross-examination concerning the statement, and the statement is (A) inconsistent with his testimony, and was given under oath subject to the penalty of perjury at a trial, hearing, or other proceeding, or in a deposition, or (B) consistent with his testimony and is offered to rebut an express or implied charge against him of recent fabrication or improper influence or motive, or (C) one of identification of a person made after perceiving him; . . . .

Fed. R. Evid. 801 (d)(1). Rule 801(d)(2) provides that a statement is not hearsay if:

    [t]he statement is offered against a party and is (A) his own statement, in either his individual or a representative capacity or (B) a statement of which he has manifested his adoption or belief in its truth, or (C) a statement by a person authorized by him to make a statement concerning the subject, or (D) a statement by his agent or servant concerning a matter within the scope of his agency or employment, made during the existence of the relationship, or (E) a statement by a coconspirator of a party during the course and in furtherance of the conspiracy.

Fed. R. Evid. 801(d)(2).

curred), (2) recordation and recollection (the witness' memory of the event), (3) narration (ambiguity in the witness' description of the event), and (4) sincerity (the possibility of fabrication).[13] To protect against these four risks, the law provides that a witness may testify at trial only as to matters within his personal knowledge (1) under oath or affirmation, (2) in person, so that the trier of fact may observe the witness' demeanor, and (3) subject to contemporaneous cross-examination.

Each of these four risks is also present in a hearsay statement. Thus, the trier of fact must evaluate risks of perception, recordation and recollection, narration, and sincerity when it determines the trustworthiness of the hearsay statement. When the statement was made out-of-court, however, the trier of fact does not have the benefit of having the declarant before it, under oath, and subject to contemporaneous cross-examination. Because the trier of fact lacks these essential tests with which it may ascertain the trustworthiness of the statement,[14]

---

13. *See, e.g.*, 4 WEINSTEIN'S EVIDENCE ¶ 800[01], 800-9 to 800-10 (1979):

When a witness testifies about an event he is saying that he perceived a particular fact, remembered it up to the moment of testifying and is now accurately expressing his memory in words. Error, deliberate or unconscious, can enter this process anywhere between the initial perception and the in-court narration. For instance, the witness may not have perceived the event at all, or he may have seen it without understanding, or his impression may have been affected by his emotional and intellectual condition at the moment, or he may have seen it so fleetingly that no accurate impression has remained. Or even if he accurately perceived the event when it occurred, the passage of time may have dulled his recollection or replaced the remembered facts with others. He may be deliberately lying in court, or be honestly mistaken, or be incapable of translating his memory into language that will have the same meaning to his listeners.

The Advisory Committee's introductory note to Article VIII of the Federal Rules of Evidence limits the factors to be considered in evaluating testimony of a witness to perception, memory and narration, taking the position that sincerity is merely an aspect of the other three. *See* FED. R. EVID. art. VIII advisory committee introductory note. However, given the importance of the risk of sincerity it clearly seems better to express the risk of sincerity as an independent factor for consideration. *See* Morgan, *Hearsay Dangers and the Application of the Hearsay Concept*, 62 HARV. L. REV. 177, 218 (1948) ("'[S]hould we not recognize that the rational basis for the hearsay classification is not the formula, 'assertions offered for the truth of the matter asserted,' but rather the presence of substantial risks of insincerity and faulty narration, memory, and perception?"); Tribe, *Triangulating Hearsay*, 87 HARV. L. REV. 957, 958 n.8 (1974) ("In an inexplicable comment, McCormick states that sincerity is 'only an aspect of' the other three infirmities. C. McCORMICK, EVIDENCE § 245, at 581 (E. Cleary 2d ed. 1972)").

14. E. MORGAN, BASIC PROBLEMS OF EVIDENCE 243-44 (1961) illustrates the burdens on the trier of fact:

If we assume that P, the proponent of the witness W, desires to persuade the trier T, to find the existence of fact A, P, through his attorney, will utter a series of sounds to which W will respond with another series of sounds. T must interpret these sounds and in doing so, must rely upon his sense of hearing aided by his sense of sight and his capacity for understanding and interpreting W's language. Suppose that he determines that the sounds uttered by W make up the sentence, "I perceived A." In order to put a proper value on this utterance as tending to prove the existence of A, T must either consciously or instinctively go through the following mental operations: (1) He must ask whether W by the use of this sentence means to convey to T what T would have meant if T had used the same words. If not, just what does he mean to convey? The answer will depend upon T's deduction as to W's use of language. (2) If T decides that W wants to have T believe that W perceived A, T must then ask whether W believes what he had said to be the truth. If not, T will not use the utterance as evidence of its truth. If so, T has concluded that W believes that he now remembers that

hearsay is excluded.[15]

The definition of hearsay, along with the four risks discussed relating to the trustworthiness of a hearsay statement, is depicted in the following "Stickperson Hearsay" diagrams.[16] Figure A portrays the hearsay risks associated with an oral statement of an out-of-court de-

---

he perceived A. (3) But what about the validity of this belief? Does W really remember or is he deceiving himself by attributing to himself the experience of another. If he has had a personal experience, how much of what he relates is he remembering and how much is he reconstructing? T must determine to what extent, if at all, he can rely upon W's memory. (4) After determining how far W's memory is reliable, T must then decide to what extent W's mental impression at the time of his perception corresponded to what was then open to his perception. T's decision will depend upon his conclusion as to W's capacity and opportunity for accurate perception, and the stimuli for using that capacity at the relevant time. All this means only that T must use his own capacity for accurate observation and his ability to interpret what is happening in his presence and must determine to what extent he can rely upon W's use of language, sincerity, memory and perception.

Now if T decides that the series of sounds uttered by W make up the sentence: "Declarant told me that he perceived A," it is obvious that T's mental operations will concern only W's auditory experience and will furnish no basis for a conclusion by T as to Declarant's use of language, sincerity, memory, or perception in his communication to W, except possibly what T can gather from W's description of the details of W's auditory experience. In a word, upon the issue of the existence or non-existence of A, Declarant is the witness and W is only the means by which Declarant's testimony is brought to T. W is telling only what he heard Declarant say, and W's testimony is hearsay.

Since we are assuming that the investigation as to the existence of A is in an Anglo-American court, Declarant, if present, would not be heard unless he spoke under oath or an equivalent sanction and subject to cross-examination. It would seem too clear for argument that P cannot avoid the imposition of these conditions upon his witness by the device of transmitting Declarant's testimony through W. And, generally speaking, he cannot do so. Hearsay is *prima facie* inadmissible.

15. Anderson v. United States, 417 U.S. 211, 220 (1974) ("The primary justification for the exclusion of hearsay is the lack of any opportunity for the adversary to cross-examine the absent declarant whose out-of-court statement is introduced into evidence."). *See also* FED. R. EVID. art. VIII advisory committee introductory note:

Emphasis on the basis of the hearsay rule today tends to center upon the condition of cross-examination. All may not agree with Wigmore that cross-examination is "beyond doubt the greatest legal engine ever invented for the discovery of truth," but all will agree with his statement that it has become a "vital feature" of the Anglo-American system. 5 WIGMORE, § 1376, at 29. The belief, or perhaps hope, that cross-examination is effective in exposing imperfections of perception, memory, and narration is fundamental. Morgan, *foreward* to MODEL CODE OF EVIDENCE 37 (1942).

Professor McCormick observed:

Morgan analyzed the protective function of cross-examination and concluded (1) that while the fear of exposure of falsehoods on cross-examination is a stimulus to truth-telling by the witness, actual exposure of wilful falsehood is rarely accomplished in actual practice and (2) that the most important service of cross-examination in present day conditions is in affording the opportunity to expose faults in the perception and memory of the witness.

C. McCORMICK, EVIDENCE § 245, at 583 (E. Cleary 2d ed. 1972).

16. Other commentators have developed heuristic devices for explaining hearsay. *See, e.g.*, Tribe, *Triangulating Hearsay*, 87 HARV. L. REV. 957 (1974). Professor Tribe explains his "testimonial triangle" thus:

The basic hearsay problem is that of forging a reliable chain of inferences, from an act or utterance of a person not subject to contemporaneous in-court cross-examination about that act or utterance, to an event that the act or utterance is supposed to reflect. Typically, the first link in the required chain of inferences is the link from the act or utterance to the belief it is thought to express or indicate. It is helpful to think of this link as involving a "trip" into the head of the person responsible for the act or utterance (the declarant) to see what he or she was really thinking when the act occurred. The second link is the one from the declarant's assumed belief to a conclusion about some external event that is supposed to have triggered the belief, or that is linked to the belief in some other way. This link involves a trip out of the

clarant. Figure B portrays the hearsay risks associated with the introduction of a written or recorded statement of an out-of-court declarant.

head of the declarant, in order to match the declarant's assumed belief with the external
reality sought to be demonstrated.

   The trier must obviously employ such a chain of inferences whenever a witness testifies
in court. But the process has long been regarded as particularly suspect when the act or
utterance is not one made in court, under oath, by a person whose demeanor at the time is
witnessed by the trier, and under circumstances permitting immediate cross-examination by
counsel in order to probe possible inaccuracies in the inferential chain. These inaccuracies
are usually attributed to the four testimonial infirmities of ambiguity, insincerity, faulty perception, and erroneous memory. In the absence of special reasons, the perceived untrustworthiness of such an out-of-court act or utterance has led the Anglo-Saxon legal system to
exclude it as hearsay despite its potentially probative value.

   There exists a rather simple way of schematizing all of this in terms of an elementary
geometric construct that serves to structure its several related elements. The construct might
be called the Testimonial Triangle. By making graphic the path of inferences, and by functionally grouping the problems encountered along the path, the triangle makes it easier both
to identify when a hearsay problem exists and to structure consideration of the appropriateness of exceptions to the rule that bars hearsay inferences.

   The diagram is as follows:

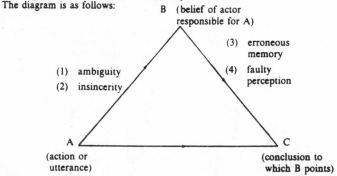

If we use the diagram to trace the inferential path the trier must follow, we begin at the
lower left vertex of the triangle (A), which represents the declarant's (X's) act or assertion.
The path first takes us to the upper vertex (B), representing X's belief in what his or her act or
assertion suggests, and then takes us to the lower right vertex (C), representing the external
reality suggested by X's belief. When "A" is used to prove "C" along the path through "B," a
traditional hearsay problem exists and the use of the act or assertion as evidence is disallowed
upon proper objection in the absence of some special reason to permit it.

   It is of course a simple matter to locate the four testimonial infirmities on the triangle to
show where and how they might impede the process of inference. To go from "A" to "B," the
declarant's belief, one must remove the obstacles of (1) ambiguity and (2) insincerity. To go
from "B" to "C," the external fact, one must further remove the obstacles of (3) erroneous
memory and (4) faulty perception.

   When it is possible to go directly from "A" to "C" with no detour through "B," there is
no hearsay problem unless the validity of the trier's conclusion depends upon an implicit path
through "B." Suppose, for example, that the issue in a lawsuit is whether the Government
took adequate safety precautions in connection with the nuclear test at Amchitka in 1971.
James Schlesinger, then Chairman of the Atomic Energy Commission, "told reporters at El-
mendorf Air Force Base outside Anchorage that he was taking his wife . . . and daughters
. . . with him [to the site of the Amchitka blast] in response to Alaska Gov. William E.
Egan's invitation. Egan strongly disapprove[d] of the test." In these circumstances, the trip
from "A," the Chairman's proposed travel with his family to the site of the blast, to "C," the
conclusion that the blast was reasonably safe, may appear at first to be purely "circumstantial," but in fact that trip requires a journey into the Chairman's head and out again—a
journey through the belief "B" suggested by his willingness to be near the blast with his
family. The journey from "A" to "B" involves problems of possible ambiguity and of insincerity in that the Chairman was apparently seeking to dispel fears of danger, so that his act
may not bespeak an actual belief in the test's safety. And the journey from "B" to "C"

involves problems of memory and perception in that he may not have recalled all the relevant data and may have misperceived such data in the first instance, so that his belief in the test's safety, even if we assume the journey from "A" to "B" safely completed, may not correspond to the facts sought to be demonstrated. On both legs of the triangle, therefore, there are testimonial infirmities that cross-examination contemporaneous with the act "A" could help to expose.

By contrast, when the trier's inference can proceed from "A" directly to "C," the infirmities of hearsay do not arise. For example, the out-of-court statement "I can speak" would be admissible as nonhearsay to prove that the declarant was capable of speech, for it is the fact of his speaking rather than the content of the statement which permits the inference, and that involves no problems of the statement's ambiguity, or of sincerity, memory, or perception.

Id. at 958-61. *Compare id. with* Saltzburg, *A Special Aspect of Relevance: Countering Negative Inferences Associated with the Absence of Evidence*, 66 CALIF. L. REV. 1011, 1034 n.84 (1978):

Professor Laurence Tribe has offered a useful device, the testimonial triangle, for examining and understanding this hearsay definition. Tribe, *Triangulating Hearsay*, 87 HARV. L. REV. 957 (1974). The following figure represents a modification of Tribe's triangle; it is designed to depict the hearsay definition as clearly as possible:

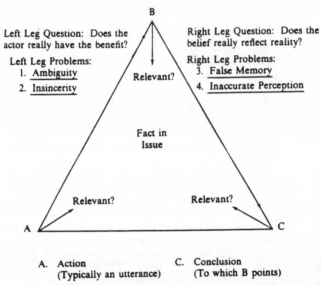

B. Belief (Of actor responsible for A)

B

Left Leg Question: Does the actor really have the benefit?

Left Leg Problems:
1. Ambiguity
2. Insincerity

Relevant?

Right Leg Question: Does the belief really reflect reality?

Right Leg Problems:
3. False Memory
4. Inaccurate Perception

Fact in Issue

Relevant?   Relevant?

A   C

A. Action   C. Conclusion
    (Typically an utterance)   (To which B points)

True hearsay, as identified in the test above, is a statement that requires the factfinder to move from A through B to C in order to find that the statement is relevant evidence. If the factfinder need only move from A to B or can rely on the fact of utterance alone (A), then the statement is not hearsay.

A linear analysis, such as the following, is also helpful and may be clearer than Tribe's triangle:

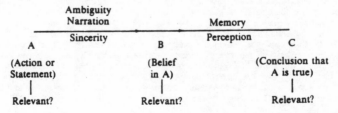

          Ambiguity
          Narration   Memory
          Sincerity   Perception
A   B   C

(Action or   (Belief   (Conclusion that
Statement)   in A)   A is true)
    | | |
Relevant?   Relevant?   Relevant?

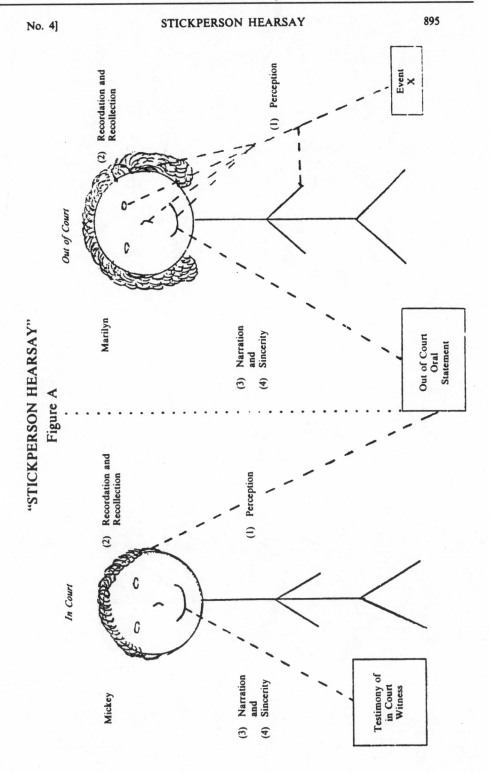

"STICKPERSON HEARSAY"
Figure A

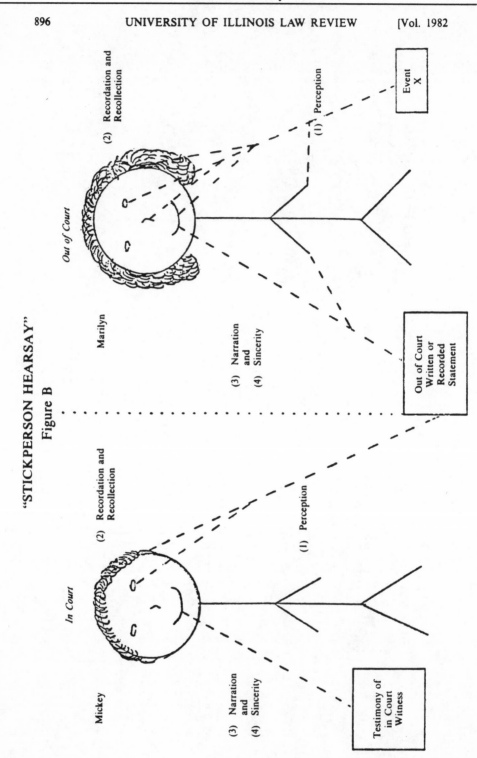

"STICKPERSON HEARSAY"
Figure B

To illustrate use of the "Stickperson Hearsay" diagram as a means of understanding the definition of hearsay, consider in-court testimony by Mickey that Marilyn either said the following in his presence, wrote the following in a letter, or recorded the following on a tape: "I saw the car go through a red light." Marilyn's declaration is a statement, as defined in rule 801(a)(1), because it is oral or written conduct intended by Marilyn as an assertion. Marilyn is the declarant.[17] Figure A represents Mickey testifying in court under oath, subject to contemporaneous cross-examination. Mickey's testimony consists of repeating the contents of his out-of-court conversation with Marilyn, during which Marilyn detailed her perceptions of Event X. In the illustration, Event X corresponds to the car actually going through a red light. Figure B represents Mickey authenticating, in court, a written or recorded statement of Marilyn describing the same Event X.

The testimonial risks associated with Mickey's in-court testimony, and the hearsay risks associated with Marilyn's out-of-court statement, are illustrated by following the dashed lines. The dashed lines on Mickey's half of the diagram represent the testimonial risks present when an in-court declarant testifies to a fact of which he has personal knowledge, in this case Marilyn's *making* of the oral, written or recorded statement. The dashed lines on Marilyn's half of the diagram represent the hearsay risks associated with an out-of-court declarant's hearsay statement—Marilyn's oral, written, or recorded statement that the car went through a red light. These hearsay risks are present when Marilyn's statement is offered to prove the truth of the matter asserted, that the car actually went through a red light.

When Marilyn's statement is relevant irrespective of its truth, it is only necesary to look to Mickey's half of the diagram, which is represented by movement from the left of the diagram along the dashed lines to the dotted line. For example, if the litigation concerns whether, following the accident, Marilyn is still capable of coherent speech, her statement's relevance does not depend upon the truth of the matter asserted. Marilyn's statement, authenticated by Mickey, is therefore not hearsay. Mickey is in court, under oath, and subject to cross-examination regarding the testimonial risks involved in his testimony that Marilyn made the statement.

On the other hand, if Marilyn's statement is offered for the truth of

---

This might be called "Straightening out Hearsay." The linear diagram has several advantages. It makes it clear that one cannot go from A to C without passing through B and that one must reach C to find that a statement is hearsay. Thus, when the words of an oral contract are important, testimony about an out-of-court declaration is admissible because there is no need to leave A, the actual utterance of the words, to decide that the evidence is relevant. And if the words are circumstantial evidence of something other than their truth, it is not necessary to go beyond A or B. Finally, the linear diagram shows that if one travels from A through B to a conclusion not asserted by the declarant, some of the traditional hearsay problems still exist even though modern codes would not treat such a statement as hearsay. *See also* R. LEMPERT & S. SALTZBURG, A MODERN APPROACH TO EVIDENCE 333 (1974).

17. *See* FED. R. EVID. 801(b).

the matter asserted—that the car ran the red light — Mickey's testimony repeating or authenticating that statement is represented by movement from the left of the diagram along the dashed lines to the right of the dotted line. If relevance of Marilyn's statement requires movement beyond the dotted line to Marilyn's dashed lines, either to her head (belief—two hearsay risks) or further down the right side (Event X—four hearsay risks), the statement is hearsay. Therefore, anytime an out-of-court statement is offered to prove the truth of the matter asserted in the statement, the statement's relevance depends upon movement along the dashed lines from the in-court testimony of Mickey to the right of the dotted line, and the statement is hearsay.[18] Conversely, to the extent that the statement is relevant simply because Mickey repeats his personal knowledge of the *making* of the oral assertion (Figure A), or authenticates Marilyn's written or recorded assertion (Figure B), movement proceeds from Mickey's in-court testimony, along the dashed lines, only *to* the dotted line. Marilyn's statement, therefore, is not hearsay. Such a statement is not being offered to prove the truth of the matter stated; it is offered solely for the fact it was said.

Hearsay statements present risks of sincerity, perception, recordation and recollection, and narration, even if the statement's relevance depends on its falsity, rather than its truth. To highlight the hearsay nature of a statement offered to prove falsity, assume that Able is charged with an offense in Chicago. The police talk to Able's wife, who tells them that Able was with her in Miami on the date and time in question. The prosecution is prepared to prove that her statement is false. The prosecution desires to offer Mrs. Able's statement to support its argument that she knew that her husband was guilty and that she lied to protect him. The wife's statement is relevant for the purpose offered by the prosecution only if she knew her statement was false. Because determining whether she knew the statement was false brings

---

18. In reversing a conviction from a bench trial for possession of heroin, the U.S. Supreme Court stated:

There can be no doubt that the informant's out-of-court declaration that the apartment in question was "Moore's apartment," either as related in the search warrant affidavit or as reiterated in live testimony by the police officers, was hearsay and thus inadmissible in evidence on the issue of Moore's guilt. Introduction of this testimony deprived Moore of the opportunity to cross-examine the informant as to exactly what he meant by 'Moore's apartment' and what factual basis, if any, there was for believing that Moore was a tenant or regular resident there. Moore was similarly deprived of the chance to show that the witness' recollection was erroneous or that he was not credible. The informant's declaration falls within no exception to the hearsay rule recognized in the Federal Rules of Evidence, and reliance on this hearsay statement in determining petitioner's guilt or innocence was error.

Moore v. United States, 429 U.S. 20, 21-22 (1976). *See also* Inventive Music Ltd. v. Cohen, 617 F.2d 29, 32 (3d Cir. 1980) (testimony in which the witness testified to what the declarant said was "a classic example of hearsay" because statement offered for truth of the matter asserted); Wathen v. United States, 527 F.2d 1191, 1199 (Ct. Cl. 1975), *cert. denied*, 429 U.S. 821 (1976) (newspaper account that an agent of the Internal Revenue Service fatally shot a woman was hearsay when considered for its truth).

her perception, recordation and recollection, narration, and sincerity into issue, the statement is hearsay.

Under the definition of hearsay employed at common law as well as that contained in rule 801(c), when a statement which is offered to prove the truth of the matter asserted is made "other than . . . by the declarant while testifying at the trial or hearing," the statement is hearsay regardless of whether the out-of-court declarant testifies at the trial or hearing. Thus, the definition of hearsay applies to all statements which are not made under oath at the trial or hearing, and are not made subject to contemporaneous cross-examination before the trier of fact.[19] When the out-of-court declarant also testifies at trial, cross-examination or direct and redirect examination provides an opportunity for the party disputing the truth of the statement to explore the truth of the assertion before the trier of fact. Nevertheless, neither the common law nor the Federal Rules of Evidence provide for the general admissibility of prior statements of in-court witnesses.[20]

Occasionally, whether the party against whom a statement is offered was present when the statement was made has a bearing upon whether the statement is hearsay or is defined as "not hearsay." Thus, an oral statement used to prove notice cannot have been effective as such unless the statement was made in the presence of the person sought to be charged with notice. Similarly, the presence of the party is essential if it is claimed that he admitted the truth of an oral statement by failing to deny it. Aside from such situations, the presence or absence of the party against whom an extrajudicial statement is offered generally has no bearing upon either the statement's status as hearsay or its admissibility; an objection based on such absence betrays a basic lack of understanding of the nature of hearsay.[21] Accordingly, arguments which base admissibility upon the presence of a party fail to address questions relevant to admissibility under the hearsay rule.

---

19. United States v. Summers, 598 F.2d 450, 459 n.11 (5th Cir. 1979) (even though declarants were present and testified at trial, their out-of-court statements were still hearsay). *See also* United States v. Sisto, 534 F.2d 616, 621 n.5 (5th Cir. 1976); FED. R. EVID. 801(c).

20. Unlike the common law, the Federal Rules of Evidence provide for limited admissibility of certain prior consistent and inconsistent statements by defining these declarations as "not hearsay." FED. R. EVID. 801(d)(1)(A)-(B). In addition, statements involving prior identification are also defined as "not hearsay." FED. R. EVID. 801(d)(1)(C). A discussion of the rationale denying generally substantive admissibility of out-of-court statements of declarants who testify in court is beyond the scope of this article.

21. "Seemingly, this type of objection, frequently appearing in the trial records before this court, arises from a misconception of the rules of evidence, and a belief that any statement or conversation occurring in the absence of defendant is inadmissible. Such is not the law." People v. Carpenter, 28 Ill. 2d 116, 120, 190 N.E.2d 738, 741 (1963). *See also* Giblin v. United States, 523 F.2d 42 (8th Cir.), *cert. denied*, 424 U.S. 971 (1975):

At trial the government defended the statements because they were "made in the presence of the defendant." While the defendant's presence may under some circumstances make the evidence material to his knowledge or intent . . . not every third party statement made in the presence of the defendant is admissible as an exception to the hearsay rule.

Id. at 45 n.5.

IV. "STICKPERSON HEARSAY" ANALYSIS IN ACTION

A. *Everyday Applications*

1. *Nonverbal Conduct Intended as an Assertion*

Nonverbal conduct of an individual may occasionally be intended as an assertion. The declarant's conduct is hearsay if offered to prove the truth of the matter contained in the nonverbal assertion. Deliberate actions such as nodding, pointing, and the sign language of the dumb are as plainly assertions as are spoken words.[22] A motion picture in which an injured plaintiff exhibits his disability by performing certain tasks also is hearsay if the movie is offered to prove the plaintiff's injury.[23]

2. *Nonverbal Conduct Not Intended as an Assertion*

Nonverbal conduct of an individual which is not intended as an assertion is not hearsay under the Federal Rules of Evidence. Rule 801(a)(2), which declares that nonverbal conduct that is not intended as an assertion is not a hearsay statement, resolves a long-standing controversy among commentators. The controversy, however, rarely has been the subject of judicial inquiry, because the litigants frequently have not perceived the hearsay question involved.

When the litigation concerns the occurrence of an event, an actor's nonverbal conduct which evidences his belief that the event actually occurred sometimes has been analogized to an express statement of the declarant's belief in such an occurrence. When this conduct is used to prove the occurrence of the event, this analogy would indicate that the statement is hearsay. Analysis based on hearsay risks, however, necessitates a rejection of this analogy between the inference arising from the actor's conduct, sometimes called an "implied assertion,"[24] and an express declaration. When a person acts without intending to communicate a belief, his sincerity is not directly at issue. Furthermore, there is often a guarantee of the trustworthiness for the inference, because the actor has based his actions on the correctness of his belief.

---

22. United States v. Ross, 321 F.2d 61 (2d Cir.), *cert. denied*, 375 U.S. 894 (1963) (testimony of an investigator that employee pointed to list in response to a question as to a salesman's number is hearsay); United States v. Caro, 569 F.2d 411 (5th Cir. 1978) (the pointing out of a vehicle by a person is assertive conduct subject to the hearsay rule). *See also* C. McCORMICK, EVIDENCE § 250, at 596 (E. Cleary 2d ed. 1972) ("No one would contend, if, in response to a question 'Who did it?', one of the auditors held up his hand, that this gesture could be treated as different from an oral or written statement, in the application of the hearsay rule, any more than could the sign-speech of the dumb.").

23. Grimes v. Employers Mut. Liab. Ins. Co., 73 F.R.D. 607, 611 (D. Alaska 1977) (film of conduct of injured person is "like a witness testifying about assertive conduct.").

24. Unfortunately, the term "implied assertion" applies not only to nonverbal conduct not intended as an assertion, but also applies to assertive statements that are offered as a basis for inferring something other than the truth of the matter asserted. C. McCORMICK, EVIDENCE § 250, at 596-600 (E. Cleary 2d ed. 1972). *See infra* text accompanying notes 40-50 for a discussion of statements offered to infer other than the truth of the matter asserted.

Consider, for example, a person who is observed opening an umbrella. This action could be offered for the inference that it is raining. While the inference to be drawn from such nonverbal conduct is the same as in the case of a direct assertion, the actor, however, intends no assertion. Thus, the sincerity danger inherent in hearsay is virtually absent. Although the sincerity risk is removed, the accuracy of the actor's perception and recollection remain untested by cross-examination. The actor may have made an honest mistake. In many instances similar to the umbrella illustration, conduct will accompany, or follow shortly, the fact to be inferred, thus reducing the risk of faulty recollection. Reliance by the actor upon his perception of the event is also likely to indicate greater trustworthiness, because an actor usually has a greater interest in ensuring correct perception than a casual observer. Moreover, the risks of error in these situations are more sensibly factors to be used in evaluating weight and credibility, rather than as grounds for exclusion.[25]

The court must be satisfied with the probative value of the offered proof in light of accompanying trial concerns. Thus, the inference of the actor's belief or the inference of the truth of the impliedly-asserted fact may be too ambiguous to warrant submitting the evidence to the jury. The inference's probative value may be so slight when compared with the possibility of unfair prejudice and misleading of the jury that exclusion pursuant to rule 403 is proper.[26] Thus, if the person opening an umbrella was known to be exiting a store that sells umbrellas, and was superstitious about opening umbrellas indoors, the ambiguity associated with offering such evidence to establish that it was raining would certainly be exacerbated. Whether exclusion is warranted under rule 403, would, of course, depend upon examination of all relevant circumstances.

When nonverbal conduct is at issue, it is not always perfectly clear whether an assertion was intended by the person whose conduct is in question. If evidence of conduct is offered on the theory that it is not intended as an assertion, and hence not hearsay, the question of the actor's intention is for the court under rule 104(a).[27]

---

25. Grimes v. Employers Mut. Liab. Ins. Co., 73 F.R.D. 607 (D. Alaska 1977) (films taken of unconscious plaintiff to show pain and suffering are not hearsay because they involve observations of nonassertive conduct); Cole v. United States, 327 F.2d 360 (9th Cir. 1964) (to establish that a robbery was accomplished by intimidation, testimony that bank teller was pale and shaking was not hearsay).

26. Rule 403 provides: "Although relevant, evidence may be excluded if its probative value is substantially outweighed by the danger of unfair prejudice, confusion of the issues, or misleading the jury, or by considerations of undue delay, waste of time, or needless presentation of cumulative evidence." FED. R. EVID. 403.

27. FED. R. EVID. 104(a). *See* FED. R. EVID. 801 advisory committee note, which provides: When evidence of conduct is offered on the theory that it is not a statement, and hence not hearsay, a preliminary determination will be required to determine whether an assertion is intended. The rule is so worded as to place the burden upon the party claiming that the intention existed; ambiguous and doubtful cases will be resolved against him and in favor of

Also included within the category of nonverbal conduct that is not intended as an assertion, and thus is not a hearsay statement, is silence or inaction which involves a failure to speak or act, when such a failure serves as the basis for an inference that conditions were such as not to evoke speech or action in a reasonable person.[28] Illustrations of this category are the failure of other passengers on a train to complain offered for the inference that the temperature of the train was not too low,[29] and the absence of complaints from others who had occupied a motel room, offered for the inference that the gas heater in the room was not defective.[30]

Nonverbal conduct not intended as an assertion is frequently, but incorrectly, treated as an admission of a party opponent. Both flight and the fabrication or suppression of evidence fall within this category.[31]

---

admissibility. The determination involves no greater difficulty than many other preliminary questions of fact.

Maguire, The Hearsay System: Around and Through the Thicket, 14 VAND. L. REV. 741, 765-67 (1961). *See also* 4 WEINSTEIN'S EVIDENCE § 801(a)[02] at 801-62 (1979):

The trial judge will also have to make a preliminary determination on the question of intent. When evidence of conduct is offered, the definition of statement in Rule 801(a) requires that a finding be made whether an assertion was intended. . . . Again, the proponent of the evidence must make a minimum showing. He must at least indicate the conduct he intends to prove and the inference he intends to draw. If at this point the judge is satisfied that the conduct was not intended as an assertion of the matter sought to be proved, the burden of demonstrating the contrary shifts to the opponent of the evidence.

Rules 104(a) and (b) provide:

(a) Questions of admissibility generally. Preliminary questions concerning the qualification of a person to be a witness, the existence of a privilege, or the admissibility of evidence shall be determined by the court, subject to the provisions of subdivision (b). In making its determination it is not bound by the rules of evidence except those with respect to privileges.

(b) Relevancy conditioned on fact. When the relevancy of evidence depends upon the fulfillment of a condition of fact, the judge shall admit it upon, or subject to, the introduction of evidence sufficient to support a finding of the fulfillment of the condition.

FED. R. EVID. 104(a), (b).

28. McCormick gives examples of situations in which such issues are likely to arise. Probably most of these cases fall in the following classes:

(a) on an issue as to defects in goods, or unwholesomeness of food served, evidence is offered by the seller that goods or food of the same quality have been sold or served to other customers and that there has been no complaint by the other customers, (b) on the question of the existence of an injury or injurious situation, or the happening of an injurious event, evidence is offered of the absence of complaint by other persons affected, and (c) on the issue of the happening of some event affecting a member of the family, or a claim to or disposition of property by such member, evidence is offered from other members of the family that he never mentioned such matter.

C. MCCORMICK, EVIDENCE § 250, at 600 (E. Cleary 2d ed. 1972).

29. Silver v. New York Cent. Ry. Co., 329 Mass. 14, 105 N.E.2d 923 (1952).

30. Cain v. George, 411 F.2d 572 (5th Cir. 1969).

31. "[F]light, even though nonverbal conduct, has been said to be an assertion (in the form of an admission) of guilt and is therefore treated by some authorities as an exception to the hearsay rule. . . . Preferably it is to be viewed as conduct offered as circumstantial evidence rather than for its assertive, testimonial value." United States v. Lobo, 516 F.2d 883, 884 n.1 (2d Cir.), *cert. denied*, 423 U.S. 837 (1975). *See also* C. MCCORMICK, EVIDENCE § 271, at 655 (E. Cleary 2d ed. 1972):

"The wicked flee when no man pursueth." Many acts of a defendant after the crime seeking to escape the toils of the law are uncritically received as admissions by conduct, constituting circumstantial evidence of consciousness of guilt and hence of the fact of guilt itself. In this

3. Oral or Written Conduct Not Intended as an Assertion

For the same reasons that nonverbal nonassertive conduct is not hearsay, oral or written conduct not intended as an assertion is not hearsay. Examples of such conduct are screams of pain, outbursts of laughter, singing a song, and uttering or writing an expletive. Of course, any of the foregoing may be intended as an assertion, and thus become hearsay, if the statement is offered to prove the truth of the matter asserted.[32]

4. Statements Offered Other Than to Prove the Truth of the Matter Asserted

Hearsay does not encompass all extrajudicial statements, but only those offered for the purpose of proving the truth of the matter asserted in the statement.[33] Therefore, when the mere making of the statement is relevant to establish a fact of consequence, hearsay is not involved. Such statements are offered solely for the fact they were said, not for the truth of their contents.[34]

a. Verbal Act

In one group of extrajudicial statements, the statement itself, as a verbal act, has independent legal significance. Thus, under the objective standard of contract, statements of offer and acceptance constitute binding legal acts without regard to the declarants' belief in the truth of the statements.[35] Other illustrations of verbal acts are statements which

---

class are flight from the scene or from one's usual haunts after the crime, assuming a false name, shaving off a beard, resisting arrest, attempting to bribe arresting officers, forfeiture of bond by failure to appear, escapes or attempted escapes from confinement, and attempts of the accused to take his own life.

32. People v. Nitti, 312 Ill. 73, 94, 143 N.E. 448, 456 (1924) (defendant, when accused of murder, responded "bullshit," by which the court said he meant to characterize the accusation as "absurd or fanciful").

33. FED. R. EVID. 801(c).

34. M.F. Patterson Dental Supply Co. v. Wadley, 401 F.2d 167, 172 (10th Cir. 1968) ("[T]estimony is not hearsay when it is offered to prove only that a statement was made and not the truth of the statement."); United States v. Sanders, 639 F.2d 268, 270 (5th Cir. 1981) ("[I]f the statement was offered on a non-assertive basis, i.e., for proof only of the fact it was said, the statement would not be subject to the hearsay objection.").

35. See Creaghe v. Iowa Home Mut. Cas. Co., 323 F.2d 981 (10th Cir. 1963):

The hearsay rule does not exclude *relevant* testimony as to what the contracting parties said with respect to the making or the terms of an oral agreement. The presence or absence of such words and statements of themselves are part of the issues in the case. This use of such testimony does not require a reliance by the jury or the judge upon the competency of the person who originally made the statements for the truth of their content. Neither the truth of the statements nor their accuracy are then involved. In the case at bar we are not concerned with whether the insured was truthful or not when he told the agent he wanted the policy cancelled and that he did not need it any more. It is enough for the issues here presented to determine only whether or not he made such statements to the agent. The fact that these statements were made was testified to by the agent, and his competency and truthfulness as to this testimony was subject to testing through cross-examination by counsel for appellant, and this was done at considerable length.

Id. at 984 (emphasis in original). *See also* United States v. Boyd, 566 F.2d 929, 937 (5th Cir. 1978)

are evidence of defamation and a principal's statement granting another authority to act as the principal's agent.

b. Characterizing Act

Also included in the group of statements comprising operative legal acts are assertions which relate to and characterize an independently relevant act.[36] Thus, for example, when an instrument which designated a decedent's wife as his beneficiary was unclear as to whether his wife was to be either the beneficiary of his insurance policy or of a six month gratuity payment, oral statements accompanying delivery of the instrument which resolved the ambiguity were not hearsay.[37]

c. Effect on Listener

A statement that is made by one person and becomes known to another is not hearsay when the statement is offered to prove the circumstances under which the latter acted. Thus, a law enforcement official's explanation for being at the scene of a crime—that he proceeded to a particular location in response to a radio call—is not hearsay. A statement is also not hearsay when offered for the purpose of showing that the listener was placed on notice or had knowledge of a given fact. Thus, in a negligence action to recover damages for personal injury sustained in a fall, a statement by the manager of a food store to a customer that the floor in aisle 2 was wet is not hearsay, provided the statement is offered to show the unreasonableness of the customer's conduct in skipping down aisle 2. The same statement, if offered to

---

(tape recorded conversations of illegal gambling are not hearsay but "constitute verbal acts and can be considered part of the offense in question"); United States v. Calaway, 524 F.2d 609, 613 (9th Cir. 1975), *cert. denied*, 424 U.S. 967 (1976). The *Calaway* court held that out-of-court statements of the defendants themselves were not hearsay on the question of their participation in conspiracy but were verbal acts. Such statements were not received to establish the truth of what the defendants said, but to show their own verbal acts.

36.   6 J. WIGMORE, EVIDENCE § 1773 (J. Chadbourn rev. ed. 1976) ("[T]he conduct that is to be made definite must be *independently material and provable under the issues*, either as a fact directly in issue or as incidentally or evidentially relevant to the issue. The use of the words is wholly subsidiary and appurtenant to the use of the conduct. The former without the latter have no place in the case, and could only serve as a hearsay assertion in direct violation of the rule. . . ."). *Id.* at 268 (emphasis in original).

37.   Shapiro v. United States, 166 F.2d 240 (2d Cir.), *cert. denied*, 334 U.S. 859 (1948). *See also* Hanson v. Johnson, 161 Minn. 229, 201 N.W. 322 (1924). In this case, the plaintiff, John Hanson, owned and leased a farm to a tenant farmer named Schrick. The terms of the lease gave Hanson two-fifths of the corn grown. When the tenant was nearly through husking the corn, he pointed to the corn in question and stated, "Mr. Hanson, here is your corn for this year, this double crib here and this single crib here is your share for this year's corn; this belongs to you, Mr. Hanson." *Id.* at 230, 201 N.W. at 322. The Minnesota Supreme Court held that the statements of the tenant were not hearsay, because "[t]he language of the tenant was the very fact necessary to be proved. The verbal part of the transaction . . . was necessary to prove the fact. The words were verbal acts. They aid in giving legal significance to the conduct of the parties. They accompanied the conduct." *Id. Accord* Morgan, *A Suggested Classification of Utterances Admissible as Res Gestae*, 31 YALE L.J. 229, 232 (1922).

show the floor was wet, is hearsay. Similarly, threats made to the defendant which bear on the reasonableness of his apprehension of danger, or which conversely provide a reason for his conduct, are not hearsay when offered to explain the defendant's actions.[38] Finally, a statement that is offered only to place another's statement in context is not hearsay.[39]

d. Impeachment

Prior statements of a witness that are inconsistent with the witness' in-court testimony are not hearsay when offered solely for impeachment.[40] The fact that the witness made a prior inconsistent statement is

---

38. See United States v. Walker, 636 F.2d 194 (8th Cir. 1980) (Drug Enforcement Administration agent's testimony that after receiving a telephone call from a confidential informant, he proceeded to a particular location was not hearsay); United States v. Bright, 630 F.2d 804, 815, n.18 (5th Cir. 1980) (testimony concerning protection pay-off negotiations was not hearsay when used to explain the witness' subsequent conduct); United States v. Herrera, 600 F.2d 502 (5th Cir. 1979) (where defendant alleges duress as a defense, statements threatening defendant and her two small children were not hearsay when offered to show defendant's state of mind); United States v. Jenkins, 579 F.2d 840 (4th Cir.), cert. denied, 439 U.S. 967 (1978) (statements on the telephone that a person was ready to complete narcotics deal were not hearsay when offered to show state of mind of the person hearing message); N.L.R.B. v. Custom Excavating, Inc., 575 F.2d 102 (7th Cir. 1978) (the testimony of a union representative that two former employees told him they were not paid overtime, and that they were required to submit two time cards, one in detail and the other blank, so that the employer could use the blank card to reconstruct the hours to comply with the bargaining agreement, that was not offered to show truth or falsity of employer's records but, to show instead that the union had a basis for its request for employer's customer list, was not hearsay); United States v. Wellendorf, 574 F.2d 1289 (5th Cir. 1978) (in a prosecution for income tax violation, evidence as to advice received by defendant at tax protestors meeting was not hearsay when offered to prove intent); Gibbs v. State Farm Mut. Ins. Co., 544 F.2d 423 (9th Cir. 1976) (in an action brought against a tort-feasor liability insurer on theory of a bad-faith failure to settle, letters from the tort-feasor stating that Gibbs would settle for the amount of medical bills are not hearsay when offered for the limited purpose of proving that State Farm had received the information); United States v. Hyde, 448 F.2d 815, 845 (5th Cir. 1971), cert. denied, 404 U.S. 1058 (1972) ("The victim's fearful state of mind is a crucial element in proving extortion. The testimony . . . is admitted not for the truth of the information in the statements but for the fact that the victim heard them and that they would have tended to produce fear in his mind."); Moody v. United States, 376 F.2d 525 (9th Cir. 1967) (statement in the presence of defendant that declarant and defendant would get caught only if somebody informed on them was not hearsay when offered to show defendant knew he was engaged in illegal enterprise); Emich Motors Corp. v. General Motors Corp., 181 F.2d 70 (7th Cir. 1950), rev'd on other grounds, 340 U.S. 558, reh'g denied, 341 U.S. 906 (1951) (letters of complaint from customers were not hearsay when offered to show that the dealer's franchise was not cancelled because of its refusal to finance sales through defendant).

39. See N.L.R.B. v. National Car Rental Sys., Inc., 672 F.2d 1182 (3d Cir. 1982), in which the court held that a manager's statement that employees who were being laid off would not be transferred to the company's other facility is not hearsay when offered to show that employees asked about transfers. The court specified that the statements were not offered to show that the employees desired to transfer, nor did the relevance of the statements depend on the truth of the matter asserted. Id. at 1186-87.

40. Rule 613 of the Federal Rules of Evidence provides:

(a) Examining witness concerning prior statement. In examining a witness concerning a prior statement made by him, whether written or not, the statement need not be shown nor its contents disclosed to him at that time, but on request the same shall be shown or disclosed to opposing counsel.

(b) Extrinsic evidence of prior inconsistent statement of witness. Extrinsic evidence of a prior inconsistent statement by a witness is not admissible unless the witness is afforded an oppor-

impeaching without regard to whether the prior statement is true. A prior statement inconsistent with the witness' in-court testimony tends to establish that the witness first speaks one way and then another. This raises doubts as to the truthfulness of the witness' in-court testimony.

B. Problem Areas in Defining Hearsay

Many of the statements that present difficult questions involving interpretation of the hearsay definition may be viewed as falling into one of two categories. The first type of statement is one offered not for the truth of the matter asserted but rather as the basis for drawing a nonasserted inference. The second difficult area involves statements offered not for the truth of the matter asserted but rather as circumstantial evidence of a fact of consequence. Each of the two categories, nonasserted inference and circumstantial use, will be discussed in turn.[41]

1. Statements Offered for Nonasserted Inference

a. Reduced Risk of Sincerity

If a statement, although assertive in form, is offered as a basis for inferring something other than the truth of the matter directly asserted, the Advisory Committee's note to rule 801(a) indicates that the statement is "excluded from the definition of hearsay by the language of subdivision (c)." The Advisory Committee's claim rests on the assumption that such statements present a reduced sincerity risk similar to that associated with nonverbal conduct which is not intended as an assertion.[42] It is extremely doubtful, however, whether these statements pos-

---

tunity to explain or deny the same and the opposite party is afforded an opportunity to interrogate him thereon, or the interests of justice otherwise require. This provision does not apply to admissions of a party-opponent as defined in Rule 801(d)(2).

41. Part IV of the article presents an interpretation of the hearsay definition which is consistent with the hearsay definition contained in the federal rules and at the common law, but which highlights in an easily understood manner a theoretically sound approach to applying the hearsay definition to all categories of statements.

42. The Advisory Committee's note to Rule 801(a) provides:

It can scarcely be doubted that an assertion made in words is intended by the declarant to be an assertion. Hence verbal assertions readily fall into the category of "statement." Whether nonverbal conduct should be regarded as a statement for purposes of defining hearsay requires further consideration. Some nonverbal conduct, such as the act of pointing to identify a suspect in a lineup, is clearly the equivalent of words, assertive in nature, and to be regarded as a statement. Other nonverbal conduct, however, may be offered as evidence that the person acted as he did because of his belief in the existence of the condition sought to be proved, from which belief the existence of the condition may be inferred. This sequence is, arguably, in effect an assertion of the existence of the condition and hence properly includable within the hearsay concept. . . . Admittedly evidence of this character is untested with respect to the perception, memory, and narration (or their equivalents) of the actor, but the Advisory Committee is of the view that these dangers are minimal in the absence of an intent to assert and do not justify the loss of the evidence on hearsay grounds. No class of evidence is free of the possibility of fabrication, but the likelihood is less with nonverbal than with assertive verbal conduct. The situations giving rise to the nonverbal conduct are such as

sess a reduced sincerity risk, much less a sincerity risk sufficiently diminished to warrant non-hearsay treatment. If such a reduced sincerity risk is absent, a statement offered as a basis for inferring something other than the matter directly asserted clearly must be considered hearsay under both the common law and rule 801(c) definitions, notwithstanding the Advisory Committee's note.

The famous English case of *Wright v. Doe d. Tatham*[43] is a good example of this problem. In *Tatham*, plaintiff's lessor claimed the right to inherit as an heir of John Marsden. Defendant Marsden's steward claimed a portion of the estate as the devisee. The case hinged upon the testamentary capacity of Marsden. Defendant offered in evidence certain letters Marsden received from persons who had subsequently died. The first letter, dated October 12, 1784, was from Marsden's cousin, who recounted the details of a sea voyage, described conditions at the destination, and wished Marsden good health. The second letter, dated May 20, 1786, was from Reverend Marton, a vicar, who requested Marsden to direct his attorney to propose some terms for a settlement of a dispute between Marsden and the parish or township. A third was a letter of gratitude, dated October 3, 1799, sent by Reverend Ellershaw upon resigning a curacy to which Marsden had appointed him. The will and codicil were made in 1822 and 1824 respectively. At trial, the letters were excluded. A verdict was returned for plaintiff's lessor, and defendant sued out a writ of error to the Exchequer Chamber. The judgment was affirmed by an equally divided court. On further writ of error, the House of Lords also affirmed.[44] Baron Parke, in the Exchequer Chamber, summarized the applicable rule:

> [P]roof of a particular fact, which is not of itself a matter in issue, but which is relevant only as implying a statement or opinion of a third person on the matter in issue, is inadmissible in all cases where such a statement or opinion not on oath would be of itself inadmissible.[45]

---

virtually to eliminate questions of sincerity. Motivation, the nature of the conduct, and the presence or absence of reliance will bear heavily upon the weight to be given the evidence. . . . Similar considerations govern nonassertive verbal conduct and verbal conduct which is assertive but offered as a basis for inferring something other than the matter asserted, also excluded from the definition of hearsay by the language of subdivision (c).

See C. McCORMICK, EVIDENCE § 249 at 590 n.92 (E. Cleary 2d ed. 1972) ("Admittedly the uncross-examined statement is subject to all the hearsay dangers, except to the extent that deliberate falsification diminishes when a statement is not used to prove anything asserted therein."). *See also supra* text accompanying notes 23-30.

43. 5 Cl. & F. 559, 47 Rev. Rep. 136 (1838).

44. *Id.*

45. Wright v. Tatham, 7 Adolphus & E. 313, 388-89, 112 Eng. Rep. 488, 516-17 (1837). "Were the rule otherwise, the hearsay rule could easily be circumvented through clever questioning and coaching of witnesses, so that answers were framed as implied rather than as direct assertions." M. GRAHAM, HANDBOOK OF FEDERAL EVIDENCE 700 n.55 (1981). With few exceptions, federal courts characterize implied assertions as hearsay. *See, e.g.*, Krulewitch v. United States, 336 U.S. 440, 442 (1949); United States v. Pacelli, 491 F.2d 1108, 1116-17 (2d Cir. 1974).

In *Tatham*, each of the three letters written to the testator, Marsden, and offered by the proponents of his will and codicil were not of a kind that would likely have been written to a mentally defective person. This implies that the writers believed him to be sane, which in turn justifies the inference that he was sane. Both the Exchequer Chamber and the House of Lords ruled the letters inadmissible hearsay as "implied assertions." These courts rejected the argument that since the out-of-court declarant did not intend to assert the matter for which the statement was being offered—the competency of the testator—a sufficient reduction in the likelihood of conscious fabrication warranted non-hearsay treatment.

The Advisory Committee's apparent attempted rejection of *Wright v. Doe d. Tatham*[46] is unfortunate. When a statement is offered to imply the declarant's state of mind, and from that to imply a given fact in the form of an opinion or otherwise, the truth of the matter directly asserted must be assumed in order for the nonasserted inference to be drawn; *the statement, therefore, is properly classified as hearsay under the language of rule 801(c)*. Because the matter directly asserted in the statement must be true, a reduction in the risk of sincerity is not present. Thus, if Reverend Ellershaw were to testify in court, he would be required to lay a foundation establishing his personal knowledge of facts forming the basis of his opinion before he could render that opinion. If a sufficient foundation of personal knowledge was not established, Reverend Ellershaw would not be permitted to state his opinion as to Marsden's testamentary capacity. Similarly, for Reverend Ellershaw's letter to be offered for the further inference that he believed Marsden possessed testamentary capacity, the existence of each of the facts relied upon by Reverend Ellershaw, regardless of whether he expressed them in the letter, must be within his personal knowledge in order for the opinion to be admissible. Moreover, Reverend Ellershaw must have sincerely intended his expression of gratitude. Because the basis for Reverend Ellershaw's expression of gratitude, in addition to the expression itself, must be true to support any inference of testamentary capacity, all four hearsay risks are present. Finally, because the matters directly asserted by the statement must themselves be true for the desired inference to be relevant, the sincerity risk remains unabated. Because the foregoing sincerity risk is fully present, the statement is hearsay, even though the sincerity risk may arguably be reduced with respect to the inference to be drawn once the truth of the matter directly asserted is assumed. Even this reduction in sincerity risk would not be present where the declarant intended that the nonasserted inference be drawn, such as in the case of statements made to accomplish a fraud.

The Advisory Committee apparently believed that statements of-

---

46. FED. R. EVID. 801(c) advisory committee note.

fered for a nonasserted inference possess minimal sincerity risks.[47] Such a position fails to appreciate that the statement's relevance depends on the truth of the matter asserted. This can be illustrated by the following example. Assume that a company president on his return home tells his wife that he had a dull time on his weekend business cruise on the company ship. The ship is damaged by a fire later in the week. The president's statement is offered to show that the president believed the ship was seaworthy, for the further inference that it was, in fact, seaworthy. If, instead, the company president really had taken his secretary with him that weekend by airplane to Las Vegas, where is the reduced risk of sincerity? Compare the situation of the company president who, after inspecting the ship, actually goes out to sea. The former is a statement offered for a different inference, sometimes called an "implied assertion,"[48] where no reduced sincerity risk is present. The latter is nonverbal nonassertive conduct, in which a reduction in the risk of fabrication results from an absence of intent to assert anything. Thus, although the Advisory Committee was correct with respect to a reduced risk of fabrication associated with *nonverbal* conduct which is not intended as an assertion, the Committee did not fully consider the consequences of extension of this concept to cases involving *verbal* statements offered as a basis for inferring something other than the matter asserted.

Even if one assumes that a reduced risk of sincerity does result when an assertive verbal statement is used to infer something other than the truth of the matter directly asserted, the practical importance of the concept nevertheless is small when compared to the analytical confusion which results from the concept's use. This confusion

---

47. Reliance on an implied assertion involves the following reasoning process. The fact finder is informed by testimony that X engaged in certain conduct. This conduct is not a direct assertion of f, the disputed fact, but the fact finder is asked to infer from the conduct that X believes f to be true. Having made this inference, the finder must then infer from X's belief in f that f is true. This inference from belief to truth will be sound only if X's belief faithfully reflects the fact, and the reflection will be faithful only if X's perception of the fact and his recollection of that perception were accurate. Reliance on implied assertions, therefore, necessarily entails reliance on memory and perception. On the other hand, since an implied assertion by definition consists of conduct *not* intended as an assertion concerning f, there is no danger that the actor is being insincere about f. A person who did not intend to make *any* statement about f could not have intended to make a misleading statement about f. Similarly, since the actor's conduct does not consist of words expressly stating f, there is no danger that language apparently affirming or denying f, and so understood by the fact finder, was in reality intended to convey a different meaning. In brief, while reliance on uncross-examined express assertions would expose the fact finder to the dangers of faulty narration, insincerity, inaccurate perception, and erroneous memory, only the perception and memory dangers seem to be posed by uncross-examined implied assertions. Because implied assertions entail fewer dangers than express assertions—especially because implied assertions raise no problem of insincerity—it is argued that they should be classified as nonhearsay. Finman, *Implied Assertions as Hearsay: Some Criticism of the Uniform Rules of Evidence,* 14 STAN. L. REV. 682, 685-86 (1962) (citations omitted).

48. The term "implied assertion" applies not only to assertive statements offered for a purpose other than the truth of the matter asserted, but to nonverbal conduct not intended as an assertion as well. C. McCORMICK, EVIDENCE § 250, at 596-600 (E. Cleary 2d ed. 1972). *See also supra* text accompanying notes 23-30.

strongly supports rejection of the concept. Moreover, many statements potentially falling within the category of statements offered for a different inference are admissible under rule 803(3) as a hearsay exception for current state of mind.[49] Thus, whenever the state of mind of the declarant is itself a fact of consequence in the litigation, discussion of whether the statement is hearsay is of no practical importance. However, where the inferred state of mind of the declarant is not of consequence but is itself used to infer the truth of a nonasserted fact, such as the competency of another in *Wright v. Doe d. Tatham*, the state of mind exception is not available. In such circumstances, if the statement possesses sufficient guarantees of trustworthiness, and is necessary in the context of the litigation, the statement may nevertheless be admissible under the other hearsay exceptions of rules 803(24) and 804(b)(5).

b.   Breadth of Concept

The three letters in *Tatham* illustrate statements offered not for the truth of the matter directly asserted, but as a basis for drawing a nonasserted inference. Not all statements offered in evidence for a further inference, however, fall within the breadth of the argued for concept of a statement used as a basis for drawing a nonasserted inference. In the previous discussion, the initial inference as to the state of mind of the declarant follows from the statement, but is not asserted by it. When the state of mind is directly asserted, the statement is clearly hearsay. Thus, if Reverend Ellershaw had written Marsden's attorney stating that he believed Marsden possessed testamentary capacity, the letter clearly would be hearsay. Similarly, when the declarant necessarily intended to express the inference for which the statement is offered, i.e., the inference is implicitly being asserted, the statement is tantamount to a direct assertion and therefore is hearsay.[50] The closer the inference to be drawn is to the matter directly asserted, the more likely the declarant intended to assert the inference for which the statement is offered as proof.

---

49. Rule 803(3) provides a hearsay exception, even if the declarant is available to testify, for a statement of the declarant's then existing "state of mind, emotion, sensation, or physical condition (such as intent, plan, motive, design, mental feeling, pain, and bodily health), but not including a statement of memory or belief to prove the fact remembered or believed unless it relates to the execution, revocation, identification, or terms of declarant's will." FED. R. EVID. 803(3) (1981).

50. The declarant necessarily intends to assert, i.e., implicitly asserts, matters forming the foundation for matters directly expressed in the sense that such additional matters must be assumed to be true to give meaning to the matters directly expressed in the context in which the statement was made. To illustrate, the question "Do you think it will stop raining in one hour?" contains the implicit assertion that it is currently raining. The fact that it is currently raining is a necessary foundation fact which must be assumed true for the question asked to make sense. A matter which is implicitly asserted as true is hearsay. *See* SALTZBURG & REDDEN, FEDERAL RULES OF EVIDENCE MANUAL 511 (2d ed. 1977) ("[T]o the extent that one fact must be being asserted if another that is directly asserted is to be taken as true, both should be treated as hearsay when the direct assertion is offered to prove the other."); 4 LOUISELL & MUELLER, FEDERAL EVIDENCE § 416 (1980). *See also infra* note 75.

The concept of a statement offered to infer something other than the truth of the matter asserted applies, if ever, only when the declarant's statement is used to infer the truth of an implied assertion of the declarant and not when the inference merely flows from assuming the truth of the matter actually asserted. For example, the nonasserted inference doctrine does not support a claim that a statement by a witness that a car was going 80 miles per hour five blocks from the site of the accident offered to infer speed at the time of the accident is not hearsay.[51]

---

51. *See* United States v. Ariza-Ibarra, 605 F.2d 1216, 1223 (1st Cir. 1979); Park v. Huff, 493 F.2d 923, *withdrawn on other grounds*, 506 F.2d 849 (5th Cir. 1974) (en banc), *cert. denied*, 423 U.S. 824 (1975); United States v. Pacelli, 491 F.2d 1108, 1115-18 (2d Cir.), *cert. denied*, 419 U.S. 826 (1974). *Park, supra*, involved a habeas petition by A.C. Park, an alleged bootlegger in Jackson County, Georgia, who was convicted as the "prime mover" in a contract to murder the local prosecutor. Park was convicted of murder on the "crucial" testimony of one of the co-conspirators, who had no personal knowledge of Park's identity, but repeated out-of-court statements of two other co-conspirators which implied that Park was behind the murder contract.

The court overturned the conviction because the statements related by the co-conspirator were hearsay, not falling within a proper exception. Judge Wisdom stated:

Implied assertions may, in certain circumstances carry less danger of insincerity or untrustworthiness than direct assertions . . . but not always. The danger of insincerity or untrustworthiness is decreased only where there is no possibility that the declarant intended to leave a particular impression. . . . When the possibility is real that an out-of-court statement which implies the existence of the ultimate fact in issue was made with assertive intent, it is essential that the statement be treated as hearsay if a direct declaration of that fact would be so treated.

Id. at 927-28. Thus, Judge Wisdom adopted the reasoning of Baron Parke in *Wright v. Doe d. Tatham, supra* text accompanying note 45.

In *Pacelli, supra*, the court reversed Vincent Pacelli's conviction for violating the civil rights of one Patsy Parks by murdering her. The court held that the trial judge had erroneously failed to exclude crucial hearsay, not falling within a valid exception. A party to the crime was permitted to testify over Pacelli's objections about conduct and statements by Pacelli's friends and relatives after the murder which implied that they knew Pacelli had committed the deed. The trial court permitted the accomplice to testify how Pacelli's friends and relatives had criticized the inept hiding of the body, and how they had urged the accomplice to flee shortly after Pacelli's arrest. The appellate court held that the testimony containing these extra-judicial statements "clearly implied knowledge and belief on the part of third person declarants not available for cross-examination as to the source of their knowledge regarding the ultimate fact in issue, i.e., whether Pacelli killed Parks, [the accomplice's] testimony as to them was excludable hearsay evidence." *Id.* at 1116.

The *Pacelli* court cited Krulewitch v. United States, 336 U.S. 440 (1949). In *Krulewitch*, the defendant was prosecuted for inducing a woman to cross state lines for immoral purposes. The trial court permitted the complaining witness (the woman induced by the defendant) to testify that subsequent to the crime the defendant's co-conspirator had suggested that the complaining witness and the co-conspirator should take the blame, since the defendant "couldn't stand it." *Id.* at 441.

The Supreme Court held that admission of this hearsay statement was reversible error; since it was outside of the conspiracy, it was simply "an unsworn, out-of-court declaration of petitioner's guilt." The admitted statement "plainly implied that petitioner was guilty of the crime for which he was on trial." *Id.* at 442.

Based on *Krulewitch*, the *Pacelli* court considered it irrelevant that the out-of-court declarants may not have intended to communicate their belief that Pacelli murdered Parks. 491 F.2d at 1116. Although Judge Wisdom in *Park v. Huff, supra*, stressed the sincerity risk inherent in intended out-of-court implied assertions, the *Pacelli* court stated:

While the danger of insincerity may be reduced where implied rather than express assertions of third parties are involved . . . there is the added danger of misinterpretation of the declarant's belief. Moreover, the declarant's opportunity and capacity for accurate perception or his sources of information remain of crucial importance. . . . Here, for instance, there is no

2. *Statements as Circumstantial Evidence*

Circumstantial evidence has occasionally been the subject of discussion in reported cases involving the application of the rule against hearsay. When such discussions have occurred they have tended to be confusing, and more often than not, theoretically unsound. The main reason for this inaccuracy is that in most such instances, although the evidence under consideration was highly probative, highly necessary, and highly trustworthy, no applicable hearsay exception existed at common law. Not surprisingly, even those courts possessing a correct understanding of the rule against hearsay were prone to squeeze unreasonably the definition of hearsay to admit such evidence. With the enactment of the "other exception" provisions of rules 803(24) and 804(b)(5) in the federal courts, and comparable provisions in states which have adopted similar rules,[52] however, resort to distortion of the hearsay definition in the interests of justice is no longer necessary. Although questions concerning application of the definition of hearsay arise in many contexts with respect to circumstantial evidence, certain distinct and recurring situations merit detailed discussion.

a. *Mechanical Traces*

The presence of something upon a person or premises may constitute circumstantial evidence tending to establish that a person performed an act which is associated with those circumstances. Such items, referred to by Wigmore as "mechanical traces,"[53] include: (1) the presences upon a person or premises of articles, fragments, stains, or tools; (2) brands on animals or timber; (3) tags, signs, and numbers on automobiles, railroad cars, or other vehicles or premises; and (4) postmarks, fingerprints, and footprints. Mechanical traces are frequently relevant as backward-looking circumstantial evidence that show the occurrence or non-occurrence of some act.

Hearsay questions arise only when the relevance of the circumstantial evidence, such as a tag or sign, stems solely from the *truth of the matter asserted* in a statement associated with the mechanical trace. For example, consider the situation in which a briefcase tag bears the name "Bill Snow." The relevance of the tag to link the defendant Bill Snow with the briefcase to which the tag is attached depends on the

---

suggestion that the declarants actually observed Pacelli commit the crimes with which he was charged. Thus their extra-judicial implied assertions have even less indicia of reliability than the implied assertion involved in *Krulewitch*, which was held inadmissible. Pacelli was entitled to cross-examine the third party declarants in order to test the validity of the inference—which the government sought to have the jury draw—that he had told the declarants he had killed Parks.

Id. at 1117.

52. *See supra* text accompanying note 1.

53. 1 J. WIGMORE, EVIDENCE §§ 149-57 (3d ed. 1940). Wigmore maintains that whenever a mechanical trace is offered as circumstantial evidence, it is not hearsay. As developed in the text, Wigmore's position is incorrect.

truth of the assertion made on the tag, that this briefcase belongs to Bill Snow. Thus, as all four hearsay risks are present, the tag is hearsay. To hold that the tag is a mechanical trace admissible as circumstantial evidence of ownership improperly ignores the definition of hearsay.[54] Similarly, to conclude that notebooks referring to drug trafficking are not hearsay because "declarations in the notebooks [are] utterances, used *circumstantially*, giving rise to the indirect inference that the apartment was the scene of drug sales and drug related activity,"[55] is incorrect for the same reason. That the tag is extremely probative evidence of ownership merely illustrates that hearsay evidence may be extremely probative and trustworthy.

The analysis is different when the relevance of the mechanical trace does not arise from the truth of the statement itself. Consider a book of matches bearing the name Red Fox Inn found on a defendant who is accused of a murder committed at the Red Fox Inn. If authenticated solely as having been taken from the defendant, the matchbook is hearsay, because its relevance depends on the truth of the statement on the matchbook that its origin is the Red Fox Inn. Now assume that the owner of the Red Fox Inn testifies that the matchbook found on the defendant is identical to the matchbooks he places on tables for use by customers. At this juncture, the relevance of the matchbook is no longer dependent on the truth of the matter asserted. This point can be more easily appreciated by changing the cover of the matchbook to a modern design bearing no lettering at all. When the owner of the Red Fox Inn testifies that this matchbook is identical to those distributed at his bar, the nonhearsay nature of the physical evidence is highlighted.[56]

54. United States v. Snow, 517 F.2d 441, 443-44 (9th Cir. 1975). In *Snow*, the trial court followed Wigmore's incorrect position, *supra* note 53, and the circuit court affirmed, stating that the name tape on Bill Snow's briefcase was "an evidentiary fact, other than an assertion 'from which the truth of the matter asserted is desired to be inferred.'" *Id.* at 443. In reality, the name tape was totally irrelevant unless its assertion was true.

55. United States v. Wilson, 532 F.2d 641, 646 (8th Cir.), *cert. denied*, 429 U.S. 846 (1976). In *Wilson*, the court permitted admission of notebooks referring to drug trafficking, demonstrating the same misunderstanding of hearsay as seen in United States v. Snow, 517 F.2d 441 (9th Cir. 1975). *See supra* note 54. For a correct interpretation, see Flores v. United States, 551 F.2d 1169, 1173 (9th Cir. 1977) ("The Government's rather tortuous claim that Buenrostro's assertion of ownership [in a letter] is admissible as circumstantial evidence of Beltran's ownership is without any merit whatsoever.").

56. *See, e.g.*, United States v. Lieberman, 637 F.2d 95, 101 (2d Cir. 1980) (hotel card held admissible to show that someone by defendant's name registered at the hotel, provided the card was admitted with other evidence showing that the card contained correct information). *See also* United States v. Canieso, 470 F.2d 1224, 1232 (2d Cir. 1972):

   Chou's [the defendant's] argument must be weighed against some facts not yet stated. Two letters, written in Chinese, were found in Chou's pockets. One letter, not dated or signed, instructed that on reaching New York, the recipient should "go outside the airport and wait for him. And then take a car together and go to the hotel. And live in the same room." The letter also instructed the party to "tell him to cable me. He has the cable number." The recipient was also told whom to contact in New York, to be sure to take the address of the hotel if he went out so that he would not get lost, and to remit the money soon in a way that was described. The second letter, dated November 1, related that the writer had already established contact about "the textile goods," sought to clarify "the basic price of

b. Character of an Establishment

McCormick classifies as not hearsay situations where "the charac-

---

$6,000," and contained other language which the jury could have found to constitute a veiled reference to narcotics. . . .

The letter, not signed or dated and in rather garbled English, which was found in Canieso's [an accomplice's] wallet, dovetailed with the first of the letters on Chou's person just described. It instructed that "[a]fter arriving in New York, everything is all right, my relatives will wait for you outside of the airport. You can get a taxi with him together and then go to the hotel. You can stay with him together." It asked that, immediately upon arrival at the hotel, the recipient should cable an address in Bangkok giving the name of the hotel, the number of the room, and the telephone number. It reminded him that "the man follow you he cannot speak English," that the recipient should "[k]indly take care of him," that the man would "go to find his friend immediately," and that the man should be reminded to take "the card of the hotel" on going out so that he could instruct the taxidriver where to return.

We have some doubt whether the Canieso letter is within the ban of the hearsay rule at all. It made no assertion about what the defendants had done; rather it told what they were to do. Its relevancy as against Chou was as circumstantial proof that he was linked with Canieso, the carrier of the narcotics, in much the same way as their common possession of cards giving the Bangkok cable address and the names of the prospective New York contacts would have done. The only way in which the letter can be deemed hearsay is by inserting in it a statement that the writer had entrusted Chou with the task of making the needed contacts in New York. We see no particular reason for doing this simply to create a hearsay problem that would not otherwise exist—even though the jury would doubtless draw exactly this inference. Here the resemblance of the letter found in Canieso's wallet to the one found on Chou's person affords a considerably stronger basis for a conclusion that the Canieso letter was receivable *"circumstantially,"* as giving rise to indirect inferences, but not as assertions to prove the matter asserted," 6 WIGMORE, EVIDENCE § 1766, at 180 (3d ed. 1940). . . .

This concept, however, has caused some difficulty. In United States v. Mejias, 552 F.2d 435 (2d Cir.), *cert. denied,* 434 U.S. 847 (1977), the court failed to explain the importance, if any, of the truth of the assertions, and whether the documents in question were authenticated properly. In *Mejias,* the defendant claimed that the admission against him of a hotel receipt, a luggage invoice, and a travel agency business card was reversible error because the items were hearsay and improperly authenticated as business records. The court stated that:

These documents were not offered to prove either the payment of a hotel bill or the purchase of a piece of luggage, but were circumstantial evidence of Padilla's connection with the Skyline Motor Inn and the attache case seized therefrom. The business card. . . noted Padilla's name and a flight schedule for April 27, 1974 to Curacao and Colombia on the reverse side. The fact that Padilla possessed this card showed a relationship between Padilla and Perez, who testified that Padilla was in Colombia after April 27. Because these documents were not offered to prove the truth of their contents, they were not hearsay, Fed.R. Evid. 801(c); and the jury could consider them circumstantially to corroborate other evidence in the case.

Id. at 446.

In United States v. Mazyak, 650 F.2d 788 (5th Cir. 1981), a prosecution for conspiracy to import marijuana, the court admitted nautical charts, a letter, and four receipts found when the coast guard boarded defendant's ship. The court held that they were not hearsay. The letter was found in the ship's wheelhouse. It was addressed to all four defendants and read in full: "Dear Grand Banks Lady. I say to you farewell your journey for you carry my greatest treasure. On precious cargo my thoughts are with you. I bid you farewell. Love, Julie." The court held that admission of the letter was proper because:

The government offered the letter for the limited purpose of linking the appellants with the vessel and with one another. The use of the letter for this limited purpose was not hearsay. The letter was not introduced to prove the truth of the matter asserted; rather, it was introduced as circumstantial proof that the appellants were associated with each other and the boat.

Id. at 792. Moreover, the court held that because the government did not claim that a person named Julie had written the appellants a letter regarding their importation of marijuana, the government did not have to authenticate the contents of the letter. *Id.*

The trial court also admitted fuel, repair, hotel, and equipment receipts. These receipts were not hearsay, according to the appellate court, because "the government did not offer these docu-

ter of an establishment is sought to be proved by evidence of statements made in connection with activities taking place on the premises."[57] The classic illustration of McCormick's position involves placing telephone calls to an establishment alleged to harbor gambling.[58] To enhance the probative value and trustworthiness of the statements under consideration, assume 20 policemen, accompanied by 20 clergymen of various denominations, place tape recorders on 40 telephones and record 100 calls. Each call is answered by a police officer or clergyman, and proceeds something like, "This is Tom, put $2 to win on Acne Pimple in the third at Belmont." Occasionally such statements have been held to be not hearsay, either because the statement characterizes an act, or because the statement is circumstantial evidence offered not for its truth but only for the fact that the statement was made.[59]

Despite these elaborate attempts to avoid the hearsay problem, such statements fall clearly within the definition of hearsay. There is no independently relevant act, apart from the act of placing a bet, for the statements to characterize. The statements are irrelevant if offered solely for the fact that they were said. For the telephone calls to prove that the establishment was a betting parlor, the person who placed the telephone call must have intended to call the number reached. Moreover, the declarant must have believed that the number dialed was a betting parlor. In addition, the declarant must have intended to place a bet, instead of, for example, playing a practical joke. Finally, and most importantly, the declarant's intention must be based upon previously acquired personal knowledge that the number which he dialed is in fact a betting parlor. Thus, the phone call is relevant only when it is offered to prove the truth of the matter necessarily and implicitly being asserted: that the establishment called by the out-of-court declarant is in fact a betting parlor.[60]

Analysis would vary if the witness overheard the entire conversation between the bookie and the bettor. In the illustration, the police officers and clergymen answered the telephone calls and only overheard requests to bet. If a police officer had overheard a person work-

---

ments to prove the truth of the matter asserted, *i.e.* that a payment for work repairs, a hotel room, fuel, and equipment additions actually occurred." *Id.*

As authenticated, however, the charts, the letter, and the receipts are hearsay. In each instance the relevancy of the item depends upon the matter asserted being true. As authenticated, however, each item could have been admitted under rule 804(b)(5).

57. C. McCormick, Evidence § 249, at 589 (E. Cleary 2d ed. 1972).

58. *Id.* at 589 n.81 ("For example, statements and conversations indicative of gambling are admissible under this theory. The evidence may consist of incoming telephone calls from unidentified persons seeking to place bets.").

59. *See* State v. Tolisano, 136 Conn. 210, 214-15, 70 A.2d 118, 120 (1949) ("The telephone calls are admissible as evidence that bets were being placed but not that the statements made to the officers were true. The evidence is admitted, not as exception to the hearsay rule, but because it is not within the rule.") *See also* People v. Barnhart, 66 Cal. App. 2d 714, 714-23, 153 P.2d 214, 219 (1944) (Doran, J., concurring).

60. The calls, although hearsay, would be admissible by virtue of Fed. R. Evid. 803(24) & 804(b)(5). *See also supra* notes 2 & 50; *infra* note 75.

ing at the establishment respond to the statement "This is Tom, put $2 to win on Acne Pimple in the third at Belmont," with "You got it, settle up as usual," the situation would be entirely different. The statement's relevance no longer depends on its truth; the statement accepting the bet would be a verbal act possessing independent significance under applicable substantive criminal law.[61]

c. Personal Knowledge of Independently Established Facts

When facts have been established by independent evidence, on rare occasions a party may wish to introduce statements to prove the declarant's personal knowledge of these facts. The declarant's personal knowledge may be relevant to establish prior presence at a particular location. Consider, for example, the case of *Bridges v. State*.[62] In *Bridges*, the defendant was convicted of taking indecent liberties with a seven-year-old girl named Sharon S. The crime occurred at the assailant's house, and the case centered on the identification of defendant as the assailant. This identification depended in part upon whether the house to which the assailant had taken the child was the house in which defendant resided at the time of the attack. The trial court admitted Sharon's statements to her mother and to police officers made prior to discovery of the location of defendant's house. These statements contained descriptions of the general appearance of the steps to the porch, the front door, and the room to which the assailant had taken her, and of various items contained in this room. The Supreme Court of Wisconsin upheld the trial court's admission of the girl's statements, holding them to be circumstantial evidence of her personal knowledge; Sharon's statements were not offered to prove the truth of the matter asserted.[63]

---

61. *See* W. LaFave & A. Scott, Criminal Law 177-82 (1972), *supra* note 35.
62. 247 Wis. 350, 19 N.W.2d 529 (1945).
63. 247 Wis. at 363-66, 19 N.W.2d at 535-36. The court's holding evidences a misunderstanding of the nature of hearsay. The court simply ignored the fact that Sharon's out-of-court declarations were relevant only if true:

There is testimony by police officers and also [by the child's mother] as to statements which were made to them by Sharon . . . to ascertain the identity of the man who committed the offense and of the house and room in which it was committed. In those statements she spoke, as hereinbefore stated, of various matters and features which she remembered and which were descriptive of the exterior and surroundings of the house; and of the room and various articles and the location thereof therein. It is true that testimony as to such statements was hearsay and, as such, inadmissible if the purpose for which it was received had been to establish thereby that there were in fact the stated articles in the room, or that they were located as stated, or that the exterior features or surroundings of the house were as Sharon stated. That, however, was not in this case the purpose for which the evidence as to those statements was admitted. It was admissible in so far as the fact that she had made the statements can be deemed to tend to show that at the time those statements were made, which was a month prior to the subsequent discovery of the room and house at 125 East Johnson Street, she had knowledge as to articles and descriptive features which, as was proven by other evidence, were in fact in or about that room and house. If in relation thereto Sharon made the statements as to which the officers and her mother testified, then those statements—although they were extrajudicial utterances—constituted at least circumstantial evidence that she then had

Notwithstanding the court's holding, Sharon's statements are hearsay. Her statements were offered as being made under circumstances indicating that she acquired her memory in a manner consistent with the events described in her statement. As so offered, all four hearsay risks are present. It is certainly possible, albeit unlikely, that the child created a description of the house out of whole cloth.[64] More likely, she could have in good faith provided a description of a house where she had been on an occasion unconnected to the assault. Finally, Sharon may have described a house that the police or someone else had suggested to her earlier as being the house where she had been taken. Admittedly, the magnitude of the hearsay risks is small. Nevertheless, because the risks of perception, recordation and recollection, narration, and sincerity are present in Sharon's statements, the statements fall within the definition of hearsay when they are offered to prove Sharon's personal knowledge of objects in defendant's residence and therefore to establish that the incident took place at that location.[65] The relevance of the child's statements involve all four hearsay risks located on the right of the dotted line in the "Stickperson Hearsay" diagram.[66]

d. Circumstantial Use of Utterances to Show State of Mind

McCormick asserts that although a statement which is a direct

---

such knowledge; and that such state of mind on her part was acquired by reason of her having been in that room and house prior to making the statements. . . .

So in this case the proof that Sharon made the statements in question before there was any possibility of having what she stated she remembered about the house, and room, and articles therein, from her first contact therewith, affected or changed by what she learned after the discovery and location thereof, at 125 East Johnson street [sic], is material and significant in so far as it tended to show that she had knowledge of certain things in and about the house and room. The existence of those things in fact could not, however, be established by her hearsay statements, but had to be proven by other evidence which was competent. In other words, although proof of her extrajudicial assertions was competent to show such knowledge on her part, it could not be deemed to prove the facts asserted thereby. When, for instance, it was proven that Sharon stated during the evening after the alleged assault that there was a picture of the lady in the room, her statement did not constitute competent evidence to prove that there was such a picture in the room. But her statement was competent as evidence to prove that she had knowledge of such an object in the room and for this purpose the utterance is not inadmissible hearsay, but is a circumstantial fact indicating knowledge on the part of [the child] at a particular time.
Id. at 366.

64. The risk of sincerity may be said to be as great as that asserted with placing a monkey in a room with a typewriter and paper and returning in two weeks to see if the monkey had produced *Hamlet*.

65. Sharon's statements are admissible, however, as an exception to the hearsay rule. Although her statement may initially appear to fall into the exception for statements evidencing existing mental, emotional, or physical condition, the statement involves her belief as a fact offered to prove the fact she believed; her statement therefore does not fit the exception. *See* FED. R. EVID. 803(3), *supra* note 49. Her statements, however, would be admissible under the general exceptions contained in FED. R. EVID. 803(24) & 804(b)(5).

66. Additional illustrations are contained in Kinder v. Commonwealth, 306 S.W.2d 265 (Ky. Ct. App. 1957) and State v. Galvan, 297 N.W.2d 344 (Iowa 1980). For an excellent discussion of the problem, see Judge Weinstein's opinion in United States v. Muscato, 534 F. Supp. 969, 974 (E.D.N.Y. 1982).

declaration of the declarant's state of mind or feeling is hearsay when it is offered to prove that state of mind or feeling, declarations which only impliedly, indirectly, inferentially, or otherwise circumstantially indicate the declarant's state of mind or feeling are not hearsay. A statement which is not a direct assertion of a state of mind or feeling of the declarant is often stated to fall outside of the hearsay definition on the ground that the statement is not being offered to prove the truth of the matter asserted. McCormick employs the following illustration:

> In a contested will case the proponent might seek to support the validity of testator's bequest to his son Harold against the charge of undue influence by showing that long before the time when the alleged influence was exerted, the testator had shown a special fondness for Harold. For this purpose evidence might be offered (a) that the testator had paid the expenses of Harold, and for none other of his children, in completing a college course, (b) that the testator said, 'Harold is the finest of my sons,' and (c) that he said, 'I care more for Harold than for any of my other children.' When offered to show the testator's feelings toward his son, under the suggested definition item (a) would present no hearsay question, item (b) would be considered a non-hearsay declaration raising a circumstantial inference as to the testator's feelings, and (c) a direct statement offered to prove the fact stated, and hence dependent for its value upon the veracity of the declarant, would be considered hearsay.[67]

McCormick justifies this distinction by asserting that such statements possess a reduced risk of sincerity, the same notion used to support classifying as non-hearsay statements which are offered as a basis for a nonasserted inference.[68]

The statement "Harold is the finest of my sons" offered as circumstantial evidence to prove that the testator cares more for Harold than any of his other children is properly classified as hearsay. The party offering this statement, which expresses directly the declarant's state of mind, uses the statement to imply an additional state of mind of the declarant. Because the trier of fact must assume the declarant's belief in the truth of the matter directly asserted, "Harold is the finest," for the trier to infer the nonasserted statement, "I care more for Harold," *the statement is hearsay according to the language of rule 801(c)* and the common law definition of hearsay;[69] the statement's relevancy depends on the truth of the matter being asserted. Because the declarant's statement, which is tantamount to "I believe Harold is the finest," must be true, i.e., the statement is being offered to prove the truth of the matter

---

67. C. MCCORMICK, EVIDENCE § 249, at 590-91 (E. Cleary 2d ed. 1972) (citations omitted).

68. *Id.* at 590 n.92 ("Admittedly the uncross-examined statement is subject to all the hearsay dangers, except to the extent that deliberate falsification diminishes when a statement is not used to prove anything asserted therein. *See* E. MORGAN, BASIC PROBLEMS OF EVIDENCE 249 (1962). The same problem exists when the non-assertive conduct is nonverbal.").

69. *See supra* text accompanying notes 2-4.

asserted, the sincerity risk remains unabated. Reliance on an analogy to nonverbal nonassertive conduct, in which a reduced risk of fabrication results from declarant's lack of intent to assert anything, is thus misplaced.

For some unexplainable reason, McCormick abandons his position that direct assertions of the existence of the relevant state of mind or feeling are themselves hearsay when the statement is offered to establish the declarant's mental incompetency. McCormick concludes that the claim "I believe that I am King Henry the Eighth," which undeniably falls squarely within the definition of hearsay, may be classified as nonhearsay on the theory of verbal conduct offered circumstantially because the statement is offered to show mental incompetency.[70] Professor Hinton correctly exposed the errors of McCormick's ways many years ago:

> It has sometimes been argued by judges and writers that, where the issue is the sanity of the testator, and some absurd statement by him is proved, e.g., 'I am the Emperor Napoleon,' no hearsay use is involved because we are not seeking to prove that he really was Napoleon, and hence that we are making a purely circumstantial use of his words to prove his irrational belief. The difficulty is that this view ignores the implied assertion of belief. If the statement had taken the form, 'I believe that I am Napoleon,' and were offered to prove that the testator so believed, it would be generally conceded [but not by McCormick] that the statement was hearsay, and receivable only because of an exception to the rule. The former assertion is simply a short method of stating the speaker's opinion or belief. Implied assertions seem to fall within the hearsay category as well as express assertions.[71]

For the statement to possess any relevance on the issue of the declarant's mental competence, the declarant must believe his statement is true. Therefore, whether the statement is "Harold is the finest of my sons" or "I am Napoleon," the hearsay risks of sincerity and narration are present. Such statements are classified properly as hearsay; their relevance depends upon movement on the "Stickperson Hearsay" diagram to the right of the dotted line. Although these statements do not possess the hearsay risks of perception and recollection, the hearsay risks of narration and, most critically, sincerity persist.

Determining whether such statements are hearsay has often been said to be important only to theorists, because the hearsay exception in rule 803(3) for statements of a declarant's then existing mental, emo-

---

70. C. McCORMICK, EVIDENCE § 249, at 593 (E. Cleary 2d ed. 1972). *See also* Park, *McCormick on Evidence and the Concept of Hearsay: A Critical Analysis Followed by Suggestions to Law Teachers*, 65 MINN. L. REV. 423 (1980).

71. Hinton, *States of Mind and the Hearsay Rule*, U. CHI. L. REV. 394, 397-98 (1934) (citation omitted).

tional, or physical condition permits admission of the statements.[72]
Nevertheless, the confusion in the overall analysis of hearsay resulting
from the overly-broad use of the concept of circumstantial evidence
persists needlessly. Moreover, statements involving "mechanical
traces," the "character of an establishment," and "facts independently
established," which meet the definition of hearsay, do not conveniently
fall within a common law hearsay exception. Characterizing assertive
statements as circumstantial evidence is simply irrelevant when ad-
dressing the definitional framework of hearsay set forth in rules 801(a)-
(c). The practice should be discontinued.

V. REFORMULATING THE DEFINITION OF HEARSAY

Courts and commentators have struggled with the definition of
hearsay because under the pigeonhole theory of exceptions to the hearsay rule many trustworthy and probative statements would be excluded
at trial if they were classified as hearsay. Attempts to expand admissibility through novel interpretations of the definition of hearsay are the
natural result of this dilemma. Such novel interpretations have resulted in holdings that "I believe I am Napoleon" and statements offered to infer something other than the truth of the matter asserted are
not hearsay. While such interpretations are clearly novel, they are incorrect interpretations of the definition of hearsay and do not comport
with the analysis of risks that the hearsay rule seeks to control. Besides
being incorrect, such novel interpretations have greatly confused not
only many practitioners and courts, but thousands of law students each
year. Whatever value these novel interpretations once had no longer
exists in the federal courts and in those states adopting rules of evidence modeled on the Federal Rules of Evidence. With the availability
of the other hearsay exceptions of rules 803(24) and 804(b)(5), trustworthy and necessary hearsay is no longer inadmissible simply because it
fails to fit neatly into one of the pigeonholed hearsay exceptions.

Clarity would be fostered, and confusion eliminated, if the definition of hearsay was revised in form but not content, to declare that
hearsay includes: (1) a statement which is relevant only if the declarant
believes the matter asserted to be true or false, whether that statement
is "I am Napoleon" or "I believe that I am Napoleon"; and (2) a statement whose relevance depends upon the matter asserted being true,
without reference to whether a further inference is then going to be
drawn. As discussed above, statements offered as circumstantial evidence of a state of mind, and statements offered for a further inference,
are currently properly classified as hearsay at common law and under
rule 801(c). Any contrary suggestion in the Advisory Committee's note
regarding statements forming the basis for a nonasserted inference is

---

72. FED. R. EVID. 803(3). *See supra* note 49.

incorrect.[73] Couching the definition of hearsay in terms of relevance also demonstrates clearly that statements offered circumstantially as mechanical traces, as characterizing an establishment, or as proving personal knowledge of facts independently established, are hearsay when the statement's relevance depends upon the truth of the matter directly asserted. As provided in rules 801(a)-(c) and the common law definition of hearsay, a statement is hearsay whenever the statement is relevant in the context of the litigation only when offered to prove the truth of the matter asserted; a statement that is relevant only if the matter asserted is true rests "for its value upon the credibility of the out-of-court assertion."[74]

An alternative formulation of rule 801(c), identical in content, although highlighting the hearsay nature of statements offered as a basis for a non-asserted inference, and statements offered as circumstantial evidence including statements of state of mind, is as follows:

> (c) Hearsay: "Hearsay" is a statement offered in evidence, other than one made by the declarant while testifying at the trial or hearing, to the extent relevance depends upon (1) the truth of the matter asserted or (2) the declarant's belief in the truth or falsity of the matter asserted.[75]

---

73. *See supra* text accompanying notes 42-50.

74. C. McCORMICK, EVIDENCE § 246, at 584 (E. Cleary 2d ed. 1972). *Accord* United States v. Parry, 649 F.2d 292, 294 (5th Cir. 1981):

> Rule 801(c) of the Federal Rules of Evidence defines hearsay as "a statement, other than one made by the declarant while testifying at the trial or hearing, offered in evidence to prove the truth of the matter asserted." The reasons for excluding hearsay are clear: when an out-of-court statement is offered as a testimonial assertion of the truth of the matter stated, we are vitally interested in the credibility of the out-of-court declarant. Because a statement made out of court is not exposed to the normal credibility safeguards of oath, presence at trial, and cross-examination, the jury has no basis for evaluating the declarant's trustworthiness and thus his statement is considered unreliable.

75. This proposal was previously set forth in my HANDBOOK OF FEDERAL EVIDENCE § 801.10 (1981). A similar but much less complete discussion of *Wright v. Doe d. Tatham* was presented in § 801.7. In an article entitled *The Definition of Hearsay in the Federal Rules of Evidence*, 61 TEX. L. REV. 49 (1982), Professor Wellborn, while agreeing with the conclusion that a statement offered for a different inference should be hearsay, offers certain criticism as to the approach taken in the *Handbook* and thus in this article. *Id*. at 82-83. This footnote responds to Professor Wellborn's remarks. In keeping with the concept of this article, no attempt will be put forth to evaluate the many other positions taken by Professor Wellborn in his article nor his assertions made with respect to positions taken by other commentators.

Three criticisms are addressed to the proposed revision in form but not content of rule 801(c) as it relates to a statement offered for a different inference. Professor Wellborn argues first that rejection of the Advisory Committee's position would set an "undesirable precedent that would undermine the very real and considerable usefulness to judges, lawyers, and scholars of the Committee's commentary on other rules." *Id*. at 82. First, the Advisory Committee's notes do not have the force of law. The language of the Federal Rules of Evidence, passed as a statute by Congress, control. As developed in this article, the language of rule 801(c), "offered in evidence to prove the truth of the matter asserted," properly understood, mandates the conclusion that statements offered for a different inference are hearsay. The language of an interpretive comment, whether by an Advisory Committee or a commentator, cannot override the language of the rule itself. As Professor Wellborn himself acknowledges, *id*. at 83, federal courts have themselves tended to treat *Wright v. Doe d. Tatham* as representing the proper interpretation of rule 801(c). Moreover, the argument concerning an "undesirable precedent" is simply untenable. Nobody is always correct—not even the Advisory Committee. Removal of a rotten apple from the barrel helps, not harms, the remaining apples.

Professor Wellborn argues next that my proposed reformulation of the definition of hearsay, i.e., whether a statement's relevance depends upon the truth of the matter, does not encompass "all of the cases Graham seems to have in mind." *Id.* Professor Wellborn provides three supposed illustrations of instances of statements he believes should be classified as hearsay (I agree) where he states that the truth of the matter asserted need not be assumed for the nonasserted inference to be drawn.

Before turning to those illustrations as developed in this article, *supra* at 910, and as Professor Wellborn himself fuly accepts in his article, *id.* at 78, *all* of the commentators agree that the concept of "intend to assert" includes matters necessarily implicitly asserted as well as those directly asserted. Professor Seligman, stated the following with respect to the statement "it will stop raining in any hour":

> In addition to the express assertion, there is in that case a necessary implication of an assertion that it is now raining and will continue to rain for an hour. As far as the intent of the speaker is concerned, while it is principally to give his thought as to cessation of the rain, it is incidentally without doubt to asserts its present existence and continuance. It is due only to a chance use of words that he did not say "the rain that is now falling will continue for an hour," in which case the express and implied assertions would have changed places, while the speaker's intent would have been undoubtedly the same. It would seem, therefore, that . . . implied assertions are hearsay. . . .

Seligman, *An Exception to the Hearsay rule*, 26 HARV. L. REV. 146, 150-51 n.13 (1912). *See also* S. SALTZBURG & K. REDDEN, FEDERAL RULES OF EVIDENCE MANUAL 511 (2d ed. 1977) ("[T]o the extent that one fact must be being asserted if another that is directly asserted is to be taken as true, both should be treated as hearsay when the direct assertion is offered to prove the other."); 4 D. LOUISELL & C. MUELLER, FEDERAL EVIDENCE § 416 (1980). This question is also discussed at *supra* note 50.

Now the illustrations:

(1) "The light was red" inferred from the statement "that driver is color blind." In making the statement concerning color blindness the declarant clearly intended to convey expressly to the hearer that the declarant observed the driver act in an improper manner. Since the "matter asserted" in the proposed rule obviously includes matter that the declarant necessarily intended to assert, the truth of the matter asserted, *i.e.*, direct and necessarily implicit, must be assumed for the statement to be relevant. Thus the illustration is not an instance of a statement offered for a different inference but rather a statement necessarily intended by the declarant to be an assertion of the truth of the inference for which the statement is offered—the inference is implicitly being asserted. Professor Wellborn, *id.* at 79, seems to agree: "the inference from 'That driver is color blind!' to 'The light is red,' while probably likewise involving only interpreting an intended meaning. . . ." In short, this is not a *Wright v. Doe d. Tatham* problem at all but rather one of simply determining the breadth of the declarant's intended assertion.

(2) The second illustration offered is the statement "It will stop raining in an hour." This illustration requires little discussion. The reader is simply referred to the quote of Seligman, *supra*, concerning the same statement. Once again the illustration does not relate to a statement offered for a different inference. The statement simply illustrates the wisdom of including necessarily implicit assertions, *i.e.*, that it is currently raining, in determining the breadth of intended assertions. Since the term "truth of the matter asserted" in the proposed rule is taken without change from current rule 801(c), there is no doubt that the statement "It will stop raining in an hour," which everyone, including apparently Professor Wellborn, considers hearsay when offered to prove it is currently raining, will retain its hearsay character. In short, Professor Wellborn is once again incorrectly using an illustration of a necessarily implicit intention to assert in considering the hearsay nature of a statement offered in evidence not for the truth of the matter asserted but rather as a basis for drawing a nonasserted inference.

(3) The last illustration involves the statement of a woman while looking in a mirror that "My boyfriend certainly has strong arms," offered to establish that her boyfriend beat her. As Professor Wellborn himself states, to argue that the statement is being offered for a different inference requires "assuming that the woman did not intend by her expression to communicate a belief that the defendant assaulted her." *Id.* at 65. One may ask whether when looking at her wounds in the mirror any conclusion othe than that the statement evidences that the declarant necessarily intended to assert that her boyfriend beat her is possible. If one were to assume no intent to assert, then the truth of the fact that her boyfriend has strong arms must be assumed to be true before the

nonasserted inference can be drawn. The problem is that absent an intent to assert that her boyfriend beat her, the statement is not relevant. Her belief that her boyfriend has strong arms based upon personal knowledge of his arm strength not acquired as a result of the beating does not make it more probable than without this evidence that he beat her. To illustrate, establishing that someone won an arm wrestling contest does not make it more likely that he inflicted a beating that could have easily been inflicted by any man of average strength. On the other hand, if one assumes personal knowledge of strength based upon the beating inflicted, then the fact that the boyfriend inflicted the beating is being implicitly asserted. In any event, once again the illustration fails to demonstrate that when a statement is in fact offered not as a direct or necessarily implicit assertion of the declarant but as a statement offered as a basis for drawing a nonasserted inference that the matter actually asserted, both direct and necessarily implicit, need not be true for the statement to be relevant.

The final contention of Professor Wellborn is clearly the most surprising. Professor Wellborn argues tht the word "assert" as defined in *Webster's Dictionary* means "to state or affirm positively, assuredly, plainly, or strongly," and from this definition that "it would seem that only a declarative sentence can be 'assertion.'" *Supra* at 72. Professor Wellborn calls such statements "nonassertive verbal conduct." *Id*. The conclusion reached is that any statement not in the form of a declarative sentence is not hearsay. *Id*. at 82-83, 92-93 n.191. To illustrate, Professor Wellborn would thus be forced to maintain that a question such as "Do you think it will stop raining in an hour?" is not hearsay. This conclusion is incorrect. Professor Wellborn fails to cite a single case in support of his contention. The term "assert" has been used in the definition of hearsay for well over one hundred years. While the alternative of "stated" as employed in Uniform Rule 62(1), "expressed," or even Professor Wellborn's term "communication" may be more accurate as a matter of semantics, the term "assert" clearly has its own meaning in law. Professor Wellborn stands alone in arguing that the statement "Do you think it will stop raining in an hour?", when offered to show it is currently raining, it not hearsay at common law or under the Federal Rules of Evidence. I stand by the proposed revision in form but not content of rule 801(a)-(c).

Part VIII
Extrinsic Probative Policy

[23]

WASHINGTON LAW REVIEW JURISPRUDENTIAL LECTURE SERIES*

EXCESSIVE SANCTIONS FOR GOVERNMENTAL MISCONDUCT IN CRIMINAL CASES

Richard A. Posner**

The fourth amendment, as is well known, forbids unreasonable searches and seizures by government officers;[1] if the government tries to introduce evidence in a criminal trial that was seized in violation of the fourth amendment, the defendant can get the evidence suppressed. If the evidence is vital to conviction, this means that the defendant will be acquitted simply because the evidence was obtained illegally. This is the famous exclusionary rule of the law of search and seizure.[2] The exclusionary rule is one example[3] of a sanction for governmental miconduct: evidence that may be essential to convicting a dangerous criminal is suppressed to punish or to deter the government's violation of a law, here the fourth amendment.

Issues concerning sanctions for governmental misconduct may seem quintessentially legal, but they also have an economic dimension. I shall argue, building on an earlier paper in which I analyzed the fourth amendment's exclusionary rule,[4] that economics can yield valuable insights into when sanctions for governmental misconduct are excessive.

These economic insights have two possible uses. One, of course, is to point the way to reform. The other, which is less obvious but from an

   * The Washington Law Review Lecture Series, now in its ninth year, is designed to bring outstanding speakers to the Law School to discuss contemporary legal issues. The *Review* gratefully acknowledges the generous financial assistance provided by the Evans Bunker Memorial Fund.

   ** Judge, U.S. Court of Appeals for the Seventh Circuit; Senior Lecturer, University of Chicago Law School. The research assistance of J. Gregory Sidak is gratefully acknowledged. The views expressed here are of course personal rather than official.

   1. The fourth amendment provides:
The right of the people to be secure in their persons, houses, papers, and effects, against unreasonable searches and seizures, shall not be violated, and no Warrants shall issue, but upon probable cause, supported by Oath or affirmation, and particularly describing the place to be searched, and the persons or things to be seized.
U.S. CONST. amend. IV.

   2. *See, e.g.*, Weeks v. United States, 232 U.S. 383 (1914) (applying exclusionary rule in federal criminal prosecutions); Mapp v. Ohio, 367 U.S. 643 (1961) (applying exclusionary rule in state criminal prosecutions).

   3. *See* part III *infra*, for other examples of governmental misconduct which are redressed by sanctions.

   4. Posner, *Rethinking the Fourth Amendment*, 1981 SUP. CT. REV. 49.

Washington Law Review   Vol. 57:635, 1982

academic standpoint more interesting, is to explain the law as it is. The branch of legal scholarship with which I have been strongly identified has tried to explain the common law on the hypothesis that the law is designed to maximize economic efficiency.[5]

The hypothesis I shall explore in this article is that the common-law remedies for governmental misconduct in criminal cases are best explained by assuming that judges are preeminently concerned with economic efficiency, even though the underlying norms defining that misconduct are often not economic. My hypothesis does not pretend to explain how judges *think* about these cases; it is designed merely to explain the outcomes of a decisional process that judges usually rationalize in noneconomic terms. But just as economists consider it nonessential to the validity of their empirical results whether businessmen and consumers speak or think in the language of economics, so I believe it nonessential whether judges explicitly speak or think in that language.

I. THE TWO TYPES OF EXCESSIVE SANCTION

A sanction can be excessive from an economic standpoint in two ways. First, it can violate the Pareto criterion of efficiency[6] by creating an avoidable deadweight loss. To explain the concept of "deadweight loss," I will use an example from the economics of sanctions for private (as distinct from governmental) misconduct: the choice between fines and imprisonment as the punishment for crime. To achieve a desired level of deterrence, society can, in principle at least, choose a fine that will be the exact equivalent of a term of imprisonment in the sense that the fine will impose the same private cost on the criminal. The social cost of the fine, however, will be smaller than the social cost of the equivalent term of imprisonment. The fine is just a transfer payment, whereas the term of imprisonment imposes deadweight losses—that is, losses not received as gains by anyone else—in the form of the criminal's forgone legitimate earnings and the costs of guarding him. Therefore, from an economic standpoint anyway, the fine is preferable.[7]

---

5. *See, e.g.*, Landes & Posner, *The Positive Economic Theory of Tort Law*, 15 GA. L. REV. 851 (1981).

6. The Pareto optimum is a state in which no person can be benefited without a corresponding detriment to another person. If it is possible through a transaction to benefit one without detriment to any other, then the situation is not a Pareto optimum. *See generally* V. PARETO, MANUAL OF POLITICAL ECONOMY 103–80 (Schwier trans. 1971) (Pareto's theory of economic equilibrium).

7. *See* Becker, *Crime and Punishment: An Economic Approach*, 76 J. POL. ECON. 169 (1968). *See also* Posner, *Optimal Sentences for White-Collar Criminals*, 17 AM. CRIM. L. REV. 409, 410 (1980) (arguing that fines are usually preferable to imprisonment for white-collar offenders because of the deadweight losses imposed by imprisonment).

Excessive Sanctions

Of course if the criminal is insolvent—as in the real world he often will be—this solution will not work. But if solvency is no problem, then a fine is Pareto-superior to imprisonment; that is simply the principle that I am interested in asserting here.

The second way in which a sanction may be economically excessive is that it may overdeter. The difference between this concern and the first can be seen most easily by imagining a choice between two fines, both collectible at zero cost from the defendant. If the smaller fine is set equal to the social cost of the defendant's crime, divided by the probability that he will be apprehended and convicted (which is simply to say, if the smaller fine is set at the optimal level), then the larger fine will be excessive. But it will be excessive not in the Paretian sense of directly imposing an avoidable social cost—for I am treating the fine as a pure, costless, transfer payment—but in the sense of creating incentives for inefficient behavior.

Now in a world of perfect certainty, to be sure, fines could be infinitely large without imposing any social cost at all; the threat of having to pay the fine would deter anyone from engaging in the forbidden activity, and so the fine would never be imposed. But when the unrealistic assumption of perfect certainty is dropped, it becomes apparent that the threat of a very large fine (or of some other Draconian punishment) will induce people to avoid lawful behavior at the edge of the ''forbidden zone'' in order to minimize the probability of being falsely accused and convicted of the offense. The benefits of the lawful behavior that is avoided because of this risk are social opportunity costs of the excessive fine.[8] Those costs provide the economic reason, or at least one important economic reason, for not imposing the death penalty on speeders; people would drive too slowly.

But it would be a mistake to conclude that a sanction really must be inefficient if it imposes an expected punishment cost greater than the formula for optimal punishment generates. The fine example makes it seem that all ''excessive'' fines are inefficient, but this is only because a fine is so easy to calibrate. But a fine is not always an available remedy, and the alternative sanction may not lend itself so easily to calibration as a sanction specified in dollars. In such a case it is necessary to compare the costs of overdeterrence with the costs of underdeterrence; if the latter costs are greater, the ''excessive'' sanction may not be excessive in a broader economic sense after all. The choice, then, is not between overdeterrence

---

8. *See* United States v. United States Gypsum Co.. 438 U.S. 422, 440–43 (1978); Block & Sidak. *The Cost of Antitrust Deterrence: Why Not Hang A Price Fixer Now and Then?*. 68 Geo. L.J. 1131, 1136–39 (1980).

Washington Law Review   Vol. 57:635, 1982

and underdeterrence but between the optimal amount of deterrence and too much deterrence.

II. THE FOURTH AMENDMENT EXCLUSIONARY RULE

The exclusionary rule applied in fourth amendment cases illustrates both senses in which a sanction may be excessive from an economic standpoint. First, it violates the Pareto-superiority criterion because it imposes a deadweight loss—the suppression of socially valuable evidence—that would have been avoided if the misbehaving government official (the policeman who had made the illegal search) had been fined instead. Second, it produces overdeterrence because the private (and social) cost imposed on the government may greatly exceed the social cost of the misconduct.

To illustrate the latter, less obvious point, suppose that evidence that is indispensable to convicting a criminal is seized as an incident to some illegal search. Further suppose that the illegal search imposes a cost of $100 on the person searched in terms of lost time spent cleaning up after the searching officers, but that the loss to society from not being able to convict him can be valued at $10,000. If the probability of apprehending and convicting the illegal searcher is one, a fine of $100 would provide optimal (which is not to say 100 percent) deterrence of such illegal searches. The much larger "fine" that is actually imposed will overdeter, causing the government to steer too far clear of the amorphous boundaries of the fourth amendment compared to what it would do at the optimal fine level. The lawful searches that are forgone and the convictions of the guilty which those searches would have produced are social opportunity costs that the lower fine would have avoided.

These problems have long been recognized, and it is immaterial that they have not been formulated in explicitly economic terms. So we must ask why the exclusionary rule was ever adopted. The answer is consistent with economic analysis: the rule was adopted because until recently there was no alternative sanction for violations of the fourth amendment that did not cause severe underdeterrence.[9] For reasons explained many years ago in an article by Caleb Foote,[10] the natural (and superficially optimal) alternative remedy to the exclusionary rule—a tort action for damages against the government or its officers who engage in an illegal search—was for a long time unavailable. This unavailability was due to limitations ranging from lack of imagination by the courts in valuing intangible

---

9. *See* Foote, *Tort Remedies for Police Violations of Individual Rights,* 39 MINN. L. REV. 493 (1955).

10. *Id.*

Excessive Sanctions

losses in damage actions to broad concepts of official and sovereign immunity that usually made the judgments in these actions uncollectible.[11]

Recent developments in tort law in general, and in the immunity doctrines regarding tort actions against governments and their officers in particular, have gone far toward solving these problems.[12] The tort remedy has thus become a more practical alternative to the exclusionary rule. Admittedly, the tort remedy is not perfect. There remains in particular the problem of the loss that is large when aggregated over the large number of persons who may sustain it yet too small to give any one person an incentive to sue.[13] An obvious remedy for this problem, though it has not yet been tried, is to set some minimum liquidated damage figure[14] to which any plaintiff would be entitled (perhaps along with attorney's fees) in any case where liability is established. The minimum damages figure should optimally be set at the level that would induce just enough people to sue to make the total damages obtained equal to the total social costs inflicted by the police misconduct. To illustrate, suppose that the total costs of the misconduct to its victims is $10,000, that there are 1000 victims, each incurring an average cost of $10, and that if the minimum damages figure were set at $100, one in every ten victims would sue. Then 100 victims would sue, and the damages, $10,000 ($100 × 100), would just equal the total social costs of the police misconduct.[15]

Thus, the tort remedy for unlawful searches and seizures is now practical where once it was practically unavailable. As a remedy for police misconduct the tort remedy has the characteristics of the optimal fine that I discussed earlier.[16] It is a transfer payment, and thus involves no (or more realistically, relatively little) deadweight loss. It also can be, and to some extent is, calibrated by judges and juries to yield the desired level of deterrence. As a result of the growing practical availability of the tort remedy, I would predict a shift away from the exclusionary rule.

In suggesting that economic analysis provides an explanation, and not just a criticism, of the law of sanctions for violating the fourth amendment, I derive additional support from an important traditional exception to the exclusionary rule: the refusal to bar prosecution on the basis of an

---

11. *Id.* at 496–504.

12. *See* Posner, *supra* note 4, at 64–68.

13. A general campaign of police harassment of some subgroup of the population would be an example of such a situation.

14. *See* Foote, *supra* note 9, at 496.

15. Of course, a drawback of this proposal is that it would give police officers no incentives to inflict costs of less than $100 on each victim of misconduct. Since the minimum penalty is $100, the officer might as well get his money's worth and do the full $100 of damage.

16. *See* note 4 and accompanying text *supra*.

Washington Law Review Vol. 57:635, 1982

illegal arrest.[17] A literal application of the exclusionary concept to the law of the fourth amendment would lead easily to a conclusion that if a person is arrested in violation of the fourth amendment he cannot be prosecuted. Take the case where someone is illegally arrested but not searched or even questioned, so that the arrest has no "fruits" of the kind that could be excluded from the prosecution's evidence at trial.[18] Suppose further that had the person not been arrested, he would not have been prosecuted.[19] In this case, barring prosecution might seem to be the logical sanction for the illegal arrest, because it would correspond to suppressing the fruits of an illegal arrest. But barring prosecution would cause overdeterrence of an even more costly sort than the exclusionary rule involves.

Because the exclusionary rule only suppresses particular evidence, it does not prevent the prosecution from going forward if the prosecution has enough lawfully obtained evidence to convict the defendant. Barring prosecution altogether solely because the arrest was illegal would impose far greater social costs: not only the suppression of evidence that sometimes is (though often is not) indispensable to conviction, but also the dismissal of the charges in every case of illegal arrest. The law has stopped short of pushing the rationale of the exclusionary rule this far, and, as I have suggested, for a good economic reason.

I have argued that the overdeterrence problem that the exclusionary rule has created in search and seizure cases is solvable today because there is now a feasible tort alternative: a damage action against the misbehaving officer (or the government agency employing him) in which the court can nicely calibrate the damages to yield the optimal amount of deterrence. But in truth the tort approach has its own problem of overdeterrence. Police and other law-enforcement personnel are compensated on a salaried rather than piece-rate basis, so that even if they perform their duties with extraordinary zeal and effectiveness they do not receive financial rewards commensurate with their performance. At the same time, if their zeal leads them occasionally to violate a person's constitutional rights, then the tort remedy will impose on these officers the full social costs of their error. There is thus an imbalance: zealous police officers bear the full social costs of their mistakes through the tort system but do not receive the full social benefits of their successes through the compensation system.

---

17. *See, e.g.,* United States v. Crews, 445 U.S. 463, 474 (1980) ("An illegal arrest, without more, has never been viewed as a bar to subsequent prosecution . . . .").

18. "Fruits" here refers to evidence that must be excluded under the "fruits of the poisonous tree" doctrine, because the evidence was obtained through an illegal search and seizure. *See* Nardone v. United States, 308 U.S. 338, 341 (1939).

19. For example, assume the government could not have discovered who or where he was but for some illegal dragnet that resulted in the illegal arrest.

Excessive Sanctions

We can fix this problem by immunizing police officers from tort liability, thereby externalizing some costs in order to eliminate a disincentive for the police to produce external benefits. But can we do this without also underdeterring police misconduct? We can—by ensuring that an officer's immunity for misconduct (committed in good faith) is not extended to the agency employing him. This rule would essentially be one of respondeat superior without the employer's usual right to indemnification: the agency would be fully liable though its employees would not. This rule would give the agency an incentive to prevent misconduct by its officers.[20]

III. EXCLUSION OF COERCED CONFESSIONS AND INVOLUNTARY GUILTY PLEAS

There are types of governmental misconduct where a tort remedy will not work and where, therefore, the exclusionary concept may be optimal despite its inherent overdeterrence. A good example is the coerced confession or involuntary guilty plea, extracted in violation of the fifth amendment's self-incrimination or due process clause.[21]

Suppose that a criminal defendant could not exclude a coerced confession from evidence in his criminal trial but could (as, in principle at least, he can) bring a tort action seeking damages for the violation of his rights. Consider two distinct types of tort case. In the first, the criminal defendant proves that the confession is unreliable because it was coerced, and that the other evidence was insufficient to sustain his conviction. In such a case the appropriate measure of his tort damages would be the costs to him of whatever punishment had been imposed. But obviously the cheaper and more efficacious remedy in this case is simply to bar the use of the coerced confession from evidence at his criminal trial. That obviates the punishment, and so avoids the difficult and uncertain task of measuring the costs of punishment to the unjustly imprisoned defendant.

This case differs from a search and seizure case in that the latter involves no issue of reliability of evidence and hence no issue of guilt. In the search and seizure context, the private costs of punishment are not

---

20. *See* Posner, *supra* note 4, at 64–68, for a fuller discussion.

21. The fifth amendment provides in part: "No person . . . shall be compelled in any criminal case to be a witness against himself, nor be deprived of life, liberty, or property, without due process of law . . . ." U.S. CONST. amend. V, cl. 3.

Purists would limit the self-incrimination clause to in-court statements, thus excluding confessions coerced by the police before trial though introduced into evidence at trial. But that would not alter my analysis here.

Because my analysis of involuntary guilty pleas is symmetrical to that of coerced confessions. I will confine my discussion to the latter.

Washington Law Review   Vol. 57:635, 1982

equal to, and usually are much greater than, the social costs of the government's misconduct. Where the defendant is not in fact guilty of a crime, the private and social costs of punishment coincide and become the proper measure of damages; more simply, this convergence provides a reason for excluding the evidence from trial.

The harder case is where the confession, although coerced, is reliable evidence. Perhaps the confession was corroborated, or perhaps the coercion was not so great as to have made the defendant confess unless he really was guilty. In this case, suppressing the confession at trial would overdeter just as much as would excluding evidence obtained by an illegal search.

There are three possible responses to this problem:

Option 1: Limit the substantive right under the fifth amendment to cases where the presence of coercion throws a serious doubt on the reliability of the confession. Then no violation would occur when the confession was corroborated or when the coercion was too mild to create a substantial doubt that the confession was true.

Option 2: Limit the tort remedy to the defendant's lawful interests, narrowly defined, as in the search and seizure case. Hence, if the police used the "third degree" to extract a confession that was corroborated or otherwise validated, the defendant could not suppress the confession in his criminal trial; but he could obtain damages for deprivation of food or sleep or for any other injury to his incontrovertibly lawful interests that resulted from the third-degree methods used to extract the confession.

Option 3: Apply the exclusionary rule. This, of course, is the current approach of the law.

Option 1 exceeds the scope of this paper; it probably also exceeds the realistic scope of judicial authority to reexamine settled doctrines. It may well be that the fundamental concern underlying the fifth amendment is with the reliability of the guilt-determining process; that the Framers thought an inquisatorial system of justice less reliable than an adversary one.[22] But the fifth amendment also reflects a view that a person should not be forced to assist in his own conviction even if he is guilty.[23]

The origin of this view is in Hobbes, who argued that because a person agrees to subject himself to the authority of the state only for the sake of self-preservation, the agreement lapses if the state tries to take away his life.[24] Even if limited to capital cases, this is not a persuasive argument.

---

22. *See* United States v. Yurasovich, 580 F.2d 1212, 1215 (3rd Cir. 1978).

23. *E.g.,* Tehan v. United States *ex rel.* Shott, 382 U.S. 406, 415 (1966) (privilege against self-incrimination premised on the philosophy that even the guilty should not be convicted unless the prosecution carries the burden of proving guilt).

24. Hobbes wrote: "If a man be interrogated by the sovereign, or his authority, concerning a

Excessive Sanctions

If coerced confessions were particularly effective in reducing crime and thereby increasing personal security *ex ante*, we might say that by joining in a civilized society a person really does waive any right to refuse to cooperate in his own destruction.

But all this is merely to concede that the underlying norms which define governmental misconduct in criminal cases are not merely economic norms. This places a constraint on remedial policy. Concretely, it forecloses Option 2. If a conviction that rests upon a coerced confession is unjust even if the defendant is clearly guilty, then no relief will be adequate that does not undo the effects of the conviction.

Some think a conviction based on illegally seized evidence also unjust despite the fact that there usually is no question about the reliability of such evidence. If they are right, the exclusionary rule cannot fairly be criticized as producing overdeterrence. But I assume that they are wrong—that the objection to unreasonable searches and seizures is not that they render criminal proceedings which use their fruits unfair, but that they invade collateral interests in property and tranquility which now can be fully protected by tort remedies.

The coerced confession and involuntary guilty plea are of course only two examples of procedural concepts designed to ensure the reliability and fairness of the criminal justice system. The same analysis that led me to conclude that exclusion is the natural and not the overdeterrent remedy for violations of the rules forbidding coerced confessions and involuntary guilty pleas compels a similar conclusion in the case of other rules—rules allowing the criminal defendant to be present at his trial, to have counsel to assist him in his defense, to be allowed to confront the witnesses against him, and so on.

But in all of these areas, including the coerced confession and involuntary guilty plea problems with which I began, there is a principle limiting the use of exclusion as a remedy. That principle, the doctrine of harmless error, is the last subject I shall discuss in this paper.

IV. HARMLESS ERROR

Suppose that the judge in a criminal trial admitted, in violation of the rules of evidence, certain hearsay evidence damaging to the defendant, but that so much admissible evidence of guilt was presented at the trial that the probability was very slight that excluding the hearsay evidence would have led to the defendant's being acquitted. In such a case the ap-

---

crime done by himself, he is not bound, without assurance of pardon to confess it; because no man . . . can be obliged by covenant to accuse himself." T. Hobbes, Leviathan, pt. 2, ch. 21 (Collier ed. 1962).

Washington Law Review   Vol. 57:635, 1982

pellate court would invoke the doctrine of harmless error to uphold the conviction notwithstanding the trial judge's error.[25]

A superficially attractive justification for this result within the economic framework of this paper is that if the outcome of a retrial really is foreordained, then reversing the conviction will have a single Pareto-inferior consequence: to impose a deadweight loss consisting of the expenses of the retrial, a pure debit on the social books. But this analysis is artificial, for if the result of a retrial really is foreordained, then the criminal defendant's only possible incentive for seeking a retrial is to give the prosecutor an incentive to plea bargain by delaying the prisoner's incarceration and imposing costs on the prosecutor. And because settlement is always cheaper than litigation when the outcome of litigation is known with certainty, all of these cases will be settled; none will be retried.

The more interesting case, and no doubt the empirically more important one, is where there is some residue of uncertainty whether the defendant will be convicted when retried. Here retrial is more than a hypothetical possibility, because if the prosecution and defense cannot converge in their estimates of the probability of conviction on retrial they may find it cheaper in an expected-value sense to litigate than to settle.

How can the cost of retrial be a deadweight loss when by hypothesis some probability exists that this time the defendant will be acquitted? The answer lies in the fact that the probability that the defendant will be acquitted on retrial exceeds the probability that he is innocent. The reason for this divergence between the two probabilities is not the heavy burden of proof in a criminal case, for no one would propose to invoke the harmless-error rule unless the evidence that remained after setting aside the improperly admitted evidence proved the defendant's guilt beyond a reasonable doubt. The reason rather is that a nontrivial possibility always exists that a jury (or even a judge) will acquit a guilty person—because the jury either does not like the law,[26] does not understand it, or cannot apply it correctly to the facts of the case.

The *power* of the jury to acquit is absolute; our system of laws contains no such thing as a motion for a directed verdict by the prosecutor. But the *right* of the jury to acquit is more limited, for the jury has only the power—and never the right—to acquit on grounds that the law does not recognize.[27] Therefore, there is no paradox in stating that the acquittal of a guilty person imposes social costs, even though the acquittal cannot be corrected by appeal to the trial judge or to a higher court.

---

25. *See* FED. R. CRIM. P. 52.

26. *See, e.g.*, Michael & Wechsler, *A Rationale of the Law of Homicide*, pt. 2, 37 COLUM. L. REV. 1261, 1265 (1937).

27. This distinction is stressed in P. DEVLIN, THE JUDGE 117–48 (1979).

Excessive Sanctions

All this is prefatory to interpreting the significance of the harmless-error rule. Its significance is that if the evidence which remains in the case after all erroneously admitted evidence is laid aside shows conclusively that the defendant is guilty notwithstanding what an errant judge or jury might conclude on retrial, the conviction will be affirmed. The reason, I think, has to be the concern with overdeterrence. If a person is guilty beyond a reasonable doubt on the basis of evidence both reliable and just, then a retrial will impose either a deadweight loss in the form of litigation expenses that will not change the outcome of the first trial, or an equally or (probably) more serious social cost resulting from the acquittal of a guilty person and consequent reduction in the deterrent and incapacitative effects of criminal punishment. These costs are excessive relative to the governmental misconduct, which by definition is slight since the defendant would in all probability have been convicted anyway.

What the harmless-error rule does, then, is to identify a type of governmental misconduct whose social costs are much lower than the social costs of attempting to deter the misconduct by overturning the conviction and forcing a retrial. This functional definition has the value of guiding the rule's application more dependably than by chewing over the connotations of the word "harmless." The functional approach implies, for example, that the rule should be interpreted more liberally for grave crimes.

The graver the crime, the more the parties are likely to invest in the litigation process itself, and that greater investment should increase the accuracy of the guilt-determining process. Thus, if the trial court concludes that the untainted evidence proves the defendant's guilt beyond a reasonable doubt, this judgment is likely to be more reliable in a case of serious crime than in a trivial one. The appellate court's finding of harmless error will thus be more firmly based in such a case.

Therefore appellate courts can be expected to hold more errors harmless in grave rather than in trivial crimes. This counterintuitive implication follows directly from what I have called the functional, which is to say the economic, approach to analyzing the harmless-error rule, and it is an empirically testable implication of that approach.[28]

---

28. An initial effort to test the implication has not, however, been very successful. A random sample of recent federal court of appeals criminal decisions involving harmless-error issues yielded 42 usable observations, in 25 of which the harmless-error doctrine was applied, and in the remaining 17 of which the error was deemed reversible. Using length of sentence as the measure of the severity of the cases, I found that the average length of sentence in the first group was 11.36 years and in the second 12.42—which is contrary to my hypothesis. Details of the study are available from the author, and are on file with the *Washington Law Review*.

Washington Law Review   Vol. 57:635, 1982

V. CONCLUSION

In devising remedies for governmental misconduct in criminal cases, courts, I have argued, have been guided by concerns articulable, if rarely articulated, in terms of economic efficiency. The underlying substantive concepts that define governmental misconduct need not be economic, and in the case of rules protecting the fifth amendement's self-incrimination clause seem not to be economic at all. But the remedial scheme that courts have created seems responsive to efficiency concerns. If so, this is further evidence that economics has profoundly influenced the structure of the law.

[24]

THE EXCLUSIONARY RULE, DETERRENCE AND POSNER'S ECONOMIC ANALYSIS OF LAW

Arval A. Morris*

Judge Posner holds economic theory demonstrates that the fourth amendment's exclusionary rule and other judicially developed doctrines implementing the Constitution impose excessive sanctions for governmental misconduct in criminal cases. This Article, focusing on the exclusionary rule, aims to place his economic argument in historical context and to assess it.

I. THE CONSTITUTIONAL DIMENSION OF THE EXCLUSIONARY RULE

The exclusionary rule, as I understand it, is of constitutional origin, and can be modified only by constitutional amendment or Supreme Court decision.

The exclusionary rule was born almost seventy years ago in *Weeks v. United States*,[1] which focused on judicial integrity and the constitutional necessity of effectively enforcing the fourth amendment. Writing for the Court, Justice Day emphasized constitutional fidelity, stating:

> The effect of the 4th Amendment is to put the courts of the United States and Federal officials, in the exercise of their power and authority, under limitations and restraints as to the exercise of such power and authority . . . . This protection reaches all alike, whether accused of crime or not, and *the duty of giving to it force and effect is obligatory upon all intrusted under our Federal system with the enforcement of the laws.* The tendency of those who execute the criminal laws of the country to obtain conviction by means of unlawful seizures and enforced confessions, the latter often obtained after subjecting accused persons to unwarranted practices destructive of rights secured by the Federal Constitution, *should find no sanction in the judgments of the courts,* which are charged at all times with the support of the Constitution, and to which people of all conditions have a right to appeal for the maintenance of such fundamental rights.[2]

Judicial fidelity to the Constitution was emphatically declared in 1961

---

*   Professor of Law, University of Washington.
1.   232 U.S. 383 (1914).
2.   *Id.* at 391–92 (emphasis added).

Washington Law Review   Vol. 57:647, 1982

to be the basis of the exclusionary rule when the Supreme Court made it applicable to the states in *Mapp v. Ohio:*[3]

> We hold that all evidence obtained by searches and seizures in violation of the Constitution is, *by that same authority,* inadmissible in a state court
> . . . .
>
> . . . .
>
> Moreover, our holding *that the exclusionary rule is an essential part of both the Fourth and Fourteenth Amendments* is not only the logical dictate of prior cases, but it also makes very good sense.[4]

Even Chief Justice Burger, an enemy of the exclusionary rule, acknowledges that it is of constitutional dimension.[5] Although the rule has occasionally been limited by the Supreme Court, the Court has not disavowed the rule's constitutional foundation. It may be a "judicially created remedy,"[6] but the exclusionary rule's constitutional underpinnings are clear.

II. THE RATIONALE OF THE EXCLUSIONARY RULE

Over the years, judges have asserted that not one, but two primary justifying considerations undergird the exclusionary rule. The first, and most important, is the principle of judicial integrity and faithfulness to the fourth amendment. This principle is sufficient to justify the existence of the rule by itself. It appeared early in the rule's history in *Weeks v. United States.*[7] Justice Day further stated the principle of judicial fidelity to the fourth amendment for excluding illegally seized evidence: "To sanction such proceedings would be to affirm by judicial decision a manifest neglect, if not an open defiance, of the prohibitions of the Constitution, in-

---

3. 367 U.S. 643 (1961). Prior to *Mapp,* the Federal courts (and the FBI) had operated successfully under the exclusionary rule for almost half a century, but the states, under Wolf v. Colorado, 338 U.S. 25 (1949), were held free to admit unconstitutionally seized materials into evidence in state courts. This pre-*Mapp* asymmetry, permitting state courts to admit illegally seized evidence, served to encourage state police and state courts to disobey the very Federal Constitution which they previously had sworn to uphold. As Justice Brandeis stated in Olmstead v. U.S., 277 U.S. 438 (1928): "Our Government is the potent, the omnipresent teacher . . . . If the Government becomes a lawbreaker, it breeds contempt for law; it invites every man to become a law unto himself; it invites anarchy." *Id.* at 485 (dissenting opinion).

4. 367 U.S. at 655, 657 (emphasis added).

5. Bivens v. Six Unknown Named Agents, 403 U.S. 388, 415 (1971) (dissenting opinion).

6. United States v. Calandra, 414 U.S. 338, 348 (1974); *cf.* Schrock & Welsh, *Up From Calandra: The Exclusionary Rule as a Constitutional Requirement,* 59 MINN. L. REV. 251 (1974) (discussing the constitutional premises underlying the *Calandra* theories of the exclusionary rule).

7. 232 U.S. 383 (1914).

The Exclusionary Rule and Posner's Analysis

tended for the protection of the people against such unauthorized action."[8]

One of our finest scholars, Professor Francis Allen, has declared that the *Weeks* opinion "contains no language that expressly justifies the rule by reference to a supposed deterrent effect on police officials."[9] As the *Weeks* Court saw it, if a court could not authorize ("sanction") a search or seizure in the first place, before the event occurred, because, for example, the police may have lacked probable cause or failed to describe with sufficient particularity the item sought, then a court could not later "affirm" ("sanction") the search or seizure after the event took place: "The efforts of the courts and their officials to bring the guilty to punishment . . . are not to be aided by the sacrifice of [fourth amendment] principles . . . ."[10]

In *Silverthorne Lumber Co. v. United States*,[11] Justice Holmes, joined by Brandeis and five other justices, stated that unless the use of the exclusionary rule were available to suppress evidence obtained by means of an unconstitutional search and seizure, "the Fourth Amendment [would be reduced] to a form of words."[12] Thus, fidelity to the Constitution defined the parameters of judicial integrity and necessitated the exclusionary rule, for "[n]othing can destroy a government more quickly than its failure to observe its own laws, or worse, its disregard of the charter of its own existence."[13] If illegally seized evidence were permitted to be introduced into evidence, we would have "an instance where one may be . . . imprisoned on evidence *obtained* in violation of due process *and yet not be deprived* of life or liberty without due process of

---

8.   *Id.* at 394.

9.   Allen, *The Judicial Quest for Penal Justice: The Warren Court and the Criminal Cases*, 1975 U. ILL. L.F. 518, 536 n.90.

10.   232 U.S. at 393.

11.   251 U.S. 385 (1920); *see also* Nardone v. United States, 308 U.S. 338, 340 (1939) (recognizing that the purpose of the exclusionary rule is to protect constitutional rights to privacy); Henderson, *Justice in the eighties: the exclusionary rule and the principle of judicial integrity*, 65 JUDICATURE 354, 356 (1982) (original basis for the rule was "the principle that judicial integrity requires the exclusionary rule lest courts become accomplices in the violation of the Constitution they are sworn to uphold").

12.   251 U.S. at 392. The Court further observed that:

The essence of a provision forbidding the acquisition of evidence in a certain way is that not merely evidence so acquired shall not be used before the Court but that it shall not be used at all. Of course this does not mean that the facts thus obtained become sacred and inaccessible. If knowledge of them is gained from an independent source they may be proved like any others, but the knowledge gained by the Government's own wrong cannot be used by it in the way proposed.

Id.

13.   Mapp v. Ohio, 367 U.S. 643, 659 (1961).

Washington Law Review   Vol. 57:647, 1982

law after all."[14] But judicial fidelity to the fourth amendment has fallen
on hard times lately.

The second justification, deterrence, has been advanced primarily by
opponents of the exclusionary rule, who often seek to minimize or undermine the principle of the judicial-fidelity-to-the-Constitution rationale.[15]
Particularly, in the writings of the rule's opponents, the pragmatic concern with deterrence completely replaces the principle of judicial fidelity
to the Constitution. The sole justification for the rule that they offer is a
pragmatic, police-practice rationale, the efficacy of which, in principle, is
subject to empirical measurement. The groundwork for this perspective
was laid down by the Burger Court, which has spearheaded the attack on
the exclusionary rule. Chief Justice Burger himself has led the attack,
writing that:

> the exclusionary rule has rested on the deterrent rationale—the hope that
> law enforcement officials would be deterred from unlawful searches and
> seizures if the illegally seized, albeit trustworthy, evidence was suppressed
> often enough and the courts persistently enough deprived them of any bene-
> fits they might have gained from their illegal conduct.[16]

Once the exclusionary rule's opponents have given it an exclusively
empirical foundation, they can attack it. They erroneously claim the
exclusionary rule extracts an unusually "high price" from society—"the
release of countless guilty criminals."[17] Then, ignoring the constitutional
dimension, they seek to shift the burden by demanding that in light of

---

14.   Kamisar, Wolf *and* Lustig *Ten Years Later: Illegal State Evidence In State and Federal
Courts*, 43 MINN. L. REV. 1083, 1108 (1959).

15.   *See, e.g.*, Chief Justice Burger's comment:
[T]he exclusionary rule does not ineluctably flow from a desire to insure that government plays
the "game" according to the rules. If an effective alternative remedy is available, concern for
official observance of the law does not require adherence to the exclusionary rule. Nor is it easy
to understand how a court can be thought to endorse a violation of the Fourth Amendment by
allowing illegally seized evidence to be introduced against a defendant if an effective remedy is
provided against the government.
Bivens v. Six Unknown Named Agents, 403 U.S. 388, 414 (1971) (dissenting opinion).

16.   *Id.* at 415 (Burger, C.J., dissenting). The notion that the exclusionary rule's purpose is to
deter police illegality was probably introduced into fourth amendment law in Wolf v. Colorado, 338
U.S. 25 (1949). *Wolf* held that states were not bound by the exclusionary rule as federal courts were;
the case was overruled in Mapp v. Ohio, 367 U.S. 643 (1961), which applied the fourth amendment's exclusionary rule to the states. *See* McKay, *Mapp v. Ohio, The Exclusionary Rule and the
Right of Privacy*, 15 ARIZ. L. REV. 327 (1973). The clear motivating factor in *Mapp* was judicial
integrity; thus, *Mapp* declared the exclusionary rule to be compelled by constitutional principle and
secondarily supported by pragmatic considerations of deterrence. This view has been so much turned
upside down by the Burger Court that Justice Powell could write in United States v. Calandra, 414
U.S. 338, 348 (1974) that "[i]n sum, the rule is a judicially created remedy designed to safeguard
Fourth Amendment rights generally through its deterrent effect."

17.   Bivens v. Six Unknown Named Agents, 403 U.S. at 416 (Burger, C.J., dissenting).

The Exclusionary Rule and Posner's Analysis

such a "high price,"[18] the rule's proponents must produce some "clear demonstration of the benefits and effectiveness of the exclusionary rule."[19] Finally, the rule's opponents rise up and triumphantly declare that "there is no empirical evidence to support the claim that the rule actually deters illegal conduct of law enforcement officials."[20]

---

18.   There are considerable grounds leading one to question whether the "price" is high at all: In *Impact of the Exclusionary Rule On Federal Criminal Prosecutions* (Report of the Comptroller General, April 19, 1979), an empirical study of cases handled in 38 U.S. Attorneys' Offices from July 1–August 31, 1978, it was found that of 2,804 charged defendants only 30% involved a search or seizure and only 11% filed a motion to suppress on Fourth Amendment grounds. These motions were denied in the "overwhelming majority" of cases, so that in only 1.3% of the 2,804 defendant cases was evidence excluded as a result of a Fourth Amendment suppression motion. Moreover, over half of the defendants whose motions were granted in total or in part were convicted nonetheless. As for the cases during the sample period which the U.S. Attorneys declined to prosecute, in only 0.4% of them was a search and seizure problem the primary reason. Similarly, in Brosi, *A Cross-City Comparison of Felony Case Processing* 18–20 (1979), an LEAA-sponsored empirical study of state felony cases in various jurisdictions, it was found that "due process related reasons accounted for only a small portion of the rejections at [prosecutor] screening—from 1 to 9 percent." The rate ranged from 13% to 42% in drug cases, but in "felony cases other than drugs, less than 2 percent of the rejections in each city involved abrogations of due process." As for post-filing dismissals and nolles, "due process problems again accounted for little of the attrition, and again most of the due process problems were accounted for by the drug cases."
Y. KAMISAR, W. LAFAVE & J. ISRAEL, MODERN CRIMINAL PROCEDURE 221–22 n.c (5th ed. 1980).
   It is obvious that our current treatment of drugs and illegal searches and seizures are linked. Stephen H. Sachs, Attorney General of Maryland, who has had 20 years' experience with the exclusionary rule—half of it as a prosecutor—states:
   I believe a fair summary of the Maryland experience to be that the rule has small effect on declinations by prosecutors, or loss at trial, in almost all categories of crime, including violent crime, except for a significantly higher incidence of suppression motions granted in drug possession cases resulting from spontaneous street encounters.
The Exclusionary Rule Bills, 1981: Hearings on S. 101 and S. 751 Before the Subcomm. on Criminal Law of the Senate Comm. on the Judiciary, 97th Cong., 1st Sess. (1981) (statement of Stephen H. Sachs) (official transcripts not yet printed at time of publication), *reprinted in* YALE L.REP., Winter 1981–82, at 71, 72 [hereinafter cited as *Hearings*]. In an important sense, an application of the exclusionary rule only serves to put the police in the same position that they would have been in if they had obeyed the Constitution in the first place.
19.   Bivens v. Six Unknown Named Agents, 403 U.S. 388, 416 (1971) (Burger, C.J., dissenting). *See also* Elkins v. U.S., 364 U.S. 206, 217 (1960) (statistics unable to demonstrate effectiveness of the exclusionary rule).
20.   Bivens v. Six Unknown Named Agents, 403 U.S. at 416 (Burger, C.J., dissenting). The favorite citation supporting this conclusion is always Oaks, *Studying the Exclusionary Rule in Search and Seizure*, 37 U. CHI. L. REV. 665, 667 (1970). *See* Posner, *Rethinking the Fourth Amendment*, 1981 SUP. CT. REV. 49, 54. *But cf.* Critique, *On the Limitations of Empirical Evaluations of the Exclusionary Rule: A Critique of the Spiotto Research and United States v. Calandra*, 69 NW. U.L. REV. 740, 743–44 (1974) (criticizing a 1973 study which purported to demonstrate that the exclusionary rule was ineffective as a deterrent) [hereinafter cited as Critique, *Empirical Research on the Exclusionary Rule*].

III. EMPIRICAL RESEARCH AND THE EXCLUSIONARY RULE

It is true that the commentators are in considerable disagreement on whether the available social science studies prove or disprove that the exclusionary rule actually deters illegal conduct.[21] There is, however, unequivocal testimony from some former prosecutors on the rule's deterrence ability. For example, Maryland's Attorney General, Stephen H. Sachs, has had twenty years' experience with the exclusionary rule, ten of those as a prosecutor. In his congressional testimony this year, he stated:

> I have watched the rule deter, routinely, throughout my years as a prosecutor. When an Assistant United States Attorney, for example, advises an FBI agent that he lacks probable cause to search for bank loot in a parked automobile unless he gets a better "make" on the car; or that he has a "staleness" problem with the probable cause to believe that the ski masks used in the robbery are still in the suspect's girl friend's apartment; or that he should apply for a search warrant from a magistrate and not rely on the "consent" of the suspect's kid sister to search his home—the rule is working. The principal, perhaps the only, reason those conversations occur is that the assistant and the agent want the search to stand up in court.[22]

Opponents of the exclusionary rule refuse to accept testimonial evidence, such as Mr. Sachs', on the deterrent impact of the exclusionary rule. Instead, they demand that the rule's proponents present ironclad,

---

21. *E.g.*, Cannon, *The exclusionary rule: have critics proven that it doesn't deter police?*, 62 JUDICATURE 398 (1979); Kamisar, *The exclusionary rule in historical perspective: the struggle to make the Fourth Amendment more than "an empty blessing,"* 62 JUDICATURE 337 (1979); Kamisar, *Is the exclusionary rule an "illogical" or "unnatural" interpretation of the Fourth Amendment?*, 62 JUDICATURE 66 (1978); Schlesinger, *The exclusionary rule: have proponents proven that it is a deterrent to police?*, 62 JUDICATURE 404 (1979); Wilkey, *A call for alternatives to the exclusionary rule*, 62 JUDICATURE 351 (1979); Wilkey, *The exclusionary rule: why suppress valid evidence?*, 62 JUDICATURE 214 (1978). A useful survey of earlier literature is found in Comment, *Trends in Legal Commentary on the Exclusionary Rule*, 65 J. CRIM. L. & CRIMINOLOGY 373 (1974).

22. *Hearings, supra* note 18 (statement of Stephen H. Sachs), *reprinted in* YALE L.REP., Winter 1981–82, at 73. Mr. Sachs also states that he does not "doubt that the rule works less well in street encounters. But here, too, the rule is at work because of the enormous increase in police training and education about constitutional rights directly attributable to the exclusion sanction." *Id., reprinted in* YALE L.REP., Winter 1981–82, at 74.

New York City Police Commissioner Michael Murphy described part of the case's deterrent impact—not unique to New York—when he said that after *Mapp v. Ohio* came down, he "was immediately caught up in the entire problem of reevaluating our procedures . . . and modifying, amending, and creating new policies and new instructions for the implementation of *Mapp.*" Murphy, *The Problem of Compliance by Police Departments*, 44 TEX. L. REV. 939, 941 (1966). He indicated that "[r]etraining sessions had to be held from the very top administrators down to each of the thousands of foot patrolmen and detectives engaged in the daily basic enforcement function." *Id.* He believed that "the framework of limitation" had been put there by the exclusionary rule: "[f]lowing from the *Mapp* case is the issue of defining probable cause to constitute a lawful arrest and subsequent search and seizure." *Id.* at 943.

The Exclusionary Rule and Posner's Analysis

empirical studies which are a "clear demonstration of the benefits and effectiveness of the Exclusionary Rule."[23] When no impeccably sound social science study is found, they then declare that "there is no empirical evidence to support the claim that the rule actually deters."[24] But the basic demand of the rule's opponents is flawed because it neglects a fundamental consideration: no impeccably sound study will ever be produced that will meet the demands of the rule's opponents because, while such a study is possible in principle, it is impossible in fact.

There are several reasons why no conclusively sound social science study of the exclusionary rule's deterrent effect will actually be produced. First, the "design" of such a research project is more than a simple compendium of the setting and circumstances of data collection. The "design" of an empirical study provides the theoretical structure upon which the validity of inferences, deductions, and conclusions are grounded.[25] If a "design" is faulty, then the study's conclusions are unreliable. The importance of "design" in an empirical study cannot be overemphasized. A design for a study of the exclusionary rule, to qualify as "impeccable," would have to be quantitative, not qualitative. The quantitative requirement presents a formidable problem because the investigator would have to quantify non-events. Police compliance with the exclusionary rule produces a non-event which is not directly observable—it consists of *not* conducting an illegal search. Although empirical research is theoretically neutral, the simple truth is that some kinds of phenomena can be measured more easily than others, which in turn means that direct observation, or its impossibility, aids only one side. And that is the case with the exclusionary rule.

Since compliance with the exclusionary rule produces a limitation on police behavior not directly visible to an impartial observer, its deterrent impact can only be gleaned indirectly and inferentially from trends of other data. The act of drawing a valid inference can be the Achilles heel of an empirical study. The most promising research design compares change in police practices (i.e., illegal searches) through time, before and

---

23. Bivens v. Six Unknown Named Agents, 403 U.S. at 416 (Burger, C.J., dissenting). They also refuse to accept testimony such as that of Detective Ken Anderson of St. Paul, Minn., on police practices prior to *Mapp v. Ohio*. There is no reason to believe the practices were unique to Minnesota:

[N]o police officer lied upon the witness stand. If you were asked how you got your evidence you told the truth. You had broken down a door or pried a window open . . . oftentimes we picked locks . . . . The Supreme Court of Minnesota sustained this time after time after time. . . . [The] judiciary o.k.'d it; they knew what the facts were.

Quoted in Kamisar, *On the Tactics of Police-Prosecution Oriented Critics of the Courts,* 49 CORNELL L.Q. 436, 443 (1964).

24. Bivens v. Six Unknown Named Agents, 403 U.S. at 416 (Burger, C.J., dissenting).

25. *See, e.g.,* D. CAMPBELL & J. STANLEY, EXPERIMENTAL AND QUASI-EXPERIMENTAL DESIGNS FOR RESEARCH (1966).

Washington Law Review Vol. 57:647, 1982

after the introduction of the exclusionary rule.[26] Without the earlier pre-exclusionary rule statistics on illegal police searches, it is impossible validly to interpret the significance of the post-rule statistics on illegal searches. Under this design, an investigator first gathers data on the rate of illegal searches before the introduction of the exclusionary rule; then, assuming the same rate of pre-rule illegal searches to continue, she projects a "baseline" into the post-rule time period; finally, the investigator gathers data on illegal searches occurring after the introduction of the exclusionary rule and compares them with the baseline. If the frequency of illegal searches occurring during the post-rule period declines from the "baseline" projected into the post-rule period, the investigator may conclude that deterrence has occurred, *ceteris paribus*.[27]

Since direct data are uncollectible non-events, the problem becomes this: what circumstantial measure shall be collected which will yield valid inferences about pre- and post-rule illegal searches?[28] Rather clearly, mo-

---

26. I draw here on Critique, *Empirical Research on the Exclusionary Rule, supra* note 20, and thank my colleague, Professor Wallace Loh, for calling it to my attention.

27.

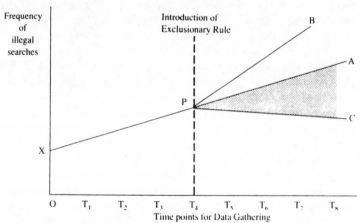

X-P represents the frequency of illegal searches during the pre-rule period. P-A represents the projected "baseline"; i.e., the continuation of X-P into the post-rule period. If post-rule collected data also fell along line P-A, then the introduction of the exclusionary rule might be viewed as having no deterrent effect. If data fell on line P-B, the conclusion might be that the exclusionary rule's effect was not deterring, but worsening the situation and therefore counterproductive. If data fell along line P-C, the conclusion might be that the exclusionary rule has a deterrent effect. Examples of research using this type of design are Campbell & Ross, *The Connecticut Crackdown on Speeding: Time-Series Data In Quasi-Experimental Analysis*, 3 LAW & SOC'Y REV. 33 (1968) and Ross, Campbell & Glass, *Determining The Social Effects of a Legal Reform: The British "Breathalyzer" Crackdown of 1967*, 13 AM. BEHAVIORAL SCIENTIST 493 (1970).

28. The necessary characteristics of the measure are: (1) it must genuinely indicate illegal searches; that is, it must not be too remote from the actual searches and it must not be substantially influenced by factors other than police searches; (2) it must be uninfluenced by the introduction of the rule; that is, it must be a consistent measure before and after the rule is introduced, and (3) it must

The Exclusionary Rule and Posner's Analysis

tions to suppress evidence cannot be used because they do not accurately measure illegal searches before the introduction of the fourth amendment's exclusionary rule.[29] Jerome Skolnick has demonstrated that direct observation of police behavior in the field might provide a way of gathering data on the current operation of the exclusionary rule.[30] His investigation was not quantitative, but Albert J. Reiss' work indicates that a quantification approach can be used with direct observation in the field.[31] Skillfully used, this methodology could identify the present (post-rule) level of illegal police searches in a given area. But current field observations cannot identify the pre-exclusionary rule level of illegal searches, which is crucial to evaluating the rule's deterrent effects validly. Thus, the method of field research must be jettisoned.

If fieldwork is not possible, the search for a useful measure of illegal searches turns to the existing records of the criminal justice system to generate the pre- and post-rule data. The viable candidates identified by Dallin Oaks[32]—search warrants,[33] arrest and conviction statistics,[34] stolen property recovered statistics,[35] and contraband seized statistics[36]—present substantial and disabling problems. After carefully analyzing Oaks' four data sources, as used by Oaks and by other researchers, one commentator concluded:

> None completely meet the requirements for valid indicators of illegal searches. Further, the sources that have been utilized in extensive research present a complex maze of data. Variations exist everywhere. Each side can find statistics from some cities that will support its position. Clearly, local factors play an important role in the efficacy of the exclusionary rule. Yet, our knowledge of the linkages between the characteristics of local govern-

---

exist in some relatively permanent way so that subsequent researchers can check the research; that is, regenerate the pre- and post-rule data. A valid empirical assessment of the deterrent effects of the exclusionary rule is not possible without identifying a measure of illegal searches that reasonably meets these three requirements.

29. Rochin v. California, 342 U.S. 165 (1951); *cf.* Irvine v. California, 347 U.S. 128 (1954) (police entered locked home to plant microphone and eavesdropped on conversations within the home; admission of evidence thus obtained held not violative of the fourth amendment under the *Rochin* "shocks the conscience" test although the evidence would be inadmissible under the exclusionary rule).

30. J. SKOLNICK, JUSTICE WITHOUT TRIAL 211–29 (2d ed. 1966).

31. A. REISS, THE POLICE AND THE PUBLIC (1971).

32. Oaks, *Studying the Exclusionary Rule In Search and Seizure*, 37 U. CHI. L. REV. 665 (1970).

33. *Id.* at 713–14.

34. *Id.* at 689–91.

35. *Id.* at 692–93.

36. *Id.* at 693–96.

ments, court systems, and police behavior is still in its infancy. It is unlikely that the puzzle will be sorted out in the near future.[37]

No research design yet conceived is capable of distinguishing between the number of nonoccurring illegal searches that can be attributed to police policies and the number of nonoccurrences correctly attributed solely to the effect of the exclusionary rule. Surely, the force of these complex, intertwined factors will vary depending upon whether a police unit is located in an upper-middle-class, small residential, or suburban city or whether it is located in a major metropolitan city like Los Angeles. But the exclusionary rule is of national application, and "impeccable" empirical research must draw valid national conclusions. The actual research task is factually hopeless. In short, "[w]hen all factors are considered, there is virtually no likelihood that the Court is going to receive any 'relevant statistics' which objectively measure the 'practical efficacy' of the exclusionary rule."[38]

IV. POSNER'S ECONOMIC ANALYSIS AND THE EXCLUSIONARY RULE

Judge Posner, a scholar of law and economics, and an opponent of the exclusionary rule, enters the controversy at this point. He boldly advances a general economic point of view which, if adopted, would transform the entire study of law from an investigation into complex and interconnected social issues of fact, value, principle, and legal doctrine into a straight forward application of two "simple," economic hypotheses, one normative and one descriptive: (1) law ought to be efficient, and (2) the law is efficient.[39]

---

37. Critique, *Empirical Research on the Exclusionary Rule, supra* note 20, at 762. For a further discussion, see *id.* at 758-62.

38. *Id.* at 763–64.

39. *See* R. POSNER, ECONOMIC ANALYSIS OF LAW (2d ed. 1977).

The key concepts for Posner's economic analysis of law, including analysis of the exclusionary rule, are efficiency and value. They are very technical terms, which are not commonly used, in Posner's sense, by judges. " 'Efficiency' means exploiting economic resources in such a way that 'value'—human satisfaction *as measured by aggregate consumer willingness to pay* for goods and services—is maximized." *Id.* at 10. Willingness to pay, "the basis of the efficiency and value concepts," is materially affected by the existing distribution of wealth and income. Thus, the poor and lower-middle classes have less to say about what counts as an "efficient" allocation of economic resources than do the upper-middle classes and the rich. They have fewer "dollar ballots" in "marketplace voting." Economic resources are deemed to be "efficiently" allocated when a few lavish garden apartments are built, and the rich buy them. But, these same resources are not "efficiently" allocated by building many low income apartments if the poor buy them at a price lower than that which would otherwise be paid for the garden apartments. "Efficiency," Posner has declared, is "determined by willingness to pay" and where "resources are shifted pursuant to a voluntary transaction, we can be reasonably confident that the shift involves a net increase in efficiency." *Id.* at 11.

The Exclusionary Rule and Posner's Analysis

Economic analysis of law is practiced in at least two quite different ways. One way consists of analyzing and evaluating legal rules to identify which of them would be the most economically efficient in obtaining a specified outcome. For example, different tort rules might be assessed to identify which of them would be most efficient in obtaining a particular level of accidents specified by some noneconomic authority as optimal under real-life circumstances. But economic analysts of this type would insist that they have no economic criteria for recommending that any level of accidents be considered "good," "optimal," or "desirable." Goals are none of their economic concern. Their analytic task is to accept the goal given to them, make certain assumptions, and then identify which legal rule would be efficient in the abstract. This type of economic analysis of law consists of purely abstract, technical efficiency analysis. It is not normative, and it has nothing to say about the policies that government should or should not adopt, or about judicial decisions judges should make or opinions they should hold.[40]

A second way of doing economic analysis of law is to make efficiency *and* normative judgments. These economic analysts believe that economic efficiency, as defined by an economic theory, is the proper and only policy prescription for social policy and judicial behavior. They recommend that government produce social change by intervening in social or human affairs, rearranging legal and political institutions, in order to achieve economic efficiency. These practitioners of economic analysis of law have much more to justify than the first group. In addition to their technical efficiency analyses, they can be required to justify their policy recommendations in social policy terms. We properly can expect them to provide an answer to the question: Why should we care whether our rules of legal liability are economically efficient? Surely, in some situations, there are other values to achieve.

Much, but not all, of Posner's work in economic analysis of law falls into this second category. He approves of the efficiency-normative-policy approach. Posner also believes that economic analysis "best" explains the law: that is, it also describes the law "best." When presenting his economic explanation/description of law, Posner relies on the principle of economic efficiency as the explanatory tool by which existing legal rules and judicial decisions might be rationalized or comprehended. He does

This assumes, however, that each person affected by the transaction must be a party to it, and as Posner recognizes and then dismisses: "strictly speaking, this requirement is almost never satisfied." *Id.* at 11 n.3.

40. For good examples of this way of practicing economic analysis of law, see Brown & Holahan, *Taxes and Legal Rules for the Control of Externalities When There are Strategic Responses*, 9 J. LEGAL STUD 165 (1980); Polinsky, *Private versus Public Enforcement of Fines*, 9 J. LEGAL STUD 105 (1980); Shavell, *Strict Liability versus Negligence*, 9 J. LEGAL STUD 1 (1980).

Washington Law Review   Vol. 57:647, 1982

not claim that judges expressly articulate and apply the principle of economic efficiency when they decide cases. Instead, he claims that his economic explanation/description can "best" account for judicial decisions or legal rules; that is, they can best be reconstructed or rationalized by observers in light of his economic theory of adjudication. In the paper under review, Posner's claim is strong. Stating that economic analysis of law has two possible uses, he contends:

> One, of course, is to point the way to reform [the Normative]. The other, which is less obvious but from an academic standpoint more interesting, is to explain the law as it is. . . .[the Descriptive/Explanatory]
>
> The hypothesis I shall explore . . . is that the common law remedies for governmental misconduct in criminal cases are best explained by assuming that judges are preeminently concerned with economic efficiency, even though the underlying norms defining that misconduct are often not economic.[41]

Posner nowhere argues for his claim of economic superiority, i.e., that legal remedies for governmental misconduct such as the exclusionary rule, are *best* explained by assuming judges are preeminently concerned with economic efficiency. There are other ways to explain the exclusionary rule as the first part of this Article demonstrates. Nor is it self-evident or intuitively obvious that the economist's explanation is superior to that of a humanist, a sociologist, an anthropologist, a psychologist, or a lawyer. Like economists, they all have said some shrewd things from time to time about law which can be ignored only at the law's peril. Like economists, other intelligent persons in other disciplines, honestly groping for understanding, have placed other matrices against the fabric of law and society, and have produced significant insights based on other assumptions, definitions, and expectations. I know of no argument—and Posner advances none—to suggest the primacy, or greater virtue or power, of economic explanation of judicial decision or legal rule over any of the explanations offered by lawyers, humanists, and social scientists. Thus, until convincing argument to the contrary is forthcoming, one must conclude that Posner's economic explanation of law and the exclusionary rule, if it explains law at all, is not the "best," but only one possible explanation among others.

Despite his claim that judge-made "remedies for governmental misconduct in criminal cases . . . are best explained by assuming that judges are preeminently concerned with economic efficiency,"[42] Posner

---

41. Posner, *Excessive Sanctions for Governmental Misconduct in Criminal Cases*, 57 WASH. L. REV. 635, 635–36 (1982).

42. *Id.* at 636.

The Exclusionary Rule and Posner's Analysis

does not present an economic explanation for the reasons accounting for the original, judicial adoption of the exclusionary rule. He puts a straightforward historical question: "So we must ask why the exclusionary rule was ever adopted."[43] Posner then asserts that the actual, historical answer is "consistent" with economic analysis. He does not give us a description/explanation that is the result of economic analysis: "The answer is consistent with economic analysis: the rule was adopted because until recently there was no alternative sanction for violations of the fourth amendment that did not cause severe underdeterrence."[44]

Posner's answer functions to shift the focus of the exclusionary rule onto deterrence, but as a matter of historical accuracy, his answer is simply wrong. As demonstrated in the first part of this paper, the judicial origins of the exclusionary rule in *Weeks*, *Silverthorne* and *Nardone* were not based on the deterrence rationale, but instead, the exclusionary rule's origins were premised on reasons that I have described as "the judicial-fidelity-to-the-Constitution rationale." It is only in recent years, due to the decisions of the Burger Court, that the exclusionary rule is seen as based on a deterrence rationale. Posner has not given us an economic explanation of the original exclusionary rule decisions or their reasons. I know of no way by which reasons such as "judicial integrity" can be "explained" by economic analysis, which does not purport to explain notions like integrity, love, or honor. This is not surprising since economic analysis was invented to explain quite different things. An economy is only one part of a total human society, and one should not expect its theory to explain the greater whole.

By placing the exclusionary rule solely onto a deterrence foundation and then attacking that foundation, Posner aligns himself with the foes of the rule. But his attack is different from others. They claim the exclusionary rule does not actually deter. Posner uses economic analysis normatively to recommend social change:[45] namely, that the exclusionary rule ought to be abandoned for two reasons, first, because it overdeters and second, because it produces a deadweight loss.

V.   THE ECONOMIC OVERDETERRENCE ARGUMENT

When Posner uses the word "overdeters," as his first ground for aban-

---

43.   *Id.* at 638.

44.   *Id.*

45.   *But cf.*: "The economist's competence in a discussion of the legal system thus is strictly limited. He can predict the effect of legal rules and arrangements on value and efficiency, in their strict technical senses, and on the existing distribution of income and wealth. *He cannot prescribe social change.*" R. POSNER, *supra* note 39, at 10 (emphasis added).

Washington Law Review   Vol. 57:647, 1982

doning the exclusionary rule, he does not mean to use "deter" in its customary empirical sense, as it was used in the first part of this Article. He assumes the exclusionary rule "deters" in that sense. Posner uses "deter" in a technical, more limited, "economic" sense relating arbitrarily assigned dollar amounts to each other in order to conclude that the rule "overdeters":

> [the exclusionary rule] produces overdeterrence because the private (and social) cost imposed on the government may greatly exceed the social cost of the misconduct.
>
>   . . . [Suppose an] illegal search imposes a cost of $100 on the person searched in terms of lost time spent cleaning up after the searching officers, but that the loss to society from not being able to convict him can be valued at $10,000. If the probability of apprehending and convicting the illegal searcher is one, a fine of $100 would prove optimal . . . deterrence of such illegal searches. The much larger "fine" that is actually imposed will overdeter, causing the government to steer too far clear of the amorphous boundaries of the fourth amendment compared to what it would do at the optimal fine level.[46]

This example needs to be "unpacked." For Posner, it contains the correct standard, i.e., the "optimal fine," for identifying the desirable amount of deterrence that should be put behind the fourth amendment's prohibition of illegal searches and seizures. The standard is the economic cost to society of the police officer's misconduct when he illegally searches (assuming the probability of apprehending and convicting the illegal searcher is one). The economic cost to society; i.e., the lost production of goods and services because of the illegal search is, for Posner, measured by the loss to society of the victim's economic production. It is the "lost time spent cleaning up after the searching officers," or the "lost" economic time of hired housecleaners if the victim does not do the cleanup. In any event, the dollar value of that "lost" economically productive time, occasioned by the illegal search, will not be high, and that weights the economic scale. Posner arbitrarily assigns it the value of $100.00, and this becomes the dollar amount of the "private and [social cost] of the misconduct." Given his apprehending-and-convicting assumption, it equals the amount of the optimal fine that should be assessed against a police officer who illegally searches in violation of the fourth amendment. The real harm to society[47] is ignored, and the victim's "lost time cleaning up" controls. That, then, is all the deterrence Posner believes the fourth amendment is entitled to—the cleanup cost.

---

46. Posner, *supra* note 41, at 638.

47. The real harm to society is the loss of judicial integrity. *See* notes 7–14 and accompanying text *supra*.

The Exclusionary Rule and Posner's Analysis

The amount of deterrence that Posner's "optimal fine" would actually produce is not necessarily related to any realistic factor or consideration that may be necessary actually to deter police from making illegal searches. Indeed, it is only tangentially and indirectly linked to the police. Instead, the optimal fine is linked directly to "lost" economic production by the victim occasioned by the unlawful search, without any consideration of factors that may deter police from making illegal searches. It is obvious that the actual amount of deterrence obtained by Posner's "optimal fine" would be accidental, and it could be none. It will vary from police officer to police officer, depending on many factors. Consider the deterrence of police officers produced by Posner's "optimal fine" when the police are persons who neither destroy anything when gaining entry to search, nor leave an untidy mess to be cleaned up later, or who are willing to (and do) clean up the mess on their own "private," off-working-hours time. In such circumstances, on Posner's assumptions, the amount of deterrence secured by his optimal fine would be zero. If a police officer believed an illegal search would break a case and result in an increase in his salary, or his promotion, worth more to him than the "optimal fine," then a "rational" economic maximizing police officer would simply see payment of the fine as the price of getting ahead. He would illegally search and pay the fine. Again, the amount of deterrence would be zero. In no case would Posner's recommendation of an economically "optimal fine" place more than only low levels of deterrence behind the exclusionary rule, and in some cases it would place none.

Posner does not come forth openly and identify any underlying justificatory reason lying behind his policy. Instead, his policy recommendation to abandon the exclusionary rule is couched solely in economic analysis terms. His justification for it cannot be "economic efficiency" because that does not tell us why we should be socially concerned with economic efficiency and adopt it as social policy in this instance. After all, we do not follow the dictates of economic efficiency when we practice representative democracy as our constitutional form of government. Representative democracy may be economically inefficient, but we keep it for other reasons. Posner has offered us no policy reason on why courts ought to adopt his version of economic efficiency as controlling when enforcing the Constitution's fourth amendment.

Several more things must be noticed about Posner's economic example of overdeterrence. First, it is hypothetical and arbitrary. If his arbitrarily assigned dollar amounts were reversed, so, too, would be his conclusion. The exclusionary rule, then, would economically underdeter. Posner presents neither evidence of the actual dollar amounts that realistically might be assigned to his economic deterrence formula nor any method whereby

Washington Law Review   Vol. 57:647, 1982

they might reliably be ascertained. Without reliably ascertained actual dollar amounts to factor into Posner's formula, even accepting his mode of economic analysis, his assertion that the exclusionary rule "produces overdeterrence" rests only on his arbitrary decision to assign the dollar amounts as he did, and proves nothing about the real world.

Second, is Posner's formula workable in fact? Can one reliably place a nonarbitrary dollar amount on such things as judicial integrity in enforcing the fourth amendment or on one's interest and society's interest in freedom from illegal searches and seizures? Clearly, Posner's suggestion of the cost of an illegal search—the victim's lost time in cleaning up—doesn't even begin to cope with the actual social costs created by illegal searches and seizures. And where might we obtain actual, reliable figures of the "probability of apprehending and convicting the illegal searcher" which we must use to calculate the "optimal fine"? Posner offers nothing here. It is not apparent that Posner's formula is workable in fact.

Third, Posner's "overdeterrence" caused by the exclusionary rule rests squarely on the "high cost" case where conviction cannot occur unless the illegally seized evidence is used at trial. Unfortunately for Posner, that case is not nearly as common as opponents of the exclusionary rule proclaim and, therefore, the "price" of the rule is not nearly as high.[48]

Ultimately, Posner's argument of overdeterrence boils down to an assessment of actually existing alternatives to the exclusionary rule and their actual deterrent effects. The important point, for him, is that "the tort remedy for unlawful searches and seizures is now practical where once it was practically unavailable."[49] Posner cites and relies only on his recent article,[50] claiming that "[a]s a result of the growing practical availability of the tort remedy, I would predict a shift away from the exclusionary rule."[51] He "doubt[s] that the rule will survive in anything like its present form much longer."[52] But, in his earlier article, Posner was not nearly so sure that the tort remedy is efficacious. He wrote:

> If the principle of *Norton* is rejected, if punitive damages are awarded in proper cases, if judges deal firmly with jury prejudice, if imagination is used in valuing intangible items of damage such as loss of mental repose, and if class-action treatment and injunctive relief are granted in appropriate cases, then, I believe, the tort remedy will bring us closer to optimum deterrence of Fourth Amendment violations than the exclusionary rule.[53]

48. *See* note 18 *supra.*
49. Posner, *supra* note 41, at 639.
50. Posner, *Rethinking the Fourth Amendment*, 1981 Sup. Ct. Rev. 49.
51. Posner, *supra* note 41, at 639.
52. *Id.*
53. Posner, *Rethinking the Fourth Amendment*, 1981 Sup. Ct. Rev. 49, 68. The case referred to

The Exclusionary Rule and Posner's Analysis

If ever there were a grudging admission that, currently, the tort remedy is grossly inadequate, the above quotation is it. Moreover, there is grave doubt that the tort remedy will ever become adequate. Consider again the testimony of Maryland's Attorney General, Stephen Sachs:

> Exclusion from evidence is almost certainly the only effective deterrent in the vast majority of unconstitutional intrusions. Even critics of the rule are quick to acknowledge the severe limitations of police self-discipline or court damage actions as deterrents when crime fighting police officers are in the dock. In rare cases involving especially gross misconduct, a police disciplinary board or a court or jury in a damage action might, *might,* impose sanctions, at least if the victim of the trespass is innocent and the police misconduct truly outrageous.
>
> But most of the suppression cases do not deal with such outrageous conduct. They deal with undramatic Fourth Amendment concerns—the sufficiency of "probable cause" in a given case, whether "exigent circumstances" excuse the necessity of a warrant, whether there is a sufficient corroboration of the tip of an anonymous informer to justify intrusion into a suspect's apartment. These requirements are not the stuff to move police disciplinary boards, or judges and juries accustomed to awarding damages on the basis of "fault." But they are our constitutional rules of the road and only the suppression sanction, the exclusionary rule, will force prosecutors and police to obey them.[54]

VI. THE ECONOMIC "DEADWEIGHT LOSS" ARGUMENT

Posner's second reason why the exclusionary rule should be abandoned is that from an economic point of view it is excessive in that "it violates the Pareto-superiority criterion because it imposes a deadweight loss— the suppression of socially valuable evidence—that would have been avoided if the misbehaving government official . . . had been fined instead."[55]

---

is Norton v. United States, 581 F.2d 390 (4th Cir. 1978), holding under the Federal Torts Claims Act a governmental agency's liability is purely derivative from the governmental agent's, so that the agency can assert any defense the agent had.

54. *Hearings, supra* note 18 (statement of Stephen H. Sachs), *reprinted in* YALE L. REP., Winter 1981–82, at 73. This was recognized in Mapp v. Ohio, 367 U.S. 643, 652 (1961): "The experience of California that such other remedies have been worthless and futile is buttressed by the experience of other States. The obvious futility of relegating the Fourth Amendment to the protection of other remedies has, moreover, been recognized by this Court since Wolf. *See Irvine v. California,* 347 U.S. 128, 137. . . ." *Id.* at 652–53.

55. Posner, *supra* note 41, at 638. This simply will not do as an economic explanation of current legal reality because it does not explain existing legal institutions and it creates a new one. No system of "fines" currently exists to levy against the offending police, and, admittedly, existing tort remedies are highly inadequate. Thus, it appears that one of Posner's necessary bases for his economic comparison ("fines") is simply not actually available, and his "economic explanation," therefore, does not follow. Moreover, as developed above, Posner's attempt to provide for an "opti-

Washington Law Review   Vol. 57:647, 1982

Posner makes odd use of the Paretian criteria when he claims that the exclusionary rule imposes an economic "deadweight" loss. Paretian superiority, as I understand it, involves a version of welfare economics and refers exclusively to the situation of individuals. It states that one specific allocation of society's goods and services is superior to another if at least one person is better off under the first allocation than under a second and if no one is made worse off.[56] The second allocation is Paretian inferior, and the first is Paretian superior. The change to a Paretian superior allocation must result in a net increase in aggregate utility in a society, since no one is made worse off by the new distribution of goods and services and at least one person is made better off by the change. Paretian superior allocations produce winners but no losers. When society's resources are allocated in a way that any further redistribution of them can only benefit one person at the expense of another, we have reached Paretian optimality. No further Paretian superiority allocation exists. Paretian optimal distributions are also Paretian efficient.

There are crucially important distinctions between individual-preference theories, total-utility theories and social-welfare theories.[57] Judgments flowing from Pareto's superiority criterion are expressed solely in terms of individual human preference orderings; that is, each person is assumed to have his or her own specific order of preferences for all goods and services. Thus, to declare that one allocation of society's goods and services is Paretian superior to some other allocation is only to say that, under the preferred allocation, one person would be placed higher along his or her preference ranking with no one else made worse off on his or her preference ranking. The existence of individual preference rankings is critical to the concept of Paretian superiority. They give us a standard of

---

mal fine" scheme is sorely lacking. This is not to say that a system of fines could not be instituted, although it may be an insuperable problem to assure they will be levied and to identify their amounts so as necessarily to achieve actual police deterrence equal to that of the exclusionary rule. If Posner is recommending that a system of fines be legislated sometime in the future, then he must be more realistic than merely to recommend an "optimal fine" equal to the cleanup costs after an illegal search. He must present an operational, real-world basis for the amounts of the fines that are empirically linked to deterring police behavior. More important, he must identify and defend openly the social policies that lie behind his recommendation. Posner's economic reasoning leading to a policy recommendation that future legislation create a system of fines as exclusive sanctions for illegal searches and seizures divorces him from current reality and catapults him into the realm of amorphous hypothetical conjecture, and consequently, cannot be accepted either as an economic explanation of existing legal reality or as an acceptable policy recommendation in its present form.

56. A good discussion of Paretian ethics can be found in Coleman, *Efficiency, Exchange and Auction: Philosophic Aspects of the Economic Approach to Law*, 68 CALIF. L. REV 221 (1980). *See also* C. PRICE. WELFARE ECONOMICS IN THEORY AND PRACTICE (1977); V. TARASCIO. PARETO'S METHODOLOGICAL APPROACH TO ECONOMICS (1968).

57. *See generally* A. SEN. COLLECTIVE CHOICE AND SOCIAL WELFARE (1970) (discussing these theories).

The Exclusionary Rule and Posner's Analysis

comparison enabling us to bring the discrete judgments about the relative standing of individuals to their preference orderings into a single judgement about aggregate utility existing in a given society at a given moment in time. Pareto's concepts require human beings with preference schedules.

Earlier in his paper Posner explains his notion of an economic "deadweight loss." Here he gives a somewhat different reason why the exclusionary rule can be economically excessive—"it can violate the Pareto criterion of efficiency"[58] and produce a deadweight loss. Posner illustrates what he means by an economic "deadweight loss" by assuming a situation where a fine levied against a criminal would produce as much deterrence as a prison sentence, but the prison term would also impose a deadweight economic loss "in the form of the criminal's forgone legitimate earnings and the costs of guarding him."[59] Therefore, on Posner's assumptions, the fine is economically preferable under his view of Pareto's efficiency concept because an equal amount of deterrence is achieved more cheaply, and society need not incur the "deadweight losses" of forgoing the criminal's "legitimate" productivity during the time he would have been in prison, or incur the costs of guarding him. Assuming an exclusive system of fines is adopted and the criminal's "legitimate" production of goods and services (represented by the criminal's legitimate earnings) are now available for social distribution, the actual distribution of the criminal's production will necessarily serve to advance one or more persons along his or her preference schedules because the total amount of society's goods and services available for distribution would have been increased by the amount "legitimately" produced by the criminal who had not been imprisoned.

On this analysis, the "deadweight loss" concept necessarily is tied to notions of productive, allocative economic efficiency, which, under certain circumstances, can be the same as Paretian efficiency.[60] Posner asks

---

58. Posner, *supra* note 41, at 636.

59. *Id.*

60. The concept of economic efficiency is quite complex and widely misunderstood. Economic efficiency can refer to at least four notions of efficiency—production-allocative efficiency; Paretian optimality; Paretian superiority; and Kaldor-Hicks efficiency. This list is incomplete because there possibly may be added a Posnerian standard of wealth optimizing. *See* sources cited in note 61 *infra*. Moreover, production-allocative efficiency on which Coase's theorem of externalities is based, *see*, Coase, *The Problem of Social Cost*, 3 J.L. & Econ. 1 (1960), (and which asserts that allocative efficiency, or the maximum productive use of society's resources, does not ultimately depend on the initial assignment of legal entitlements, assuming perfect market competition and zero transaction costs) can be consistent and perhaps interchangeable, under certain circumstances, with Paretian optimality. See particularly the discussion of "Pareto Optimality and Allocative Efficiency" in Coleman, *Efficiency, Exchange, and Auction: Philosophic Aspects of the Economic Approach to Law*, 68 Calif. L. Rev. 221, 226–37 (1980).

Washington Law Review   Vol. 57:647, 1982

us to compare two ways of achieving the same level of deterrence—a system of fines and prison sentences—and to choose the more efficient method, which turns out, on Posner's assumptions, to be a system of fines. By adopting a system of fines instead of prison terms, we avoid the economic "deadweight loss" which consists of the prisoner's lost production and the economic costs incurred by guarding him. The "deadweight losses" would have been incurred if we had chosen imprisonment.

Is this analysis applicable to the exclusionary rule? Posner seems to indulge in similar assumptions and reasoning about it. For example, if one makes the assumption that the exclusionary rule and fines are equal, or sufficiently equal, deterrents of illegal searches, then one might claim that the exclusionary rule imposes an economic "deadweight loss" because the illegally seized evidence cannot be used at trial, as it could have been under an exclusive scheme of fines. But this is to speak metaphorically, and the economic claim is false. It is no longer the economic analysis of law because the term "deadweight loss" now no longer carries economic meaning. It no longer is directly connected to forgone, i.e., lost, "legitimate" economic productivity of goods and services which qualified as the economic loss in Posner's example about fines and prison terms. What is "lost" now is only the police officer's *illegitimate* production of illegally seized evidence. I know of no way in which this *illegitimate* "production" by the police officer could be distributed so as to advance anyone along his or her preference schedule. The police officer has not produced "legitimate" economic goods and services which can be distributed, as did the criminal who was gainfully employed after avoiding imprisonment in Posner's fine/imprisonment example. Thus, the analogy between imprisonment and the exclusionary rule fails, and the exclusionary rule does not impose a "deadweight loss" in the same economic sense as does imprisonment. Furthermore, Posner's basic assumption has no basis in current legal fact. No system of fines currently exists that is equal, or sufficiently equal, in deterrent effect to the exclusionary rule. Also, as indicated above, it is unlikely that such an equally deterring system of fines will ever exist, although a legislature may enact a system of fines. Finally, Posner offers us nothing about the judicial-fidelity-to-the-Constitution basis for the exclusionary rule, which simply cannot be dismissed. The constitutional dimension must be faced and accounted for if one is to account fully in economic terms for the exclusionary rule.

VII. CONCLUSION

In summary, Posner does not use economic analysis to explain the ori-

The Exclusionary Rule and Posner's Analysis

gins of the exclusionary rule. Nor does he analyze its empirical reality. A strong policy recommendation is loud and clear—abandon the exclusionary rule—but his recommendation rests on inadequate theoretical and practical grounds. Posner makes no attempt to justify his policy recommendation on grounds of social policy beyond his claims of theoretical "economic efficiency." Finally, he never attempts to answer the crucial question: Why should our constitutional policy on illegal searches and seizures be based *exclusively* on economic efficiency grounds?[61] Until these serious deficiencies are remedied, we might believe that the claim of excessive sanctions for governmental misconduct in criminal cases is unproved, and justifiably remain quite skeptical about normative claims derived from the economic analysis of law.

---

61. Although he formerly embraced it, Posner has recently disavowed classical utilitarianism as the ultimate ground of justification for economic efficiency. Posner, *Utilitarianism, Economics and Legal Theory*, 8 J. LEGAL STUD. 103, 111–19 (1979). Instead, he embraced a system of wealth maximization which requires people to act so as to increase social wealth—defined as the dollar value equivalents of everything in society. His definition of wealth in its relationship to a system of wealth maximization is:

> The value in . . . dollar equivalents . . . of everything in society. It is measured by what people are willing to pay for something or, if they already own it, what they demand in money to give it up. [Everything, for Posner, has its price.] The only kind of preference that counts in a system of wealth maximization is thus one that is backed up by money—in other words, that is registered in a market.

Id. at 119. But, if there were no prices, Posner's scheme of wealth maximization collapses. If I trade you an apple for your orange, there is no wealth maximization under Posner's new wealth maximization criterion. But, if I pay you a dollar for your orange, and you pay me a dollar for my apple, then we have prices, and wealth maximization under Posner's new criterion. Unfortunately for Posner, it has been convincingly shown that wealth maximization fails as a normatively defensible first principle, which is what Posner must supply to justify his economic efficiency criterion. Coleman, *Efficiency, Utility, and Wealth Maximization*, 8 HOFSTRA L. REV 509, 520–40 (1980); *see also*, Dworkin, *Is Wealth A Value?*, 9 J. LEGAL STUD 191, 194–97 (1980).

Part IX
Protection of the Accused

[25]

ISRAEL LAW REVIEW

| Vol. 9 | January, 1974 | No. 1 |

AN ATTEMPT TO UPDATE THE LAW OF EVIDENCE*

THE 11TH REPORT OF THE ENGLISH CRIMINAL LAW REVISION COMMITTEE

*By Rupert Cross***

1. *Introduction*

When Dean Feller did me the honour of inviting me to give the Lionel Cohen lecture for 1973 one of the subjects I submitted, and the one accepted by him, was "Reforming the Law of Evidence—The English Experience". For me those were the halcyon days before the publication of the 11th Report of the Criminal Law Revision Committee; the law of evidence in civil cases had been modernised by the Civil Evidence Acts of 1968 and 1972, and I pictured the draft Criminal Evidence Bill annexed to the 11th Report going merrily through Parliament, if not without some protest and amendment, at least with celerity and the certitude of becoming law. Alas, this was not to be. To describe the reception of the Report as "unenthusiastic" would be the understatement of the century; but, although I must confess to considerable pessimism concerning the questions when and to what extent the draft Bill will become law in England, I am pleased that it should continue to be the subject of my lecture, although the title of the latter had perforce to undergo some change in order to cater for the fact that the English experience of reforming the law of evidence is too incomplete to allow for profitable discussion.

My contention is that, if the Bill were to become law just as it is, England would have the best rules of evidence in criminal cases in the common law world. Of course I do not say that they would be perfect; indeed I shall be indicating points at which I think they could be improved upon, but, even after allowance has been made for this limitation, my contention is a bold one. Some of the criticism of the 11th Report has been well informed, many

---

* Sections 1–3 of this article are an expanded version of the Lionel Cohen lecture delivered at the Hebrew University of Jerusalem on June 12, 1973; section 4 is based on a talk given to a seminar at the Hebrew University on June 19, 1973.

** D.C.L., F.B.A., Vinerian Professor of English Law, University of Oxford.

of the Committee's recommendations run counter to recent decisions of the United States Supreme Court and there are excellent sets of rules of evidence that claim favourable comparison with those recommended by the Criminal Law Revision Committee. Notable among these are the United States Federal Rules of Evidence adopted by the Supreme Court by a majority last December with a direction that they should come into force on July 13, 1973,[1] a date which has, however, since been deferred by Act of Congress, and the lesser known but equally good rules of evidence proposed by the Ghana Law Reform Commission. I shall be referring to both these sets of rules as well as the older American Law Institute's Model Code of Evidence published in 1942, and Uniform Rules of Evidence published in 1953.

A few preliminary words about the Criminal Law Revision Committee and the terms in which the law of evidence was referred to it may not come amiss. The Committee was set up as a standing committee in 1959 "To examine such aspects of the criminal law of England and Wales as the Home Secretary may from time to time refer to the Committee, to consider whether the law requires revision and to make recommendations." The Committee consists of judges, practitioners and academics; at present there are 14 members, assisted by a secretary and assistant secretary who are civil servants. The first chairman was Sir Frederick Sellers (Sellers L. J. until the end of 1967) and he was succeeded in 1969 by Edmund Davies L. J. The Committee has published 12 reports on subjects as varied as the right of reply and the penalty for murder. The 8th Report which resulted in the Theft Act 1968 recommended drastic simplification and modernisation of the law of theft; but the 11th Report on "Evidence (General)"[2] is the most controversial as well as the most massive of the Committee's productions.

In 1964 the Home Secretary asked the Committee "To review the law of evidence in criminal cases and to consider whether any changes are desirable in the interests of the fair and efficient administration of justice; and in particular what provision should be made for modifying rules which have ceased to be appropriate in modern conditions." Work on this reference was not begun until the end of 1965 and the 11th Report was published in the middle of 1972. The law of evidence in civil cases was referred to the Law Reform Committee in terms similar to those which have just been quoted. The Law Reform Committee is appointed by the Lord Chancellor, and its functions are similar in relation to the civil law to those performed in relation to the criminal law by the Criminal Law Revision Committee. It was able to complete its work on evidence far more speedily than its counterpart, and its reports on hearsay evidence in civil proceedings,[3] the rule in *Hollington* v. *Hewthorn* under which convictions of crime were inadmissible in subsequent

---

[1] 34 L. Ed. 2d no. 5.

[2] Cmnd. 4991, 1972.

[3] Cmnd. 2964, 1966.

civil proceedings as evidence of the facts on which they were founded,[4] privilege in civil proceedings[5] and evidence of opinion[6] have resulted in the Civil Evidence Acts of 1968 and 1972.

I was a coopted member of the Criminal Law Revision Committee from the beginning of its deliberations on evidence and became a full member in 1970; I was also a coopted member of the sub-committee of the Law Reform Committee which prepared the reports to which I have referred. I can therefore assure you that the greater amount of time taken over the 11th Report was in no way due to lack of assiduity on the part of the members of the Criminal Law Revision Committee. It was entirely the outcome of the greater significance of the role played by the law of evidence in criminal cases. If one excludes arguments about the construction of such statutes as the Evidence Act, 1938 and the Civil Evidence Act, 1968, it is comparatively rarely that a dispute concerning the admissibility of evidence is fought à outrance at the trial of a civil action in England. On the other hand, points on evidence are a fertile source of appeals in criminal cases. An important function of the law of evidence is rightly thought to be the protection of the accused from the risk of an unjust conviction. To what extent should confessions made by him be admissible? Should the prosecution be allowed to give evidence of his misconduct on other occasions? If the accused has a criminal record, should he be liable to cross-examination on that subject? These are the kind of questions which consumed the time of the Criminal Law Revision Committee.

The Home Secretary's request that the Committee should consider what provision ought to be made for modifying rules which have ceased to be appropriate in modern conditions is highly significant. The question of what changes in conditions are relevant to the rules of evidence is to some extent one of opinion; but there is no room for denying that a whole mass of rules of evidence could have been reconsidered with advantage when the accused was made a competent witness in all criminal cases in 1898. They were not reconsidered then and the argument for considering them together with the working of the Criminal Evidence Act 1898 had become unanswerable by 1964. Included in the mass of rules calling for re-examination were those concerning police interrogations and the admissibility of hearsay for, in the days when the accused could not testify, it would have been grossly unfair to have attached as much weight to what he did or did not say to the police as might be done under a system in which the accused is a competent witness with regard to these matters; and the argument for the inadmissibility of what was said "behind the accused's back" loses some of its force once the accused is in a position to answer it in court. Such questions as those connected with the accused's failure to give evidence and the cross-examination

[4] Cmnd. 3391, 1967.
[5] Cmnd. 3472, 1967.
[6] Cmnd. 4489, 1970.

of an accused with a criminal record clearly called for consideration in connection with the working of the Act of 1898. What was needed was a comprehensive review of the law of evidence in criminal cases and that was what it got.

Considerations of space preclude my discussing all the results of that review. I will begin by dealing with the effects of the accused not giving evidence, police interrogations and confessions, three matters commonly believed to raise issues concerning the right to silence; after a brief excursus on the cross-examination of the accused, I deal with hearsay and conclude with a reference to what I regard as one of the major perils of the common law of evidence in criminal cases—its propensity to produce distinctions without differences. I realise that, from the Israeli point of view, a discussion of proposals for change in the English law may be robbed of some of its significance by the fact that there is no jury trial in Israel, but I don't think this deprives the detailed provisions of the English draft Bill of all interest to an Israeli lawyer. Therefore I have not scrupled to set some of the clauses out and even to draw attention to the phraseology of similar provisions in other common law jurisdictions. Some of you may yet live to see the time when the comparison and contrast of the aims and drafting of statutory provisions is regarded as more important than the study of the minutiae of case-law.

2. *The right to silence*

(a) *The accused's failure to give evidence*

Clause 5(3) of the draft Bill reads:

"If the accused —

(a) after being called upon by the court to give evidence in pursuance of this section, or after he or counsel or solicitor representing him has informed the court that he will give evidence, refuses to be sworn or

(b) having been sworn, without good cause refuses to answer any question, the court or jury in determining whether the accused is guilty of the offence charged, may draw such inferences from the failure as appear proper; and the failure may, on the basis of such inferences, be treated as, or as capable of amounting to, corroboration of any evidence given on behalf of the prosecution."

Clause 5(3)(a) refers back to the proposal, embodied in clauses 5(1) and 5(2), that the accused should be formally called upon to give evidence before any evidence is given for the defence, unless the court has previously been informed by the accused, his counsel or solicitor, that he will testify. This is a procedural innovation which is not to everyone's taste; because there are those who regard it as something of a gimmick; but everyone recognizes the necessity of an explanation by the court to an unrepresented defendant of the effect of clause 5(3).

A more important point is that clause 5(4) provides that nothing in the whole clause shall be taken to render the accused compellable to give evidence on his own behalf; therefore he could not be sent to prison for contempt of court in refusing to be sworn. The Bill does not subject him to what has been rhetorically described as "the cruel trilemma of self-accusation, perjury or contempt".[7] The trilemma would be self-accusation, perjury or, on appropriate facts, the risk of adverse inferences. If it be thought that this trilemma is cruel, I would have no objection to the abolition of the accused's liability to be prosecuted for perjury in giving false evidence on his own behalf. Such prosecutions are rare in England, and many Europeans think that even the possibility of proceedings of this nature is an Anglo-Saxon absurdity. If, for the loaded phrase "self-accusation" we were to substitute "liability to cross-examination", the defendant at a criminal trial would be confronted with the choice between giving the court his version of the facts with the possibility of a cross-examination which might or might not be unpleasant, and running the risk of adverse inferences being drawn from his failure to testify, a risk the magnitude of which would vary considerably from case to case. If, as I shall suggest he should be,[8] an accused with a criminal record is adequately protected from cross-examination on that subject, I fail to see how the choice can realistically be described as a cruel one. I also fail to see how human dignity enters into the question, and the suggestion that putting a certain amount of pressure on the accused to testify is tantamount to making him dig his own grave leaves me cold.[9]

Clause 4(2) of the draft Bill would deprive the accused of the right which he enjoys under the present English law of making an unsworn statement from the dock.[10] I regard this right as an historical anomaly, a survival of the bad old days when the accused could not give evidence and the judges did what they could to ameliorate his lot. I don't feel like shedding tears over the suggestion that it should be abolished or wasting time in further discussion of the subject.

Another right, currently enjoyed by the accused under sec. 1(b) of the Criminal Evidence Act 1898, which would be forfeited if the Bill were to become law, is immunity from comment by the prosecution on his failure to give evidence. As things are, the accused's failure to testify may be the subject of comment by the judge and by a co-accused; this is the result of case-law based on the absence of any prohibition on comment from these sources in our Act of 1898.[11] The decisions on what the judge may or may

---

[7] Goldberg J. in *Murphy* v. *Waterfront Commission of New York Harbour* 378 U.S. 52 at p. 55.

[8] Section 3 *infra*.

[9] See Goldberg in *Murphy's* case *supra,* and Griswold, *The Fifth Amendment To-day,* p. 7.   [10] Criminal Evidence Act, 1898 sec. 1(h).

[11] The authorities are reviewed in *R.* v. *Mutch*, [1973] 1 All E.R. 178 and *R.* v. *Sparrow,* [1973] 1 W.L.R. 488; the co-accused's right to comment is established by *R.* v. *Wickham, Ferrara and Bean* (1971) 55 Cr. App. Rep. 199.

not say to the jury by way of comment show that everything depends on the facts of the particular case. If there are undisputed or clearly established facts calling for an explanation[12] the judge may go so far as to tell the jury that they are entitled to draw inferences adverse to the accused from his failure to testify; if the defendant says that, though he did agree to participate in robberies with his co-defendant, he never agreed to the use of a gun, a very strong comment on his failure to support this allegation from the witness box at his trial for being a party to murder is called for.[13] On the other hand, if the defence takes the form of a general denial, the judge should, if he comments on the matter at all, do no more than say that, by exercising his right not to give evidence, the accused has deprived the jury of the opportunity of hearing him tell his full story subject to cross-examination.[14] What the judge must never do is to say anything which might lead the jury to suppose that they can draw a direct inference of guilt from the accused's failure to testify.

This would continue to be the case under clause 5(3) of the draft Bill because such an inference would not "appear proper". The prosecution must prove the accused's guilt beyond reasonable doubt, and it is not difficult to imagine cases in which the accused's failure to testify should have little if any effect on the degree of conviction of his guilt entertained by the jury. For example, if he was admittedly in a crowd one of whom assaulted the prosecutor, the jury might not be satisfied with the evidence of identification; or, whatever be the nature of the case, the witnesses for the prosecution might have been badly shaken in cross-examination.[15] By way of contrast there would be the murder charge against someone who was the last person seen with the deceased and very shortly before his or her death at that; the supposition that the accused left the victim alive and well to be done to death by a person unknown could be discounted with much greater confidence if he did not give evidence.[16] Similarly it might be proper to draw an inference against the availability of such defences suggested by the evidence as non-complicity in the use of firearms, self-defence or, if the charge be one of rape, consent, where the accused declines to go into the witness box. The adverse inference does not have to be drawn, but many cases can be put in which it would be a perfectly proper one.

Precisely what, it may be asked, would be the effect of clause 5(3) of

---

12 As in *R. v. Corrie* (1904) 20 T.L.R. 365.

13 *R. v. Sparrow supra.*

14 *R. v. Mutch supra.*

15 *R. v. Adams* (1957); extracts from the summing-up in this *cause célèbre* are given in Glanville Williams, *The Proof of Guilt* (3rd ed.) 60. See also Sybil Bedford, *The Best We Can Do.* Had the draft Bill been in force at the time of *Dr. Adams'* trial, it would not have been proper for the judge to have directed the jury that they might draw adverse inferences from the accused's failure to testify.

16 *R. v. Nodder* (1937); *Proof of Guilt* 59.

the draft Bill? There would be an obvious change in the law with regard to corroboration to which I shall be referring shortly; apart from that, all I can say is that, in appropriate cases, when commenting on the accused's failure to give evidence, the judge will be able to be more explicit about the types of inference which would be proper in the particular circumstances. It would of course also be possible for the prosecution to draw attention to inferences which might properly be drawn; but those who consider that the change would be a vast one are labouring under the delusion that there is, in this context, a real distinction between commenting and pointing to inferences. The only reason for commenting is to draw attention to possible legitimate inferences. To take as an example the most moderate judicial comment sanctioned by the English case-law:

"The accused is not bound to give evidence. He can sit back and see if the prosecution have proved their case; it is true that you have been deprived of the opportunity of hearing his story tested in cross-examination, but you must on no account assume that the accused is guilty because he has not gone into the witness box."[17]

What is this but a concise way of stressing that, though the accused admits nothing by exercising his right not to testify, it is permissible to infer from that fact that his defence, supported, it may be, by questions put to witnesses for the prosecution, or even by witnesses called by him, is not a good one? The attempt to draw a distinction between comment and the suggestion that inferences may be drawn from the accused's failure to give evidence makes no more sense than the attempt, rejected by the English Court of Appeal,[18] to distinguish between describing such a failure as an "evidential factor" and a "material matter".

Sec. 129(3) of the Ghana Criminal Procedure Code, 1960 provides that "the failure of any person charged with an offence to give evidence ... may be the subject of comment by the judge, the prosecution or the defence". Part 7 rule (11)(d) of the proposed Ghana Rules of Evidence reads "If an accused in a criminal action does not testify on his own behalf, the court, the prosecution and the defence may comment on the accused's failure to testify, and the tribunal of fact may draw all reasonable inferences therefrom". It follows from what I have been saying that I do not consider that there is any real distinction between the two provisions except that the latter is more honest because fuller than the former, and less likely to lead to dark case-law concerning which side of a mysterious line a particular comment falls.[19]

---

[17] *R.* v. *Bathurst,* [1968] 2 Q.B. 99.

[18] *R.* v. *Sparrow,* [1973] 1 W.L.R. at p. 493.

[19] "Since the first decade of this century, there have been many cases in which this court and its predecessor have had to rule whether comments about the accused's silence from the witness box or a failure to disclose a defence when questioned by the police were permissible, and as Salmon L. J. pointed out in *R.* v. *Sullivan*

Rule 201(3) of the American Law Institute's Model Code of Evidence is in substantially the same terms as those of the proposed Ghana Rules;[20] but the Federal Rules contain no such provision. Plainly this is due to the intervening decision of the majority of the United States Supreme Court in *Griffin* v. *California*[21] in which comment by the prosecutor or the court on the accused's failure to testify was held to violate the requirement of the Fifth Amendment of the United States Constitution that no person shall be compelled to be a witness against himself. We have not got a Bill of Rights, either in England or in Israel, and this is not the occasion for a consideration of the merits of having one, or of the inclusion therein of a clause like the Fifth Amendment, or, if such a clause were included, of the weight to be attached to the majority and minority views on the question whether permission to comment on the accused's failure to testify would infringe it.

Two points commonly urged against a provision that adverse inferences may be drawn from the accused's failure to give evidence are first, that it would lighten the burden of proof borne by the prosecution, and secondly, that it fails to take account of the manifold reasons which may cause a person not to testify.

So far as the first point is concerned, the burden was lightened by the granting to the accused of the option to testify. The very last thing I want to do is to question the propriety of this course, but it would be idle to deny that any provision converting an hitherto incompetent accused into a competent witness is bound to lead to the drawing of adverse inferences against someone who does not avail himself of that provision. This is recognised by the courts of the United States to such an extent that it has been held that the jury should only be instructed to disregard the accused's failure to testify when a request for such an instruction has been made because it draws the jury's attention to the fact that the accused has not given evidence when he might have done so.[22] When I say that the burden borne by the

---

(51 Cr. App. Rep. 102 at p. 105): 'The line dividing what may be said and what may not be said is a very fine one and it is perhaps doubtful whether in a case like the present it would be even perceptible to the members of any ordinary jury'. Nevertheless, as long as the law recognises the so-called right to silence, judges must keep their comments on the correct side of the line, even though the differences between what is permissible and what is not may have little significance for many jurors" (*per* Lawton L. J. in *R.* v. *Mutch*, [1973] 1 All E.R. at p. 181).

[20] "If an accused in a criminal action does not testify, [the judge and] counsel may comment upon accused's failure to testify, and the trier of fact may draw all reasonable inferences therefrom". The words in square brackets are omitted from r. 23(4) of the Uniform Rules.

[21] 380 U.S. 609.

[22] *U.S.* v. *Woodmansee* 354 Fed. 2d 235.

prosecution was "lightened" by the permission given to the accused to testify, I do not, of course, wish to suggest that it is any less true today than it was before 1898 that the prosecution must prove the accused's guilt beyond reasonable doubt; all that has happened is that the accused has been deprived of one means of raising such a doubt—the fact that the jury was to a large extent left in the dark, through no fault of his, about his account of the facts. In spite of the occasional suggestion to the contrary, there is no doubt that the accused gained more than he lost by the Act of 1898 for he was given the opportunity, previously denied to him, of raising a reasonable doubt by means of his testimony.

As to the manifold reasons other than guilt which may impel an accused person not to testify, I think that the fact that he has a criminal record and is fearful of cross-examination on it requires special consideration,[23] and Bentham disposed of the rest long before the accused was given the right to testify:

"Innocent himself, a man chooses to be treated as if he were guilty, rather than to expose the secrets of a mistress or a friend: an act of martyrdom perfectly heroical, and the more heroical, the fitter a subject for a play or a romance. But the more heroical, the more rare; and therefore less fit a subject to constitute a ground for the steps of the legislator ... probabilities and not improbabilities constitute the true ground for legislative practice".[24]

I have said that, if clause 5(3) were to be enacted, there would be a change in the English law with regard to corroboration. That this would be so is made plain by the case of *R. v. Jackson*[25] in which Lord Goddard C. J. speaking for the Court of Criminal Appeal said:

"...one cannot say that the fact that a prisoner had not gone into the witness box is of itself corroboration of accomplices' evidence. It is a matter which the jury very properly could, and very probably would, take into account, but it should clearly be understood that the direction [that failure to testify can amount to corroboration] is wrong in law".

I submit that the distinction between a matter which can very properly be taken into account by the jury and something which corroborates other evidence, is a distinction without a difference, of the kind which has been exposed by the House of Lords in a more recent case concerning corroboration. In *Director of Public Prosecutions* v. *Kilbourne*[26] the House disposed of a distinction which had crept into English law in relation to the question whether evidence of an accomplice in another crime which could properly be proved against the accused could corroborate the evidence of an accomplice in the crime charged. Earlier decisions had given a negative

[23] See section 3 *infra*.
[24] *Works* (Bowring edition) vol. vii, p. 27.
[25] [1953] 1 All E.R. 872.
[26] [1973] 1 All E.R. 440.

answer while holding that the evidence might nevertheless help the jury to determine the truth. The House of Lords held that the evidence of the accomplice in the other crime could corroborate that of the accomplice in the crime charged and in effect characterised the distinction drawn in the earlier cases as absurd and incapable of explanation to a jury. It is sometimes said that, though failure to testify cannot be regarded as an independent item of evidence against the accused, it adds to the weight of the evidence against him; what is this if it is not corroboration?

I conclude therefore that clause 5(3) has all the merits of rule 11 of part 7 of the proposed Ghana Rules of Evidence and of rule 201(3) of the American Law Institute's Model Code of Evidence, with the addition that it makes it plain that failure to testify can be used as corroboration of other evidence where this is appropriate.

(b) *Police interrogations and the admissibility of confessions*

Clause 1(1) of the draft Bill reads

"Where in any proceedings against a person for an offence evidence is given that the accused —

(a) at any time before he was charged with the offence, on being questioned by a police officer trying to discover whether or by whom the offence had been committed, failed to mention any fact relied on in his defence in those proceedings; or

(b) on being charged with the offence or officially informed that he might be prosecuted for it, failed to mention any such fact, being a fact which in the circumstances existing at the time he could reasonably have been expected to mention when so questioned, charged or informed, as the case may be, the court, when determining whether to commit the accused for trial or whether there is a case to answer, and the court or jury, in determining whether the accused is guilty of the offence charged, may draw such inferences from the failure as appear proper; and the failure may, on the basis of such inferences, be treated as, or as capable of amounting to, corroboration of any evidence given against the accused in relation to which the failure is material".

I have dealt with clause 5(3) before clause 1(1) because, if inferences could not be drawn from the accused's failure to give evidence, it would be very odd if they might yet be drawn from the belated nature of the defence. Anything resembling clause 1(1) would of course have been out of the question until the accused had become a competent witness, for it is essential that he should have an opportunity of explaining his failure to mention a fact at his police interrogation. I am unaware of any statutory provision analogous to clause 1(1) in any common law jurisdiction; but I don't think its adoption would entail a drastic change in English law while it would get rid of yet another of those distinctions without a difference which have come to disfigure our law of evidence.

The supposed distinction was described by Lord Hewart C.J. in the following words in *R*. v. *Littleboy*:[27]

"There is a great difference between making the comment that silence on the part of the prisoner is unfortunate and a matter to be regarded with reference to the weight of the defence, when the defence of alibi is raised, and saying that the fact that the prisoner was silent may be treated as evidence against him or as corroborating the evidence of an accomplice".

The distinction between "a matter to be regarded with reference to the weight of the defence" and something which may be treated as evidence against the accused is like the distinctions without a difference between a material matter and an evidential factor, or evidence which may help in determining the truth and evidence which can corroborate the testimony of an accomplice, which have already been rejected by the English courts. If, as common sense dictates, the fact that an alibi was belated may detract from its weight even to the extent of rendering it incredible, what is that fact if it is not evidence against the accused? Why should it not be capable of corroborating the evidence of an accomplice?

Of course it would be wrong for the jury to draw, or to be directed to draw, a direct inference of guilt from the accused's silence under interrogation, but it can hardly be suggested that anything of the sort is sanctioned by clause 1(1). I therefore commend it for serious consideration by all those who are interested in the rationalisation of the common law of evidence.[28]

The sub-clause has, however, been the subject of bitter attack. No doubt it was the provision that was uppermost in Professor Dworkin's mind when he said that those who will suffer from the changes recommended in the 11th Report are "the confused and inarticulate, including immigrants, who are insecure in the language, bewildered by legal complexities, and frightened of formal authority".[29] The possibility that someone would fail to mention a fact because he was shocked by the accusation is envisaged in the Report and met by the observation that "It will be for the court or (with the help of the judge's direction) for the jury to decide whether in all the circumstances they are justified in drawing an adverse inference".[30] Surely Professor Dworkin's fears can be allayed in the same way.

Even the most cursory consideration of police interrogations should devote some attention to the question of the admissibility of confessions. The present English law is stated under head (e) of the introductory principles of the 1964 Judges' Rules:

[27] [1934] 2 K.B. 408 at p. 414.

[28] In a jurisdiction in which there are provisions like the English Judges' Rules under which suspects must be cautioned in terms telling them that they are not obliged to say anything, provision would of course have to be made for a modification of the practice. This matter is dealt with in paras. 43–7 of the Report.

[29] Letter to *The Times*, July 3, 1972.

[30] Para. 35.

"It is a fundamental condition of the admissibility in evidence against any person, equally of any oral answer given by that person to a question put by a police officer and of any statement made by that person, that it shall have been voluntary, in the sense that it has not been obtained from him by fear of prejudice, or hope of advantage, exercised or held out by a person in authority or by oppression".

Two comparatively minor changes would be effected by clause 2(2) of the draft Bill if it were adopted. In the first place, the threat or inducement would not have to emanate from someone in authority in order that it should render a confession inadmissible; it might come from a friend or a fellow prisoner, for instance. Secondly, the threat or inducement would have to be likely, in the circumstances, to render the confession unreliable. The existing procedure of a trial within the trial to determine the question of admissibility would be preserved. I am in favour of the proposed changes, but I don't think they go far enough and I wish to draw your attention to more drastic possibilities. As a prelude I mention the two major principles underlying the present English law. In the 11th Report they are described as the "reliability" and "disciplinary" principles respectively.

According to the first, the dominant consideration is that a confession which was not made voluntarily is likely to be unreliable. If this is the governing principle, there is no justification, now that the accused can give evidence, for either the trial within the trial or the legal technicalities concerning voluntariness according to which the mildest inducements which are most unlikely to have caused the utterance of an untruth render the confession inadmissible. In the days when it was not possible for the accused to testify concerning the circumstances in which the confession was made, there was a lot to be said for what amounted to a double check on reliability—the trial within the trial and the trial proper;[31] but why should the reliability of confessions be treated differently today from the reliability of any other hearsay statement such as an informal admission? The reliability of evidence is essentially a matter for the tribunal of fact. Trials within the trial are a nuisance in jury cases and something of an unreality when the judge sits alone.

It is customary to answer the question I have just put in terms of the disciplinary principle according to which one of the objects of the law governing voluntariness is the discouragement of improper police methods. Of course I am all in favour of the object, but I doubt whether the law of evidence is a suitable instrument for its achievement. Those who do not share my doubts maintain that, as the police would not be zealous to prosecute each other for the use of improper methods of investigation, even when such methods amounted to crimes, and as improper methods of obtaining con-

---

[31] A full history of the trial within the trial has yet to be written. Some of the pre-1898 decisions with regard to the admissibility of confessions appear to have been made in the presence of the jury.

fessions are not always criminal, the only way to insure propriety is to make it plain to a police officer contemplating the contrary that he will not benefit from his iniquity because the resulting confession will be inadmissible. The argument seems to me to be naive in the extreme. The police officer resorting to improper methods believes that his version of what took place at the interrogation will be preferred to that of the accused, and the officer's version will not be a tale of impropriety. If the existence of impropriety comes to light, it is likely to be the subject of judicial comment calling for action, by the prosecuting authority where a crime may well have been committed, and by a police authority where this is not the case. These possibilities, rather than the rejection of the improperly obtained confession, are more likely to influence the police officer obtaining a confession in this way.

If, as I think it is, the disciplinary principle is something which does not make sense in this context, there is a lot to be said for abolishing the trial within the trial in the case of confessions and treating all confessions as admissible as a matter of law, their weight being a question for the tribunal of fact, a question to which the method of obtaining the confession is highly relevant. This is the course canvassed by a minority of the Criminal Law Revision Committee. It is not as draconian as it sounds because a judge who thinks that a confession may have been obtained by "conduct of which the Crown ought not to take advantage"[32] would retain his existing discretion to exclude the confession, discharging the jury and ordering a fresh trial where necessary.

Sec. 6 of the Northern Ireland (Emergency Provsions) Act, 1973 may be of interest to those who both prefer something more definite than "conduct of which the Crown ought not to take advantage" and require that some improperly obtained confessions should continue to be inadmissible as a matter of law. It reads

(1) "In any criminal proceedings ... a statement made by the accused may be given in evidence by the prosecution in so far as it is relevant to any matter in issue in the proceedings and is not excluded by the court in pursuance of subsection (2) below".

(2) "If, in any such proceedings, where the prosecution proposes to give in evidence a statement made by the accused, *prima facie* evidence is adduced that the accused was subjected to torture or to inhuman or degrading treatment[33] in order to induce him to make the statement, the court shall, unless the prosecution satisfied them that the statement was not so obtained, exclude the statement or, if it has been received in evidence, shall either continue the trial, disregarding the statement, or direct that the trial shall be restarted before a differently constituted court (before whom the statement shall be inadmissible)".

[32] *King v. The Queen*, [1969] 1 A.C. 304 at p 319.
[33] "Torture or inhuman or degrading treatment" are the words used in the European Convention on Human Rights.

The Act gives effect to the recommendations of the Diplock Commission concerning the administration of justice in Northern Ireland during the emergency.[34] One of these recommendations was that trial by jury for certain offences should be suspended, and the provision with regard to confessions is accordingly drafted for trial by judge alone. Even if it could not be adapted to jury cases in such a way as to eliminate the trial within the trial, its adoption for such cases would have the double merit of reducing the number of such trials and allowing the reliability of confessions obtained by pressures falling short of torture or inhuman or degrading treatment to be assessed, like the reliability of all other evidence, by the jury.

Like most English lawyers who are interested in these matters (perhaps I could add like most Commonwealth, American or Israeli lawyers with similar interests), I am much concerned about the recording of police interrogations. I suspect that the number of those among us who object to clause 1(1) of the draft Bill and to proposals concerning confessions such as those I have just mentioned would be very considerably reduced if we were sure that the courts could always ascertain exactly what was done and said at the police station. With this end in view the majority of the Criminal Law Revision Committee recommends experiments with tape recording; a minority would go further and provide that clause 1 should not come into effect until tape recorders are installed in the principal police stations, and then statements made by a suspect under interrogation would only be admissible evidence at his trial if they had been recorded. Other suggestions are that statements should only be received if the interrogation took place before a Magistrate or some other independent person.[35] Of course none of these suggestions is foolproof. An evilly disposed police officer could always "put on the verbals", i.e. attribute spontaneous remarks to the accused, detrimen-

---

[34] The report of the Commission recommended the placing of the burden of proving torture or inhuman or degrading treatment on the accused, and the Northern Ireland (Emergency Provisions) Bill was drafted accordingly. Placing the burden of proof on the accused was something which could only be justified, if at all, by a state of emergency, and, as a member of the Commission, I must confess to some pleasure at the fact that Parliament felt able to apply the ordinary principle that, once an issue has been raised by the evidence, the burden of proof should be borne by the prosecution. This principle is consistently applied in the 11th Report of the Criminal Law Revision Committee (paras. 137–42).

[35] The proposal concerning the magistrate stems from the Indian Evidence Act, 1872. It is embodied in the proposed Ghana Rules, but I understand that they have been amended so as to provide for interrogation before an independent person chosen by the accused. This was due to the insufficiency of magistrates in parts of Ghana. A further objection is that the proposal for interrogation before a magistrate might have the effect of making it appear that the judiciary participates in the process of investigation. It is open to question whether the proposal for interrogation before an independent person is practicable. Will such a person always be readily available? What if the suspect objects to all those who are available?

tal to his case, before he got to the station; but it would at least be necessary for the interrogator at the station to refer to the alleged verbal in order that any credence should be given to it.

To my mind a far more serious objection to proposals such as those mentioned in the last paragraph relates to the undesirability of publicising certain portions of some police interrogations, notably those relating to other suspects still at large. It may be that we are confronted with a choice between having, on the one hand, provisions like clause 1(1) subject to a condition of complete recording, with the attendant risk of undesirable publicity, and having, on the other hand, something like the present law and practice under which, through fear of an abuse of police powers, in the absence of recording, inferences may not be drawn from a suspect's failure to answer questions, and statements by an accused are only admissible if made after caution that nothing need be said, and subject to highly technical requirements of voluntariness. I am not sufficiently conversant with the ways of the police and their suspects to express an informed view with regard to this choice; but, if the ultimate decision has to be in favour of the status quo, it will not be based on a fundamental right to silence or privilege against self-incrimination, but rather on the difficulty of providing and the undesirability of fully publicising a complete record of what goes on in a police station. In other words, the decision will be one of expediency. It will be based on the view that more crime than would otherwise be the case is likely to be detected if the suspect and the police are allowed to have conversations "off the record".

3.   *The accused with a criminal record*

When considering the possibility that an accused person might have reasons for not giving evidence other than his guilt of the offence charged, I said that the man with a criminal record required special consideration. This is because he might well be deterred from testifying by fear of cross-examination to credit on his record although innocent of the offence charged. The danger of a miscarriage of justice on this score is present in all systems which permit the accused to testify without prohibiting cross-examination on his previous convictions when he refrains from setting up his good character; but the danger would no doubt be enhanced by the adoption of clause 5(3) of the draft Bill.[36] To my mind the only satisfactory way to meet the danger is to take a leaf out of Israel's book and impose the prohibition to which I have just referred.[37] This is the course contemplated in the American Law In-

---

[36] See the beginning of section 2 of this article for this clause.

[37] Criminal Procedure Law, 1965 sec. 146 (19 L.S.I. 158): "Where an accused has chosen to testify, he shall not be asked in cross-examination any question relating to his previous convictions, unless he has testified to his good character or submitted other evidence to that effect either in his own case or on cross-examination of wit-

stitute's Model Code of Evidence[38] and the proposed Ghana Rules of Evidence under each of which adverse inferences may be drawn from the accused's absence from the witness box; but it only gained the approval of a minority of the Criminal Law Revision Committee. Another minority was in favour of a change in the English law which would have enhanced the danger I have mentioned. This change would have involved taking a leaf out of Canada's book and leaving the accused in the same position with regard to cross-examination to credit as any other witness; it would mean that he would have no protection against cross-examination on his record apart from the possibility of the exercise of the trial judge's discretion in his favour. The majority of the Committee was, however, in favour of a change in the English law which would, if adopted, be more favourable to the accused than the present compromise established by proviso (f) to sec. 1 of the Criminal Evidence Act, 1898.

Proviso (f) prohibits cross-examination of the accused on his previous convictions subject to exceptions of which the most important are cases in which he gives or seeks to elicit evidence of his good character, and cases in which "the nature or conduct of the defence is such as to involve imputations on the character of the prosecutor or the witnesses for the prosecution". This latter exception has been literally construed by the House of Lords with the result that, as a matter of law, an accused who raises a defence such as self-defence which necessarily involves an imputation on the character of the prosecutor is liable to be cross-examined on his record.[39] The effect of clause 6(4) of the draft Bill is to modify the second exception to sec. 1(f) of the Act of 1898 mentioned above by providing that the accused shall only be liable to cross-examination on his previous convictions when the court is of opinion that the main purpose of questions put by him to witnesses for the prosecution about their misdeeds was "to raise an issue as to the witness's credibility". In other words the accused would only be liable to cross-examination to credit under the sub-clause if he cross-examined the witnesses for the prosecution as to their credit. The adoption of the proposal would make

---

nesses for the prosecution" (translation as in the American series of Foreign Penal Codes). I have set the section out for the benefit of non-Israeli readers and for the sake of comparison with the corresponding provision of the American Model Code.

[38] "If an accused who testifies at the trial introduces no evidence for the sole purpose of supporting his credibility, no evidence concerning his commission or conviction of crime shall, for the sole purpose of impairing his credibility, be elicited on his cross-examination or be otherwise introduced against him" (Model Code r. 106(3)). "Evidence of the conviction of a witness for a crime not involving dishonesty or false statement shall be inadmissible for the purpose of impairing his credibility. If the witness be the accused in a criminal proceeding, no evidence of his conviction of a crime shall be admissible for the sole purpose of impairing his credibility unless he has first introduced evidence admissible solely for the purpose of supporting his credibility" (Uniform Rules r. 21).

[39] *Selvey* v. *Director of Public Prosecutions*, [1970] A.C. 304.

English law the same as the present law of Ghana.[40] I have no doubt that it would represent an improvement on the present position, and I strongly suspect that it is the furthest that the great majority of English practising lawyers would wish to go, but this is a matter of considerable regret to me.

My main reason for this regret is that the modification is, like the present English practice, based on the assumption that it is possible to draw a valid distinction between cross-examining an accused to his credit and cross-examining him to the issue.[41] Though difficult to draw on some occasions, the distinction is logically defensible when applied to an ordinary witness[42] because the fact that he is shown by cross-examination to credit to have been lying when, for example, he swore that, at the material time, he saw the accused near or at a place remote from the scene of the crime, does not necessarily point to the guilt or innocence of the accused who may have been where the witness falsely swore that he saw him; but, in the case of an accused who testifies, the rejection of his evidence must point to his guilt. If the evidence was the contradictory of a fact essential to the prosecution's case, the affirmation of consent on a charge of rape, for example, its rejection entails the acceptance of that fact (absence of consent in the case supposed).[43] If the evidence was the contrary of a fact alleged by the prosecution, an alibi for example, its negation points (though not conclusively) to the guilt of the accused because innocent people do not normally invent false alibis. The distinction beween cross-examining the accused to credit and to the issue is yet another of those distinctions without a difference which disfigure the present English law of evidence. It obliges the judge to direct the jury in something like the following terms:

"You must not infer from the fact that the accused has numerous con-

---

[40] Under sec. 129(5)(c) of the Ghana Criminal Procedure Code 1960, an accused who testifies is liable to be cross-examined on his previous convictions when "the nature or conduct of the defence is such as to involve imputations against the character of the prosecutor or the witnesses for the prosecution which are not reasonably necessary for the conduct of the defence". Both in Ghana and under the English draft Bill (clause 7) an accused who adduces or elicits evidence of good character is liable to cross-examination on his previous convictions.

[41] For a recent example of insistence on the distinction by the English Court of Appeal see *R. v. Vickers* [1972] Crim.L.R. 101.

[42] It is not so defensible when applied to the victim as a witness in a criminal case, or to the parties in civil proceedings. The distinction antedated the competence of parties and persons interested and was assumed, without, so far as I am aware, any discussion, to be applicable to parties when testifying in civil suits, and to the victim and accused when testifying in criminal cases.

[43] In practice the usual effect of cross-examination to credit is no doubt to lead the tribunal of fact to conclude that it would be unsafe to act on the testimony rather than to be convinced that it would be proper to act on the contradictory, but the soundness of the distinction under consideration must be tested on the assumption that the cross-examination achieves everything it set out to achieve.

victions that he is guilty because he is the kind of man who would commit
this crime but, when considering the weight to be attached to his testimony
to the effect that he did not commit this crime, you must remember that it is
rendered less trustworthy than would otherwise be the case by the fact that
he has numerous convictions".

4. *Hearsay*

Clause 30(1) of the draft Bill reads

"In any [criminal] proceedings a statement other than one made by a
person while giving oral evidence in those proceedings shall be admissible as
evidence of any fact stated therein to the extent that it is so admissible by
virtue of any provision of this act or any other statutory provision, ... but not
otherwise".

Clause 31(1) provides that "a statement made whether orally or in a
document or otherwise, by any person" shall be admissible as evidence of
any fact stated therein of which direct oral evidence by him would be admissible, provided he is called as a witness or is unavailable for a variety of
reasons including the usual ones of death, illness or absence abroad.

At first glance this may seem to be an odd way of legislating. Clause 30(1)
conflates three common law rules, the rule prohibiting the proof of the previous statements of a witness consistent with his testimony, the rule according to which the previous statements of a non-party witness inconsistent with
his testimony are inadmissible as evidence of the facts stated and the rule
against hearsay according to which statements of persons other than the
witness who is testifying are inadmissible as evidence of the facts stated.[44]
There are a few exceptions to the first rule, none to the second and a lot to
the third. The terms of clause 30(1) might lead the reader to suppose that
the scheme was first to convert the common law exclusionary rules into
statutory prohibitions, and then to state the exceptions, if any, in the suc-
ceeding clauses; but clause 31(1) appears to permit precisely what clause
30(1) prohibits. The truth is that the intention of the Bill is to abolish the
three common law rules and to render the statements covered by them admissible as evidence of the facts stated subject to certain safeguards to be
mentioned shortly. The form of the legislation was to some extent dictated
by the necessity of abolishing the exceptions to the common law rules as
well as the rules themselves. If this part of the Bill were to become law, the
correct way of stating the position with regard to the admissibility as evidence
of the facts stated of statements which do not form part of a witness's testimony would be to say that they are admissible provided certain conditions
are fulfilled. This would mean that the law students and lawyers of the future
would be relieved of the necessity of cluttering up their minds with the nice-

---

[44] All three rules are frequently subsumed under the rule against hearsay (see for
example 13th Report of the Law Reform Committee para. 5).

ties of the rule against hearsay as we know it, with all its elaborate and ill-defined exceptions.

The legislative scheme is largely that of the Civil Evidence Act, 1968 which is now in force in England. It is also to a large extent the scheme of the American Law Institute's Model Code of Evidence; but I prefer the English scheme because it contains safeguards against inaccuracy and abuse which are lacking in the American. In the first place, when the previous statement of a witness consists of a proof of the evidence he is prepared to give, it will only be admissible with the leave of the court which must, before admitting the statement, be of opinion that it is in the interests of justice that the witness' oral evidence should be supplemented in this way;[45] secondly, where the statement to be proved is not made in a document, and the maker is not called as a witness, it can only be proved by someone who heard or otherwise perceived it being made, in other words "hearsay upon hearsay" or "double" or "secondhand" hearsay will generally be excluded;[46] thirdly, statements made by persons who are beyond the seas, unidentifiable or untraceable will be inadmissible if made after the accused was charged;[47] finally, a statement made by someone who is unavailable as a witness will only be admissible at a trial on indictment if due notice is given to his opponent by the party wishing to tender it in evidence.[48] It is true that the Model Code also restricts the admissibility of double hearsay, but there is no counterpart to the other safeguards I have mentioned, and they are not unimportant.[49]

An alternative scheme is that of the American Uniform and Federal Rules under which the existing exceptions to the rule against hearsay are modernised and enlarged. The Federal Rules contain a final exception of "a statement not specifically covered by any of the foregoing exceptions but having comparable circumstantial guarantees of trustworthiness;[50] nevertheless I prefer the thoroughgoing method of dealing with the rule against hearsay contemplated by the English draft Bill. It seems to me that troublesome questions are bound to arise concerning the applicability of a particular exception. For example, at the hearing of an appeal governed by the common law the

[45] Clause 32(3) of the English draft Bill.
[46] *Ibid.* clause 31(5). Provision is made for the reception of records which frequently consist of hearsay upon hearsay in clauses 34 and 35.
[47] Clause 32(1).
[48] Clause 32(4).
[49] A further objection to the Model Code which can also be made against the Uniform and Federal Rules is the existence of sub-clauses under which hearsay declarations may be proved in the absence of the maker, although he is available. The examination-in-chief of a witness is often as revealing as the cross-examination. This is why sec. 2(2) of the English Civil Evidence Act, 1968 provides that the previous consistent statements of a witness shall only be admissible with the leave of the court which shall not in general be given before the end of the examination-in-chief.
[50] R. 803(24); r. 804(6).

Judicial Committee of the Privy Council held that an inscription on goods as to their place of origin was inadmissible evidence of that fact.[51] The answer to the question whether the case would be covered by the "business entries" exception to the prohibition on hearsay in the Uniform and Federal Rules depends on whether the inscription was a "memorandum, report or record";[52] it certainly fits more naturally into the category of "statement" and it would be admissible under the English draft Bill as that of a person who cannot be identified after all reasonable steps have been taken.[53]

I now wish to exemplify the advantages of the hearsay provisions of the draft Bill over the common law by referring to four fairly commonly recurring situations.

(a) *The consistent witness*

W. is the agent of a company charged with obtaining money by means of a fraudulent advertisement concerning property for sale. The defence is that the property was sold by W. on behalf of the company before the advertisement appeared and the money was therefore obtained in consequence of the anterior contract of sale. W. testifies to the conclusion of the contract, and the original of a letter written by W. to the company's solicitor before the date of the advertisement is produced. The letter refers to the conclusion of the contract, but it is inadmissible in-chief at common law.[54] Surely it should be admissible, and it would be admissible as evidence of the facts stated under the draft Bill. The reason commonly given for the present rule is that the previous consistent statement of the witness could easily be manufactured, and yet, if his cross-examiner is so imprudent as to suggest that the evidence-in-chief is a recent fabrication, the previous statement becomes admissible in re-examination to negative the suggestion but never as evidence of the facts stated. The distinction is of course quite absurd because, in situations like that mentioned in the example, the real significance of the statement is that it adds considerably to the weight of the testimony and is nothing if it is not evidence of the facts stated, viz. the conclusion of the contract on a particular day.

(b) *The turncoat witness*

W. tells the police that he saw the accused near the scene of the crime; at the trial he swears that he did not see the accused near the scene of the crime and, when his previous inconsistent statement is put to him in cross-examination, he admits that he made it but says that he did so because he had quarrelled with the accused. In most cases the only safe course for the

---

[51] *Patel* v. *Comptroller General of Customs,* [1966] A.C. 356.
[52] Uniform Rules r. 63(13); Federal Rules r. 803(6).
[53] Clause 31 (1) (c) (iv).
[54] *Gillie* v. *Posho Ltd.* [1939] 2 All E.R. 196.

tribunal of fact will be to ignore W.'s evidence; but what if there is other evidence to suggest that W. had been "got at"? What if it is obvious that W.'s testimony concerning the quarrel is false? Surely it is wrong that there should be an absolute rule that the previous inconsistent statement of a non-party witness is admissible for the sole purpose of impeaching his credit? At times it must seem absurd to the layman that the law should permit an inconsistent statement to be received for the purpose of neutralising the maker's testimony, although it may never be acted upon, even when it is the contradictory of that testimony, and even when there is every reason to suppose that the statement was true. This is yet another of those distinctions which do little credit to the law of evidence. The possibility of treating the statement as evidence of the truth of its contents is recognized in the draft Bill.[55]

(c)   *The unavailable witness*

If, in the examples just given under heads (a) and (b), W. were unavailable, ought his letter to the solicitors and his statement to the police to be admissible? I would unhesitatingly answer "yes", and I applaud the fact that they would be admissible under the draft Bill; but there are undoubtedly those who would reply "let it be granted that the law could be liberalized with advantage when the maker of the extrajudicial statement is called as a witness and cross-examined, it would be too risky to allow the statement to be proved when the maker is not available. After all, the maker of a statement to the reliability of which good sight is essential might have been short sighted, a congenital liar and an imbecile". This is true, but provision can be made for the proof of such facts,[56] the person to whom the statement was made can be asked about all relevant circumstances, and, above all, allowance must be made for the cumulative nature of the evidence in almost every case. In *R. v. McLean*,[57] for instance, M. had been convicted of a robbery from G. whose assailant made off in a car. G. made a mental note of the number of the car which he dictated to C. some 3 minutes after the crime had been committed. G. gave evidence at the trial but was unable to recollect the number of the car and the circumstances were not such as to enable him, according to English law, to refresh his memory from the note taken by C.[58] C. was nonetheless allowed to produce the note at the trial. The Criminal Division of the English Court of Appeal felt constrained to quash the conviction because the hearsay rule had been infringed

---

[55] Clause 33(1).
[56] This is done by clause 39 of the English draft Bill.
[57] (1968) 52 Cr. App. Rep. 80.
[58] G had neither checked the document nor seen C. write the number down. It seems that in South Africa G. could have refreshed his memory with the aid of the note provided C. swore that he wrote down the number dictated by G. (*R. v. O'Linn* 1960 (1) S.A. 545).

as C. had been allowed to prove the number of the car dictated to him by G. in order to complete the latter's evidence that a car with the number had been used in the robbery. This happened to be a matter of crucial importance because there was evidence tending to show that a car with the number in question had previously been hired by the accused. The note taken by C. should surely have been admissible even if G. had ceased to be available by the time of the trial. It would of course be inadmissible under the present law, but provision is made for the reception of such a document in the draft Bill.[59] The probative value of the note might have been slightly decreased by the absence of G., but, owing to the other evidence associating M. with a car with the number mentioned in the note that document would have been of the greatest evidential significance. Of course hearsay is not the best evidence, but this does not mean that it ought to be excluded because, taken by itself, it would frequently be of no great weight.

(d) *The co-accused's confession*

A. and B. are being tried together for an offence. A. has made a voluntary confession which implicates B. as well as A. himself. It is trite learning that, at common law, the confession is evidence against A. but not against B., even when a finding of guilt against A. necessarily entails the guilt of B., as when the crime is incest or abortion. This is surely one of those distinctions which do little credit to the law. Under the English draft Bill, A.'s confession implicating B. is admissible evidence against the latter.[60]

5. *Conclusion*

I hope I have shown that there are at least the makings of a case for my claim that, if the draft Bill attached to the 11th Report of the Criminal Law Revision Committee were adopted by the English Parliament just as it is, England would have the best rules of evidence in criminal cases in the common law world; but I hope even more that I have provoked thought concerning the tenability of some of the distinctions underlying the present law of evidence. These include the distinction between commenting on the accused's failure to testify and pointing to inferences which may be drawn from it; the distinction between treating such failure as a matter which may properly be taken into account by the jury and as something which could corroborate evidence against the accused; the distinction between treating the accused's silence under interrogation by the police as something which affects the weight of the defence and as evidence against the accused; the distinction between cross-examining the accused to credit and to the issue;

---

[59] Clause 31(6).

[60] Clause 2(4). The American Model Code, Uniform Rules and Federal Rules are to the same effect as are the proposed Ghana Rules of evidence.

the distinction between admitting the previous statements of witnesses as evidence to confirm or impugn their testimony and as evidence of the facts stated; and the distinction between treating A.'s confession implicating his co-accused B. as evidence against A. and as evidence against B. This list is a formidable one, so is my contention that each and every one of the distinctions is, at least when stated in inflexible terms, as they always are stated, untenable. The first four distinctions are the outcome of an attempt to ensure that the accused should not be prejudiced by the permission to testify, the fifth distinction is probably attributable to the antiquated objection to receiving statements not made on oath as evidence of the facts stated, while the sixth is probably the outcome of a combination of the two causes. Whatever the cause, it seems to me that these purported distinctions are enough to show that the present law of evidence is rooted in illogicality. At this point, some ominous words of Lord Devlin come to mind:

"The common law is tolerant of much illogicality especially on the surface; but no system of law can be workable if it has not got logic at the root of it".[61] It is because the recommendations of the 11th Report would go a good way towards eliminating the illogicality in which the law of evidence has come to be rooted that I regret so deeply the fact that the Report has probably been put on the shelf, if not into its coffin, in England.

---

[61] *Hedley Byrne and Co. Ltd.* v. *Heller and Partners Ltd.,* [1964] A.C. 465 at p. 516.

Name Index